GLOBAL POLITICAL ECONOMY

GLOBAL POLITICAL ECONOMY

THEORY AND PRACTICE

Third Edition

Theodore H. Cohn
Simon Fraser University

PEARSON
Longman

New York   San Francisco   Boston
London   Toronto   Sydney   Tokyo   Singapore   Madrid
Mexico City   Munich   Paris   Cape Town   Hong Kong   Montreal

To Shirley

Vice President and Publisher: Priscilla McGeehon
Acquisitions Editor: Edward Costello
Senior Marketing Manager: Elizabeth Fogarty
Production Manager: Denise Phillip
Project Coordination, Text Design, and Electronic Page Makeup: Shepherd, Inc.
Cover Designer/Manager: Wendy Ann Fredericks
Cover Images: Globe art: Riley & Riley Photography, Inc./Pictureesque, Inc./Workbookstock;
   background photo: Baron Wolman/Getty Images, Inc.-Stone Allstock
Manufacturing Buyer: Lucy Hebard
Printer and Binder: R.R. Donnelley and Sons
Cover Printer: Coral Graphics Services

For permission to use copyrighted material, grateful acknowledgment is made to the copyright holders on pp. 447–471, which are hereby made part of this copyright page.

Library of Congress Cataloging-in-Publication Data

Cohn, Theodore H., 1940–
    Global political economy : theory and practice / Theodore H. Cohn.—3rd ed.
        p. cm.
    Includes bibliographical references and index.
    ISBN 0-321-20949-4
    1. International economic relations. 2. International trade. 3. International finance.
    I. Title
    HF1359.C654 2005
    337—dc22

                                                                    2004044560

Please visit our website at http://www.ablongman.com

ISBN 0-321-20949-4

1 2 3 4 5 6 7 8 9 10—DOC—07 06 05 04

Contents

Preface

This book introduces undergraduate students and beginning graduate students to the complex and important issues of global political economy. I wrote the book because of a long-held conviction that it is only possible for students to understand the broader implications of international political economy (IPE) issues by examining them in a theoretical context. Without the organizing framework of theory, it is difficult to make sense of the growing body of IPE facts and statistics and to interpret events in the global political economy. Thus, the text takes a comprehensive approach to the study of IPE, focusing on both theory and practice. To help draw connections between theory and the substantive issues, the book focuses on three major themes or challenges: globalization, North-North relations (among developed countries), and North-South relations (among developed countries of the North and developing countries of the South). Considerable space is also devoted to the transition economies of China and the former Soviet bloc and Soviet Union, which are becoming increasingly integrated in the capitalist global political economy.

Although a major theme of the text is globalization, I do *not* claim that globalization is leading to a world society or world government. Indeed, considerable space is devoted to the increasing importance of regional blocs and organizations such as the European Union, the North American Free Trade Agreement, and Mercosur, and Chapter 9 is devoted to the subject of regionalism. Furthermore, there is discussion throughout the text of the interconnections between economic and security issues, and between domestic and international issues. Domestic-international interactions are generally more important in the study of IPE than in the study of security issues.

CHANGES IN THE THIRD EDITION

The third edition of this book is revised throughout. Some of the most important changes including the following:

- The text and tables/figures are revised and updated to account for important changes in the global political economy.
- The book devotes more attention to the relationship between economic and security issues.

- The book devotes more attention to the rivalries and differences among the developed countries, especially with the end of the Cold War and the growing concerns about terrorist activity.
- The theoretical chapters (Chapters 3 to 5) have been updated to incorporate recent theoretical developments. For example, Chapter 4 contains a discussion comparing international regime theory with the concept of global governance.
- Chapter 6 devotes more discussion to the new European currency—the Euro—and assesses the euro's role in relation to the U.S. dollar.
- The title of Chapter 7 has been changed to "Foreign Debt and Financial Crises," and a major new section has been added to the chapter comparing the debt and financial crises and discussing efforts to develop a new international financial architecture.
- Chapter 8 examines North-South and U.S.-European tensions since the GATT Uruguay Round as well as the problems with the current WTO Doha Round of trade negotiations.
- Chapter 9 points to important new trends in the regionalization of the global economy, such as the increase in bilateral free trade agreements, and updates the discussion of the main regional trade agreements.
- Chapter 10 discusses recent developments in efforts to negotiate international investment rules.
- Chapter 11 contains a more detailed discussion of the World Bank's efforts to alter its development policies, and additional discussion of current tensions in North-South relations.
- Chapter 12 contains some discussion of "newer" IPE-related issues including migration, health, and illegal activity.

ACKNOWLEDGMENTS

I am grateful for the comments, advice, and support of a number of individuals in writing and revising this book. First, I want to thank Mark Zacher of the University of British Columbia, Michael Webb of the University of Victoria, and Benjamin Cohen of the University of California-Santa Barbara for providing helpful advice and comments with regard to the organization and content of earlier editions of this book. I also want to recognize the contribution the late Harold K. Jacobson of the University of Michigan made to my studies. The emphasis of this IPE text on international institutions and governance owes a great deal to the interest I developed in the subject years ago when Professor Jacobson was my Ph.D. supervisor. I am indebted to the following external reviewers whose helpful comments provided major contributions to the various editions of this book: Sherry L. Bennett, Rice University; Vicki Birchfield, Georgia Institute of Technology; Kurt Burch, University of Delaware; Jeffrey Cason, Middlebury College; Vincent Ferraro, Mount Holyoke College; David N. Gibbs, University of Arizona; Vicki L. Golich, California State University-San Marcos; Robert Griffiths, University of North Carolina at Greensboro; Beverly G. Hawk, University of Alabama at

Birmingham; Michael J. Hiscox, University of California-San Diego; Matthias Kael-berer, University of Northern Iowa; Quan Li, Florida State University; Dr. Waltraud Q. Morales, University of Central Florida; Thomas Oatley, University of North Carolina at Chapel Hill; Howard Richards, Earlham College; David E. Spiro, University of Ari-zona; Kenneth P. Thomas, University of Missouri-St. Louis; and Robert S. Walters, University of Pittsburgh. In addition, thanks are due to several colleagues at Simon Fraser University with whom I discussed various aspects of the text, including Stephen McBride, Michael Howlett, Tsuyoshi Kawasaki, James Busumtwi-Sam, Anil Hira, and Sandra MacLean.

The competent editorial staff at Longman Publishers has given active support to this book. I appreciate the work that Jennie Errickson, Ellen MacElree, and Anita Castro put into earlier editions. I especially want to thank Edward Costello, Ken Har-rell (of Shepherd Incorporated), and Kent Martin for their careful work on the third edition. Two individuals at Longman who have been especially helpful for all three editions of the book are Eric Stano and Megan Galvin-Fak. Finally, I appreciate the careful attention the copyeditors gave to the various editions of the text.

My acknowledgments would not be complete without mentioning the important role my students have played over the years in asking insightful questions, raising im-portant issues, and giving me feedback as to what aspects of IPE they found clear or confusing. I also want to thank a friend, Ken Abramson, for his computer help at vari-ous crucial junctures. My sons Daniel and Frank gave me assistance in a variety of ar-eas, and I appreciate their patience with my extended working hours. Finally, I am ded-icating this book to my wife Shirley, for her caring advice, support, and encouragement.

Theodore H. Cohn

Acronyms and Abbreviations

AASM: Associated African States and Madagascar

ABB: Asea Brown Boveri

ACP: African, Caribbean, and Pacific

ADDs: antidumping duties

AFTA: ASEAN Free Trade Area

AID: Agency for International Development

AMF: Asian Monetary Fund

APEC: Asia-Pacific Economic Cooperation

ASEAN: Association of Southeast Asian Nations

BIS: Bank for International Settlements

BITs: bilateral investment treaties

CACM: Central American Common Market

CAP: Common Agricultural Policy

CARIBCAN: Canadian Trade, Investment, and Industrial Cooperation program

CARICOM: Caribbean Community and Common Market

CDF: Comprehensive Development Framework

CEECs: Central and Eastern European countries

CFIUS: Committee on Foreign Investment in the United States

CIA: Central Intelligence Agency

CMEA: Council for Mutual Economic Assistance

COCOM: Coordinating Committee

CPE: centrally planned economy

CRTA: Committee on Regional Trade Agreements

CU: customs union

CUSFTA: Canada-U.S. Free Trade Agreement

CVDs: countervailing duties

DC: developed country

DISC: Domestic International Sales Corporation

EAI: Enterprise for the Americas Initiative

EC: European Community

ECB: European Central Bank

ECLA: Economic Commission for Latin America

ECSC: European Coal and Steel Community

ECU: European currency unit

EFTA: European Free Trade Association

EMS: European Monetary System

EMU: European Economic and Monetary Union

ERM: exchange rate mechanism

EU: European Union

FAIR: Federation for American Immigration Reform

FCN: Friendship, Commerce, and Navigation

FDI: foreign direct investment

FIRA: Foreign Investment Review Agency

FSU: former Soviet Union

FTA: free trade area

FTAA: Free Trade Area of the Americas

G-5: Group of Five

G-7: Group of Seven

G-8: Group of Eight

G-10: Group of Ten

G-24: Group of 24

G-77: Group of 77

GAB: General Arrangements to Borrow

GATS: General Agreement on Trade in Services

GATT: General Agreement on Tariffs and Trade

GDI: gender-related development index

GDP: gross domestic product
GEM: gender empowerment measure
GNP: gross national product
GSP: generalized system of preference
HDI: human development index
HIPC: Heavily Indebted Poor Countries (initiative)
IBRD: International Bank for Reconstruction and Development
ICSID: International Centre for Settlement of Investment Disputes
IDA: International Development Association
IDB: Inter-American Development Bank
IFC: International Finance Corporation
IMF: International Monetary Fund
IO: international organization
IPC: Integrated Program for Commodities
IPE: international political economy
IR: international relations
ISI: import-substituting industrialization
ITO: International Trade Organization
ITT: International Telephone and Telegraph Corporation
KIEOs: keystone international economic organizations
LAFTA: Latin American Free Trade Association
LDC: less developed country
LIC: low-income country
LLDC: least developed country
M&As: mergers and acquisitions
MAI: Multilateral Agreement on Investment
MFA: Multi-Fiber Arrangement
MFN: most favored nation
MIC: middle-income country
MIGA: Multilateral Investment Guarantee Agency
MNC: multinational corporation
MTNs: multilateral trade negotiations
NAB: New Arrangements to Borrow
NAFTA: North American Free Trade Agreement
NATO: North Atlantic Treaty Organization
NEM: New Economic Mechanism
NEP: National Energy Program
NGO: nongovernmental organization
NIE: newly industrializing economy
NIEO: New International Economic Order

NTB: nontariff barrier
OA: official aid
ODA: official development assistance
ODF: official development finance
OECD: Organization for Economic Cooperation and Development
OEEC: Organization for European Economic Cooperation
OPEC: Organization of Petroleum Exporting Countries
PPP: purchasing power parity
PRC: People's Republic of China
PTA: preferential trading arrangement
Quad: Quadrilateral Group
R&D: research and development
RTA: regional trade agreement
RTAA: Reciprocal Trade Agreements Act
S&D: special and differential (treatment)
SAL: structural adjustment loan
SAP: structural adjustment program
SDRs: special drawing rights
SEA: Single European Act
SPARTECA: South Pacific Regional Trade and Economic Cooperation Agreement
TOA: Treaty of Asunción
TRIMs: Trade-Related Investment Measures
TRIPs: Trade-Related Intellectual Property Rights
UN: United Nations
UNCTAD: United Nations Conference on Trade and Development
UNCTC: United Nations Center on Transnational Corporations
UNDP: United Nations Development Program
UNFPA: United Nations Fund for Population Activities
UNHCR: United Nations High Commissioner for Refugees
UNICEF: United Nations Children's Fund
UNIFEM: United Nations Development Fund for Women
UR Understanding: Uruguay Round Understanding on the Interpretation of GATT Article 24
USIA: United States Information Agency
WTO: World Trade Organization

P A R T I

Introduction
and Overview

The field of international relations (IR) traditionally focused mainly on political-security issues and largely ignored economic issues, but it has become increasingly evident that the political, economic, and social aspects of IR are closely intertwined. As a result, *international political economy (IPE)* has emerged as an important area of study. Chapter 1 provides answers to some basic questions such as "What is IPE?" and "Why is IPE a relatively new area of study?" It then discusses the themes of this book and introduces the main theoretical perspectives. Chapter 2 has a brief historical discussion beginning from the fifteenth century and then provides a general overview of the world economy since World War II with emphasis on the institutions developed to manage international economic relations. For ease of reference, all terms defined in the glossary as well as the text of this book are initially in **bold print,** while terms defined only in the text are in italics.

Introduction

Ⅰn July 1944, while World War II was still raging in Europe and the Pacific, delegates from 44 countries held a conference in the small resort town of Bretton
Woods, New Hampshire, to reach a broad-ranging agreement for economic cooperation. The **Bretton Woods system** that emerged from the conference helped shape
international economic relations in the postwar era. After World War II, however, the
emergence of the Cold War between the United States and the Soviet Union became
the central concern of Western policymakers. Thus, postwar IR scholars viewed security issues related to the Cold War as most important, or *high politics;* and they considered international economic issues to be less important, or *low politics.* As this book
discusses, by the late 1960s to early 1970s policymakers and academics became increasingly aware that they had underestimated the political importance of economic
issues. Indeed, some of the most contentious international issues of the 1970s were
both economic and political by nature. It was at about this time that IPE emerged as
an important field of study. Some examples of major issues and events clearly demonstrate how international politics and economics are often closely intertwined.

Military Actions Against Iraq   In August 1990, Iraq invaded its much smaller neighbor Kuwait and was in a position to control about one-fifth of the Organization of Petroleum Exporting Countries' (OPEC's) oil production. The Western industrial states and
Japan were concerned not only about the strategic implications of Iraq's invasion, but
also about the economic effects in view of their dependence on Middle East oil. When
Iraq failed to withdraw from Kuwait by a specified date, the United Nations (UN) Security Council endorsed the use of force by a U.S.-led military coalition. Because one
Communist regime after another in Eastern Europe had disintegrated in 1989 and the
Soviet Union itself was on the verge of dissolution, the United States was able to engage
in military actions against Iraq without concerns about any counteraction from the Soviets. Nevertheless, the U.S. *economic* position was no longer as predominant as it had
been in the 1950s and 1960s, and Japan, Germany, Saudi Arabia, and Kuwait provided a
substantial amount of funding to help finance the Gulf War effort.

The reasons for the second U.S.-led war against Iraq, which began in March 2003,
were more complex and contentious and resulted in serious U.S. and British differences with some other major Western states such as France, Germany, and Canada.
The economic costs of the second conflict were greater for the United States because

some U.S. allies were more reluctant to provide support, and the goal of installing a new Iraqi regime after the downfall of Saddam Hussein resulted in a longer-term U.S. occupation in Iraq. Projections indicated that the United States would have a record budget deficit of about $455 billion in 2003 as a result of the U.S. operations in Iraq, a decrease in U.S. income taxes, and increased U.S. efforts to deter terrorists. A close relationship exists between economic "wealth" and political "power" internationally, and differences between the two conflicts with Iraq demonstrate that even a predominant military power such as the United States must consider the economic costs (and benefits) of engaging in military operations.

European Integration   In 1951, six Western European countries (France, West Germany, Italy, Belgium, the Netherlands, and Luxembourg) formed the **European Coal and Steel Community (ECSC),** which was designed to coordinate the member states' policies and reduce their trade barriers in coal and steel. Although the ECSC resulted in the *economic* integration of the members' coal and steel resources, the reasons for its formation in 1951 were primarily *political.* France's foreign minister, Robert Schuman, developed plans for the ECSC for two major reasons: first, to meet U.S. demands that West Germany be rebuilt to help deter aggression by the Soviet Union, and second, to allay France's fears of renewed aggression by a rearmed Germany. Over the centuries, Germany and France had repeatedly fought over access to coal and steel resources in border areas such as Alsace-Lorraine. It was therefore felt that a sharing of these resources in the ECSC would help rebuild Germany and also make future wars between France and Germany virtually impossible. Thus, the ECSC treaty preamble states that the member countries wish "to create, by establishing an economic community, the basis for a broader and deeper community among peoples long divided by bloody conflicts."[1]

After the the six member states integrated their coal and steel resources, they agreed to extend the ECSC to a full-scale regional integration agreement by forming the European Economic Community (EC) in 1957. Today, this community—which is now called the **European Union (EU)**—has 15 full members and a large number of associate member states. One of the original purposes of economic integration in Europe—to end armed hostilities between France and Germany—has certainly been achieved.

World Bank Loans to Developing Countries   This book shows that politics and economics are often linked in the decision making of international economic organizations. Such linkages are evident in the lending activities of the *World Bank* (or the *Bank*), which is the largest source of multilateral development finance for economically less developed countries (LDCs). The Bank *Articles of Agreement* state that it "shall not interfere in the political affairs of any member" and that "only economic considerations shall be relevant" to its lending decisions.[2] Many analysts argue, however, that the Bank's loans are based on political as well as economic considerations. For example, the Bank has preferred to lend to countries that promote private enterprise, and this preference became far more pronounced after the LDC foreign debt crisis during the 1980s (see Chapter 7). Although Bank officials argue that countries with a private market orientation are more likely to be economically efficient, the Bank's preference for private enterprise is also based on the political and ideological leanings of its most powerful members—the advanced industrial states. During the 1950s to 1970s, the Bank gave some support to LDC development strategies that combined state action with private entrepreneurship, and it provided finance for **infrastructure** projects such as roads, railways, airports, water systems, and public utilities that involved state-owned corporations. However, even during these early years the Bank showed a definite preference for private enterprise; one noted analyst has written that Eugene Black, the Bank's president from 1949 to 1962, was "inclined to talk as if there were some kind of exclusive relationship between political freedom and private enterprise, and as if he believed that his main task is therefore to defend the only true economic faith throughout the world."[3]

In the 1980s the Bank followed national leaders such as British Prime Minister Margaret Thatcher and U.S. President Ronald Reagan in a shift to the political Right, and it was far more inclined to view governments and public enterprise as hindrances to growth. Thus, the Bank's structural adjustment loans (SALs) to indebted LDCs in the 1980s and 1990s were linked with the agreement of these countries to promote privatization, deregulation, and trade liberalization. In sum, politics and economics have been so intertwined in the international development area that the World Bank has been both unwilling and unable to fully follow the directive of its Articles of Agreements that its loans should be based solely on economic considerations.

The Boeing Company's Merger with McDonnell Douglas Corporation   This book demonstrates that economic activities of private actors such as international banks and multinational corporations (MNCs) often have major political implications. A prime example of such political-economic linkages is evident in the decision of two U.S. aircraft companies—Boeing and McDonnell Douglas—to merge their operations in early 1997. When the merger proposal was first announced, the EU strongly protested and threatened to retaliate against Boeing, which was based in Seattle, Washington (Boeing headquarters later moved to Chicago, Illinois). Boeing had a much larger market share for commercial aircraft than Europe's Airbus, and the EU feared that McDonnell Douglas' experience with defense production and an increase in public funding for defense-related research would solidify Boeing's domination of the civil aircraft business. Furthermore, the EU objected to 20-year contracts with exclusive-supplier provisions that Boeing signed with three U.S. airlines—Delta, American, and Continental. Although the U.S. Federal Trade Commission approved the merger, Boeing had to be concerned about retaliation. The Europeans could not block a merger between two U.S. companies, but they threatened to impose fines for violation of their competition rules that would make it difficult for Boeing to operate in Europe. They also threatened to withdraw from the 1992 U.S.-EU bilateral civil aircraft agreement, which limited direct and indirect subsidies in the aircraft sector. To avoid these actions, Boeing eventually agreed not to enforce its exclusive-supplier provisions with the U.S. airlines, to supply information to the EU about indirect subsidies it received from government-sponsored research, and to provide some benefits to European companies.

The United States has had similar complaints about Airbus. After years of disputes over European government subsidies to Airbus, which contributed to its growing sales vis-à-vis Boeing, the United States pressured the EU to sign the 1992 agreement limiting Airbus subsidies. In recent years the competition has become fierce, as airline carriers have suffered financial losses and the market for jets has declined. Furthermore, Airbus has steadily caught up with Boeing, and in 2003 it overtook Boeing in both orders and output for the first time. Boeing has become less dependent on civil jet sales as its defense and space interests have increased, but it has accused Airbus of using aggressive and unethical tactics. Airbus has returned the accusations. The civil airline industry has been described as "the most politicized in the world—apart from the defense industry," with which it is closely tied.[4] However, as global competition increases in many economic areas, conflicts of this nature will become more frequent. Because governments often feel a stake in the welfare of their home-based MNCs, disputes over economic market share can be highly politicized.

The "Nixon Economic Shocks"   This book shows that economics and politics are closely intertwined in foreign policymaking. On August 15, 1971, President Richard Nixon responded to growing U.S. balance of payments deficits by suspending the convertibility of the U.S. dollar into gold and imposing a 10 percent surcharge on all dutiable imports. These "Nixon shocks" are explained in Chapters 6 and 8. Of interest here is the reaction of Henry Kissinger, who was President Nixon's national security adviser (and later secretary of state), to the crisis with Europe and Japan surrounding the Nixon shocks. Kissinger later wrote in his memoirs:

> My own participation in the economic deliberations during this period was peripheral. From the start I had not expected to play a major role in international economics, which—to put it mildly—had not been a central field of study for me. Only later did I learn that the key economic policy decisions are not technical but political. At first I thought that I had enough on my hands keeping watch on the State and Defense Departments and the Central Intelligence Agency without also taking on Treasury, Commerce, and Agriculture. I took a crash 'tutorial' from Professor Richard N. Cooper of Yale University to learn the rudiments of the subject. I appointed the brilliant economists Fred Bergsten and Robert Hormats to my staff.[5]

The foregoing examples demonstrate that politics and economics are often inextricably linked in the real world of IR. Before discussing the purposes and themes of this book, we address two important questions: What is IPE? And why is IPE a relatively new area of study?

WHAT IS INTERNATIONAL POLITICAL ECONOMY?

As a field of study that bridges the disciplines of politics and economics, IPE is concerned with the interaction between "the state" and "the market." The state is associated with the political pursuit of power, and the market with the economic pursuit of wealth. However, the state also has concerns related to the accumulation of wealth, and the market is not totally removed from power considerations. As the political component of IPE, the **state** is a sovereign, territorial unit with a government and population. As the economic component, the **market** is a coordinating mechanism where sellers and buyers exchange goods and services at prices and output levels determined by supply and demand.

An inherent tension often exists between the state and the market. While the state is concerned with preserving national sovereignty and unity, the market is associated with economic openness and the breaking down of state barriers.[6] For example, the 1988 **Canada-U.S. Free Trade Agreement (CUSFTA)** contributed to an open market between the two countries, which some Canadians considered a threat to their national sovereignty in energy, foreign investment, and cultural industries. When CUSFTA was extended to form the **North American Free Trade Agreement (NAFTA)** in 1994, Mexicans were concerned that NAFTA might encroach on their sovereignty in energy and agriculture. Although the United States is the largest economy in North America, many Americans feared that NAFTA would threaten national control over employment and the environment.

Despite the tensions between states and markets, they also have a complementary relationship. Domestically, states establish rules to protect private property rights and provide infrastructure such as transportation and communications required for market transactions. Internationally, states form international agreements and organizations to promote economic openness and stability. Furthermore, there is often a close relationship between a state's wealth and market size and its military and political power. As interdependence has increased, states have been drawn into the competitive forces of the world economy. Thus, states today are sometimes called *competition states* because they are involved in supporting research and development (R&D) in high-technology sectors, restructuring industry, and deregulating financial markets.[7] The impressive economic growth rates of some states seem to be closely related to their success in fostering a symbiotic relationship with the competitive marketplace. As we discuss, Japan and the newly industrializing economies (NIEs) of East Asia (Hong Kong, Singapore, South Korea, and Taiwan) successfully fostered state-market relationships from the 1960s to 1980s.

Although state-market interactions are the core issue in the study of IPE, other types of organizational relationships are also of concern. Primary among these is the interaction between states and MNCs—also referred to as transnational corporations. The MNC is the main nonstate actor with which the state must contend. The 600 largest MNCs each benefit from worldwide sales of more than $1 billion, and together they produce more than 25 percent of world gross domestic product; the 350 largest MNCs account for about 40 percent of world trade. As is the case with states and markets, there are inherent tensions between states and MNCs, but they can also have cooperative relations.

The traditional view is that an MNC is closely linked with the "home" state where its headquarters are located. Although an MNC opens foreign branch plants in "host" states, its main financial and R&D activities remain firmly planted in the home state. The home state also provides the basic environment and legal structure within which its MNCs must function; and directors and shareholders in the home state retain primary responsibility for managing the MNC's foreign operations. However, this traditional model has been supplemented by two other models in which the host state gains more control over its MNC branch plant operations or the MNC extricates itself from control by any single state. This latter type is sometimes referred to as a "stateless" corporation, because its ownership and board of directors become internationalized. Some MNCs follow a deliberate strategy of internationalizing their operations to increase their freedom of operation. Although stateless corporations must take different national markets into account in their production and marketing strategies, they are no longer beholden to any single state. As discussed in Chapter 10, IPE scholars differ over the importance they attach to these three models of MNC-state relations.[8]

Whether one focuses on state-market, state-MNC, or power-wealth interactions, there is general agreement that IPE is interdisciplinary and draws on contributions from political scientists, economists, sociologists, anthropologists, historians, and geographers. IPE theorists also seek to overcome limitations imposed by the current disciplinary boundaries. On the one hand, they criticize some economists for **economism**; i.e., for overestimating the importance of the economic sphere and underestimating the importance and autonomy of the political sphere. On the other hand, IPE theorists criticize some political scientists for **politicism;** i.e., for devoting too much attention to politics and power and too little attention to economic structures and processes.[9]

The challenge of engaging in interdisciplinary study is magnified when political economy is examined at the international level. How does one develop an IPE theory that examines international influences and accounts for social, cultural, economic, political, and developmental variations across nation-states? Furthermore, it is more essential for IPE than security scholars to focus on international-domestic linkages. Defense officials normally have considerable leeway in dealing with security matters because domestic groups are generally willing to leave decision making on these issues to the government experts. In contrast, domestic groups often see a close relationship between their economic welfare and international issues such as trade and foreign investment, and they therefore demand a greater role in government decision making in economic areas. Thus, "effective international economic cooperation depends not only on the external interests and actions of states, but on their ability to manage, channel, or circumvent domestic political pressures as well."[10] IPE scholars have the daunting tasks of focusing on both IR and domestic relations and of crossing the boundaries between a number of social science disciplines.

WHY IS IPE A RELATIVELY NEW AREA OF STUDY?

The relative newness of IPE as an academic area of study is ironic, because of the close interaction between politics and economics and because awareness of these linkages extends back to ancient times. Thucydides (471–400 B.C.), who is often described as the founder of IR, demonstrated an acute awareness of the linkages between power and wealth. In his *History of the Peloponnesian War* dealing with conflict among the Greek city-states, he wrote that "war is a matter not so much of arms as of money, which makes arms of use."[11] The earlier discussion of the cost-sharing arrangements during the 1990s Persian Gulf War demonstrates that Thucydides' work continues to be relevant. Aristotle (384–322 B.C.) also demonstrated a sensitivity to political-economic interactions, and he in fact subsumed economics under the study of politics.[12]

Despite this early awareness of linkages between politics and economics, several factors led to the tendency in modern times to view them as distinct areas of study: the influence of the liberal school of thought, the hierarchy of international concerns after World War II, and the organization of university disciplines. As discussed in Chapter 4, liberal-economic theorists such as Adam Smith (1723–1790) considered economic and political matters to be largely separable. In Smith's view, economic activity operates under a naturally harmonious system of laws, whereas politics does not obey natural laws and is not harmonious. As a result, Smith is associated with calls for laissez-faire capitalism, in which the economic system functions best with minimal government interference. The liberal view that politics is separable from economics and that the state should have a minimal role in operation of the market contributed to a turning away from the study of political economy.

In the post-World War II period, the most pressing international concerns were in the security area. The rapid emergence of the Cold War led scholars to view the questions of war and peace as the truly important ones, or high politics. Postwar international economic relations, by contrast, were relatively stable and cooperative under U.S. leadership, and scholars viewed international economic matters as being outside the realm of high diplomacy, or as low politics.[13] IR specialists in the postwar period therefore accepted the liberal dictum that politics is separable from economics, but one could say that they "turned Adam Smith on his head," and gave priority to political security over economic issues. A perusal of IR textbooks from the 1950s to the 1970s and even later clearly demonstrates the lack of attention given to political-economic interactions.[14]

Beginning in the late 1960s to 1970s, several factors contributed to a reversal of these trends and to new interest in IPE among both policymakers and academics. On the one hand, détente between the United States and Soviet Union ushered in a period of decreased tension over global security matters. On the other hand, the relative decline of U.S. economic power, combined with economic threats resulting from the OPEC oil price increases in the 1970s and the foreign debt crisis in the 1980s heightened concerns about international economic stability. Thus, it was evident that international economic issues had become high politics and required urgent attention.

Since the mid-1970s, the North American academic community has made great strides in developing the IPE field. Nevertheless, the social sciences in most universities continue to be organized in separate disciplines, with political science, economics, sociology, anthropology, and geography in different departments. These disciplinary divisions have considerable influence over "rewards, interactions, and the flow of thought itself."[15] It is evident that despite the obstacles posed by the inflexibility of academia, world events are making the study of IPE increasingly relevant. With the end of the Cold War, industrial states in the North, LDCs in the South, and emerging economies in Eastern Europe and the former Soviet Union (FSU) are all directing more attention to economic problems.

In sum, IPE, like security studies, is now a recognized academic field of study. However, international security and IPE specialists can be faulted for devoting too little attention to the *linkages* between security and economic issues. Some of the most striking recent events in IR have had both security and economic implications. For example, the breakup of the Soviet bloc and end of the Cold War have contributed to increased economic tensions among the United States, EU, and Japan; and the terrorist attacks on New York's World Trade Center on September 11, 2001 had major economic as well as security implications.[16] While IPE and international security are now each important areas of study, "we should expect scholarship that links economics and security to become increasingly prominent in the post-Cold War IR literature."[17]

PURPOSES AND THEMES OF THIS BOOK

This book provides a comprehensive approach to the study of IPE. Part II introduces students to the main theoretical perspectives in the field, and Part III examines substantive issues including monetary and financial relations, foreign debt, trade, investment, and international development. We can only understand the broader implications of these IPE issues by examining them in a theoretical context. The substantive chapters in Part III therefore regularly direct the reader to the interaction between theory and practice. To help draw connections between theory and the substantive issues, this book focuses on three major themes: globalization, North-North relations, and North-South relations.

Globalization

Globalization involves the broadening and deepening of interactions and interdependence among peoples and countries of the world. Broadening refers to the extension of geographic linkages to encompass virtually all major societies and states. Thus, events and policies adopted in one part of the world can have a significant impact on distant locations. Deepening refers to an increase in the frequency and intensity of state and societal interactions. Although the state continues to be the most important actor in IR, developments linked with globalization such as modern telecommunications and rapid transportation increase interconnections among people with less regard to territorial boundaries. Thus, states are confronting a more complex international environment in which international organizations (IOs), governmental subunits, MNCs and nongovernmental organizations (NGOs) have more important roles.[18] Although this book focuses on IPE, it takes account of the fact that there is often close interaction between economic aspects of globalization such as trade and foreign investment, and non-economic aspects of globalization such as the environment (e.g., climate change), migration, disease (e.g., AIDS and SARS), and security issues (e.g., terrorism). The chapters in Part III point to indications of globalization in various aspects of IPE. For example, the *daily* volume of foreign exchange trading in currencies rose from about $1 billion in the mid-1970s to $1.2 trillion in the mid-1990s; foreign direct investment (FDI) flows reached $315 billion in 1995, nearly a sixfold increase over the 1981–85 level; and global trade grew twelvefold during the postwar period, amounting to more than $4 trillion a year by 1995.[19]

Globalization can be both a dependent and an independent variable, and this book is concerned with both the causes and effects of globalization.[20] In terms of causes, we are interested in such factors as technological advances and the spread of market economies. In terms of effects, we are interested in the impact of globalization on interactions among states, between states and markets, and between states and MNCs. For example, state policies that were traditionally considered to be domestic now often have a significant impact on other states and on international business. Pressures have therefore increased to subject "domestic" factors such as competition policies, subsidies, and financial market activity to international regulation. MNCs are also demanding nondiscriminatory trade and investment rules so they can operate without restrictions internationally, and these new rules could impose additional restrictions on the policymaking autonomy of states.

Globalization is a controversial term because some extreme globalists claim we are entering a "borderless world" in which MNCs are losing their national identities and distinct national economies are being subsumed under the global marketplace.[21] Although this book considers globalization to be a significant development, it adopts a less extreme version of globalization in four respects. First, globalization is not a uniform process throughout the world. The effects of globalization are more evident in major urban centers than in rural areas, remote islands, and underdeveloped LDC areas. Second, globalization is *not* causing the state to wither away. Although the state's autonomy in implementing economic policies is eroding in some important respects, states are also adopting new and more complex functions to deal with a highly interdependent world. Governments continue to have choices in how they respond to globalization. When domestic groups appeal for assistance in dealing with global competition, some states resort to trade protectionism, others adopt industrial policies to promote competitiveness, and still others permit the market to function without interference.[22]

Third, globalization is *not* leading to a world government. Indeed, globalization can result in fragmentation and conflict as well as unity and cooperation. For example, some writers argue that the increase in global **competitiveness** is contributing to the formation of three economic blocs centered in Europe, North America, and Japan/East Asia. Opinions differ as to whether the relationship among these blocs will become more cooperative or conflictual. Fourth, interdependence and globalization are not unique to the present-day period. Historically, interdependence has fluctuated over time, and it is possible that international events could eventually reverse the current moves toward globalization. For example, before World War I there was a high degree of interdependence in trade, foreign investment, and other areas. In 17 industrial countries for which there are comparative data, exports as a share of the total value of goods and services they produced averaged 12.9 percent in 1913, which is comparable to the 1993 level of 14.5 percent; and the migration of people around the world was more extensive in some earlier periods than it is today. The interdependent linkages of the nineteenth and early twentieth centuries declined during World War I, and virtually collapsed in the interwar period as a result of increased nationalism and the Great Depression. Only after World War II did global economic ties begin to increase again.[23]

Despite the historical fluctuations in interdependence, globalization is more encompassing today than it was at any time in the past. With advances in technology, communications, and transportation, state activities are being internationalized to a degree not previously experienced. In communications, for example, the cost of international telephone calls fell by more than 90 percent from 1970 to 1990, telecommunications traffic increased by 20 percent a year in the 1980s, and more than 50 million people were using the Internet by the late 1990s. Indeed, the spread of ideas through the media, television, videos, and the Internet seems to be contributing to the emergence of a global culture. In transportation, shipping costs fell by more than two-thirds between 1920 and 1990, and airline operating costs per mile fell by 60 percent from 1960 to 1990.[24] Global interdependence today is also qualitatively different than it was in the past. Although a number of corporations globalized their activities during the nineteenth century, the role of MNCs in generating foreign investment, trade, and technology is a modern-day phenomenon. By 1988, there were about 19,000 MNCs, which accounted for 25 to 30 percent of the productive output of all market economies and for 80 percent of the trade in managerial and technology skills.[25]

The geographic reach of the capitalist economic system today is also encompassing virtually the entire globe, with LDCs becoming more actively involved in the global economy and the emerging centrally planned economies (CPEs) of Eastern Europe and the former Soviet Union liberalizing their economies since the demise of communism. Thus, for the first time, membership in the **International Monetary Fund (IMF)**, World Bank, and **World Trade Organization (WTO)** is becoming truly global in scope.[26] This book examines the implications of these changes as well as the differing attitudes of theorists, government officials, and the broader public as to whether globalization is a positive or negative phenomenon. Regarding the public reaction to globalization, we discuss the dramatic increase in **civil society** activism in recent years. The term "civil society" was an old idea that emphasized civic responsibility and community service by voluntary associations or NGOs, including caring for the poor and sick, and filling gaps in social services. "Civil society" refers not only to these operational functions, but also to political advocacy functions of NGOs. This book emphasizes the political advocacy functions and defines civil society as a wide range of nongovernmental, noncommercial organizations outside of official circles that seek to either reinforce or alter existing norms, rules, and social structures.[27] Of particular interest are environmental, labor, women's, development, and human rights groups, and other social movements.

North-North Relations

The second theme of this book concerns relations among advanced industrial states or developed countries (DCs) in the North. As globalization has increased, countries have found it more difficult to manage their economic affairs individually, and they have been inclined to seek regional and global solutions. The DCs in Western Europe, North America, and Japan are the only countries with the wealth and power to look after international management of the global economy. Thus, international management is primarily a North-North issue. This book discusses two factors IPE scholars have focused on as contributing to international economic management: hegemony and international institutions.

Because of its combined economic and military power, the United States was the undisputed leader or *hegemon* in the early post-World War II period. One important measure of economic power is the **gross domestic product (GDP)**, the total value of goods and services produced within a country's borders during a given year. GDP counts income in terms of where it is earned rather than who owns the factors of production. While the GDP includes all the interest and profits foreign individuals and companies earn in a country, it does *not* include the income the country's residents earn abroad. Alternatively, some economists measure a country's total output in terms of its **gross national product (GNP).** The GNP is the total value of goods and services produced by domestically owned factors of production in a given year. In contrast to GDP, GNP counts income according to who owns the factors of production rather than where the income is earned. GNP is derived by adding the income a country's residents earn from foreign activity to the GDP and subtracting the income foreigners earn from activity in the country. For example, the income a U.S. resident earns in France is part of the U.S. GNP but not the U.S. GDP. On the other hand, this income is included in the French GDP but not in the French GNP. It is also necessary to mention a third indicator of total output, the **gross national income (GNI),** because a number of states and international organizations such as the World Bank now use it instead of the GNP. Suffice it to say that *the GNI is equal to the GNP*—it simply measures the income produced by the GNP rather than the value of the product itself.[28]

This book usually uses the term GDP, because it is the best measure of economic activity within a country's borders. However, a country's GDP and GNP (or GNI) normally do not differ greatly, and data are given in terms of all three of these measures, depending on the source of the data. Regardless of whether GDP, GNP, or GNI is used as a measure, the United States was clearly the economic hegemon after World War II. During the war the U.S. GDP had increased by about 50 percent, whereas Western European countries had lost one-quarter of their GDPs on average and the economies of the Soviet Union and Japan were severely damaged. Thus, in 1950 the U.S. GDP was about 3 times larger than the Soviet Union's, 5 times larger than Britain's, and 20 times larger than Japan's. Western Europe and Japan at this time were also highly dependent on U.S. aid and foreign investment for postwar reconstruction.[29]

In the 1950s-60s, the *relative* economic position of the United States vis-à-vis other DCs began to decline as Western Europe and Japan recovered from the war. The extent of the U.S. economic decline and the possibilities for a renewal of U.S. predominance are matters of intense debate. The debate is confused by the fact that IR theorists sometimes focus on different aspects of hegemony. For example, in the *security* area U.S. hegemony has clearly increased since the breakup of the Soviet Union and the decline of the Cold War. However, almost all would agree that U.S. *economic* power relative to the power of other DCs has fallen since the end of World War II. For example, the U.S. dollar continued to be the top currency for international economic transactions, but the Japanese yen and German mark gained in importance, and the Euro emerged as a new currency challenging the dollar; in 1971 the United States shifted from having annual balance-of-trade surpluses to having balance-of-trade deficits (i.e., imports greater than exports); the United States increasingly became a recipient as well as a source of foreign direct investment; and in 1989 Japan surpassed the United States as the largest single donor of development assistance to LDCs. This book examines the effects of the relative U.S. economic decline on global economic management.

The second factor in global management of interest is the role of international institutions. Under U.S. and British leadership, three international economic organizations were established to help manage the global economy at the end of World War II: the IMF, the International Bank for Reconstruction and Development (IBRD or World Bank), and the **General Agreement on Tariffs and Trade (GATT).** Because DCs have been the dominant powers influencing the policies of these organizations, institutional management of the global economy has been largely a North-North issue. This book examines the role of these institutions in the management of the global economy.

Although the DCs have often acted in concert to look after global economic management, there are also significant differences among them. With the demise of the Cold War and the relative decline of U.S. economic hegemony, three major economic blocs have emerged: in Europe, North America, and East Asia. Because much of the world's economic, technological, scientific, and military power is encompassed in these three blocs, the competitiveness among them has major consequences for the future of the global economy.[30] In addition, differences over security issues such as the U.S.-led war against Iraq in March 2003 further exacerbated divisions among the DCs on economic issues. Thus, the second theme of this text relates to both the linkages and divisions among the DCs of the North.

North-South Relations

This book uses the term LDCs to refer to countries in the South that often have colonial histories and low levels of economic and social development. Economically, LDCs generally have low per capita incomes, inadequate infrastructure facilities (e.g., transportation and communications), and limited availability of modern technology. Poorer LDCs have widespread poverty and malnutrition. LDCs' lack of economic resources also limits their ability to foster social development. Thus, many LDCs have limited educational facilities, low literacy rates, and inadequate health and sanitary facilities. Assessing political development in a country is a difficult and contentious issue. However, LDCs are more likely than DCs to have unstable and authoritarian governments.[31] It is important to note that many IOs and development theorists today prefer the term "developing countries" to LDCs because they believe the LDC term suggests that these countries are inferior or are expected to follow the same path to development as the DCs. However, LDCs is used as an abbreviation in this book simply to indicate that these countries are *economically* less-developed. LDCs may have histories and cultures as rich or richer than those of DCs. As this book shows, LDCs are also a very diverse group of countries that do not all follow the same development path.

Some analysts in fact question whether it is meaningful to speak of the South or LDCs as a group of countries with common characteristics in view of the major differences in their levels of income and economic development. On the one hand, the East Asian NIEs—South Korea, Taiwan, Singapore, and Hong Kong—have relatively high per capita incomes and literacy rates, and they are quite competitive with DCs in some areas. On the other hand, the UN list of 49 least developed countries (LLDCs)—mostly in sub-Saharan Africa and South Asia—have extremely low per capita incomes and literacy rates, and formidable economic problems.[32] Despite the disparities in socio-economic development, it is meaningful to generalize about LDC problems because the East Asian NIEs tend to be the exception rather than the rule. Two of the four East Asian NIEs—Singapore and Hong Kong—have a unique status; they are so small geographically that they are more akin to city-states, and Hong Kong was a British crown colony before it was incorporated into mainland China. Furthermore, even some East Asian NIEs have been vulnerable to financial and currency crises in recent years (see Chapter 11). Thus, a major characteristic of the global economy today is the marked inequality in wealth and power between the DCs in the North, and the *great majority* of LDCs in the South.

The South includes almost all the countries of Latin America and the Caribbean, Asia and Oceania, and Africa and the Middle East. In 1950 the South accounted for almost 65 percent of the total world population, and by 1996 the South's population had climbed to almost 80 percent of the world total. A number of previously Communist countries in Eastern Europe and the former Soviet Union are now receiving foreign debt and development financing from the DCs and are in effect also a part of the South. When we speak of the world, we therefore must give a great deal of attention to the South.[33] Although our main concern when discussing international inequality is with the differences between DCs in the North and LDCs in the South, the global economy is also marked by differences in the wealth and power of individuals *within* states. As noted in Chapter 11, some groups within LDCs such as women and children are often in especially disadvantageous positions. (Disparities in wealth of course are also prevalent within DCs.) This book discusses the effects of changes in the global economy, such as the liberalization of trade and financial flows, on inequalities between rich and poor both within states and among states.

The South has relatively little influence in setting the agenda and making decisions regarding the global political economy. This is evident, for example, in important international economic organizations such as the WTO, IMF, and World Bank. Over the years, a variety of strategies have been followed to promote economic development, and the LDCs have also sought to increase their power and influence over international economic issues. Although a relatively small number of LDCs—particularly in East and Southeast Asia and Latin America—have improved their economic positions, the great majority of LDCs have been frustrated in their efforts to promote development and exert more influence. Even among the more successful LDCs in East Asia and Latin America, recent events indicate that their economic progress may be precarious.[34] Thus, the United Nations Development Program reported in 1996 that "the world has become more polarized, and the gulf between the poor and rich of the world has widened even further."[35] This book examines competing views as to why most LDCs continue to be poor and why they continue to have little influence on IPE issues, and it explores the strategies LDCs have employed to promote economic development and increase their influence.

Finally, considerable space is devoted to the emerging economies or former CPEs that are liberalizing as a result of the breakup of the Soviet bloc and Soviet Union. (Chapter 7, for example, discusses the major impact that the foreign debt crisis has had on transition economies as well as LDCs.) Nevertheless, East-West relations is not a major theme of this book because the Cold War has virtually ended, and the former CPEs are becoming increasingly involved in the capitalist global political economy. The more developed transition economies, such as the Czech Republic and Hungary, are approaching the level of development of some DCs in the North, and the poorer transition economies are essentially becoming members of the South.

THE IPE THEORETICAL PERSPECTIVES

Many students tend to avoid "theory," and this seems to be particularly the case in the study of IPE. Without theory, however, we are basically compiling a series of facts, and we are unable to assess the broader implications of these facts for international political and economic relations in general. One might argue that the facts speak for themselves, but in reality a person interprets the facts quite differently depending on whether he or she is viewing them "from a bank office in Zurich, a *maquiladora* [border factory] in Mexico, a shantytown in Peru, a rice paddy in Sri Lanka . . . [or] a trade office in Washington, D.C."[36] Our interpretation of the facts depends on our theoretical views of the world, and the only choice is whether our views remain implicit or whether we explicitly examine the theories we use to interpret issues and events.

A scholar's choice of theoretical perspective also determines which facts he or she chooses to focus on or ignore. For example, theorists writing from the realist perspective place considerable emphasis on the struggle for power in IR, and some realists claim that "power is the essence of politics."[37] Although realists provide many useful insights regarding relations among the most powerful DCs, they normally have little interest in examining the conditions of the poorest and weakest LDCs. Only when LDC entities such as OPEC or the NIEs challenge the predominant position of the North do realists usually take notice. Dependency theorists writing from the historical structuralist perspective, by contrast, devote most of their attention to the conditions of LDCs in the periphery of the global economy. However, they are so concerned with examining the North's exploitation of the South that they often fail to look at purely *domestic* factors in LDCs that interfere with their development.

IPE is a field of study in which scholars apply a wide range of theories and analytical methods. Three theoretical perspectives have been most prominent: the realist, liberal, and historical structuralist perspectives. Realism is the oldest theoretical perspective in both IR and IPE. According to realists, the state is the principal or dominant actor in international politics. Realists view the international system as a "self-help" system without a centralized authority, in which each state must build up its own power to prevent being dominated by other states. Realists also tend to characterize IR as a *zero-sum game,* in which one state's gain is another state's loss. *Relative gains,* or the gains a state achieves in relation to the gains achieved by other states, are therefore extremely important to realists. Each state can be expected to manipulate the market to capture relative gains vis-à-vis other states.

Although realism has been the most important perspective in IR, liberalism is the most important perspective in IPE. To avoid confusion, it is important to note that the term *liberal* is used differently in IPE and in U.S. domestic politics. In the United States, "liberals" support greater government involvement in the market to prevent inequalities and stimulate growth. "Conservatives" in the United States, by contrast, are committed to free markets and minimal intervention by the government. Orthodox liberals in IPE are more akin to U.S. conservatives; they emphasize the importance of free markets and private property rights and favor only a limited government role in economic activities. However, Chapter 4 discusses the fact that some nonorthodox liberals are more accepting of government intervention. Liberals are more optimistic than realists about the prospects for cooperation among states, and they believe that IOs and other international institutions can help promote such cooperation. Thus, in the liberal view economic relationships are a *positive-sum game* in which all states benefit, even if they do not benefit equally.

This book uses the term *historical structuralism* for the third perspective because scholars in this group argue that history has been marked by structural means of exploitation, in which one class dominates another.[38] The main characteristic of the current system is the dominance of capitalist relations of production, with the capitalist class (the bourgeoisie) exploiting the workers (the proletariat). Some historical structuralists, such as dependency and world-systems theorists, focus on the exploitation of LDCs in the periphery by advanced capitalist states in the core of the global economy. Unlike liberals and realists, who generally support the capitalist system, historical structuralists typically advocate a transformation to socialism as the key to an end to exploitation.

Becoming familiar with realism, liberalism, and historical structuralism is an important starting point in developing alternative lenses for viewing the substantive issue areas (such as trade and monetary relations) in IPE. However, the field of IPE is not neatly divided into these three perspectives for several reasons. First, the margins separating these perspectives have become blurred as they have evolved and influenced each other over time. Second, some of the most important IPE theoretical approaches, such as regime theory and hegemonic stability theory, are hybrid theories that draw on more than one of the three perspectives. Third, much of the recent literature examining the relationship between domestic institutions and IPE does not fit easily into any one of the three traditional perspectives. In addition to the three main theoretical perspectives, this book looks at the hybrid theories and at domestic-international interactions. For example, the chapters in Part III discuss the fact that major decisions and events in monetary relations, trade, foreign investment, and international development are affected by domestic as well as international interests and developments. Finally, some perspectives of growing importance such as constructivist, feminist, and environmentalist perspectives are not adequately covered by the three traditional perspectives. After developing a solid background in the three main IPE perspectives, the student is encouraged to examine the more varied range of perspectives in the field.[39]

A growing range of theoretical perspectives and approaches are used in the study of IPE. Some social scientists view this diversity as an indication of our failure to develop an all-embracing theory. However, the existence of different perspectives and theories should not be viewed as a weakness. Social science theory "is always *for* someone and *for* some purpose,"[40] and because the three major IPE perspectives are based on different sets of values, it is unlikely that they will ever be entirely compatible. The three IPE perspectives have differing interpretations of the main themes in this book relating to globalization, North-North relations, and North-South relations. In regard to the first theme, realists emphasize the importance of the nation-state and question whether significant globalization is in fact occurring; liberals believe there is a significant level of globalization, which they view as a positive development; and historical structuralists also believe globalization is significant, but they believe this has negative consequences for lower classes and LDCs in the periphery of the global economy. In regard to the second theme, liberals are far more inclined than realists or historical structuralists to argue that international institutions can play an important role in promoting international economic cooperation. In regard to the third theme, historical structuralists place more emphasis than liberals or realists on inequalities between the North and the South and on the North's exploitation of the South.

FOCUS OF THIS BOOK

This book introduces undergraduate students and beginning graduate students to the study of IPE. Several distinguishing features of the book have already been discussed. First, it provides an in-depth background to IPE theory, a discussion of current IPE issues in historical perspective, and an examination of the interplay of theory and practice. Without the organizing framework of theory, discussions about trade, foreign investment, development, and other substantive IPE issues simply become a series of disparate facts. Second, the book focuses on three major themes relating to globalization, North-North relations, and North-South relations.

Third, this book emphasizes the role of international economic organizations such as the WTO, IMF, and World Bank in the management of the global political economy. It also devotes considerable attention to important regional organizations such as the EU, NAFTA, and the Southern Common Market Treaty (Mercosur). Most IPE textbooks devote some space to IOs, but the coverage is very limited and unsystematic. This is a reflection of the lack of emphasis on IOs in the field of IR in general. Early scholarship on IOs had a strong idealistic and legal focus on the bodies, rules, and procedures in the League of Nations and then the UN. Post-World War II realists understandably felt that these legalistic studies provided little information about the real world of power politics, and they turned away from the study of IOs. In recent years, however, a number of scholars have recognized the importance of studying IOs as part of, rather than divorced from, the realities of international politics. It is especially important that we devote more attention to IOs in the case of IPE, where the WTO, IMF, World Bank, EU, NAFTA, and other organizations have significant roles.[41]

This book does *not* attempt to glorify IOs, and it discusses their limitations and problems as well as their possibilities. IOs are to a considerable degree creatures of the states that created them, even though IO leaders have some leeway in formulating objectives and conducting operations. Furthermore, IOs are having great difficulty managing the international economy in an age of globalization. Indeed, the total resources of the UN, World Bank, and IMF are far smaller than the daily flows of foreign exchange on global markets. Despite their limitations, IOs often serve as important fora for negotiation, and they assist in upholding critical principles, norms, and rules of the global political economy.

A fourth emphasis of this book is on regional as well as global relations in IPE. Most IPE texts focus almost exclusively on global issues and contain no systematic discussion of trends toward regionalism. Yet these trends are inevitably affecting the management of the global political economy, and this book therefore devotes a full chapter to regionalism and globalism in trade. With the formation of NAFTA, "the trade and economic relations of the two largest markets in world trade—the European Community and the United States—are increasingly conditioned by regional agreements."[42] LDCs have also been establishing their own regional trade agreements, and two of the largest South American countries, Brazil and Argentina, are members of Mercosur. In Asia, APEC (which includes Japan and China as well as the United States) has a goal of establishing a free and open trade and investment arena for DC members by 2010 and for LDC members by 2020. Regionalism of course affects other areas in addition to trade, and Part III devotes some attention to regional trends in the chapters on monetary relations, foreign investment, and international development. This book focuses mainly on the *relationship between* regionalism and globalism in the international economy.

A fifth focus of this book is on North-South issues. Instead of discussing these issues in a separate section, the book integrates the North-North and North-South discussions as much as possible for several reasons. The three main theoretical perspectives should be assessed in terms of their approach to IPE as it relates to *all* countries, both rich and poor. Chapters 3 through 5 therefore discuss each perspective's approach to North-South as well as North-North issues. The historical structuralist perspective (discussed in Chapter 5) focuses almost exclusively on the weaker and exploited classes and countries, and an adequate examination of it necessarily includes a discussion of the South. Part III also integrates the discussion of North-North and North-South relations because the process of globalization in trade, foreign investment, and monetary relations is affecting all areas of the globe. Two chapters are largely devoted to the South. Chapter 7 on the foreign debt and financial crises deals with issues that affected LDCs, but even this chapter includes a discussion of Eastern Europe and the FSU. Chapter 11 is devoted to a detailed discussion of alternative strategies to promote LDC development.

Sixth, this book provides substantial coverage of the emerging states of Eastern Europe, the FSU, and China. These countries are undergoing a transition from CPEs to more market-oriented economies, which has often been a difficult process. As part of this change, they are establishing closer economic ties with the advanced industrial states and becoming more active members of international economic organizations. The transition CPEs are discussed along with other countries in Part III. Finally, although this book of necessity focuses almost wholly on the many facets of IPE, some attention is given to discussing linkages between international security and economic issues. Recent events such as the end of the Cold War and the terrorist attacks on New York's World Trade Center have highlighted the degree to which security and economic issues can be closely intertwined.

In summary, political leaders and IR scholars have devoted much more attention to international economic issues in recent years, particularly since the decline of the Cold War. This book focuses on the major theoretical perspectives and substantive issues in IPE and on the interaction between theory and practice. To assess some of the changes occurring in the international economy, we focus on three major themes: globalization, North-North relations, and North-South relations. Chapter 2 provides an overview of the historical development of the global political economy, with an emphasis on the development of post-World War II institutions. Chapters 3 through 5 discuss the basic assumptions and historical evolution of the three main IPE theoretical perspectives and examine how each perspective approaches North-South as well as North-North relations. Chapters 6 through 11 cover monetary relations, foreign debt and financial crises, global trade, trade regionalism, MNCs, and international development.

NOTES

1. Preamble to *Treaty Establishing the European Coal and Steel Community*, Paris, April 18, 1951 (London: Her Majesty's Stationery Office, 1972).
2. International Bank for Reconstruction and Development, *Articles of Agreement* as amended effective February 16, 1989 (Washington, DC: World Bank, August 1991), Article 4, section 10.
3. Andrew Shonfield, *The Attack on World Poverty* (New York: Random House, 1960), p.147. On the World Bank's political leanings see David A. Baldwin, "The International Bank in Political Perspective," *World Politics* 18 (October 1965), pp.68–81; Theodore H. Cohn, "Politics in the World Bank: The Question of Loans to the Asian Giants," *International Organization* 28-3 (Summer 1974), pp.561–571; and Luiz Carlos Bresser Pereira, "Development Economics and the World Bank's Identity Crisis," *Review of International Political Economy* 2-2 (Spring 1995), pp.211–247.
4. "Boeing v. Airbus," *The Economist*, July 26, 1997, pp.59–61; "Asleep in Seattle? Airbus and Boeing," *The Economist*, January 18, 2003, pp. 63–64. The Boeing-Airbus dispute highlights U.S.-EU differences over legal and economic approaches. See Eric J. Stock, "Explaining the Differing U.S. and EU Positions on the Boeing/McDonnell-Douglas Merger: Avoiding Another Near-Miss," *University of Pennsylvania Journal of International Economic Law* 20-4 (Winter 1999), pp.825–909.
5. Henry Kissinger, *White House Years* (Boston: Little, Brown and Company, 1979), p.950.
6. Robert Gilpin, with Jean M. Gilpin, *The Political Economy of International Relations* (Princeton: Princeton University Press, 1987), pp.8–11. State-market tensions are reflected in some IPE book titles such as Robert Boyer and Daniel Drache, eds., *States Against Markets: The Limits of Globalization* (London: Routledge, 1996); and Herman M. Schwartz, *States Versus Markets: The Emergence of a Global Economy*, 2nd ed., (New York: St. Martin's Press, 2000).
7. Philip G. Cerny, *The Changing Architecture of Politics: Structure, Agency and the Future of the State* (London: Sage, 1990), pp.228–229.
8. Lorraine Eden, "Bringing the Firm Back in: Multinationals in International Political Economy," in Lorraine Eden and Evan H. Potter, eds., *Multinationals in the Global Political Economy* (New York: St. Martin's Press, 1993), pp.25–26; Stephen D. Krasner, "Power Politics, Institutions, and Transnational Relations," in Thomas Risse-Kappen, ed., *Bringing Transnational Relations Back In: Non-State Actors, Domestic Structures and International Institutions* (Cambridge: Cambridge University Press, 1995), pp.277–279; Wyn Grant, "Perspectives on Globalization and Economic Coordination," in J. Rogers Hollingsworth, ed., *Contemporary Capitalism: The Embeddedness of Institutions* (Cambridge: Cambridge University Press, 1997), pp.322–325.
9. Richard K. Ashley, "Three Modes of Economism," *International Studies Quarterly* 27-4 (December 1983), p.463; Colin Hay and David Marsh, "Introduction: Towards a New (International) Political Economy?," *New Political Economy* 4-1 (1999), pp.9–10.
10. Michael Mastanduno, David A. Lake, and G. John Ikenberry, "Toward a Realist Theory of State Action," *International Studies Quarterly* 33-4 (December 1989), p.458.
11. Thucydides, *The History of the Peloponnesian War*, translated by Richard Crawley (London: Dent & Sons, Everyman's Library, 1910), p.41.
12. Martin Staniland, *What Is Political Economy? A Study of Social Theory and Underdevelopment* (New Haven: Yale University Press, 1985), p.11; Aristotle, *Politics*, translated by Benjamin Jowett (New York: Modern Library, 1943).

13. Postwar IR scholars were more inclined than government officials to differentiate between high and low politics. See Richard N. Cooper, "Trade Policy Is Foreign Policy," *Foreign Policy* 9 (Winter 1972–73), p.18.

14. Some scholars called for greater emphasis on the study of IPE from an early period. See Klaus Knorr, "Economics and International Relations: A Problem in Teaching," *Political Science Quarterly* 62-4 (December 1947), p.560; Susan Strange, "International Economics and International Relations: A Case of Mutual Neglect," *International Affairs* 46 (April 1970), p.307; and Christopher Brown, "International Political Economy: Some Problems of an Interdisciplinary Enterprise," *International Affairs* 49-1 (January 1973), p.52.

15. Michael Mastanduno, "Economics and Security in Statecraft and Scholarship," *International Organization* 52–4 (Autumn 1998), p.853. See also James A. Caporaso, "False Divisions: Security Studies and Global Political Economy," *Mershon International Studies Review* 39-1 (April 1995), pp.117–122.

16. See, for example, International Monetary Fund, *World Economic Outlook—December 2001: The Global Economy After September 11* (Washington, D.C.: IMF, 2001).

17. Mastanduno, "Economics and Security in Statecraft and Scholarship," p.853.

18. See Jan Aart Scholte, *Globalization: A Critical Introduction* (New York: St. Martin's Press, 2000).

19. United Nations Development Program (UNDP), *Human Development Report—1997* (New York: Oxford University Press, 1997), p.83.

20. See Aseem Prakash and Jeffrey A. Hart, "Globalization and Governance: An Introduction," in Aseem Prakash and Jeffrey A. Hart, eds., *Globalization and Governance* (London: Routledge, 1999), pp.4–17.

21. Paul Hirst and Grahame Thompson, *Globalization in Question: The International Economy and the Possibilities of Governance* (Cambridge: Polity Press, 1996), ch. 1; Kenichi Ohmae, *The Borderless World: Power and Strategy in the Interlinked Economy* (New York: Harper Perennial, 1990).

22. Philip G. Cerny, "Globalization and Other Stories: The Search for a New Paradigm for International Relations," *International Journal* 51-4 (Autumn 1996), pp.617–637; Ethan B. Kapstein, *Governing the Global Market: International Finance and the State* (Cambridge: Harvard University Press, 1994), p.7.

23. For a historical discussion of globalization see Paul Bairoch, "Globalization Myths and Realities: One Century of External Trade and Foreign Investment," in Boyer and Drache, eds., *States Against Markets,* pp.173–192. Hirst and Thompson question how extensive globalization is today in *Globalization in Question.*

24. UNDP, *Human Development Report 1997*, p.83.

25. John H. Dunning, *Multinational Enterprises and the Global Economy* (Wokingham: Addison-Wesley, 1993), pp.14–15.

26. Russia is not yet a WTO member, but it is actively seeking to join.

27. Jan Aart Scholte with Robert O'Brien and Marc Williams, "The WTO and Civil Society," *Journal of World Trade* 33-1 (February 1999), p.109; David Robertson, "Civil Society and the WTO," *World Economy* 23-9 (September 2000), p.1121–1123.

28. For a discussion of the GNP and GNI, see Organization for Economic Cooperation and Development, *System of National Accounts, 1993—Glossary* (Paris: OECD, 2000), p.23; World Bank, *World Development Report — 2003* (Washington, D.C.: World Bank, 2003), pp.233 and 245.

29. Joseph S. Nye, Jr., *Bound to Lead: The Changing Nature of American Power* (New York: Basic Books, 1990), p.70.

30. See Lester Thurow, *Head to Head: The Coming Economic Battle Among Japan, Europe, and America* (New York: Morrow, 1992).

31. Howard Handelman, *The Challenge of Third World Development* (Upper Saddle River: Prentice-Hall, 1996), pp.3–10.

32. See United Nations Conference on Trade and Development (UNCTAD), *The Least Developed Countries, Annual Reports* (New York: United Nations).

33. Mike Mason, *Development and Disorder: A History of the Third World Since 1945* (Toronto: Between the Lines, 1997), p.1.

34. See "South-East Asia Loses Its Grip," *The Economist,* July 19, 1997, p.15; and Edward A. Gargan, "Currency Assault Unnerves Asians," *New York Times,* July 29, 1997, pp.A1, C15.

35. UNDP, *Human Development Report 1996* (New York: Oxford University Press, 1996), p.2.

36. James A. Caporaso, "Global Political Economy," in Ada Finifter, ed., *Political Science: The State of the Discipline II* (Washington, DC: American Political Science Association, 1993), p.451.

37. Hans J. Morgenthau, revised by Kenneth W. Thompson, *Politics Among Nations: The Struggle for Power and Peace,* 6th ed. (New York: Knopf, 1985), p.10.

38. The term *historical structuralism* emerged in discussions with a colleague, James Busumtwi-Sam, for which I am grateful.

39. See Ronen Palan, ed., *Global Political Economy: Contemporary Theories* (London: Routledge, 2000).

40. Robert W. Cox, "Social Forces, States and World Orders: Beyond International Theory," *Millennium* 10-2 (1981), p.128. See also Roger Tooze, "Perspectives and Theory: A Consumer's Guide," in Susan Strange, ed., *Paths to International Political Economy* (London: Allen & Unwin, 1984), pp.3–4.

41. For a discussion of the inadequate attention given to IOs, see J. Martin Rochester, "The Rise and Fall of International Organization as a Field of Study," *International Organization* 40-4 (Autumn 1986), pp.777–813; Pierre de Senarclens, "Regime Theory and the Study of International Organizations," *International Social Science Journal* 45-138 (November 1993), pp.453–462; and J. Martin Rochester, "The United Nations in a New World Order: Reviving the Theory and Practice of International Organization," in Charles W. Kegley, Jr., ed., *Controversies in International Relations Theory: Realism and the Neoliberal Challenge* (New York: St. Martin's Press, 1995), pp.199–221.

42. World Trade Organization, *Regionalism and the World Trading System* (Geneva: WTO, April 1995), p.27.

Managing the Global Economy Since World War II: The Institutional Framework

After three years of preliminary negotiations, delegates from 44 countries met in July 1944 in Bretton Woods, New Hampshire, to convene the United Nations Monetary and Financial Conference, also known as the Bretton Woods conference. Within 22 days, the delegates endorsed agreements to institute a framework for international economic cooperation after World War II. These Bretton Woods agreements marked "the first successful attempt consciously undertaken by a large group of nations to shape and control their economic relations."[1] The Bretton Woods conference led directly to the establishment of two new international economic organizations—the IMF and IBRD or World Bank. Several years later, GATT was to become the main global trade organization. These three organizations became part of a complex institutional framework to help manage the postwar global economy.

The critical negotiations preceding the Bretton Woods conference, and the conference itself, were in fact "very much an Anglo-American affair, with Canada playing a useful mediating role."[2] Other major countries had less important roles in the conference or did not even attend the meetings: Although a French delegation participated in the conference, France was still occupied by Germany at the time of Bretton Woods; Germany, Italy, and Japan, as enemy countries, were not represented; and the Soviet Union had only a limited role in the conference and did not sign the final agreements. Twenty-seven LDCs were present (19 of them Latin American), but their role was marginal. The chief conference planners were Harry Dexter White of the U.S. Treasury and John Maynard Keynes of Britain. Although the delegates had some fundamental differences of outlook, they generally agreed on the type of institutional order required for the postwar period. They particularly wanted to avoid a repetition of the disastrous events of the interwar period, when increased exchange controls and trade protectionism had contributed to the Great Depression of the 1930s and to World War II itself. Although this chapter focuses on global economic management after World War II, it first provides some historical background on global economic relations in earlier periods.

Global Economic Relations Before World War II

The substantive chapters in this text begin with some historical background on each issue area such as trade and monetary relations. This section simply identifies important historical benchmarks, including the mercantilist period, the Industrial Revolution and British hegemony, the decline of British hegemony and World War I, and the interwar period. It also discusses the institutional framework established from 1815 to World War II to deal with international economic issues.

The Mercantilist Period

The origins of IPE are closely associated with the development of the modern European state system and its global markets.[3] The modern European state gained official recognition at the 1648 Treaty of Westphalia, marking the end of the Thirty Years War during which mostly Protestant countries in Northern Europe defeated the Catholic Hapsburg countries. The Peace of Westphalia institutionalized changes that had been occurring for at least 150 years by upholding the sovereignty and territorial integrity of states. The Westphalian view of each state as an equal and independent member of the international system legitimized the idea that external religious and secular authorities (e.g., the Pope, Holy Roman Emperor, and other states) should not interfere in a state's internal affairs.

A major factor contributing to the establishment of central state authority vis-à-vis internal and external forces was the development of **mercantilism.** The term mercantilism was first used by Adam Smith, an eighteenth century economist, in reference to much of the economic thought and practice in Europe from about 1500 to 1750.[4] (As discussed later, Smith as a liberal economist strongly criticized the mercantilists.) Mercantilists were acutely aware of the linkage between politics and economics; they believed that power and wealth were closely related, and that both were legitimate goals of national policy. In the mercantilist view, a state's power depended on the amount of gold and silver it could accumulate in the public treasury. With these precious metals, the state could build up its armed forces, hire mercenaries, and influence its enemies and allies. Mercantilist states therefore took all necessary measures to accumulate gold and silver by increasing their exports and decreasing their imports. They increased exports of manufactured goods and restricted exports of raw materials and technology to limit the ability of others to develop their own manufacturing capabilities. They also limited imports of manufactured goods, and only imported raw materials that would reduce costs for their own manufacturers.

Colonialism was an integral part of mercantilism, with the colonies providing the metropole with revenues and raw materials for processing, and serving as markets for the metropole's manufactures. Thus, the metropole prohibited manufacturing in the colonies. Liberals such as Smith strongly criticized mercantilists for following beggar-thy-neighbor policies that would inevitably lead to international conflict because it is impossible for all states to have a balance-of-trade surplus (i.e., more exports than imports).[5] Nevertheless, mercantilism served an important function in building up state authority and territorial unification through its emphasis on national power. The establishment of the sovereign European state system in turn was a major factor contributing to the development of the global political economy.[6]

Although sovereignty at least in principle gives states supreme authority within their own territory, there is a pecking order in which some states are more powerful than others. A number of scholars have examined the role of successive dominant or *hegemonic* powers in leading the international system, and in Chapter 3 we discuss and critique hegemonic stability theory, which many scholars have applied to the study of IPE. Some scholars have examined the role of "world powers," including Portugal, Spain, the Netherlands, and Britain, during the mercantilist period. However, there is considerable debate as to which (if any) of these countries were dominant enough to be considered hegemonic.[7] Most hegemonic stability theorists maintain that only two global hegemons have existed, both of them after the mercantilist period: Britain in the nineteenth century and the United States in the twentieth century.

The Industrial Revolution and British Hegemony

Mercantilism as the term is used in this book, is a preindustrial doctrine. The Industrial Revolution enhanced "the position of a country [Britain] already made supremely successful in the preindustrial, mercantilist struggles of the eighteenth century," and transformed "it into a different sort of power."[8] The Industrial Revolution was a gradual process that began about 1780, affected only some manufactures and means of production, and progressed from region to region rather than involving entire countries. Nevertheless, Britain was basically the first country to industrialize, and this helps explain why it became a hegemonic power in the nineteenth century. By 1860 Britain accounted for about 37 percent of total European industrial production and for 20 percent of world industrial production. In view of its lead in technology, about 80 percent of newer technology industries were located in Britain.[9]

Britain's competitive edge, combined with domestic changes, caused it to alter its mercantilist policies and shift toward free trade. By the 1830s Britain had removed most of its industrial trade restrictions, but it continued to impose barriers to agricultural trade. In 1846 Britain finally abolished its *Corn Laws*, which restricted agricultural imports, and this decision contributed to an extended period of free trade during the nineteenth century.[10] Both domestic and external factors accounted for Britain's agricultural trade liberalization. Domestically, legislative and demographic changes caused industrial groups to gain in representation vis-à-vis landed agricultural groups in the British Parliament. Because the agricultural elite's influence in Parliament declined, it was unable to prevent the repeal of the Corn Laws. Externally, Britain opened its markets to agricultural and raw material imports so foreign countries would accept its manufactured goods. The resultant division of labor, in which Britain specialized in industrial exports, clearly served its hegemonic interests. Britain's hegemony resulted partly from the fact that its import market was large enough to cause others to orient their production in line with British preferences. In addition to the repeal of the Corn Laws, another free-trade landmark was the 1860 *Cobden-Chevalier Treaty* between Britain and France, which resulted in a network of commercial treaties lowering tariff barriers throughout Europe.[11]

The Decline of British Hegemony and World War I

By the late nineteenth century, industrial protectionism on the European continent, depressed economic conditions, and a decline of British hegemony in trade and industrial production slowed the growth of trade liberalization. Major Western European states abandoned free trade during the 1870s-80s, and after 1890 even Britain turned increasingly to its colonial markets. Britain's share of world trade fell from 24 percent in 1870 to 14.1 percent in 1913, whereas Germany's share rose from 9.7 to 12.2 percent and the U.S. share rose from 8.8 to 11.1 percent. In view of its declining export competitiveness, Britain was less able to serve as a market of last resort for other countries' exports.[12] Britain's decreased trade competitiveness resulted largely from the relative decline of its productivity vis-à-vis its two main competitors: the United States and Germany. Banks and the state (including U.S. state governments) played a significant role in promoting U.S. and German productivity through investment in infrastructure such as railroads and canals and in industrial production, and the two countries used trade protectionism to build up their infant industries so they could challenge British industry in global markets.[13] By 1913, on the eve of World War I, the United States had become the largest industrial power, accounting for about 32 percent of world industrial output.[14]

Despite Britain's decline in trade and industrial power, it continued to dominate in international finance until World War I. The city of London was the main center of the international financial system, the British pound was the international currency, and in 1913 the British accounted for $19.5 billion or about 43 percent of the world's foreign investment.[15] World War I marked "the shift in financial preeminence from London to New York," and hastened Britain's decline as a hegemonic power.[16] The war increased Britain's foreign liabilities, marked the emergence of the United States as a net creditor for the first time, and further disrupted the prewar trade and monetary regimes that Britain had helped to maintain.

The Interwar Period

The United States emerged from World War I as the world's largest industrial power and the only major net creditor nation. Although it lent about $10 billion to cash-short countries during the 1920s, some U.S. policies did not facilitate a return to an open, liberal economy. As the largest creditor nation in the interwar period, the United States initially insisted that European states repay all their war debts, even though this added to their financial problems. Britain and France had the largest war debts to the United States, amounting to almost $5 billion and more than $4 billion, respectively (before interest multiplied the totals).[17] The United States also imposed trade barriers during this period, which made it difficult for the Europeans to gain needed revenues from exports. The U.S. Congress responded to a recession with the Fordney-McCumber Act of 1922, which raised customs duties on agricultural and other products. When the U.S. economy moved into depression after the 1929 stock market crash, Congress passed the 1930 Smoot-Hawley Act, which increased U.S. tariffs to their highest level in the twentieth century.[18] European countries rushed to retaliate with their own import restrictions, and world trade declined from $35 billion in 1929 to $12 billion in 1933.[19]

The disastrous experience of the interwar period resulted partly from a lack of economic leadership, and hegemonic stability theorists argue that a global hegemon increases the likelihood that there will be a more stable, open international economy. According to these theorists, Britain was the global hegemon in the nineteenth century. During the interwar period, however, Britain was no longer able, and the United States was not yet willing, to assume the hegemonic duties of promoting freer trade and an open, stable economic system.[20] (Debates over the validity of hegemonic stability theory are discussed in Chapter 3.) Other theorists argue that domestic politics was a major factor explaining the economic disarray and conflict. For example, the U.S. policy-making system contributed to the rise in U.S. tariffs despite the growing economic power of the United States. The U.S. Constitution gives Congress authority to regulate foreign commerce, but Congress is a large, unwieldy body subject to special interests, and it was unable to resist constituent demands for greater protection.[21]

In efforts to reverse the damage caused by the increased trade restrictions, the U.S. Congress passed the *Reciprocal Trade Agreements Act (RTAA)* in 1934. The RTAA delegated tariff-setting policy to the president, who could resist the pressures of special interests and negotiate a reduction in tariffs more effectively than Congress. Despite the RTAA, however, the United States was not yet willing to "adopt the policies of a hegemonic leader," and "protection at home remained an important goal of American trade strategy."[22] Thus, the RTAA reflected a U.S. conviction that lower tariffs abroad and an ability to bargain bilaterally for these reductions would help restore U.S. export markets. The RTAA resulted in a number of U.S. bilateral trade agreements with other countries, but tariff rates were so high in the early 1930s that these agreements were not sufficient to stem the forces of trade protectionism.

The Institutional Framework Before World War II

European states established most of the IOs formed from 1815 to 1914, and Europeans were the main members of these organizations. Most IOs created during this period had economic objectives: to promote economic regulation, facilitate commerce, and take advantage of technological innovations. The first permanent functional intergovernmental organization of the modern era was the Central Commission for the Navigation of the Rhine, created in 1815 during the Congress of Vienna to maximize the use of the river for commerce. To gain commercial advantages from the technological innovation of the steamship, the Commission sought to ensure that states did not interfere with the free flow of traffic on the Rhine. The invention of the telegraph led to the creation of the International Telegraph Union in 1865, and the Universal Postal Union was established in 1874 to promote speed and efficiency in postal deliveries.[23]

After World War I, the League of Nations Covenant (Article 23e) called on member states to "make provision to secure and maintain freedom of communications and of transit and equitable treatment for the commerce of all Members of the League."[24] Thus, IOs continued to facilitate transportation, communications, and commerce. The first financial IO was also established in the interwar period (in 1930): the **Bank for International Settlements (BIS).** Located in Basle, Switzerland, the BIS was formed to oversee the settlement of German reparations after World War I. The main purpose of the BIS, however, was to promote cooperation among central banks in developing financial policies. (The BIS is discussed in Chapter 6.)[25]

Other than the BIS, economic IOs in the interwar period were mainly concerned with promoting international *coordination,* or the standardization of basic facilities, equipment, and installations required for the functioning and growth of the global economy. These organizations were ill equipped to deal directly with major economic problems such as the Great Depression. As economic differences increased in the 1920s–1930s, several conferences were convened in efforts to jointly confront trade and financial problems. For example, an international conference in Genoa, Italy in 1922 called on central banks to cooperate in managing currency exchange rates and to use currencies such as the pound sterling that were convertible into gold. However, these conferences failed to resolve the central problems related to war reparations and debt, disorderly exchange conditions among currencies, and a decline in world trade. When the gold exchange standard regime collapsed, the 1933 world economic and monetary conference in London failed to reach agreement on a dollar-sterling rate of exchange. (The gold exchange standard is discussed in Chapter 6.) It was not until 1936 that Britain, the United States, and France reached a tripartite agreement to recognize international responsibility for exchange rates.[26] This experience demonstrated that permanent international economic organizations promoting *collaboration* as well as coordination were needed to support open and stable economic relations after World War II. The IMF, World Bank, and GATT were established to promote collaboration in the areas of monetary, financial, and trade relations.[27]

THE FUNCTIONS OF THE **IMF, WORLD BANK,** AND **GATT**

In contrast to the interwar period, the United States emerged as a more mature power at the end of World War II, both willing and able to assume a leadership position. In addition, the major powers established an institutional framework to help prevent a recurrence of the interwar problems. Although some writers refer to the IMF, World Bank, and GATT as Bretton Woods institutions, GATT was in fact established several years after the Bretton Woods conference. This book refers to these three IOs as *keystone international economic organizations (KIEOs)* because of their central role in international finance, trade, and monetary relations.[28]

The IMF was created to support international monetary stability and the elimination of currency exchange restrictions. To promote monetary stability, the IMF monitored a system of fixed or pegged exchange rates, in which currencies were given official exchange rates in relation to gold and the U.S. dollar. The pegged exchange rate system was designed to avoid the competitive devaluation of currencies which had led to trade wars during the interwar period. **Devaluation** refers to a reduction in the official rate at which one currency is exchanged for another. When a country devalues its currency, its imported goods and services become more expensive, and its exports become less expensive to foreigners. Countries with **balance of payments** deficits (i.e., with more money leaving than entering the country) are inclined to devalue their currencies to increase their export revenue. The IMF was authorized to provide short-term loans to help countries deal with temporary balance-of-payments deficits and maintain the **fixed exchange rates** of their currencies.

The IBRD or World Bank was created to provide long-term loans (unlike the IMF's short-term loans) for postwar reconstruction in Europe and economic development in LDCs. The Bank, like the IMF, sought to prevent problems that had occurred in the interwar period. After World War I, the cost of servicing war debts and stimulating economic recovery had contributed to economic tension and conflict. To prevent a recurrence of these problems after World War II, the Bank provided long-term loans for postwar reconstruction and development. GATT was designed to lower countries' tariffs in multilateral negotiations so they could not use protectionist trade barriers as they had during the interwar period. In addition to providing a forum for trade negotiations, GATT established rules for conducting international trade relations and developed procedures for settling members' trade disputes.

Because the IMF, the Bank, and GATT were established partly to avoid problems of an earlier period (the interwar years), the functions of these institutions inevitably evolved as changes occured after World War II. For example, European reconstruction proved to be a larger task than originally anticipated, and the United States established the European Recovery Program (the Marshall Plan) in 1948 to give **bilateral aid** to Western Europe. As a result, the Bank played only a minor role in European reconstruction and shifted its attention almost completely to providing loans for economic development. As for the IMF, it lost one of its main functions when the fixed-exchange-rate system for currencies collapsed in the early 1970s and was replaced by **floating exchange rates.** However, the IMF's profile increased again in the early 1980s when it became the lead international agency for the foreign debt crisis, which began when Mexico threatened to default on its loans in 1982 (see Chapter 7). The Bank also provides finance to LDC foreign debtors, and recipients of IMF and Bank loans include countries in Eastern Europe and the FSU.

GATT was created under special circumstances, and to understand its evolution it is necessary to be aware of its origins. Negotiations were held for several years after the Bretton Woods conference to create an international trade organization (ITO) comparable in strength to the IMF and the Bank. However, trade is one of the most sensitive economic issues, and the U.S. Congress refused to support the formation of the ITO (see Chapter 8). As a result, the "temporary" GATT, signed by 23 governments in 1947 to initiate postwar trade negotiations, became the main global trade organization by default. Because GATT was designed to be only a provisional treaty, it never became a fully developed IO. Indeed, countries joining GATT became contracting parties rather than formal members of the agreement (this book uses the term *GATT members* for the sake of brevity). Despite its humble origins, GATT was quite effective for a number of years in liberalizing trade. However, members were able to circumvent a number of GATT regulations, the GATT dispute settlement system was weak, and GATT was not well equipped to deal with many new areas of trade. In January 1995 GATT was superseded by a new WTO, a full-fledged IO. Unlike GATT, the WTO deals not only with trade in goods, but also with trade in services, intellectual property rights, and trade-related investment measures.

INTERNATIONAL ECONOMIC ORGANIZATIONS AND THE UNITED NATIONS

Figure 2.1 shows that the IMF and the Bank are specialized agencies theoretically under the UN Economic and Social Council (ECOSOC), which is one of the six principal organs of the UN. When the WTO was established in 1995, the members decided it should not be a specialized agency.[29] Thus, the WTO is listed as a related organization in Figure 2.1, and does not report to the ECOSOC. As Figure 2.1 shows, the Bank today is in fact a **World Bank group** of five institutions (see Chapter 11).

Although the IMF and the Bank are specialized agencies, the UN in fact has little authority over them—and the same applies to the WTO. The UN signed an agreement with the Bank when it was formed (and a similar agreement with the IMF), acknowledging that "it would be sound policy to refrain from making recommendations to the Bank with respect to particular loans or with respect to terms or conditions of financing."[30] The UN General Assembly has on occasion tried to influence World Bank lending decisions, but it has been largely unsuccessful.[31] A major reason for the lack of UN leverage is that the IMF and the Bank are more financially sound than the UN. In September 1995 the UN even indicated it might try to borrow money from the Bank to deal with its deficits, but some major UN member states vetoed this idea. Chapters 6 and 11 discuss the IMF and the Bank weighted voting systems in which the rich Northern states have the most votes. This contrasts with the one-nation, one-vote system of many UN bodies. Because the DCs prefer weighted voting, they have directed most of their funding for multilateral economic management away from the UN and toward the IMF and the Bank.[32]

Although the KIEOs generally act independently of the UN, UN bodies have sometimes induced them to revise their policies and adopt new programs. Examples include the UN's role in the Bank's creation of a soft-loan agency (see Chapter 11), the IMF's establishment of a compensatory financing facility (see Chapter 6), and the IMF and Bank decisions to introduce human and social dimensions in their lending programs. The Bank has also cooperated with a number of UN bodies in providing development assistance.[33]

POSTWAR ECONOMIC INSTITUTIONS AND THE NORTH

The North's role in the global political economy is marked by three main characteristics, which are also evident in the management of the KIEOs. First, the United States continues to be the most powerful single state, but its economic hegemony is gradually giving way to a three-way predominance by a *triad* composed of North America, Western Europe, and Japan-East Asia. (The chapters in Part III demonstrate how influential the triad is in substantive IPE areas.) Second, the DC-led triad is responsible for the largest share of international economic transactions today, including foreign investment, trade in manufactures and services, and **capital** flows. For example, in 1995 the DCs were the largest source *and* the largest recipients of foreign direct investment (FDI), accounting for 92.1 percent of outward stocks and 71.9 percent of inward stocks of FDI. In 1995, North America, Western Europe, and Asia also accounted for almost 93 percent of world exports of manufactures and for 89.3 percent of world exports of commercial services.[34]

The third characteristic is that countries within the triad conduct most of their international economic transactions with each other, and their trade and investment flows with other parts of the world are relatively small. U.S. MNCs have shown a strong preference for investing in Europe, intra-European investment has accelerated, and Japan and Western European countries have invested heavily in the United States. Thus, the DCs occupy the dominant position in the global political economy. Although LDCs and emerging countries of Eastern Europe and the FSU are increasing their linkages with the DCs, they continue to occupy peripheral economic positions.

The IMF, World Bank, and WTO

In view of their role in global economic transactions, DCs have the most influence in determining the agenda and operations of the KIEOs. For example, DCs provide most of the funding for IMF and Bank loans and have the most votes in these weighted-voting institutions. The five countries with the largest number of votes in the IMF and the Bank are the United States, Japan, Germany, France, and Britain. Although the WTO has a one-nation, one-vote system, the major trading nations, which are mainly DCs, have the largest role in setting the agenda in multilateral trade negotiations. Northern dominance in these institutions is also evident from the nationalities of their chief executive officers. By tacit agreement, the Bank president has always been an American, and the IMF managing director has always been a European. All the GATT and WTO directors general from 1948 to September 2002 were also from DCs. On September 1, 2002, Supachai Panitchpakdi of Thailand became the first WTO director general from an LDC. The South has been underrepresented on the professional staffs of all three KIEOs, and most Communist countries were not members of the KIEOs from the 1940s to the 1970s.[35]

The Bretton Woods system and its institutions are often credited with contributing "to almost unprecedented global economic growth and change over the past five decades."[36] However, the type of growth these institutions foster has closely followed the prescriptions of the United States and other DCs. The KIEOs support a liberal economic approach to growth, which holds that international prosperity and peace are most likely when there is a free flow of goods and capital throughout the world. As discussed in Chapter 5, historical structuralists argue that this liberal economic approach to growth benefits wealthy capitalist countries in the core of the global economy but disadvantages the lower classes and poorer countries in the periphery.

UNITED NATIONS

The UNITED

PRINCIPAL ORGANS OF

INTERNATIONAL COURT OF JUSTICE	SECURITY COUNCIL	GENERAL ASSEMBLY

Security Council subsidiary bodies:

Military Staff Committee

Standing Committees and ad hoc bodies

International Criminal Tribunal for the Former Yugoslavia

International Criminal Tribunal for Rwanda

UN Monitoring, Verification, and Inspection Commission (Iraq)

Peacekeeping Operations and Missions

General Assembly subsidiary bodies:

Main committees

Other sessional committees

Standing committees and ad hoc bodies

Other subsidary organs

PROGRAMMES AND FUNDS

UNCTAD
United Nations Conference on Trade and Development

  ITC
  International Trade Center
  (UNCTAD/WTO)

UNDCP
United Nations Drug Control Programme

UNEP
United Nations Environment Programme

UNDP
United Nations Development Programme

  UNIFEM
  United Nations Development Fund for Women

  UNV
  United Nations Volunteers

UNFPA
United Nations Population Fund

UNHCR
Office of the United Nations High Commissioner for Refugees

UNICEF
United Nations Children's Fund

WFP
World Food Programme

UNRWA**
United Nations Relief and Works Agency for Palestine Refugees in the Near East

OTHER UN ENTITIES

OHCHR
Office of the United Nations High Commissioner for Human Rights

UNCHS
United Nations Centre for Human Settlements (Habitat)

UNOPS
United Nations Office for Project Services

UNU
United Nations University

RESEARCH AND TRAINING INSTITUTES

INSTRAW
International Research and Training Institute for the Advancement of Women

UNICRI
United Nations Interregional Crime and Justice Research Institute

UNITAR
United Nations Institute for Training and Research

UNRISD
United Nations Research Institute for Social Development

UNIDIR**
United Nations Institute for Disarmament Research

* Autonomous organizations working with the United Nations and each other through the coordinating machinery of the Economic and Social Council.
** Report only to the General Assembly.

Figure 2.1 The United Nations System

Source: From United Nations, DPI/2299—February 2003, © United Nations

NATIONS system

THE UNITED NATIONS

| ECONOMIC AND SOCIAL COUNCIL | TRUSTEESHIP COUNCIL | SECRETARIAT |

FUNCTIONAL COMMISSIONS

Commission for Social Development

Commission on Human Rights

Commission on Narcotic Drugs

Commisson on Crime Prevention and Criminal Justice

Commisson on Science And Technology for Development

Commission on Sustainable Development

Commisson on the Status of Women

Commision on Population and Development

Statistical Commission

REGIONAL COMMISSIONS

Economic Commission for Africa (ECA)

Economic Commission for Europe (ECE)

Economic Commission for Latin America and the Caribbean (ECLAC)

Economic and Social Commission for Asia and the Pacific (ESCAP)

Economic and Social Commission for Western Asia (ESCWA)

Sessional and Standing Committies

Expert, ad hoc and related bodies

RELATED ORGANIZATIONS

IAEA
International Atomic Energy Agency

WTO
World Trade Organization

CTBTO
Comprehensive Nuclear-Test-Ban-Treaty Organization

OPCW
Organization for the Prohibition of Chemical Weapons

WTO
World Tourism Organization

SPECIALIZED AGENCIES*

ILO
International Labour Organization

FAO
Food and Agriculture Organization of the United Nations

UNESCO
United Nations Educational, Scientific, and Cultural Organization

WHO
World Health Organization

WORLD BANK GROUP

IBRD	International Bank for Reconstruction and Development
IDA	International Development Association
IFC	International Finance Corporation
MIGA	Muitilateral Investment Guarantee Agency
ICSID	International Centre for Settlement of Investment Disputes

IMF
International Monetary Fund

ICAO
International Civil Aviation Organization

IMO
International Maritime Organizaton

ITU
International Telecommunication Union

UPU
Universal Postal Union

WMO
World Meteorological Organization

WIPO
World Intellectual Property Organization

IFAD
International Fund for Agricultural Development

UNIDO
United Nations Industrial Development Organization

SECRETARIAT

OSG
Office of the Secretary-General

OIOS
Office of Internal Oversight Services

OLA
Office of Legal Affairs

DPA
Department of Political Affairs

DDA
Department for Disarmament Affairs

DPKO
Department of Peacekeeping Operations

OCHA
Office for the Coordination of Humanitarian Affairs

DESA
Department of Economic and Social Affairs

DGAACS
Department of General Assembly Affairs and Conference Services

DPI
Department of Public Information

DM
Department of Management

OIP
Office of the Iraq Programme

UNSECOORD
Office of the United Nations Security Coordinator

ODCCP
Office for Drug Control and Crime Prevention

UNOG
UN Office at Geneva

UNOV
UN Office at Vienna

UNON
UN Office at Nairobi

Judged by liberal economic criteria, the KIEOs were quite effective in the 1950s–1960s in promoting economic liberalization, growth, and stability. A number of factors help to account for their effectiveness. First, the Cold War increased the incentive of the United States to cooperate economically with Western Europe and Japan; vigorous economic recovery was viewed as a prerequisite for a strong anti-Soviet alliance system. Second, the United States as global hegemon was able and willing to provide leadership in establishing principles and rules for the conduct of postwar trade, financial, and monetary relations. Third, a relatively small number of politically and economically like-minded countries that accepted U.S. leadership were involved in developing the postwar economic system. Finally, the postwar international institutions were designed so governments could pursue domestic policy objectives such as full employment and also abide by international rules and obligations.[37]

Despite the early effectiveness of the KIEOs, they encountered increasing problems in managing the global economy. With Europe and Japan growing faster than the United States in the 1960s, the United States became less confident about its economic dominance and less inclined to support economic liberalism. For example, pressures for trade protectionism increased in the United States when its balance of trade shifted to a deficit position in 1971. Europe and Japan also began to question U.S. leadership, and the decline of the Cold War permitted frictions among advanced capitalist states to increase. A second factor posing a challenge to the KIEOs was the increased influence of the South. LDCs had long been dissatisfied with the policies of the KIEOs, and during the 1970s they were able to put some force behind their protests. A critical turning point was the first oil shock after the October 1973 Middle East War. At this time, the members of OPEC limited the supply of Persian Gulf oil, and its price increased by more than 400 percent. The subsequent disruption in the global economy challenged the management capabilities of DCs and the KIEOs.

A third challenge to the KIEOs resulted from the forces of globalization, such as increased capital flows. As discussed in Part III, increased capital mobility has made it difficult for the KIEOs to manage, and even to monitor, many activities in the global economy. The total economic resources of the KIEOs "pale in comparison to daily market-driven foreign exchange cash flows,"[38] and no IO effectively oversees the activities of MNCs and international banks, which are major contributors to these massive capital flows. As a result, a number of analysts are skeptical that the KIEOs are able to oversee the effective management of the global economy.[39] Finally, the growing membership of the KIEOs with the influx of LDCs and former Soviet bloc countries has also interfered with their management capabilities. By mid-2003, there were 184 members of the IMF, 184 members of the Bank, and 146 members of the WTO. Although some argue that the KIEOs must become more broadly representative, others point to the problems of decision making in such large, unwieldy institutions. The large, diverse memberships of these organizations can contribute to serious difficulties and frustrations in consultation, coordination, decision-making, and the supervision of policies.

The IMF, the Bank, and the WTO continue to have important functions in the global economy, but their large memberships have led some liberal analysts to argue that "they must be led by a much smaller core group whose weight confers on them the responsibility of leadership."[40] In the postwar period, DCs have in fact often con-

ORGANIZATION FOR ECONOMIC COOPERATION AND DEVELOPMENT
(YEAR OF ADMISSION)

Australia	1971	Hungary	1996	Poland	1996
Austria	1961	Iceland	1961	Portugal	1961
Belgium	1961	Ireland	1961	Slovak Republic	2000
Canada	1961	Italy	1962	South Korea	1996
Czech Republic	1995	Japan	1964	Spain	1961
Denmark	1961	Luxembourg	1961	Sweden	1961
Finland	1969	Mexico	1994	Switzerland	1961
France	1961	Netherlands	1961	Turkey	1961
Germany	1961	New Zealand	1973	United Kingdom	1961
Greece	1961	Norway	1961	United States	1961

SMALLER GROUPS

United States
Japan
Germany   **G-5**
France
United Kingdom
                              G-7*
Italy
Canada
                                          G-10**
Belgium
Netherlands
Sweden
Switzerland

*The G-8 also includes Russia, but Russia is not in the G-10 or OECD.
**Currently the G-10 has 11 members

Figure 2.2   Groups of Developed Countries

ferred among themselves in smaller groups before seeking endorsement of their policies by the larger KIEOs.[41] As Figure 2.2 shows, these groups include the Organization for Economic Cooperation and Development (OECD), **Group of Ten (G-10), Group of Five (G-5),** and **Group of Seven (G-7).** These smaller groups are more manageable for dealing with coordination of policies among the advanced industrial states in an age of globalization and power sharing among the United States, Europe, and Japan. Furthermore, DCs can meet in these groups without sharing information and decision-making power with the LDCs. Unlike liberal economists, who view these smaller groups as essential for promoting economic leadership and stability, historical structuralists argue that the groups permit the most powerful capitalist states to exclude peripheral states from the decision-making process. Although the IMF and the Bank have weighted voting, they are nevertheless preferable to the smaller groups from this perspective because the LDCs are at least present at the bargaining table.

The OECD

The Organization for Economic Cooperation and Development (OECD) is a group of mainly DCs based in Paris, France. As Figure 2.2 shows, the OECD had 30 member countries as of 2003, which produce about two-thirds of the world's goods and services.[42] From the time of its creation in 1961, the OECD has been committed to liberalizing international transactions such as trade and capital flows. The OECD is well known for its policy studies of economic and social issues, but it also serves as a forum for DCs to discuss members' economic policies, review common problems, and promote cooperation and policy coordination. In an age of globalization, a country's domestic policies can often have international consequences, and OECD members seek to achieve a consensus on implementing domestic policies that will minimize conflict. Although the OECD has the authority to adopt binding as well as nonbinding agreements, it usually operates through a system of mutual persuasion, in which governments exert peer pressure on each other to meet their commitments.[43]

The advanced industrial states use the OECD not only to promote cooperation but also to develop a more unified position on issues of interest to DCs in the IMF, the Bank, and the WTO. For example, as early as 1963, an OECD report recommended that the Bank establish an international agency to guarantee funds that private investors direct to LDCs. This report eventually served as the basis for the Bank's decision to establish the Multilateral Investment Guarantee Agency (MIGA) in 1988. The OECD's work on liberalization of trade in services also led to the decision that the new WTO should be responsible for trade in services as well as goods.[44]

Less frequently, the OECD has been *directly* involved in negotiating agreements in areas where the DCs have a special interest. For example, the OECD has negotiated agreements on *export credit,* "an insurance, guarantee or financing arrangement which enables a foreign buyer of exported goods and/or services to defer payment over a period of time."[45] Almost all export credit is provided by OECD countries, and the OECD agreements seek to prevent cut-throat competition among the export credit providers. In 1995 the OECD also began negotiations to conclude a Multilateral Agreement on Investment (MAI), which was designed primarily to protect foreign investors. Because many LDCs in the WTO were opposed to such an agreement, the DCs decided to negotiate the MAI in the OECD. Nevertheless, the MAI negotiations were suspended in 1998 because of divisions among OECD members and strong opposition by LDCs and civil society groups (see Chapter 10).

Although OECD membership was for years generally limited to the DCs, a debate in the early 1990s resulted in a decision that the organization should be open to some enlargement. Thus, Figure 2.2 shows that six countries outside the industrial core group have become OECD members since the 1990s: Mexico in 1994; the Czech Republic in 1995; Hungary, Poland, and South Korea in 1996; and the Slovak Republic in 2000. The OECD now involves about 70 nonmember states in its work, and other states are seeking membership in the organization. Although some OECD countries are open to enlargement, others warn that "transforming the OECD into a mini-United Nations could well jeopardize its ability to achieve high quality agreements among like-minded countries."[46]

Three smaller groupings limited to the most important countries in the OECD—the G-10, G-5, and G-7—have taken on significant functions in recent years. The G-10 was the first of these groups to be formed, in 1962. As Figure 2.2 shows, the G-10 now includes 11 countries: the United States, Japan, Germany, France, Britain, Italy, Canada, Belgium, the Netherlands, Sweden, and Switzerland. As discussed in Chapter 6, the quota subscriptions of IMF members are the main source of financial resources for the IMF. However, the IMF lacked sufficient funding in the early 1960s to meet the borrowing requirements of its members. The G-10 countries therefore established the General Arrangements to Borrow (GAB) in 1962, under which they agreed to provide supplementary loans to the IMF in their own currencies when needed. After a financial crisis in Mexico in 1994, it was evident that substantially more resources might be needed to respond to future crises. In 1997, the G-10 therefore agreed to supplement the GAB with New Arrangements to Borrow (NAB). The NAB are credit arrangements between the IMF and 25 member states and institutions (including the G-10) prepared to supply the IMF with supplementary resources. The decision to create the NAB rather than enlarging membership in the GAB stemmed from the desire of G-10 governments to retain their overall control. Thus, the GAB continues to exist alongside the NAB.[47]

Although the OECD and G-10 continue to be involved in coordinating DC economic policies, the main focus of policy coordination shifted to two smaller groups in the 1970s: the G-5 and G-7. With the growing membership in the IMF, the Bank, and the WTO, the G-5 and G-7 have had some special advantages in policy coordination: They have a small number of members, they include the most powerful DCs in the global economy, they are flexible groupings without formal constitutions, and top political leaders with authority to implement agreements often attend their meetings.[48]

The G-5, G-7, and G-8

The G-5 includes the finance ministers and **central bank** governors of the United States, Japan, Germany, France, and Britain (see Figure 2.2). These are the five largest industrial economies, and have the most votes in the IMF and World Bank policymaking bodies. After the G-5 first met in 1967 to informally discuss international monetary issues, they agreed that such meetings were useful and should be continued. In 1975, the G-5 agreed to hold more formal summit meetings during which their heads of government or state could discuss international economic issues. The interest in formal meetings came after major changes in the global economy, including the need for more collective leadership with the decline of U.S. hegemony, the growing interdependence among DCs, the OPEC oil crisis, and the world economic recession. Italy was invited to attend the first summit along with the G-5 countries in 1975, and Canada was invited to the second summit in 1976. Once invited they continued attending, and the G-7 was created. Although the G-7 summit is not a decision-making forum, members seek to reach a consensus on key issues at the highest political level.[49]

From 1975 to 1986, the G-5 and G-7 met as two largely separate entities. While the G-5 finance ministers and central bank governors held informal and confidential meetings on monetary and financial issues, the G-7 heads of state and government held highly publicized meetings on political as well as economic matters. In 1986, the G-7 largely displaced the G-5, and today the G-7 has two different layers: At the top are the heads of state or government who meet in annual summits, and the second level contains the finance ministers and central bank governors.

The G-5 and G-7 performed some critical functions in the 1970s and 1980s, coordinating **macroeconomic**, currency, and monetary policies among the advanced industrial states. (Macroeconomic policies deal with problems such as employment income and prices in the economy as a whole, and microeconomic policies refer to decisions of individual households and firms.) The meetings were also important in arranging financing and other measures to deal with East-West economic issues, global energy problems, and the 1980s foreign debt crisis. Furthermore, the G-7 summit agenda has expanded to include discussions of a wide range of "microeconomic, environmental, transnational and political-security subjects."[50] In 1991 the G-7 invited the Russian president Mikhail Gorbachev for the first time to meet with them at their summit meeting in London. The invitation was designed to help Russia come to terms with its loss of superpower status after the breakup of the Soviet Union, and to encourage it to continue with economic and political reform. Russia gradually became more involved in the G-7 summits, and in 1997 U.S. President Bill Clinton made the G-7 summit in Denver the first "Summit of the Eight," in which Russia participated alongside G-7 countries from the outset. The G-7 has therefore become a **Group of Eight (G-8)** with Russia participating. Nevertheless, Russia is more involved in the political than the economic discussions, and in some economic areas such as finance the main actors are effectively the G-7 countries.[51]

Some analysts argue that the G-7 meetings of finance ministers and central bank governors have become less effective in recent years, and they raise serious concerns about "the apparent inability of G-7 macroeconomic cooperation to ensure stability in the markets, or to sustain global economic growth."[52] They attribute the G-7's decline to two central factors. First, with the demise of the Cold War, capitalist states feel less urgency to coordinate their economic policies, and conflicts among the G-7 countries have increased. The lack of a common purpose has been exacerbated by the United States' decreased ability and willingness to exert economic leadership. The second reason for the G-7 decline relates to its difficulties in coping with globalization pressures. For example, massive international private capital flows interfere with the ability of G-7 monetary authorities to influence currency markets.

In the view of some scholars and policymakers, continued G-7/G-8 leadership is essential for international economic stability and prosperity. To regain its influence, the G-7/G-8 must make the necessary transition from unilateral U.S. leadership to effective collective leadership. This involves both U.S. willingness to share decision making and the willingness of countries such as Japan and Germany to assume more global responsibilities. The G-7/G-8 must also address the question of its legitimacy among countries outside its select group. Indeed, it is striking that the G-7/G-8 has no LDC members, considering the size and economic importance of such countries as China, India, Brazil, and Indonesia. The G-7/G-8 also has no OPEC country as a member (e.g., Saudi Arabia), despite the effect of petroleum on economic developments since the 1970s. Although the G-7/G-8 is not likely to expand its membership in the near future, countries such as China, India, and Brazil cannot be ignored, and the G-7/G-8 must be willing to consult with nonmembers more seriously.[53]

Divisions Within the North

To this point, we have focused mainly on groups in which the DCs cooperate and co-ordinate their policies on a global basis. Even in these groups, divisions have increased as U.S. economic hegemony has declined and as differences have developed as a result of security events such as the end of the Cold War, the U.S. reaction to the September 2001 terrorist attacks on the World Trade Center, and the U.S.-led conflict with Iraq in 2003. Globalization has also had the dual effect of creating pressures for coopera-tion and coordination of policymaking on the one hand, and contributing to conflict as states seek to preserve their autonomy on the other hand. This book discusses numer-ous instances of divisions among the DCs. The following examples relate to the post-war economic institutions.

In recent years, some industrial states have expressed dissatisfaction with their level of representation in the KIEOs. Critics in Germany and Japan in particular have argued that their countries' influence in these organizations has not kept pace with their growing economic importance. Thus, a German representative at the 1988 an-nual meetings of the IMF-Bank boards of governors asserted that "the Americans have the power, the French get the top jobs, and the Germans and the Japanese come up with the money."[54] None of the chief executive officers of the three KIEOs (the Bank president, IMF managing director, and GATT/WTO director general) was from Germany or Japan until March 2000, when the IMF executive board selected Ger-man national Horst Köhler as its new managing director.[55] Even the United States was dissatisfied with the fact that all the GATT directors general were European. When it came time to select the first WTO director general in 1995, the United States supported a Mexican for the post. As discussed in Chapter 8, the Mexican was not se-lected, but New Zealander Mike Moore became the first non-European WTO direc-tor general in September 1999.

The most important institutional sign of divisions among DCs in recent years has been the proliferation of regional trade agreements (RTAs). Whereas some analysts view RTAs as stepping-stones to global cooperation, others argue that they promote divisiveness and interfere with globalism. Many factors account for this turn to region-alism, including impatience with decision making in the large, heterogeneous global organizations; the growing U.S. interest in regionalism as its global hegemonic position has declined; and increased competitiveness among three major regional blocs cen-tered in the European Union, the United States, and Japan-East Asia. (see Chapter 9.) The EU has advanced to a further stage of integration than most other RTAs such as NAFTA, and to understand the phenomenon of regionalism it is necessary to discuss the stages of regional economic integration.

The Stages of Regional Economic Integration   As Figure 2.3 shows, there are five levels of regional economic integration.

1. **Free trade area (FTA).** In an FTA, member countries progressively elimi-nate tariffs on substantially all trade with each other. Every FTA member re-tains the right, however, to follow its own trade policies toward nonmember states. As a result, an FTA poses less of a threat to national sovereignty and is more acceptable to countries with politically sensitive relationships. One of

	Free Trade Area (FTA)	Customs Union (CU)	Common Market	Economic Union	Political Union
Removal of all tariffs among members	X	X	X	X	X
Common external tariff		X	X	X	X
Free movement of factors (labor and capital)			X	X	X
Harmonization of economic policies				X	X
Political unification					X

Figure 2.3   Stages of Regional Economic Integration

the most important FTAs established in recent years is NAFTA. Most economic integration agreements are FTAs.

2. **Customs union (CU).** A CU has the same characteristics as an FTA *plus* a common external tariff toward outside countries. Because a CU involves common tariff barriers, member countries must surrender more ability to make independent decisions. Thus, Britain was originally unwilling to join the EC (a customs union) because it wanted to retain its Commonwealth preference system with countries such as India, Canada, and Australia. Britain's trade became increasingly European oriented, and it eventually joined the EC in 1973 and agreed to phase out its Commonwealth preferences. Compared with FTAs, the number of customs unions is relatively small.

3. **Common market.** A common market has the same characteristics as a customs union *plus* the free mobility of factors of production (labor and capital) among member countries. Because a common market has increased labor mobility, there is a tendency to establish similar health, safety, educational, and social security standards so that no country's workers have a competitive advantage. The EU has generally progressed to the common market stage.

4. **Economic union.** An economic union has the characteristics of a common market, and also involves the harmonization of industrial, regional, transport, fiscal, monetary, and other economic and social policies. A full economic union also includes a monetary union, with the adoption of a common currency. In January 1999, 11 EU members formed an economic and monetary union, and moved to adopt a new currency—the Euro—in place of their national currencies. Greece joined the EMU in January 2001. (The 12 EMU members are identified by an asterisk in Figure 2.4.)

Year of Membership	Members
1957	*France Germany (Federal Republic) *Italy *Belgium *Netherlands *Luxembourg
1973	Britain Denmark } First enlargement *Ireland
1979	*Greece
1986	*Spain } Second enlargement *Portugal
1990	*Germany unified
1995	*Austria *Finland } Third enlargement Sweden

*Members of the European Economic and Monetary Union.

Figure 2.4   Expanding Membership of the European Union

5. **Political union.** A political union has all the characteristics of an economic union but extends from the economic area to political areas such as foreign and defense policy. A fully developed political union is more akin to a federal political system than to an agreement among sovereign states.

It is important to note that these stages of regional integration are pure models that do not fully describe reality. NAFTA, for example, is primarily at stage 1 (an FTA); but it contains some provisions requiring more openness toward foreign investment normally identified with stage 3 (a common market).

The Growing Impact of Regionalism   It is possible to identify two major phases in the growth of regionalism during the postwar period. The first phase began in 1957, when six countries formed the EC, now called the EU (see Figure 2.4). Following the EC example, a number of LDCs sought to establish their own RTAs in the 1960s. However, this first phase of regionalism "had virtually died by the end of the [1960s] decade, except for the original European Community."[56] In the 1980s there was a revival of regionalism, and many analysts believe this second phase of regionalism is likely to be far more enduring. The United States had refused to join RTAs in the first phase but became more supportive of regionalism in the second phase. In the 1980s the United States concluded FTAs with Israel and Canada, in the early 1990s it formed NAFTA with Canada and Mexico, and since the late 1990s it has been negotiating to establish a range of bilateral free trade agreements and a possible Free Trade Area of the Americas (FTAA).

Several factors account for the U.S. willingness to participate in RTAs since the 1980s. First, the United States was reacting to the broadening and deepening of EU integration, an expanding trade bloc from which it was excluded. As Figure 2.4 shows, membership in the EU grew from 6 states in 1957 to 15 in 1995. In December 2002 the European Council approved the accession of 10 Central and Eastern European States to the EU—the Czech Republic, Hungary, Poland, Slovakia, Slovenia, Estonia, Latvia, Lithuania, Cyprus, and Malta. These states are scheduled to become full members of the EU in 2004. A second related factor is that the EU and a number of other U.S. trading partners were negotiating FTAs that did not include the United States. These FTAs threatened to put U.S. business firms that did not benefit from the freeing of trade and investment regulations at a competitive disadvantage. Third, the United States was dissatisfied with the slow progress of multilateral trade negotiations. Thus, it was during the protracted eighth round of GATT negotiations (the Uruguay Round) that the United States established its FTAs with Israel, Canada, and Mexico. A fourth factor relates to the relative decline in U.S. economic hegemony. During the first phase of regionalism, the United States as economic hegemon took the main responsibility for upholding the global trade regime as the best path to trade liberalization. However, frustration over its chronic trade deficits pushed the United States to seek regionalism as another possible route to expanding its export markets.

As discussed in Chapter 9, some U.S. domestic groups strongly oppose NAFTA and any other U.S. attempts to form FTAs. Nevertheless, the great majority of WTO members are parties to one or more RTAs, and the number of RTAs has continued to increase rapidly since the early 1990s. About 250 RTAs were notified to the GATT/WTO as of December 2002, 130 of which were notified after January 1995. More than 170 of these RTAs are currently in force, and an additional 70 are considered to be operational, even though they have not yet been notified to the WTO (see Chapter 9). Thus, pressure on the major traders to continue forming RTAs is likely to continue.

What is the significance of the proliferation of RTAs for relations among the advanced industrial states? Some observers view this as a period of open regionalism that will serve as a stepping-stone to global trade and investment cooperation. Others consider regionalism to be a divisive force that could split the world into three major economic blocs based in Europe, the Western Hemisphere, and East Asia. Political security changes such as the end of the Cold War, the September 11, 2001 terrorist attacks, and the U.S.-led conflicts with Iraq have added to concerns that the growth of economic regionalism may be yet another source of divisiveness within the North. Nevertheless, the DCs have normally been able to cooperate when necessary to preserve their predominant influence vis-à-vis the LDCs in the IMF, the Bank, and the WTO. It is therefore important to examine why the South has had so little influence in these institutions and what actions it has attempted to take to remedy this situation.

POSTWAR ECONOMIC INSTITUTIONS AND THE SOUTH

The Bretton Woods system and its institutions are often credited with contributing "to almost unprecedented global economic growth and change over the past five decades."[57] However, this economic growth has not been shared by all. Poverty and its attendant problems such as disease and hunger are prevalent in much of the world, and there is a major gulf between the rich states of the North and the poor states of the South. LDCs are characterized not only by low levels of economic development, but also by low levels of social development.

Finding measures to compare the economic development of states is a difficult process. The most common economic development measure economists use is *per-capita GDP* or *per capita income* (a country's GDP or national income divided by its total population). **Exchange rates,** or the rates at which currencies are exchanged for one another, are used to convert per capita income figures in other currencies into the base currency, the U.S. dollar. However, comparing countries' per capita GDPs in U.S. dollars does not provide an adequate basis for comparing their standards of living because the exchange rate does not accurately reflect the purchasing power of the local currency in each country. Price levels of comparable goods differ significantly in different countries, and in general price levels are lower in LDCs than in the United States. In converting per capita GDP figures to U.S. dollars, a number of international organizations such as the United Nations Development Program (UNDP) and World Bank therefore use **purchasing power parity (PPP)** exchange rates. PPP rates are "the number of units of a country's currency required to buy the same amount of goods and services in the domestic market as a United States dollar would buy in the United States."[58] For example, since 1986 *The Economist* has used a "Big Mac index" to compare PPP rates for Big Mac hamburgers. If a Big Mac costs 2.74 Euros in countries that use the Euro and costs $2.65 in the United States, the PPP exchange rate for Big Macs would be 2.75/2.65, or 1.0377.[59] The PPP rate differs depending on the goods and services being compared, and many goods and services are looked at and weighted according to their importance in the economy.

PPP exchange rates do have some limitations. For example, PPP estimates are based on price comparisons of comparable items, but not all items are of the same quality across countries and over time. Services are especially difficult to compare because many services are not sold on the open market in various countries.

Nevertheless, PPP rates are generally considered to be more accurate in comparing living standards, and when possible this book provides per capita GDP or per capita income rates in PPP terms (for example, see Table 2.1).

Although PPP-adjusted per capita GDP figures take account of different price levels, it is important to note that they only provide a measure of a country's *economic* development. Since 1990 the UNDP has been publishing a *Human Development Report* with a **human development index (HDI),** which compares the development of countries on the basis of social as well as economic dimensions. The HDI indicators have been revised over time, and today they measure countries' achievements based on three dimensions: a long and healthy life measured by life expectancy at birth; knowledge measured by the adult literacy rate and by primary, secondary, and tertiary school enrollments; and a decent standard of living measured by PPP-adjusted per capita GDPs. One of the biggest problems with the HDI index is collecting reliable data. For example, the UNDP excluded 18 countries from its HDI index in 2002 for which it lacked reliable data.[60]

Table 2.1 compares HDI values and per capita GDPs for a number of countries during 2000. As Table 2.1 shows, both the per capita GDPs and HDI values tend to be substantially higher for DCs than for LDCs. Some differences in rankings for the two values do exist; for example, Norway ranked first in the HDI in 2000 but not in GDP per capita. However, the differences in HDI values for the four DCs—Norway, the

Table 2.1

HUMAN DEVELOPMENT INDEX (HDI) VALUE AND GROSS DOMESTIC PRODUCT (GDP) PER CAPITA, 2000

Country	HDI Value	GDP Per Capita (PPP* U.S.$)
Norway	0.942	29,918
United States	0.939	34,142
Japan	0.933	26,755
France	0.928	24,223
Korea, Republic of	0.882	17,380
Hungary	0.835	12,416
Mexico	0.796	9,023
Russian Federation	0.781	8,377
Brazil	0.757	7,625
China	0.726	3,976
South Africa	0.695	9,401
Indonesia	0.684	3,043
India	0.577	2,358
Bangladesh	0.478	1,602
Nigeria	0.462	896
Sierra Leone	0.275	490

*purchasing power parity

Source: From Human Development Report 2002 by United Nations Development Programme, copyright 2002 by the United Nations Development Programme. Used by permission of Oxford University Press, Inc..

United States, Japan, and France—are insignificant. Table 2.1 also shows some other differences in rankings; for example, China scores higher and South Africa scores lower on HDI values than one would expect on the basis of their per capita GDPs. Nevertheless, the table shows that LDCs not only have lower levels of economic development, but also less opportunities for adequate health care and education. (The HDI does not measure political aspects of human rights such as freedom of speech.)

The following examples show that the North-South economic gap is not only great but is widening.

- In 1993 the global GDP amounted to about $23 trillion. Of this $23 trillion, LDCs with almost 80 percent of the world's population accounted for only $5 trillion, whereas DCs accounted for $18 trillion.
- The share of global income of the poorest 20 percent of the world's population declined from 2.3 percent in 1963 to 1.4 percent in 1993, whereas the share of the richest 20 percent increased from 70 to 85 percent.
- The gap in per capita income between the DCs and the LDCs almost tripled from $5,700 in 1960 to $15,400 in 1993.[61]

Although the North-South economic gap has generally increased in recent years, there are also growing divisions *within* the South. Thus, Table 2.2 shows that East Asian and Latin American states generally score higher in terms of economic and so-

Table 2.2

HUMAN DEVELOPMENT INDICATORS

Region	Real GDP Per Capita (U.S.$)		Infant Mortality Rate (per 1,000 live births)		Adult Expectancy at Birth (%)		Adult Literacy Rate (%)	
	1960	1998	1960	1998	1970–1975	1995–2000	1970	1998
Sub-Saharan Africa	$ 990	$ 1,607	166	106	45.0	48.9	27	58.5
South Asia	$ 698	$ 2,112	163	72	50.1	62.7	32	54.3
East Asia	$ 729	$ 3,564	146	37	63.2	70.0	88	83.4
East Asia excluding China	$ 869	$13,635	84	10	63.3	72.8	88	96.3
Southeast Asia and Pacific	$ 732	$ 3,234	127	41	52.3	65.9	65	88.2
Latin America and Caribbean	$2,137	$ 6,510	107	32	61.1	69.5	72	87.7
Arab States	$ 931	$ 4,140	166	55	52.4	65.6	30	59.7
All LDCs	$ 915	$ 3,270	149	64	55.6	64.4	43	72.3

Source: From Human Development Report 2002 by United Nations Development Programme, copyright 2002 by the United Nations Development Programme. Used by permission of Oxford University Press, Inc.

cial indicators than South Asian and sub-Saharan African states. Sub-Saharan Africans and East Asians demonstrate the most striking differences in development. The per capita GDP in sub-Saharan Africa in 1960 ($990) was slightly higher than the per capita GDP in East Asia excluding China ($869). By 1998, however, the per capita GDP in East Asia excluding China ($13,635) was more than eight times higher than the per capita GDP in sub-Saharan Africa ($1,607). Sub-Saharan Africa also registered lower levels of development than most other regions on social measures such as infant mortality, life expectancy, and literacy rates, whereas the development level for East Asia excluding China was well above the average in these areas. The infant mortality rate of 106 per 1,000 live births for sub-Saharan Africa in 1998 in fact increased from a mortality rate of 97 per 1,000 live births in 1994.

Recognizing the major divisions among LDCs, the UN in 1971 compiled a list of 24 least developed countries or LLDCs, and this list has grown to 49 countries. The UN has singled out the LLDCs for special attention because they generally have extremely low per capita GDPs, literacy rates, and shares of manufacturing. As Table 2.3 shows, almost three-quarters of the 49 LLDCs are in Africa, and there are also a substantial number in the Asia/Pacific. The third column in the table shows that 20 of the 44 LLDCs for which statistics are available had *negative* GDP per capita growth rates from 1990 to 1999.

Although a relatively small number of LDCs—particularly in East and Southeast Asia—have improved their economic positions, most LDCs have been frustrated in their efforts to promote development and exert more influence. As discussed in Chapter 11, even East and Southeast Asian states such as South Korea, Indonesia, Malaysia, and Thailand, which had been viewed as exemplars of economic development, confronted a financial crisis in the late 1990s. The most significant gap in socio-economic

Table 2.3

DEVELOPMENT INDICATORS OF THE LEAST DEVELOPED COUNTRIES (LLDCS)

LLDCs	1999 GDP Per Capita (in 1999 dollars)	1999 Population (millions)	1990–1999 Annual Average Growth Rates of Per Capita Real GDP (%)
Afghanistan	—	21.9	—
Angola	685	12.5	−3.0
Bangladesh	361	126.9	3.1
Benin	405	5.9	1.9
Bhutan	733	0.6	4.0
Burkina Faso	228	11.6	1.0
Burundi	107	6.6	−4.9
Cambodia	285	10.9	2.1
Cape Verde	1389	0.4	3.0
Central African Republic	297	3.5	−0.3
Chad	211	7.5	−1.3
Comoros	291	0.7	−3.3
Dem. Rep. of the Congo	115	50.3	−8.3
Djibouti	—	0.6	—
Equatorial Guinea	1575	0.4	−1.2
Eritrea	180	3.7	1.6*
Ethiopia	107	61.1	1.9
Gambia	345	1.3	−0.8
Guinea	502	7.4	1.3
Guinea-Bissau	186	1.2	−1.8
Haiti	485	8.1	−2.8
Kiribati	732	0.1	1.8
Lao People's Democratic Republic	259	5.3	3.7
Lesotho	415	2.1	2.0
Liberia	—	2.9	—
Madagascar	241	15.5	−1.6
Malawi	171	10.6	2.6
Maldives	1359	0.3	4.4
Mali	248	11.0	1.0
Mauritania	369	2.6	1.3
Mozambique	209	19.3	2.5
Myanmar	—	45.1	—
Nepal	210	23.4	2.2
Niger	199	10.4	−0.9
Rwanda	270	7.2	−1.3
Samoa	1250	0.2	0.8
Sao Tome and Principe	328	0.1	−0.4
Senegal	519	9.2	0.7
Sierra Leone	142	4.7	−6.4
Solomon Islands	806	0.4	0.3
Somalia	—	9.7	—

Table 2.3

(continued)

LLDCs	1999 GDP Per Capita (in 1999 dollars)	1999 Population (millions)	1990–1999 Annual Average Growth Rates of Per Capita Real GDP (%)
Sudan	345	28.9	6.1
Togo	334	4.5	−0.4
Tuvalu	1931	—**	2.2
Uganda	300	21.1	4.3
United Republic of Tanzania	268	32.8	−0.9
Vanuatu	1327	0.2	−0.3
Yemen	387	17.5	−0.7
Zambia	370	9.0	−2.1

*1993–1999.
**Tuvalu's population is 11,000.
Source: United Nations Conference on Trade and Development, *The Least Developed Countries 2002 Report,* Annex Table 1, p.247.

development therefore continues to be the division between DCs in the North on the one hand and the large majority of LDCs in the South on the other. Because most LDCs are in a weak position individually, only collective action has provided some opportunity for extracting costly concessions from the North. Thus, the South has often attempted to present a unified front vis-à-vis the North.

LDC Efforts to Alter the Institutional Framework

Many LDCs have been dissatisfied because of their lack of influence in the KIEOs. From the LDC perspective, the KIEOs often promote policies that either do not contribute to, or pose major obstacles to economic development.[62] This chapter briefly discusses LDC efforts to bring about changes in the postwar international institutions and to create new institutions that would increase their influence and development prospects. Subsequent chapters examine the position of LDCs on issues such as foreign debt and foreign investment, and Chapter 11 outlines alternative strategies LDCs have followed for promoting development.

The 1950s   An early target of LDC dissatisfaction was the IBRD or World Bank, which provides long-term loans for economic development. As discussed in Chapter 11, the IBRD provides *hard loans,* with higher interest rates and shorter repayment periods; for example, the interest rate on IBRD loans in 1995 was about 7.1 percent. Because the poorest LDCs require **concessional** or **soft loans**, IBRD funding is available mainly to middle-income LDCs. The South was also dissatisfied with the IBRD's weighted voting system, which favors the rich Northern states. In 1997, for example, the 26 DCs had 61.6 percent of the votes in the Bank board of governors, and the G-7 countries alone had 47.8 percent of the votes. The 163 LDC members of the Bank had only 38.4 percent of the votes.[63]

Throughout the 1950s, the South repeatedly pressured the UN to establish a new agency with a more equitable voting system than the Bank that would provide grants or soft loans (with low or no interest and long repayment periods) to LDCs. These proposals repeatedly failed, however, because of opposition from the North. Because of decolonization and growing LDC needs for capital, the North finally agreed to establish a soft-loan aid agency, the *International Development Association (IDA)* in 1960. As is often the case, however, the North did not accede to Southern demands for greater power over decision making, and it insisted that the IDA become a part of the World Bank group with its weighted voting system (see Figure 2.1). Furthermore, the largest share of Bank group loans continues to be hard loans provided by the IBRD. The soft IDA loans or "credits" are more limited in amount and available only to poorer LDCs. In fiscal 2000, for example, IBRD loan disbursements totaled about $13.3 billion, whereas IDA credit disbursements amounted to $5.2 billion.[64]

The 1960s   In the 1960s decolonization transformed North-South relations as many new African and Asian LDCs gained political independence and joined the UN. (Most Latin American LDCs had become independent in the nineteenth century.) Thus, the number of African and Asian states in the UN increased from 10 in 1955 to 55 in 1966, when they accounted for about 45 percent of UN members.[65] In 1964, the 77 LDCs in the UN from Africa, Asia, and Latin America ("the Third World") met to express their dissatisfaction with the KIEOs and to prepare for a major conference on trade and development.[66] Although this caucus now has well over 100 members, it is still referred to as the **Group of 77 (G-77).**

The conference the G-77 organized in Geneva in March 1964 was the first **United Nations Conference on Trade and Development (UNCTAD).** In view of the growing numbers of LDCs in the UN, the G-77 was able to convene UNCTAD I despite the initial opposition—and then the grudging acceptance—of the North. UNCTAD I was "the first institutional response in the economic sphere to the entry of the Third World on the international scene," and UNCTAD subsequently became a permanent organ of the UN General Assembly (see Figure 2.1).[67] Although all UN members are members of UNCTAD, the LDCs with their greater numbers have had the predominant role in setting UNCTAD's agenda and work program. In marked contrast to the KIEOs, the UNCTAD secretariat has openly supported LDC interests, and the UNCTAD secretary general has always been from the South. UNCTAD experienced some success in espousing an alternative approach to trade and economic development, in inducing GATT to give more priority to Southern trade interests, and in overseeing the establishment of international commodity agreements. However, GATT/WTO continues to be the unrivaled international organization in the global trade regime. Because UNCTAD's orientation posed a direct challenge to the liberal-economic order and the power position of the North, the DCs refused to accept it as a major forum for trade negotiations. Thus, UNCTAD's main role has not been in international management but in serving as a pressure group for Southern interests.

The 1970s   Although the South attempted to improve its position vis-à-vis the North in the 1960s, its stance became far more militant in the 1970s when OPEC drastically increased oil prices. A number of factors contributed to OPEC's success in raising prices, including the North's growing dependence on Middle East oil and the unifying effect on Arab OPEC members of the October 1973 Middle East War. LDC oil importers as well as DCs were hurt by the OPEC price increases, but most LDCs nevertheless viewed OPEC as an example of what they might also do to increase their power and wealth vis-à-vis the North. Thus, the OPEC example, along with increased prices of a number of commodities that LDCs exported, led to LDC calls for a **New International Economic Order (NIEO)** in the 1970s. The NIEO was a multilateral strategy to increase the South's economic and political power and to gain major economic concessions from the North.

The North was willing to join in NIEO negotiations with the South in the 1970s because of its concerns about OPEC's increased leverage. Indeed, implicit linkages were drawn between Northern willingness to discuss the NIEO demands on the one hand and guaranteed supplies of OPEC oil at lower prices on the other. Southern demands in the NIEO negotiations were numerous, including an increase in **foreign aid,** LDC control over their economies and natural resources, increased LDC control over foreign direct investment, more access to Northern technology on easier terms, preferential treatment for LDC exports to the North, international commodity agreements, and increased LDC decision-making power in the IMF and the Bank.[68]

The South did register some gains during the NIEO negotiations. For example, the voting shares of OPEC countries increased somewhat in the IMF and the Bank, and the North eventually agreed to a generalized system of preferences (GSP) for LDC exports (see Chapter 8). These gains, however, were clearly limited, and the North became less willing to make concessions as it gradually regained its bargaining power. Oil proved to be a unique commodity, since LDC producers of other commodities could not acquire similar marketing power. The North also gradually gained access to other sources of oil and became less dependent on OPEC producers. The most significant factor shifting the balance of power back toward the North, however, was the foreign debt crisis in the 1980s.

The 1980s and 1990s   As discussed in Chapter 7, the foreign debt crisis of the 1980s was closely related to the OPEC oil price increases of the 1970s. OPEC countries deposited a large share of their oil revenues in international banks, which recycled these "petrodollars" by extending massive loans to LDC oil importers. A combination of imprudent lending and borrowing and unexpected international events contributed to overborrowing by many LDCs in the 1970s and to Southern dependence on debt relief assistance in the 1980s and 1990s. In return for extending structural adjustment loans to LDC debtors, the IMF and the Bank, backed by the North, imposed conditions requiring LDCs to open their economies to trade and foreign investment. Thus, the South has generally taken a more conciliatory approach toward the North since the 1980s, and it has been more willing to accept Northern demands for such policies as liberalization, privatization, and deregulation.

This shift in the balance of power toward the North is evident in UNCTAD, which has been "the principal focus of Third World efforts to obtain changes in the trade and other economic relationships between developed and developing countries."[69] UNCTAD's pressures on behalf of the South had increased during the 1970s when it was demanding a NIEO. By the late 1980s, however, UNCTAD began to shift toward a more conciliatory approach because of threats that it could become totally irrelevant. This change was evident in UNCTAD's relationship with GATT, which shifted from an emphasis on conflicting to complementary interests between the two organizations. The change was also evident in UNCTAD conferences, held about once every four years. The sixth UNCTAD conference (UNCTAD VI) in 1983 was marked by confrontation, but UNCTADs VII and VIII in 1987 and 1992 were notable for efforts to identify common North-South interests. Because it was the first UNCTAD conference since the breakup of the Soviet bloc, UNCTAD VIII "brought together a virtually universal view that economic policies based on market forces were the best basis for achieving development."[70] UNCTAD's policy reversal was only one indication that most LDCs in the 1990s saw little alternative to operating within the framework of the DCs' liberal-economic system. Nevertheless, this book discusses clear indications that North-South conflict could increase again if greater economic openness does not produce socioeconomic benefits for the South.

POSTWAR ECONOMIC INSTITUTIONS AND THE CENTRALLY PLANNED ECONOMIES

The IMF, World Bank, and GATT/WTO are considered to be universal membership organizations, in which all states can become members.[71] For much of the history of these organizations, however, the CPEs of Eastern Europe, the Soviet Union, and China either were nonmembers or played a very limited role. At the end of World War II there was an institutional division of labor, with the UN concentrating primarily on political security matters and the Bretton Woods institutions taking responsibility for economic cooperation. Nevertheless, political security issues were inevitably a factor in the deliberations of the KIEOs.[72] The Western allies generally thought that universalism was the best approach to create a more secure environment, and Harry Dexter White of the U.S. Treasury Department wrote in his April 1942 draft Bretton Woods plan that "to exclude a country such as Russia would be an egregious error. Russia, despite her socialist economy could both contribute and profit by participation."[73] The allied governments also expected that the Eastern European states, which previously had close economic ties with the West, would become full members of the Bretton Woods organizations.[74]

Although the Soviet Union was fearful of capitalist encirclement, it wanted access to financial aid to reconstruct its war-damaged economy. The Soviets were therefore actively involved in the deliberations leading up to and including the Bretton Woods conference. As the only Communist state at Bretton Woods (Poland and Czechoslovakia were not yet Communist), the Soviet Union expressed concerns regarding such issues as special consideration for state-trading countries, the IMF and the Bank's paid-in subscriptions and voting procedures, and the amount of information the IMF and the Bank would require of member states. The major Western countries made limited concessions to the Soviets in the *IMF Articles of Agreement* concerning subscription payments and the provision of information to the IMF, and the Soviet Union signed the Bretton Woods agreements. However, it continued to oppose the method of allocating the IMF and Bank votes, the transfer of gold to U.S. territory, and the conditions the IMF would place on its loans. After the first IMF/Bank board of governors meeting in March 1946, the Soviet Union stopped participating, and it did not become a member of these organizations. By this time, Cold War issues were intruding (e.g., disputes over the administration of Berlin and the Soviet occupation of Eastern Europe), and both the Soviet Union and the West backed away from the goal of universality. Thus, the Soviet Union did not even attend the conferences to develop a global trade organization.[75]

In 1947, the United States responded to the continuing economic problems in Western Europe—the near exhaustion of foreign exchange reserves for purchasing needed food, energy, and raw materials—with the European Recovery Program, or Marshall Plan. When U.S. Secretary of State George C. Marshall introduced the plan, he invited the Soviet Union and Eastern Europe to participate. However, the Soviets refused to join in and vetoed the idea of East European participation. They especially objected to U.S. requirements that the United States have some advisory authority over the internal budgets of Marshall Plan aid recipients, that the European countries cooperate with each other in using Marshall Plan aid, and that most of the aid be used to purchase U.S. exports. Only Western European states therefore joined with the United States in the Marshall Plan, and the Soviets established the *Council for Mutual Economic Assistance (CMEA)* in January 1949 as a counterweight. Composed of the Soviet Union and Eastern European states other than Yugoslavia, CMEA solidified the economic and political divisions between Eastern and Western Europe.[76]

The Soviet-led CMEA engaged in a number of economic activities such as technical cooperation and joint planning, and its strategies for promoting cooperation among the CPEs sharply differentiated it from the market-oriented Bretton Woods system. For example, CMEA emphasized central planning for almost all economic decisions such as resource allocation; the nationalization of the factors of production, including capital, natural resources, and in most cases land; the collectivization of agriculture; and a rather rigid separation of the domestic economy from external economic influences. CMEA's main goals were to reorient Eastern European trade away from the West and to solidify economic linkages between the Soviet Union and Eastern Europe. Thus, CMEA established two institutions, the International Bank for Economic Cooperation (in 1964) and the International Investment Bank (in 1971), which were to assume functions similar to those of the IMF and World Bank. These two CMEA banks were very inadequate substitutes, however, because they were associated with increased bilateralism, inward-looking policies, and a currency (the ruble) with unrealistic conversion rates that limited trade.[77]

The growing East–West economic rift resulted from policies of the United States as well as the Soviet Union. For example, the United States restricted trade with Communist countries from 1948, and the 1949 U.S. Export Control Act authorized the president to establish a licensing system regulating exports to the Communist states. The United States also pressured its allies to join in the *Coordinating Committee (COCOM),* which was established to coordinate Western embargoes of strategic goods to the Soviet bloc. COCOM was an effort to limit the Soviet Union's military advances, by hurting it economically and isolating it politically. Furthermore, the U.S. Congress passed the Trade Agreements Extension Act in 1951, which withdrew trade concessions previously granted to all Communist countries other than Yugoslavia. The liberal-economic orientation of the KIEOs was another factor contributing to the East-West split. Theoretically, IMF and Bank lending decisions are to be nonpolitical, and the IBRD Articles of Agreement explicitly state that "only economic considerations shall be relevant" to the Bank's decisions.[78] A number of analysts argue, however, that these institutions are committed to a capitalist world economy and make decisions on the basis of political and ideological as well as economic considerations.[79] Even when these organizations do not consciously promote Western-style capitalism, the values of their professional staff members, who have received their education and training mainly in Western capitalist countries, affect the decision-making process.[80]

In view of the major East-West divisions, most linkages between Communist states and the KIEOs were severed during the 1950s. Although Czechoslovakia, Poland, Yugoslavia, China, and Cuba had been founding members of the IMF and the Bank, their membership ended or their status changed after they became Communist states (the sole exception was Yugoslavia). As Table 2.4 shows, Poland withdrew from the IMF and the Bank in 1950, charging that these institutions were largely controlled by the U.S. government. The Bank and the IMF expelled Czechoslovakia in 1954; the ostensible reasons for expulsion were related to Czechoslovakia's failure to pay part of its capital subscription to the Bank and its refusal to provide information to the IMF.[81] Yugoslavia was the only Eastern European state remaining in the IMF and the Bank in the 1950s, but it was a special case because of its independence from the Soviet Union. The Republic of China (Taiwan) occupied the China seat in these institutions after the People's Republic of China took over the mainland in October 1949, and Cuba under Fidel Castro withdrew from the Bank in 1960 and the IMF in 1964.

Table 2.4 shows that China and Czechoslovakia were founding members of GATT in 1948, but the Chiang Kai-shek government (which had fled from the mainland to Taiwan) withdrew from the organization in 1950, purportedly on behalf of China. Czechoslovakia remained a member of GATT (but not of the IMF and the Bank), even though its membership was inactive for a number of years. Czechoslovakia was able to retain membership because of GATT's status as a highly informal organization.

As nonmembers of the KIEOs, the Soviet bloc countries joined the South in supporting the formation of alternative organizations in which the advanced capitalist states would have less control. Thus, the Soviet Union strongly endorsed the formation of UNCTAD. By the late 1960s, however, the Soviet bloc countries became less interested in UNCTAD and other alternative organizations for a number of reasons. These included the emergence of East-West détente, increased tensions and economic problems within the Eastern bloc's CMEA, the growing dependence of Eastern European countries on Western markets for their exports, and the political desire of Eastern Europeans to gain more independence from the Soviet Union. Thus, Table 2.4 shows that some Eastern European states (Poland, Romania, and Hungary) joined the KIEOs beginning in the late 1960s, and the People's Republic of China replaced Taiwan in the IMF and the Bank in 1980. The most far-reaching change occurred in the early 1990s after the breakup of the Soviet

Table 2.4

MEMBERSHIP OF TRANSITION ECONOMIES IN THE KEYSTONE INTERNATIONAL ECONOMIC ORGANIZATIONS

	IMF	World Bank	GATT/WTO
1946	Poland, Czechoslovakia, Yugoslavia & China (founding members of IMF and World Bank)		
1948			Czechoslovakia and China (founding members)
1950	Poland withdraws from IMF and World Bank		Republic of China (Taiwan) withdraws from GATT
1954	Czechoslovakia ousted from the IMF and World Bank		
1966			Yugoslavia
1967			Poland
1971			Romania
1972	Romania	Romania	
1973			Hungary
1980	People's Republic of China (replaces Taiwan in the IMF and World Bank)		
1982	Hungary	Hungary	
1986	Poland	Poland	
1990	Bulgaria, Czechoslovakia	Bulgaria	East Germany accedes to GATT by virtue of reunification
1991	Albania, Lithuania	Albania Czechoslovakia	
1992 to 1996	Russian Federation, other FSU* republics, Croatia, Slovenia, Macedonia, Bosnia and Herzegovina, Czech Republic, Slovak Republic (IMF & World Bank)		Bulgaria, Czech Republic, Slovak Republic, Slovenia
1998 to 2001	Federal Republic of Yugoslavia (IMF & World Bank)		Kyrgyz Republic, Estonia, Croatia, Albania, Georgia, Lithuania, Moldova, China
2002			Taiwan
2003			Armenia, Macedonia

*FSU: Former Soviet Union republics
Sources: International Monetary Fund, *Annual Report of the Executive Board,* (Washington, D.C.: IMF, various years); *World Bank Annual Report,* (Washington, D.C.: World Bank, various years); General Agreement on Tariffs and Trade, *GATT Activities* (Geneva, Switzerland: GATT, various years).

Union, when Russia and other FSU republics joined the IMF and the Bank and a number of former East bloc countries joined GATT. Another momentuous change occurred when China and Taiwan became members of the WTO in December 2001 and January 2002, respectively. Of the major emerging economies, only Russia has not yet become a WTO member. The emerging economies have had to accept market reforms when joining the KIEOs, and the KIEOs in turn have had to become open to some degree of central planning. Later chapters discuss in detail the emerging economies' moves toward integration with the IMF, the Bank, and the GATT/WTO.

POSTWAR ECONOMIC INSTITUTIONS AND CIVIL SOCIETY

Although LDCs have been the main disadvantaged group, a wide range of NGOs focusing on the environment, women, labor, development, and human rights have also been largely excluded from positions of power. These NGOs are extremely diverse but are often categorized together under the "civil society" label. Operational NGOs emphasize the provision of voluntary social services, whereas advocacy NGOs are politically active and seek to influence decision making in governments and international organizations. This book refers primarily to the advocacy functions of NGOs. Critics sometimes argue that advocacy NGOs describe themselves as civil society groups because the term connotes civic duty and responsibility and therefore masks their political ambitions. Supporters counter that advocacy NGOs are compensating for a "democracy deficit" by expressing the views of disadvantaged and underrepresented groups, but critics maintain that these NGOs are self-appointed and not necessarily representative of broader public concerns.[82] Although a majority of these groups express their views primarily by peaceful means, demonstrations at gatherings such as the November 1999 WTO ministerial conference in Seattle show that a minority of these groups either engage in violent protest or condone such violence. The term civil society in this book refers to groups that are generally committed to peaceful discussion and protest. Among the major groups that often feel excluded from decision making in the KIEOs, women's, environmental, labor, and development groups are especially prominent.

Women's Groups

Women's groups have expressed concerns regarding the small number of women in influential positions in IOs and the failure of these organizations to take sufficient account of gender issues in their deliberations and policy decisions. Article 8 of the UN Charter states that the UN "shall place no restrictions on the eligibility of men and women to participate in any capacity and under conditions of equality in its principle and subsidiary organs."[83] Although this article was included to legitimize the hiring of women as permanent IO staff members, it is phrased in prohibitive terms rather than as an affirmative obligation to hire women. Women have always constituted a majority of clerical workers but a minority of professional staff in the UN and its specialized agencies.

After decades of pressure by women's groups, the UN secretary general appointed a Coordinator for the Improvement of the Status of Women in 1985 and set goals for increasing women's representation. As a result, women's representation on the UN professional staff increased from 19 percent in 1980 to 39 percent in 1999. Women in the UN nevertheless have fewer positions at higher levels. In 1999, 48 percent of junior professionals but only 21 percent of senior managers on the UN professional staff were women. Of 21 under-secretary generals, two were women. Women's representation on the professional staff of the UN specialized agencies in 1998 was 32 percent, and among senior managers 16 percent, lower than in the UN secretariat. Women have been appointed to head some UN agencies, including the UN Children's Fund (UNICEF), the UN Development Fund for Women (UNIFEM), the office of the UN High Commissioner for Refugees (UNHCR), and the UN Fund for Population Activities (UNFPA), but these agencies deal primarily with social issues which are often identified as women's areas. No head of the major international economic organizations—the IMF, World Bank, WTO, or OECD—has been a woman.[84]

Some feminist theorists argue that the small number of women in high IO positions is "symptomatic of a much deeper issue . . . the extent to which international politics is such a thoroughly masculinized sphere of activity that women's voices are considered inauthentic."[85] They also maintain that these institutions often make decisions that disadvantage women and merely reinforce the gendered divisions of labor and power in society. However, some IOs are becoming more attuned to the need to address gender differences in their member states. Since the human development index (HDI) only assesses average achievements, the UNDP introduced a gender-related development index (GDI) in 1995, which adjusts the HDI for inequalities in achievements of men and women. For example, in 2001 the GDI showed that male literacy rates were at least 15 percentage points higher than female rates in 43 countries. The UNDP also introduced a gender empowerment measure (GEM) in 1995 to assess gender inequality in economic and political opportunities.[86] Despite growing awareness of the need to deal with gender differences in society, IOs continue to have serious shortcomings in this area. Chapter 11 discusses the gender-related effects of World Bank structural adjustment loans to LDCs.

Environmental and Labor Groups

Environmental and labor groups also contend that they are excluded from positions of influence in major international economic institutions, and that these institutions largely ignore environmental and labor considerations in their decision making. For example, a considerable amount of literature exists on the exclusion of environmental NGOs from a formal role at the WTO, and the WTO has been criticized for not taking sufficient account of environmental and labor issues in its dispute settlement and rule-making procedures. Furthermore, a wide array of literature is critical of the Bank's failure to give higher priority to the environment in its development projects. Although the KIEOs have in varying degrees sought to address these concerns, many environmental and labor groups argue that the KIEO efforts have been insufficient.[87]

Development Groups

It is important to note that the concerns of labor and environmental groups sometimes run counter to the perceived interests of LDCs. For example, many LDCs argue that environmental and labor standards can be used by the North as an excuse for imposing trade barriers against Southern exports. LDCs maintain that their economic development prospects will be severely jeopardized if they must adhere to the same environmental and labor standards as the DCs. A number of civil society groups have been concerned specifically with promoting development in the South. For example, some groups have called for more foreign debt relief for low-income LDCs through accelerating the relief process, broadening the eligibility criteria, and increasing the amount of assistance. Civil society groups have also called for drastic reform of IMF and the Bank structural adjustment loans to LDCs. These development groups are discussed in Chapters 7 and 11.

CONCLUSION

This chapter has examined the changing institutional framework for managing the postwar global economy. The states at the 1944 Bretton Woods conference had great faith in the establishment of international institutions to prevent a recurrence of the problems of the interwar years, and the three KIEOs have been important contributors to postwar prosperity. Nevertheless, there is a hierarchy of states within the IMF, the Bank, and the WTO, and postwar prosperity has not been equally distributed among states and peoples. The United States and other DCs have been at the top of the hierarchy, in a position to establish the principles and rules for the functioning of the global economic order. LDCs have sought to alter the KIEOs and establish alternative organizations such as UNCTAD. However, their gains have been limited, and events such as the 1980s foreign debt crisis have greatly weakened their position.

Unlike the LDCs, the centrally planned economies for many years were nonparticipants in the KIEOs, and the Soviet Union established the CMEA as an alternative organization for the Eastern bloc. However, economic problems, political tensions, and growing dependence on the advanced capitalist states gradually pushed the Eastern bloc countries to join the Western-dominated KIEOs. The breakup of the Soviet bloc has sped up this integration process. The foreign debt and financial crises have similarly forced many LDCs to become more dependent on IMF and Bank loans and to become more closely integrated with the capitalist economic order.

The globalization process has contributed to the increase in membership of the IMF, the Bank, and the WTO, and for the first time they are in fact becoming universal membership organizations. Although globalization has contributed to the increased size of the KIEOs, it has also made it more difficult for them to manage global economic relations. The rapid movement of capital around the world is simply one indication of the pervasive influence of private actors such as MNCs and international banks in an age of "cascading interdependence."[88] These changes are posing an increasing challenge not only to the KIEOs' management capabilities but also to the states that support them. In efforts to coordinate their activities, the advanced capitalist states have therefore often turned to smaller, more informal groupings such as the G-7/G-8.

Although globalization challenges the management capabilities of states and IOs, it is *not* leading to a borderless world. In fact, states are seeking to survive and prosper in the new age of global competitiveness. With the demise of the Cold War, new economic power centers have emerged in Europe and East Asia, posing a challenge to U.S. economic hegemony. These three regional blocs have extended competitiveness among the DCs to the global level, and security issues such as the end of the Cold War have sometimes exacerbated the regional differences. Despite these regional divisions, however, one can argue that the advanced capitalist states "are still committed through the G7, the IMF, the World Bank, and the World Trade Organisation to continue to manage the international system."[89]

Divisions have become more evident not only within the North but also within the South. Indeed, the South has fragmented into a number of groups, with the largest gap developing between the LLDCs and the East Asian NIEs. The South has also been fragmenting on a regional basis, with some LDCs joining with DCs in regional groupings. Notable examples include the associate membership of African, Caribbean, and Pacific countries in the EU; Mexico's membership in NAFTA; and the joining of DCs and LDCs in APEC. In recent years, divisions have also become far more prominent between the KIEOs and civil society groups representing women, the environment, labor, and development interests. As globalization has increased, these groups have been concerned that the KIEOs are subordinating "issues such as environmental protection, gender equality, and labour rights to a liberalisation drive."[90] How this challenge from civil society groups plays out will have a major impact on global economic management in the twenty-first century.

Notes

1. Armand Van Dormael, *Bretton Woods: Birth of a Monetary System* (London: Macmillan, 1978), p.ix.
2. Richard N. Gardner, "The Political Setting," in A. L. K. Acheson, J. F. Chant, and M. F. J. Prochowny, eds., *Bretton Woods Revisited* (Toronto: University of Toronto Press, 1972), p.20.
3. Herman M. Schwartz, *States versus Markets: The Emergence of a Global Economy*, 2nd ed., (New York: St. Martin's Press, 2000), p.11.
4. Adam Smith used the term mercantile system, and German writers in the 1860s used the term Merkantilismus. Only afterward did the term *mercantilism* become standard in the English language. See Jacob Viner, "Mercantilist Thought," in David L. Sills, ed., *International Encyclopedia of the Social Sciences,* (New York: Free Press, 1968), 4, p.436; and David A. Baldwin, *Economic Statecraft* (Princeton: Princeton University Press, 1985), p.72.
5. Adam Smith, *The Wealth of Nations* (London: Dent, Everyman's Library no. 412, 1910), vol. 1, bk. 4, p.436.
6. Classic studies of mercantilism include Eli F. Heckscher, *Mercantilism*, vols. 1 and 2, rev. 2nd ed. translated by Mendel Shapiro (London: George Allen & Unwin, 1955); and Jacob Viner, *Studies in the Theory of International Trade* (New York: Augustus M. Kelley, 1965), chs. 1 and 2.

7. For competing views on world powers during the mercantilist period, see George Model-ski, "The Long Cycle of Global Politics and the Nation-State," *Comparative Studies in Society and History* 20-2 (April 1978), pp.214–235; Immanuel Wallerstein, "The Three Instances of Hegemony in the History of the Capitalist World-Economy," in *The Politics of the World-Economy: The States, the Movements and the Civilizations* (London: Cambridge University Press, 1984), pp.37–46; George Modelski, *Long Cycles in World Politics* (Seattle: University of Washington Press, 1987), ch. 2; Joshua S. Goldstein, *Long Cycles: Prosperity and War in the Modern Age* (New Haven: Yale University Press, 1988), pp.99–147.

8. Paul Kennedy, *The Rise and Fall of the Great Powers: Economic Change and Military Conflict from 1500 to 2000* (New York: Random House, 1987), p.151.

9. Paul Bairoch, "International Industrialization Levels from 1750 to 1980," *Journal of European Economic History* 11-2 (Fall 1982), pp.291–292.

10. Some writers argue that Britain's contribution to freer trade in the nineteenth century is overestimated. See Timothy J. McKeown, "Hegemonic Stability Theory and 19th Century Tariff Levels in Europe," *International Organization* 37-1 (Winter 1983), pp.73–91.

11. Edward John Ray, "Changing Patterns of Protectionism: The Fall in Tariffs and the Rise in Non-Tariff Barriers," *Northwestern Journal of International Law & Business*, 8 (1987), pp.294–295; Stephen D. Krasner, "State Power and the Structure of International Trade," *World Politics* 28-3 (April, 1976), pp.330–335.

12. David A. Lake, *Power, Protection, and Free Trade: International Sources of U.S. Commercial Strategy, 1887–1939* (Ithaca: Cornell University Press, 1988), p.31.

13. On the role of banks and the state in promoting industrialization in late industrializers, see Alexander Gerschenkron, *Economic Backwardness in Historical Perspective* (Cambridge: Harvard University Press, 1962). In the nineteenth century the United States and Germany were late industrializers relative to Britain.

14. Lake, *Power, Protection, and Free Trade*, pp.30–32; Bairoch, "International Industrialization Levels from 1750 to 1980," pp.292–293 and 297.

15. Kennedy, *The Rise and Fall of the Great Powers*, p.230.

16. Albert Fishlow, "Lessons from the Past: Capital Markets during the 19th Century and the Interwar Period," *International Organization* 39-3 (Summer 1985), p.390; David A. Lake, "British and American Hegemony Compared: Lessons for the Current Era of Decline," in Michael Fry, ed., *History, The White House and The Kremlin: Statesmen as Historians* (London: Pinter, 1991), p.108.

17. Sally Marks, *The Illusion of Peace: International Relations in Europe 1918–1933* (New York: St. Martin's Press, 1976), p.47; Charles P. Kindleberger, *The World in Depression 1929–1939*, rev. and enlarged ed. (Berkeley: University of California Press, 1986), pp.23–26.

18. Robert A. Pastor, *Congress and the Politics of U.S. Foreign Economic Policy, 1929–1976* (Berkeley: University of California Press, 1980), p.78; John M. Dobson, *Two Centuries of Tariffs: The Background and Emergence of the U.S. International Trade Commission* (Washington, DC: U.S. International Trade Commission, 1976), p.32.

19. On the 1930 U.S. tariff see Joseph M. Jones, Jr., *Tariff Retaliation: Repercussions of the Hawley-Smoot Bill* (Philadelphia: University of Pennsylvania Press, 1934).

20. See Kindleberger, *The World in Depression*.

21. The classic study of domestic pressures on the U.S. Congress during the interwar period is E. E. Schattschneider, *Politics, Pressures and the Tariff: A Study of Free Private Enterprise in Pressure Politics, as Shown in the 1929–1930 Revision of the Tariff* (Hamden: Archon Books, 1963, unaltered from the 1935 edition). See also Helen V. Milner, *Resisting Protectionism: Global Industries and the Politics of International Trade* (Princeton: Princeton University Press, 1988).

22. Lake, *Power, Protection, and Free Trade*, p.204.

23. Harold K. Jacobson, *Networks of Interdependence: International Organizations and the Global Political System* (New York: Alfred A. Knopf, 1979), pp.230–231; Javed A. Ansari, *The Political Economy of International Economic Organization* (Sussex: Wheatsheaf, 1986), pp.6–7; Kelly-Kate S. Pease, *International Organizations: Perspectives on Governance in the Twenty-First Century* (Upper Saddle River: Prentice-Hall, 1999), pp.18–19.

24. *Covenant of the League of Nations*, Article 23e.

25. For a discussion of the BIS see Age F. P. Bakker, *International Financial Institutions* (New York: Longman, 1996), ch. 6; and Hazel J. Johnson, *Global Financial Institutions and Markets* (Oxford: Blackwell, 2000), pp.410–411.

26. Margaret Garritsen de Vries, "The Bretton Woods Conferences and the Birth of the International Monetary Fund," in Orin Kirshner, ed., *The Bretton Woods-GATT System: Retrospect and Prospect After Fifty Years* (Armonk: M. E. Sharpe, 1996), pp.3–4.

27. On the difference between coordination and collaboration, see Arthur Stein, "Coordination and Collaboration: Regimes in an Anarchic World," in David A. Baldwin, ed., *Neorealism and Neoliberalism: The Contemporary Debate* (New York: Columbia University Press, 1993), pp.41–45.

28. The term *KIEOs* is used in Harold Jacobson and Michel Oksenberg, *China's Participation in the IMF, the World Bank, and GATT: Toward a Global Economic Order* (Ann Arbor: University of Michigan Press, 1990).

29. Communication from a Counsellor, External Relations Division, WTO, November 8, 2001.

30. Quoted in Sidney Dell, "Relations Between the United Nations and the Bretton Woods Institutions," *Development* 4 (1989), p.28.

31. See Samuel A. Bleicher, "UN v. IBRD: A Dilemma of Functionalism," *International Organization* 24-1 (Winter 1970), pp.31–47.

32. "United Nations-Bretton Woods Collaboration: How Much Is Enough?" *Report of the Twenty-Sixth United Nations Issues Conference* (Muscatine: Stanley Foundation, February 24–26, 1995), p.18.

33. See Dell, "Relations Between the United Nations and the Bretton Woods Institutions," pp.27–38; and Edward S. Mason and Robert E. Asher, *The World Bank Since Bretton Woods* (Washington, DC: Brookings Institution), pp.566–576.

34. UNCTAD, *World Investment Report 1996* (New York: UN, 1996), pp.239–247; World Trade Organization, *WTO Annual Report 1996* (Geneva: WTO, 1996), vol. 2, pp.24, 67.

35. LDCs have been underrepresented on the KIEO professional staffs for a number of reasons. See Theodore Cohn, "Developing Countries in the International Civil Service: The Case of the World Bank Group," *International Review of Administrative Sciences* 41-1 (1975), pp.47–56.

36. Bretton Woods Commission, *Bretton Woods: Looking to the Future* (Washington, DC: Bretton Woods Committee, July 1994), p.B–3.

37. Barry Eichengreen and Peter B. Kenen, "Managing the World Economy under the Bretton Woods System: An Overview," in Peter B. Kenen, ed., *Managing the World Economy: Fifty Years After Bretton Woods* (Washington, DC: Institute for International Economics, 1944), pp.5–6; John Gerard Ruggie, "International Regimes, Transactions, and Change: Embedded Liberalism in the Postwar Economic Order," in Stephen D. Krasner, ed., *International Regimes* (Ithaca: Cornell University Press), pp.195–231.

38. "United Nations-Bretton Woods Collaboration: How Much Is Enough?" p.2.

39. Aaron Segal, "Managing the World Economy," *International Political Science Review* 11-3 (1990), p.367.

40. C. Fred Bergsten and C. Randall Henning, *Global Economic Leadership and the Group of Seven* (Washington, DC: Institute for International Economics, 1996), p.15.

41. For a discussion of the smaller DC-led groups in the global trade regime see Theodore H. Cohn, *Governing Global Trade: International Institutions in Conflict and Convergence* (Aldershot: Ashgate, 2002).

42. The European Union is a special member of the OECD.

43. Organization for Economic Cooperation and Development, *The OECD in the 1990s* (Paris: OECD, 1994), p.9; David Henderson, "The Role of the OECD in Liberalising International Trade and Capital Flows," in Sven Arndt and Chris Miller, eds., Special issue of *The World Economy* on "Global Trade Policy" (1996), pp.11–28.

44. Bernard Colas, "The OECD's Legal Influence in a Global Economy," *World Economic Affairs* 1-3 (Spring/Summer 1997), pp.66–67; William J. Drake and Kalypso Nicolaïdis, "Ideas, Interests, and Institutionalization: 'Trade in Services' and The Uruguay Round," *International Organization* 46-1 (Winter 1992) pp.37–100.

45. OECD, Export Credit Financing Systems in OECD Member and Non-Member Countries—1999 Supplement (Paris: OECD, 1999), p.1. See also Andrew M. Moravcsik, "Disciplining Trade Finance: The OECD Export Credit Arrangement," *International Organization* (Winter 1989), pp.173–205; and Cohn, *Governing Global Trade*, chs. 3-4.

46. Colas, "The OECD's Legal Influence in a Global Economy," p.67; Henderson, "The Role of the OECD," pp.21–22.

47. Peter B. Kenen, *The International Financial Architecture: What's New? What's Missing?* (Washington, D.C.: Institute for International Economics, 2001), p. 4; International Monetary Fund, "IMF Survey Supplement," vol. 30, September 2001, p.18.

48. Michael C. Webb, *The Political Economy of Policy Coordination: International Adjustment Since 1945* (Ithaca: Cornell University Press, 1995), pp.176–177.

49. Michael P. Blackwell, "From G-5 to G-77: International Forums for Discussion of Economic Issues," *Finance & Development* 23-4 (December 1986), p.40; Robert D. Putnam and Nicholas Bayne, *Hanging Together: Cooperation and Conflict in the Seven-Power Summits*, rev. ed. (London: Sage, 1987), pp.150–154.

50. John Kirton, "The Diplomacy of Concert: Canada, the G7 and the Halifx Summit," *Canadian Foreign Policy* 3-1 (Spring 1995), p.66. See also Nicholas Bayne, *Hanging in There: The G7 and G8 Summit in Maturity and Renewal* (Aldershot: Ashgate, 2000).

51. Bayne, *Hanging in There*, pp.116–118.

52. Stephen Gill, "Global Finance, Monetary Policy and Cooperation Among the Group of Seven, 1944–92," in Philip G. Cerny, ed., *Finance and World Politics: Markets, Regimes and States in the Post-Hegemonic Era* (London: Elgar, 1993), p.104; C. Fred Bergsten, "A Clinton Round or a Pacific Free Trade Area?" *New Perspectives Quarterly* 10-2 (Spring 1993), pp.19–22.

53. Bergsten and Henning, *Global Economic Leadership and the Group of Seven*, pp.6–7 and 43-49.

54. Quoted in Klaus Engelen, "Comment," in Kenen, ed., *Managing the World Economy*, p.79. See also Klaus C. Engelen, "Anger and Angst: Why the Germans Hate the World Bank and the IMF," *The International Economy* 2-5 (Sept./Oct. 1988), pp.74–78.

55. Despite some U.S. opposition to the Köhler nomination, the German Chancellor (Gerhard Schröder) was "determined to have a German succeed Michel Camdessus of France" as IMF Managing Director. (Edmund L. Andrews, "New Candidate Proposed for I.M.F.," *New York Times*, March 8, 2000, p.C4.)

56. Jagdish Bhagwati, "Regionalism and Multilateralism: An Overview," in Jaime de Melo and Arvind Panagariya, eds., *New Dimensions in Regional Integration* (Cambridge: Cambridge University Press, 1993), p.29.

57. Bretton Woods Commission, *Bretton Woods*, p.B-3.

58. World Bank, *World Development Indicators— 2001* (Washington, D.C.: World Bank, 2001), p. 293. See also Michelle A. Vachris and James Thomas, "International Price Comparisons Based on Purchasing Power Parity," *Monthly Labor Review*, October 1999, pp. 3–12.

59. For example, see "Big MacCurrencies," *The Economist,* April 11, 1998, p. 58.
60. UNDP, *Human Development Report 2002* (New York: Oxford University Press, 2002), pp.143–144.
61. UNDP, *Human Development Report 1996* (New York: Oxford University Press, 1996), p.2.
62. See, for example, Kevin Danaher, ed., *Fifty Years Is Enough: The Case Against the World Bank and the International Monetary Fund* (Boston: South End Press, 1994); John Cavanagh, Daphne Wysham, and Marcos Arruda, eds., *Beyond Bretton Woods: Alternatives to the Global Economic Order* (London: Pluto Press, 1994); and Stephen D. Krasner, *Structural Conflict: The Third World Against Global Liberalism* (Berkeley: University of California Press, 1985).
63. *World Bank Annual Report 1997* (Washington, DC: World Bank, 1997), pp.227–230.
64. *World Bank Annual Report 2000* (Washington, D.C.: World Bank, 2001), p.1.
65. David A. Kay, *The New Nations in the United Nations, 1960–1967* (New York: Columbia University Press, 1970), pp.2–3.
66. The term *Third World* was apparently first used by a French demographer, Alfred Sauvy, in 1952.
67. Michael Zammit Cutajar, ed., *UNCTAD and the North-South Dialogue: The First Twenty Years* (Oxford: Permagon Press, 1985), p.vii.
68. Jeffrey A. Hart, *The New International Economic Order: Conflict and Cooperation in North-South Economic Relations, 1974–77* (London: Macmillan, 1983); and Ervin Laszlo, et al., *The Obstacles to the New International Economic Order* (New York: Pergamon Press, 1980).
69. Tyrone Ferguson, *The Third World and Decision Making in the International Monetary Fund: The Quest for Full and Effective Participation* (London: Pinter Publishers, 1988), p.33.
70. Grant B. Taplin, "Revitalizing UNCTAD," *Finance & Development* 29-2 (June 1992), pp.36–37; Marc Williams, *International Economic Organizations and the Third World* (New York: Harvester Wheatsheet, 1994), p.192; Carlston B. Boucher and Wolfgang E. Siebeck, "UNCTAD VII: New Spirit in North-South Relations?" *Finance & Development* 24-4 (December 1987), p.14.
71. Harold K. Jacobson, *Networks of Interdependence: International Organizations and the Global Political System* (New York: Knopf, 1979), p.13.
72. Henry Morgenthau, Jr., "Bretton Woods and International Cooperation," *Foreign Affairs* 23-2 (January 1945), p.186.
73. Quoted in Joseph Gold, *Membership and Nonmembership in the International Monetary Fund: A Study in International Law and Organization* (Washington, DC: IMF, 1974), p.129.
74. Jozef M. van Brabant, *The Planned Economies and International Economic Organizations* (Cambridge: Cambridge University Press, 1991).
75. Valerie J. Assetto, *The Soviet Bloc in the IMF and the IBRD* (Boulder: Westview Press, 1988), pp.56–66, 185; Brabant, *The Planned Economies and International Economic Organizations,* pp.45–48; Laszlo Lang, "International Regimes and the Political Economy of East-West Relations," *Occasional Paper Series* No. 13 (New York: Institute for East-West Security Studies, 1989), pp.19–22.
76. On the relationship between the Marshall Plan and the formation of the CMEA (also called COMECON), see William R. Keylor, *The Twentieth Century World—An International History* (New York: Oxford University Press, 1984), pp.274–275, 359; and Michael Kaser, *Comecon: Integration Problems of the Planned Economies* (London: Oxford University Press, 1965), pp.9–12.
77. Klaus Schröder, "The IMF and the Countries of the Council for Mutual Economic Assistance," *Intereconomics* 2 (March/April 1982), p.87; Brabant, *The Planned Economies and International Economic Organizations,* p.70.
78. *IBRD—Articles of Agreement,* as amended effective February 16, 1989 (Washington, DC: IBRD, August 1991), Article 4, section 10.

79. See David A. Baldwin, "The International Bank in Political Perspective," *World Politics* 18-1 (October 1965), pp.68–81; and Theodore H. Cohn, "Politics in the World Bank Group: The Question of Loans to the Asian Giants," *International Organization* 28-3 (Summer 1974), pp.561–571. For critiques of the IMF and World Bank's political/ideological orientation from a historical structuralist perspective, see Cheryl Payer, *The Debt Trap: The IMF and the Third World* (Middlesex: Penguin, 1974); and Teresa Hayter, *Aid as Imperialism* (Middlesex: Penguin, 1971).

80. Assetto, *The Soviet Bloc in the IMF and the IBRD,* pp.53–54.

81. Gold, *Membership and Nonmembership in the International Monetary Fund,* pp.342–379; Marie Lavigne, "Eastern European Countries and the IMF," in Béla Csikós-Nagy and David G. Young, eds., *East-West Economic Relations in the Changing Global Environment* (London: Macmillan, 1986), p.298; and Assetto, *The Soviet Bloc in the IMF and the IBRD,* pp.69–93.

82. David Robertson, "Civil Society and the WTO," *World Economy* 23-9 (September 2000), pp.1119–1123.

83. *Charter of the United Nations,* Chapter III, Article 8.

84. UN Department of Social and Economic Affairs, *The World's Women—2000* (New York: UN, 2000), pp.167–168; Hilary Charlesworth, Christine Chinkin, and Shelley Wright, "Feminist Approaches to International Law," *American Journal of International Law* 85-4 (October 1991), pp.621—626; V. Spike Peterson and Anne Sisson Runyan, *Global Gender Issues,* 2nd ed. (Boulder: Westview Press, 1999), pp.74—81.

85. J. Ann Tickner, *Gender in International Relations: Feminist Perspectives on Achieving Global Security* (New York: Columbia University Press, 1992), p.4.

86. UNDP, *Human Development Report 2001* (New York: Oxford University Press), pp.15–16.

87. See, for example, Daniel C. Esty, "Non-Governmental Organizations at the World Trade Organization: Cooperation, Competition, or Exclusion," *Journal of International Economic Law* 1-1 (March 1998), pp.123–147; Jim Rollo and J. Alan Winters, "Subsidiarity and Governance Challenges for the WTO: Environmental and Labour Standards," *World Economy* 23-4 (April 2000), pp.561–576; Ibrahim F. I. Shihata, "Implementation, Enforcement and Compliance with International Environmental Agreements—Practical Suggesions in Light of the World Bank's Experience," *Georgetown International Environmental Law Review* 9-1 (1996), pp.37–51; Robert O'Brien et al., *Contesting Global Governance: Multilateral Economic Institutions and Global Social Movements* (Cambridge: Cambridge University Press, 2000).

88. See James N. Rosenau, "The State in an Era of Cascading Politics: Wavering Concept, Widening Competence, Withering Colossus, or Weathering Change?" *Comparative Political Studies* 21-1 (April 1988), pp.13–44.

89. Andrew Gamble and Anthony Payne, "Conclusion: The New Regionalism," in Andrew Gamble and Anthony Payne, eds., *Regionalism and World Order* (London: Macmillan, 1996), p.253.

90. O'Brien et al. *Contesting Global Governance,* p.21.

PART II

Theoretical Perspectives

art II of this book focuses on the three main theoretical perspectives in the study of IPE: realism, liberalism, and historical structuralism. Before discussing these perspectives, it is necessary to make some general points about them. First, the three main perspectives are not mutually exclusive ideologies. Although the perspectives remain distinctive, they have interacted and influenced one another over time, and the margins between them are sometimes blurred. Many IPE theories such as regime theory, hegemonic stability theory, and the business conflict model also are hybrids that draw on more than one perspective. In addition, scholarly research on the intersection of domestic and foreign policy variables in IPE cannot be neatly classified under one of the three traditional perspectives. Chapters 3 through 5 discuss some of these hybrid theories under the perspective with which they are most closely identified.

Second, it is somewhat simplistic to state that there are three main IPE perspectives, because each perspective contains a wide diversity of writings. Liberalism is perhaps the most broad ranging of the perspectives, and historical structuralism encompasses writings ranging from classical Marxism to dependency theory and world-systems theory. Nevertheless, a diversity of writings can be grouped within each school of thought because the authors generally agree on a core set of assumptions.* Third, the three perspectives do not adequately address some newer issues in IPE relating to the environment, gender, technology, and migration. Nevertheless, no new theoretical approaches to this point have posed a major challenge to the three traditional IPE perspectives in terms of the scope and importance of their explanations.** Becoming familiar with these perspectives is an important starting point in the study of IPE.

It is useful to provide a brief preview here of the organization of Chapters 3 to 5. To compare the main IPE perspectives, each chapter begins with a discussion of how

---

*Thomas J. Biersteker, "Evolving Perspectives on International Political Economy: Twentieth-Century Contexts and Discontinuities," *International Political Science Review* 14-1 (January 1993), pp.7–33.

**Stephen D. Krasner, "International Political Economy: Abiding Discord," *Review of International Political Economy* 1-1 (Spring 1994), pp.13–14.

the perspective deals with three key questions: (1) What is the role of domestic actors, particularly the individual, the state, and societal groups? (2) What are the nature and purpose of international economic relations? and (3) What is the relationship between politics and economics? Although these three questions provide a basis for comparing the IPE perspectives, they gloss over the differences among writers *within* each perspective. The second part of each chapter therefore examines the historical development of the perspective, with particular emphasis on the diversity of views within the perspective. Each chapter concludes with a discussion of the perspective's approach to North-South relations.

C H A P T E R 3

The Realist Perspective

Part II begins with a discussion of the realist perspective, the oldest school of thought in international relations. Indeed, Thucydides (ca. 471–400 B.C.) is often credited with writing the first important work on IR—*The History of the Peloponnesian War* on war between the Greek city-states—and also with being the first writer in the realist tradition.[1] In addition to being the oldest school of thought, realism was also the most influential school affecting the views of American foreign policy leaders after World War II. Despite realism's prominence in IR in general, it has been far less important than the liberal perspective in the subfield of IPE, for several reasons. First, realists have developed their theories by drawing mainly on politics and history rather than on economics; and second, the realists' emphasis on power has most often directed their attention to security rather than economic issues. Nevertheless, the realist emphasis on the role of the state and power is of considerable importance in the study of IPE.

There are variations among writers in all three main IPE perspectives. Thus, we can identify two major strains of realism, one that has largely neglected economic matters and a second that has been far more attuned to economic-political interactions. The first strain was evident in the views of Niccolò Machiavelli, an Italian philosopher and diplomat who lived from 1469 to 1527. Machiavelli is best known for his classic work *The Prince*, in which he provided advice to leaders on how to gain and maintain power. Machiavelli saw little connection between economics and politics, and he wrote, "Fortune has decreed that, as I do not know how to reason either about the art of silk or about the art of wool, either about profits or about losses, it befits me to reason about the state."[2] Machiavelli also considered military strength to be far more important than wealth in making war because "gold alone will not procure good soldiers, but good soldiers will always procure gold."[3] An important writer on security-economic linkages has argued that Machiavelli's work should be supplemented with economic advice for the modern prince "on the most efficient use of quotas, exchange controls, capital investment, and other instruments of economic warfare."[4] As discussed in this chapter, postwar American realists, like Machiavelli, relegated economics to a relatively low level of importance.

The other strain of realism, stemming from Thucydides and the mercantilists, has been associated with a distinctive realist approach to IPE. Theorists in this strain draw close linkages between traditional realist concerns with power and security on the one hand and economic relations on the other. In *The History of the Peloponnesian War*, for example, Thucydides attributed war among the Greek city-states to a number of economic changes, including the growth of trade, the emergence of new commercial powers such as Athens and Corinth, and the use of money in traditional agrarian economies. Unlike Machiavelli, Thucydides considered wealth to be a vitally important source of military strength, and he wrote that "war is a matter not so much of arms as of money, which makes arms of use."[5] Although Thucydides often referred to economic issues, it was the classical mercantilists of the sixteenth to nineteenth centuries who first engaged in *systematic* theorizing on IPE from a realist perspective.[6] The emphasis of mercantilists on the linkages between power and wealth was critical to the establishment of a realist perspective on IPE.

BASIC TENETS OF THE REALIST PERSPECTIVE

The Role of the Individual, the State, and Societal Groups

Realists assert that the international system is anarchic because there is no central authority above nation-states. Unlike most domestic societies, IR is a self-help system in which each state must look after its own interests.[7] Thus, realists consider the state to be the principal or dominant actor in IR, and they place considerable emphasis on the preservation of national sovereignty. A state has internal sovereignty when it has a monopoly on the legitimate use of force within its territory, and it has external sovereignty when it is free of control by any outside authority.[8] To retain its sovereignty, a state must have sufficient power to defend its interests. Some realists assert that "power is always the immediate aim" of international politics,[9] while others argue that state "security is the highest end."[10] Whether realists give top priority to power or security, they all place considerable emphasis on the ability of the state to survive and pursue its national interest.

The state, according to realists, is not only the most important international actor but also a unitary actor. Realists studying foreign economic policymaking recognize the need to discuss subnational and transnational actors in explaining a state's policies.[11] Nevertheless, most modern-day realists continue to emphasize the unitary nature of the state on important international issues; in the realist view, nonstate actors generally operate within the rubric of state policies. Realists also assume that states are rational actors concerned with maximizing the benefits and minimizing the costs of pursuing national objectives. They acknowledge that policy-makers may be affected by bias and misperceptions and may lack information and capabilities required to make the best decisions. Instead of making *value-maximizing* decisions, states may settle for *value-satisficing* decisions that are satisfactory but not optimal.[12] Nevertheless, the state is essentially a rational decision maker. Because realists assume that states are rational, unitary actors, they have been at the forefront in developing *parsimonious* theories that simplify explanations by explaining a great deal with a small number of concepts and variables.

The Nature and Purpose of International Economic Relations

Because IR is a self-help system, each state in the realist view must look after its own survival and security. Nevertheless, a *security dilemma* results when each state takes actions to bolster its own security because such actions increase the fear and insecurity of other states. For example, a state may build up its armaments solely for defensive purposes, but this action may raise the fears of others and contribute to an arms race. In view of the security dilemma, realists argue that each state is most concerned about *relative gains,* or its position vis-à-vis other states. Thus, realists contend that "even though two states may be gaining absolutely in wealth, in political terms it is the effect of these gains on relative power positions which is of primary importance."[13] Unlike realists, liberals concentrate more on *absolute gains,* in which each state seeks to maximize its own gains and is less concerned about the gains or losses of others.

The realists' emphasis on relative gains stems from their view that IR is often a *zero-sum game* in which one group's gain equals another group's loss. This contrasts with the liberal view that IR is a *variable-sum game* in which different groups may gain or lose together. The liberal versus realist view of international institutions provides a prime example of this difference in outlook. Liberals assume that international economic organizations—the IMF, World Bank, and WTO—are politically neutral and benefit all states that adhere to their liberal-economic guidelines. Realists, by contrast, believe that the most powerful states shape the rules of these organizations to fit their own particular national interests and that IOs serve primarily as "arenas for acting out power relationships."[14]

Although realists believe that all states are concerned with relative gains, the objectives of states may be either offensive or defensive in nature. Aggressive states may use the international economy to promote imperialist expansion or extend their national power over others, whereas defensive states may simply seek to maintain their economic positions in the system. Whether a state is more aggressive or defensive, its interests and policies are determined by its power position in the international system. Thus, realists believe that a hegemonic state with dominant power is likely to have very different interests and policies than less powerful states.

Despite the realist attention to relative gains, historical structuralists argue that realists are mainly concerned with redistribution of power *within* the capitalist system and that they share the commitment of liberals to capitalism. Historical structuralists, by contrast, believe that a more equitable distribution of wealth and power is not possible under capitalism, and they therefore question the capitalist system itself. In the historical structuralist view, there are only "two main modes of development in contemporary history: capitalist and redistributive," and they group realism along with liberalism in the capitalist mode.[15]

The Relationship Between Politics and Economics

Realists give priority to politics over economics and assume that powerful states can structure economic relations at the international level. Thus, they are critical of liberal theorists who argue that increasing interdependence and globalization are eroding state control. Some realists question the premise that interdependence and globalization are increasing.[16] Others acknowledge that globalization may be occurring, but they disagree with liberals about the causes and consequences of this phenomenon. Whereas liberals attach considerable importance to technological change and advances in communications and transportation as factors behind globalization, realists believe that globalization (to the extent that it is occurring) increases only because states permit it to increase. Thus, the largest states have the capability of either opening or closing world markets, and they can use globalization to improve their power positions vis-à-vis smaller and weaker states.[17] Realists also place considerable emphasis on a hegemonic state's ability to create an open and stable economic order that can further the globalization process. (Hegemonic stability theory is discussed later in this chapter.)

THE MERCANTILISTS

The term **mercantilism** was first used by Adam Smith, the eighteenth century economist and philosopher, in reference to much of the economic thought and practice in Europe from about 1500 to 1750.[18] As discussed in Chapter 2, mercantilism played an important role in state building and territorial unification after the demise of feudalism through its emphasis on national power. Mercantilists believed that a state's power depended on the amount of gold and silver it could accumulate in the public treasury. With these precious metals, the state could build up its armed forces, hire mercenaries, and influence both its enemies and its allies. Mercantilist states therefore took all necessary measures to accumulate gold by increasing their exports and decreasing their imports. Since it is impossible for all states to have a balance-of-trade surplus, mercantilists believed that conflict was central to IR and that relative gains were more important than absolute gains. Thus, the mercantilists stood firmly within the realist school of thought.

A number of writers from different countries contributed to classical mercantilist thought over several centuries; thus, it is not surprising that there are different interpretations of their ideas. For example, some analysts argue that classical mercantilists considered national power to be the most important goal and viewed the acquisition of wealth as simply a means of gaining power—the ultimate objective. Others maintain that the mercantilists placed power and wealth on equal footing, viewing them both as "proper ultimate ends of national policy."[19] Despite these differences of view, analysts agree that mercantilism focused on the national interest and on the pursuit of wealth as well as power by the state.

In the late eighteenth century, important thinkers began to develop comprehensive critiques of mercantilism on political and ethical as well as economic grounds. They criticized mercantilists, for example, for not guaranteeing the freedom of the individual from intrusive state regulation and for contributing to the continuous cycle of wars in

Europe. Adam Smith launched a vigorous economic attack on mercantilism, arguing that it encouraged states to engage in "beggaring all their neighbours" and caused trade and commerce to become a "fertile source of discord and animosity."[20] These criticisms of mercantilism were highly effective, and liberal views of free trade became dominant in England—the major power of the time—for much of the nineteenth century.

It is important to note that some authors use the term *mercantilism* in a more general sense in reference to realist thought and practice in IPE. Thus, they refer not only to the mercantilist period in the sixteenth to eighteenth centuries but also to "neomercantilist" states today, which rely on government involvement and various forms of protectionism to promote self-sufficiency and increase their power and wealth. To avoid confusion, this book uses the term *realism* in reference to the general school of thought in IPE; it uses the term *mercantilism* to refer only to the specific period when states sought to accumulate precious metals and increase their national power in the sixteenth to eighteenth centuries.

REALISM AND THE INDUSTRIAL REVOLUTION

Although the liberal critics of mercantilism were highly successful, some thinkers and policymakers continued to emphasize realist practices. Mercantilism was a preindustrial doctrine, and the advent of the Industrial Revolution gave a new impetus to realist thought. Industrialization in the realist view had become a central requirement for countries seeking to gain national security, military power, and economic self-sufficiency. Foremost among the realist thinkers at this time were the first U.S. Secretary of the Treasury, Alexander Hamilton (1755–1804), and a German civil servant, professor, and politician who was imprisoned and exiled for his dissident political views, Friedrich List (1789–1846).

Although the classical mercantilists were the first to engage in systematic realist theorizing on IPE, Hamilton's 1791 *Report on the Subject of Manufactures* "contains the intellectual origins of modern economic nationalism and the classic defense of economic protectionism."[21] Hamilton believed that the preservation of U.S. national independence and security depended on the strengthening of the economy and the promotion of economic development. His preferred policies to achieve economic growth were largely realist, including an emphasis on industry over agriculture, economic self-sufficiency, government intervention, and trade protectionism. Although Hamilton realized that agriculture was important, he believed that manufacturing was more essential for diversifying the U.S. economy and decreasing its vulnerability to external forces. In his *Report on Manufactures*, Hamilton wrote:

> Not only the wealth; but the independence and security of a Country, appear to be materially connected with the prosperity of manufactures. . . . The extreme embarrassments of the United States during the late War, from an incapacity of supplying themselves, are still matter of keen recollection.[22]

Because the British government had discouraged manufacturing in the American colonies, Hamilton felt that U.S. government intervention was necessary to establish an industrial base. To counter the advantages of British over American industries, Hamilton argued that the U.S. government should encourage the introduction of foreign technology, capital, and skilled labor. The government should also adopt protectionist trade policies, including tariffs, quotas, and bounties, to bolster its fledgling industries. However, Hamilton's advocacy of protectionism differed from classical mercantilism because he did not consider the accumulation of gold and a positive balance of trade to be the primary objectives. Instead, he emphasized the development of a strong manufacturing economy.

List was strongly influenced by Hamilton's ideas, and like Hamilton he emphasized the importance of manufacturing industries for a country's economic development. Indeed, in his seminal work *The National System of Political Economy* (1841), List wrote that "a nation which exchanges agricultural products for foreign manufactured goods is an individual with *one* arm, which is supported by a foreign arm."[23] List had lived in the United States as well as Germany, and he argued that these two countries would never equal Britain's wealth and power if they did not develop their manufacturing industries. As strategies to increase manufacturing, List placed particular emphasis on the imposition of trade barriers, the promotion of national unity, and the development of "human capital."

If Germany and the United States were to catch up with Britain, List argued, they would have to provide some trade protection for their infant industries. Indeed, Britain itself had attained manufacturing supremacy by adopting a protective commercial policy, and it supported free trade only after it became the economic leader. By turning to a free trade policy during the nineteenth century, Britain promoted a division of labor that enabled it to retain its supremacy in industry and technology. Thus, trade between Britain and the United States in the first half of the nineteenth century consisted mainly of the exchange of British manufactured products for U.S. wool and cotton. Although states can benefit from free trade in the long term, List argued, U.S. and German economic development would be constrained in an open competitive economy as long as they lagged behind Britain. It was therefore necessary for the United States and Germany to adopt some protective trade policies as a means of building up their productive potential.

List also emphasized the importance of national unity, which would enable the state to implement policies promoting economic development. List's preoccupation with national unification was understandable because of the prevalence of internal duties on trade within Germany at the time. A strong, unified state was necessary, List believed, not only to impose external trade barriers and engage in national projects such as building railroads but also to promote the development of human capital. List attributed British leadership in manufacturing and trade to the superiority of the British educational system, and he argued that governments had special responsibilities for educating their citizens.[24]

As a realist, List strongly criticized the views of liberal economist Adam Smith, who favored a division of labor and free trade. In List's view, liberals like Smith overemphasized the existence of natural harmony and peace and underestimated the extent to which the world is divided by national rivalries and conflict. It is important to note, however, that List believed a division of labor and free trade were valuable *in the long term.* In the short term, he argued that government involvement in developing human capital and protecting infant industries was necessary in countries such as

Germany and the United States. Only when these less advanced nations could be "raised by artificial measure," as the British had been, wrote List, could "freedom of trade . . . operate naturally."[25]

REALISM IN THE INTERWAR PERIOD

As discussed in Chapter 2, Britain repealed its Corn Laws in 1846, opening its markets to agricultural imports and ushering in a period of free trade that continued until the latter part of the nineteenth century. However, changes occurring in the late nineteenth century caused liberal free trade ideas to lose some of their appeal. Under the pressures of World War I and the economic crises and conflicts of the interwar years, there was a virtual breakdown of cooperative relations based on liberalism. Realist ideas gained more influence as countries seeking to protect their national interests turned to policies of protectionism, competitive currency devaluations, and foreign exchange controls. The dire economic circumstances also encouraged extremists, especially on the right, who "took advantage of the economic dislocation to attack the entire liberal-capitalist system and to call for assertive 'national' policies, backed if necessary by the sword."[26]

The experience of extreme nationalism and trade protectionism during the interwar years and its linkage with the Great Depression and the outbreak of World War II provided an impetus for leaders at the Bretton Woods conference to establish a more liberal economic system. Thus, liberalism became the dominant school of thought in the postwar international economic system. In the postwar international *political* system, however, realist thought was to reign supreme. Unlike the earlier mercantilists, the postwar realist scholars were largely unconcerned with economic matters.

REALISM IN THE POST–WORLD WAR II PERIOD

Although realists such as Thucydides, the mercantilists, Hamilton, and List had been highly attuned to economic issues, U.S. realist scholars after World War II focused almost exclusively on security issues. Security matters were a major preoccupation with the rapid emergence of the Cold War, and international economic issues by contrast seemed to have little political importance. Under U.S. leadership, a consensus had developed at Bretton Woods that seemed to usher in a period of economic stability and prosperity. LDCs thought that their interests received too little attention at Bretton Woods, but they had little ability to influence postwar economic policies. The Cold War was also largely excluded from the postwar economic system because most Soviet bloc countries were not members of the KIEOs (the IMF, World Bank, and GATT). Their nonparticipation did not interfere with the functioning of these organizations because the Eastern bloc accounted for only a small share of global economic interactions. The KIEOs were largely dominated by the Western DCs and espoused liberal principles; thus realists felt they were involved with "low politics" and therefore not worthy of much attention.[27]

Postwar realist scholars were also influenced by liberal views on the separability of economics and politics. However, unlike liberals such as Adam Smith, who supported the idea of a laissez-faire economy free of political constraints, the realists emphasized political forces and largely ignored economics. Traditional U.S. views that there *should be* a clear separation between the state and the economy were yet another source of influence on postwar realists. Government involvement in military and defense matters was fully accepted in the United States, but state involvement in the economy was viewed as somehow less legitimate. Finally, the superpower status of the United States led U.S. realists to fix their attention so firmly on the power struggle with the Soviet Union that they "overlooked the economic relations beneath the flux of political relations."[28] As a result, liberalism and Marxism clearly overshadowed realism as schools of thought in IPE during the 1950s–1960s.

THE REVIVAL OF REALIST IPE

In the 1970s–1980s, some realist writers began to return "to a realist conception of the relationship of economics and politics that had disappeared from postwar American writings."[29] For example, Robert Gilpin, who was a leading scholar in the realist rediscovery of IPE, devoted an entire book to the study of U.S. power and the MNC in 1975.[30] Two factors contributed to the reemergence of realism as a major perspective on IPE. First, the decline of the Cold War and increasing disarray in the global economy forced many realists to broaden their focus beyond security issues; and second, realists were highly critical of liberal and Marxist economic analyses of IPE.

Although Western monetary, trade, and aid relations had prospered under U.S. leadership during the 1950s–1960s, major changes occurred in the 1970s–1980s with destabilizing consequences for the global economy. These changes included the emergence of OPEC as a powerful new world actor; the relative decline of U.S. economic hegemony; the increase in economic frictions and competitiveness among the United States, the EC, and Japan; and the emergence of a foreign debt crisis in many LDCs. The new sources of economic instability forced realists to confront the fact that economic issues were of central importance and could no longer be considered low politics.

Realists also criticized liberal and Marxist students of IPE for being *economistic;* i.e., for exaggerating the importance of economics and underestimating the importance of politics.[31] A number of developments during the postwar period demonstrated the necessity for realist studies of IPE, with emphasis on political issues and the role of the state. For example, the "Keynesian Revolution" from the 1930s–1950s caused DC governments to become heavily involved in macroeconomic management and public social expenditures; the breakdown of colonialism led to the establishment of many newly independent states that developed forms of government quite different from the Western liberal democratic model; and growing international competition facing the United States in the 1970s–1980s led to protestations that the state should be doing more to promote U.S. industry. An updated realist perspective was therefore needed to "bring the state back in" to the study of IPE.[32]

In their approach to IPE, the newer realists posed a direct challenge to liberal interpretations of economic change. According to liberals, international economic relations had flourished after World War II because of the growth of interdependence. This interdependence was closely linked with advances in communications and transportation, and with the increased role of nongovernmental actors such as MNCs. Realists, by contrast, with their emphasis on the state and power, argued that *the distribution of power among states* (not advances in transportation and communications) is the most important factor determining whether international economic relations will flourish. A major factor to consider in power distribution is whether there is a global hegemonic state with predominant power willing and able to provide leadership. Thus, the later realists were strong advocates of hegemonic stability theory, which draws linkages between the existence of a hegemonic state and the nature of global economic relationships.[33]

Although hegemonic stability theory is closely tied with the realist school of thought, it is a hybrid theory that also draws on the liberal and historical structuralist perspectives. The discussion that follows demonstrates that hegemonic stability theory cannot be neatly categorized. Nevertheless, the main aspects of hegemonic stability theory are discussed in this chapter because it forms such a central part of the realist approach to IPE.

HEGEMONIC STABILITY THEORY

Hegemonic stability theory asserts that the international economic system is most likely to be open and stable when there is a single dominant or hegemonic state with two characteristics: it has a sufficiently large share of resources that it is *able* to provide leadership, and it is *willing* to pursue policies necessary to create and maintain a liberal economic order. In addition to being willing and able to lead, the hegemon must follow policies that other major actors believe are relatively beneficial. When a global hegemon is lacking or declining in power, economic openness and stability are more difficult—but not impossible—to maintain. It is generally agreed that hegemonic conditions have occurred at least twice—under Britain during the nineteenth century and under the United States after World War II. Some writers maintain that there were other world powers before the nineteenth century, including Portugal, Spain, the United Provinces or the present-day Netherlands, and (again) the British.[34] However, most scholars believe that these countries did not have international influence comparable to British and American influence during the nineteenth and twentieth centuries.

Hegemonic stability theory has spawned a vast array of literature as well as lively discussion and debate in the field of IPE. Scholars have critiqued virtually all aspects of the theory, some simply calling for revisions and others questioning its basic assumptions. In response, hegemonic stability theorists have defended the theory and revised certain aspects of it. Many of the criticisms are based on empirical grounds. For example, critics question whether theorists can draw meaningful generalizations about hegemonic behavior based on the experiences of only a small number of global hegemons during limited historical periods. There is also disagreement as to the definition and measurement of hegemony, with different authors focusing variously on the military, political, economic, and cultural aspects. In view of these differences, disagreements among analysts over when British hegemony declined and over whether U.S. hegemony is declining are not surprising. Even theorists who agree that the United States is a declining hegemon have different views about timing. Furthermore, some critics question one of the basic premises of the theory: that a global hegemon contributes to economic openness and stability. Rather than examining the numerous studies critiquing and defending hegemonic stability theory, four questions focus on the major sources of division:

1. What is hegemony?
2. What are the strategies and motives of hegemonic states?
3. Is hegemony necessary and/or sufficient to produce an open, stable economic system?
4. What is the status of U.S. hegemony?

What Is Hegemony?

The distribution of power among major states is rarely equal. Indeed, realists and some historical structuralists (such as world-systems theorists, discussed in Chapter 5) believe that the international system is marked by unequal growth, with some states increasing and others declining in power. The term **hegemony** is used when the distribution of power is *extremely* unequal, and realists view hegemony in state-centric terms. For example, one important realist writer describes the international system as imperial or hegemonic when "a single powerful state controls or dominates the lesser states in the system."[35] A definition of this sort, however, does not provide us with answers as to how much control, and what types of control, are necessary for a state to be hegemonic. Can a state attain hegemony based on military or economic power alone, or must it achieve a leadership position in both areas? Most theorists have rather stringent conditions for hegemonic status, and they therefore believe that hegemonic conditions have been fulfilled on only two or three occasions. Thus, one prominent definition limits hegemony to a relationship among states that is so unbalanced that "one power can largely impose its rules and wishes (at the very least by effective veto power) in the economic, political, military, diplomatic and even cultural arenas."[36]

Although most theorists define hegemony in state-centric terms, *Gramscian* theorists use the term hegemony in a cultural sense to connote the complex of *ideas* that social groups use to assert their legitimacy and authority. (Gramscian analysis, which stems from the writings of Antonio Gramsci, an Italian Marxist, is discussed in Chapter 5.[37]) Thus, Gramscians refer to the hegemony of ideas such as capitalism and to the global predominance of American culture. According to Gramscians, the capitalist class agreed to provide a wide range of concessions—such as welfare payments, unemployment insurance, and workers' rights to organize—to subordinate social classes. In return for these concessions, subordinate social classes viewed the hegemony of the capitalist class as acceptable and legitimate. This hegemony is difficult to overcome because opposing groups must first make the subordinate classes aware that they are being oppressed. As globalization has proceeded in such areas as trade, foreign investment, and finance, some Gramscians assert that a "transnational capitalist class" is establishing its hegemony at the global level. This transnational capitalist class is ensuring that all impediments to the free flow of capital around the world are being removed.[38]

The Gramscian views enrich our understanding by focusing on aspects of hegemony that are not adequately covered in the state-centric definitions. Nevertheless, most writers involved in debates over hegemonic stability theory use a state-centric definition.

What Are the Strategies and Motives of Hegemonic States?

Although hegemonic stability theorists agree that a hegemon must be willing and able to lead, they have differing views regarding the hegemon's leadership methods and goals. Thus, authors refer to three models of hegemony, ranging from benevolent at one end of the spectrum to coercive at the other end.[39] In the first model, the hegemon is benevolent in both its methods and goals. It is more concerned about promoting generalized benefits than its self-interest, and it relies on rewards rather than threats to ensure compliance by other states. In the second, mixed model, the hegemon has an interest in general as well as personal benefits, but it relies on coercive methods when necessary to achieve its objectives. In the third model, the hegemon is exploitative. It exerts leadership out of self-interest, and is more inclined than hegemons in the first two models to use coercion to enforce compliance. Benvolent hegemons are more concerned with absolute gains, coercive hegemons are more concerned with relative gains, and hegemons with mixed motives and methods are interested in both absolute and relative gains.

Liberals view hegemony in the most benevolent terms, emphasizing the degree to which the hegemon is willing to "take on an undue share of the burdens of the system."[40] According to liberals, the hegemon provides public goods in order to create and maintain open, stable economic regimes. **Public goods** have two characteristics: they are nonexcludable and nonrival. Nonexcludability means that others can benefit from the good, even if they do not contribute to its provision. For example, a sidewalk is nonexcludable because even individuals who have not helped pay for it through taxes are free to use it. Nonrivalness means that a state's (or individual's) use of the good does not seriously decrease the amount available to others. Again, a sidewalk is nonrival because many individuals can simultaneously benefit from using it.

In the liberal view, a benevolent hegemon is willing to provide a wide range of public goods to ensure there is economic openness and stability. At the end of World War II, the United States provided security as a public good through the U.S. nuclear umbrella so that Western Europe and Japan could concentrate on their postwar economic recovery. The United States as global hegemon has also permitted its currency to be used as the principal reserve asset, supplied adequate U.S. dollars to permit the growth of international trade, provided financing for economic growth of LDCs, and maintained a relatively open market for other countries' exports. There are very few pure public goods because a hegemon may be able to at least partially exclude some countries. In contrast to public goods, private goods are both excludable and rival.[41] Because states receive a public good even if they do not help provide it, they tend to become noncontributors or *free riders,* and public goods are underproduced in relation to private goods.

Realists are more inclined than liberals to portray the hegemon as furthering its national self-interest rather than the general good. In the realist view, a rising hegemonic state prefers an open international system because such openness can contribute to its economic growth, national income, and political power.[42] Realists are also more likely than liberals to portray the hegemon as coercive, threatening to cut off trade, investment, and aid in efforts to force other states to share the costs of public goods. Nevertheless, many realists indicate that hegemonic states may have mixed motives and that the overall effects of hegemony can be beneficial. For example, one realist writer asserts:

> There is no question that the creation of a system of multilateral trade relations was in the interests of the United States. . . . It does not follow from this fact, however, that American efforts to achieve such a system were solely self-serving. . . . Nor does it follow that what is good for the United States is contrary to the general welfare of other nations.[43]

Among proponents of the three main IPE perspectives, historical structuralists are the least likely to view a hegemon as benevolent. Some historical structuralists argue that the hegemon coordinates the responses of DCs in the core of the global economy, enabling them to solidify their dominance over LDCs in the periphery. Only when the hegemon declines is there disarray among the leading capitalist states, which undermines their ability to continue extracting surplus from the periphery. Thus, Gramscian theorists advocate the development of a "counterhegemony" among disadvantaged groups in the periphery as a means of extricating themselves from subservience to the hegemonic forces in the core.[44]

Is Hegemony Necessary and/or Sufficient to Produce an Open, Stable Economic System?

Hegemonic stability theorists believe the existence of a hegemonic state increases the likelihood that the international economy will be open and stable. A hegemon often promotes openness and stability by helping to create and maintain liberal international regimes (discussed in detail in Chapter 4). International **regimes** are "sets of implicit or explicit principles, norms, rules, and decision-making procedures around which actors' expectations converge in a given area of international relations."[45] In other words, the regime concept addresses the fact that a degree of governance exists above the nation-state level in specific areas of IR, even without a centralized world government. Members of the WTO, for example, abide by certain trade regime principles, such as nondiscrimination, reciprocity, and trade liberalization, and they follow trade regime rules and engage in trade negotiations to uphold these principles.

According to hegemonic stability theorists, the United States as global hegemon has helped create and maintain open and stable monetary, trade, and aid regimes since the end of World War II. Through the provision of public goods and rewards and the use of coercion, the United States as global leader gives other states the incentive to abide by the regime principles, norms, and rules. Thus, hegemonic stability theorists assume that open, stable economic regimes are more difficult to maintain if a hegemonic state is declining or there is no hegemon. On the basis of these assumptions, hegemonic stability theorists have made a number of assertions about the liberalizing effects of British and U.S. hegemony:

- British hegemony was a major factor contributing to trade liberalization in the nineteenth century.
- The decline of British hegemony after 1875 led to a decline in free trade.
- The lack of a hegemon willing and able to lead between World Wars I and II resulted in increased protectionism culminating in the Great Depression.
- The emergence of the United States as global hegemon after World War II resulted in the re-emergence of open and stable international economic regimes.

A number of empirical studies, however, have questioned the assumption that hegemony is necessary and/or sufficient to produce economic openness. For example, many writers agree that Britain was a declining hegemon after 1875. However, some empirical findings reveal that there was no widespread return to protectionism after 1875 and that it was World War I, *not* Britain's hegemonic decline, "that sounded the death knell for liberalized international trade."[46] Some liberal critics concede that a hegemonic state may play an important role in creating open international economic regimes but argue that these regimes will not necessarily weaken after the hegemon declines. Open economic regimes can have beneficial effects on other states, which may have the incentive to maintain these regimes through cooperative efforts even after the hegemon declines. Thus, it is important to ask not only whether a hegemon is available to *supply* open regimes but also whether there is sufficient *demand* to maintain such regimes in a posthegemonic period.[47] Some liberal theorists go even further and argue that hegemony is not necessary for either the creation or maintenance of regimes. In addition to regimes imposed or supplied by a hegemon, it is possible to have *negotiated regimes* that arise through negotiations among willing states that are relatively equal in stature. *Spontaneous regimes* may also be formed when countries' expectations converge without their conscious efforts to negotiate an explicit agreement; for example, spontaneous orders relating to language systems and ethical values sometimes develop within many societies, and the same can occur among states.[48]

Others point out that hegemonic states are not uniformly committed to open economic regimes because domestic groups or individuals can favor barriers to the free flow of goods, services, or capital. As noted in Chapter 6, although the United States generally supported an open international trade regime in the 1940s, it did *not* endorse an open, liberal international financial order. Instead, the United States joined European countries in supporting the use of national controls on capital flows. Even in the trade area, the United States was not uniformly liberal in the postwar era. In response to domestic interests, the United States insisted that GATT provide several major exceptions for agriculture and supported the creation of a restrictive Multi-Fiber Agreement to limit textile imports.[49]

Some writers also maintain that factors other than hegemony can account for economic openness and stability. For example, general world prosperity can result in open economic regimes, whereas economic downturns can cause countries to adopt more closed, protectionist policies. Furthermore, industries are more inclined to pressure for trade protectionism when they produce surpluses and are more likely to support trade openness during periods of shortages.[50] In sum, many critics concede that there may be *some* connection between hegemony and economic openness. However, they question whether hegemony is necessary and/or sufficient to create and maintain open, liberal economic regimes.

What Is the Status of U.S. Hegemony?

One of the most vigorous debates focuses on the current status of U.S. hegemony. This debate stems from the fact that there is no clear consensus or criteria for determining when a state is hegemonic. Debate continues to this day over the timing of Britain's hegemonic decline. Although some authors date Britain's declining hegemony in trade and industrial competitiveness from about 1875, others note that Britain maintained its hegemonic position in finance until World War I (this issue is discussed in Chapter 2).[51] In regard to the United States, a number of theorists are "declinists" who argue that hegemony is inherently unstable and that "one of the most important features of American hegemony was its brevity."[52] Declinists often draw parallels between the United States and Britain and note that Germany and Japan's erosion of U.S. dominance in the 1970s-1980s had similarities with U.S. and German erosion of British dominance in the 1890s. There is often a sense of inevitability in the declinist literature, with one noted historian writing that "the only answer to the question increasingly debated by the public of whether the United States can preserve its existing position is 'no'—for it simply has not been given to any one society to remain *permanently* ahead of all the others."[53] Declinists cite various reasons for U.S. hegemonic decline, including the hegemon's tendency to overextend itself in military and economic terms (or imperial overstretch),[54] the tendency of free riders to gain more than the hegemon from economic openness, and the emergence of dynamic and competitive economies that challenge the hegemon's predominant position. Although declinists believe that U.S. hegemony will not persist, they often predict the United States will continue to be a significant power in a multipolar world.[55]

Pitted against declinists are "renewalists" who challenge the assumption that the United States is declining. Although most renewalists concede that U.S. economic power has declined in a relative sense since 1945, they argue that this has not had a significant effect on U.S. hegemony. U.S. predominance at the end of the war was so great that its relative position was bound to decline as a result of economic reconstruction in Europe and Japan. Nevertheless, U.S. economic power continues to be "quite enormous when compared to that of any other country, and has an international aspect which gives the U.S. government a unique prerogative *vis-à-vis* the rest of the world."[56] As evidence of its continued hegemony, renewalists maintain that the United States has a considerable amount of *structural* or *soft power*: it is often successful in getting "other countries to *want* what it wants."[57] Thus, the United States continues to have a large degree of control over setting the global agenda and determining how issues are dealt with in IR. In explaining the continued U.S. influence, renewalists criticize declinists for failing to consider noneconomic factors. U.S. television, movies, and magazines have an enormous effect on cultural tastes and habits around the world, despite the efforts of some countries to limit such influences, and U.S. supremacy in the military-security area also permits it to exercise power in the economic sphere. Although the decline of the Cold War has decreased the scope of security threats to Western Europe and Japan, new global security threats are likely to emerge, and the breakup of the Soviet bloc has solidified U.S. military-security predominance.[58]

Recent events in the security and economic areas have resulted in an upsurge of writings by renewalists. In the security sphere, the end of the Cold War has led some writers to refer to the United States as the only superpower and a unipolar power. These analysts have examined the effects of U.S. military supremacy on its relations with the EU, Japan, and other major actors on economic as well as security issues.[59] In the economic sphere, the financial crisis in East and Southeast Asia in the late 1990s and Japan's inability to assume a leadership role and revive its own lackluster economy has led renewalists to argue that the United States is also regaining its economic predominance. Compared with East Asia and Japan, the United States was experiencing high economic growth and low unemployment and inflation rates. Although the United States had lost market share to Japan in many industrial goods such as automobiles and in some high technology products, "the renovation of U.S. manufacturing, the U.S. services offensive, and the inherent limitations of the Japanese model created a complex situation by the end of the 1990s."[60]

However, renewalist arguments that the United States is the unchallenged hegemon are more convincing in the military-security area than the economic area. Declinists reject the idea that U.S. economic revival in the 1990s is a long-term structural phenomenon, and argue instead that it was a sign of short-term cyclical fluctuations. In the declinist view, the mid- to long-term trend is operating against U.S. economic hegemony.[61] Thus, declinists point to the fact that the EU is a larger international trading entity than the United States (see Chapter 8) and assert that the formation of the European Economic and Monetary Union (EMU) and adoption of a new currency—*the euro*—in place of 12 EU members' national currencies "offers the prospect of a new bipolar international economic order that could replace America's hegemony since World War II"[62] (see Chapter 6). This continuing debate raises questions as to whether those focusing on the security and economic aspects of hegemony are communicating with one another (only a small number of scholars are seriously examining both aspects of hegemony).

Thus, there is a need for IPE scholars to do more to integrate the study of security and economic issues. For example, one issue to examine is whether U.S. military predominance in the post-Cold War era has in fact detracted from U.S. soft or structural power in both the security and economic areas. Whereas many countries during the Cold War "welcomed the United States as their protector against the other superpower," with the end of the Cold War some argue that other major powers are more likely to view the only remaining superpower as a threat to their interests.[63] Thus, there has been considerable unease in Europe with "the idea of unrivalled American power," and attention is now being given "to strengthening European military capacity, and forging an inner core within an enlarged European Union, as a balance to American power."[64] Another issue to examine is the longer-term effects of U.S. actions in the security sphere on its economic position and relations with Europe and East Asia.

In 1989 two IR theorists described hegemonic stability theory as "the most prominent approach among American political scientists for explaining patterns of economic relations among the advanced capitalist countries since 1945."[65] However, this discussion has shown that the tenets of hegemonic stability theory are controversial, and in recent years a number of IPE scholars have devoted more attention to other theories. Although

realists at first turned to hegemonic stability theory partly as a response to liberal interpretations of IPE, liberal versions of the theory have also been prominent, and historical
structuralists (e.g., world-systems and Gramscian theorists) have also focused on hegemony. It is not surprising that realists have been particularly interested in hegemonic stability because of their preoccupation with interactions among the most powerful states.

REALIST CONTRIBUTIONS TO THE STUDY OF IPE

An examination of hegemonic stability theory has pointed to two areas where realists
provide important contributions to IPE: their preoccupation with security issues and
with the role of the state. As discussed, the realist emphasis on security is important in
directing the attention of IPE scholars to the interconnections between security and
economic issues. The realist emphasis on the state and the liberal emphasis on the
market and MNCs are both essential for the study of IPE. For example, technological
change is an important source of economic growth, and to understand the role of technological innovation we must draw on both the liberal and realist perspectives. Most
technological innovation occurs within business enterprises, but "the institutional environment is key to understanding whether firms will be successful or not in creating
new products and processes."[66] Thus, to understand the sources of technological innovation it is important to examine the interaction among three institutional spheres:
industry, government, and academia.[67] A major contribution of realism continues to be
its role in bringing "the state back in" to the study of IPE.[68]

REALISM AND NORTH-SOUTH RELATIONS

Although realists are very concerned about relative gains, their preoccupation with
power and influence usually leads them to examine distributional issues only among
the most powerful states; i.e., among Northern DCs. In security studies, for example,
realists during the Cold War were far less concerned about conflicts in the South (Korea, Vietnam, and the Middle East were exceptions) than about possible conflict "in
Europe, where fear of the catastrophic escalation potential of any East-West confrontations prevented even the most minor form of warfare between the two power
blocs."[69] Indeed, superpower intervention in LDC conflicts was often viewed as a permissible safety valve not available in Europe. In IPE, the realist tendency to ignore
Southern interests extends back to the nineteenth century writings of Friedrich List.
As discussed, List believed that Northern countries such as Germany and the United
States should develop their manufacturing industries so they could compete with
Britain. However, List did not consider industrialization to be a legitimate objective
for colonial territories of the South, which served as a source of raw materials and agri-
cultural goods for the North. In *The National System of Political Economy*, List wrote
that Northern countries were "specially fitted by nature for manufacturing" and that

Southern countries should provide the North with "colonial produce in exchange for their manufactured goods."[70]

As a result, realist IR scholars have until recently only rarely focused on North-South relations.[71] Realists in IPE have written more studies on North-South relations in recent years, but this is primarily because some LDCs have posed a challenge to the power position of the North. In the 1970s, for example, realists became interested in OPEC when it wrested control over oil prices and production levels from the international oil companies and launched "the most effective exercise of power by the South against the North since the conclusion of the Second World War."[72] (Membership in OPEC is limited to LDCs.) When OPEC supported the G-77's demands in the UN for a New International Economic Order, realists also wrote studies on the NIEO's possible impact. In the 1980s–1990s, realists became less interested in OPEC as its ability to control oil supplies and prices declined. Instead, they devoted attention to the East Asian NIEs, which seemed to pose a new challenge to the power position of the North. Thus, realists engaged in a vigorous debate with liberals: Were the economic successes of East Asian NIEs (South Korea, Taiwan, Singapore, and Hong Kong) due more to their market orientation (the liberal view) or to government-business cooperation and government involvement in the market (the realist view)? Even when realists study North-South relations, they generally do not have a sustained interest in LDC development as a legitimate area of inquiry. Thus, the author of a 1977 realist study on North-South relations warned that his book dealt with issues that do not normally fall within the domain of IR.[73]

The realist and liberal perspectives on North-South relations differ in some important respects. Whereas liberals assert that LDCs are primarily interested in economic growth and prosperity, realists argue that LDCs seek increased power as well as wealth in efforts to decrease their vulnerability to the North. In the realist view, LDC problems can be traced not only to their poverty but also to their weak position in the international system. Even when LDCs experience absolute economic gains, they continue to feel vulnerable because of their weak position vis-à-vis the North.[74] The section that follows briefly discusses three strategies realists claim LDCs employ to decrease their vulnerability. (These strategies are discussed further in Part III.)

First, LDCs employ collective action vis-à-vis the North based on their greater numbers, because they have little power individually. For example, LDCs formed the G-77 in the early 1960s (see Chapter 2). This caucus, which now has well over 100 members, has served as a major vehicle pressuring for Southern interests. Other joint actions by LDCs to strengthen their positions include producer associations such as OPEC and regional trade agreements (see Chapter 9). Second, LDCs depend on government involvement to promote their development. As discussed in later chapters, LDCs have often opted for economic development policies such as import substitution and export-led growth in which the government supplements the market. These policies draw on the assumption of Hamilton and List that late industrializers will never be able to catch up if there is open competition. Thus, for late industrializers the state often takes responsibility for actively promoting development.[75] Third, LDCs try to alter international economic regimes and organizations. At the end of World War II, the United States used its hegemonic position to establish international regimes upholding liberal principles, norms, rules, and decision-making procedures. However, LDCs prefer more authoritative, less market-oriented regimes in which IOs would make decisions redirecting power and wealth from the North to the South. LDCs also prefer international economic organizations (such as UNCTAD) based on a one-nation, one-vote principle rather than weighted-voting organizations such as the IMF and World Bank. As discussed in Chapter 11, LDC efforts to alter market-oriented regimes were most evident in their demands for a NIEO in the 1970s.[76]

Although realists, unlike liberals, focus on the North-South struggle for a redistribution of power and wealth, they assume that such a redistribution is fully possible within the capitalist system. In other words, both realists and liberals generally accept capitalism as the most desirable system for conducting economic relations. As discussed in Chapter 5, historical structuralists such as dependency and world-systems theorists by contrast believe that a significant redistribution of power and wealth between the North and the South is impossible under capitalism and can occur only under socialism.

CRITIQUE OF THE REALIST PERSPECTIVE

This discussion focuses on important general criticisms of the realist perspective. Realists often correctly criticize both liberals and historical structuralists for "economism," or for exaggerating the importance of economics and underestimating the importance of politics. In seeking to remedy this deficiency, however, realists sometimes overemphasize the centrality of politics in relation to economics. The preoccupation of U.S. realists in the early postwar period with international security and their almost total neglect of economic issues was a prime example of this error. Since the 1970s–1980s, some writers have revitalized the realist study of IPE, for example, with the realist approach to hegemonic stability theory and the role of the state in IPE. Nevertheless, these theorists often continue to downgrade the importance of economic issues that are not closely related to realist concerns with power, security, and relative gains. For example, this chapter notes that realists have not had a sustained interest in North-South relations and that liberal and historical structuralist analyses have therefore been more important in this area.

Realists often pride themselves on being the most parsimonious IR theorists, and their simplifying assumptions regarding the rational, unitary state have enabled them to develop some elegant theories. Nevertheless, the "state as unitary actor" view is probably the most controversial of the realist assumptions.[77] As interdependence and globalization increase, domestic processes and nongovernmental actors have a greater role in foreign policy, but the realist perspective is less attuned to this vision of the state. Since transnational actors such as MNCs and international banks are particularly important in IPE, the parsimonious habits of realists sometimes limit their analyses of economic issues. In recent years, some students of foreign economic policymaking have tried to develop a realist theory of state action that takes account of domestic as well as international variables.[78] However, liberal IPE theorists continue to be far more attuned than realists to domestic variables.[79]

Realists also place more emphasis on relative than absolute gains because of their concern with state survival and security in an anarchic self-help system. Relative gains are clearly of primary concern in some interstate relationships, such as U.S.-Soviet relations during the Cold War. However, absolute gains are often of greater concern in interdependent relationships in which states cooperate and do not threaten each other with force.[80] Even when realists study international economic organizations, they are more attuned to concerns about relative than absolute gains. For example, one realist study of the EU concludes that "the weaker but still influential partners will seek to ensure that the rules" established give them the opportunity "to voice their concerns and interests and thereby prevent their domination by stronger partners."[81] The preoccupation of realists with relative gains causes them to be highly skeptical about the influence of international institutions. If states are always concerned that they may gain less than others, realists argue, they will be very reluctant to transfer significant authority to these IOs. Nevertheless, international and regional economic organizations such as the IMF, World Bank, WTO, EU, and NAFTA have a significant effect in some areas of IPE.

Although the realist perspective has had remarkable longevity and success in IR in general, its preoccupation with security issues has limited its influence in the study of IPE. This book now turns to a discussion of liberalism, which has been the most important IPE theoretical perspective.

NOTES

1. For a discussion of Thucydides and realism, see Michael W. Doyle, "Thucydidean Realism," *Review of International Studies* 16-3 (1990), pp.223–237; and Laurie M. Johnson Bagby, "The Use and Abuse of Thucydides in International Relations," *International Organization* 48-1 (Winter 1994), pp.131–153.
2. Quoted in Albert O. Hirschman, *National Power and the Structure of Foreign Trade,* exp. ed., (Berkeley: University of California Press, 1980), p.xv.
3. Niccolò Machiavelli, *The Prince and the Discourses* (New York: Modern Library, 1940), pp.308–310.
4. Hirschman, *National Power and the Structure of Foreign Trade,* p.xv.
5. Thucydides, *The History of the Peloponnesian War,* translated by Richard Crawley (London: Dent, Everyman's Library, 1910), p.41; Robert G. Gilpin, "The Richness of the Tradition of Political Realism," *International Organization* 38-2 (Spring 1984), p.293.
6. Thomas J. Biersteker, "Evolving Perspectives on International Political Economy: Twentieth-Century Contexts and Discontinuities," *International Political Science Review* 14-1 (1993), p.25.
7. On a self-help system, see Kenneth N. Waltz, *Theory of International Politics* (Reading: Addison-Wesley, 1979), pp.105–107.
8. For a discussion of the forms of sovereignty see Stephen D. Krasner, *Sovereignty: Organized Hypocrisy* (Princeton: Princeton University Press, 1999), pp.9–25.
9. Hans J. Morgenthau, revised by Kenneth W. Thompson, *Politics Among Nations: The Struggle for Power and Peace,* 6th ed., (New York: Knopf, 1985), p.31.
10. Waltz, *Theory of International Politics,* p.126.
11. See Stephen D. Krasner, *Defending the National Interest: Raw Materials Investments and U.S. Foreign Policy* (Princeton: Princeton University Press, 1978); and Michael Mastanduno, David A. Lake, and G. John Ikenberry, "Toward a Realist Theory of State Action," *International Studies Quarterly* 33-4 (December 1989), pp.457–474.
12. On the "satisficing" terminology see Herbert A. Simon, "A Behavioral Model of Rational Choice," in Herbert A. Simon, ed., *Models of Man: Social and Rational* (New York: John

Wiley & Sons, 1957), pp.20–21. For a realist view of satisficing strategies see Robert Gilpin, *War and Change in World Politics* (Cambridge: Cambridge University Press, 1981), pp.20–21.

13. Robert Gilpin, *U.S. Power and the Multinational Corporation: The Political Economy of Foreign Direct Investment* (New York: Basic Books, 1975), p.34. See also Waltz, *Theory of International Politics*, p.126; and Joseph M. Grieco, "Anarchy and the Limits of Cooperation: A Realist Critique of the Newest Liberal Institutionalism," *International Organization* 42-3 (Summer 1988), p.498.

14. Tony Evans and Peter Wilson, "Regime Theory and the English School of International Relations: A Comparison," *Millennium* 21-3 (Winter 1992), p.330.

15. Robert W. Cox, *Production, Power, and World Order: Social Forces in the Making of History* (New York: Columbia University Press, 1987), p.6.

16. See Kenneth N. Waltz, "The Myth of National Interdependence," in Charles P. Kindleberger, ed., *The International Corporation* (Cambridge: MIT Press, 1970), pp.222–223; Janice E. Thomson and Stephen D. Krasner, "Global Transactions and the Consolidation of Sovereignty," in Ernst-Otto Czempiel and James N. Rosenau, eds., *Global Changes and Theoretical Challenges: Approaches to World Politics for the 1990s* (Lexington: Heath, 1989), p.197.

17. Andrew Hurrell and Ngaire Woods, "Globalisation and Inequality," *Millennium* 24-3 (1995), p.458.

18. Adam Smith used the term *mercantile system,* and German writers during the 1860s used the term *Merkantilismus* to describe this doctrine. Only afterward did the term *mercantilism* become standard in the English language. See Jacob Viner, "Mercantilist Thought," in David L. Sills, ed., *International Encyclopedia of the Social Sciences* (New York: Free Press, 1968), vol.4, p.436; and David A. Baldwin, *Economic Statecraft* (Princeton: Princeton University Press, 1985), p.72.

19. Jacob Viner, "Power Versus Plenty as Objectives of Foreign Policy in the Seventeenth and Eighteenth Centuries," *World Politics* 1 (October 1948), pp.10, 17; Eli F. Heckscher, *Mercantilism* (London: Allen and Unwin, 1934), vol. 2, p.17.

20. Adam Smith, *The Wealth of Nations* (London: Dent & Sons, Everyman's Library No. 412, 1910), vol.1, bk.4, p.436.

21. Robert Gilpin with Jean M. Gilpin, *The Political Economy of International Relations* (Princeton: Princeton University Press, 1987), p.180.

22. Alexander Hamilton, *The Report on the Subject of Manufactures,* December 5, 1791, in Harold C. Syrett, ed., *The Papers of Alexander Hamilton,* Vol. 10 (New York: Columbia University Press, 1966), p.291.

23. Friedrich List, *The National System of Political Economy,* translated by Sampson S. Lloyd (London: Longmans, Green 1916), p.130.

24. David Levi-Faur, "Friedrich List and the Political Economy of the Nation-State," *Review of International Political Economy* 4-1 (Spring 1997), pp.154–178.

25. List, *The National System of Political Economy,* p.107. On the greater role of government in late industrializers see Alexander Gerschenkron, *Economic Backwardness in Historical Perspective: A Book of Essays* (Cambridge: Harvard University Press, 1962).

26. Paul Kennedy, *The Rise and Fall of the Great Powers: Economic Change and Military Conflict from 1500 to 2000* (New York: Random House, 1987), p.283.

27. Michael Mastanduno differentiates realist government officials from scholars in the early postwar period. Although U.S. officials were active in international economic policy and provided leadership in creating the KIEOs, they subordinated their economic initiatives to U.S. security objectives. U.S. realist scholars in the early postwar period, by contrast, devoted scant attention to economic issues, and "analyses of the interplay between economics and security . . . were conspicuous by their absence." (Michael Mastanduno, "Economics and Security in Statecraft and Scholarship," *International Organization* 52-4 [Autumn 1998], p.835.)

28. Gilpin, "The Richness of the Tradition of Political Realism," p.294.

29. Gilpin, *The Political Economy of International Relations*, p.xii.

30. See Gilpin, *U. S. Power and the Multinational Corporation.*

31. Richard K. Ashley, "Three Modes of Economism," *International Studies Quarterly* 27-4 (December 1983), p.463.

32. Theda Skocpol, "Bringing the State Back In: Strategies of Analysis in Current Research," in Peter B. Evans, Dietrich Rueschemeyer, and Theda Skocpol, eds., *Bringing the State Back In* (Cambridge: Cambridge University Press, 1985), pp.6–7.

33. The first realists writing about hegemonic stability theory were Robert Gilpin and Stephen Krasner.

34. See George Modelski, "The Long Cycle of Global Politics and the Nation-State," *Comparative Studies in Society and History* 20-2 (April 1978), pp.214–235; Immanuel Wallerstein, "The Three Instances of Hegemony in the History of the Capitalist World-Economy," in *The Politics of the World-Economy: The States, the Movements and the Civilizations* (London: Cambridge University Press, 1984), pp.37–46; George Modelski, *Long Cycles in World Politics* (Seattle: University of Washington Press, 1987), ch. 2; Joshua S. Goldstein, *Long Cycles: Prosperity and War in the Modern Age* (New Haven: Yale University Press, 1988), pp.126–133.

35. Robert Gilpin, *War and Change in World Politics* (Cambridge: Cambridge University Press, 1981), p.29; Joseph S. Nye, Jr., *Bound to Lead: The Changing Nature of American Power* (New York: Basic Books, 1990), pp.37–40.

36. Wallerstein, "The Three Instances of Hegemony in the History of the Capitalist World-Economy," p.38.

37. See Antonio Gramsci, *Selections from the Prison Notebooks of Antonio Gramsci*, edited and translated by Quintin Hoare and Geoffrey Nowell Smith (New York: International Publishers, 1971).

38. See Stephen Gill, ed., *Gramsci, Historical Materialism and International Relations* (Cambridge: Cambridge University Press, 1993).

39. See Duncan Snidal, "The Limits of Hegemonic Stability Theory," *International Organization* 39-4 (Autumn 1985), pp.585–586.

40. Charles P. Kindleberger, *The World in Depression 1929–1939* (Berkeley: University of California Press, 1973), p.28.

41. James A. Caporaso, "Global Political Economy," in Ada Finifer, ed., *Political Science: The State of the Discipline II* (Washington, DC: American Political Science Association, 1993), p.453; Snidal, "The Limits of Hegemonic Stability Theory," pp.590–592; Charles P. Kindleberger, "Dominance and Leadership in the International Economy," *International Studies Quarterly* 25-2 (June 1981), p.244; Mancur Olson, *The Logic of Collective Action: Public Goods and the Theory of Groups* (Cambridge: Harvard University Press, 1965), pp.14–15.

42. Stephen D. Krasner, "State Power and the Structure of International Trade," *World Politics* 28 (April 1976), p.322.

43. Robert Gilpin, "The Politics of Transnational Economic Relations," in Robert O. Keohane and Joseph S. Nye, Jr., eds., *Transnational Relations and World Politics* (Cambridge: Harvard University Press, 1972), p.58.

44. Wallerstein, "The Three Instances of Hegemony in the History of the Capitalist World-Economy," pp.44–46; Robert W. Cox, "Gramsci, Hegemony and International Relations: An Essay in Method," in Stephen Gill, ed., *Gramsci, Historical Materialism and International Relations* (Cambridge: Cambridge University Press, 1993), pp.64–65.

45. Stephen D. Krasner, "Structural Causes and Regime Consequences: Regimes as Intervening Variables," in Stephen D. Krasner, ed., *International Regimes* (Ithaca: Cornell University Press, 1983), p.2.

46. Arthur A. Stein, "The Hegemon's Dilemma: Great Britain, the United States and the International Economic Order," *International Organization* 38-2 (Spring 1984), p.373.

47. Robert O. Keohane, *After Hegemony: Cooperation and Discord in the World Political Economy* (Princeton: Princeton University Press, 1984); and Robert O. Keohane, "The Demand for International Regimes," in Krasner, ed., *International Regimes,* pp.141–171.

48. Oran R. Young, "Regime Dynamics: The Rise and Fall of International Regimes," in Krasner, ed., *International Regimes,* pp.98–101; Mark A. Levy, Oran R. Young, and Michael Zürn, "The Study of International Regimes," *European Journal of International Relations* 1-3 (1995), p. 286.

49. Eric Helleiner, *States and the Reemergence of Global Finance: From Bretton Woods to the 1990s* (Ithaca: Cornell University Press), p.4; Theodore H. Cohn, "The Changing Role of the United States in the Global Agricultural Trade Regime," in William P. Avery, ed., *World Agriculture and the GATT, International Political Economy Yearbook* (Boulder: Rienner, 1993) vol. 7, pp.20–24; Vinod K. Aggarwal, *Liberal Protectionism: The International Politics of Organized Textile Trade* (Berkeley: University of California Press, 1985), pp.77–81.

50. Timothy J. McKeown, "Hegemonic Stability Theory and Nineteenth Century Tariff Levels in Europe," *International Organization* 37-1 (Winter 1983), p.89; Peter F. Cowhey and Edward Long, "Testing Theories of Regime Change: Hegemonic Decline or Surplus Capacity?" *International Organization* 37-2 (Spring 1983), pp.157–188.

51. David A. Lake, *Power, Protection, and Free Trade: International Sources of U.S. Commercial Strategy, 1887–1939* (Ithaca: Cornell University Press, 1988), pp.30–32; Albert Fishlow, "Lessons from the Past: Capital Markets during the 19th Century and the Interwar Period," *International Organization* 39-3 (Summer 1985), p.390.

52. Robert O. Keohane, *After Hegemony: Cooperation and Discord in the World Political Economy* (Princeton: Princeton University Press, 1984), p.139. The IPE literature is replete with statements about U.S. hegemonic decline. See Michael C. Webb and Stephen D. Krasner, "Hegemonic Stability Theory: An Empirical Assessment," *Review of International Studies* 15 (Spring 1989), p.185; and Wallerstein, "The Three Instances of Hegemony in the History of the Capitalist World-Economy," p.46. Other declinist literature includes Kennedy, *The Rise and Fall of the Great Powers;* David P. Calleo, *Beyond American Hegemony: The Future of the Western Alliance* (New York: Basic Books, 1987); and Walter Russel Mead, *Mortal Splendor: The American Empire in Transition* (Boston: Houghton Mifflin, 1987).

53. Kennedy, *The Rise and Fall of the Great Powers,* p.533.

54. Kennedy, *The Rise and Fall of the Great Powers,* p.515.

55. See, for example, Samuel P. Huntington, "The Lonely Superpower," *Foreign Affairs* 78-2 (March/April 1999), pp. 35–49.

56. Stephen Gill, "American Hegemony: Its Limits and Prospects in the Reagan Era," *Millennium* 15-3 (Winter 1986), p.331. See also Samuel Huntington, "The U.S.—Decline or Renewal?" *Foreign Affairs* 67-2 (Winter 1988–89), pp.76–96.

57. Joseph S. Nye, Jr., "Soft Power," *Foreign Policy* 80 (Fall 1990), p.166. See also Nye, *Bound to Lead;* and Susan Strange, "The Persistent Myth of Lost Hegemony," *International Organization* 41-4 (Autumn 1987), pp.551–574.

58. Bruce Russett, "The Mysterious Case of Vanishing Hegemony; or, Is Mark Twain Really Dead?" *International Organization* 39-2 (Spring 1985), p.230; Susan Strange, "The Future of the American Empire," *Journal of International Affairs* 42 (Fall 1988), pp.1–17.

59. See, for example, Christopher Layne, "Unipolar Illusion: Why Great Powers will Rise," *International Security* 17-4 (Spring 1993), pp.5–51; Christopher Layne and Benjamin Schwarz, "American Hegemony without an Enemy," *Foreign Policy* 92 (Fall 1993), pp.5–23; David N. Gibbs, "Washington's New Interventionism: U.S. Hegemony and Inter-Imperialist Rivalries," *Monthly Review* 53-4 (September 2001), pp.15–37.

60. Herman M. Schwartz, *States versus Markets: The Emergence of a Global Economy*, 2nd ed., (New York: St. Martin's Press, 2000), p.298.

61. For differing views of the 1990s U.S. economic revival, see Mortimer B. Zuckerman, "A Second American Century," *Foreign Affairs* 77-3 (May/June 1998), pp.18–31; Paul Krugman, "America the Boastful," *Foreign Affairs* 77-3 (May/June 1998), pp.32–45; and "United States: Too Triumphalist by Half," *The Economist*, April 25, 1998, pp.29–30.

62. C. Fred Bergsten, "America and Europe: Clash of the Titans?," *Foreign Affairs* 78-2 (March/April 1999), p. 20.

63. Huntington, "The Lonely Superpower," p. 43.

64. "Which Way Now for French Policy?," *The Economist*, July 26, 2003, pp.47–48. See also Stephen M. Walt, "The Ties that Fray: Why Europe and America are Drifting Apart," *National Interest* 54 (Winter, 1998/99), pp.3–11.

65. Webb and Krasner, "Hegemonic Stability Theory," p.183.

66. Jorge Niosi, "Canada's National R&D System," in Robert Anderson, Theodore Cohn, Chad Day, Michael Howlett and Catherine Murray, eds., *Innovation Systems in a Global Context: The North American Experience* (Montreal: McGill-Queen's University Press, 1998), p.91.

67. Henry Etzkowitz, "The Triple Helix of Academia-Industry-Government: The U.S. National Innovation System," in Anderson, et al., *Innovation Systems in a Global Context*, pp.127–147.

68. Skocpol, "Bringing the State Back In," pp.6–7.

69. Amitav Acharya, "Beyond Anarchy: Third World Instability and International Order after the Cold War," in Stephanie G. Neuman, ed., *International Relations Theory and the Third World* (New York: St. Martin's Press, 1998), p.165.

70. List, *The National System of Political Economy*, p.154.

71. David A. Lake, "Power and the Third World: Toward a Realist Political Economy of North-South Relations," *International Studies Quarterly* 31-2 (June 1987), p.217.

72. Stephen D. Krasner, *Structural Conflict: The Third World Against Global Liberalism* (Berkeley: University of California Press, 1985), pp.108–109.

73. Robert L. Rothstein, *The Weak in the World of the Strong: The Developing Countries in the International System* (New York: Columbia University Press, 1977), p.ix.

74. Krasner, *Structural Conflict*, p.3; Rothstein, *The Weak in the World of the Strong*, p.8.

75. Chalmers Johnson, *MITI and the Japanese Miracle: The Growth of Industrial Policy, 1925–1975* (Stanford: Stanford University Press, 1982), p.19. On the role of government involvement for late industrializers, see Alexander Gerschenkron, *Economic Backwardness in Historical Perspective: A Book of Essays* (Cambridge: Harvard University Press, 1962).

76. Krasner, *Structural Conflict*, p.7.

77. Joseph M. Grieco, "Realist International Theory and the Study of World Politics," in Michael W. Doyle and G. John Ikenberry, eds., *New Thinking in International Relations Theory* (Boulder: Westview Press, 1997), p.168.

78. See Mastanduno, Lake, and Ikenberry, "Toward a Realist Theory of State Action," pp.457–474.

79. For an alternative view, see Jennifer Sterling-Folker, "Realist Environment, Liberal Process, and Domestic-Level Variables," *International Studies Quarterly* 41-1 (March 1997), pp.1–25.

80. Robert O. Keohane, "Neoliberal Institutionalism: A Perspective on World Politics," in Robert O. Keohane, *International Institutions and State Power: Essays in International Relations Theory* (Boulder: Westview Press, 1989), pp.10–11.

81. Joseph M. Grieco, "The Maastricht Treaty, Economic and Monetary Union and the Neorealist Research Programme," *Review of International Studies* 21 (January 1995), p.34.

C H A P T E R   4

The Liberal Perspective

L iberalism is the most influential perspective in IPE. Most important international economic organizations and the economic policies of most states today are
strongly influenced by liberal principles. The term *liberal,* however, is used differently in IPE than in U.S. domestic politics. Liberalism in the United States is often
contrasted with conservatism. Whereas U.S. conservatives are committed to free markets and minimal government intervention, U.S. liberals are inclined to support
greater government involvement in the market to prevent inequalities and stimulate
growth. Liberal economists, by contrast, have many similarities with U.S. conservatives; they emphasize the importance of the free market and private property rights
and call for only a limited government role in economic affairs. However, there are
also variations among economic liberals. Although some liberal economists favor as little government involvement in the economy as possible, others believe that a degree
of government intervention is necessary for the effective functioning of markets.

BASIC TENETS OF THE LIBERAL PERSPECTIVE

Liberal international theory is exceedingly diverse in nature, and it is difficult to provide a single "core statement of the liberal credo."[1] Compared with the liberal perspective, the core statements in realism and Marxism are easier to identify. A major
reason for this difference is that realists and Marxists place more emphasis than liberals on developing parsimonious theories that rely on a small number of concepts and
variables. Whereas realists oversimplify by focusing on the rational, unitary state,
Marxists view the world in terms of class relations. Liberals are pluralist by nature, so
they focus on a wider range of actors and levels of analysis. Although this broader outlook enables liberals to capture many of the complexities of IR that realists and Marxists overlook, it also interferes with the development of a coherent and encompassing
liberal international theory.

　　This chapter focuses on three variants of liberalism that are directly relevant to
the study of IPE: orthodox, interventionist, and institutional liberalism.[2] *Orthodox liberals* are concerned with promoting "negative freedom," or freedom of the private sector and the market to function with minimal interference from the state. The earliest

economic liberals, such as Adam Smith and David Ricardo, adhered to liberal ortho-doxy. *Interventionist liberals* believe that an exclusive focus on negative freedom is too narrow because it is not always certain that the private sector and the market will be progressive and produce widespread benefits. Interventionist liberals therefore see benefits from some government involvement to promote more equality, fairness, and justice in a free **market economy.** *Institutional liberals* also believe that some outside involvement is necessary to supplement the functioning of the market, and they favor the development of strong international institutions such as the WTO, IMF, and World Bank. Orthodox liberals often do not devote sufficient attention to institutions because of the emphasis they place on the market.

The Role of the Individual, the State, and Societal Groups

The liberal perspective takes a bottom-up approach to politics and gives primacy of place in society to the individual consumer, firm, or entrepreneur.[3] In the liberal view, individuals have inalienable natural rights that must be protected from private and public collectivities such as labor unions, churches, and the state. If individuals are free to pursue their own political and economic interests, the welfare of society and its inhabitants is most likely to be achieved. Thus, Adam Smith, an orthodox liberal writ-ing during the eighteenth century, discussed the "invisible hand," which converts the individual's selfish interest into advantage for society as a whole:

> Every individual is continually exerting himself to find out the most advanta-geous employment for whatever capital he can command. It is his own advan-tage, indeed, and not that of the society, which he has in view. But the study of his own advantage naturally, or rather necessarily, leads him to prefer that employment which is most advantageous to the society.[4]

Because the hidden hand of the market performs so efficiently, society can regu-late itself best with minimal interference from the state. Some liberals even reject the idea that the state is an autonomous actor, with motivations and resources different from those of other societal institutions. Instead, they view the state as simply an ag-gregation of private interests, with public policy resulting from a struggle among inter-est groups.[5] Interventionist liberals, however, point to the limitations of markets in dealing with some economic problems, such as unemployment, and foresee some role for the government in these situations.

The Nature and Purpose of International Economic Relations

The three KIEOs—the IMF, World Bank, and GATT/WTO—are all based on liberal-economic principles, and it is therefore not surprising that liberals have a rather posi-tive view of international economic relations as currently structured. They maintain that the KIEOs' formal rules are politically neutral and that all states' economic growth and efficiency benefit when their policies conform to the liberal principles of the KIEOs. If existing international relationships do not result in growth and efficient allocation of resources, liberals often argue that the problem is not with the international economic system but with the unwillingness of governments to pursue rational liberal economic policies.

Liberalism assumes that international economic interactions can be mutually beneficial, or a positive-sum game, if they are permitted to operate freely. All states and individuals are likely to gain from open economic relationships, even if they do not gain equally. In view of the overall positive effect of economic relations, liberals are often less concerned with *distributional* issues and less likely to differentiate between rich versus poor or large versus small states. Certainly, liberalism encompasses a range of views on distributional issues, with interventionist liberals emphasizing equality and social democracy as well as liberty and efficiency. All liberals believe, however, that the international economic system functions most efficiently if it ultimately depends on the price mechanism and the market. This emphasis on the market causes liberals to be more preoccupied with such values as liberty and efficiency.

Many liberals believe that LDCs today face basically the same challenges that countries in Europe and North America did during the nineteenth century. Unlike the nineteenth century, however, contemporary LDCs can benefit from a diffusion of advanced technology and modern forms of organization from the advanced industrial states. Integration with the centers of modern economic and political activity therefore spurs LDC modernization and economic growth, whereas relative isolation from these centers of activity results in LDC backwardness. In sum, liberals believe that all states, including LDCs, can benefit from the growth of interdependence and globalization if they follow open, liberal policies.

According to the liberals, the purpose of international economic activity is to achieve the optimum or most efficient use of the world's scarce resources and to maximize economic growth and efficiency. Liberals are therefore primarily concerned with aggregate measures of economic performance such as the growth of GDP, trade, foreign investment, and per capita income. Absolute gains in the level of foreign trade and investment are more important to liberals than relative gains among states.

The Relationship Between Politics and Economics

Liberals tend to view politics and economics as separable and autonomous areas of activity.[6] Since competition among self-interested individuals in the market can produce aggregate social benefits, many liberals believe that governments should not interfere in domestic and international economic transactions. To the extent that government has a role, it should be to create an open environment in which individuals and private firms can freely express their economic preferences. Thus, the state should prevent restraints on competition and free trade and should provide public goods such as national defense and infrastructure, including roads and railways to facilitate production and the transport of goods and people. Everyone benefits from the more efficient use of the world's scarce resources if government restrictions do not impede freer trade and investment flows. If governments permit the market to operate freely, a natural division of labor develops in which each country specializes in producing those goods for which it has a comparative advantage. As this chapter discusses later, intervention-ist liberals accept a greater degree of government involvement than orthodox liberals.

ORTHODOX LIBERALISM

The liberal tradition dates back at least to the writings of John Locke (1632–1704) dur-ing the seventeenth century. Although Locke believed that governments should be able to take limited enforcement actions to levy taxes and require military service, he argued that the primary role of the state was to ensure the *"Preservation* of . . . [peo-ples'] Lives, Liberties and Estates, which I call by the general Name, *Property.*"[7] Locke predated Adam Smith (1723–1790) by almost a century, but Smith is consid-ered to be the central figure adopting the orthodox liberal approach to political econ-omy. Unlike Locke, who based his support for the minimal state largely on political doctrines, Smith emphasized laissez-faire economics and led the way in opposing mer-cantilist economic thought (see Chapter 3). Smith argued that freely operating mar-kets based on a division of labor maximize efficiency and prosperity, and that the pro-ductive gains are likely to be positive-sum in nature. (A positive-sum game is a form of variable-sum game in which all states gain together.) The mercantilists believed that a country could gain wealth and power only at the expense of other countries, but Smith cautioned against such views:

> By such maxims as these . . . nations have been taught that their interest consisted in beggaring all their neighbours. Each nation has been made to look with an invidious eye upon the prosperity of all the nations with which it trades, and to consider their gain as its own loss. Commerce, which ought nat-urally to be, among nations, as among individuals, a bond of union and friend-ship, has become the most fertile source of discord and animosity.[8]

As a strong free trade advocate, Smith opposed the barriers of mercantilist states against the free exchange of goods and enlargement of markets. Although Smith real-ized that merchants who benefited from protectionism would try to retain their advan-tages, he differentiated such specific groups from the populace in general who would benefit from freer trade. Smith's arguments for free trade were based on the princi-ples of division of labor and economic interdependence. Each state in an unregulated international economy would find a productive niche based on **absolute advantage;** i.e., it would benefit by specializing in those goods it produced most efficiently and by trading with other states. David Ricardo (1772–1823) subsequently strengthened the free trade defense by arguing that two countries would benefit from trade based on **comparative advantage.** Even if one of the countries had no absolute advantage in the production of any good, it should specialize in and export those products for which it had a *relative* advantage (i.e., the least cost disadvantage). The concepts of absolute and comparative advantage are explained in detail in Chapter 8.

Although Smith was a strong supporter of free trade, he did not believe it should be a unilateral or unconditional policy. For example, he thought a country should be able to impose limits on free trade to meet national security requirements and retaliate against unfair trade restrictions of others. Smith also believed that a government could give domestic industry and labor groups time to adjust to international competition by implementing free trade gradually. Furthermore, Smith tempered his arguments for limited government intervention with an awareness of political realities. Thus, he indicated that the state should perform three important but circumscribed functions: to provide for national defense, protect members of society from injustice or oppression, and provide public works and institutions (i.e., public goods), which private individuals and groups would not provide on their own.[9] Despite their openness to some government involvement, Smith and other orthodox liberals believed this involvement should be limited mainly to actions that would promote the functioning of the market.

THE INFLUENCE OF JOHN MAYNARD KEYNES

John Maynard Keynes (1883–1946) once wrote that "the ideas of economists and political philosophers, both when they are right and when they are wrong, are more powerful than is commonly understood."[10] Keynes's ideas certainly had a powerful influence on the theory and practice of political economy, and some scholars argue that he was "the most influential economist of his generation."[11] Although Keynes was a liberal economist, he called for a greater degree of government interventionism than did the orthodox liberals. Keynes strongly opposed the extreme level of nationalism and beggar-thy-neighbor policies of the interwar years associated with realism. However, he also viewed the Great Depression as an indication that orthodox liberals overestimated the degree of convergence between self-interest and the public interest. Orthodox liberal theory provided virtually no guidance or remedies for dealing with the high unemployment levels of the 1930s, which had devastating economic and social consequences.

In contrast to the orthodox liberal view that markets tend inherently toward a socially beneficial equilibrium, Keynes argued that market-generated equilibrium between production and consumption might occur at a point where labor and capital are underutilized. Producer organizations, the variability of business confidence, and other factors that introduce rigidities into markets, can contribute to instability in the private economy and prolonged stagnation and unemployment. For example, Keynes noted that economic adjustment tended to result in unemployment rather than wage cuts because labor unions resisted the downward movement of wages. This rise of unemployment in turn led to decreased demand and a reduction in production and investment. Governments could remedy this situation, in Keynes's view, by becoming involved in the management of aggregate demand. Thus, Keynes emphasized the need for governments to implement fiscal policies (and to a lesser extent monetary policies) to increase demand, and he supported government investment when necessary in public projects. In his major work *The General Theory of Employment, Interest, and Money*, Keynes wrote that "the central controls necessary to ensure full employment will, of course, involve a large extension of the traditional functions of government."[12] Keynes's view that the state should intervene regularly in the economy of course marked a divergence from the laissez-faire doctrine of orthodox liberals.

Keynes's support for government involvement resulted in a greater "willingness to accept public sector deficits in order to finance public works or other spending programs designed to lower unemployment."[13] His emphasis on full employment also caused him to place less priority than orthodox liberals on specialization and international trade. Indeed, he argued that it was sometimes justifiable to limit imports to bolster domestic employment, even if the goods could be produced more cheaply abroad. When unemployment levels reached record highs in the 1930s, Keynes wrote that goods should "be homespun whenever it is reasonably and conveniently possible."[14] After World War II, Keynes moved toward supporting more multilateral, internationalist solutions in the Bretton Woods negotiations, but this was largely because he foresaw the possibility of planning on a global scale (the United States basically overruled this objective). Keynes's concessions to multilateralism were also a response to Britain's financial problems. As Britain's chief postwar negotiator, he pressured the Labour government to pursue open liberal policies, and in return the United States provided the British with $3.75 billion in loans.[15]

Keynes's support for economic management at the national and international levels had a major impact on liberal-economic thought. Because markets often behave differently than orthodox liberals predicted, Keynes explicitly called for the state to play a role in combating unemployment. Nevertheless, Keynes considered his macroeconomic management techniques to be alternatives to more extreme forms of state intervention. Despite his divergence from liberal orthodoxy, Keynes remained firmly within the liberal-economic tradition, believing in the importance of individual initiative and the inherent efficiency of the market. Greater management, in Keynes's view, would facilitate rather than impede the efficient functioning of market forces. Thus, Keynes favored government intervention, not to replace capitalism but to rescue and revitalize it. Keynes's views calling for greater government intervention in the economy gave rise to the interventionist strand of liberalism.[16]

LIBERALISM IN THE POSTWAR PERIOD

In seeking to avoid the economic problems of the interwar years (including trade wars, financial crises, and the Depression), postwar economic planners were influenced not only by Keynes, but also by Karl Polanyi. In his classic 1944 work *The Great Transformation,* Polanyi warned of the dangers of the orthodox liberal commitment to the "self-regulating market," with little concern about the effects on society. In Polanyi's view, society would move to protect itself from unregulated market activities, because disasters such as the Depression of the interwar years would result if society was unprotected.[17] Influenced by Keynes's and Polanyi's ideas, the postwar planners designed the international economic order on the basis of an interventionist or "embedded liberal compromise." "Embedded liberalism" refers to the fact that postwar efforts to maintain an open liberal international economy were embedded in societal efforts to provide domestic security and stability for the populace.[18] Thus, movement toward greater openness in the international economy included measures to cushion domestic economies from external disruptions, and policies to provide domestic stability in turn were designed to minimize interference with the expansion of global economic relations. In trade policy, for example, Western leaders called for multilateral tariff reductions, but they also permitted countries to use safeguards and exemptions from the trade regulations to protect their balance of payments and promote full employment.

Underlying the postwar interventionist liberal compromise was a domestic class compromise between business and labor. Thus, labor unions largely abandoned their demands that the economy be socialized, and in return they benefited from collective bargaining, the welfare state, and political acceptance. Business for its part agreed to a greater role for the government, welfare, and collective bargaining, and in return it won broad societal acceptance of freer international trade, private ownership, private profit, and the market.[19] In sum, most liberals in the postwar period viewed government intervention as necessary to counteract socially unacceptable aspects of the market. These interventionist liberals, however, opted for government measures that would reinforce rather than replace the market, and they looked to the market as the preferred means of determining production and distribution.

A RETURN TO ORTHODOX LIBERALISM

Although Western policymakers in the postwar period were highly supportive of interventionist liberalism, orthodox liberal theorists retained some influence in certain circles. In 1947 Friedrich Hayek organized the first meeting of what became known as the Mont Pelerin Society, a transnational private forum of scholars and political figures committed to orthodox liberal ideas. Proponents of a return to orthodox liberalism, such as Hayek, Ludwig von Mises, and Milton Friedman, placed the highest priority on competitive markets and the efficient allocation of resources, and often viewed economics and politics as being even more separable than did Adam Smith and David Ricardo. Thus, Friedman (b. 1912) wrote in 1962 that "the kind of economic organization that provides economic freedom directly, namely, competitive capitalism, also promotes political freedom because it separates economic power from political power."[20] Hayek and Friedman also expressed extremely negative views of state interference with the market. For example, Milton Friedman and Rose Friedman argued:

> Wherever we find any large element of individual freedom, some measure of progress in the material comforts at the disposal of ordinary citizens, and widespread hope of further progress in the future, there we also find that economic activity is organized mainly through the free market. Wherever the state undertakes to control in detail the economic activities of its citizens . . . there ordinary citizens are in political fetters, have a low standard of living, and have little power to control their own destiny.[21]

Proponents of orthodox liberalism also rejected the idea that free market policies contribute to inequality, and they criticized Keynes's emphasis on government involvement to combat unemployment. Private initiative and free enterprise rather than government intervention, in their view, were most likely to result in full employment, rising wages, and a higher standard of living for the average person.[22]

Despite the persistence of orthodox views, most Western leaders followed interventionist liberal policies during the expansive years of the 1950s-1960s. However, the OPEC oil price shock in 1973 and the prolonged global recession after 1974 made it more costly for governments to continue with welfare and full-employment policies, and the contradictions between capital accumulation and the redistribution of wealth became more evident. Orthodox writings of Hayek and Friedman therefore experienced a revival in the late 1970s-1980s and began to exert more influence over government policies. Foremost among political leaders pushing for this revival were British Prime Minister Margaret Thatcher and U.S. President Ronald Reagan.

In the view of many critics, the Thatcher-Reagan policies concentrated on revitalizing the confidence of business in government, largely rejecting the attempt to ease the effects of liberalism on vulnerable groups. These policies therefore resulted in open conflict with government employees, trade unions, and welfare recipients. As the changes initiated under Reagan and Thatcher spread to other countries, there were growing pressures on governments in the 1980s-1990s, to adopt orthodox liberal policies with an emphasis on privatization, deregulation, and the promotion of free trade and foreign investment. To legitimize their confrontational approach toward excluded groups, the newer orthodox leaders sometimes appealed to traditional values such as "the work ethic, family, neighborhood, and patriotism."[23]

This return to orthodox liberalism differs from the liberalism of Adam Smith in certain respects. Most importantly, pressures for liberal orthodoxy are now global in extent, for several reasons. First, advances in technology, communications, and transportation have enabled MNCs and international banks to shift their activities and funds throughout the world. Second, the IMF, World Bank, and DCs have provided LDC debtors with financing since the foreign debt crisis erupted in 1982, but the conditions on this financing have included pressures for LDCs to privatize, deregulate, and liberalize their economies. Third, with the breakup of the Soviet bloc, orthodox liberal pressures have also spread to the former CPEs. To differentiate this new liberal orthodoxy from the liberalism of Smith and Ricardo, scholars often use the term "neoliberalism."

LIBERALISM AND INSTITUTIONS

As discussed in Chapter 1, theorists point to "hegemony" and "institutions" as two important mechanisms for managing the global political economy. Two types of institutions are of interest here: international regimes and IOs.[24] Regime theory is the main theoretical approach of IR scholars to the study of institutions. Although hegemonic stability theory draws on more than one IPE perspective, it was covered in Chapter 3 because of its close links with realism. Regime theory also draws on more than one IPE perspective. Although a liberal scholar first used the "regime" term in an IPE context, a realist scholar edited a definitive volume on regimes.[25] However, institutions and regimes are discussed in this chapter because liberals attach more importance to these concepts than do realists. Because international regimes help promote cooperation in issue areas such as trade and monetary relations where there is a high degree of interdependence, we begin with a discussion of interdependence theory.[26]

Interdependence Theory

Interdependence can be defined as "mutual dependence," in which "there are reciprocal (although not necessarily symmetrical) costly effects of transactions."[27] Interdependence is not a new phenomenon in IR, and a number of theorists wrote studies on the subject in the early 1900s.[28] During the 1940s, scholars wrote works on interdependence in trade and monetary relations.[29] Despite these early studies, Richard Cooper's book *The Economics of Interdependence* (1968) is the first systematic study of the growing economic interdependence among states.[30] Cooper argues that growing economic interdependence as a result of advances in transportation, communications, and technology "negates the sharp distinction between internal and external policies that underlies the present political organization of the world," and increasingly circumscribes "the ability of nation-states to achieve their desired aims, regardless of their formal retention of sovereignty."[31] The response of states to their loss of autonomy may be passive, exploitative, defensive, aggressive, or constructive. The *constructive* response to growing interdependence in Cooper's view is the attempt by governments to jointly develop and implement their policies. This coordination of actions could include "a wide range of policies concerning taxation, the regulation of business structure and activity, the framing of monetary policy, and other 'domestic' policies."[32]

Although Cooper views cooperation as the best response to interdependence, he does not explicitly consider how *political* conditions can promote or undermine international cooperation. In their seminal work *Power and Interdependence*, published almost a decade after Cooper's study, Robert Keohane and Joseph Nye go a step further and analyze how interdependence transforms international politics. Although Keohane and Nye agree with Cooper that interdependence offers new opportunities for cooperation, they caution against an overly optimistic view of global harmony. Instead of negating politics, they argue that interdependence creates a new type of politics:

> Asymmetrical interdependence [i.e., mutual dependence that is not evenly balanced] can be a source of power. . . . A less dependent actor in a relationship often has a significant political resource, because changes in the relationship . . . will be less costly to that actor than to its partners.[33]

Nevertheless, Keohane and Nye have a rather benign view of the effects of asymmetrical interdependence on smaller states. Thus, they argue that interdependent relationships increase the opportunities for bargaining and permit smaller states to achieve their objectives in disputes with larger states more often than one might anticipate. In a study of asymmetrical interdependence between the United States and Canada, Keohane and Nye conclude that Canada's ability to successfully confront the United States in conflicts results largely from the highly interdependent relationship between the two countries. In their view, Canada benefits from "complex interdependence" with the United States, in which multiple channels connect societies, there is an absence of hierarchy among issues (military security does not dominate the agenda), and one government (the United States) does not use military force against another (Canada).[34] Some Canadian foreign policy analysts, however, strongly disagree with these conclusions. The United States as the larger power, they argue, is not content to let market transactions dictate its interdependence with Canada and instead is inclined to demand a wide array of "side payments." For example, Canadian side payments in exchange for free trade with the United States include concessions to U.S. demands regarding sharing of energy resources and openness to foreign investment (see Chapter 9).[35] A small number of Canadian analysts go even further and characterize Canada's relationship with the United States as dependence rather than interdependence.[36]

Interdependence theorists explicitly question the realist assumptions that states are unitary rational actors, that states are the only important actors in IR, and that military force is always useful for promoting a state's national interest. They also maintain that the scope of IR has expanded dramatically beyond the areas that realists emphasize, encompassing "new" issues such as environmental pollution, human rights, immigration, monetary and trade instabilities, and **sustainable development.** These new issues are more *intermestic* (domestic as well as international) than traditional security issues.[37] Thus, interdependence theorists often criticize realists for overemphasizing the divisions between international and domestic politics. Although interdependence theorists are critical of many realist assumptions, they view their model as supplementing rather than replacing realism. They consider realism to be the best model for understanding many security situations where power and force are of prime importance, but they argue that interdependence theory is often more applicable than realism in explaining international economic relations.

The Liberal Approach to Cooperation

Achieving cooperation in a world of nation-states is problematic because there is no centralized international authority to establish and enforce rules for state behavior. Game theory is useful for assessing the prospects for cooperation among states, and **prisoners' dilemma** is the game most often used by IR theorists. Prisoners' dilemma examines situations where states have an incentive to cheat even though cooperation provides them with mutual benefits if they can rely on each other to honor agreements.

The term *prisoners' dilemma* derives from the story used to describe the game: The police arrest two individuals, actors A and B, for committing fraud. The police suspect that A and B have also committed robbery, but they cannot prove it without a confession. The police question A and B in different cells where they cannot communicate with each other. In Figure 4.1, prisoners A and B "cooperate" with each other if they do not confess to committing robbery, and they "defect" (or cheat on each other) if they confess. The prisoners receive "payoffs" (i.e., benefits or losses) depending on the decisions they make. The numbers in bold at the top right-hand corner of the squares in Figure 4.1 are A's payoff figures, and the numbers at the bottom left-hand corners are B's payoffs. The police make a tempting offer to induce A to confess (i.e., defect). They inform A that conviction for fraud is certain and will result in a 1-year sentence for both prisoners if they do not confess (square II). However, if A confesses to robbery (defects) and B does not (cooperates), A will go free and B will get 10 years imprisonment (square I). If both A and B defect and confess to robbery, they will get a reduced sentence of 5 years (square III). Finally, if A does not confess to robbery (cooperates) but B confesses (defects), A will get 10 years imprisonment and B will go free (square IV). The police provide the same offer to B.

The question is, what will the prisoners do? According to *individual* rationality, if B defects, A is better off defecting (a payoff of −10) than cooperating (−40). If B coop-

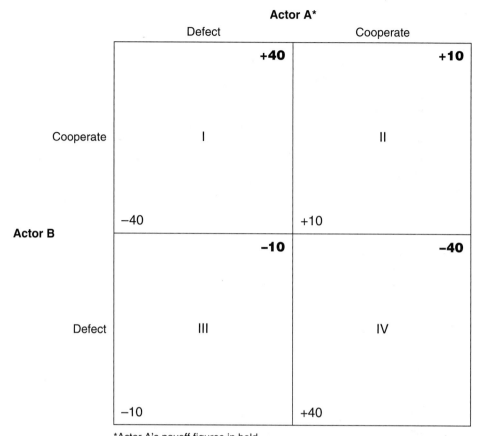

*Actor A's payoff figures in bold

Figure 4.1   Prisoner's Dilemma

erates, A is also better off defecting (+40) than cooperating (+10). Thus, whatever B does, it seems rational for A to defect! The same reasoning applies to B's decisions. A fears that B will defect, and wants to avoid ending up with the worst possible penalty by cooperating (−40 in square IV); thus, A is almost certain to defect, and B who mistrusts A, is also likely to defect. A and B are therefore both likely to defect and end up with the third-best outcome (square III), even though both would have been better off cooperating and ending up with the second-best outcome (square II). Square III is a *Pareto-suboptimal* or *Pareto-deficient* outcome because *all* actors (A and B) would prefer another outcome (II). Square II, by contrast, is the **Pareto-optimal** outcome or the best collective outcome for A and B; no single actor can be made better off without making someone else worse off (i.e., if A's payoff increases to +40 in square I, B's payoff decreases to −40).[38]

The dilemma in this game is that individual rationality differs from collective rationality and leads to a Pareto-suboptimal outcome (square III) for both prisoners.[39] In IR we ask how (and whether) states can move from a Pareto-suboptimal outcome (mutual defection or DD) to a Pareto-optimal outcome (mutual cooperation or CC). In the view of liberals, "cheating" by states can inhibit cooperation, but the move to mutual cooperation is often possible if cheating can be controlled. The existence of a global hegemon and international institutions can limit cheating and facilitate movement toward mutual cooperation. A global hegemon prevents cheating by providing public goods and coercing other states to abide by agreed rules and principles. Institutions such as IOs prevent cheating simply by bringing states together on a regular basis. A state that interacts regularly with other states is less likely to cheat because the other states will have many opportunities to retaliate. International institutions also enforce principles and rules to ensure that cheaters are punished, and collect information on member states' policies, increasing transparency or confidence that cheaters will be discovered. Finally, international institutions contribute to a mutual learning process in which states become aware that mutual gains can result from cooperation.[40]

Realists are far more skeptical than liberals that international institutions can play a significant role in moving states to a Pareto-optimal (CC) outcome. In the realist view, institutions serve the interests of the most powerful states rather than inducing them to seek cooperative solutions with weaker states. Realists also argue that state concerns with *relative gains* pose a major obstacle to cooperation, and they are highly skeptical of the liberal view that international institutions can refocus a state's interests toward absolute, mutual gains. Because of their basic interests in survival and security, states continue to be concerned about their capabilities *relative to* those of other states. Even when two states have common interests, they may be unwilling to cooperate because of each state's concern that the other will receive greater gains. Institutions may have a significant role in promoting cooperation, according to many realists, only if they can ensure that member-state gains are balanced and equitable. However, this is extremely difficult to achieve because gains are rarely equal. As is the case with all three schools of thought, there are gradations of view, and some realists are more willing to concede that institutions may have an important role in specific instances.[41] Robert Gilpin, for example, maintains that international economic organizations can be important when they "do not infringe on the security interests of powerful states."[42] Nevertheless, realists are generally less inclined than liberals to attribute an important role to international institutions.

Regime Theory

Although realists point out that the international system is anarchic because a central authority above nation-states is lacking, regime theory first developed from efforts to explain why international interactions seem to be more orderly in some issue areas than in others.[43] With the growth of interdependence, states have established some principles, norms, and rules to regulate each others' behavior in such areas as trade, aid, and monetary relations. Thus, *regimes* can be defined as "sets of implicit or explicit principles, norms, rules, and decision-making procedures around which actors' expectations converge in a given area of international relations."[44] International regimes are normally associated with IOs. For example, the WTO is embedded in the global trade regime, and the IMF is embedded in the global monetary regime. Regime *principles* and *norms* refer to general beliefs and standards of behavior that determine how relations are conducted in a specific issue area. Important principles of the global trade regime, for example, include trade liberalization, reciprocity, and non-discrimination.⁴⁵ Regime *rules,* which are more specific than principles and norms, refer to the types of behavior considered to be permissible. Rules and decision-making procedures stem from the broader principles and norms, which are the most central components of a regime. For example, "trade liberalization" is an important principle of the global trade regime. To promote this principle, the WTO upholds rules and decision-making procedures that limit trade protectionism. The sections that follow briefly examine some of the research done on the formation and consequences of regimes.

Regime studies have generally focused on three major themes. One theme concerns the *formation* of international regimes. As discussed in detail in Chapter 3, researchers disagree as to whether a hegemon is necessary for the creation of regimes. Other issues that researchers examine are the strategies and processes that lead to successful regime creation, and the role of international organizations in the creation of regimes. A second theme concerns the *maintenance* of regimes. Many theorists have been impressed by the durability of regimes even after the interest and power structures that led to their creation have changed. Thus, some writers argue that it is easier to maintain regimes than to establish them, and that countries benefiting from a regime may be willing to maintain it even after a hegemonic state declines (see Chapter 3).⁴⁶ Others relate the durability of regimes to their adaptability, and examine the process of change in regimes over time. Regime analysis has often been criticized for devoting inadequate attention to the third theme regarding the *results* of regimes; that is, do regimes "make a difference" in IR. In assessing regime results, researchers examine whether member states regularly abide by regime principles, norms, and rules; whether regimes cause states to broaden their perceptions of self-interest; and whether regimes adequately manage international problems.⁴⁷

Traditional realists believe that it is uncertain whether regimes exist, and that even if they do exist they have little effect. The most powerful states, in their view, have the most influence in establishing regime principles, norms, and rules that fit with their national objectives. However, these states will not adhere to the regime principles, norms, and rules if they come into conflict with their national interests. As global interdependence increased, some realists acknowledged that regimes may have importance, but only in certain areas (e.g., in trade and monetary relations) and under rather restrictive conditions. Compared with modified realists, liberals are more likely to view regimes as a pervasive and significant phenomenon in IR.⁴⁸

This book assumes that regimes have a significant impact on international behavior in certain issue areas. Regime principles, norms, and rules help to establish standards in these areas, which states and nonstate actors can use to assess each others' actions. In setting standards, regimes provide countries with reliable information, decrease misunderstandings, and increase possibilities for cooperation. Regimes also induce states to follow consistent policies, limit actions that adversely affect others, and become less responsive to special interest groups. To say that regimes and their IOs influence international behavior does not indicate that their effect is always positive. As realists and historical structuralists point out, a regime's principles, norms, and rules may reflect or further the interests of the most powerful actors, and pressure may be greatest on the least powerful actors to abide by them.⁴⁹

Despite the value of regime analysis, some liberal theorists have argued that it has some serious shortcomings, and have turned their attention to a study of *global governance*. The next section discusses the problems with regime analysis and draws comparisons between the concepts of regimes and global governance.

LIBERALISM, GLOBAL GOVERNANCE, AND REGIMES

The term **governance** refers to formal and informal processes and institutions that organize collective action. The term **global governance** describes formal and informal arrangements developed to produce a degree of order and collective action above the nation-state level in the absence of an international government. In other words, global governance is an encompassing term that involves a wide range of collective actions, including the creation of regimes and other institutions that "do not require centralized political organizations to administer them."[50] As globalization has increased, global governance has become a central issue in IPE for two major reasons. First, it is more difficult for states to manage their economic affairs individually, and public and private actors therefore often seek regional and global solutions. Second, with the growth of interdependence, self-regarding actions of states increasingly affect others, and governance is necessary to decrease conflict and promote cooperation.[51]

Some liberal theorists argue that the global governance concept avoids the problems of regime analysis. First, regime studies have traditionally been state-centric, devoting too little attention to the role of nonstate actors. Global governance by contrast is described as a multilayered process involving national, international, subnational, public, private, formal, and informal actors and institutions. Second, the issue-area focus of regimes has caused analysts to overlook broader issues of global management. For example, most regime studies on trade do not examine the linkages between the global trade and environment regimes, despite the current constant interaction between trade and environmental issues. Because the global governance concept is more encompassing, it is better able than regime theory to examine the linkages among issue areas.

It is important to note that some theorists have been altering their studies in recent years in response to the criticisms of regime analysis. For example, one theorist discusses both *international regimes* whose members are states and *transnational regimes* whose members are nonstate actors. Most regimes are in fact arrangements among both state and nonstate actors, and there is no reason why regime studies cannot become less state-centric.[52] Furthermore, some regime analysts have broadened their studies and devoted more attention to the linkage among issue areas. Thus, "the concept of international regimes is not . . . incompatible with the concept of global governance; on the contrary, although they differ in emphasis, both concepts recognize the signficance of nonstate actors and the relationships between issue areas."[53] Regime theory has a major advantage in that it permits us to engage in in-depth analysis of explicitly delineated issue areas. Thus, Part III of this book examines the role of regimes and IOs in regard to specific IPE issue areas. However, this book is also attuned to the criticisms of regime analysis and refers to some of the broader issues of global governance.

LIBERALISM AND DOMESTIC-INTERNATIONAL INTERACTIONS

IPE scholars are more likely than security specialists to focus on domestic-international interactions, because domestic groups and individuals often see a close relationship between international economic issues (such as trade and foreign investment) and their own welfare. Although much of the literature on domestic structure and IPE cannot be neatly categorized under any one of the three IPE perspectives, liberals most closely adhere to the view that domestic societal pressures affect state policy (some Marxists view the state as an "instrument" of the dominant capitalist class; see Chapter 5).

One area in which IPE specialists have examined domestic-international interactions extensively is foreign economic policymaking. A state's foreign economic policy clearly results from domestic as well as international factors.[54] For example, some analysts argue that more centralized states such as Japan and France often respond more decisively to external events than decentralized states such as the United States. The U.S. separation of powers between the president and Congress, and the division of powers between the federal government and the states make the U.S. government more vulnerable to interest group pressures and less able to respond to international economic crises. Thus, France promptly took actions to increase its security of energy supplies after the 1973 OPEC oil price increases by supporting French oil companies, promoting special relations with former French colonies that had oil, and developing nuclear energy as an alternative energy source. The decentralized U.S. government, by contrast, was less decisive because it was subject to competing societal pressures from oil companies, environmentalists, and other groups.[55]

Although the strong state/weak state distinction may be helpful in comparing DC policies in a general sense, more recent studies argue that states are not uniformly strong or weak across different issue areas and time periods.[56] Thus, the U.S. executive has been able to implement monetary policy more easily than trade policy because societal groups see their economic fortunes as being more affected by trade. Although societal groups exert pressures on Congress on controversial trade issues such as NAFTA, they give government leaders considerable latitude in formulating and implementing monetary policy. States such as Japan, which are considered to be highly centralized, also do not act decisively in regard to every issue. When a financial crisis affected East and Southeast Asia in the late 1990s, Japan had great difficulty in adopting the bold policy measures required to alleviate the crisis (see Chapter 11).

When variations in issue areas and time periods are accounted for, domestic structure can be an important factor in explaining a country's foreign economic policies. For example, hegemonic stability theorists look at U.S. economic and political resources, but they largely ignore the *domestic* constraints confronting U.S. policymakers. The domestic divisions within both the U.S. polity (e.g., between the president and Congress) and U.S. society can make it difficult for the United States to provide international leadership *even if* it has the external strength one associates with a hegemon. Japan, by contrast, with fewer external power resources, benefits from a greater unity of purpose in its polity and society under certain circumstances.

IR specialists also focus on domestic-international interactions when examining international economic negotiations. For example, theorists often view international negotiations as a "two-level game" involving the relationship between a state's international interests and obligations (level 1) on one hand and its domestic interactions (level 2) on the other.[57] At the international level, state representatives bargain with each other to reach an agreement. At the domestic level, these representatives bargain with their own domestic constituencies, whose concurrence is often needed to arrive at legitimate and effective agreements. A degree of consistency must develop between the international and domestic interests if agreements are to be signed and implemented. The two-level game framework is especially useful in examining issues such as agricultural trade, in which a wide range of domestic interests come into conflict with a state's international interests and obligations.[58]

In addition to examining foreign economic policymaking and international negotiations, IPE specialists seek to explain international economic cooperation and conflict in terms of domestic variables.[59] Chapters 6 and 8, for example, refer to arguments that domestic factors are more important than the existence of a hegemon in explaining cooperation and conflict in global monetary and trade issues. There is a wealth of literature on domestic interactions in IPE; this book can only begin to discuss the subject.

LIBERALISM AND NORTH-SOUTH RELATIONS

Liberals generally agree that the key factors in development are the efficient use of scarce resources and economic growth, which is often defined as an increase in a country's per capita income. Beyond these broad areas of agreement, however, the liberal development school "lacks a central unifying, theoretical argument."[60] The division between orthodox and interventionist liberals discussed earlier is also evident among liberal development theorists.

Orthodox Liberals and North-South Relations

Orthodox liberals are not particularly concerned with North-South distributional issues, because they consider international economic relations to be a positive-sum game and believe that interdependence has a mutually beneficial effect on states. Indeed, orthodox liberals often argue that North-South linkages provide even more benefits to LDCs than to DCs. LDC economic problems, in the orthodox liberal view, stem from irrational or inefficient domestic policies and not from their unfavorable position in the global economy. The sections that follow outline the views of orthodox liberals regarding domestic and external determinants of development.

Domestic Development Factors   Orthodox liberals assume that development problems of LDCs stem largely from their irrational or inefficient policies. In the 1950s-1960s, liberal *modernization theorists* compared traditional and modern societies and traced the development process from traditionalism to modernity. Although modernization theory was considered to be largely passé by the 1970s, its precepts continue to influence orthodox liberal thought. Modernization theory asserts that Northern DCs achieved economic development by abandoning traditional methods of organizing society and that their development experience serves as an indispensable guide to development for the South. From the modernization perspective, LDCs must replace their traditional values, institutions, and activities if they are to overcome the obstacles to development. The individual and societal changes required may produce considerable dislocation and hardship, but the rewards and opportunities in societies that successfully modernize are also great. A system of rewards for innovation is essential for modernization because innovation and other internal mechanisms for generating surpluses contribute to increased investment and thus to self-sustaining growth.[61]

It is generally conceded that modernization theory's concepts of "traditional" and "modern" were imprecise, that the two concepts are not mutually exclusive, and that modern values and practices are not always superior to traditional ones. Nevertheless, orthodox liberals continue to believe that the main factors hindering LDC development are domestic. For example, they argue that Western European countries that protected private property rights experienced early success in industrialization and development, and that LDCs that do not enforce these rights hinder foreign investment and the adoption of new technologies. In the orthodox liberal view, LDC governments should permit private producers to operate freely through the price mechanism and should limit their own involvement to providing public goods such as national security, education, and services designed to improve the functioning of markets.[62]

Paths to Development   A number of modernization theorists were deterministic, advising the South to follow the same path to development that was previously taken by the North. For example, one theorist wrote during the 1960s that the Western development model "reappears in virtually all modernizing societies of all continents of the world, regardless of variations of race, color, or creed."[63] The best-known study prescribing a single development path is Walt Rostow's *The Stages of Economic Growth,* which received widespread attention from the time of its publication. Rostow takes a highly deterministic position, claiming that societies move through five specific stages on their way to modernity: traditional society, the preconditions for takeoff, the takeoff, the drive to maturity, and the age of high mass consumption.[64] Despite the initial influence of Rostow's model, his predictions regarding LDC growth were unduly optimistic, and it was difficult to apply his stages to specific LDCs. For example, Rostow argued that an LDC reaching the takeoff stage would be transformed in such a way that its growth would become self-sustaining. Such predictions raised false hopes that LDC economic development was readily achievable and irreversible. Although some modernization theorists were more open to the idea that LDCs could follow different routes to development, much modernization theory was deterministic.[65]

Critics of modernization theory strongly criticize the view that all countries can or should follow similar development paths, because the challenges facing LDCs today are very different from those confronting early developers. The forces of globalization, the need to compete with the North, and the proliferation of MNCs all indicate that Southern development cannot simply be a repetition of the earlier Western model.[66] Nevertheless, even after modernization theory was considered passé, orthodox liberals continued to view the Western model as the only legitimate path to development. In the 1970s, orthodox liberals strongly opposed OPEC's strategy to raise oil prices because it interfered with market-oriented pricing, and they opposed the South's demand for an NIEO because it would redistribute wealth and power on the basis of political pressure rather than efficient economic performance.[67] Orthodox liberals became even more assertive after the breakup of the Soviet bloc. Thus, in the late 1980s–1990s, some theorists wrote that "third-world countries are much like those of the first world and will, with a modicum of external aid and internal stability, follow in the path of their predecessors," and that "what we may be witnessing is not just the end of the Cold War" but "the universalization of Western liberal democracy as the final form of human government."[68]

External Development Factors   Internationally, orthodox liberals view North-South relations as a positive-sum game that benefits the South, and they strongly reject the idea that the North is responsible for poverty in the South. On the contrary, orthodox liberals often argue that "the late-comers to modern economic growth tend to catch up with the early-comers."[69] Whereas LDCs that achieve development are closely integrated in the global economy through freer trade and capital flows, the poorest and least developed LDCs have few trade and foreign investment linkages with the North. Because LDCs have shortages of capital and technology, they require foreign investment and the diffusion of advanced technologies. Exports are also of critical importance to LDCs because of their small domestic markets, and international trade permits LDCs to specialize in the goods they can produce most efficiently. Thus, two orthodox liberal economists have written that "such economic development as has taken place [in Tanzania] is in large measure due to access to Western markets and to Western enterprise, capital, and ideas."[70]

Because orthodox liberals advocate free trade, they were extremely critical of the South's **import-substituting industrialization (ISI)** policies in the 1950s-1960s. (Some Latin American LDCs continued to follow ISI policies during the 1970s and early 1980s.) These policies involved protection of local industry through a wide array of tariffs and **nontariff barriers (NTBs),** with an emphasis on production for the domestic market over production for export. In the orthodox liberal view, ISI causes economic distortions in LDC economies and fosters uncompetitive industries with high prices and low-quality products.[71] Orthodox liberals, by contrast, attributed the economic success of East Asian NIEs to their export-led development model, which they viewed as clearly preferable to ISI. As its name implies, **export-led growth** relies on deep involvement in international trade as a "motor" to development. Thus, orthodox liberals argued that "Malaysia, Singapore, Korea, Taiwan, Hong Kong, and Japan—all relying extensively on private markets, are thriving" while "India, Indonesia, and Communist China, all relying heavily on central planning, have experienced economic stagnation and political repression."[72] As discussed in Chapter 3, realists dispute the liberal view that the East Asian NIEs' success in exporting depended on market-oriented policies. Instead, realists argue that government-business cooperation and selective government involvement was the key to East Asian economic development. Chapter 11 examines this debate in greater detail.

Interventionist Liberals and North-South Relations

Interventionist liberals begin with the same basic assumptions as orthodox liberals that LDCs with efficient, market-oriented policies are most likely to achieve economic growth. In contrast to orthodox liberals, however, interventionists point to the pronounced inequalities between North and South, and they call on the DCs to give more consideration to the special needs of LDCs. The interventionists believe that "economic forces left entirely to themselves tend to produce growing inequality," especially when North-South income distribution is highly distorted.[73] They therefore recommend a variety of changes that involve some degree of intervention in the market, including the removal of DC trade barriers to LDCs while permitting some degree of protectionism for LDC industries, the provision of increased IMF and World Bank financial resources to indebted LDCs, and the assurance that MNCs will not take undue advantage of LDC needs for foreign investment and technology. Interventionists believe that Northern assistance to the South is a matter of enlightened self-interest because "the countries of the North, given their increasing interdependence with the South, themselves need international economic reform to ensure their own future prosperity."[74]

Although interventionists argue that corrective devices are needed to provide for the South's special needs, they believe that the necessary changes can occur within the international liberal order and that a radical redistribution of wealth and power between North and South is not necessary. They also share the faith of other liberals in private enterprise, believing that private sector interactions between North and South should be encouraged. Finally, interventionist and orthodox liberals agree that many Southern development problems are rooted in domestic inefficiencies and that LDCs therefore have the primary responsibility for facilitating their development.[75]

CRITIQUE OF THE LIBERAL PERSPECTIVE

It is impossible to provide a detailed critique of the liberal perspective here. This section focuses mainly on some important general criticisms of the liberals by realists and historical structuralists. As this chapter notes, liberals believe that all countries benefit from trade, foreign investment, and other economic linkages in a competitive market. Because these exchange relations produce mutual benefits, orthodox liberals are not particularly concerned about the fact that all countries do not benefit equally. Although interventionist liberals point out that unemployment can occur under market conditions and that LDCs may require special treatment, they believe these problems can be resolved by supplementing rather than replacing the liberal-economic system.

Both realists and historical structuralists criticize liberals for their inattention to power and distributional issues. In contrast to liberals who emphasize the mutual gains from exchange, realists argue that the relative distribution of gains is more important, with the more powerful states capturing a larger share of the benefits. Realists believe that economic exchanges are rarely free and equal and that bargaining power based on monopoly and coercion can have important political effects. Thus, more powerful states can injure weaker states simply by reducing or terminating linkages in such areas as trade, aid, and foreign investment.[76] Historical structuralists often accuse liberals of seeking to legitimize inequalities and exploitation. Domestically, liberals mislead the working class into believing that it will reap the benefits of economic prosperity along with the capitalist class, and internationally, liberals disguise exploitation and imperialism under the cloak of "interdependence."

Critics also question the liberal view that technology rather than global redistribution can solve the world's most urgent economic and environmental problems. Even with technological advances, the liberal international order that seemed so positive-sum in the immediate postwar years is becoming more intensely competitive as global resources become less abundant. Furthermore, orthodox liberals underestimate the degree to which technological advances may contribute to greater North-South inequalities. *Endogenous growth theory* posits that technological change is not simply the result of fortunate breakthroughs in knowledge that are exogenous to the factors of production determining economic growth. Instead, technological knowledge is an important endogenous factor of production along with labor and capital. The more rapid technological advances in DC firms produce increases in the productivity of labor and capital, making "it possible for a large and rich economy to grow indefinitely at a faster pace than a small and poor economy."[77] Although some claims of endogenous growth theorists are controversial and not yet proven, they raise important questions about the orthodox liberal assumption that "the late-comers to modern economic growth tend to catch up with the early-comers."[78]

Orthodox liberals also simply assume that open economic policies will improve LDC opportunities, without considering North-South political power relationships. Aside from some aberrant cases such as OPEC and the East Asian NIEs, critics argue, North-South relationships are highly asymmetrical, with LDCs far more dependent on DCs than vice versa. Thus, Tanzania's President Julius Nyerere remarked to a G-77 ministerial meeting in February 1979 that:

> . . . What we have in common is that we are all, in relation to the developed world, dependent—not interdependent—nations. Each of our economies has developed as a by-product and a subsidiary of development in the industrialized North, and is externally oriented.[79]

It is evident that this dependent relationship provides the North with a potent source of power over the South. The liberal perspective, however, tends to avoid the subject of power, discounting the effects of North-South asymmetries by arguing that North-South relations are a positive-sum game in which everyone benefits. One liberal assessment of NAFTA, for example, indicates that the United States, Canada, and Mexico agreed to "a partial surrender of autonomy in order to achieve the benefits that are available from mutual relaxation of protectionism."[80] However, orthodox liberals avoid asking whether Southern states (i.e., Mexico in NAFTA) must surrender more autonomy than Northern states (the United States and Canada).

Liberals are also criticized for putting too much faith in the market and for disregarding the role of the state. Although Adam Smith recognized that the state had to perform certain essential functions, orthodox liberalism generally provides for a minimal role for the state. Interventionist liberals such as Keynes have viewed states as performing various corrective functions, but even interventionists are criticized for undertheorizing the role of the state. Liberal theory portrays the state as simply performing functions not performed by the market, and it does not sufficiently explore the capacities or constraints of the state. Thus, realists argue that we should "bring the state back in" to our research because of its central role in policymaking.[81]

Chapters 3 and 4 demonstrate that realists and liberals have different perceptions regarding a wide range of IPE issues. However, these two schools of thought are much closer together than the third school—historical structuralists—in one important respect. Whereas liberals and realists accept the capitalist system as a given, historical structuralists view capitalism as an exploitative system that should—and will—eventually be replaced by socialism. It is to the historical structuralists that this book now turns.

NOTES

1. R. D. McKinlay and R. Little, *Global Problems and World Order* (London: Pinter, 1986), p.41. Andrew Moravcsik attempts to identify the core propositions of liberalism in "Taking Preferences Seriously: A Liberal Theory of International Politics," *International Organization* 51-4 (Autumn 1997), pp.513–553.
2. For a discussion of the forms of liberalism, see Mark W. Zacher and Richard A. Matthew, "Liberal International Theory: Common Threads, Divergent Strands," in Charles W. Kegley, Jr., ed., *Controversies in International Relations Theory: Realism and the Neoliberal Challenge* (New York: St. Martin's Press, 1995), pp.107–150.
3. Moravcsik, "Taking Preferences Seriously," p.517.
4. Adam Smith, *The Wealth of Nations* (London: Dent, Everyman's Library no. 412, 1910), vol. 1, bk. 4, p.398.
5. See E. E. Schattschneider, *Politics, Pressures and the Tariff: A Study of Free Enterprise in Pressure Politics, as Shown in the 1929–1930 Revision of the Tariff* (Hamden: Archon Books, 1963, reprint of the 1935 edition).
6. See Michael Walzer, "Liberalism and the Art of Separation," *Political Theory* 12-3 (August 1984), pp. 315–330.
7. John Locke, *Two Treatises of Government* (Cambridge: Cambridge University Press, 1964), ch. 9 of the Second Treatise, p.368.
8. Adam Smith, *The Wealth of Nations*, vol. 1, bk. 4, p.436.
9. Smith, *The Wealth of Nations,* vol. 2, bk. 4, pp.180–181. For an alternative view of Smith see A. Wyatt-Walter, "Adam Smith and the Liberal Tradition in International Relations," *Review of International Studies* 22-1 (1996), pp. 142–172.
10. John Maynard Keynes, *The General Theory of Employment, Interest, and Money* (New York: Harcourt, Brace & World, 1936), p.383.
11. Peter A. Hall, "Introduction," in Peter A. Hall, ed., *The Political Power of Economic Ideas: Keynesianism across Nations* (Princeton: Princeton University Press, 1989), p.4.
12. Keynes, *The General Theory of Employment, Interest, and Money,* pp.378–379.
13. Hall, "Introduction," p.7.
14. John Maynard Keynes, "National Self-Sufficiency," *The Yale Review* 22 (1933), p.758. For a discussion of Keynes's changing view of trade protection, see Barry Eichengreen, "Keynes and Protection," *Journal of Economic History* 44-2 (June 1984), pp.363–373.

15. Fred L. Block, *The Origins of International Economic Disorder: A Study of United States International Monetary Policy from World War II to the Present* (Berkeley: University of California Press, 1977), pp.62–69; D. E. Moggridge, *Keynes* (London: Macmillan, 1976), p.147.

16. Anthony Arblaster, *The Rise and Decline of Western Liberalism* (New York: Basil Blackwell, 1984), p.292; B. Greenwald and J. E. Stiglits, "Keynesian, New Keynesian and New Classical Economics," *Oxford Economic Papers* 39-1 (1987), p.119; Donald Winch, "Keynes, Keynesianism, and State Intervention," in Hall, ed., *The Political Power of Economic Ideas*, pp.109–110.

17. Karl Polanyi, *The Great Transformation* (Boston: Beacon Press, sixth printing, 1965).

18. John Gerard Ruggie coined the term "embedded liberalism compromise" in his important article "International Regimes, Transactions, and Change: Embedded Liberalism in the Postwar Economic Order," in Stephen D. Krasner, ed., *International Regimes* (Ithaca: Cornell University Press, 1983), pp.204–214.

19. Peter Gourevitch, *Politics in Hard Times: Comparative Responses to International Economic Crises* (Ithaca: Cornell University Press, 1986), pp.166–169; Adam Przeworski, *Capitalism and Social Democracy* (Cambridge: Cambridge University Press, 1985), pp.205–211.

20. Milton Friedman, *Capitalism and Freedom* (Chicago: University of Chicago Press, 1962), p.9.

21. Milton Friedman and Rose Friedman, *Free to Choose: A Personal Statement* (New York: Harcourt Brace Jovanovich, 1980), pp.54–55.

22. See Friedman, *Capitalism and Freedom*, pp.171–172; F. A. Hayek, *New Studies in Philosophy, Politics, Economics and the History of Ideas* (Chicago: University of Chicago Press, 1978), p.209; and Ludwig von Mises, *Planning for Freedom* (South Holland: Libertarian Press, 1974), p.17.

23. Robert Cox, *Production, Power, and World Order: Social Forces in the Making of History* (New York: Columbia University Press, 1987), pp.286–288; Alain Lipietz, *Towards a New Economic Order: Postfordism, Ecology and Democracy,* translated by Malcolm Slater (New York: Oxford University Press, 1992), pp.30–31.

24. Robert Keohane identifies three types of international institutions: IOs, regimes, and conventions. See Keohane's "Neoliberal Institutionalism: A Perspective on World Politics," in Robert O. Keohane, *International Institutions and State Power: Essays in International Relations Theory* (Boulder: Westview Press, 1989), pp.3–4.

25. In IPE, John Gerard Ruggie first used the regime term in his article "International Responses to Technology: Concepts and Trends," *International Organization* 29-3 (Summer 1975), pp.570–573. Stephen Krasner edited the volume *International Regimes.*

26. Ernst B. Haas, "Words Can Hurt You; or, Who Said What to Whom About Regimes," in Krasner, ed., *International Regimes*, p.27.

27. Robert O. Keohane and Joseph S. Nye, *Power and Interdependence*, 2nd ed. (Glenview: Scott, Foresman, 1989), pp.8–9.

28. See Sir Norman Angell, *The Foundations of International Polity* (London: Heinemann, 1914); Francis Delaisi, *Political Myths and Economic Realities* (London: Douglas, 1925); Ramsay Muir, *The Interdependent World and Its Problems* (Boston: Houghton Mifflin, 1933); and David A. Baldwin, "Interdependence and Power: A Conceptual Analysis," *International Organization* 34-4 (Autumn 1980), pp.481–482.

29. See W. A. Brown, Jr., *The International Gold Standard Reinterpreted, 1914–1934,* 2 vols. (New York: National Bureau of Economic Research, 1940); and Albert O. Hirschman, *National Power and the Structure of Foreign Trade* (Berkeley: University of California Press, 1945).

30. Richard N. Cooper, *The Economics of Interdependence: Economic Policy in the Atlantic Community* (New York: McGraw-Hill, 1968).

31. Richard N. Cooper, "Economic Interdependence and Foreign Policy in the Seventies," *World Politics* 24 (January 1972), p.179.

32. Cooper, "Economic Interdependence and Foreign Policy in the Seventies," pp.170–171.
33. Keohane and Nye, *Power and Interdependence,* p.11. See also George T. Crane and Abla Amawi, eds., *The Theoretical Evolution of International Political Economy* (New York: Oxford University Press, 1997), pp.14, 107–109.
34. See Keohane and Nye, *Power and Interdependence,* pp.24–29 and ch. 7.
35. See, for example, Ricardo Grinspun and Maxwell A. Cameron, eds., *The Political Economy of North American Free Trade* (Montreal: McGill-Queen's University Press, 1993).
36. See Wallace Clement, *Continental Corporate Power: Economic Linkage Between Canada and the United States* (Toronto: McClelland and Stewart, 1976); Glen Williams, "On Determining Canada's Location Within the International Political Economy," *Studies in Political Economy* 25 (Spring 1988), pp.107–140; and Duncan Cameron and Mel Watkins, eds., *Canada Under Free Trade* (Toronto: Lorimer, 1993).
37. Bayless Manning coined the term *intermestic* in "The Congress, The Executive and Intermestic Affairs: Three Proposals," *Foreign Affairs* 55 (June 1977), pp.306–324.
38. The term *Pareto-optimal* is named after an Italian sociologist, Vilfredo Pareto (1848–1923).
39. Robert Axelrod, *The Evolution of Cooperation* (New York: Basic Books, 1984), p.9.
40. Keohane, "Neoliberal Institutionalism," pp.1–20; Robert Axelrod and Robert O. Keohane, "Achieving Cooperation Under Anarchy: Strategies and Institutions," in Kenneth A. Oye, ed., *Cooperation Under Anarchy* (Princeton: Princeton University Press, 1986), pp.226–254.
41. For example, John J. Mearsheimer expresses a hardline realist position in "The False Promise of International Institutions," *International Security* 19-3 (Winter 1994–1995), pp.5–49. Joseph Grieco's view is somewhat less extreme in *Cooperation Among Nations: Europe, America, and Non-Tariff Barriers to Trade* (Ithaca: Cornell University Press, 1990).
42. Robert Gilpin with Jean M. Gilpin, *Global Political Economy: Understanding the International Economic Order* (Princeton: Princeton University Press, 2001), p.83, fn. 13.
43. Mark W. Zacher with Brent A. Sutton, *Governing Global Networks: International Regimes for Transportation and Communications* (Cambridge: Cambridge University Press, 1996), p.1.
44. Krasner, "Structural Causes and Regime Consequences," in Krasner, ed., *International Regimes,* p.2.
45. One criticism of regime theory is that a consensus on the difference between regime principles and norms is lacking. For example, in an important article on the global trade regime, Mark Zacher and Jock Finlayson describe nondiscrimination, trade liberalization, and reciprocity as "norms." In a subsequent article, Zacher decides it is better to view these as "principles." See Jock A. Finlayson and Mark W. Zacher, "The GATT and the Regulation of Trade Barriers: Regime Dynamics and Function," in Krasner, ed., *International Regimes,* pp.273–314; Mark W. Zacher, "Trade Gaps, Analytical Gaps: Regime Analysis and International Commodity Trade Regulation," *International Organization* 41-2 (Spring 1987), p.176, fn. 8.
46. Robert O. Keohane, *After Hegemony: Cooperation and Discord in the World Political Economy* (Princeton: Princeton University Press, 1984), pp.49, 244–245.
47. Olav Schram Stokke, "Regimes as Governance Systems," in Oran R. Young, ed., *Global Governance: Drawing Insights from the Environmental Experience* (Cambridge: MIT Press, 1997), pp. 27–63. On the need for more studies of regime results see Robert O. Keohane, "The Analysis of International Regimes: Towards a European-American Research Programme," in Volker Rittberger, ed., with Peter Mayer, *Regime Theory and International Relations* (Oxford: Clarendon Press, 1993), pp.32–34; Volker Rittberger and Michael Zürn, "Towards Regulated Anarchy in East-West Relations: Causes and Consequences of East-West Regimes," in Volker Rittberger, ed., *International Regimes in East-West Politics* (London: Pinter, 1990), pp.20–22.

48. See Krasner, "Structural Causes and Regime Consequences," pp.5–10. An often cited traditional realist critique of regime theory is Susan Strange, "Cave! Hic Dragones: A Critique of Regime Analysis," in Krasner, ed., *International Regimes*, pp.337–354.

49. For a discussion of the historical structuralist perspective and regime theory see Fred Gale, "Cave 'Cave! Hic dragones': A Neo-Gramscian Deconstruction and Reconstruction of International Regime Theory," *Review of International Political Economy* 5-2 (Summer 1998), pp.252–283.

50. Oran R. Young, *Governance in World Affairs* (Ithaca: Cornell University Press, 1999), p.2.

51. Leon Gordenker and Thomas G. Weiss, "Pluralizing Global Governance: Analytical Approaches and Dimensions," in Thomas G. Weiss and Leon Gordenker, eds., *NGOs, the UN, and Global Governance* (Boulder: Lynne Rienner, 1996), p. 17; David A. Lake, "Global Governance: A Relational Contracting Approach," in Prakash and Hart, eds., *Globalization and Governance*, pp.31–53; Robert O. Keohane and Joseph S. Nye, Jr., "Introduction," in Joseph S. Nye, Jr. and John D. Donahue, eds., *Governance in a Globalizing World* (Washington, D.C.: Brookings Institution, 2000), pp.1–41; James N. Rosenau and Ernst-Otto Czempiel, eds., *Governance without Government: Order and Change in World Politics* (Cambridge: Cambridge University Press, 1992).

52. Young, *Governance in World Affairs*, p.11; Virginia Haufler, "Crossing the Boundary between Public and Private: International Regimes and Non-State Actors," in Rittberger with Mayer, eds., *Regime Theory and International Relations*, pp.94–111.

53. Olav Schram Stokke, "Regimes as Governance Systems," in Oran R. Young, ed., *Global Governance: Drawing Insights from the Environmental Experience* (Cambridge: MIT Press, 1997), p.31. Stokke's article provides a detailed comparison of the regime and global governance concepts.

54. Even realists who examine foreign economic policy must be attuned to domestic factors. See Stephen D. Krasner, *Defending the National Interest: Raw Materials Investments and U.S. Foreign Policy* (Princeton: Princeton University Press, 1978), pp.12–13; and Michael Mastanduno, David A. Lake, and G. John Ikenberry, "Toward a Realist Theory of State Action," *International Studies Quarterly* 33-4 (December 1989), pp.457–474.

55. Peter J. Katzenstein, "International Relations and Domestic Structures: Foreign Economic Policies of the Advanced Industrial States," *International Organization* 30-1 (Winter 1976), pp.41–42; Peter J. Katzenstein, ed., *Between Power and Plenty: Foreign Economic Policies of Advanced Industrial States*, special issue of *International Organization* 31-4 (Autumn 1977); Matthew Evangelista, "Domestic Structure and International Change," in Michael W. Doyle and G. John Ikenberry, eds., *New Thinking in International Relations Theory* (Boulder: Westview Press, 1997), pp.206–208.

56. G. John Ikenberry, David A. Lake, and Michael Mastanduno, ed., *The State and American Foreign Economic Policy*, special issue of *International Organization* 42-1 (Winter 1988); William D. Coleman and Grace Skogstad, *Policy Communities and Public Policy in Canada: A Structural Approach* (Mississauga: Copp Clark Pitman, 1990), p.ix.

57. Robert D. Putnam, "Diplomacy and Domestic Politics: The Logic of Two-Level Games," *International Organization* 42-3 (Summer 1988), pp.427–460; and Peter B. Evans, Harold K. Jacobson, Robert D. Putnam, eds., *Double-Edged Diplomacy: International Bargaining and Domestic Politics* (Berkeley: University of California Press, 1993).

58. William P. Avery, ed., *World Agriculture and the GATT* (Boulder: Rienner, 1993); Theodore H. Cohn, "The Intersection of Domestic and Foreign Policy in the NAFTA Agricultural Negotiations," *Canadian-American Public Policy*, no. 14 (Orono: University of Maine, September 1993); William P. Avery, "American Agricultural and Trade Policymaking: Two-Level Bargaining in the North American Free Trade Agreement," *Policy Sciences* 29 (1996), pp.113–136.

59. Peter Alexis Gourevitch, "Squaring the Circle: The Domestic Sources of International Co-operation," *International Organization* 50-2 (Spring 1996), pp.349–373.

60. David A. Lake, "Power and the Third World: Toward a Realist Political Economy of North-South Relations," *International Studies Quarterly* 31-2 (June 1987), p.218.

61. C. E. Black, *The Dynamics of Modernization: A Study in Comparative History* (New York: Harper & Row, 1966), p.27; Daniel Lerner, "Modernization: Social Aspects," in David Sills, ed., *International Encyclopedia of the Social Sciences* (New York: Macmillan, 1968) vol. 10, pp.386–388.

62. Robert Wade, *Governing the Market: Economic Theory and the Role of Government in East Asian Industrialization* (Princeton: Princeton University Press, 1990), pp.11–14.

63. Daniel Lerner, *The Passing of Traditional Society: Modernizing the Middle East* (New York: Free Press, 1964), pp.viii–ix. (This quotation appears in the preface to the paperback edition.)

64. W. W. Rostow, *The Stages of Economic Growth: A Non-Communist Manifesto* (Cambridge: Cambridge University Press, 1960), pp.4–92.

65. Less deterministic studies include Gabriel A. Almond and James S. Coleman, eds., *The Politics of the Developing Areas* (Princeton: Princeton University Press, 1960); Samuel P. Huntington, *Political Order in Changing Societies* (New Haven: Yale University Press, 1968); and Alexander Gerschenkron, *Economic Backwardness in Historical Perspective: A Book of Essays* (Cambridge: Harvard University Press, 1962).

66. Alejandro Portes, "On the Sociology of National Development: Theories and Issues," *American Journal of Sociology* 82-1 (July 1976), p.60.

67. McKinlay and Little, *Global Problems and World Order*, p.96; Peter T. Bauer and Basil S. Yamey, "World Wealth Redistribution: Anatomy of the New Order," in Karl Brunner, ed., *The First World and the Third World: Essays on the New International Economic Order* (Rochester: University of Rochester Policy Center Publications, 1978), p.193.

68. Lloyd G. Reynolds, *Economic Growth in the Third World, 1850–1980* (New Haven: Yale University Press, 1985), p.6; Francis Fukuyama, "The End of History?" *The National Interest* 16 (Summer 1989), p.4.

69. W. W. Rostow, *Why the Poor Get Richer and the Rich Slow Down* (Austin: University of Texas Press, 1980), p.259.

70. P. T. Bauer and B. S. Yamey, "Against the New Economic Order," *Commentary* 63-4 (April 1977), p.27.

71. For a survey of literature criticizing ISI policies, see Carlos F. Díaz-Alejandro, "Trade Policies and Economic Development," in Peter B. Kenen, ed., *International Trade and Finance: Frontiers for Research* (London: Cambridge University Press, 1975), pp.112–116.

72. Milton Friedman and Rose Friedman, *Free to Choose: A Personal Statement* (New York: Harcourt Brace Jovanovich, 1980), p.57. See also Bela Balassa, "The Process of Industrial Development and Alternative Development Strategies," in Bela Balassa, ed., *The Newly Industrializing Countries in the World Economy* (New York: Pergamon Press), pp.16–17.

73. Independent Commission on International Development Issues (henceforth, Brandt Commission I), *North-South, A Program for Survival* (Cambridge: MIT Press, 1980), pp.103–104.

74. Brandt Commission I, *North-South*, p.33. See also Albert Fishlow, "A New International Economic Order: What Kind?" in Albert Fishlow, Carlos F. Díaz-Alejandro, Richard R. Fagen, and Roger D. Hansen, *Rich and Poor Nations in the World Economy* (New York: McGraw-Hill, 1978), pp.51–76.

75. Stephen D. Krasner, *Structural Conflict: The Third World Against Global Liberalism* (Berkeley: University of California Press, 1985), pp.22–25.

76. Charles E. Lindblom, *Politics and Markets: The World's Political-Economic Systems* (New York: Basic Books, 1977), p.48.

77. Michael Parkin and Robin Bade, *Modern Macroeconomics,* 4th edition (Scarborough: Prentice-Hall, 1995), p.255. On endogenous growth theory, see Paul M. Romer, "Increasing Returns and Long-Run Growth," *Journal of Political Economy* 94-5 (October 1986), pp.1002–1037; Paul M. Romer, "Endogenous Technological Change," *Journal of Political Economy* 98-5 (October 1990), pp.S71–S102; Philippe Aghion and Peter Howitt, *Endogenous Growth Theory* (Cambridge: MIT Press, 1998).

78. Rostow, *Why the Poor Get Richer and the Rich Slow Down,* p.259.

79. "Address by His Excellency Mwalima Julius K Nyerere, President of the United Republic of Tanzania, to the Fourth Ministerial Meeting of the Group of 77," Arusha, 12–16 February 1979, in Karl P. Sauvant, *The Group of 77: Evolution, Structure, Organization* (New York: Oceana Publications, 1981), p.133.

80. Steven Globerman and Michael Walker, "Overview," in Steven Globerman and Michael Walker, eds., *Assessing NAFTA: A Trinational Analysis* (Vancouver: The Fraser Institute, 1993), p.ix.

81. Theda Skocpol, "Bringing the State Back In: Strategies of Analysis in Current Research," in Peter B. Evans, Dietrich Rueschemeyer, and Theda Skocpol, eds., *Bringing the State Back In* (Cambridge: Cambridge University Press, 1985), p.6.

C H A P T E R   5

The Historical Structuralist Perspective

The term *historical structuralism* encompasses a wide range of theoretical approaches, including Marxism, dependency theory, world-systems theory, and Gramscian analysis. All these approaches have some roots in Marxism, but some have diverged quite substantially from mainstream Marxist ideas. For example, certain Marxists accuse dependency and world-systems theorists of not being sufficiently Marxist and of being mistaken in their interpretation of the South's development. There are several reasons why this book refers to the third IPE perspective as historical structuralism. The term *structuralist* reflects the perspective's focus on structural means of exploitation, in which one class dominates another, or rich Northern states in the core of the global economy dominate poorer Southern states in the periphery. However, some realists are also structuralists because they believe that structural factors such as a state's power and position in the international system have a critical effect on its behavior.[1] To differentiate the third perspective from structural realism, we add the word *historical* to indicate that theorists in this perspective take a historical approach to the study of IPE.[2] According to these theorists, history has been marked by exploitation, and the main characteristic of the current system is the dominance of capitalism, with the capitalist class (the *bourgeoisie*) exploiting the workers (the *proletariat*). Thus, the term *historical structuralism* best describes this school of thought.

It is difficult to generalize about the basic tenets of the third IPE perspective because of the diversity of historical structuralist approaches. Thus, the discussion of theoretical developments provides some indication of the wide differences among writers in this school of thought. There is no separate section on North-South relations in this chapter because some historical structuralists such as dependency theorists focus almost exclusively on North-South issues.

Basic Tenets of the Historical Structuralist Perspective

The Role of the Individual, the State, and Societal Groups

Marxists identify the relationship among classes as the main factor affecting the economic and political order. Each mode of production (e.g., feudalism and capitalism) is associated with two opposing classes: an exploiting nonproducing class and an exploited class of producers. Classes are absent only in the simplest mode of production, the primitive-communal, and in the future Communist mode. Thus, Karl Marx and Friedrich Engels write in *The Communist Manifesto:*

> The history of all hitherto existing society is the history of class struggles. . . .
> The modern bourgeois society that has sprouted from the ruins of feudal society,
> has not done away with class antagonisms. It has but established new classes,
> new conditions of oppression, new forms of struggle in place of the old ones.[3]

In most of Marx and Engels's writings, they depict the state as being nothing more than an agent of the dominant class—in capitalism, the bourgeoisie. Thus, the bourgeoisie uses the state as an instrument for the exploitation of wage labor. Marx and Engels suggest that under certain conditions, the state may have some autonomy from a dominant class; for example, the state's autonomy may increase temporarily during transition periods, when the power of warring classes is more equally balanced.[4] However, Marx and Engels argue that the state cannot escape from its dependence on the capitalist class in the longer term. Only when the proletarian revolution eliminates private ownership and class distinctions will the state no longer be needed as an instrument of class oppression. A number of later writers, both within and outside the Marxist tradition, have been highly critical of Marx and Engels's position that state actions simply reflect the views of the dominant class (see the following discussion).

The Nature and Purpose of International Economic Relations

Whereas liberals consider economic relations to be a positive-sum game, historical structuralists and realists view economic relations as being basically conflictual and zero-sum in nature. Thus, Marx and Engels argue that "one fact is common to all past ages, *viz.*, the exploitation of one part of society by the other."[5] This exploitation takes the form of a class struggle, with capitalism being the most advanced stage. Under capitalism, a class of private owners of the means of production extracts surplus value from a class of free but propertyless wage laborers. The private owners then convert this surplus value into capital, which is invested in new means of production.

It is well known that the views of historical structuralists evolved along with changes in the international system. Thus, Marx and Engels initially predicted that contradictions within the capitalist system would contribute to the absolute poverty of the working class, surplus production, economic downturns, and the eventual collapse of capitalism. When this dire prediction was not realized, Lenin asserted that *imperialism* explained the continued survival of capitalism.[6] Imperialism delayed the downfall of capitalism because colonies provided the "metropole" states with a cheap source of agricultural and raw materials, and a market for the metropoles' surplus capital and manufactured goods. When decolonization marked an end to the age of imperialism, capitalism continued to demonstrate resilience, and some historical structuralists turned their attention from colonialism to *neocolonialism* as an explanation. Although the imperial powers had ceded political control over their former colonies, they continued to control the newly independent LDCs economically.[7] Others who have sought to explain the persistence of capitalism and LDC underdevelopment include dependency and world-systems theorists. *Dependency theorists* argue that the world is hierarchically organized, with the leading capitalist states in the core of the global economy exploiting poor states in the periphery. Only the core states can make autonomous choices about domestic and foreign economic policies, and market mechanisms simply reinforce the economic and political inequalities. Some early dependency theorists asserted that the core states *underdeveloped* the peripheral states, but LDC success stories such as the emergence of the NIEs caused later theorists to acknowledge that development is possible in some LDCs. Nevertheless, these theorists argue that LDC economic growth takes the form of *dependent development*, which involves a close association between elites in the core and the periphery.

Because historical structuralists focus on the exploitative nature of capitalism, like realists they place considerable emphasis on the redistribution of power and wealth. Unlike realists, however, historical structuralists reject the idea that a meaningful redistribution of wealth and power can occur under capitalism. Actively taking the side of the poor and less powerful, historical structuralists argue that the inequalities under capitalism will disappear only after there is a transformation to socialism. The ultimate goal of exploited states and classes, according to historical structuralists, should be to break linkages with the capitalist states or to overthrow the capitalist system.

The Relationship Between Politics and Economics

Marx describes history as a dialectical process in which there is a contradiction between evolving economic modes of production (e.g., feudalism, capitalism, and socialism) on one hand and the political system on the other. This contradiction is resolved when changes in the mode and relations of production eventually cause the political "superstructure" to undergo similar changes. Marx viewed politics as subordinate to economics, and his writings provided the foundation for the instrumentalist tradition in Marxist thought.[8] **Instrumental Marxism,** like liberal pluralism, perceives formal government institutions as responding in a rather passive manner to socioeconomic pressures. Liberals, however, believe that any societal group may have political influence, whereas instrumental Marxists believe the state's policies reflect the interests of the capitalist class. To support their position, instrumental Marxists point to the personal ties between leading capitalists and public officials and to the movement of individuals between business and government. One instrumental Marxist, for example, argues that the individuals in *"all* command positions in the state system have largely, and in many cases overwhelmingly, been drawn from the world of business and property, or from the professional middle classes."[9]

After World War II, many Marxist as well as non-Marxist scholars strongly criticized the instrumental Marxist views because industrial states were adopting a number of social policies such as welfare and unemployment insurance *despite* the opposition of important business groups. As a result, a second tradition of **structural Marxism** emerged. In contrast to the instrumentalists, structural Marxists argue that the state is relatively autonomous from direct political pressure by the capitalist class. Thus, the state may adopt some policies that provide benefits to all major groups in society, including the working class. Although capitalists may oppose these state policies in the short term, they have internal divisions and are less well placed than the state to recognize that these policies serve their long-term interests. By providing welfare and other benefits, the state often placates the workers and gains their support for the continuance of capitalism.[10]

Although they consider the state to be relatively autonomous, structural Marxists differ from realists in some important respects. The state is not under the direct control of the bourgeoisie in the structural Marxist view, but it shares with that class a commitment to the long-term maintenance of the capitalist system. Realists, by contrast, believe the state has genuine independence from the economic interests of any societal group. Thus, the state in the realist view is free to take those actions it deems necessary to further the "national interest."

Karl Marx and IPE

Karl Marx (1818–1883) did not write systematically about international relations, but his theory of capitalism and class struggle provided the basic framework for historical structuralist approaches to IPE. Although Marx wrote a number of articles about the effect of Western capitalism on non-European areas, his knowledge of economically less developed areas outside Europe was in fact quite limited. At the time Marx was writing, "relatively few sources of information" on non-European areas "were available to him."[11] Marx's specific references to present-day LDCs focused primarily on India and China.[12]

Marx believed it was no accident that capitalism first emerged in Europe, where the feudal mode of production was prevalent. Because feudal landholdings were private, they could be converted into private bourgeois property when capitalism replaced the feudal mode of production. In contrast to Europe, Marx described India and China as having an "Asiatic" mode of production that was outside the mainstream of Western development. The state's presence was much greater in the Asiatic mode because climate and geography made centralized irrigation important in agriculture. Thus, strong central governments in China and India developed large public work projects to provide water over extensive land areas. At the local level, Marx portrayed India and China as having small, self-sufficient village communities in which there was communal rather than individual ownership. Because communal property (locally) and public property (centrally) overshadowed private property in the Asiatic mode, Marx saw no basis for a transformation from private feudal landholdings to private capitalist holdings. As a result, Marx believed that "oriental societies" such as China and India had no internal mechanisms for change and that external pressure from Western imperialism was necessary if these countries were to progress to capitalism—and then to socialism.[13]

Marx certainly does not glorify British imperialism in India in his writings. Indeed, he harshly criticizes England's role in destroying the Indian handicraft textile industry, first by preventing India from exporting cotton to the European market and then by inundating India with British textiles. Nevertheless, Marx views the stagnant Asiatic society as being even worse than capitalism because it lacked capitalism's capacity for development. He therefore asserts that India's village communities "restrained the human mind within the smallest possible compass, making it the unresisting tool of superstition, enslaving it beneath traditional rule, depriving it of all grandeur and historical energies."[14]

In contrast to his view of stagnating Asiatic societies, Marx considered capitalism to be a dynamic, expansive system with a historical mission to move the development process forward throughout the world. Thus, Marx viewed England as performing a dual function in India—first, in destroying the old Asiatic society, and second, in providing the foundation for Western society in Asia. Without this introduction of Western capitalism, Marx reasoned, the conditions for a Communist revolution in Asia would not be met:

> Can mankind fulfill its destiny without a fundamental revolution in the social state of Asia? If not, whatever may have been the crimes of England, she was the unconscious tool of history in bringing about that revolution.[15]

Although Marx strongly criticized the exploitative nature of British imperialism, he nevertheless viewed it as enabling India to move from the stagnant Asiatic mode to the dynamic capitalist mode. This move was a necessary evil as a prerequisite for subsequent moves to socialism and communism. It is important to note that there were major defects in Marx's analysis of Asiatic societies, due to his lack of first-hand knowledge and his Eurocentric prejudices. Later in his life Marx in fact repudiated some of his own ideas regarding the Asiatic mode and the role of imperialism in promoting capitalism in the East. Despite his apparent change of view, Marx never explained how capitalism could develop in the Asiatic villages without Western imperialism.[16]

MARXIST STUDIES OF IMPERIALISM

Although Marx raised some important—and contentious—questions about the impact of Western capitalism on non-European societies, systematic studies of imperialism depended on later writers. In contrast to most liberal theories that emphasize the mutual benefits of international interactions, theories of imperialism portray the world as hierarchically organized, with some societies engaging in conquest and control over others. Most non-Marxists have used the term *imperialism* in reference to political rather than economic relationships between metropolitan countries and their colonies. It is therefore ironic that a non-Marxist English economist, John A. Hobson (1858–1940), developed one of the most influential economic theories of imperialism. Hobson argued that three major problems plague capitalist societies: low wages and underconsumption by workers, oversaving by capitalists, and overproduction. Although capitalism is highly efficient, private owners increase their profits by paying extremely low wages to their workers. As a result, workers in the capitalist countries have very limited purchasing power, and the capitalists must look to countries abroad as an outlet for their surplus goods and profits. Their forays into what is now termed the South give rise to imperialism.[17]

Despite the influence of Hobson's writings, the most important theories of imperialism are Marxist. Thus, *Imperialism: The Highest Stage of Capitalism* by Vladimir Lenin (1870–1924) became the most widely cited work in this area, even though Lenin borrowed many of his ideas from earlier Marxist and non-Marxist writers.[18] Lenin was interested in the new, expanded form of imperialism of the late nineteenth century, "in which the dominance of monopolies and finance capital [had] established itself" and "the division of all territories of the globe among the great capitalist powers [had] been completed."[19] Writing in the Marxist tradition, Lenin took a more doctrinaire approach than Hobson. Although Hobson and Lenin agreed that imperialism resulted from low wages and underconsumption by workers, they prescribed very different solutions. As a liberal, Hobson believed that imperialism would be less essential as an outlet for surpluses if wages increased and income was redistributed *within* the capitalist system. As a Marxist, Lenin by contrast believed that exploitation of the workers and imperialism were *inevitable* outcomes of the highest stage of capitalism, and that imperialism could disappear only with the advent of socialism.

Like Marx, Lenin argued that capitalism contributes to overproduction and underconsumption, lower wages and unemployment for the working class, and falling rates of profit for the capitalists. However, Marx had predicted that the growing misery of the proletariat would lead to revolution in the advanced capitalist states, and Lenin turned to imperialism to explain why the revolution had not occurred. Under imperialism, the export of capital and goods to colonial areas provided new "superprofits" for capitalist firms, which helped them avert economic crises. By using part of these superprofits to bribe the working class (or "labor aristocracy") in their home countries with higher wages, the capitalists were able to delay the revolution. However, Lenin argued that imperialism did not mark an end to capitalism's underlying contradictions and that the revolution was still inevitable. Once the capitalist states had divided up the globe into colonial areas, competition among them would lead to interimperialist wars and the downfall of capitalism.

Lenin's position on the effects of colonialism on capitalist development was somewhat ambivalent. On one hand, Lenin predicted that capitalist monopolies would oppose industrialization in the colonies, using them as sources of raw materials and markets for their manufactures. On the other hand, Lenin agreed with Marx that colonialism was a progressive force essential for Southern development. Indeed, Lenin maintained that capitalism has an inherent contradiction: it develops rather than underdevelops the South. As Western capitalist states export capital and technology to their colonies, they help create foreign competitors with lower wages that can outcompete them in world markets. The increase of economic competition between rising and declining capitalist powers eventually leads to conflict and imperial rivalries.

Although Marx and Lenin viewed colonialism as a necessary evil that would bring capitalist development to the colonies, industrialization and development did not occur as anticipated. Even after most Latin American colonies gained their independence from Spain and Portugal in the early nineteenth century, they continued to produce more primary products than industrial goods, and they were highly dependent on capital and technology from the advanced industrial states. The failure to bring about capitalist development in the colonies and former colonies led to major rifts among the Marxists. Most notably, Otto Kuusinen, a Finnish member at the Sixth Congress of the Communist International in 1928, argued that imperialism was economically regressive rather than progressive as Lenin had maintained. The views of Marxists such as Kuusinen subsequently provided a basis for the arguments of Latin American dependency theorists after World War II.[20] As the following discussion demonstrates, dependency theorists "turned classical Marxism on its head" and focused on capitalism's role in hindering rather than facilitating the South's development.

DEPENDENCY THEORY

Dependency theorists (or *dependencistas*) were originally Latin American or focused on Latin America, and **dependency theory** became the dominant approach to development among Latin American intellectuals during the 1960s. Some of the important early studies were published only in Spanish, and it was not until a number of years later that they were translated for English-speaking scholars. Dependency theorists reject the optimism of liberal modernization theorists (discussed in Chapter 4) and argue that the advanced capitalist countries either underdevelop LDCs or prevent them from achieving genuine autonomous development. The discussion here examines the origins, basic tenets, and criticisms of dependency theory. However, it is important to note that there is considerable diversity among the writers identified as dependency theorists.[21]

The Origins of Dependency Theory

Dependency theory is based on two major theoretical traditions: Marxism and Latin American structuralism. Some of the most prominent writers on dependency explicitly express their allegiance to Marxism.[22] Dependency theorists, like Marxists, limit their studies almost exclusively to capitalist development, and they adopt many of the terms used by Marxists such as *class, mode of production,* and *imperialism.* Dependency theorists and Marxists also are committed to taking political action as well as to conveying ideas, and both groups advocate the replacement of capitalism with socialism. However, Marxists take a more doctrinaire approach than many dependency theorists in regard to the inevitability of socialism.[23]

A fundamental difference between Marxism and dependency theory is that dependency theorists focus almost exclusively on North-South relations and development problems in the South. Dependency theorists also reject Marxist views that Northern DCs are performing a service to LDCs in the long term by contributing to the spread of capitalism. Paul Baran was a key figure in the transition from classical Marxism to dependency theory. He was the first important Marxist theorist to view the South as a major area of study, and he differed from his predecessors in arguing that capitalist development was a fundamentally different process in advanced and underdeveloped countries. Unlike Marx, who argued that colonialism enabled countries such as India to advance from the Asiatic to the capitalist mode of production, Baran believed that the objectives of advanced capitalist states were harmful to the development of the "backward" nations. Thus, Baran wrote that:

> . . . Economic development in underdeveloped countries is profoundly inimical to the dominant interests in the advanced capitalist countries. Supplying many important raw materials to the industrialized countries, providing their corporations with vast profits and investment outlets, the backward world has always represented the indispensable hinterland of the highly developed capitalist West. Thus the ruling class in the United States (and elsewhere) is bitterly opposed to the industrialization of the so-called 'source countries.'[24]

Baran further maintained that Northern capitalists form alliances with Southern elites to prevent LDC industrialization. These elites include feudal landed interests and a *comprador class* comprised of merchants who import manufactured goods from the North. Thus, Baran diverged from the Marxists, arguing that capitalist development in the North occurs *at the expense of* autonomous development in the South. His view was to become a fundamental tenet of the dependency approach.

In addition to its roots in Marxism, dependency theory originates from Latin American structuralism, particularly the ideas of the Argentinian economist Raúl Prebisch, who became director of the United Nations Economic Commission for Latin America (ECLA) in the late 1940s. Prebisch and his followers were called structuralists because they focused on the structural obstacles to LDC development. Prebisch particularly questioned the liberal assumptions that everyone benefits from freer trade, and argued instead that LDCs in the periphery of the global economy suffer from declining **terms of trade** with DCs in the center or core. (Prebisch began to use the terms "center" and "periphery" as early as the 1950s.) LDCs, according to Prebisch, are at a marked disadvantage because they export mainly primary commodities and import finished goods from the core. Whereas demand for finished goods increases with rising incomes, demand for primary products remains relatively constant (e.g., wealthy individuals drink only so much coffee or tea, regardless of their incomes). Furthermore, the North can often develop substitute or synthetic products if LDCs attempt to charge higher prices for their raw materials.

According to Prebisch, LDCs could develop only if their governments acted to promote industrialization and decrease dependence on trade with the North. Thus, he advised LDCs to adopt import substitution (ISI) policies to protect their infant industries, imposing tariff and nontariff barriers and emphasizing domestic production of manufactures to satisfy demand previously met by imports.[25] Prebisch's structuralist views influenced a number of LDCs, especially in Latin America, and they adopted ISI policies in the 1950s-1960s. However, these ISI policies eventually contributed to a wide range of problems for LDCs, including uncompetitive industries and growing balance-of-payments deficits (see Chapter 11). Scholars challenged the Prebisch approach from the right and the left, and many left-leaning scholars turned to dependency theory. Dependency theorists adopted many of Prebisch's ideas, but their views of the problems and solutions for the South were more extreme than those of Prebisch. Unlike Prebisch, dependency theorists did not believe that the core would ever willingly transfer resources to the periphery. A number of dependency theorists therefore called for a domestic social revolution in LDCs and a severing of contacts with the North.[26]

The Basic Tenets of Dependency Theory

A discussion of the tenets of dependency theory is complicated by the fact that there is considerable variation among writers. Two major strains of dependency theory are of particular importance. The first strain, which is closely identified with two Latin Americans—Fernando Henrique Cardoso and Enzo Faletto—took a less doctrinaire and more variegated position to North-South relations. Because Cardoso and Faletto's seminal book, *Dependency and Development in Latin America,* was not available in English until a number of years after it was published, much of the early North American "consumption" of dependency theory relied on a second strain which drew its inspiration from André Gunder Frank.[27] This second strain, which became influential in the United States at an early stage, took a more radical, doctrinaire position regarding both the impact of dependency on the South and the proposed solutions. To organize the discussion and draw comparisons, the next sections examine dependency views regarding the source of LDC problems, possibilities for development in the periphery, and prescriptions for change. When relevant, this book differentiates between the two main strains of dependency theory.

The Source of LDC Problems   Dependency theorists reject the views of liberal theorists that LDC economic problems result primarily from inefficient domestic policies and that greater North-South interdependence promotes LDC development. In contrast, dependency theorists argue that external factors related to the global capitalist economy are primarily responsible for constraining development possibilities in the South. Whereas core countries in the North benefit from their global capitalist linkages and experience dynamic development based on internal needs, development in peripheral countries of the South is severely constrained as a result of their interaction with the core. Although dependency theorists attach primary importance to external constraints on development, there has been some variation among authors. Whereas the Gunder Frank strain placed far more emphasis on external forces, the Cardoso-Faletto strain was sensitive "to local as well as international variations in dependency relations and to the independent significance of internal structures even in an approach that highlights external conditioning."[28]

Class struggle is one factor that links external and internal forces, and a number of dependency theorists have examined the class linkages between individuals within core and peripheral states. Thus, they describe the development of a class alignment in the South, where elites in LDCs (*compradores*) act as intermediaries between the capitalist international order on one hand and the subjected local peoples on the other. Although this collaborating *comprador* class may have local concerns, it ultimately depends on the international economic order to ensure its survival as a class. Because the main political alliances of the *compradores* are with foreign capitalists in the North, they often take actions that reinforce the pattern of LDC dependency.[29]

LDC Possibilities for Development   Dependency theorists have had differing views regarding LDC possibilities for development. Those in the Gunder Frank strain argued that the development of capitalist economies in the core *required* the underdevelopment of the periphery. These theorists were highly deterministic; they believed that LDCs could not escape from underdevelopment as long as they maintained linkages with the core. Although LDCs may have been *un*developed in the past, they were not *under*developed because they were not yet part of the periphery in the global capitalist economy. When these undeveloped countries became part of the periphery, they became underdeveloped *as a result of* their involvement with countries in the capitalist core.[30]

Theorists in the Cardoso-Faletto strain took a more nuanced approach, arguing that in some cases development was possible in the periphery. However, this was "associated dependent development" in which dependency linkages were maintained.[31] The Cardoso-Faletto view gained support over time because theorists who viewed underdevelopment as the only possible fate for peripheral countries found it difficult to explain why industrialization *was* occurring in some LDCs. Liberals, realists, and some Marxists all pointed to the fact that NIEs such as South Korea, Taiwan, Brazil, and Mexico were experiencing impressive economic growth rates. Furthermore, NIEs such as South Korea and Taiwan had close linkages with the global capitalist structure in the core. A number of dependency studies in the late 1970s and 1980s therefore followed the Cardoso-Faletto example and focused on "dependent development" rather than "underdevelopment."[32] Gunder Frank's writings evolved, and by the 1980s even he was writing about dependent development.[33]

Those who write about dependent development are more attuned to variations in local conditions and dependency relations in the South. Thus, certain LDCs can undergo development when a particularly favorable alliance forms between foreign capital, domestic capital, and the LDC. This alliance enables the LDC to benefit from capital accumulation and a degree of industrialization. Despite recognizing the diversity of LDC situations, however, these authors maintain that even the more favored LDCs remain fundamentally dependent and cannot attain genuine autonomous development. Those LDCs experiencing dependent development cannot escape from their dependent linkages with core countries, and their development is therefore conditioned by requirements of the core. Dependency theorists argue that although the NIEs seem to be success stories, workers in these countries often receive low wages and produce less technologically sophisticated goods than those of DCs in the core. The production of capital goods in these countries is also limited, and ultimately they depend on imports of machinery, technology, and foreign investment from the core.[34]

Prescriptions for Change   Dependency theorists believe that LDCs cannot escape from their dependent position in the capitalist system; thus, they often prescribe a breaking of linkages with the core countries and a socialist revolution to bring about more social justice and equality. However, the goals of autonomy and socialism are not necessarily compatible, and theorists do not explicitly state which of these goals is more important for decreasing dependency. Those who emphasize autonomy call for nationalistic and antiforeign actions such as the cutting of linkages with the DC core states. Such actions do not ensure that the other goal of dependency theorists will be achieved; policies that increase a state's autonomy do not ensure that there will be social justice or equality for the bulk of the population. Nevertheless, dependency theorists at least hope that an end to dependent linkages will lead a country to "emphasize distribution and participation rather than accumulation and exclusion."[35]

Critiques of Dependency Theory

Dependency theory became a favorite target of criticism in the 1970s and 1980s, and other theories have subsequently become more important in the historical structuralist school. One major criticism is that dependency theorists do not adequately define their basic concepts. For example, theorists tend to view countries in dichotomous terms as either dependent or not dependent, and it is unclear how to measure lesser or greater *degrees* of dependence. There are also different *forms* of dependence, such as military, economic, and cultural, but these different forms are not usually identified. Furthermore, "developed versus underdeveloped" or "core versus periphery" are broad categories that include a wide range of countries. What does the term *periphery* signify when it includes countries as diverse as Brazil, India, and Haiti? How does one justify including Portugal along with the United States, Japan, and Germany in the core? Critics argue that these concepts are too vague to make the distinctions required for good theorizing.[36]

A second criticism relates to the preoccupation of dependency theorists with capitalism and their failure to consider other forms of exploitation. Some critics argue that the most important factor in dependency is not capitalism (as dependency theorists maintain) but unequal power among states. As long as power is unequal, larger states are able to impose dependence on smaller states.[37] Thus, some scholars have done studies of the former Soviet bloc to demonstrate that dependency relations can also exist in noncapitalist systems. These studies show some marked differences between the Soviet and Western systems. For example, postwar Soviet dominance contributed to rapid industrialization with an emphasis on heavy industry in Eastern Europe, which was quite different from the Western model in the South; and political linkages were more important in the Soviet bloc, whereas economic linkages were central to the West's relations with the South. Despite the differences, however, both the Soviet and capitalist systems were marked by "asymmetric and unequal linkages between a dominant center and its weaker dependencies."[38] Dependency theorists also did not usually examine the role socialist states played in the capitalist world economy, and since the collapse of the Soviet Union they have not explored where countries such as North Korea and Cuba fit in a world of core and peripheral countries.[39]

A third criticism is that dependency theory attaches too much importance to the international system and too little to domestic policies as a source of LDC development problems. Although dependency theorists in the Cardoso-Faletto strain do focus on domestic structures in LDCs, they continue to give primacy to the importance of external factors. Dependency theorists therefore tend to portray LDCs as being virtually helpless vis-à-vis outside forces, and they cannot adequately explain why LDCs sometimes respond in very different ways to similar external constraints. To explain such differences, critics charge, it is necessary to give more consideration to domestic economic and political factors.[40] A fourth criticism is that dependency theory's predictions regarding LDC development prospects are often simply incorrect. For example, China was initially held up as a model of agrarian self-reliance, but in 1976 it turned to a policy of openness rather than closure to promote national development. This change in policy contributed to rapid economic growth in China, and LDCs that are the most integrated in the world economy are sometimes the fastest growing countries.

A fifth criticism is that dependency theorists' prescriptions for change are rather vague and ill defined. Although dependency theorists call for socialism as one of their two main goals, they do not clearly indicate what they mean by the term, they do not explain how a socialist revolution will enable countries to escape dependency, and they do not describe how the revolution will occur. Dependency theorists also do not explain how peripheral countries can become more autonomous from the core countries. The vague prescriptions in dependency theory relate partly to the tension between the goals of autonomy and socialism and partly to the fact that Marxist predictions regarding a socialist revolution in the most advanced industrial states proved to be inaccurate.

Finally, some of the strongest criticisms of dependency theory come from within the Marxist tradition. The U.S. social scientist Bill Warren, for example, presented updated arguments to support Marx's thesis regarding LDC development. Although imperialism contributed to exploitation and inequality, Warren argued, it also provided the conditions for capitalist development in the South. In the postwar period, LDCs could use the East-West conflict and competition among Western industrial states and MNCs to promote their own capitalist national development (on the way to socialism). In contrast to dependency theorists, Warren maintained that the obstacles to this development "originate not in current imperialist-Third World relationships, but almost entirely from the internal contradictions of the Third World itself."[41] Some Marxist scholars also criticize dependency theorists for being overly nationalistic and not sufficiently Marxist. They insist that the most fundamental problem is not *foreign* control or domination, as dependency theorists maintain, but *private* control of the means of production. Thus, they criticize dependency theorists for putting more emphasis on "relations of exchange" (between core and peripheral states) than on "relations of production" (between classes—the proletariat and bourgeoisie).[42]

The numerous criticisms of dependency theory from both the right and the left have had a telling effect. Unfortunately, the criticisms were often aimed at the most extreme, doctrinaire versions of dependency theory and did not do justice to the less extreme forms in the Cardoso-Faletto strain. Thus, a noted dependency theorist predicted in 1985 that the dependency label would disappear because the term was "too closely associated with simplistic hypotheses of external determination" and "the impossibility of either capitalism or democracy on the periphery."[43] Although writers only rarely identify themselves as dependency theorists today, development theorists in fact continue to draw on many aspects of dependency theory in their studies of Latin America, Africa, and Asia.[44] The case for continuing to use some of the basic ideas and concepts of dependency theory is strengthened by the further marginalization of some peripheral LDCs as globalization pressures increase. Thus, one noted development economist considers it a misconception to believe "that the dependency debate is dead forever and that it has no relevance in the modern world. . . . There are indeed many issues and areas of development where dependency plays a major role."[45] The next section raises questions about the future of the historical structuralist perspective in IPE in view of the breakup of the Soviet bloc, and the final sections of the chapter discuss some historical structuralist approaches that seem to be particularly promising.

WHITHER THE HISTORICAL STRUCTURALIST SCHOOL OF IPE?

With the failed predictions of Marxist-Leninists regarding the downfall of capitalism and the strong criticisms of dependency theory, numerous questions were raised about the vitality of the historical structuralist perspective. Since the breakup of the Soviet bloc and the end of the Cold War during the late 1980s–1990s, some mainstream theorists have even claimed that the historical structuralist perspective is no longer relevant. For example, one liberal theorist argues that "the implosion of the Soviet Union, and domestic changes in Eastern Europe, have eliminated the significance of the socialist economic model," and another claims that the discrediting of Marxism-Leninism is leading to "an unabashed victory of economic and political liberalism."[46] Many observers are also referring to the "triumph" of liberalism in the South. Although LDCs had turned to economic nationalism, state socialism, and trade protectionism in the 1960s–1970s, their policies have changed markedly. For reasons discussed in this book, LDCs since the 1980s have been moving en masse toward liberal policies of reduced state intervention in the economy, increased reliance on the market, and liberalized trade and foreign investment policies.[47]

Despite these negative prognostications about historical structuralism, it continues to have major relevance. Most importantly, historical structuralists devote considerable attention to the poorest and weakest individuals and states and to distributive justice issues, which are not dealt with adequately by liberals and realists. The end of the Soviet threat has also caused growing divisions in the West by reducing

> the self-restraint of capitalist nations. Without the Soviets, commercial conflicts are free to grow more and more venemous, and tendencies toward cartels and blocs are harder to resist. The present situation, it must be noticed, is rather amenable to Marxist interpretations.[48]

Although liberals and realists accept the capitalist system largely as a given, historical structuralists raise serious questions about inequality and exploitation under capitalism, and discuss the possibilities of alternative systems. Thus, historical structuralism continues to be an important IPE perspective, and the following sections discuss three theoretical approaches with linkages to this perspective that continue to be of interest: world-systems theory, Gramscian theory, and the business conflict model.

World-Systems Theory

World-systems theory has many similarities with dependency theory, and some former dependency theorists now identify themselves as world-systems theorists. Both groups of theorists view capitalism as basically exploitative and advocate major changes in global economic relations. Nevertheless, world-systems theory is accepted as more relevant than dependency theory because it is more broad ranging and flexible. Instead of limiting their inquiry to the effects of the core on peripheral states, world-systems theorists focus on the entire world system, including relationships among states in the core and the rise and decline of hegemonic states. Furthermore, they delve more deeply than dependency theorists into the historical development of capitalism in attempts to explain the core's exploitation of the periphery. Much world-systems analysis examines world economic structure and cyclical fluctuations ranging from depressions to recessions and economic upswings extending back to at least the sixteenth century. Finally, world-systems analysts introduce the concept of "semiperiphery" and question dependency theorists' view that all LDCs are permanently relegated to the periphery.[49]

Only a brief discussion of world-systems theory is provided here, and students interested in the subject should refer to more detailed sources.[50] Immanuel Wallerstein is the originator of the world-systems perspective and its most important contributor, but there are also other important world-systems theorists, such as Christopher Chase-Dunn. Some former dependency theorists such as Samir Amin and Gunder Frank have also incorporated some of Wallerstein's ideas in their analyses.[51] World-systems theorists have differences of view on a number of issues, including the definition and boundaries of world-systems, when the transition occurred to the modern capitalist world system, how many core states have been hegemonic and for how long, and the nature of linkages between economic cycles, wars, and hegemony.[52] The discussion that follows refers primarily to the writings of Wallerstein.

The main unit of analysis in world-systems theory is the world-system, which is "a unit with a single division of labor and multiple cultural systems."[53] World-systems can be of two major types: *world-empires,* which have a common political system, and *world-economies,* which do not have a common political system. In world-empires, a single political entity (such as ancient Rome or China) often used coercive power to control the economic division of labor between core and peripheral regions. The modern world-system is a world-economy rather than a world-empire, because no single state has been able to conquer the entire core region. Instead, states in the core engage in a "hegemonic sequence," in which various hegemonic states (the Netherlands, Britain, and the United States) rise and fall. Today there is only one world-system, a world-economy that is capitalist in form. Since the modern world-economy consists of numerous political systems, power hierarchy is achieved mainly through market mechanisms, and the core states engage in force only when peripheral states pose a major challenge to the market rules that help sustain the core's dominance. The main features of the capitalist world-economy, which emerged in Europe during the "long" sixteenth century (1450–1640), are production for sale in a market with the goal of realizing the maximum profit, and unequal exchange relations which strong core states enforce on weak peripheral areas. Thus, Wallerstein argues that "capitalism involves not only appropriation of the surplus value by an owner from a laborer, but an appropriation of surplus of the whole world-economy by core areas."[54]

Because world-systems theorists take the capitalist world-economy as their main unit of analysis, they do not consider states to be meaningful actors apart from their position in the world-economy.[55] Thus, long before the breakup of the Soviet Union Wallerstein argued that there are "no socialist systems in the world-economy any more than there are feudal systems because there is *one* world-system" that is capitalist in form.[56] World-systems theorists also believe that the internal and external strength of a state cannot be viewed separately from its position in the world-economy. Core states are therefore relatively strong states by definition, and peripheral states are relatively weak.

World-systems theorists responded to the fact that some LDCs—the East Asian and Latin American NIEs—were industrializing by introducing a third category of countries between the periphery and the core: the *semiperiphery*. Semiperipheral states have more capital-intensive industry than peripheral states but less than core states and are stronger and more autonomous from the core than peripheral states.[57] World-systems theorists believe it is sometimes possible for states to move upward or downward on the core/semiperiphery/periphery hierarchy. Examples of economies that have moved upward in the past include the United States, Japan, Taiwan, Singapore, South Korea, Hong Kong, and China. Nevertheless, world-systems theorists are far more pessimistic than liberals about the future prospects for today's LDCs, and they believe that a country's ascent from the periphery is relatively rare. Although some states in the semiperiphery seem to be models of economic success, world-systems theorists view them as simply "the more advanced exemplars of dependent development."[58] Thus, they consider the division of the world-economy into the core, periphery, and semiperiphery to be an enduring feature of the capitalist world-economy.[59]

In the world-systems view, the existence of the semiperiphery contributes to the stability of the capitalist world-economy and to the continued predominance of DCs in the core. Because the distribution of wealth and power in the capitalist world-economy is highly unequal, it would be natural for peripheral countries to directly confront the core countries. The periphery includes the overwhelming majority of states, and a rebellion against the minority of states within the core would have a good chance of success if the periphery remained united. However, the semiperiphery divides the majority in the periphery so that the core states do not face a unified opposition. Even though the core takes advantage of semiperipheral states, they "tend to think of themselves primarily as better off than the lower sector rather than as worse off than the upper sector."[60] They therefore have a dual role as both exploiter and exploited, effectively dividing the periphery and stabilizing the capitalist world-economy. Despite this apparent political stability, however, the capitalist world-economy continues to have contradictions that could threaten its long-term survival. World-systems theorists therefore raise the prospect of the decline of capitalism and its replacement by socialism, but their predictions regarding the timing of these changes are surprisingly vague. For example, Wallerstein asserts that the internal contradictions in the capitalist world-economy should "bring it to an end in the twenty-first or twenty-second century."[61]

Liberal, realist, and Marxist scholars express numerous criticisms of world-systems theory. Some classical Marxists charge that world-systems theorists (like dependency theorists) place more emphasis on "relations of exchange" among core, semiperipheral, and peripheral states than on "relations of production" between capitalists and workers. Writers from all three schools argue that world-systems theorists place far more emphasis on external than internal factors in explaining conditions in the periphery. Indeed, Wallerstein moved even farther away from examining individual states than dependency theorists such as Gunder Frank. Wallerstein's interest in individual states "is limited to showing how they are incorporated into . . . [the world-economy] and the subsequent effect upon their social, political and economic systems."[62] Realists are especially critical of world-systems theorists for undertheorizing the role of the state. Thus, they accuse Wallerstein of rather simplistically assuming that "strong states" naturally are in the core and "weak states" are in the periphery. Many authors have provided counterexamples to challenge such statements. For example, they note that some of the strongest states in the sixteenth century, Spain and

Sweden, were in the periphery, whereas the core states of this period, Holland and England, had relatively weak state structures. They also note that late industrializers have often demonstrated successful development because of strong state leadership. This was true of Russia and Germany in the past, and it is true of the East Asian NIEs (the semiperiphery) today. Finally, some writers argue that the United States, the leading economic and military power, has a relatively weak state because of its separation and division of powers.[63]

Despite the numerous criticisms of world-systems theory, it provides an important alternative approach to the study of IPE. World-systems theorists offer a long-term historical view of social, economic, and political change, unlike many realists and liberals who either are ahistorical in their approach or devote too little attention to historical change. For example, the views of liberal modernization theorists that LDCs could and should follow the development path of DCs proved to be misguided, but many liberals still adhere to a more sophisticated version of these views. Critics understandably argue that liberals underestimate the importance of historical differences between the industrializing countries in the past and LDCs today. In view of historical and other changes, LDCs today may not choose to, or be able to, follow the development path Western DCs have taken in the past. World-systems theory also avoids some pitfalls of dependency theory by asserting that countries can sometimes ascend from the periphery to the semiperiphery and core. However, world-systems theorists avoid the overoptimism of liberal theorists regarding the prospects for ascent from the periphery. Unlike realists and liberals, world-systems theorists focus on the poorest and weakest in society and on the core's exploitation of the periphery. Although world-systems theorists may be accused of overestimating the degree to which external exploitation causes LDC problems, realists and liberals err in the opposite direction by largely ignoring the role of external exploitation of the poor and weak in the capitalist world-economy. Even those realists and liberals who are critical of some aspects of capitalism accept it largely as a given. In sum, world-systems theorists have proved to be a dynamic group, able to adjust their theoretical views in response to criticism.[64]

Gramscian Analysis

Antonio Gramsci, a former leader of the Italian Communist party, drew many of his ideas from Marxism. Gramsci argued, however, that Marxism was economistic; that is, it exaggerated the importance of economics relative to political, social, and cultural factors. Thus, classical Marxists were unable to explain crucial aspects of political and social reality during Gramsci's time, such as the role of Catholicism and the rise of Mussolini in Italy. The domination of capitalism, Gramsci asserted, depends only partly on economic factors such as private ownership of the means of production. To understand capitalist domination, one must also be familiar with the political, ideological, and cultural aspects of class struggle. Similarly, it is necessary to consider politics and culture as well as economics when discussing the reorganization of society under socialism. Thus, Gramsci placed more emphasis than classical Marxists on the role of culture, ideas, and institutions in explaining societal organization and change.[65]

As noted in Chapter 3, the Gramscian and realist views of hegemony are quite different. Unlike the realists, who identify hegemony solely with the predominant power of a state (or a group of states), Gramscians also view hegemony in terms of class relationships. If the dominant class rules almost exclusively by coercion, this is *not* the Gramscian idea of hegemony. In such societies the overthrow of the dominant class is possible simply by using physical force because the roots of its power do not penetrate into all aspects of social life. A dominant class has hegemony, by contrast, when it legitimates its power through institutions and makes concessions to encourage subordinate groups to support the existing social structure. Thus, hegemonic rule is based more on social-moral leadership than on coercion. The ruling class gains the active consent of subordinate classes on the basis of shared values, ideas, and material interests. The bourgeoisie often achieve such a consensus by providing the subordinate classes with a range of limited concessions, such as social and economic benefits and support for workers' efforts to organize labor unions. In return, the subordinate classes are accepting or even supportive of continued leadership by the bourgeoisie.

Gramscian theorists use the term *historic bloc* to refer to the congruence between state power on the one hand and the prevailing ideas guiding the society and the economy on the other. The historic bloc established under bourgeois hegemony is difficult for subordinate groups to replace because it is supported not only by physical power but also by the power of ideas. Like the classical Marxists, Gramsci was committed to political action as well as theory, and he wrote about the importance of building a *counterhegemony* among subordinate groups. A counterhegemony is an alternative ethical view of society that poses a challenge to the dominant bourgeois-led view. If subordinate groups become sufficiently dissatisfied, a counterhegemony organized around socialist ideas could pose a challenge to the hegemony organized around capitalism. For example, the propensity of governments to decrease socioeconomic benefits to subordinate classes in this age of global competitiveness might eventually cause disadvantaged groups to pose such a counterhegemonic challenge. If the proletariat succeeded in supplanting bourgeois hegemony with their own counterhegemony, they would create a new historic bloc based on socialism.[66]

Whereas Gramsci's analysis focused primarily on the domestic level, writers such as Robert Cox and Stephen Gill have extended his ideas and applied them to IR. For example, Cox refers to the 1945–1965 period as a hegemonic world order under the United States. During this period, U.S.-dominated institutions such as the UN Security Council, IMF, World Bank, and GATT legitimized U.S. hegemony and minimized the need for force by upholding the system's liberal norms and values.[67] Cox and Gill also argue that in this age of globalized production and exchange a *transnational historic bloc* may be developing. The main institutions in this bloc are the largest MNCs, international banks, IOs such as the IMF and World Bank, and international business groups in the most powerful capitalist states. With the development of a transnational historic bloc, class relations can now be viewed on a global scale. As discussed in Chapter 4, the predominant strand of liberalism after World War II was interventionist because countries balanced movement toward greater openness in the international economy with measures to cushion the effects on vulnerable groups through such measures as welfare and unemployment insurance. According to Gramscian theorists, the developing transnational historic bloc is threatening this interventionist liberal compromise.

A crucial element of the current transnational historic bloc is the power and mobility of transnational capital, which is putting both national labor unions and national business groups on the defensive. As discussed in Chapter 6 on monetary relations, the advanced industrial states imposed controls on capital flows in the 1950s–1960s, but these controls were gradually removed beginning in the 1970s. The increased ability of transnational capital and MNCs to shift location from one country to another enables them to play off national labor groups—which are relatively immobile—against one another. Workers employed by MNCs in both the core and the periphery also tend to identify their own interests with those of transnational capital, and this divides the working class and further limits its ability to build a counterhegemony. Furthermore, the transnational historic bloc is posing a threat to the ability of elected governments to make autonomous policy decisions. The recessionary conditions during the 1980s, for example, induced states to engage in competitive deregulation of their national **capital markets** in efforts to attract more foreign investment, accelerating the reduction of barriers to capital mobility. Further solidifying this transnational historic bloc is a hegemonic ideology, which portrays capital mobility as contributing to economic efficiency, consumer welfare, and economic growth.[68]

Despite the solid foundations of the transnational historic bloc, dissatisfaction with the transnational liberal forces could eventually stimulate a counterhegemonic response. For example, IMF and World Bank structural adjustment loans (discussed in Chapters 7 and 11), which are linked to pressures for privatization, deregulation, and trade liberalization, are creating resentment in some LDC recipients, and there is disillusionment with moves toward a market economy in Eastern European and FSU countries. Although transnational capital is currently in the ascendancy, Gramscian theorists argue that this may not continue indefinitely. In discussing a possible reaction to the transnational historic bloc, Gramscians often refer to *civil society*. Gramsci's analysis of civil society has been viewed as one of his most important theoretical contributions. Civil society in his *Prison Notebooks* has different meanings, including both "the realm in which the existing social order is grounded," and "the realm in which a new social order can be founded."[69] In other words, civil society can help sustain the bourgeoisie's hegemony and can also be the source of a counterhegemony. In supporting bourgeois hegemony, civil society is part of a top-down process in which the dominant capitalist class gains acquiescence from most of the population. As part of a counterhegemony, civil society is part of a bottom-up process in which disadvantaged elements of the population try to displace the hegemonic capitalist order. Gramsci's analysis has considerable relevance for discussions of recent civil society protests at meetings of the IMF, World Bank, and WTO. Although the protests have "certainly not attained the status of a counterhegemonic alliance of forces on the world scale," they demonstrate considerable concern about the effects of orthodox liberalism and globalization on people's lives today.[70]

Gramscian analysis has been criticized on a number of grounds. For example, critics charge that Gramscians (like some other historical structuralists) are so preoccupied with examining the problems of capitalism and the hegemony of transnational capital that they do not explore the potential problems of dominance and subordination in other possible global systems (e.g., socialism). Gramscians avoid some of the pitfalls of classical Marxists who often made unrealized predictions regarding the downfall of capitalism. However, Gramscians also provide little guidance as to when a counterhegemony might develop and what form it might take; thus they are better at pointing to the problems with the capitalist system than in offering solutions. Despite these criticisms, Gramscian analysis has many strengths. For example, the Gramscian view of hegemony has some advantages over the realist and liberal views. As discussed, realists and liberals define hegemony in state-centric terms, and they can identify only two or three times when there was a hegemonic state (Britain, the United States, and perhaps the Netherlands). Their ability to examine the effects of hegemony is therefore limited to a small number of relatively brief historical periods. Gramscian theorists, by contrast, use the term *hegemony* in a cultural sense to connote the complex of *ideas* social groups use to assert their legitimacy and authority, and they extend the concept of hegemony to include nonstate actors such as MNCs and international banks as well as nation-states. Thus, we can use the Gramscian concept of hegemony to examine a wider range of events in the global economy. The Gramscian concept of *counterhegemony* is also useful for examining the diverse range of groups protesting against globalization today. Gramscians ask whether these groups are likely to coalesce sufficiently to form a counterhegemony that would challenge the current hegemonic ideology.[71]

The Business Conflict Model

The business conflict model, like hegemonic stability theory and regime theory, is a hybrid approach that draws on more than one theoretical perspective (in this case, historical structuralism and liberalism).[72] According to business conflict theorists, business groups—especially large corporations—are the most important societal groups affecting government policymaking, but there are major cleavages within the business community over policy issues. The cleavages include "divisions among corporations of different nationalities, among corporations of the same nationality, and among internationally owned corporations."[73] These divisions lead to conflicts within and among states that have a major impact on government policy processes and output.

The business conflict model is discussed with historical structuralism because it emphasizes class (i.e., business) as a major factor in foreign policymaking and views business firms as being motivated primarily by profit. Nevertheless, there are significant differences between business conflict theorists and instrumental Marxists, who argue that "the state serves the interests of the capitalist class because it is controlled by this class."[74] Instrumental Marxists simply assume that the capitalist class is united in furthering its interests, whereas business conflict theorists maintain that divisions among capitalists are pervasive. Business conflict theorists are also highly critical of structural Marxists, who believe that the state (though committed to ensuring the long-term survival of capitalism) is relatively autonomous from direct political pressure of the capitalist class. In the view of business conflict theorists, the state does not have relative autonomy from business group pressures, even in the short term.[75] The business conflict model has some similarity to liberal pluralism. Both are society-centered theories that emphasize the role of interest groups in government policymaking. In the pluralist view, however, no single interest group or class dominates society and the state. Business conflict theorists, by contrast, believe that "business groups have often been able to shape and direct . . . foreign investment and trade strategy independent of other pressure groups."[76]

In the view of business conflict theorists, the most significant division in the business community is between internationalist and nationalist business groups.[77] Whereas nationalist firms are smaller and oriented primarily to the domestic market, internationalist firms are larger, more competitive, and heavily involved with foreign trade and investment. The diverse positions of nationalist and internationalist firms give them different vested interests in policymaking. For example, nationalist firms often feel threatened by imports and favor trade protectionism, whereas internationalist firms with integrated multinational operations and substantial dependence on exports resist protectionism and favor open international markets.[78]

In pressuring for more open foreign trade and investment policies, internationalist firms usually benefit from a close working relationship with the U.S. executive branch. Business internationalists also form organizations to influence and work with U.S. foreign policy officials, who are more likely to listen to the internationalists than to other groups. Smaller domestic business groups, which are more inclined to favor economic closure and protectionism, do not benefit from such connections with the U.S. foreign policy establishment. As a result, business nationalists often attempt to influence congressional committees involved with foreign policy issues. Although domestic businesses lack the wealth, connections, and expertise of the business internationalists, the diverse membership of Congress permits domestic business to gain influence by targeting individual representatives. Thus, protectionist pressures from domestic business in Congress often collide with business internationalist pressures for liberalization in the executive branch.

Even internationalist business groups are sometimes divided among themselves over foreign economic strategies, and this can affect their ability to influence policymaking. For example, internationalist firms that depend extensively on labor-intensive production in LDCs often favor military force to quell leftist insurgencies, and support military governments that discipline the domestic labor force and ensure that wages are low. Internationalist firms that are less labor intensive, by contrast, are less likely to support military action.[79] The business conflict model postulates that divisions between business nationalists and internationalists and divisions among internationalists are reflected in foreign policy outcomes. The model is a promising new approach to foreign economic policymaking that draws on both historical structuralism and liberal pluralism.

CONCLUSION

The influence of the three major perspectives on IPE as a discipline varies over time. The historical structuralist perspective may have faltered in recent years, but there are a number of promising new theoretical approaches in this school of thought. It is also certainly possible that the historical structuralist perspective could gain more influence in the future. Current pressures to replace postwar interventionist liberalism with a return to liberal orthodoxy is causing considerable dissatisfaction among many "have-nots" in society, providing a stimulus to a possible revival of historical structuralism. Furthermore, although some historical structuralist approaches such as dependency theory have been discredited in recent years, many of the concerns of dependency theorists continue to be relevant. Recent advances in world-systems, Gramscian, business conflict, and other theories in this school indicate that historical structuralism provides an important alternative perspective to the liberal and realist views.

NOTES

1. The seminal structural realist (or neorealist) study is Kenneth N. Waltz, *Theory of International Politics* (Reading: Addison-Wesley, 1979). See also Robert O. Keohane, "Theory of World Politics: Structural Realism and Beyond," in Robert O. Keohane, ed., *Neorealism and Its Critics* (New York: Columbia University Press, 1986), pp.158–203.
2. The term *historical structuralism* emerged in discussions with a colleague, Professor James Busumtwi-Sam, for which I am grateful.
3. Karl Marx and Friedrich Engels, *The Communist Manifesto* (New York: International Publishers, 1948), p.9.
4. For a discussion of the two strands of Marxist writing on the state, see Bob Jessop, *The Capitalist State: Marxist Theories and Methods* (Oxford: Martin Robertson, 1982), pp.1–31; and David Held, *Models of Democracy* (Cambridge: Polity Press, 1987), pp.113–121.
5. Marx and Engels, *The Communist Manifesto*, p.29.
6. See V. I. Lenin, *Imperialism: The Highest Stage of Capitalism*, rev. trans. (New York: International Publishers, 1939).
7. Jack Woddis, *An Introduction to Neo-Colonialism* (London: Lawrence & Wishart, 1967); Harry Magdoff, "Imperialism Without Colonies," in Roger Owen and Bob Sutcliffe, eds., *Studies in the Theory of Imperialism* (London: Longman, 1981), pp.144–169.
8. Some authors argue that Marx was not a strict economic determinist. See David McLellan, *Marx*, (7th ed. London: Fontana/Collins, 1980), p.41; and Gabriel Palma, "Dependency: A Formal Theory of Underdevelopment or a Methodology for the Analysis of Concrete Situations of Underdevelopment?" *World Development* 6-7/8 (July/August 1978), pp.883–884.
9. Ralph Miliband, *The State in Capitalist Society* (New York: Basic Books, 1969), p.66. On instrumental Marxism, see David A. Gold, Clarence Y. H. Lo, and Erik Olin Wright, "Recent Developments in Marxist Theories of the Capitalist State," *Monthly Review* 27-5 (October 1975), pp.32–35.
10. On structural Marxism see Gold, Lo, and Wright, "Recent Developments in Marxist Theories of the Capitalist State," pp.35–40; and Pat McGowan and Stephen G. Walker, "Radical and Conventional Models of U.S. Foreign Economic Policy Making," *World Politics* 33-3 (April 1981), pp.357–360.
11. James H. Mittelman and Mustapha Kamal Pasha, *Out from Underdevelopment Revisited: Changing Global Structures and the Remaking of the Third World* (London: Macmillan, 1997), pp.90–91.
12. For Marx's writings on the non-European world see Shlomo Avineri, ed., *Karl Marx on Colonialism and Modernization: His Dispatches and Other Writings on China, India, Mexico, the Middle East and North Africa* (Garden City: Doubleday, 1968). For conflicting interpretations of Marx's views of the South see Carlos Johnson, "Ideologies in Theories of Imperialism and Dependency," in Ronald H. Chilcote and Dale L. Johnson, eds., *Theories of Development: Mode of Production or Dependency?* (Beverly Hills: Sage, 1983), pp.75–104.
13. Brendan O'Leary, *The Asiatic Mode of Production: Oriental Despotism, Historical Materialism and Indian History* (Oxford: Basil Blackwell, 1989), p.263; Anthony Giddens, *Capitalism and Modern Social Theory: An Analysis of the Writings of Marx, Durkheim and Max Weber* (Cambridge: Cambridge University Press, 1971), pp.24–27; Lawrence Krader, *The*

Asiatic Mode of Production: Sources, Development and Critique in the Writings of Karl Marx (Assen: Van Grocum & Comp., 1975); Timothy Brook, ed., *The Asiatic Mode of Production in China* (Armonk: M.E. Sharpe, 1989).

14. Karl Marx, "The British Rule in India," in Avineri, ed., *Karl Marx on Colonialism and Modernization,* pp.86–88.

15. Marx, "The British Rule in India," p.481.

16. B. N. Ghosh, *Dependency Theory Revisited* (Aldershot: Ashgate, 2001), p.19.

17. J. A. Hobson, *Imperialism: A Study* (Ann Arbor: University of Michigan Press, 1965), p.81.

18. For differing views of Lenin's contribution to the study of imperialism, see Anthony Brewer, *Marxist Theories of Imperialism: A Critical Survey,* (2nd ed. London: Routledge, 1990), p.116; and Tom Kemp, "The Marxist Theory of Imperialism," in Roger Owen and Bob Sutcliffe, eds., *Studies in the Theory of Imperialism* (London: Longman, 1972), pp.26–30.

19. Lenin, *Imperialism: The Highest Stage of Capitalism,* p.89.

20. Thomas Biersteker, "Evolving Perspectives on International Political Economy: Twentieth-Century Discontinuities," *International Political Science Review* 14-1 (January 1993), p.12; Palma, "Dependency," pp.896–897.

21. Thomas B. Gold, *State and Society in the Taiwan Miracle* (Armonk: M.E. Sharpe, 1986), pp.13–17.

22. See Peter Evans, "After Dependency: Recent Studies of Class, State, and Industrialization," *Latin American Research Review* 20-2 (1985), p.159; and Fernando Henrique Cardoso and Enzo Faletto, *Dependency and Development in Latin America,* translated by Marjory Mattingly Urquidi (Berkeley: University of California Press, 1979), p.ix.

23. Aidan Foster-Carter, "From Rostow to Gunder Frank: Conflicting Paradigms in the Analysis of Underdevelopment," *World Development* 4-3 (March 1976), p.175.

24. Paul A. Baran, *The Political Economy of Growth* (New York: Monthly Review Press, 1962), pp.11–12.

25. Raúl Prebisch, "The Economic Development of Latin America and Its Principal Problems," *Economic Bulletin for Latin America* 7-1 (February 1962), pp.1–22 (first published in Spanish in May 1950).

26. Joseph L. Love, "The Origins of Dependency Analysis," *Journal of Latin American Studies* 22 (February 1990), pp.143–160.

27. Fernando Henrique Cardoso, "The Consumption of Dependency Theory in the United States," *Latin American Research Review* 12–3 (1977), pp.7–24. Cardoso and Faletto's *Dependencia y desarrollo en América Latina* was published in 1971, but it was not available in English until eight years later. See Cardoso and Faletto, *Dependency and Development in Latin America.*

28. Gary Gereffi, *The Pharmaceutical Industry and Dependency in the Third World* (Princeton: Princeton University Press, 1983), p.18; Gold, *State and Society in the Taiwan Miracle,* pp.14–15. Despite his far greater emphasis on external forces, even Gunder Frank recognized the need to examine external-internal interactions.

29. Tony Smith, "Requiem or New Agenda for Third World Studies?" *World Politics* 37-4 (July 1985), pp.546–547.

30. See André Gunder Frank, "The Development of Underdevelopment," *Monthly Review* 18-4 (September 1966), pp.17–31.

31. Cardoso and Faletto, *Dependency and Development in Latin America,* p.174.

32. Peter Evans, *Dependent Development: The Alliance of Multinational, State, and Local Capital in Brazil* (Princeton: Princeton University Press, 1979); Gereffi, *The Pharmaceutical Industry and Dependency in the Third World;* Gold, *State and Society in the Taiwan Miracle.*

33. André Gunder Frank, "Asia's Exclusive Models," *Far Eastern Economic Review* 116-26 (June 25, 1982), pp.22–23.

34. Gunder Frank, "Asia's Exclusive Models," p.23.
35. Evans, *Dependent Development*, p.329. See also Gereffi, *The Pharmaceutical Industry and Dependency in the Third World*, p.24; Cardoso and Faletto, *Dependency and Development in Latin America.*
36. Colin Leys, "Underdevelopment and Dependency: Critical Notes," *Journal of Contemporary Asia* 7-1 (1977), pp.92–107.
37. David Ray, "The Dependency Model of Latin American Underdevelopment: Three Basic Fallacies," *Journal of Interamerican Studies and World Affairs* 15-1 (February 1973), pp.7–8. Although some dependency theorists acknowledge that dependent relationships can exist between socialist countries, they generally limit their analyses to the capitalist system.
38. Cal Clark and Donna Bahry, "Dependent Development: A Socialist Variant," *International Studies Quarterly* 27-3 (September 1983), p.286.
39. Mittelman and Pasha, *Out from Underdevelopment Revisited*, p.46.
40. Tony Smith, "The Underdevelopment of Development Literature: The Case of Dependency Theory," *World Politics* 31-2 (January 1979), pp.257–258; Stephan Haggard, "The Newly Industrializing Countries in the International System," *World Politics* 38-2 (January 1986), p.346.
41. Bill Warren, "Imperialism and Capitalist Industrialization," *New Left Review* 81 (September–October 1973), p.4. See also Bill Warren, *Imperialism: Pioneer of Capitalism* (London: New Left Books and Verso, 1980), edited by John Sender after Warren's death in 1978.
42. Ernesto Laclau, "Feudalism and Capitalism in Latin America," *New Left Review* 67 (May–June, 1971), p.25.
43. Evans, "After Dependency," p.158.
44. See articles in the journal *Latin American Perspectives;* writings by James Petras and Ronald Chilcote; Ghosh, *Dependency Theory Revisited;* Jill Hills, "Dependency Theory and Its Relevance Today: International Institutions in Telecommunications and Structural Power," *Review of International Studies* 20-2 (April, 1994), pp.169–186; David L. Blaney, "Reconceptualizing Autonomy: The Difference Dependency Theory Makes," *Review of International Political Economy* 3-3 (Autumn 1996), pp.457–497.
45. Ghosh, *Dependency Theory Revisited*, p.133.
46. John Gerard Ruggie, "Multilateralism: The Anatomy of an Institution," in John Gerard Ruggie, ed., *Multilateralism Matters: The Theory and Praxis of an Institutional Form* (New York: Columbia University Press, 1993), p.33; Francis Fukuyama, "The End of History?" *The National Interest* 16 (Summer 1989), pp.3, 11.
47. Thomas J. Biersteker, "The 'Triumph' of Neoclassical Economics in the Developing World: Policy Convergence and Bases of Governance in the International Economic Order," in James N. Rosenau and Ernst-Otto Czempiel, eds., *Governance Without Government: Order and Change in World Politics* (Cambridge: Cambridge University Press, 1992), pp.102–131.
48. David P. Calleo, "Restarting the Marxist Clock? The Economic Fragility of the West," *World Policy Journal* 13-2 (Summer 1996), p. 63.
49. For a discussion of the differences between dependency and world-systems theory, see Peter Evans, "Beyond Center and Periphery: A Comment on the Contribution of the World System Approach to the Study of Development," *Sociological Inquiry* 49-4 (1979), pp.15–20.
50. A good introduction to world-systems theory is Thomas R. Shannon, *An Introduction to the World-System Perspective*, 2nd ed. (Boulder: Westview Press, 1996). Recent research from this perspective is contained in the online *Journal of World-Systems Research* (http://csf.colorado.edu/jwsr).
51. See Samir Amin, *Empire of Chaos*, translated by W. H. Locke Anderson, (New York: Monthly Review Press, 1992).

52. For a discussion of these differences see Christopher Chase-Dunn and Peter Grimes, "World-Systems Analysis," *Annual Review of Sociology* 21 (1995), pp.387–417.

53. Immanuel Wallerstein, "The Rise and Future Demise of the World Capitalist System: Concepts for Comparative Analysis," in Immanuel Wallerstein, *The Capitalist World-Economy* (New York: Cambridge University Press, 1979), p.5.

54. Wallerstein, "The Rise and Future Demise of the World Capitalist System," pp.18–19. See also Chase-Dunn and Grimes, "World-Systems Analysis," pp. 390–397.

55. Immanuel Wallerstein, "Class Formation in the Capitalist World-Economy," in Wallerstein, *The Capitalist World-Economy,* p.230.

56. Wallerstein, "The Rise and Future Demise of the World Capitalist System," p.35.

57. Wallerstein was not the first to identify a middle group between the core and periphery. Ruy Mauro Marini and Johan Galtung referred to "subimperial" and "go-between" states. See Ruy Mauro Marini *Subdesarollo y Revolución* 9th ed. (Mexico: Siglo Veintiuno, 1978); and Johan Galtung, "A Structural Theory of Imperialism," *Journal of Peace Research* 8-2 (1971), p.104.

58. Evans, *Dependent Development*, p.33.

59. Chase-Dunn and Grimes, "World-System Analysis," p.389.

60. Immanuel Wallerstein, "Dependence in an Interdependent World: The Limited Possibilities of Transformation Within the Capitalist World-Economy," in Wallerstein, *The Capitalist World-Economy,* p.69.

61. Wallerstein, "Dependence in an Interdependent World," p.67; Wallerstein, "The Rise and Future Demise of the World Capitalist System," p.35.

62. Gold, *State and Society in the Taiwan Miracle.*, pp.13–14.

63. Theda Skocpol, "Wallerstein's World Capitalist System: A Theoretical and Historical Critique," *American Journal of Sociology* 82-5 (March 1977), pp.1084–1088; Alexander Gerschenkron, "Economic Backwardness in Historical Perspective," in Alexander Gerschenkron, *Economic Backwardness in Historical Perspective: A Book of Essays* (Cambridge: Belknap Press of Harvard University Press, 1962), pp.16–21; Peter J. Katzenstein, ed., "Between Power and Plenty: Foreign Economic Policies of Advanced Industrial States," special issue of *International Organization* 31-4 (Autumn 1977).

64. See William G. Martin, "Still Partners After All These Years? Wallerstein, World Revolutions and the World-Systems Perspective," *Journal of World-Systems Research* 6-2 (Summer/Fall 2000), pp.234-263.

65. See Antonio Gramsci, *Selections from the Prison Notebooks of Antonio Gramsci*, edited and translated by Quintin Hoare and Geoffrey Nowell Smith (New York: International Publishers, 1971). See also John Merrington, "Theory and Practice in Gramsci's Marxism," in New Left Review, ed., *Western Marxism: A Critical Reader* (London: New Left Review, 1977), pp.142–150.

66. Robert W. Cox, "Gramsci, Hegemony and International Relations: An Essay in Method," *Millennium* 12-2 (1983), pp.162–175; Mark Rupert, *Producing Hegemony: The Politics of Mass Production and American Global Power* (Cambridge: Cambridge University Press, 1995), p.29.

67. Robert W. Cox, "Social Forces, States and World Orders: Beyond International Relations Theory," in Robert O. Keohane, ed., *Neorealism and Its Critics* (New York: Columbia University Press, 1986), pp.204–254; Fred Gale, "Cave 'Cave! Hic Dragones': A Neo-Gramscian Deconstruction and Reconstruction of International Regime Theory," *Review of International Political Economy* 5-2 (Summer 1998), pp.269–277.

68. Stephen Gill and David Law, "Global Hegemony and the Structural Power of Capital," in Stephen Gill, ed., *Gramsci, Historical Materialism and International Relations* (Cambridge: Cambridge University Press, 1993), pp.93–124.

69. Robert W. Cox, "Civil Society at the Turn of the Millennium: Prospects for an Alternative World Order," *Review of International Studies* 25 (1999), p.4.

70. Cox, "Civil Society at the Turn of the Millennium," p.13; Joseph A. Buttigieg, "Gramsci on Civil Society," *Boundary 2* 22–3 (Fall 1995), pp.1–32.

71. See, for example, Mark E. Rupert, "(Re) Politicizing the Global Economy: Liberal Common Sense and Ideological Struggle in the U.S. NAFTA Debate," *Review of International Political Economy* 2-4 (Autumn 1995), pp.658–692.

72. This discussion of the business conflict model relies on David N. Gibbs, *The Political Economy of Third World Intervention: Mines, Money, and U.S. Policy in the Congo Crisis* (Chicago: University of Chicago Press, 1991); Ronald W. Cox, *Power and Profits: U.S. Policy in Central America* (Lexington: University Press of Kentucky, 1994); and David Skidmore, "The Business of International Politics," *Mershon International Studies Review* 39, suppl. 2 (October 1995), pp.246–254. See also Gregory P. Nowell, *Mercantile States and the World Oil Cartel, 1900–1939* (Ithaca: Cornell University Press, 1994); and Robert Vitalis, *When Capitalists Collide: Business Conflict and the End of Empire in Egypt* (Berkeley: University of California Press, 1995).

73. Gibbs, *The Political Economy of Third World Intervention,* p.30.

74. McGowan and Walker, "Radical and Conventional Models of U.S. Foreign Economic Policy Making," p.352.

75. Gibbs, *The Political Economy of Third World Intervention,* pp.13–19.

76. Cox, *Power and Profits,* p.4.

77. Skidmore, "The Business of International Politics," p.246.

78. Helen Milner, *Resisting Protectionism: Global Industries and the Politics of International Trade* (Princeton: Princeton University Press, 1988), pp.24–25.

79. Cox, *Power and Profits,* p.15.

P A R T   I I I

The Issue Areas

Part III focuses on the main substantive issue areas in IPE. It begins with a discussion of international monetary relations in Chapter 6, because most significant transactions in the international economy—including trade, investment, and finance—depend on the availability of money and credit. Chapter 7 deals with foreign debt and international financial crises , which are closely linked with international monetary relations. The IMF has been the lead IO dealing not only with monetary issues, but also with foreign debt and financial crises. Chapters 8 and 9 examine trade relations at the global and regional levels. Regionalism affects all the substantive issue areas examined. For example, Chapter 6 on monetary relations devotes some attention to the European economic and monetary union. Chapter 10 deals with the most important private actor in the international economy, the MNC. The increase of globalization and international competitiveness has a major effect on the relationship between the MNC and the state. Chapter 11 examines the issue of international development. Whereas most of the chapters in Part III devote some attention to the South, Chapter 11 focuses specifically on alternative strategies for promoting economic development. The final section of each chapter in Part III draws linkages between the issue areas and the main themes and IPE theoretical perspectives.

C H A P T E R 6

International Monetary Relations

Interernational monetary relations is the most central issue area in IPE, because the most important transactions in the international economy—including trade, investment, and finance—all depend on the availability of money and credit. Thus, one long-term analyst of global monetary issues has stated that the most critical issue to hegemonic stability theorists should "not [be] what the hegemon does or does not do in trade . . . but what it does or fails to do to maintain peace and what it does or fails to do to keep the monetary system stable and credit flowing in a steady fashion."[1] Although international monetary relations is one of the most difficult issues for students to master, some background in this area can provide a sound basis for understanding other major IPE issues.

The sheer volume of international monetary and financial transactions is playing a major role in reshaping the global political economy. Indeed, the amount of money handled *daily* by foreign exchange markets increased from negligible amounts in the late 1950s, to $590 billion in 1989, and to $1.5 trillion in 1998. About 29 percent of the world's circulating currency is located outside the country issuing it, and during the mid-1990s at least $300 billion of the three top currencies (the U.S. dollar, German deutsch mark, and Japanese yen) were circulating outside the country of origin.[2] Liberal interdependence theorists assert that this marked increase in international financial transactions has resulted largely from advances in communications, technology, and transportation and that nation-states are finding it increasingly difficult to regulate economic activities. Realist scholars, by contrast, argue that financial transactions have increased with the permission (and sometimes the encouragement) of the most powerful states and that these states continue to dictate the terms for such transactions.[3]

Realists also point to the fact that international monetary transactions still rely primarily on the existence of separate national currencies. As discussed in this chapter, some assets such as special drawing rights are international in scope, and the establishment of a new "euro" currency for members of the European Economic and Monetary Union (EMU) is posing a major challenge to the predominance of the nationally based U.S. dollar. Nevertheless, the global monetary regime continues to function primarily in a world of separate national currencies, where states are inevitably concerned about their balance of payments—the total flow of money into and out of a state.[4] A country's balance of payments tells us not only about its overall financial position but also about its position in other areas such as trade and foreign investment. It is therefore necessary to provide some background on the balance-of-payments.

THE BALANCE OF PAYMENTS

The **balance of payments,** which records the debit and credit transactions of residents, firms, and governments of one country with foreign countries and international institutions, is composed of two broad categories: the **current account,** which includes all transactions related to a country's current expenditures and national income, and the **capital account,** which includes all movements of financial capital into and out of a country. As Table 6.1 shows, the current account comprises four types of transactions:

Table 6.1

BALANCE-OF-PAYMENTS DATA, 1992 (U.S.$ billions)

	United States	Japan
Current account		
1. Merchandise trade		
Exports	+440.14	+330.87
Imports	−536.28	−198.47
Merchandise trade balance	−96.14	+132.40
2. Services trade		
Credit	+159.40	+48.31
Debit	−117.08	−89.73
Services trade balance	+42.32	−41.42
Balance of trade (1 + 2)	−53.82	+90.98
3. Investment income and payments		
Credit	+130.95	+145.75
Debit	−110.55	−114.47
Balance	+20.40	+31.28
4. Remittances and official transactions	−32.88	−4.62
Current account balance	**−66.30**	**+117.64**
Capital account		
5. Direct investment and other long-term capital	−17.61	−30.78
6. Short-term capital	+54.19	−75.77
Capital account balance	**+36.58**	**−106.55**
Statistical discrepancy	**−12.34**	**−10.46**
Total	**−42.06**	**+0.63**
Change in reserves*	**+42.06**	**−0.63**

*Increase in reserves: −; decrease in reserves: +.
Source: International Monetary Fund, *Balance of Payments Statistics Yearbook,* vol. 44, part 1, 1993 (Washington, DC: IMF, 1993), pp.366, 742.

1. *Merchandise trade*, or the export and import of tangible goods. The difference between the value of merchandise exports and imports is the *merchandise trade balance.*
2. *Services trade*, or intangible items such as insurance, information, transportation, banking, and consulting, provided to or by foreigners. A country's merchandise and services exports minus its merchandise and services imports (items 1 and 2 in the table) are equal to its *balance of trade.*
3. *Investment income and payments* measure interest and dividend payments on investments by citizens of the home country to foreigners and by foreigners to citizens of the home country.
4. *Remittances and official transactions* include income that migrant workers or foreign companies send out of a country, military and foreign aid, and salaries and pensions paid to government employees abroad.

Table 6.1 shows that Japan had a current account *surplus* of \$117.64 billion (U.S.) in 1992, whereas the United States had a current account *deficit* of \$66.30 billion. The critical item for both countries was the merchandise trade balance, with Japan having a merchandise trade *surplus* of \$132.40 billion and the United States having a merchandise trade *deficit* of \$96.14 billion. As noted in Chapter 8, the United States has had annual merchandise trade deficits since 1971, whereas Japan has had substantial trade surpluses. The largest U.S. trade deficits are often with Japan, which has been a constant source of friction between the two countries. Table 6.1 shows that in contrast to its merchandise trade deficit, the United States had a positive balance in its *services* trade in 1992 (+\$42.32 billion). For many years the United States has been a net exporter of services, because of its many skilled consultants and its highly developed markets in insurance and banking. This helps to explain why the United States exerted strong pressure to include services trade in the NAFTA and in the 1986–1993 GATT Uruguay Round negotiations. The United States also had a positive balance for the investment income and payments item of the current account in 1992 (+\$20.40 billion) because of interest and dividend payments received on past investments, but the positive balances on services and investment income were not sufficient to overcome the large U.S. negative merchandise trade balance. Thus, the overall U.S. current account balance in 1992 was negative (−\$66.30 billion).

The second major item in the balance of payments is the *capital account*, which measures long- and short-term capital flows (items 5 and 6 in Table 6.1). A country's capital exports are *debit* items because they involve payments to foreigners and use foreign exchange; its capital imports are *credit* items because they involve payments from foreigners and earn foreign exchange. (This is the opposite of merchandise trade, in which exports are credits and imports are debits.) Short-term investments normally have a maturity of less than one year, whereas long-term investments extend beyond this period. Long-term capital flows are further subdivided into FDI and portfolio investment. FDI is capital investment in a branch plant or subsidiary of an MNC in which the investor has voting control. **Portfolio investment,** by contrast, is investment in bonds or a minority holding of shares that does not involve legal control.

Governments tend to offset their current account imbalances with changes in their capital accounts. Thus, a country with a current account deficit often seeks to offset this deficit with foreign investment or an inflow of funds into its capital account. A current account surplus, on the other hand, permits a country to have a capital account deficit through investment abroad or the accumulation of foreign assets. As Table 6.1 shows, Japan (which had a current account *surplus*) had a capital account *deficit* of $106.55 billion in 1992 and the United States (which had a current account *deficit*) had a capital account *surplus* of $36.58 billion. In view of the rapid increase in capital flows in recent years (discussed in this chapter), trade flows in some transition economies and LDCs have in fact been driven by capital flows. Thus, some of these countries during the 1990s "ran current account deficits because they were attracting capital inflows."[5] The important point to remember, however, is that a current account deficit is normally accompanied by a capital account surplus.

In addition to the current and capital accounts, the balance of payments includes two less important items. The *statistical discrepancy* item results partly from errors in collecting and computing data, but mainly from a government's failure to include all the goods, services, and capital that cross its borders. The final item is the *change in official reserves.* Each country has a **central bank** (e.g., the U.S. Federal Reserve or the Bank of Canada) that holds foreign exchange and gold reserves. When a country has a deficit in its current *and* capital accounts (the "Total" item in Table 6.1), this amount must be matched by an equivalent reduction in reserves. When a country has a surplus in its current and capital accounts, it accumulates the surplus in its reserves. The total of a country's current account, capital account, statistical discrepancy, and change in reserves always equals zero, hence the term *balance of payments.* Note in Table 6.1 that, by standard accounting procedures, a *minus* figure equals an *increase* in reserves and a *plus* figure equals a *decrease* in reserves. This is merely a bookkeeping exercise so the balance of payments will equal zero. Thus, in 1992 U.S. reserves *declined* by $42.06 billion, and Japanese reserves *increased* by $0.63 billion.

Although the balance-of-payments account always balances (i.e., equals zero) in a bookkeeping sense, this does not indicate that a country never has payments difficulties. On the contrary, a country may have a *balance-of-payments surplus* or a *balance-of-payments deficit.* These terms refer only to the current and capital accounts, and exclude any changes in official financing. A government with a balance-of-payments surplus reduces its liabilities to foreign governments and/or adds to its official reserves, whereas a government with a balance-of-payments deficit increases its liabilities and/or reduces its official reserves. The main body of the balance of payments therefore informs us about a state's overall position in terms of financial assets and liabilities.[6]

GOVERNMENT RESPONSE
TO A BALANCE-OF-PAYMENTS DEFICIT

Countries with balance-of-payments deficits normally feel more pressure to correct the imbalances than countries with balance-of-payments surpluses. A deficit country's reserves can eventually be depleted, but a surplus country can continue to increase its reserves indefinitely. Furthermore, realists believe that a balance-of-payments surplus, even if it is maintained with the help of government policy, is an indication of "superior competitive performance."[7] Surplus countries can in fact feel both economic and political pressures to correct their surpluses in the longer term. For example, excessive official reserves can lead to rising domestic prices and inflationary pressures, and large balance-of-payments surpluses can force up the value of a country's currency making its exports more expensive for foreigners. Nevertheless, surplus countries normally view their payments disequilibrium as an economic asset rather than a liability, and we therefore focus here on a country's response to a payments deficit. When governments have balance-of-payments deficits, they have two basic policy choices: to *finance* the disequilibrium or *adjust* to it. Governments often prefer financing measures because they can defer the cost of paying the debts to the future. Adjustment measures, by contrast, can have major political risks because some societal groups must bear the adjustment costs in the present.[8]

Adjustment Measures

Governments opting for adjustment measures rely on three types of policy instruments to affect the balance of payments: monetary, fiscal, and commercial policy. **Monetary policy** influences the economy through changes in the money supply. When a government uses monetary policy to deal with a balance-of-payments deficit, its central bank limits public access to funds for spending purposes and makes such funds more expensive. For example, the central bank raises interest rates to make borrowing more costly, decreases the amount of money available for loans by requiring commercial banks to hold larger reserves, and sells government bonds to withdraw money from the economy. These policies are designed to lower the payments deficit by producing a contraction of the economy and less spending on goods and services. **Fiscal policy** affects the economy through changes in taxes and government spending. When a government uses fiscal policy to deal with a payments deficit, it lowers government expenditures and raises taxes to withdraw purchasing power from the public. Economies with balance-of-payments surpluses often follow the opposite policies; for example, they adopt measures to expand the money supply, increase the budget deficit, and inflate the economy. *Commercial policy* lowers a country's payments deficit by affecting its trade flows; that is, by increasing its exports and decreasing its imports.

The combination of monetary, fiscal, and commercial policies a governments uses depends on whether it opts for external or internal adjustment measures. *External adjustment measures* impose most of the adjustment costs on foreigners by reducing payments to foreigners and increasing payments from foreigners. For example, tariffs, import quotas, export subsidies, tax incentives, and currency devaluation are used to decrease imports and foreign investment outflows, and to increase exports and foreign investment inflows. Because external adjustment measures are aimed at foreign countries, others often retaliate and everyone loses in the long run. The competitive devaluation of currencies, with every country attempting to lower the value of its currency—and thus the relative price of its exports—is an example of the results of such retaliation. Although a government may adopt external measures to avoid making politically unpopular decisions at home, even external measures impose costs on some domestic groups.

For example, a reduction in imports may promote domestic production and employment, but also adversely affects importing businesses and the range of products available to consumers. *Internal adjustment measures* cause individuals and groups at home to pay more of the adjustment costs. These are usually deflationary monetary and fiscal policies to slow down business activity in efforts to decrease the deficit; examples include higher taxes and interest rates to reduce spending by individuals, businesses, and the government. The domestic costs of internal adjustment methods include unemployment, lower living standards, business bankruptcies, and a phasing out of publicly financed programs. However, internal adjustment measures can also affect foreigners by deflating the economy and lowering the demand for foreign imports.

Financing

Instead of using adjustment measures, a country may seek *financing* to deal with its balance-of-payments deficit, by borrowing from external credit sources or decreasing its foreign exchange reserves. Governments tend to shift from adjustment to financing when reserves and access to credit are available, because it is easier to postpone difficult political decisions and opt for future over current costs. However, financing may not be available over a lengthy period; a country's reserves can be depleted, and foreigners are reluctant to invest in a country with chronic foreign debt problems.

In recent years the United States has normally depended on financing through its capital account (+$36.58 billion in 1992, in Table 6.1) to counter its current account deficit (−$66.30 billion in 1992). As Table 6.2 shows, the U.S. current account deficit has increased almost every year since 1995, and in 2002 it exceeded $500 billion dollars and accounted for more than 5 percent of the U.S. GDP. One result of this long-term deficit is that the United States changed from being a net creditor nation of $300 billion in 1980 to a net debtor of $1.5 trillion in 1998, with debt projections of 3 to 4 trillion dollars by 2005. The main factor in the growing U.S. current account deficit is the country's merchandise trade deficit. In 1999, the U.S. merchandise trade deficit amounted to $268 billion.[9]

There is debate as to whether the growing U.S. trade and current account deficits are a serious problem. Some analysts argue that these deficits are not a major concern for two reasons. First, the U.S. negative trade balance is no longer a valid measure of U.S. global sales competitiveness because corporate America "has never been better positioned to compete in the global marketplace."[10] U.S. firms often prefer to sell goods abroad through their foreign subsidiaries rather than exporting them

Table 6.2

CURRENT ACCOUNT BALANCES (U.S.$ billions)

	1995	1996	1997	1998	1999	2000	2001	2002
United States	−105.8	−117.8	−128.4	−203.8	−292.9	−410.3	−393.4	−503.7
European Union	53.2	83.2	112.7	71.1	15.4	−32.2	8.5	56.7
Japan	111.4	65.7	96.6	119.1	114.5	119.6	87.8	112.8

Source: International Monetary Fund, *World Economic Outlook, April 2003* (Washington, D.C.: IMF, 2003), Table 27, p. 206

from the United States. Thus, in 1998 U.S. foreign affiliate sales of $2.4 trillion were far greater than U.S. global exports of $933 billion. The merchandise trade deficit is not a major concern from this perspective, because U.S. firms today are highly competitive. Second, some analysts point out that the United States tends to have higher trade and current account deficits when there is a greater gap between the productivity growth rate in the United States and abroad. For example, Table 6.2 shows that the United States had growing current account deficits while Japan and the EU had current account surpluses in the latter half of the 1990s. (The U.S. trade deficit also dramatically increased during this period.) The 1990s, however, was also a decade during which the United States experienced sustained economic expansion while economic growth in the EU was largely stalled and the Japanese economy was often in recession.[11] Thus, some argue that U.S. trade and current account deficits may simply indicate that a vibrant U.S. economy is serving as the largest market for other countries' exports.

Certainly a balance of trade surplus is not the only measure of economic health, as Japan's economic problems clearly demonstrate. (Japan's problems are discussed later in this chapter and in Chapter 11.) Nevertheless, arguments that the U.S. trade and current account deficits are of little concern are not convincing. Regarding the first argument, there is considerable debate among scholars as to whether a state's competitiveness is synonymous with the competitiveness of its MNCs (see Chapter 10). In assessments of U.S. trade competitiveness (and of employment prospects for U.S. workers), it is of course not sufficient to focus only on the sales of U.S. foreign affiliates. Regarding the second argument, it is true that the United States sometimes has higher trade and current account deficits during periods of rapid economic growth, and it has been able to rely on financing to cover its deficits because its large economy and political stability attract foreign investors. Nevertheless, if a country depends on large capital inflows over time, it begins to pay out more in interest and dividends to foreigners than it receives. As a result of regular U.S. borrowing on its capital account to deal with its current account deficit, the United States' investment income and payments item under its current account (item 3 in Table 6.1) also became a negative item in 1998 (−$6.21 billion) and 1999 (−$18.48 billion).[12] Other possible problems from the long-term U.S. deficits include a protectionist backlash against U.S. liberal trade policy, a loss of U.S. disposable income, increased leverage of foreign governments with substantial U.S. dollar holdings, and disruptive market volatility against the U.S. dollar. Thus, one analyst warns that "the longer the large U.S. external deficit continues and the foreign debt increases, the more likely will be a hard landing for the dollar and the U.S. economy."[13] In sum, despite differences of view, most economists believe the persistent U.S. deficits are a problem, and in September 2002 the U.S. Institute of International Economics in Washington, D.C. held a conference stemming from concerns that "the large and potentially widening external deficit poses risks for the U.S. economy."[14]

Adjustment, Financing, and the Theoretical Perspectives

In reality, states usually employ a combination of external adjustment, internal adjustment, and financing measures to deal with their payments deficits. Liberals, realists, and historical structuralists have different preferences regarding these policy instruments. Orthodox liberals believe that payments deficits result from domestic inefficiencies and that governments should therefore adopt internal adjustment measures as a necessary form of discipline. Orthodox liberals oppose external adjustment measures because they contribute to trade barriers and distort economic interactions; and they oppose external financing because it permits countries to delay instituting necessary internal reforms. Realists and historical structuralists by contrast warn that internal adjustment methods pose a threat to domestic autonomy in policymaking. Dependency theorists argue that LDCs should not have to bear the costs of internal adjustment measures because the international system serves the interests of the rich Northern states. External adjustment measures, by contrast, are far more acceptable to both realists and historical structuralists. Realists view external measures as "fair game" in a state's efforts to improve its competitive position vis-à-vis other states, and historical structuralists believe LDCs may have to impose import controls because of their unfavorable terms of trade with DCs. Some historical structuralists also argue that the North, which benefits most from the international system, should provide LDCs with liberal financing to help alleviate their balance-of-payments problems.

In an age of interdependence and globalization, it is important to note that collective measures are sometimes required to deal with balance of payments disequilibria. For example, some analysts argue that Japan and China "have been persistently manipulating their currencies to gain an unfair competitive advantage" and that this has "had a substantial impact on exchange rates and the U.S. trade deficit."[15] Joint action is required to address this problem, because Japan and China often have the largest trade surpluses with the United States. (The relationship between exchange rates and trade are discussed later in this chapter.) Later chapters also discuss the fact that many LDCs cannot deal with their balance of payments problems individually because of a wide range of external and internal constraints. In sum both individual decisions by states regarding adjustment and financing and collective decision-making are often necessary.

INTERNATIONAL MONETARY RELATIONS BEFORE BRETTON WOODS

The literature on the modern period of international monetary relations commonly refers to the existence of four successive monetary regimes: The classical gold standard, from the 1870s to the outbreak of World War I in 1914; a gold exchange standard during the first part of the interwar period; the Bretton Woods system from 1944 to 1973; and a "non-system" of floating and fixed exchange rates from 1973 to the present.[16] This chapter focuses primarily on the third and fourth regimes, which developed after World War II. However, to understand the Bretton Woods regime it is necessary to provide some background on the first two regimes.

The Classical Gold Standard (1870s to 1914)

The classical **gold standard** was a *fixed exchange rate* regime in which governments announced and adhered to a specific exchange rate for their currencies in relation to gold. By making the national currency values more stable, the gold standard facilitated trade and other transactions between economies. For example, if the U.S. dollar and British pound were pegged at $35 and at £14.5 per ounce of gold, the exchange rate between the dollar and the pound would remain constant at $2.41 per £1 (35 divided by 14.5). Although all countries had to undergo adjustments to maintain their exchange rates, the gold standard functioned reasonably well because it was backed by British hegemony and by cooperation among the major powers (especially Britain, France, and Germany).[17] Britain assumed a leadership role in stabilizing the gold standard by providing public goods to other countries, such as investment capital, loans, and an open market for imports. Thus, Western Europe and the United States generally maintained their official gold parities for about 35 years.[18]

The gold standard was based on orthodox liberal ideas in some important respects. The primary objective was to promote monetary openness and stability through the maintenance of stable exchange rates. This was a period before John Maynard Keynes introduced interventionist liberal ideas to combat unemployment, and countries were expected to sacrifice domestic social objectives for the sake of monetary stability. Orthodox liberals sometimes refer to the gold standard in highly idealized terms, and in 1981 President Ronald Reagan even created a special commission to determine whether the United States should return to the gold standard (the commission's recommendation was negative).[19] However, critics maintain that the poorest countries and the poorest classes within countries often assumed the largest burden of adjustment under the gold standard through sacrifices in welfare and employment.

The Interwar Period (1914 to 1944)

World War I completely disrupted international monetary relations, but after the war Britain attempted to establish a *gold exchange standard* regime. A gold exchange standard, like a gold standard, is based on fixed exchange rates among currencies. However, a country's international reserves under the nineteenth century gold standard were officially held in gold, whereas official reserves under a gold exchange standard consist of both gold and reserve currencies (the British pound in the interwar period). Although central banks had in fact held reserve currencies as well as gold in earlier years, the gold exchange standard institutionalized this practice.[20] Because gold is in scarce supply and depends on new discoveries, a gold *exchange* standard permits more flexibility in increasing international reserves. (Furthermore, the largest gold producers are South Africa and Russia, which were not always the most favored countries.)

Although British efforts to maintain a gold exchange standard continued for several years, they eventually failed. Thus, monetary relations for much of the interwar period were marked by competitive devaluations, a shift to floating rather than fixed exchange rates, destabilizing speculative capital flows, and increased trade protectionism, which culminated in the Great Depression. Some theorists maintain that the failure to re-establish monetary stability in the interwar period resulted from Britain's inability as a declining hegemon to pursue effective stabilizing policies. However, others argue that the main factor in the breakdown of monetary stability was the growing reluctance of countries to sacrifice domestic goals such as full employment for the sake of currency stability. Those who argue that domestic factors were mainly responsible point to the differences in domestic politics before and after World War I. Before the war, voting in most countries was limited, labor unions were weak, farmers were not organized, and leftist parties were restricted. Thus, governments generally felt free to raise interest rates and taxes and decrease government expenditures to bolster the value of their currencies, even if these policies contributed to domestic hardships such as unemployment. By the end of World War I, however, domestic groups had gained more influence through the extension of suffrage, legalization of labor unions, organization of farmers, and development of mass political parties. It was no accident that Keynes introduced his interventionist liberal ideas at this time, positing that some government intervention is necessary to deal with domestic economic problems. Thus, governments could no longer easily sacrifice the welfare of their citizens to maintain the gold exchange standard, and one government after another responded to economic problems during the interwar period by turning away from international openness.[21]

The Formation of the Bretton Woods Monetary Regime

World War II was marked by a breakdown of monetary cooperation and a period of exchange controls, and planning for a postwar monetary regime culminated in the 1944 Bretton Woods conference. The Bretton Woods monetary regime was a gold exchange standard in which the value of each country's currency was pegged to gold or the U.S. dollar. Unlike the previous two regimes, however, the Bretton Woods system was based on the postwar interventionist liberal compromise (see Chapter 4).[22] On one hand, postwar planners assumed that the pegged exchange rates would provide sufficient monetary stability to permit a resumption of normal international trade. On the other hand, the planners ensured that there was some flexibility and assistance so that countries could pursue domestic objectives related to employment and inflation. This marked a contrast with the classical gold standard, in which long-term exchange rate stability took precedence over domestic requirements.[23]

The interventionist liberal compromise had three major elements. First, the postwar gold exchange standard was in fact an adjustable-peg exchange rate rather than a fixed exchange rate system. Although countries were to maintain the par value of their currencies in the short term, all countries other than the United States (as discussed later) could devalue or revalue their currencies under IMF guidance to correct chronic balance-of-payments problems. (Devaluation lowers the value, and revaluation raises the value of a currency.) The Bretton Woods negotiators hoped that a cooperative IMF framework for changing currency values would provide flexibility that was lacking with the classical gold standard and avoid competitive devaluations such as those of the interwar period. The second element of the interventionist liberal compromise was the IMF, which would provide short-term loans to countries with temporary balance-of-payments problems and thus alleviate domestic problems resulting from the need to maintain exchange rate stability. The third element of the compromise was support for national controls over capital flows. Speculative capital flows had contributed to great instability during the interwar period, and the postwar negotiators feared that such speculation could undermine efforts to maintain pegged exchange rates and promote freer trade under the Bretton Woods regime. The chief negotiators also believed that unrestricted capital flows would interfere with the functioning of the welfare state. If corporations and citizens could freely move capital abroad to evade taxes, this would jeopardize funding the state required for social welfare expenditures.[24]

THE INTERNATIONAL MONETARY FUND

The most important IO embedded in the Bretton Woods monetary regime was the IMF, located in Washington, D.C. The IMF was created to stabilize exchange rates and provide member states with short-term loans for temporary balance-of-payments problems. Under the IMF Articles of Agreement, members were required to peg their currencies to gold or the U.S. dollar, which was valued at $35 per ounce of gold. Member states were also to contribute to a pool of national currencies that would be available for the IMF loans to deficit countries.[25] Each IMF member was given a *quota* based on its relative economic importance, which determined the size of its *subscription* or contribution to the IMF resource pool. Under the IMF's weighted voting system, the most economically powerful states have the largest quotas and subscriptions and the most votes. At regular intervals of not more than five years, the IMF decides whether to propose adjustments in the members' quotas in accordance with changes in their relative economic positions.

The IMF approves loans to members in a series of stages, or *tranches*. In the 1980s–1990s the IMF developed a number of new programs to deal with the foreign debt and financial crises, and members can now borrow amounts far above the level of their IMF quotas. IMF **conditionality** has become central to its loan giving: members agree to adopt specific economic policies in return for IMF funding.[26] The more a member state borrows from the IMF in relation to its quota, the more stringent are the IMF's conditionality requirements. LDCs have strong pressures to abide by IMF conditionality because they depend on IMF loans and because DCs and private international banks often make the acceptance of IMF conditions a requirement for their own granting of loans and development assistance. The IMF usually requires loan recipients to adopt contractionary monetary and fiscal policies that are liberal-economic in nature. In the view of IMF officials, these requirements help ensure that borrowers correct their balance-of-payments problems so they can repay the IMF loans. From the perspective of many LDC loan recipients, however, IMF conditionality often infringes on their sovereignty and does not address the basic structural problems hindering their economic development (see Chapter 7).

The two main IMF policymaking bodies are the *board of governors* and the *executive board*. Every IMF member appoints one representative (usually the finance minister or central bank governor) to the board of governors, but the voting power of each governor depends on the IMF weighted voting system. The IMF board of governors normally meets only once a year in conjunction with the World Bank board of governors, and most of its powers are delegated to the board of executive directors (or executive board), which is in continuous session. The executive board, which also has weighted voting, is composed of 24 directors who are appointed or elected by the IMF members, and the IMF managing director who serves as chair. It carries out its work mainly on the basis of papers prepared by the IMF management and staff and is responsible for the IMF's daily business, including requests for financial assistance, economic consultations with member countries, and policy development. In addition to the boards of governors and executive directors, the IMF has an *International Monetary and Financial Committee* and a *Development Committee* (a joint committee with the World Bank), that serve as advisory bodies to the IMF at the ministerial level.

The countries with the largest subscriptions and most votes in the IMF governing bodies are the G-5—the United States, Japan, Germany, France, and Britain. In April 2002, the G-5 countries had 39.28 percent of the votes in the board of governors. The United States had 17.16 percent, followed by Japan with 6.16 percent, Germany with 6.02 percent, and France and Britain with 4.97 percent each.[27] Whereas the G-5 countries have a sufficient number of votes to appoint their own executive directors, coalitions of member states elect the other executive directors every two years.[28] In addition to having the most voting power in the IMF governing bodies, the DCs also have considerable influence in the operating staff. By tacit agreement, the top executive officer of the IMF, the managing director, has always been European, and the World Bank president has always been American.

One could argue that IMF weighted voting is of little importance because almost all IMF decisions are made by consensus. However, the legal structure of voting in fact has considerable influence because members are aware "of the likely outcome [of a vote] if the negotiation breaks down."[29] Despite the North's predominant influence, the South can influence IMF decisions through bloc voting under certain circumstances. Most IMF decisions are made with a simple majority vote, but majorities of 70 and 85 percent are required for some important decisions. The provision for these special majorities gives an effective veto to the United States, EU, and the LDCs *if* they act as a group. Although the South has on rare occasions blocked some initiatives requiring special majorities, it is not able to alter the IMF's existing structure, which clearly favors the North. Because it includes such a large, amorphous group of states, the South also has difficulty acting as a monolithic group to block IMF decisions. Not surprisingly, the South has expressed dissatisfaction with the North's dominance in the IMF, and the non-oil LDCs joined with OPEC after the 1973–1974 oil price increases to demand greater voting power. As a result of these demands, the OPEC countries benefited from a readjustment of IMF voting allocations, and LDCs were included in more of the IMF's deliberations. Nevertheless, the IMF's weighted voting system continues to favor the interests and objectives of the North.[30]

Chapter 2 noted that all the CPEs except Yugoslavia withdrew or were ousted from the IMF and World Bank in the 1950s–1960s. Membership issues in the two institutions are closely related because a country must join the IMF if it wishes to join the World Bank. This requirement deterred most Communist countries from joining the Bank for a number of years despite their interest in receiving World Bank financing because they would have been subject to IMF conditionality. Although Romania joined the IMF and World Bank in 1972, most former Soviet bloc countries did not join these institutions until the 1980s–1990s. Chapter 7 discusses the experience of Eastern European and FSU debtor countries in the Bretton Woods institutions.

THE FUNCTIONING OF THE BRETTON WOODS MONETARY REGIME

Bretton Woods was a gold exchange regime in which the main reserves were gold and the U.S. dollar. Economists generally ask three questions about the adequacy of reserve assets in upholding a monetary regime. First, are there sufficient reserves (e.g., gold and the U.S. dollar) for **liquidity,** or financing purposes? As interdependence increases, more liquidity is necessary to cover the growing number of economic transactions, but if there is a surplus of liquidity, inflation and other problems can result. Second, is there a *confidence* problem with the existing reserve assets? When countries lack confidence that an asset's value will remain reasonably stable, they are reluctant to hold that asset in their reserves. Confidence problems have led to periodic efforts to sell off British pounds and U.S. dollars. And third, what *adjustment* options do reserve-currency countries have in dealing with their balance-of-payments deficits? An effective regime should provide all deficit countries (including the top-currency country, the United States) with a sufficient range of adjustment options. The discussion that follows examines problems that developed with liquidity, confidence, and adjustment in the Bretton Woods monetary regime.[31]

The Central Role of the U.S. Dollar

Because the Bretton Woods monetary regime was based on a gold exchange standard, central banks could hold their international reserves in two forms—gold and foreign exchange—in any proportion they chose. It is ironic, however, that the original attraction of gold as a reserve asset—its scarcity—became a liability as increased trade and foreign investment led to growing demand for international reserves. With gold-mining sources limited and Western Europe recovering from World War II, the U.S. dollar was the only currency that could meet this need for increased liquidity. Monetary relations immediately after the war were more unstable than expected, with balance-of-payments deficits and lack of foreign exchange seriously hindering Europe's recovery. Thus, Western Europe was severely lacking in the main source of liquidity it required for making payments—U.S. dollars. Although it was vital to have sufficient dollars available for global liquidity purposes, large U.S. balance-of-trade surpluses in the late 1940s contributed to a dollar shortage. To remedy this problem, the United States distributed dollars throughout the world through economic aid and military expenditures from 1947 to 1958. From the liberal perspective, the United States provided *public goods* to Europeans and others during this period, opening its market to imports, providing long-term loans and grants through the European Recovery Program or Marshall Plan, and supplying the U.S. dollar as the main source of international liquidity.[32]

Under IMF guidance other countries at times changed the par value of their currencies relative to gold and the U.S. dollar, but the dollar's value was to remain fixed at the 1934 rate of $35 per ounce of gold. The fixed rate was designed to ensure that the dollar would be "as good as gold." Thus, the United States agreed to exchange all dollars held by foreign central banks and treasuries for gold at the official rate. This commitment seemed to be perfectly reasonable because the United States held a much larger share of gold reserves after the war than any other country. Most other countries in fact preferred U.S. dollars to gold for their reserves and international transactions; dollars (unlike gold) earned interest and did not have to be shipped and stored.[33] Although the United States as global hegemon was providing its currency as a public good to meet international liquidity needs, it was also receiving the private benefit of seignorage. **Seignorage** is "the profit that comes to the seigneur, or sovereign power, from the issuance of money."[34] As the supplier of the key world currency, the United States gained financial power and influence, and it was largely exempt from the discipline the international financial system imposed on other states. The United States was also able to trade and borrow in domestic currency and thus avoid exchange rate risks and transaction costs, and the dollar's leading role enabled New York City to retain its position as the world's financial capital. U.S. policy from 1947 to the late 1950s was therefore based on a mixture of altruism and self-interest, and other countries acquiesced to U.S. monetary leadership because of the benefits they received.[35]

Despite the early emergence of the United States as hegemon in the global monetary regime, several changes in the late 1950s led to concerns about its continued leadership. The United States regularly had a substantial balance-of-trade surplus in the postwar period, but it had even larger debits because of the economic and military financing it was providing through the Marshall Plan and other assistance programs. As a result, the United States had an overall balance-of-payments deficit beginning in 1950. U.S. payments deficits averaged about $1.5 billion per year for most of the decade, but they increased rapidly in the late 1950s, and observers began to speak of a dollar glut rather than a dollar shortage. In 1960, the U.S. payments deficit rose to $3.7 billion, and foreign dollar holdings exceeded U.S. gold reserves for the first time.[36] Thus, European governments, which had eagerly sought to obtain dollars, became reluctant to accumulate excessive dollar reserves.

To some economists, the dollar's declining fortunes demonstrated fundamental problems with a monetary regime that relied on a single key currency. On one hand, the need for sufficient liquidity caused the United States to spread dollars worldwide by running balance-of-payments deficits. On the other hand, these payments deficits would eventually deplete U.S. gold reserves and make it impossible for the United States to continue exchanging dollars for gold at $35 per ounce; this could lead to a collapse of confidence in the dollar as the top currency. Ironically, any U.S. actions to drastically reduce its balance-of-payments deficit to restore confidence in the dollar would contribute to a shortage of global liquidity. The **Triffin dilemma** (named after economist Robert Triffin) refers to the problem confronting a monetary regime that depends on a single key currency: Two of the main functions of the currency—the liquidity and confidence functions—would eventually come into conflict.[37]

A second major change that raised questions about U.S. control over monetary relations was the growth of the *Eurocurrency market* (or *Euromarket*). **Eurocurrencies** are national currencies traded and deposited in banks outside the home country. As the name connotes, Eurocurrencies originally developed in Europe, with London the most important location. However, Eurocurrency activity gravitates toward areas with less regulation, and in recent years it has expanded to a number of Asian countries. By the early 1990s, banks in Europe, North America, Asia, and the Caribbean had Eurocurrency deposits totalling more than $1 trillion. Over half of these were *Eurodollar* deposits held in banks outside the United States. The origins of the Eurocurrency market extend back to 1917, when the Communist government in Russia deposited its U.S. dollars in European banks to prevent the United States from seizing them. After World War II, the Soviet Union and Eastern Europe dealt in dollars as part of their efforts to develop and modernize their economies. They preferred to hold these dollars in Europe rather than the United States because of concerns that the Americans would freeze their holdings in the event of Cold War hostilities.

The Eurocurrency market as we know it developed during the 1960s when President Lyndon Johnson responded to the U.S. balance-of-payments deficits by imposing restrictions on foreign lending by American banks. To avoid these restrictions, U.S. companies began to finance their foreign operations from offshore banks, which were not subject to U.S. banking legislation. The Eurodollar market also grew because European firms involved with international trade found it easier to use the U.S. dollar as the key currency than to constantly exchange their currencies. These firms used local banks that were willing to accept dollar deposits. After 1973, a further impetus to the Eurodollar market came from the huge dollar deposits from OPEC countries as a result of the four-fold increase in the price of oil. Middle Eastern OPEC countries wanted to avoid keeping their dollar deposits in the United States because of fears the U.S. government would freeze them in a political crisis.

A major appeal of Eurodollars to depositors is that they are not subject to standard regulations governments impose on domestic banking activities. For example, the U.S. Federal Reserve has required banks to hold a certain percentage of their deposits as reserves and to impose a ceiling on interest rates they pay on deposits; but the United States does not have this control over Eurodollar deposits. The growth of the Eurocurrency market in the 1960s raised serious questions about U.S. control over monetary relations, and its rapid growth since that time has created problems for monetary relations in general. One of the most serious problems is that the Eurocurrency market makes it more difficult for governments to stabilize their domestic economies. For example, if a government attempts to restrict credit to fight inflation large firms can continue to borrow in the Eurocurrency market. Another problem is that the size and speed of Eurocurrency flows throughout the world can greatly destabilize foreign exchange rates and domestic interest rates. Regulation of the Eurocurrency market must be multilateral if it is to be effective, but strong competition for Eurobanking has thus far precluded that possibility.[38]

Liberal interdependence theorists point to the role that private actors such as international bankers played in the expansion of the Euromarket, and they view this as a natural development reflecting the increase in capital mobility, and global lending and borrowing. Some realists note that the leading states also contributed to the growth of the Euromarket because of perceived advantages it offered to them. For example, the British government allowed the Euromarket to operate without regulation in an effort to promote London as a leading financial center, and the U.S. government permitted its bankers to retain their dominant position in international finance by avoiding U.S.

capital controls and moving their international dollar business to London. In view of the declining confidence in its currency, the U.S. government also believed that the Euromarket would enhance the appeal of U.S. dollars to foreigners.[39] Nevertheless, realists warn that the central roles that the British and U.S. governments played in supporting the expansion of the Euromarket could have unintended consequences: "It may prove to have been the most important single development of the century undermining national monetary sovereignty."[40] Persistent U.S. balance-of-payments deficits, combined with the growth of the Eurodollar market in the 1960s, posed questions about the United States' ability to manage international monetary relations, and this in turn contributed to a shift toward multilateralism.

A Shift Toward Multilateralism

As U.S. balance-of-payments deficits continued to increase, the dollar slipped from top-currency to negotiated-currency status during the 1960s. A *top currency* is favored for international monetary transactions because others have confidence in the strong economic position of the issuing state. A *negotiated currency* does not benefit from this high degree of confidence, so the issuing state must offer inducements to others to continue accepting its leadership, and must be open to more multilateral management.[41] Thus, 10 DCs (the G-10) established the General Arrangements to Borrow (GAB) in 1962, under which they agreed to lend the IMF up to $6 billion in their own currencies if needed for supplementary resources to cope with international monetary problems. (The G-10 currently consists of 11 countries. See Chapter 2.) The G-10 represented a shift from unilateral U.S. management to more collective management of monetary issues because it had to approve each request for supplementary support.[42]

Another indication of the shift to multilateral management was the increased role of the *Bank for International Settlements (BIS)* in the 1960s. Located in Basle, Switzerland, the BIS is the oldest of the international financial institutions. Although the BIS was formed to help oversee the settlement of German reparations after World War I, its main purpose was to promote cooperation among central banks. The BIS became controversial during the 1930s because of allegations that it had pro-Nazi sentiments and accepted looted gold from countries occupied by Germany. As a result, the United States wanted to disband the BIS and transfer its functions to the IMF in the 1940s, but European countries would not agree to this. Although the BIS resumed operations after it made gold available to the countries from which it had been seized, the stigma of earlier BIS activities "prevented it from being accepted as a dominant international financial institution."[43] The BIS remains the main forum for cooperation and consultation among DC central bankers, and BIS meetings permit the central bankers to freely discuss international monetary conditions and problems on a confidential basis. Central banks deposit part of their official currency reserves with the BIS, which can use them to deal with exchange rate problems and provide credit to central banks that lack liquidity. When the U.S. dollar came under downward pressure in the 1960s, the BIS organized mutual lines of credit among the central banks to help stabilize exchange rates and the price of gold. The United States refused to attend the BIS monthly meetings in the 1940s–1950s, but it has been more accepting of multilateral management and has attended the BIS meetings since the 1960s.[44]

Although Western European countries viewed the creation of the G-10 and the upgrading of the BIS as a victory for collective management, LDCs were dissatisfied that they were not even represented in these groups. Despite the IMF's weighted voting, at least they were present at the bargaining table.[45] Thus, the South responded to the G-10 by setting up its own group in 1971, the **Group of 24.** The G-24 is composed of finance ministers or central bank governors from the three main LDC regions (Africa, Asia, and Latin America and the Caribbean); but all other G-77 members are welcome to attend G-24 meetings as observers, and China has been a special invitee since 1981. The G-24 regularly reviews international monetary relations, tries to coordinate LDC monetary policies and responds to G-10 reports on international monetary reform by presenting its own counterreports. Although the G-24's ideas have received some recognition, its influence (like the influence of UNCTAD and the G-77) is clearly circumscribed because it consists of borrowers rather than lenders in the IMF.[46]

The G-10 could supply a substantial amount of financial resources, but there were concerns that even G-10 resources were not sufficient to defend the dollar if it came under attack. Indeed, a rush to change dollars into gold became more likely as the U.S. balance-of-payments deficit continued to increase. A series of measures were therefore adopted to bolster the dollar, and the United States sought to improve its balance of payments by reducing capital outflows. In 1965, for example, the United States imposed limits on foreign investments and loans by U.S. firms and banks. Despite these efforts, U.S. gold stocks fell from $22.7 billion in 1950 to $10.7 billion in 1970, while dollar claims against the U.S. gold supply rose from about $5 billion to $70 billion. Thus, by 1968 the dollar in effect had become inconvertible into gold.[47]

Disagreement continues as to the causes of the U.S. balance-of-payments deficit. Some observers attribute the deficit to the public goods the United States as a global hegemon provided, such as the Marshall Plan, the U.S. dollar as the key currency, and an open market for others' exports. However, critics argue that Americans and their governments have been unwilling to balance their revenues and expenditures. During the Vietnam War, for example, the U.S. Congress refused to raise taxes to pay for the war effort, and President Johnson refused to cut domestic social programs. The United States also has a lower personal savings rate than the other G-5 countries. In 1980, for example, the personal savings ratio as a percentage of disposable income was 19.2 percent for Japan, 12.3 percent for Britain, 11 percent for France, 10.9 percent for West Germany, and only 6 percent for the United States. The difference in personal savings habits of Japanese and Americans results both from cultural factors and Japanese monetary and fiscal policies. Thus, high-saving Japan has been the source of large-scale capital flows to the low-saving United States in recent years.[48] Yet another possible reason for the U.S. balance-of-payments problem relates to the decline of U.S. competitiveness as a result of the postwar recovery in Western Europe and Japan. Under the gold exchange standard, the United States was the only country that could not devalue its currency to become more competitive. Thus, the Bretton Woods regime did not provide the United States with sufficient *adjustment* options to deal with its decreased competitiveness.

The U.S. balance-of-payments deficit was not the only problem confronting the Bretton Woods system in the 1960s and 1970s. Despite the continuance of national controls on capital flows, investors lacked confidence in the existing currency exchange rates, and speculative capital flows increased significantly. Speculative activity in the Euromarket was especially difficult to regulate, and MNCs were able to evade controls through transactions among their affiliates in different countries. Thus, MNCs became adept at moving their capital from one country to another to take advantage of interest rate spreads and expected exchange rate adjustments, and this increased capital mobility put growing pressure on states to realign their currency exchange rates. In efforts to prevent a run on their currencies, leaders often committed themselves to the established parities, severely limiting their policy options. Powerful domestic interest groups also prevented governments from instituting needed realignment of their currencies. As a result, modest changes in parities were difficult to institute, and the monetary regime became overly rigid despite the need for flexibility.[49]

To confront the problem of declining confidence in the U.S. dollar, proposals emerged in the 1960s to create a new artificial reserve asset. The United States initially opposed this idea because it wanted to maintain the dollar's reserve role, but it eventually changed its position to take pressure off the dollar in international money markets.[50] France, however, resented U.S. privileges as the top-currency state, and it wanted the United States to deal with its balance-of-payments problems before a new reserve was created. After several years of negotiation, IMF members finally agreed in 1969 to create a new international reserve, termed special drawing rights.[51]

Special drawing rights (SDRs) are artificial international reserves, created and managed by the IMF with the G-10's approval, which IMF members use in transactions to meet balance-of-payments financing needs. Decisions to allocate SDRs require approval by three-fifths of the IMF members with 85 percent of the voting power, because the EC insisted it should have a veto over SDR creation; this European veto power represented a decline in U.S. financial power. IMF members are allocated SDRs in proportion to their quotas so that those with the highest quotas (the G-5 countries) have received the most SDRs. SDRs have been allocated only twice: allocations of 9.3 billion SDRs in 1970, and of 12.6 billion SDRs in 1981. Initially, 35 SDRs were equal to $35 (U.S.) or an ounce of gold, but after the move to floating currencies (discussed later in this chapter), the SDR value was determined by a basket or weighted average of currencies: 16 currencies from 1974 to 1980; the G-5 currencies from 1981 to 2000; and the U.S. dollar, euro, Japanese yen, and British pound sterling since 2001. Because movements in different currencies tend to offset one another (i.e., some currencies rise while others fall in value), the SDR is more stable in value than any single currency in the basket. This stability makes the SDR attractive as a unit of account to the IMF and other IOs.[52]

The SDR, however, has not met the IMF's expectations as a reserve asset. At its 1976 annual meeting, the IMF set the objective of establishing the SDR as the principal reserve asset in the international monetary regime, and this decision was formalized in 1978 in the second amendment to the IMF Articles of Agreement. Nevertheless, SDRs accounted for less than 1.1 percent of IMF members' non-gold reserve assets as of December 2002. There are several reasons why the plans to make the SDR a major reserve asset were not realized. First, North-South conflict over SDRs has limited their role. When the DCs decided to create SDRs in 1969, they initially planned to limit their allocation to the G-10 states, but the IMF managing director insisted that SDRs should be allocated to all IMF members. The compromise agreement was to allocate SDRs to all IMF members, but in accordance with their quotas so that DCs received far more SDRs than LDCs. The South was obviously dissatisfied because most SDRs were allocated to large DCs that had the least need to supplement their reserves. As a result, the South proposed that a link be established between the creation of new SDRs and the transfer of resources to LDCs for development purposes. If LDCs received most of the new SDRs, this would benefit the South while providing an increase in liquidity.[53]

The DCs, however, argued that this link proposal would undermine the monetary integrity of the SDR, because it would blur the division between monetary policy and development assistance. They were particularly concerned that LDC needs for development assistance were almost limitless and might lead to the creation of an excessive amount of SDRs in terms of liquidity. The LDCs tried to allay this fear by noting that the G-10 would retain decision-making power over when to create new SDRs, but the DCs were unmoved and decided that any new SDRs should be allocated (as in the past) according to a country's IMF quota.[54] Because SDRs had been allocated only in 1970 and 1981, Eastern European and FSU countries that joined the IMF after 1981 had never received SDRs. In September 1997, the IMF Board of Governors therefore approved the fourth amendment of the Articles of Agreement to allow for a special one-time allocation of SDRs that would permit all IMF members to participate in the SDR system. However, this allocation was still not approved as of April 2003, and North-South acrimony over the method of allocating SDRs is one factor that delayed approval. (This was not the only factor, since the United States had also not endorsed the allocation of SDRs to Eastern European and FSU states as of April 2003.)[55]

A second factor limiting the role of SDRs has been the changing views of DCs. The DCs first approved the creation of SDRs in 1969 largely because they required additional liquidity to accumulate the reserves necessary to support continued growth in the global economy. However, several events discussed later in this chapter resolved the problem of inadequate liquidity and the Triffin dilemma: an end to the U.S. commitment to convert dollars into gold, a shift from fixed to flexible exchange rates, and a phasing out of controls on capital flows. Although a number of DCs have supported a one-time allocation of SDRs to the Eastern European and FSU states, DCs generally now think there is little need for SDRs. With an end to capital controls, DCs can easily borrow on capital markets to increase their reserve holdings, so they do not require the SDR system. However, some monetary experts point out that LDCs and transition economies cannot borrow as easily and require reserves such as SDRs to decrease their vulnerability to changes in international capital markets. During recent financial crises (discussed in Chapters 7 and 11), SDRs would have helped these countries "moderate the impact of capital outflows on exchange rates."[56] Despite these arguments, it is unlikely that SDRs will become an important reserve asset because of reservations in the North and because a truly international reserve unconnected with an economically powerful state or group of states such as the EU may simply be ahead of its time. Indeed, "no money has ever risen to a position of international preeminence that was not initially backed by a leading economy."[57]

The Demise of the Bretton Woods Monetary Regime

By the late 1960s, the Bretton Woods monetary regime had become untenable. France's President Charles de Gaulle was deliberately converting dollars into gold to bring about an end to U.S. hegemonic privilege as the key currency state, and the United States was making it more difficult for foreign central banks to change their dollars into gold. Although U.S. balance-of-payments deficits extended back to 1950, these deficits had resulted from foreign investment and loans the United States extended throughout the world. In 1971, however, the United States had its first balance-of-*trade* deficit since 1893, indicating that its trade competitiveness was seriously declining. On August 15, 1971, President Richard M. Nixon therefore suspended the official convertibility of the dollar into gold, and imposed a 10 percent tariff surcharge on all dutiable imports. These actions sent shockwaves throughout the world. At the time of the Nixon shocks, the U.S. share of international reserves had fallen from a postwar level of 50 percent to only 16 percent, and the EC's share had risen from 6.1 to 32.5 percent. In December 1971, the G-10 countries therefore agreed to lower the dollar's value by 10 to 20 percent vis-à-vis other major currencies through the first Smithsonian Agreement (negotiated at the Smithsonian Institution in Washington, D.C.). However, U.S. balance-of-payments deficits continued, and a second Smithsonian Agreement devaluing the dollar further was negotiated in February 1973.[58]

A multitude of problems confronted the Bretton Woods monetary regime by the early 1970s. First, although the U.S. role as the top-currency state was premised on the idea that it was an unrivaled economic hegemon, this no longer seemed to be the case. Second, as capital flows worldwide increased, the Bretton Woods system of pegged exchange rates became increasingly untenable. And third, the three requirements for adequate reserves—liquidity, confidence, and adjustment—all presented serious problems: The persistent U.S. balance-of-payments deficit contributed to a crisis of confidence in the dollar; countries were therefore reluctant to hold large supplies of U.S. dollars for liquidity purposes; and the dollar could not be adequately adjusted through devaluation when the United States became less competitive (the Smithsonian agreements were "too little, and too late"). After the first Smithsonian agreement, major DCs and LDCs held discussions in efforts to reform the international monetary regime. Two years of discussions ultimately failed, however, because of differences among the Americans, Europeans, and LDCs; destabilizing global changes such as the 1973 increase in OPEC oil prices; and Germany and France's preoccupation with establishing a European monetary system. Thus, it became evident that the Bretton Woods regime of fixed exchange rates would collapse and be replaced by a regime based on floating rates.[59]

THE REGIME OF FLOATING (OR FLEXIBLE) EXCHANGE RATES

The Bretton Woods agreement had outlawed freely floating exchange rates, so all the major trading nations were "living in sin" by 1973.[60] The IMF meeting in Jamaica in January 1976 finally legalized this situation by permitting each government to decide whether to establish a par value for its currency or to shift to floating rates. In a *free-floating* regime, member countries do not intervene in currency markets, and the market alone determines currency valuations. In recent years IMF members have in fact relied extensively on *managed floating,* in which central banks intervene to deal with disruptive conditions such as excessive fluctuations in exchange rates. Although managed floating is considered to be legitimate, the IMF calls on central banks to avoid *dirty floating,* or "manipulating exchange rates . . . in order to prevent effective balance of payments adjustment or to gain an unfair competitive advantage."[61] Today the monetary regime is mixed in nature: Major industrial countries such as the United States, Japan, and Canada (and a number of LDCs) independently float their currencies; the EU countries seek increased regional coordination of their policies; and many LDCs peg the value of their currencies to a key currency or basket of currencies. It is not surprising that some observers refer to the current system of monetary relations as a "nonsystem."[62]

The move to floating rates had an intellectual appeal for both some liberals and realists. Orthodox liberals in particular argued that floating rates were preferable because adjustment of international exchange rates would depend on market pressures rather than government involvement. Thus, as early as 1953 Milton Friedman wrote a classic article favoring the establishment of "a system of exchange rates freely determined in open markets, primarily by private transactions, and the simultaneous abandonment of direct controls over exchange transactions."[63] Although some liberals feared that floating rates would lead to instability because of speculative capital flows, as had occurred in the 1930s, Friedman argued that the instability during the 1930s had resulted more from fundamental economic and financial problems. Ironically, floating rates were also appealing to some realists because of the view that governments would be able to adopt independent monetary policies. In a fixed exchange regime, "monetary policy must be subordinated to the requirements of maintaining the peg, effectively eliminating the discretion of authorities." A floating regime by contrast "allows monetary policy to be set autonomously, as deemed appropriate in the domestic context (e.g., for stabilization purposes), and the exchange rate becomes a residual, following whatever path is consistent with the stabilization policy."[64] By the 1970s there were additional reasons for liberal economists to favor a shift to floating rates: With the marked increase in capital flows and speculative pressures, governments could no longer defend fixed exchange rates, and floating rates would contribute to rapid adjustments of international payments imbalances in response to market pressures.[65]

The results of the change to floating exchange rates, however, have not been as positive as expected. Most economists in the early 1970s underestimated the degree to which capital mobility would increase and disrupt exchange rates. Partly as a response to the return of orthodox liberalism, the United States and Britain rejected the postwar imposition of national controls on capital flows under Bretton Woods and began to allow capital to move more freely. Others soon followed the U.S. and British examples because countries were competing for the inflow of foreign investment. Thus, after the United States and Britain removed their capital controls in the 1970s, Australia, New Zealand, Japan, and the EC countries removed most of their capital controls in the 1980s. The removal of capital controls, combined with technological advances in areas such as telecommunications, contributed to a massive growth in speculative capital flows, which had far-reaching effects on the world's financial markets. Contrary to arguments of some advocates, floating exchange rates also do not necessarily permit capital-dependent emerging economies in East Asia and elsewhere to have independent monetary policies. When investors engage in massive selling of emerging economies' assets, their exchange rates are likely to fall dramatically. To prevent this, these economies have to raise their interest rates. Finally, economists underestimated the degree to which countries would engage in currency manipulation and the effect this would have on floating exchange rates.[66]

In view of these changes, two problems developed with the floating exchange rate regime: volatility and misalignment of exchange rates. *Volatility* refers to short-term instability in the exchange rate, and *misalignment* refers to the long-term departure of an exchange rate from its competitive level. The Bretton Woods pegged rate regime had limited the variability in exchange rates, but exchange rates are much more volatile under the floating system. Rapid and unexpected capital flows sometimes contribute to highly volatile exchange rates that create uncertainty, inhibit productive investments, and interfere with international trade. Misalignment, however, is more problematic than volatility because it can lead to prolonged changes in international competitiveness. Although some economists believed that misalignments would be eliminated with floating currencies, this has not been the case. Depending on whether a currency is under- or overvalued, misalignment can give a country substantial price advantages or disadvantages vis-à-vis its competitors. Both capital flows and currency manipulation contibute to the misalignment problem. For example, capital inflows into the United States as a favored investment market sometimes result in dollar overvaluation and a marked increase in the U.S. balance of trade deficit; and heavily managed floating through official large-scale purchases of currencies has enabled Japan and China to maintain lower exchange rates than market levels. As a result of capital flows and currency manipulation, exchange rate misalignment under the floating regime has been as high as 20 to 30 percent for the U.S. dollar and Japanese yen.[67]

The shift to floating rates also created a crisis of purpose for the IMF because the IMF's original role in stabilizing the pegged exchange rates under Bretton Woods largely disappeared. The DCs often held policy discussions regarding the floating regime in the G-5 and G-7, outside IMF auspices, and at G-7 summits, member governments engaged in a limited degree of policy coordination to stabilize monetary relations. For example, at the 1978 Bonn Summit the United States agreed to adopt policies to deal with its balance-of-payments deficits, and Germany and Japan agreed to adopt expansionary economic policies that would increase their demand for U.S. goods.[68] However, this limited degree of policy coordination ended with the Reagan administration, which lowered taxes and raised spending for military-defense purposes. These policies contributed to a huge U.S. government deficit, which exceeded $200 billion annually by the mid-1980s. To service its debt, the United States raised interest rates to attract foreign capital; but the increase in capital imports simply strengthened the U.S. dollar, and the U.S. balance-of-trade and payments deficits began to spiral out of control.

The Plaza-Louvre Accords

With the U.S. dollar continuing to appreciate in value and U.S. deficits climbing, the United States became far more concerned with exchange rates. In efforts to lower the value of the dollar, Treasury Secretary James Baker III assembled the G-5 finance ministers and central bank heads in New York City's Plaza Hotel in September 1985.

The G-5 agreed on joint intervention to raise the value of the major nondollar currencies through coordinated market intervention (i.e., by buying and selling currencies), and the United States in return promised to reduce government spending. Because the dollar depreciated significantly after the Plaza Agreement, the G-5 met at the Louvre in Paris in February 1987 to prevent its value from slipping even further. The major countries involved at that point were the *Group of Three*—the United States, Japan, and Germany.[69]

The Plaza and Louvre accords marked a shift to managed floating, in which the major governments intervened to correct serious volatility and misalignment of currencies. However, the major economies have not coordinated their interventions on a consistent basis since the Louvre accord. Although policy coordination is important for maintaining international currency stability, it is difficult to achieve because of the high degree of mobility of international capital flows.[70] The unwillingness of governments to accept constraints on adopting fiscal and monetary policies as they see fit also limits the degree to which policy coordination is likely to occur. Thus, the current floating monetary regime is far more unstable than liberal economists had predicted, and it is uncertain that the major DCs will coordinate their policies sufficiently to prevent future misalignment of currency rates.

ALTERNATIVES TO THE CURRENT MONETARY REGIME

With unstable global monetary relations under the flexible exchange rate regime, there has been considerable discussion about the need for monetary reform. The question therefore arises as to whether there are alternatives to floating exchange rates. A related question is whether there are alternatives to the dominance of the U.S. dollar under the current regime. Some economists point to the problems of volatility and misalignment of exchange rates under the floating regime and argue in favor of returning to some sort of pegged or fixed exchange rate regime.[71] However, a more commonly held view is that efforts "to re-establish a system of pegged but adjustable rates will . . . prove futile."[72] With the rise in international financial transactions, it has become increasingly difficult for states to defend pegged exchange rates. The only possible way to enforce capital controls at a tolerable cost would be through policy coordination among the major states, but such coordination is extremely difficult. Thus, the current global monetary regime is likely to retain its mixed characteristics, with DCs such as the United States, Japan, and Canada (and some LDCs) independently floating their currencies and with many LDCs pegging their currencies to a key currency or a basket of currencies.

In looking to alternatives to the current flexible exchange rate regime, many IPE scholars have focused on regional relationships. The most significant regional alternative is a monetary union, in which members substitute a common currency for their national currencies and cede monetary decision making to a single central agency. In addition to a few arrangements left over from the colonial era such as the Eastern Caribbean Currency Union, Europe's EMU is the only monetary union formed in recent years. Another type of regional system involves pegging the currencies of smaller states to the currency of a larger state or group of states. For example, several Latin American and Caribbean states have tied their currencies to the U.S. dollar. (This phenomenon is not only regional because some East Asian states have also linked their currencies to the U.S. dollar.) The sections that follow examine monetary relations in Europe, East Asia, and the Western Hemisphere and the likelihood of competition among the U.S. dollar, euro, and Japanese yen as international currencies.[73]

EUROPEAN MONETARY RELATIONS

With the future of global monetary relations uncertain, "the only initiative that might be held out as a serious experiment" in international monetary reform is taking place in Europe.[74] It is therefore important to examine the European approach to monetary relations. The Treaty of Rome creating the EC in 1957 provided specific details on eliminating trade barriers, but other than describing exchange rate policies as an issue of common concern, it did not identify monetary integration as one of the treaty's goals. Nevertheless, a number of practitioners and scholars have long considered monetary union in Europe to be worthy of consideration. Since the 1960s, a series of events have given concrete form to the idea of European monetary integration, and in May 1998, 11 EU members formally committed to replacing their national currencies with the euro as a single European currency. The following discussion examines the reasons why the EU established an EMU, the problems and tensions surrounding the formation of the EMU, and the implications of the EMU for Europe and the global monetary regime.

From 1958 to the late 1960s, the Bretton Woods monetary regime provided the EC with a framework for coordinating monetary policies and with some stability under the system of fixed exchange rates. Several changes in the 1960s, however, caused the EC countries to seriously consider proposals for regional monetary integration. First, growing U.S. balance-of-payments deficits resulted in decreased confidence in the U.S. dollar and a threat to exchange rate stability. This threat increased in the 1960s when President Johnson continued to pursue the Vietnam War at great expense to the United States and also launched ambitious domestic social programs. Second, rapid European progress in establishing a customs union and the development of the EC's Common Agricultural Policy increased the need for exchange rate stability among EC members.[75]

During a December 1969 EC summit meeting in The Hague, the six EC members proposed that a European monetary union be established and appointed Pierre Werner, the Luxembourg prime minister, as chair of a group to develop a detailed proposal. The 1970 Werner Report subsequently recommended the gradual completion of a monetary union by 1980 through a phased approach, including the coordination and convergence of fiscal and monetary policies and the reduction of exchange rate fluctuations among EC countries. However, the Werner Report's vagueness on policy details and the turmoil on currency markets resulting from President Nixon's decision to suspend the convertibility of the dollar into gold in August 1971 interfered with the implementation of the report. One of the few elements of the Werner plan to survive was a "snake in the tunnel" arrangement that limited exchange rates among

EC member currencies to a narrow band of +2.25 or −2.25 percent. However, the 1973–1974 oil price hike, the 1975 global recession, and different inflation rates among EC members made it impossible for countries with weaker currencies to adhere to the narrow fluctuation band. Thus, France, Ireland, Italy, and Britain soon left the snake agreement.[76]

By the late 1970s fluctuations in the value of the U.S. dollar and variability in EC exchange rates made it evident that the "snake" would require major changes if European currencies were to have a degree of stability. A *European Monetary System (EMS)* was therefore launched as a successor to the snake in March 1979, with two main features; an *exchange rate mechanism (ERM)* and a *European currency unit (ECU)*. The ERM was a form of adjustable peg system, similar to the original Bretton Woods regime. Participating countries decided on exchange rates for their currencies, setting bands beyond which the rates could not fluctuate (+2.25 to −2.25 percent for most EC countries). When the limits of a band were reached, central banks intervened to keep the exchange rates within the required levels. After consultation with other EMS members, countries could realign their currencies. The second feature, the ECU, was a new currency based on a weighted basket of the EMS countries' currencies. Although the ECU served as a common unit of account and was used in cross-border banking activity, it was not generally used for commercial transactions in goods and services.[77]

The EMS experienced a reasonable degree of success, contributing to European habits of cooperation on monetary issues from 1979 to the early 1990s. However, the EMS also had some major drawbacks because it was only a partial monetary union. For example, the EMS was subjected to frequent speculative attacks, and EC countries that could not keep their currency exchange rates within the narrow ERM band of +2.25 to −2.25 percent were permitted to move to a broader band of +6 to −6 percent. Some countries' currencies fluctuated within the broader band for most of 1979 to 1993. Britain also joined the EMS late, and some EC countries realigned their currencies more frequently than others. Furthermore, because the EMS depended largely on self-enforced rules, its credibility depended on policy leadership by the German central bank, which created political tensions with some other EC members.[78]

The EC's economic problems were not limited to monetary issues, and economic recession, declining competitiveness, and continuing barriers to intra-EC trade resulted in major efforts to increase the level of European integration in the 1980s–1990s. (European trade issues are discussed in Chapter 9.) In 1986, EC members signed the *Single European Act (SEA)* calling for completion of the internal market, or the removal of all barriers on the movement of goods, people, and capital within the EC by January 1, 1993. The SEA included a commitment to form an EMU, and in June 1988 the European Council established a committee to propose concrete steps toward this goal. The Delors Committee (chaired by Jacques Delors, president of the European Commission) proposed a three-stage process toward EMU: first, the coordination of monetary policies; second, the realignment of currency exchange rates; and third, the creation of a single currency under a new European central bank. Subsequently, negotiations resulted in the *Treaty on European Union* or *Maastricht Treaty* in December 1991, an agreement to establish an EMU in 1999. The EMU was to include the creation of a central bank and a single currency, central control over the money supply, and wide-ranging influence over national tax and financial policies.[79]

When EU members signed the Maastricht Treaty, many economists predicted that monetary integration would progress smoothly.[80] However, the steps toward monetary union have been difficult for a number of reasons. A major obstacle stemmed from the fact that the Maastricht agreement had rather rigid requirements for developing a single currency, which were included mainly at Germany's insistence. To join the EMU, countries had to have (or be showing substantial progress toward) budget deficits that did not exceed 3 percent of their GDPs, public debt no greater than 60 percent of their GDPs, and relatively low inflation rates. Only some EU countries were likely to meet these targets, and the required cuts in domestic welfare and social expenditures caused considerable discontent. For example, French workers in Paris staged massive strikes in December 1995 to protest planned cutbacks in social security programs.

Another related problem was that many Germans were fearful of sacrificing the deutsche mark, which reflected the country's economic strength, for what could be a much weaker euro. Germany accounts for about 25 percent of the EU's total economic output, and the deutsche mark was the second largest currency (after the U.S. dollar) held in official reserves of countries throughout the world. As a result, many Germans were concerned that weaker countries such as Italy could detract from the strength of the euro. Nevertheless, Germany's Chancellor Helmut Kohl strongly supported the EMU and staked his reputation on monetary integration. Other countries had different concerns. For example, Britain, Denmark, and Sweden did not seek membership in the EMU in the first wave for political as well as economic reasons. Britain in particular, was concerned about preserving its national sovereignty, and the fact that the new European Central Bank (ECB) was to be located in Frankfurt, Germany, delighted neither the British nor the French.

Despite the obstacles to implementing the Maastricht Treaty's goals, the European commitment to monetary union remained very much alive. Thus, 11 members of the EU formed an EMU in January 1999 and moved to adopt a new currency—the euro—in place of their national currencies. The 11 founding members of the EMU were Austria, Belgium, Finland, France, Germany, Ireland, Italy, Luxembourg, the Netherlands, Portugal, and Spain. Only four EU members did not participate in the agreement: Britain, Sweden, and Denmark chose not to join initially, and Greece was too weak economically. However, Greece was admitted to the EMU in January 2001. Under the EMU, the euro was introduced in wholesale financial markets first and at the retail-consumer level several years later. Although the euro became the legal currency of the EMU as of January 1, 1999, EMU member countries were not required to withdraw all national currencies until June 30, 2002.[81]

Since the EMU was formed, intense debates have continued over the benefits and costs of a common currency in Europe as well as over the possible future role of the euro as an international currency. Benefits of a monetary union include reduced exchange rate volatility and uncertainty, lower transaction costs, greater price transparency, and a better functioning internal market. The costs of a monetary union result mainly from the loss of the exchange rate as an available policy instrument; that is, an EMU member can no longer pursue an independent monetary policy by altering its exchange rate.[82] A good deal of the economic debate on costs versus benefits was framed by the work of Nobel laureate Robert Mundell many years earlier. In a 1961 article titled "A Theory of Optimum Currency Areas," Mundell posed a question that seemed radical at the time: When is it advantageous for regions to relinquish their monetary sovereignty in favor of a common currency?[83] An *optimum currency area,* which maximizes the benefits of using a common currency, has certain characteristics; for example, it is subject to common economic shocks, has a high degree of labor mobility, and has a tax system that transfers resources from economically strong to weak areas. Mundell's optimum currency area framework has been controversial, with economists differing on the policy implications for regions such as Europe. Nevertheless, the framework is highly influential because it has been used "to analyze choices between currency regimes."[84] As a strong supporter of a European common currency, Mundell has been called the "Father of the Euro."[85] Although optimum currency area studies help frame the *economic* debate on the costs and benefits of monetary integration, political factors such as the existence of a regional hegemon and a sense of community also play a major role in determining whether countries will join in a monetary union. Thus, one noted monetary specialist argues that "political conditions are most instrumental in determining the sustainability of monetary cooperation among sovereign governments."[86]

As for the issue of the euro as an international currency, the important questions are how soon will the euro emerge as a rival to the U.S. dollar, and how great a rival will it be? "Euro-enthusiasts" argue that the euro will soon emerge as a strong and stable currency that will challenge the dollar's dominant position. The euro area is one of the largest economies in the world, accounting for about 15 percent of world GNP, and its share of world exports is almost 16 percent, which is well above U.S. and Japanese shares. Furthermore, enthusiasts note that the euro zone has a strong external financial position as a large creditor area, whereas the United States now has a net foreign debt of more than $2 trillion. Investors will therefore want to diversify their portfolios from dollars into euros, and "in the long term, the emergence of a European pole may lead to the creation of a new international monetary architecture."[87]

"Euro-skeptics," on the other hand, note that Britain and thus London—Europe's major financial center—has to this point stayed out of the euro zone. Britain's reluctance to join raises questions regarding "the EU's official view that the single currency is both historically inevitable and arguably beneficial for all who adopt it."[88] Euro-skeptics also believe that risk-averse investors may be reluctant to substantially increase their euro holdings because Europe's financial markets are fragmented, and (other than the City of London) do not pose a major challenge to U.S. financial markets in terms of size, openness, and operational efficiency. It will be a long time, they argue, before European financial markets benefit from the EMU through economies of scale and lowering of costs. Furthermore, skeptics note that economic growth in the euro area has been unimpressive and that the fiscal rules designed to bind EMU members have an anti-growth bias. In addition, the governance structure of the EMU is fragmented, and no single body represents the EMU at the IMF or other international organizations (unlike trade where the European Commission represents the EU in the WTO). To this point, skeptics note, the dollar continues to be the favored vehicle for currency exchange; it is also the dominant international currency for invoicing of international trade and for financial claims, including stocks, bonds, bank deposits, and loans.[89] This book returns to a discussion of the challenge the euro poses to the U.S. dollar later in this chapter and in Chapter 12.

EAST ASIAN MONETARY RELATIONS

In contrast to Europe, formal currency links are lacking in East and Southeast Asia (usually referred to here as "Asia" for brevity). For a number of years, however, some analysts predicted that an Asian "yen bloc" would emerge because of Japan's position as a major exporter, top international creditor, and second largest national economy. When Japan experienced rapid economic growth during the 1980s, there were several indications of the yen's increasing influence. For example, the yen's share of the Eurobond market grew from about 5 percent to 13 percent from 1980 to 1993. Although the yen accounted for only 9 percent of global foreign exchange reserves, its share of reserves in Indonesia, the Philippines, Singapore, and Taiwan was more than 30 percent. Nevertheless, no country pegged its exchange rate specifically to the yen, and in East Asia most countries maintained currency links with the U.S. dollar (often with a basket of currencies in which the U.S. dollar had the most weight). Japan's traditional lack of openness in trade and finance posed obstacles to the yen's development as a major reserve for regional and global economic transactions. There were also political obstacles because Asian countries with harsh memories of Japan's occupation during World War II were reluctant to give it a more prominent role in the region. In addition, long-term rivalries between China and Japan indicated that neither would accept the other as a "regional currency hegemon."[90]

In July 1997 a financial crisis began in Thailand and then spread to much of East and Southeast Asia (see Chapters 7 and 11). The baht currency in Thailand was pegged to a basket of currencies with the U.S. dollar having the dominant weight, and some analysts thought the crisis "illustrated that the traditional exchange rate policy of pegging to the U.S. dollar can be incompatible with macroeconomic stability in the Asian countries."[91] Instead, they recommended that Asian countries peg their currencies more closely to the Japanese yen. Japan also took some actions designed to encourage regional solutions to the Asian financial problems. Most prominently, in September 1997 the Japanese government proposed that an Asian Monetary Fund (AMF) be formed to provide emergency balance-of-payments support to economies affected by the Asian financial crisis. The United States and IMF strongly opposed this move, arguing that an AMF would be lax on conditionality and therefore pose a threat to the IMF's effectiveness; but U.S. Treasury officials were in fact "even more concerned about a possible threat to the dollar in the region."[92]

Although the AMF plan was rejected, some regional monetary initiatives have appeared in East Asia, partly as a negative reaction to the conditions the IMF imposed in response to the financial crisis.[93] It is unlikely that these efforts to promote Asian monetary cooperation will take the form of a yen bloc because of Sino-Japanese rivalry and Japan's economic turnaround in recent years. Since the 1990s, Japan's economy has stagnated, largely as a result of problems with its domestic laws, customs, and institutions such as its fragile banking system. Although some analysts believe the yen's standing as an international currency could recover, others argue that the gradual decline of the yen's position is likely to continue. The yen's future prospects will depend on whether Japan can reform its banking sector and domestic economic laws and institutions and can shift to more open trade and financial policies. Japan has implemented some policies to liberalize its financial sector, but to institute additional reforms it will have to confront the vested interests of powerful domestic private and public actors.

Although a yen bloc does not seem likely, some scholars have pointed to a range of efforts to develop collective safeguards against future disruptions since the Asian financial crisis. For example, the 10 members of the Association of Southeast Asian Nations (ASEAN) have joined with Japan, China, and South Korea to discuss various plans for monetary cooperation such as the creation of a regional liquidity system. Nevertheless, it is unlikely that there is sufficient solidarity of views to form a monetary union or formal regional monetary institutions. Instead, East and Southeast Asia will probably "continue to rely primarily on informal arrangements and market processes rather than formal institutions to pursue their [monetary] objectives."[94]

THE U.S. DOLLAR AND REGIONALISM

As discussed, the U.S. dollar continues to serve as the top, albeit negotiated, international currency. The formation of the EMU has also contributed to a revival of interest in the issue of *dollarization,* or a country's decision to supplement or replace its own currency with another currency—usually within the same region. (The terminology is misleading, because the currency adopted may be not only the U.S. dollar but also the euro, yen, or some other currency.) U.S. debate over dollarization (or the use of the U.S. dollar) in Latin America stems back to the nineteenth century. From 1900 to 1915 U.S. policymakers often encouraged dollarization, but they reversed their policies and encouraged Latin American states to "de-dollarize" in the 1940s–1950s. Whereas the debate during these earlier periods concerned whether to adopt the U.S. dollar along with a country's national currency, when the debate revived in the 1990s the issue became whether to adopt the U.S. dollar as the exclusive currency of foreign countries. Indeed, Ecuador and El Salvador replaced their national currencies with the U.S. dollar in 2000 and 2001, respectively.[95]

The main attraction of dollarization to Latin American governments is association with the large dollar-based capital and goods markets and the increased foreign investment this would bring. With financial liberalization, partial dollarization has already spread to many Latin American countries, and the next step to full dollarization would therefore seem less extreme. However, there is also considerable Latin American nationalist opposition to the dollarization idea. U.S. supporters of dollarization believe it would promote U.S. trade and investment in Latin America during a period of negotiations for a Free Trade Area of the Americas (see Chapter 9). A report by Congressional staff members also indicates that dollarization would "help the dollar remain the premier international currency, a status the euro is now challenging."[96] However, U.S. support for dollarization at the highest political levels has in fact been quite limited. U.S. Federal Reserve and Treasury Department officials believe that Latin American countries benefit from some discretionary monetary authority and that dollarization could produce hostility toward the United States during difficult economic periods. The current U.S. policy of "passive neutrality" on dollarization is likely to continue unless a challenge by the euro to the dollar's top currency status triggers a competitive U.S. response.[97]

Dollarization in Latin America and Canada would be a highly asymmetrical process. In the EMU, *all* members sacrificed their currencies for a new common currency with collective managment of monetary policy, but with dollarization one country relinquishes its currency and control over monetary policy to another country. When a Latin American country adopts the U.S. dollar as legal tender, the U.S. "Federal Reserve has no responsibilities toward that country whatsoever."[98] Thus, some Canadian economists have debated the idea of forming a monetary union with the United States following the EMU model as an alternative to dollarization. However, this idea has been subject to widespread division in Canada on political as well as economic grounds, and there is no reason to believe the United States would be willing to relinquish its currency for a monetary union with its much smaller neighbor.[99]

In global monetary terms the euro is likely to pose a major challenge to the U.S. dollar in the future, and this could create serious problems for the United States. For example, the existence of a major competitor to the dollar will force the United States to pay higher interest rates to attract foreign capital to finance its large foreign debt. If U.S. policymakers believe that the euro poses such a challenge, this may cause them to become more supportive of dollarization to bolster the U.S. financial position. However, interventionist liberals would argue that regional approaches such as the EMU and dollarization are not sufficient for major economic powers such as the EU and United States, which have responsibilities for upholding the *global* monetary regime. In the current period of floating exchange rates, a degree of U.S.-EU-East Asian cooperation and policy coordination is necessary to prevent serious misalignment of currencies and to promote stability in the global monetary regime.[100]

CONCLUSION

In the 1940s the Bretton Woods negotiators opted for a monetary regime based on interventionist liberalism, in which exchange rates were pegged to the U.S. dollar and gold, the IMF provided short-term loans for balance-of-payments problems, and member states could impose controls on capital flows to maintain exchange rate stability. However, persistent U.S. balance-of-payments problems, combined with pressures for a return to orthodox liberalism, contributed to a shift from pegged to floating exchange rates in 1973 and to a gradual freeing of capital controls in the 1970s–1980s. Liberal interdependence theorists believe that advances in technology and communications have made these changes irrevocable and that to return to pegged exchange rates in "today's world of globalizing capital markets, capital controls would have to be fierce."[101] In 1973, only about $15 billion of currency was traded on world markets each day, and in 1983, the figure was still a modest $60 billion per day. Since 1983, however, currency trading has increased twenty-fold, aided by new financial instruments and advanced computers and telecommunications. Central bank reserves have grown far more slowly, and their ability to cope with currency traders has therefore decreased.[102] In the orthodox liberal view, the shift to floating currencies and the freeing of capital flows are positive developments enabling markets to function more freely, with little interference from the state.

Historical structuralists, by contrast, view the increased capital mobility as a highly negative development because the fear of capital outflows can force governments to adopt policies that adversely affect the poorest and weakest in society. If governments do not adopt capital-friendly policies, MNCs and international banks can readily shift their funds to more welcoming locations. Thus, governments are inclined to lower their tax rates on corporate income even if this means sacrificing social programs.[103] Increased capital mobility, according to historical structuralists, also adversely affects the working class. Unlike capital, labor is still largely immobile between countries, and countries with weaker labor unions will draw investment away from countries where labor unions are stronger and more independent.[104]

Many realists argue that the degree to which globalization has occurred in monetary and financial relations is greatly exaggerated. Indeed, they often present evidence to show that there was more openness to capital flows before World War I than there is today.[105] To the extent that global financial flows have increased in recent years, realists believe this has occurred with the permission and sometimes encouragement of the most powerful states, and that these states continue to dictate the terms for such transactions. Some writers combine realism with liberalism, arguing that powerful states initially adopted policies contributing to the globalization of finance, but that this globalization "has had unintended consequences for those who promoted it."[106] Thus, it may no longer be possible for states to regain control over the global market forces they unleashed. Realists also argue that states have a more important role in the current regime of floating exchange rates than many liberals would lead us to believe. Indeed, the Plaza and Louvre accords show that the DCs can manage exchange rates by intervening collectively in the market when they so choose. When this does not occur, it is because the most powerful states cannot agree on the need for, or type of, intervention, not because exchange rates are uncontrollable. Furthermore, realists remind us that this is primarily a world of *national* currencies, in which the U.S. dollar continues to be the top—albeit negotiated—currency. Efforts to increase the role of SDRs as an alternative to the dollar have been largely unsuccessful.

Despite the dollar's continued importance, confidence in the U.S. currency is problematic because of general U.S. economic decline. For example, the United States now accounts for only 20 percent of global output and 14 percent of global exports; and it is the world's largest debtor, even though countries with the world's key currencies have traditionally been international creditors.[107] In monetary relations, the U.S. percent of votes in the IMF decision-making bodies has steadily decreased from about 40 percent during the 1940s to 17.16 percent in 2002, and collective leadership has replaced unilateral U.S. leadership in some important areas of monetary and financial policy. With the relative decline in U.S. economic hegemony, some countries wishing to insulate themselves from instabilities in the flexible exchange rate regime are seeking regional alternatives. Of particular importance was the decision of most EU countries to form the EMU and replace their own currencies with the euro. There is a difference of views as to how much of a challenge the euro will pose to the U.S. dollar as the key international currency. Nevertheless, the creation of the euro has clearly shifted the playing field away from the realist world of exclusively national currencies. A number of analysts are looking not only to Europe but also to Asia and the Americas as possible future regional currency blocs. In this context, dollarization is currently being discussed in North America, but it continues to be a highly contentious issue.

Despite the relative decline of U.S. economic hegemony, it is is likely that the U.S. dollar will continue to be the top currency in at least the short- to medium-term future. Realists are concerned about the status of U.S. hegemony in the global monetary regime in the longer term, and liberals point to the need for greater trans-Atlantic monetary cooperation as the euro poses an increased challenge to the dollar. Many historical structuralists, by contrast, believe that these issues will have little significance for LDCs in the periphery of the global economy. The rich Northern states have dominated the South in global monetary relations, from this perspective, and they will continue to do so even if U.S. hegemony declines.

NOTES

1. Susan Strange, "Protectionism and World Politics," *International Organization* 39-2 (Spring 1985), p.257.
2. Benjamin J. Cohen, "Life at the Top: International Currencies in the Twenty-First Century," *Essays in International Economics,* no. 221 (Princeton: Princeton University, International Economics Section, December 2000), pp.2–4; Eric Helleiner, *States and the Reemergence of Global Finance: From Bretton Woods to the 1990s* (Ithaca: Cornell University Press, 1994), p.1; Joseph S. Nye, Jr., "Soft Power," *Foreign Policy* 80 (Fall 1990), pp.153–171.
3. Susan Strange, *Casino Capitalism* (Oxford: Basil Blackwell, 1986), p.29.
4. Benjamin J. Cohen, "Introduction," in Benjamin J. Cohen, ed., *The International Political Economy of Monetary Relations* (Aldershot: Elgar, 1993), pp.xi–xiv.
5. Peter B. Kenen, *The International Financial Architecture: What's New? What's Missing?* (Washington, D.C.: November 2001), pp.17–18.
6. Richard G. Lipsey, Douglas D. Purvis, and Peter O. Steiner, *Economics,* 5th ed. (New York: Harper & Row, 1985), pp.765–772; Benjamin J. Cohen, *Organizing the World's Money: The Political Economy of International Monetary Relations* (New York: Basic Books, 1977), pp.20–24.
7. David Calleo and Susan Strange, "Money and World Politics," in Susan Strange, ed., *Paths to International Political Economy* (London: Allen & Unwin, 1984), p.97.
8. On adjustment and financing see Mordechai E. Kreinin, *International Economics: A Policy Approach,* 6th ed. (San Diego: Harcourt Brace Jovanovich, 1991), pp.123–124; and Richard N. Cooper, *The Economics of Interdependence: Economic Policy in the Atlantic Community* (New York: McGraw-Hill, 1968), pp.13–23, chs. 7–9.
9. Ernest H. Preeg, *The Trade Deficit, the Dollar, and the U.S. National Interest* (Indianapolis: Hudson Institute, 2000), p.1; Joseph Quinlan and Marc Chandler, "The U.S. Trade Deficit: A Dangerous Obsession," *Foreign Affairs* (May/June 2001), p.87.
10. Quinlan and Chandler, "The U.S. Trade Deficit: A Dangerous Obsession," p.97.
11. William R. Cline, "The Impact of U.S. External Adjustment on Japan," and Kathryn M. Dominguez, "Foreign Exchange Intervention: Did It Work in the 1990s?," in C. Fred Bergsten and John Williamson, eds., *Dollar Overvaluation and the World Economy* (Washington, D.C.: Institute for International Economics, 2003), pp.179 and 218; Quinlan and Chandler, "The U.S. Trade Deficit: A Dangerous Obsession," p.88.

12. International Monetary Fund, *Balance of Payments Statistics Yearbook,* (Washington, DC: IMF, 2000), vol. 51, pt. 1, p.917.

13. Preeg, *The Trade Deficit, the Dollar, and the U.S. National Interest,* p.8. See also Catherine L. Mann, *Is the U.S. Trade Deficit Sustainable?* (Washington, D.C.: Institute for International Economics, 1999).

14. Cline, "The Impact of US External Adjustment on Japan," p. 176.

15. Ernest H. Preeg, "Exchange Rate Manipulation to Gain an Unfair Competitive Advantage," in Bergsten and Williamson, eds., *Dollar Overvaluation and the World Economy,* p. 270.

16. See Kenneth W. Dam, *The Rules of the Game: Reform and Evolution in the International Monetary System* (Chicago: University of Chicago Press, 1982), p.6; and Cohen, *Organizing the World's Money,* ch. 3.

17. Barry Eichengreen argues that the major powers' cooperation and willingness to undergo domestic adjustments when necessary were more important than British hegemony in maintaining the gold standard. See Barry Eichengreen, *Golden Fetters: The Gold Standard and the Great Depression, 1919–1939* (New York: Oxford University Press, 1992), ch. 2.

18. John Gerard Ruggie, "International Regimes, Transactions, and Change: Embedded Liberalism in the Postwar Economic Order," in Stephen D. Krasner, ed., *International Regimes* (Ithaca: Cornell University Press, 1983), pp.204–207; Ronald I. McKinnon, "The Rules of the Game: International Money in Historical Perspective," *Journal of Economic Literature* 31-1 (March 1993), pp.3–11.

19. Paul R. Krugman and Maurice Obstfeld, *International Economics: Theory and Policy,* 3rd ed. (New York: HarperCollins, 1994), p.507.

20. Charles P. Kindleberger, *The World in Depression* 1929–1939, rev. and enl. ed. (Berkeley: University of California Press, 1986), pp.46–49.

21. Peter Alexis Gourevitch, "Squaring the Circle: The Domestic Sources of International Cooperation," *International Organization* 50-2 (Spring 1996), pp.349–373. For arguments that domestic factors had a major role in the breakdown of monetary stability in the interwar period see Eichengreen, *Golden Fetters;* and Beth A. Simmons, *Who Adjusts? Domestic Sources of Foreign Economic Policy During the Interwar Years* (Princeton: Princeton University Press, 1994).

22. John Ruggie calls this the embedded liberal compromise. See Ruggie, "International Regimes, Transactions, and Change," pp.209–214.

23. Dam, *The Rules of the Game,* p.38; Edward M. Bernstein, "The Search for Exchange Stability: Before and After Bretton Woods," in Omar F. Hamouda, Robin Rowley, and Bernard M. Wolf, eds., *The Future of the International Monetary System: Change, Coordination or Instability?* (Aldershot: Elgar, 1989), p.29.

24. Eric Helleiner, "From Bretton Woods to Global Finance: A World Turned Upside Down," in Richard Stubbs and Geoffrey R. D. Underhill, eds., *Political Economy and the Changing Global Order* (Toronto: McClelland & Stewart, 1994), p.164; J. Keith Horsefield, ed., *The International Monetary Fund* 1945–1965: *Twenty Years of International Monetary Cooperation, Vol. 3: Documents* (Washington, DC: IMF, 1969), p.67.

25. *Articles of Agreement of the International Monetary Fund,* adopted July 22, 1944 (Washington, DC: IMF, 1993).

26. Sidney Dell, "On Being Grandmotherly: The Evolution of IMF Conditionality," *Essays in International Finance,* no. 144 (Princeton: Princeton University, October 1981); "Conditionality: Ensuring Effective Use of Revolving Resources," *IMF Survey—Supplement on the IMF,* 24 (September 1995), p.9.

27. *International Monetary Fund Annual Report—2002* (Washington, DC: IMF, 2002) p.146.

28. In 2002 Saudi Arabia, China, and Russia also appointed their own IMF executive directors, but they have fewer votes than the G-5 countries.

29. John H. Jackson, *The World Trading System: Law and Policy of International Economic Relations* (Cambridge, MIT Press, 2nd ed., 1997), p. 69.

30. Marc Williams, *International Economic Organizations and the Third World* (New York: Harvester Wheatsheaf, 1994), pp.67–68; Stephen D. Krasner, *Structural Conflict: The Third World Against Global Liberalism* (Berkeley: University of California Press, 1985), pp.138–140; Tyrone Ferguson, *The Third World and Decision Making in the International Monetary Fund: The Quest for Full and Effective Participation* (London: Pinter, 1988), pp.90–91.

31. A group of 32 economists first identified the problems of liquidity, confidence, and adjustment. See Fritz Machlup and Burton G. Malkiel, eds., *International Monetary Arrangements: The Problem of Choice: Report on the Deliberations of an International Study Group of 32 Economists* (Princeton: Princeton University, International Finance Section, 1964), p.24.

32. Dam, *The Rules of the Game*, pp.64–69; Ruggie, "International Regimes," p.223; Cohen, *Organizing the World's Money*, pp.94–97.

33. John Charles Pool, Stephen C. Stamos, and Patrice Franko Jones, *The ABCs of International Finance*, 2nd ed. (Lexington: Heath, 1991), pp.67–68; Beth V. Yarbrough and Robert M. Yarbrough, *The World Economy: Trade and Finance*, 3rd ed. (Fort Worth: Harcourt Brace, 1994), p.640.

34. Charles P. Kindleberger, "Dominance and Leadership in the International Economy: Exploitation, Public Goods and Free Rides," *International Studies Quarterly* 25-2 (June 1981), p.248.

35. Marina V. N. Whitman, "Leadership Without Hegemony," *Foreign Policy* 20 (Fall 1975), p.140; "Will the Buck Stop Here?" *The Economist*, November 12–18, 1994, p.88.

36. Robert A. Isaak, *Managing World Economic Change: International Political Economy*, 2nd ed. (Englewood Cliffs: Prentice-Hall, 1995), pp.84–85.

37. See Robert Triffin, *Gold and the Dollar Crisis: The Future of Convertibility*, rev. ed. (New Haven: Yale University Press, 1961).

38. Harold James, *International Monetary Cooperation Since Bretton Woods* (Washington, DC, and New York: IMF and Oxford University Press, 1996), pp.179–181; Dominick Salvatore, *International Economics* (Upper Saddle River: Prentice-Hall, 6th ed., 1996), pp.453–457.

39. Helleiner, *States and the Reemergence of Global Finance*, pp.81–100; Michael C. Webb, *The Political Economy of Policy Coordination: International Adjustment Since 1945* (Ithaca: Cornell University Press, 1995), p.16.

40. Susan Strange, *Sterling and British Policy: A Political Study of an International Currency in Decline* (London: Oxford University Press, 1971), p.209.

41. Strange, *Sterling and British Policy*, pp.5, 17.

42. C. Fred Bergsten and C. Randall Henning, *Global Economic Leadership and the Group of Seven* (Washington, DC: Institute for International Economic, 1996), pp.22–23.

43. Hazel J. Johnson, *Global Financial Institutions and Markets* (Oxford: Blackwell, 2000), p.411.

44. Although the United States attended meetings, it was not until September 1994 that Alan Greenspan, governor of the U.S. Federal Reserve, occupied the seat reserved for him in the BIS. See Age F. P. Bakker, *International Financial Institutions* (New York: Longman, 1996), ch. 6; Johnson, *Global Financial Institutions and Markets*, pp.410–411.

45. Keith J. Horsefield, *The International Monetary Fund, 1945–65: Twenty Years of Monetary Cooperation* (Washington, DC: IMF, 1969), vol. 1, p.514.

46. Ngaire Woods, "A Third World Voice within the IMF?" *The Round Table* 314 (April 1990), p.196. See also C. Randall Henning, "The Group of Twenty-Four: Two Decades of

Monetary and Financial Co-operation Among Developing Countries," in United Nations Conference on Trade and Development, *International Monetary and Financial Issues for the 1990s–Vol. 1* (New York: United Nations, 1992), pp.137–154.

47. Barry Eichengreen and Peter B. Kenen, "Managing the World Economy Under the Bretton Woods System: An Overview," in Peter B. Kenen, ed., *Managing the World Economy: Fifty Years After Bretton Woods* (Washington, DC: Institute for International Economics, 1994), pp.26–34.

48. Krugman and Obstfeld, *International Economics,* pp.311–313; Marin Bronfenbrenner and Yasukichi Yasuba, "Economic Welfare," in Kozo Yamamura and Yasukichi Yasuba, eds., *The Political Economy of Japan: The Domestic Transformation, Vol. 1* (Stanford: Stanford University Press, 1987), p.100.

49. Helleiner, *States and the Reemergence of Global Finance,* p.102; John Williamson and C. Randall Henning, "Managing the Monetary System," in Kenen, ed., *Managing the World Economy,* p.89.

50. For a discussion of the reasons for the U.S. policy shift, see John S. Odell, *U.S. International Monetary Policy: Markets, Power, and Ideas as Sources of Change* (Princeton: Princeton University Press, 1982), pp.79–164.

51. For a discussion of the lengthy negotiations leading to the creation of SDRs, see Susan Strange, *International Monetary Relations* (London: Oxford University Press, 1976), pp.229–262.

52. Pierre-Paul Schweitzer, "Political Aspects of Managing the International Monetary System," *International Affairs* 52-2 (April 1976), p.214; "What is the SDR?," *IMF Survey Supplement* 31 (September 2002), p.28; Graham Bird, "The Political Economy of the SDR: The Rise and Fall of an International Reserve Asset," *Global Governance* 4-3 (July 1998), p.378, fn. 10. Long before the creation of SDRs, Keynes had proposed introducing a new international reserve asset which he called "bancor"; but this proposal was rejected at the 1944 Bretton Woods conference.

53. The idea of linking development assistance to international liquidity creation was not new. Maxwell Stamp is credited with making the first linkage proposal in 1958. See Hon. Maxwell Stamp, "The Fund and the Future," *Lloyds Bank Review* (October 1958), pp.14–20.

54. Graham Bird, *The International Monetary System and the Less Developed Countries,* 2nd ed. (London: Macmillan, 1982), p.254. For a discussion of the link debate, see Williamson, *The Failure of World Monetary Reform,* pp.143–147.

55. For a discussion of the disagreements over a third allocation of SDRs see Bird, "The Political Economy of the SDR," pp.363–377.

56. Peter B. Clark, quoted in "SDRs Could Meet Growing Demand for Reserves at No Cost while Reducing Systemic Risk," *IMF Survey* 32-2 February 3, 2003, pp.28–29.

57. Cohen, "Life at the Top," pp.5–6.

58. For a discussion of President Nixon's August 1971 decision and the Smithsonian agreements, see Robert Solomon, *The International Monetary System, 1945–1981,* 2nd ed. (New York: Harper & Row, 1982), pp.176–234.

59. For a discussion of the failed negotiations, see John Williamson, *The Failure of World Monetary Reform, 1971–74* (Sunbury-on-Thames: Nelson, 1977).

60. Cohen, *Organizing the World's Money,* p.115. Unlike other countries in the Bretton Woods regime, Canada had floated its currency from 1950 to 1962. The United States (and IMF) had agreed to this exception partly because of its "special relationship" with Canada. See A. F. W. Plumptre, *Three Decades of Decision: Canada and the World Monetary System, 1944–75* (Toronto: McClelland and Stewart, 1977).

61. *Articles of Agreement of the IMF,* Article 4, section 1-iii.

62. Yusuke Kashiwagi, "Future of the International Monetary System and the Role of the IMF," in Bretton Woods Commission, *Bretton Woods: Looking to the Future, Background Papers* (Washington, DC: Bretton Woods Committee, July, 1994), p.C-1.

63. Milton Friedman, "The Case for Flexible Exchange Rates," *Essays in Positive Economics* (Chicago: University of Chicago Press, 1953), p.203.

64. J. Lawrence Broz and Jeffry A. Frieden, "The Political Economy of International Monetary Relations," in *Annual Review of Political Science 2001*, vol. 4, pp.323–324.

65. John Williamson, *The Exchange Rate System*, rev. ed. (Washington, DC: Institute for International Economics, 1985), p.9; Michael Devereux and Thomas A. Wilson, "International Co-ordination of Macroeconomic Policies: A Review," *Canadian Public Policy* 15 (February 1989), pp.S22–S23; Kashiwagi, "Future of the International Monetary System and the Role of the IMF," p.C-1.

66. Helleiner, *States and the Reemergence of Global Finance*, pp.115–116; Gordon G. Thiessen, "Foreign Exchange Markets Viewed from a Macro-Policy Perspective," *Canadian Public Policy* 15 (February 1989), p.S68; Zanny Minton Beddoes, "From EMU to AMU? The Case for Regional Currencies," *Foreign Affairs* 78-4 (July/August, 1999), p.10.

67. Williamson, *The Exchange Rate System*, pp.9–10 and 39; Preeg, "Exchange Rate Manipulation to Gain an Unfair Competitive Advantage," pp.267–284.

68. Devereux and Wilson, "International Co-ordination of Macroeconomic Policies," pp.S23–S24.

69. Williamson and Henning, "Managing the Monetary System," p.100.

70. For a discussion of the difficulties in bringing about policy coordination, see Webb, *The Political Economy of Policy Coordination*.

71. The Nobel laureate economist Robert Mundell has been a strong (and controversial) defender of fixed exchange rates and the gold standard as an anchor for price stability.

72. Barry Eichengreen, *International Monetary Arrangements for the 21st Century* (Washington, DC: Brookings Institution, 1994), p.5.

73. Benjamin J. Cohen, "Are Monetary Unions Inevitable?," *International Studies Perspectives* 4-3 (August 2003), pp.276–277; Kashiwagi, "Future of the International Monetary System and the Role of the IMF," p.C-3.

74. Barry Eichengreen, "Prerequisites for International Monetary Stability," in Bretton Woods Commission, *Bretton Woods: Looking to the Future*, p.C-50.

75. Michele Fratianni and Jürgen von Hagen, *The European Monetary System and European Monetary Union* (Boulder: Westview Press, 1992), pp.11–12.

76. David R. Cameron, "Transnational Relations and the Development of European Economic and Monetary Union," in Thomas Risse-Kappen, ed., *Bringing Transnational Relations Back In: Non-State Actors, Domestic Structures and International Institutions* (Cambridge: Cambridge University Press, 1995), pp.39–41; Andrew Britton and David Mayes, *Achieving Monetary Union in Europe* (London: Sage Publications, 1992), pp.6–9; A. J. Kondonassis and A. G. Malliaris, "Toward Monetary Union of the European Community: History and Experiences of the European Monetary System," *American Journal of Economics and Sociology* 53-3 (July 1994), pp.292–294; Helmut Schlesinger, "On the Way to a New Monetary Union: The European Monetary Union," *Federal Reserve Bank of St. Louis Review* 76-3 (May/June 1994), p.4; Malcolm Levitt and Christopher Lord, *The Political Economy of Monetary Union* (London: Macmillan, 2000), pp.29–31.

77. A common unit of account was not a new idea in Europe and dated back to the 1950s when the six EC members formed a European Payments Union and used a European unit of account. Paul De Grauwe, *The Economics of Monetary Union*, 2nd rev. ed. (Oxford: Oxford University Press, 1994), pp.98–102; Levitt and Lord, *The Political Economy of Monetary Union*, pp.31–35.

78. Levitt and Lord, *The Political Economy of Monetary Union,* pp.31–42.
79. Sylvester C. W. Eijffinger and Jakob de Haan, *European Monetary and Fiscal Policy* (Oxford: Oxford University Press, 2000), pp.4–7; Michael H. Abbey and Nicholas Bromfield, "A Practitioner's Guide to the Maastricht Treaty," *Michigan Journal of International Law* 15-4 (Summer 1994), pp.1329–1357.
80. Brian K. Kruzmann, "Challenges to Monetary Unification in the European Union: Sovereignty Reigning Supreme?" *Denver Journal of International Law and Policy* 23-1 (Fall 1994), p.158.
81. "Fanfare for the Euro," *The Economist,* May 2, 1998, p.45.
82. For a discussion of the costs and benefits of a monetary union see Eijffinger and de Haan, *European Monetary and Fiscal Policy,* pp.16–26.
83. Robert A. Mundell, "A Theory of Optimum Currency Areas," *American Economic Review* 51-4 (September 1961), pp.657–665. Other contributors to the theory of optimum currency areas in the 1960s–1970s were Ronald I. McKinnon, Peter B. Kenen, and W. Max Corden.
84. James W. Dean, "Robert A. Mundell," in Abu N. M. Wahid, ed., *The Frontiers of Economics: Nobel Laureates of the Twentieth Century* (Westport: Greenwood Press, 2002), p.383.
85. See Robert A. Mundell, "Uncommon Arguments for Common Currencies," in Harry G. Johnson and Alexander K. Swoboda, eds., *The Economics of Common Currencies* (London: Allen & Unwin, 1973), pp.114–132; C. Randall Henning and Pier Carlo Padoan, *Transatlantic Perspectives on the Euro* (Washington, DC: Brookings Institution, 2000), pp.6–12.
86. Benjamin J. Cohen, "Beyond EMU: The Problem of Sustainability," in Barry Eichengreen and Jeffry Frieden, eds., *The Political Economy of European Monetary Unification* (Boulder: Westview Press, 1994), p.152.
87. A. Bénassy, A. Italianer, and Jean Pisani-Ferry, "The External Implications of the Single Currency," *Économie et Statistique,* (1993), p.9; C. Fred Bergsten, "America and Europe: Clash of the Titans?," *Foreign Affairs* 78-2 (March/April 1999), pp.26–27.
88. "Britain and the Euro: What a Pity. What a Relief," *The Economist,* June 14, 2003, p. 46.
89. Benjamin J. Cohen, *The Geography of Money* (Ithaca: Cornell University Press, 1998), pp.156–161; Eijffinger and de Haan, *European Monetary and Fiscal Policy,* pp.165–174. Cohen, "Life at the Top," pp. 2–3.
90. David D. Hale, "Is It a Yen or a Dollar Crisis in the Currency Market?" in Brad Roberts, ed., *New Forces in the World Economy* (Cambridge: MIT Press, 1996), pp.304–320; Jeffrey A. Frankel and Shang-Jun Wei, "Is a Yen Bloc Emerging?" in symposium on "Economic Cooperation and Challenges in the Pacific," *Joint U.S.-Korea Academic Studies* 5 (1995), pp.145–175.
91. Chi Hung Kwan, "The Possibility of a Yen Bloc Revisited," *ASEAN Economic Bulletin* 17-2 (August 2000), p.218.
92. Cohen, "Life at the Top," p.18; On the AMF proposal see Chang Li Lin, "The Economics and Politics of Monetary Regionalism in Asia," *ASEAN Economic Bulletin* 18-1 (April 2001), pp.103–118.
93. For one interpretation of the East Asian reaction, see Richard Higgott, "The Asian Economic Crisis: A Study in the Politics of Resentment," *New Political Economy* 3-3 (1998), pp.333–356.
94. Cohen, "Are Monetary Unions Inevitable?," pp.286–287. For discussion of changes in East Asian attitudes toward monetary regionalism, see Heribert Dieter, "Exploring Alternative Theories of Economic Regionalism From Trade to Finance in Asian Co-operation?," *Review of International Political Economy* 10-3 (August 2003), pp.430–454; and Paul Bowles, "Asia's Post-Crisis Regionalism: Bringing the State Back In, Keeping the United States Out," *Review of International Political Economy* 9-2 (Summer 2002), pp.230–256.

95. For a historical discussion of the dollarization issue in Latin America, see Eric Helleiner, "Dollarization Diplomacy: U.S. Policy towards Latin America Coming Full Circle?," *Review of International Political Economy* 10-3 (August 2003), pp.406–429.

96. Kurt Schuler and Robert Stein, quoted in Helleiner, "Dollarization Diplomacy," p. 422; Kenneth P. Jameson, "Latin America and the Dollar Bloc in the Twenty-First Century: To Dollarize or Not?," *Latin American Politics and Society* 43-4 (Winter 2001), pp.1–35.

97. Benjamin J. Cohen, "U.S. Policy on Dollarisation: A Political Analysis," *Geopolitics* 7-1 (Summer, 2002), pp. 63–84.

98. Beddoes, "From EMU to AMU?," p.12. Even in the case of the EMU, some argue that Germany will dominate the monetary union because of its economic size. See also Willem H. Buiter, "The EMU and the NAMU: What is the Case for North American Monetary Union?" *Canadian Public Policy* 25-3 (1999), pp.285–305.

99. For Canadian views on the idea of monetary union with the United States see Herbert G. Grubel, *The Case for the Amero: The Economics and Politics of a North American Monetary Union* (Vancouver: Fraser Institute Critical Issues Bulletin, 1999); and David Laidler, "Canada's Exchange Rate Options," *Canadian Public Policy* 25-3 (1999), pp. 324–332.

100. Bergsten, "America and Europe," pp.26–29.

101. Richard G. Lipsey, "Agendas for the 1988 and Future Summits," *Canadian Public Policy* 15 (February 1989), p.S90.

102. "Big: The Foreign-Exchange Market," *The Economist,* September 23, 1995, pp.63–64.

103. The standard rate of corporate income tax in OECD countries did in fact fall from 43 percent in 1986 to 33 percent in 1995, while the average tax rate for workers increased. See "Survey: World Economy," *The Economist,* September 20, 1997, p.33.

104. Stephen Gill and David Law, "Global Hegemony and the Structural Power of Capital," in Stephen Gill, ed., *Gramsci, Historical Materialism and International Relations* (Cambridge: Cambridge University Press, 1993), p.108.

105. Paul Hirst and Grahame Thompson, *Globalization in Question: The International Economy and the Possibilities of Governance* (Cambridge: Polity Press, 1996), p.27.

106. Ethan B. Kapstein, *Governing the Global Economy: International Finance and the State* (Cambridge: Harvard University Press, 1994), p.6. See also Helleiner, *States and the Reemergence of Global Finance.*

107. "Will the Buck Stop Here?" *The Economist,* November 12, 1994, p.88.

Foreign Debt and Financial Crises

I n the early 1980s an international debt crisis erupted that was "one of the most trau-
matic international financial disturbances" of the twentieth century.[1] Debt crises
had occurred during the nineteenth century, and widespread defaults on loans in
the 1930s had severely disrupted capital flows to Latin America and Southern and
Eastern Europe. Nevertheless, the world seemed unprepared for the 1980s debt crisis, which threatened the international banking system as well as some of the largest
LDCs. This chapter focuses primarily on the origins of the 1980s debt crisis and strategies adopted to deal with it; the effects of the crisis on debtors, creditors, and international banks; and the roles of the United States, IMF, and World Bank. The latter part
of this chapter also discusses the East and Southeast Asian (henceforth "Asian") financial crisis beginning in May 1997, which resulted in the collapse of some currencies,
and a sharp decrease in capital formation and economic output. Whereas the economic development aspects of the Asian financial crisis are discussed in detail in
Chapter 11, this chapter draws comparisons between the debt and financial crises and
the impact of these crises on the global management of debt and financial problems.

WHAT IS A DEBT CRISIS?

As discussed in Chapter 6, a country has a current account deficit when its payments
abroad are greater than those it receives. A government that chooses to finance rather
than adjust to its deficits must borrow from external credit sources and/or decrease its
foreign exchange reserves. If the government continues to borrow, it may be burdened
with growing foreign debts. In determining the severity of a country's debt problem, we
need to know not only the size of the debt, but also whether the country has the ability
and commitment to service its debt repayments. A "debt crisis" results when a country
lacks sufficient foreign exchange to make the principal and/or interest payments on its
debt obligations. Debt crises vary in severity and in the length of time and types of measures required to bring about a resolution.[2] This is a standard definition of a debt crisis,

but there are also more subjective definitions. For example, the North tended to define the 1980s debt crisis as a threat to "the stability of the international financial system" resulting from "the onset of widespread difficulties in servicing the mountain of developing country debt." The South, by contrast, defined the debt crisis as "a crisis of development, one element of the deepest economic downturn since the Great Depression, which had begun for some developing countries after the first oil shock."[3]

A number of authors have examined the similarities and differences between the 1980s debt crisis and earlier crises.[4] One significant difference relates to changes in lending mechanisms. During the 1920s, most lending to Latin America occurred through the bond markets, and therefore country debt was held by numerous individual bondholders in many different countries. When LDCs defaulted on their debts in the 1930s, the losses were fragmented among the many individual bondholders. In the 1970s, by contrast, private bank lending to middle-income LDCs greatly increased. When the debtor countries threatened to default on their loans in the 1980s, the possible losses were therefore much more concentrated in the largest commercial banks, which occupied a central position in international finance. In 1982 the nine largest U.S. banks had loans outstanding to 17 highly indebted countries amounting to 194 percent of the banks' capital and reserves, and a major debt default could have affected the core of the entire banking system.

Because the 1980s debt crisis posed a serious threat to international financial stability, creditor governments felt more pressure to intervene in the debt-settlement process.[5] Thus, another historical difference relates to the role of IOs and Northern states. In earlier periods of default, international institutions to deal with debt problems were almost nonexistent, and governments were less willing to intervene. During the 1980s, by contrast, the IMF pressured private banks to continue lending to LDC debtors on one hand, and debtor countries to alter their economic policies on the other. There was also no hegemonic power to deal with the 1930s debt crisis, but the United States filled this position in the 1980s. Together, the United States and IMF orchestrated the response in the 1980s, and other actors such as the World Bank, Paris and London Clubs, and Bank for International Settlements had supporting roles.[6]

THE ORIGINS OF THE 1980S DEBT CRISIS

The debt crisis began in August 1982 when Mexico announced it could no longer service its public sector debt obligations; this produced shock waves because Mexico's external debt was estimated at $78 billion by the end of 1981. However, earlier warning signs of a possible crisis had been largely ignored. From 1976 to 1980, a number of LDCs, including Zaïre, Argentina, Peru, Sierra Leone, Sudan, and Togo, had been involved in debt rescheduling negotiations, and the external debt of LDCs in general had increased six-fold to $500 billion between 1972 and 1981. Foreign debt was also a growing problem in Eastern Europe, and Poland's indebtedness had reached serious proportions by 1981.[7] After Mexico's 1982 announcement, the debt crisis spread rapidly as private creditor banks moved to decrease their loan exposure to other LDC borrowers. Thus, 25 LDCs requested a restructuring of their commercial bank debt by late 1982, and in 1983 the World Bank reported that "almost as many developing countries have had to reschedule loans in the last two years as in the previous twenty-five years."[8]

Analysts have differing views regarding the causes of the 1980s debt crisis that stem partly from their divergent ideological perspectives. Most commonly, they attribute the crisis to unexpected changes in the global economy, irresponsible behavior of lenders, irresponsible behavior of debtors, and the South's dependence on the North.

Unexpected Changes in the Global Economy

Some observers attribute the debt crisis primarily to unexpected global economic changes.[9] The first external shocks occurred in the early 1970s, when there was a sharp rise in grain and oil prices. During the late 1960s, major surpluses of wheat and grain had accumulated, leading to a decline in international food prices and production cutback programs in the United States, Canada, and some other grain-exporting countries. As a result of these production cutbacks, the world was highly vulnerable to unanticipated events such as inclement weather and crop shortfalls in the Soviet Union, which resulted in massive Soviet grain purchases and serious foodgrain shortages. In 1972–1973, global food stocks fell to their lowest level in 20 years, the volume of food aid was drastically reduced, and there were substantial increases in foodgrain prices.[10] After the October 1973 Middle East war, the Arab countries in OPEC also managed to drastically raise the price of oil by limiting supply. Thus, LDCs that imported oil as well as food were doubly hit by the food and oil crises.

Whereas many importing states were severely hurt by the increased oil prices, the OPEC states accumulated unprecedented amounts of excess reserves or "petrodollars," which they deposited in the largest commercial banks. These banks recycled many of the petrodollars through loans to middle-income LDCs, which were considered to be creditworthy for receiving commercial bank loans. Thus, about 60 percent of external financing for non-OPEC LDCs came from commercial bank credits from 1974 to 1979.[11] A second oil shock occurred in 1979, when OPEC more than doubled its prices. The private banks provided additional loans to help LDCs pay for the new round of oil price increases, and they offered loans to oil-exporting LDCs to help develop their industries and diversify their economies.

The second oil shock contributed to a severe economic contraction in the North and to the worst global recession since the 1930s. As a result, LDCs faced a sharp decline in demand for their commodity exports, and they found it increasingly difficult to earn foreign exchange to service their debts. The 1979 oil price increases also produced inflationary pressures, which the DCs sought to control by raising interest rates. The U.S. Reagan administration's need to borrow abroad to cover its huge federal budget deficits was yet another source of upward pressure on interest rates. The creditor banks were providing short-term loans at variable interest rates, and the impact of the higher rates on LDC debt levels was rapid and severe.[12] It may seem ironic that the debt crisis began with Mexico—an oil exporter. Oil-exporting LDCs, however, had also borrowed private funds to launch ambitious development projects without anticipating that oil prices—and their oil revenues—would fall sharply after 1979. Thus, unexpected global economic changes in the 1970s–1980s contributed to external debt problems for LDC oil exporters as well as importers.

Although unanticipated global changes were an important factor in the debt crisis, this was certainly not the only cause. For example, external shocks do not explain why the East and Southeast Asians fared far better than the Latin Americans (see discussion below). Both commercial banks and debtor states often favor the external shocks explanation for the debt crisis because it awards "primary responsibility to economic policy shifts beyond their control."[13] Nevertheless, the policies of lenders and borrowers must also be considered as explanations for the crisis.

Irresponsible Behavior of Lenders

Historical structuralists and some interventionist liberals consider irresponsible behavior by creditor banks to be a major cause of the debt crisis. Commercial banks, according to this perspective, engaged in overlending without being sufficiently concerned about the creditworthiness of borrowers or the activities they were financing. When the OPEC states deposited large amounts of petrodollars in private commercial banks (mainly in New York and London), the banks aggressively sought to increase their loan activity in the South. The competition to lend funds combined with inflationary conditions meant that large commercial banks charged extremely low interest rates, which did not give LDCs adequate signals as to when to stop borrowing. By the time interest rates rose sharply in the early 1980s, LDC debtors had become overly dependent on commercial bank loans, and this heightened the severity of the crisis.[14] Thus, the commercial banks were often accused of "loan pushing" that encouraged "debtor countries to increase their liabilities."[15]

Some critics argue that the banks did not engage in overlending completely on their own, and that Northern governments shared responsibility for this development. After the first oil shock in 1973, the DCs adopted policies that encouraged the flow of private bank funds to the South. For example, in 1974 the central banks in the G-10 countries provided assurances that they would assist banks recycling petrodollars if they encountered financial difficulties. The IMF also introduced new lending programs for LDC oil importers such as the 1974 oil facility and the 1974 Extended Fund Facility, which encouraged private banks to upgrade their own lending activities. Furthermore, the gradual lifting of capital controls in the North (discussed in Chapter 6) eased the process by which U.S. and Western European banks could recycle surplus petrodollars to the South. From this perspective, both creditor banks and the DCs in which they were located shared responsibility for overlending, which was a major cause of the debt crisis.[16]

Irresponsible Behavior of Borrowers

Many liberal theorists, especially orthodox liberals, attribute primary responsibility for the debt crisis to the imprudent behavior of borrowing states. These critics argue that LDCs sought the easy route of borrowing from private banks in the 1970s to avoid the conditionality requirements of IMF loans. Unlike the IMF, private banks were not inclined (and did not have legal authority) to impose policy conditions on their loans to sovereign governments. Basic IMF principles—that indebted governments should not have unlimited access to balance-of-payments financing and should undergo adjustment measures—were jeopardized because private funds were so accessible. As a liberal-economic institution, the IMF itself endorsed this view in its 1977 *Annual Report:*

> Access to private sources of balance of payments finance may . . . in some cases permit countries to postpone the adoption of adequate domestic stabilization measures. This can exacerbate the problem of correcting payments imbalances, and can lead to adjustments that are politically and socially disruptive when the introduction of stabilization measures becomes unavoidable.[17]

Some liberals point out that LDC governments sometimes *want* IMF conditionality to help them push through unpopular economic reforms. For example, Robert Putnam argues that international negotiations are a two-level game which may enable "government leaders to do what they privately wish to do, but are powerless to do domestically." In Italy's negotiations with the IMF, Putnam notes, "domestic conservative forces exploited IMF pressure to facilitate policy moves that were otherwise infeasible internally."[18] The government of Uruguay similarly found an agreement with the IMF useful in its efforts to impose painful, unpopular economic austerity measures. IMF conditionality raised the cost to domestic interests of opposing economic reform "because a rejection was no longer a mere rejection of the [Uruguayan] president, but also of the IMF."[19] With the ready availability of private bank loans during the 1970s, governments seeking to impose unpopular reforms found it more difficult to justify to their populations a decision to seek IMF loans. Thus, governments were inclined to follow the path of least resistance and seek bank loans without instituting necessary reforms.

In addition to imprudent borrowing behavior, liberals attribute the debt crisis at least partly to the domestic policies of borrowing states. Although some LDCs used commercial bank loans wisely to finance productive investments and economic growth, a number, according to this view, used the funds to make poor investments, increase public expenditures, import consumer goods, and pay off corrupt officials. Some LDCs reacted to the debt crisis in a timely manner with readjustment policies, but many others demonstrated unwillingness or inability to change. Liberal economists often contrast the strong economic performance of Asian debtors such as South Korea and Indonesia during the 1980s with the weak performance of Latin American debtors. (The most notable exception was the weak performance of the Philippines.)

The differential economic performance of Asians and Latin Americans, from this perspective, cannot be explained by differences in external shocks or even by the amount of external borrowing. Instead, the most important differences relate to these countries' economic policies. Whereas Latin American LDCs employed import substitution policies, Asian LDCs emphasized export-led growth policies. Exports are a critical source of foreign exchange for servicing a country's debts, so the Asians' outward-oriented policies put them in a stronger position to deal with their debt problems. Overvalued exchange rates also encouraged capital flight in Latin American LDCs such as Mexico and Argentina because residents feared precipitous declines in the value of their currencies. Asian LDCs, by contrast, had realistic exchange rates and generally avoided the Latin American problem of capital flight.[20]

Table 7.1 illustrates the more favorable position of Asians vis-à-vis Latin Americans in 1982. The largest debtors in Table 7.1 are Latin American (the debts of Brazil,

Table 7.1

TOTAL DEBT AND DEBT INDICATORS, 1982 (U.S.$ millions)

	Total Debt	Debt/Exports (%)	Debt Service Ratio*(%)
Latin America			
Argentina	43,634	447.3	50.0
Brazil	92,990	396.1	81.3
Chile	17,315	335.9	71.3
Colombia	10,306	204.3	29.5
Mexico	86,019	311.5	56.8
Peru	10,712	255.9	48.7
Venezuela	32,153	159.8	29.5
East and Southeast Asia			
Indonesia	24,734	116.3	18.1
Republic of Korea	37,330	131.6	22.4
Malaysia	13,354	93.4	10.7
Philippines	24,551	297.8	42.6
Thailand	12,238	130.0	20.6

*Debt service ratio: the ratio of a country's interest and principal payments to its export income.
Source: World Bank, *World Debt Tables 1992–93, Vol. 2: Country Tables* (Washington DC.: IBRD, 1992).

Mexico, and Argentina exceeded $92 billion, $86 billion, and $43 billion, respectively); some Asian countries such as South Korea, Indonesia, and the Philippines also had substantial debt levels (exceeding $37 billion, $24 billion, and $24 billion, respectively). However, the stronger export position of the Asians (except the Philippines) enabled them to service their debts better than the Latin Americans. Economists use the **debt service ratio,** which measures the ratio of a country's interest and principal payments on its debt to its export income, to assess a country's ability to service its debt. The lower the debt service ratio (and debt-to-export ratio), the more favorable are the prospects that a country will meet its debt obligations. Thus, Table 7.1 shows that the debt service ratios of Malaysia and Indonesia were as low as 10.7 and 18.1 percent in 1982, while the debt service ratios of Brazil and Chile had reached the highly unfavorable levels of 81.3 and 71.3 percent.

The view that irresponsible LDC behavior was the major factor explaining the debt crisis, like the other perspectives, has been subjected to criticism. Critics point out that some LDC governments with good intentions lacked the political capacity and support to institute necessary economic reforms.[21] They also charge that the attribution of LDC responsibility ignores the fact that the debt crisis was *systemic* in nature. Indeed, "the simultaneous onset of the crisis in more than forty developing countries" indicates that some major contributing factors were external to the LDCs and largely beyond their control.[22] Furthermore, Asian LDCs such as Thailand, Malaysia, Indonesia, and South Korea, which liberals identified as following responsible policies during the 1980s debt crisis, experienced a severe financial crisis in the late 1990s (see discussion on pp. 209–212).

The South's Dependence on the North

Some historical structuralists argue that the 1980s debt crisis stemmed not only from proximate factors, but also from the long-term structural nature of the capitalist system. Thus, dependency and world-systems theorists view debt crises as extreme instances of a "debt trap," which exploits LDCs in the periphery and binds them to DCs in the core.[23] Some writers draw linkages between foreign debt crises and the legacy of colonialism. The colonial powers established a division of labor in which the colonies provided agricultural products and raw materials to the metropole and served in turn as markets for the metropole's manufacturers. This pattern still characterizes the export and import structures of many LDCs, preventing them from earning the foreign exchange necessary for development. Although some LDCs are industrializing, they remain dependent on MNCs and other institutions in the core for technology and finance and therefore find it impossible to escape from their indebtedness.[24]

Other historical structuralists point to foreign aid as a source of debt crises because more than half of all official development assistance is disbursed as loans. A substantial share of World Bank financing is also disbursed to the South as *hard loans* with high interest rates and relatively short repayment periods (see Chapter 11). A large percentage of multilateral and bilateral foreign aid today is therefore required simply to cover LDC repayments of past aid disbursements. Thus, development assistance is simply another mechanism by which surpluses are transferred from the periphery to the core. Many historical structuralists also view IMF and World Bank conditionality requirements as infringing on LDC sovereignty and as incorrect prescriptions for reducing LDC debt problems. Thus, IMF and World Bank loans, like commercial bank loans, serve to perpetuate LDC dependency:

> If they seek official help on softer than commercial terms, they have to accept outside scrutiny . . . and accept conditions which doom their efforts at industrial, diversified development. If they accept suppliers' credits on commercial terms in order to go through with their cherished projects, they are caught anyway when the payments come due before they are able to meet them.[25]

Like other interpretations of the debt crisis, dependency theory has been subjected to criticism. Liberals argue that dependency theorists attribute debt problems of LDCs solely to external causes beyond their control and thereby avoid looking at the *domestic* sources of LDC problems—traditional attitudes, domestic inefficiencies, corrupt political leaders, and a reluctance to follow liberal-economic policies.

It is safe to conclude that all the preceding views regarding the origins of the debt crisis have some validity. The unexpected food and oil price increases during the 1970s encouraged LDCs to increase their borrowing, and the monetary policy changes and world recession after the 1979 oil price increases added to the debt load of many LDC borrowers. Although these unexpected global changes made a debt crisis more likely, the behavior of some commercial banks, DCs, and LDCs certainly exacerbated the debt situation. Furthermore, the South's long-term structural dependency on the

North increased the vulnerability of LDCs to protracted debt problems. Mexico's minister of finance and public credit in 1982–1986 clearly identified the multiple causes of the debt crisis and the widespread failure to foresee it, when he stated:

> . . . The origin of the debt itself is clearly traceable to a decision by both developing and developed countries that . . . resulted in the channeling of tens of billions of dollars to the debtor community of today. . . . The whole world congratulated itself on the success, smoothness, and efficiency with which the recycling process was achieved. *We all were responsible.*[26]

THE FOREIGN DEBT REGIME

Before discussing the world's reaction to the 1980s debt crisis, it is necessary to describe the foreign debt regime that developed to monitor and manage the crisis. A debt regime was more evident in the 1980s than during the 1930s because a global hegemon (the United States) and a more developed institutional framework (including the IMF and World Bank) existed to deal with the 1980s crisis. Before World War II, the mechanisms for coping with a debt crisis included unilateral actions by the creditors or debtors, and two-party solutions in which the debtors and creditors reached a compromise at the bargaining table. Debt settlements in the postwar period, by contrast, have often been three-party affairs involving IOs such as the IMF and World Bank and less formal groupings such as the Paris and London Clubs (discussed later). The United States has also acted as a third party in the postwar period, using its hegemonic position to pressure for debt settlements and coordinate settlement efforts.[27]

Some regimes encompass only one sector or issue whereas others are broader in scope, and specific regimes may be nested within more diffuse regimes. For example, some authors describe the textile and agricultural trade regimes as being nested within the global trade regime.[28] Although the global trade regime principles, norms, and rules provide a general framework, textile and agricultural trade relations have their own unique characteristics and have often been treated as exceptions by the GATT/WTO. This chapter views the 1980s foreign debt regime as a specific regime nested within a more diffuse balance-of-payments financing regime because foreign debt crises are a specific, more extreme type of balance-of-payments problem.[29] Although creditors and debtors have engaged in continuous efforts to negotiate agreements during the postwar period, pressures resulting from the 1980s debt crisis produced more coordinated, longer-term efforts to establish rules and decision-making procedures that we normally associate with an international regime.

A basic principle of the balance-of-payments financing regime is that an adequate but not unlimited amount of supplementary financing should be available to states for dealing with their balance-of-payments deficits. A second principle is that those providing this financing may attach conditions to the funding to ensure that recipient states correct their balance-of-payments problems. The rules of the balance-of-payments financing regime include the explicit conditions the IMF places on borrowers.[30] In the 1970s, the balance-of-payments regime's principle of conditional lending was threatened because private banks with petrodollars to recycle provided debtor countries loans with extremely low interest rates and minimal conditions. Although these private bank loans were readily available to many middle-income countries (MICs) and NIEs during the 1970s, low-income countries (LICs) lacked creditworthiness to receive private bank loans and remained highly dependent on loans from the IMF and donor governments. Thus, Table 7.2 shows that in 1980 private bank loans accounted for only 6 percent of LIC debt but for 38 percent of MIC debt and 65 percent of NIE debt. **Official development assistance (ODA),** by contrast, accounted for 67 percent of LIC debt in 1980 but for only 25 percent of MIC debt and 4 percent of NIE debt. The willingness of private banks to provide for the financing needs of more creditworthy LDCs limited the IMF's ability to set conditions for these borrowers.

With the emergence of the 1980s debt crisis, however, private banks moved quickly to limit their loan exposure, and the MICs and NIEs therefore had to look to the IMF, World Bank, and government aid agencies for assistance with their growing debt problems. This dependence on official financing provided the IOs and the U.S. government with considerable leverage in establishing the foreign debt regime. As with the pre–1970s balance-of-payments regime, the basic principle of the debt regime revolved around conditionality—that the provision of new loans and debt rescheduling were contingent on debtor countries' commitment to market-oriented reforms. However, the 1980s debt regime was also different from the pre–1970s regime in some important respects.

First, the IMF (with U.S. backing) adopted a new role when it imposed pressures on private commercial banks in the 1980s to continue providing loans to debtor LDCs. Second, creditor groups such as the Paris and London Clubs were used much more frequently in the 1980s–1990s than during earlier periods. Third, both the IMF and World Bank provided structural adjustment loans to indebted LDCs and transition economies. These SALs were conditioned on far more demanding requirements than previously—that loan recipients adopt orthodox liberal reforms such as deregulation, privatization, and greater openness to trade and foreign investment. The changing roles of the IMF and World Bank in the foreign debt regime are examined later in this chapter. Next comes a discussion of two sets of actors whose roles were also important: the transition economies of Eastern Europe and the FSU that became major debtors along with the LDCs, and the Paris and London Clubs that rescheduled loans.

The IMF, World Bank, and Transition Economies

Chapter 2 noted that the Soviet bloc countries were not IMF and World Bank members for most of the early postwar period. Before examining the role of these countries in the foreign debt regime, this chapter discusses how they joined these two closely-related institutions: a country cannot join the World Bank (or "the Bank") without first becoming a member of the IMF. As Table 7.3 shows, Yugoslavia was a member of the IMF and the Bank from the time they were established. This is not surprising in view of Yugoslavia's defection from the Soviet Bloc in 1948 and its moves to develop an independent, nonaligned foreign policy. Yugloslavia was also adopting policies of worker self-management and market socialism that were more compatible with the liberal-economic orientation of the Bretton Woods institutions. In contrast to Yugoslavia, Poland and Czechoslovakia left the IMF and the Bank in 1950 and 1954 (Czechoslovakia was expelled for not paying its dues), because membership in these institutions was considered incompatible with their status as satellite countries in the Soviet bloc.

Table 7.2

Total Debt and Share of Debt Based on ODA and Private Bank Loans for Nonoil LDCS

Income Group	1971			1975			1980			1982		
	Total Debt*	Percentage ODA	Percentage Private Banks	Total Debt	Percentage ODA	Percentage Private Banks	Total Debt	Percentage ODA	Percentage Private Banks	Total Debt	Percentage ODA	Percentage Private Banks
LICs	$18	74	2	$40	73	7	$86	67	6	$110	69	6
MICs	$25	45	14	$40	33	29	$107	25	38	$144	24	39
NIEs	$32	16	38	$72	9	60	$192	4	65	$266	3	67

*Total debt figures in billions.

Abbreviations: ODA: official development assistance

    LICs: low-income countries

    MICs: middle-income countries

    NIEs: newly industrializing economies

Source: *External Debt of Developing Countries—1982 Survey*, p.34. Copyright © OECD, 1982. By permission of the Organization for Economic Co-operation and Development.

Table 7.3

MEMBERSHIP OF TRANSITION ECONOMIES
IN THE IMF AND WORLD BANK

	IMF	World Bank
1946	Poland, Czechoslovakia, Yugoslavia, and China (founding members of IMF and World Bank)	
1950	Poland withdraws from IMF and World Bank	
1954	Czechoslovakia ousted from the IMF and World Bank	
1972	Romania	Romania
1980	People's Republic of China (PRC) replaces Taiwan in the IMF and World Bank	
1982	Hungary	Hungary
1986	Poland	Poland
1990	Czech and Slovak Republic, Bulgaria	
1991	Albania	Albania, Bulgaria, Czech and Slovak Federal Republic
1992 to 1996	Russian Federation, and other FSU* Republics, Croatia, Slovenia, Macedonia, Czech Republic, Slovak Republic, Bosnia, and Herzegovina (IMF and World Bank)	
2000	Federal Republic of Yugoslavia (IMF and World Bank)	

*FSU: former Soviet Union

Sources: International Monetary Fund, *Annual Report of the Executive Board,* (Washington, DC.: IMF, various years); World Bank, *Annual Report,* (Washington, DC.: World Bank, various years).

Table 7.3 shows that Romania was the first CPE to join these institutions after the withdrawals or expulsions of the 1950s. Like Yugoslavia, Romania was atypical. Although Romania was still a member of the Soviet bloc, it had distanced itself politically from the Soviet Union and thought that the policies of the Soviet-led Council for Mutual Economic Assistance (CMEA) were hindering its industrialization. Membership in the IMF and the Bank would enable Romania to benefit from their loans, upgrade its economic relations with the West, and further its political objectives. Remarkably, Romania became a member of these IOs in 1972 without having to pass through a transition phase, even though its moves toward economic reform and decentralization were halting and it was building up a sizable foreign debt. Western states downgraded the importance of these economic issues because Romania's membership contributed to significant divisions within the Soviet bloc. Although Romania provided sensitive economic information to the IMF and the Bank, the two institutions abided by a special agreement not to disclose this information in their statistical reports.[31]

The People's Republic of China (PRC) was the next CPE to participate in IMF and Bank meetings, and its case was also atypical. The IMF and the Bank permitted the PRC to take over the China seat from Taiwan and thus treated the issue as one of representation rather than new membership. The PRC's decision to "return" to the

Bretton Woods institutions in 1980 followed a radical change in its policies. The Sino-Soviet dispute of the late 1950s–1960s had caused Mao Zedong's PRC to turn inward with a self-reliance policy, and China's policies became far more autarkic in 1966–1969 during the Cultural Revolution. However, the Cultural Revolution created so many political and economic problems that China became somewhat more open to the outside world. In response, the UN General Assembly voted to seat the PRC delegation in October 1971, and China's commercial contacts with the North increased. Despite some change in its foreign policy, it was not until Mao's death in 1976 and the arrest of cultural revolutionaries that the PRC launched the Four Modernizations program to increase economic productivity and efficiency and develop a more active role in the global economy. Thus, China wanted to renew its membership in the IMF and the Bank as a means of gaining access to capital for infrastructure projects essential for its economic modernization. In the negotiations that followed, several factors facilitated China's reentry application, including active support of the United States and a compromise worked out regarding Taiwan.[32]

After the PRC's takeover of the China seat in 1980, Hungary and Poland requested accession in late 1981. Unlike Romania, Hungary came much closer to meeting the IMF's normal economic requirements. In 1968, Hungary had introduced its New Economic Mechanism (NEM), designed to increase the country's economic decentralization, outward economic orientation, and competitiveness in international markets; and in the 1970s–1980s Hungary introduced other economic reforms. Hungary sought IMF membership to safeguard these reforms and obtain assistance with its foreign debt, which resulted partly from its development plans. Debt problems were far more serious for Poland, which had borrowed in international financial markets during the early 1970s instead of introducing meaningful economic reform. Poland needed to reassure the financial community that it was committed to servicing its debt in the early 1980s, and IMF membership would be helpful in this regard. Although Hungary was admitted to the IMF and the Bank in 1982, Poland's application was stalled by its imposition of martial law in December 1981; it was not until 1986 that Poland was admitted to the Bretton Woods institutions (see Table 7.3).[33]

Poland was the last Eastern European country to become an IMF and Bank member before the upheaval in the Soviet bloc transformed East-West relations. After Mikhail Gorbachev took office, he attempted to revive the Soviet economy through a combination of economic restructuring (*perestroika*) and political openness (*glasnost*). Although Gorbachev's economic efforts failed, his policies contributed to a series of revolutionary changes. Thus, the disintegration of one Communist regime after another in Eastern Europe during 1989 and the unification of Germany in June 1990 led to the decision to dissolve the CMEA in June 1991. This was followed by the Moscow coup in August 1991, which led to the independence of the Baltic states and the formal dissolution of the Soviet Union in December 1991. Czechoslovakia and Bulgaria joined the IMF and the Bank in 1990 and 1991, but the most significant change was the accession of Russia and other FSU republics in 1992–1993. Because Russia was facing an economic crisis, the IMF and Western donors offered it a $24 billion assistance package in return for Russia's commitment to decrease its budget deficit and inflation rate.[34]

The Bretton Woods institutions have worked closely together to assist the transition economies in moving toward market orientation. The IMF has taken the lead in this process, estimating financing needs, providing policy advice, and setting conditions for economic reform. The Bank has provided financing for infrastructure and has offered technical assistance and funding to promote the development of market incentives, privatization of state monopolies, and a legal framework for the emerging private sector.[35] Tensions have existed between the transition economies and the Bretton Woods institutions because of their different economic outlooks. Nevertheless, the addition of so many new countries has put pressures on IMF and Bank resources, and LDCs sometimes charge that the transition economies are receiving favored treatment. There does in fact seem to be some truth to these charges. For example, one study revealed that Romania, Poland, and Hungary have received more IMF loans than expected on the basis of economic criteria; and there is evidence that Russia was permitted to borrow more funds in relation to its IMF quota than other countries when it joined the IMF in 1992.[36] The favored treatment the IMF and its DC members sometimes give to transition economies demonstrates that security as well as economic factors play a role in their lending decisions. However, it seems that the charges of favored treatment do not apply to all transition economies. A 1990 study, for example, concluded that the IMF and the Bank have not given special funding treatment to China.[37] As noted in this chapter, the 1980s foreign debt crisis affected transition as well as LDC economies. The IMF and the Bank's expanding membership has inevitably meant that more debtors are competing for their funds. Despite the charges of special treatment, the membership of transition economies has enhanced the universality of the Bretton Woods institutions.

The Paris and London Clubs

Three major types of negotiations occurred between creditors and debtors to deal with the 1980s debt crisis. In the first type, the IMF and the Bank agreed to provide SALS to LDC debtor governments in exchange for the debtors' commitment to follow prescribed economic policies to eliminate their balance-of-payments problems. The other two types of negotiations involved meetings between the debtors and less formal creditor groups: the Paris and London Clubs. The **Paris Club** is a quasi-institutional group of creditor governments, which in most cases are members of the OECD. The **London Club** is the term informally used for private creditor committees, which are composed of the largest commercial banks. The Paris and London Clubs have no charters or formal institutional structures, and their memberships vary with each rescheduling negotiation. The ad hoc nature of these clubs stems from the creditors' view that negotiations should be low-profile in nature and that debt reschedulings should be unusual occurrences. Thus, the Paris Club has no legal status or written rules, no voting procedure (decision making occurs by consensus), and no regular office (meetings are usually held in the French Ministry of Finance).[38]

The Paris Club's first meeting in 1956 negotiated a rescheduling of Argentina's foreign debt. Argentina was in arrears to several European governments, and this meeting provided a multilateral rescheduling forum as an alternative to a series of uncoordinated bilateral reschedulings. Paris Club meetings were originally limited in number, but they became much more frequent as debt problems increased. Thus, the

Paris Club concluded more than twice as many agreements in the 7-year period from 1978 to 1984 as it did in the previous 22 years; the 1978–1984 agreements resulted in the deferment of about $27 billion of debt service obligations. Participants in Paris Club debt reschedulings include the debtor government, the governments of the main official creditors, and representatives of the IMF, the Bank, UNCTAD, and sometimes the regional development banks. In its deliberations, the Paris Club emphasizes three basic principles: imminent default, conditionality, and burden sharing.[39]

The first principle of imminent default is designed to limit requests for relief to those with a serious, justifiable need. To avoid unnecessary negotiations, the Paris Club will not even consider a request for relief unless the debtor has substantial external payments arrears and is likely to default on its payments. The second principle of conditionality stems from the creditor governments' concerns that the debtor will be able to service its debts on schedule. Thus, the debtor country must first conclude a standby arrangement with the IMF, based on IMF conditionality requirements, before the Paris Club will agree to negotiate.[40] In the small number of cases where the debtor was not an IMF member at the time of rescheduling (e.g., Poland, Cuba, and Mozambique), the Paris Club established its own conditionality program. As for the third principle of burden sharing, all creditor governments must provide relief in proportion to their loan exposure to the debtor country. The burden-sharing principle helps avoid the problem of free riding among creditors, and it also extends to the private creditor banks; thus, the Paris and London Clubs cooperate and communicate with each other regularly.

Private debt reschedulings have a number of similarities with Paris Club agreements. In both cases, rescheduling is done on a case-by-case basis by mutual agreement between a single debtor and its creditors, and the debtor must normally commit to adjustment policies as agreed with the IMF. A fundamental difference, however, is that commercial banks are far more numerous than nation-states. Whereas a relatively small number of states can agree on rescheduling loans at Paris Club meetings, the coordination problems for private creditors are more complicated. Private creditors coordinate their activities by establishing creditor committees for the various debtor countries, with the largest international banks (those holding the most loans outstanding) representing the smaller creditor banks. The international banks on a creditor committee bargain with each other and with the debtor country to establish the terms for debt rescheduling and then present the agreement to the smaller creditor banks for ratification. Although the largest creditors would like to limit their loan exposure to a troubled debtor, they realize that the debtor country could default if all creditors withheld loans. The major international banks have a common interest in successful debt restructuring because of their high loan exposure and their long-term interest in the stability of international capital markets.

Smaller creditor banks, by contrast, have fewer loans at risk and less interest in maintaining the international credit system. Thus, they are reluctant to ratify restructuring agreements that require them to provide additional loans. Because smaller creditor banks are more inclined to think on the basis of individual rationality, in line with prisoners' dilemma (see Chapter 4), there is a danger that all banks could defect and that massive debtor default could disrupt the international banking system. To prevent a Pareto-suboptimal outcome of this nature, the large international banks pressure the smaller banks to avoid free riding and to participate in the debt restructuring agreements.[41] As discussed in the next section, this system of private creditor committees worked quite effectively in earlier years but was insufficient to deal with the 1980s debt crisis.

Historical structuralists and many LDC debtors have been highly critical of the Paris and London Clubs. When a single debtor meets with all its major creditors at the bargaining table, the creditors can exert unusually strong pressures on the debtor government. The case-by-case approach of the Paris and London Clubs also prevents the debtors from developing a united front, and it ignores the systemic nature of the 1980s debt crisis by operating on the assumption that each debtor's situation can be treated individually. Furthermore, historical structuralists criticize the two clubs for the strong emphasis they place on IMF conditionality as a prerequisite for their negotiations.[42] At the UNCTAD V conference in 1979, the G-77 sought to replace the Paris and London Clubs with an international debt commission more attuned to LDC interests. Although the creditor governments agreed to invite an observer from the UNCTAD secretariat to future Paris Club negotiations, it did not accede to LDC demands for an international debt commission. Thus, the creditors continue to set the rules and procedures for Paris and London Club negotiations.

STRATEGIES TO DEAL WITH THE 1980S DEBT CRISIS

The debt crisis was more prolonged than many observers had anticipated, and the creditor states and international institutions gradually adopted more activist policies as it became evident that milder measures were insufficient. Two of the main actors involved in devising and implementing strategies were the United States and the IMF. Although the IMF had lost some importance with the collapse of the pegged exchange rate system and the increase in private bank lending in the 1970s, the 1980s debt crisis placed it "back at the center of the international financial system, first as a coordinator in a crisis, and then . . . as a source of information, advice, and warning on the mutual consistency of national policies."[43] The IMF owed its more central role largely to the support of U.S. administration officials, who believed that multilateral institutions could best implement U.S. (and Western) policies on debt issues. The IMF could exert pressure on both the private banks and LDC debtors, avoiding major protests over U.S. government interference with private sector lending and LDC sovereignty. When international debt issues came onto the agendas of G-7 summit meetings during the 1980s, the major economic powers to some extent replaced U.S. hegemony with collective responsibility for LDC debt problems.[44]

The international debt strategies had three major objectives: to prevent the collapse of the international banking and financial systems, to restore capital market access for the debtor countries, and to minimize economic dislocation and restore economic growth in the debtor countries. The strategies employed to achieve these objectives can be divided into four phases: (1) the provision of emergency loans and private "involuntary" loans to debtor countries (1982–1985); (2) the Baker Plan, which continued with private involuntary lending and placed new emphasis on official lending (1986–1988); (3) the Brady Plan, which emphasized debt reduction agreements (1989–1994); and (4) the Heavily Indebted Poor Countries Initiative (1996 to the present).

Emergency Measures and Involuntary Lending: 1982 to 1985

The first phase in dealing with the debt crisis was a "firefighting" strategy in which the United States, IMF, and other creditors provided short-term emergency loans to Mexico, Brazil, Venezuela, and other LDCs to avert a 1930s-style financial collapse. The BIS also provided some bridging finance to LDC debtor states until IMF loans were approved.[45] This emergency lending was followed by a medium-term strategy in which private banks engaged in involuntary lending. Involuntary lending, which is politely termed *concerted lending* in official circles, refers to "the increase in a bank's exposure to a borrowing nation that is in debt-servicing difficulty and that, because of a loss of creditworthiness, would be unable to attract new lending from banks not already exposed in the country."[46]

In the late 1970s–1980s, the private creditor committees were quite successful in managing the debt situation; the largest international banks induced the smaller banks to engage in involuntary lending when necessary in debt restructuring agreements. Only nine states had to restructure their commercial debts from the mid-1970s to 1982, so interbank coordination was sufficient to manage the debt situation. Although the IMF had a role in supervising debtor economic policies, its involvement was quite limited during this period. The Mexican debt crisis in August 1982, however, drastically altered the debt management system. The large international banks were unable to cope with the debt crisis because of its massive scope, and many small banks in the U.S. Southwest with loans outstanding to Mexico were unwilling to increase their loan exposure. Thus, the IMF had to intervene with an activist policy:

> In November 1982, the Fund's Managing Director . . . took the unprecedented step of establishing mandatory levels of forced private lending before the IMF would sign a stabilization agreement with Mexico. This bold action, repeated in the Brazilian case, was a turning point in the treatment of sovereign debt. It staked out a new leadership role for the Fund, and a new relationship between the Fund and private banks.[47]

In addition to pressuring creditor banks, the IMF insisted that debtor states develop adjustment programs as the price for debt rescheduling and new lending. Thus, realists point out that it was creditor *states* operating through the IMF that managed the debt crisis, and not private banks and the market. The debt crisis posed such a major threat to the international financial system that only states could mobilize sufficient resources to deal with the crisis. Furthermore, only official pressures could induce banks to continue lending to debtors on the one hand and force debtors to meet conditionality requirements on the other.[48] Liberals, by contrast, emphasize the IMF's role as an international institution in managing the debt crisis, and they disagree with the realist view that the IMF was simply following the creditor states' instructions.

The IMF and creditor states in these early years assumed that the debt crisis was only a short-term problem stemming from the temporary inability of LDCs to service their debts. However, it became evident that many LDCs could not resolve their debt problems even after adjusting their policies.[49] Although the early firefighting tactics dealt with the immediate crisis, economic activity and investment in most debtor states were declining and international pressures for adjustment programs in LDCs were interfering with their economic growth objectives. Furthermore, private commercial banks were resisting IMF pressures and reducing their loan exposure. Thus, official creditors such as the IMF rather than the private banks were assuming an increasing share of the lending risk. When James A. Baker III became U.S. Secretary of the Treasury in 1985, he therefore adopted a more structured approach to the debt crisis.

The Baker Plan: 1986 to 1988

In late 1985, Secretary Baker provided a more concrete formula for dealing with the debt crisis and extended debt repayments over a longer period; but he did not change the basic assumptions about the best strategy to follow. As was the case in the 1982–1985 period, the **Baker Plan** underestimated the insolvency problem confronting many LDCs and therefore rejected the idea that major portions of the LDC debt should be forgiven. Instead, the Baker Plan emphasized the postponement of some debt payments, the provision of new loans, and changes in debtor country policies. This strategy rested on the assumption that "principal debtor countries could grow their way out of debt and could expand their exports enough to reduce their relative debt burdens to levels compatible with a return to normal credit market access."[50]

The Baker Plan also focused mainly on Latin American debtors. When Secretary Baker referred to the heavily indebted countries, he identified 15 middle-income LDCs (later increased to 17) as the target group for international debt measures. As the asterisks in Table 7.4 show, 12 of the 17 targeted states were Latin American and Caribbean, and the "Baker-17" list did not include low-income LDCs that were heavily indebted to official (rather than private) creditors.[51] Table 7.4 lists these 17 countries in order of their gross external debt from highest to lowest in 1985, shortly before the Baker Plan was instituted (the order of countries changed somewhat in 1994). As the table shows, the four countries with the highest debts in 1985 (Brazil, Mexico, Argentina, and Venezuela) were all Latin American. However, more than gross external debt figures are needed to assess a country's debt servicing abilities. Such an assessment must also examine *debt indicators* including a country's debt service ratio (see Table 7.1) and debt as a share of GNP. Table 7.4 shows that LDCs with the highest gross external debts ranked well below some poorer and smaller LDCs in terms of debt as a percent of GNP. Thus, external debt as a percent of GNP for the three largest debtors in 1985, Brazil, Mexico, and Argentina, were 50.3, 55.2, and 84.2 percent, respectively. Six of the other debtors on the list had much higher debt-to-GNP ratios, exceeding 100 percent. The countries on the Baker-17 list with the highest external-debt-to-GNP ratios in 1985 were Jamaica (234.9 percent), Bolivia (176.6 percent), and Cote d'Ivoire (154.2 percent).

Although the Baker Plan focused mainly on middle-income LDCs and did not recognize the severity of the debt problem, it marked a turning point in one important respect. Recognizing that the debt crisis was becoming a longer term problem, the Baker Plan shifted emphasis from short-term balance-of-payments adjustment to

Table 7.4

Gross External Debt and External Debt as a Percent of GNP for the Baker-17 Countries, 1985 and 1994 (U.S.$ millions)

	1985		1994	
	Debt	**EDT/GNP%**	**Debt**	**EDT/GNP%**
*Brazil	106,148	50.3	151,104	27.9
*Mexico	96,867	55.2	128,302	35.2
*Argentina	50,946	84.2	77,388	27.8
*Venezuela	35,334	—	36,850	64.0
Philippines	26,622	89.1	39,302	59.3
Former Yugoslavia	22,251	48.2	13,557	—
*Chile	20,384	143.3	22,939	45.5
Nigeria	19,550	25.1	33,485	102.5
Morocco	16,529	136.6	22,512	76.3
*Peru	12,884	85.3	22,624	45.8
*Colombia	14,245	42.6	19,416	30.9
Cote d'Ivoire	9,745	154.2	18,452	338.9
*Ecuador	8,703	77.4	14,955	94.6
*Bolivia	4,805	176.6	4,749	89.4
*Costa Rica	4,401	120.8	3,843	47.8
*Jamaica	4,068	234.9	4,318	110.1
*Uruguay	3,919	89.7	5,099	33.2

EDT/GNP %: Total external debt to GDP.
* indicates Latin American and Caribbean countries.
Source: World Bank, World Debt Tables, 1992–93 and 1996, Vol. 2: Country Tables (Washington, DC.: IBRD, 1992 and 1996).

long-term structural change and the resumption of economic growth in the LDC debtor states. In view of the new emphasis on long-term change, the World Bank and Inter-American Development Bank (IDB)—with their longer term loans—assumed a more central role. Thus, the Baker Plan proposed that the multilateral development banks increase their lending by $10 billion to a gross level of $20 billion over three years and that the private banks also lend $20 billion to the major debtors. In return, the debtors were to institute significant liberal-economic reforms, including the liberalization of trade and foreign investment policies and the privatization of state firms. These reforms had particular significance for Latin American LDCs, which had previously followed protectionist import substitution policies.

Any possibilities that the Baker Plan could succeed were upset by unexpected changes in the global economy. For example, international oil prices collapsed shortly after the Baker Plan was announced, upsetting the recovery plans of oil-exporting debtor countries such as Mexico. The decline of oil prices also gave some oil-importing LDCs less incentive to adopt economic policy reforms that were necessary for their recovery. Thus, the Baker initiative lost much of its momentum by mid-1986. The Baker Plan also did not achieve adequate results in terms of LDC economic growth, and many LDC debtors refused to comply with IMF conditionality requirements (e.g., Brazil declared a moratorium on paying its debts in 1987). Furthermore, commercial banks sought to reduce their loan exposure, and the lending risks continued to shift from private banks to governments and multilateral agencies. The multilateral development banks also disbursed less funding than the Baker Plan had anticipated. As a result, debt repayments began to exceed the funding LDCs were receiving in new loans. The net transfer of financial resources to LDCs shifted from +$29 billion in 1982 to −$34 billion by 1987, and the net resource transfer to the Baker-17 countries shifted from +$11 billion to −$17 billion during the same period.[52]

Because the debtors' repayment requirements greatly exceeded their access to new financing, they experienced serious economic problems during the Baker Plan period. During 1981–1988, real per capita income in almost every South American LDC declined in absolute terms, and living standards in many LDCs fell to levels comparable with the 1950s–1960s. Thus, many analysts referred to the 1980s as a "lost development decade." Although the Baker Plan's failure resulted partly from unforeseen external events such as the collapse of international oil prices, historical structuralists viewed the plan as an "attempt to maintain the fiction that the debt crisis was only temporary and could be surmounted if all parties cooperated."[53] A number of debtor countries were caught in a vicious circle, in which their debt burdens interfered with their economic growth, and their slow growth in turn prevented them from overcoming their debt problems.[54]

The Brady Plan: 1989 to 1994

The Baker Plan's failure to promote economic recovery and growth posed a serious threat to U.S. exports in Latin American markets. Concerns were also voiced in the U.S. Congress about the possible negative effects of continued debt problems on the revival of democratic governments in Latin America. Serious riots in Caracas, Venezuela, in February 1989 were associated with government austerity measures, providing further evidence that the Baker measures were insufficient. In early 1989, Nicholas Brady, the new U.S. Treasury Secretary, sanctioned an approach of forgiving some debts by launching the *Brady Plan*. The idea of *debt reduction*—that some debts would not be repaid in full—was highly contentious; but the major economic powers resolved their differences on this issue at the July 1989 G-7 summit, and the IMF adopted the Brady Plan at its Fall 1989 meeting.[55] Mexico was the first LDC to conclude a Brady Plan debt reduction agreement, partly because it was liberalizing its economy after it suffered from the 1986 collapse of oil prices (e.g., it joined GATT in 1986). However, the choice of Mexico as the first beneficiary also shows that security as well as economic factors play a role in foreign debt decisions. "As usual in these matters, Mexico was in the vanguard" because of its "strategic importance to the United States."[56]

Like the Baker Plan, the Brady Plan handled debt on a case-by-case basis, with each debtor negotiating separately with its creditors; and it linked the easing of credit terms with the debtor's acceptance of IMF and World Bank conditions for liberal economic reform. However, the Brady Plan differed from the Baker Plan with its new emphasis on debt reduction, or partial forgiveness of debt. The Baker Plan had rejected debt reduction on the grounds that banks would not lend to countries if they failed to pay their debts, and that LDCs would be able to pay their debts and return to prosperity if the debt repayment period was simply extended. The Brady Plan, by contrast, recognized that LDCs could not regain creditworthiness if their debt burden was too onerous, and that extending the debt repayment period without debt reduction had not returned the debtors to economic growth. The Brady Plan therefore stipulated that U.S. private banks would receive guarantees of repayment on the remaining portion of debt if they reduced the principal or interest on the debt owed to them. The IMF and World Bank would help finance these guarantees, and Japan also committed funds for this purpose.[57]

In some respects the Brady Plan was quite successful, even though it took longer than expected to achieve results. For the Baker-17 countries, the ratio of net external debt to exports of goods and services fell from 384 percent in 1986 to 225 percent in 1993. Furthermore, as Table 7.4 shows, the external-debt-to-GNP ratio was lower in 1994 than 1985 for most Baker-17 countries other than Nigeria, Cote d'Ivoire, and Ecuador. (The IMF data were not available for Venezuela and the former Yugoslavia.) However, the Brady Plan also had some definite shortcomings. Table 7.4 shows that overall foreign debt for most Baker-17 countries increased from 1985 to 1994. As mentioned, most of these countries were Latin American, and the combined foreign debt owed by Latin American states increased from $425 billion in 1987 to more than $600 billion in 1997. In 1997, Latin America was paying about 30 percent of its export earnings to service those debts, and it owed about 45 percent of its combined GDP to foreign creditors. The Brady Plan's most serious shortcoming was that it dealt only with commercial bank debt. It offered little to low-income LDCs because most of their debt was to official creditors such as governments and international financial institutions. Although most of these low-income debtors were in sub-Saharan Africa, they were also in Asia and Latin America. In the 1990s, the debt situation was far worse for these low-income LDCs than it was for the Baker-17 countries.[58] Thus, it was necessary to develop a new debt relief plan, this time for low-income LDCs.

The Heavily Indebted Poor Countries Initiative

From 1980 to 1990, the total external debt of sub-Saharan African countries increased from $56.2 billion (U.S.) to $147 billion, and their total external debt service payments (interest and principal) on long-term loans for this period rose from $4.5 billion to $11.1 billion. Thus, it was evident by the early 1990s that debt relief was insufficient for the poorest, most heavily indebted LDCs, especially those in Africa. The 1996 G-7 summit in Lyon, France, directly addressed this problem by agreeing to establish a plan aimed specifically at the debts of the poorest LDCs to multilateral institutions, the **Heavily Indebted Poor Countries (HIPC) initiative.** The IMF and World Bank had previously refused to permit debt rescheduling of their loans because of fears this would damage their high credit ratings as international institutions. However, the presence of the IMF director general and World Bank president at the Lyon G-7 summit facilitated agreement on the HIPC initiative.[59]

The purpose of the HIPC initiative was to reduce the debts of eligible countries to a sustainable level so they could service their debts without incurring loan arrears or requiring debt rescheduling and without hindering their economic development. The HIPC countries had low enough incomes to be eligible for soft loans from the Bank group's IDA, and external debts that were more than twice their annual export earnings. (See Chapter 11 for discussion of the IDA). Forty-one countries initially met these criteria; 33 were in sub-Saharan Africa and the other eight were in the Americas and Asia.[60] The HIPC program involved a demanding two-stage process, with each stage lasting up to three years. During the first stage, the HIPC country had to implement an IMF- and Bank-supported economic reform program. If the IMF and the Bank then determined that debt relief was insufficient, the country entered the second stage, where it received some debt relief and financial support from bilateral and commercial creditors and the multilateral institutions.[61] The implementation of the HIPC initiative was therefore a slow process, and by May 1998 only eight countries had made reasonable progress. Furthermore, the debt situation of many of the poorest LDCs was not improving. For example, Honduras and Nicaragua were the only two Central American countries sufficiently poor to be on the list of 41 HIPC countries. Despite the HIPC program, economic growth was stagnant in Honduras and Nicaragua from 1990 to 1998, and in 1998 they had the largest external debt burdens in Central America. In Africa, Zambia was devoting 40 percent of its national budget to foreign debt payments in 1997. The costs of the debt crisis were also not spread evenly *within* debtor states, and there was considerable evidence that the poorest and most vulnerable people were the most adversely affected.[62] In response to the protracted debt problems of the low-income LDCs, a London-based civil society organization with worldwide connections called *Jubilee 2000* launched a debt forgiveness campaign in 1998.

Jubilee 2000 is composed of a large number of mainly religious but also some secular civil society groups from around the world. Beginning in 1998, Jubilee 2000 called for full debt relief for low-income LDCs by the year 2000 and provided detailed proposals to accelerate the HIPC process, broaden its eligibility criteria, and increase the amount of assistance to eligible countries. The rapid economic relief provided to more prosperous LDCs affected by the 1997 Asian financial crisis demonstrated that DCs could move swiftly when foreign investment and the stock market were affected, and Jubilee 2000 supporters demanded a similar rapid response to problems of the HIPCs. Jubilee 2000 also engaged in mass demonstrations; for example, it formed a human chain of 50,000 people around the convention center at the 1998 G-7 summit in Birmingham, England.

After some delay because of divisions among the G-7 countries, the 1999 G-7 summit in Cologne, Germany, finally agreed to establish an *enhanced HIPC initiative,* and in September 1999, the IMF and Bank governors adopted the major elements of the G-7 proposal. It appears that Jubilee 2000 had some influence in pressuring the North to reach this decision. The enhanced initiative more than doubled the amount of debt relief and was designed to make the existing HIPC initiative faster (permitting LDCs to receive debt relief more quickly), broader (applying to more countries), and deeper (permitting a higher amount of debt write-off). Although these changes marked a significant improvement, critics argue that the debt relief measures are still insufficient and that IMF and Bank SALs are not in the best interests of debtor LDCs (SALs are discussed later in this chapter and in Chapter 11). Even supporters of the enhanced HIPC initiative concede that "given the continued fragility of these countries, the initiative is not likely to provide recipients with a last exit from their debt problems, unless they achieve strong, sustained economic growth."[63]

Assessing the Effectiveness of the Debt Strategies

The international debt strategies had three main objectives: to prevent the collapse of the international banking and financial systems, to restore capital market access for the debtors, and to restore economic growth in the debtor countries. The Baker and Brady Plans were most successful in achieving the first two objectives. In regard to the first objective, by the late 1980s "the banks were no longer in the serious jeopardy that they faced at the outset of the debt crisis."[64] From 1982 to 1992, the loan exposure of all U.S. banks to the Baker-17 highly indebted countries fell from 130 percent of the banks' capital and reserves to only 27 percent; the loan exposure of British banks fell from 85 to 12 percent, of German banks from 31 to 19 percent, and of French banks from 135 to 23 percent. In 1988, the BIS also oversaw an agreement that commercial banks in the OECD countries must have equity and reserves amounting to at least 8 percent of their outstanding loans, and this helped restore some confidence in the international banking system.[65] In regard to the second objective, Latin American debtors were able to return to the international financial markets far more rapidly after the 1980s debt crisis than after the 1930s crisis. Liberal-economic academics and policymakers view these first two criteria as most important for assessing the effectiveness of the debt strategies, and they therefore generally considered the Baker and Brady Plans to be successful.[66]

In marked contrast, historical structuralists and some interventionist liberals believe that the third objective—restoring economic growth in LDC debtor countries—should be the most important, and they considered the Baker and Brady Plans to be largely ineffective. For example, one critic argued that the IMF and major creditor states were primarily concerned with increasing "the immediate payment capacity of the debtor nations and not their development."[67] Historical structuralists also believed that the debt strategies required far more sacrifice from LDCs than from DCs and international bankers. These critics therefore concluded that "the debt crisis is by no means over yet; a banking crisis may have been tidied up, but a development crisis is in full swing."[68]

There is in fact considerable evidence that the Baker and Brady Plans had serious shortcomings in regard to the third objective of restoring LDC economic growth. This was true for the Baker-17 countries and even more so for the poorest LDC debtors, most of whom were not on the Baker-17 list. As discussed, the Baker and Brady Plans were concerned mainly with debt to commercial banks, and they did not provide relief for debt to the IMF and World Bank. Because the poorest LDCs were highly dependent on IMF and Bank loans, the Baker and Brady Plans were of little use to them. In 1996, the North therefore instituted the HIPC initiative for the poorest states, and in 1998 the enhanced HIPC initiative was introduced. The North should be credited for gradually developing more assertive debt strategies, shifting from debt rescheduling under the Baker Plan to debt reduction under the Brady Plan to debt relief for the poorest LDCs under the HIPC initiative. However, it could be argued that it always took a new crisis before the IMF, the

Bank, and DCs upgraded their debt relief efforts, and it remains to be seen whether the latest HIPC initiative is sufficient to deal with the debt problems of the poorest LDCs.

Historical structuralists have reserved special criticism for the IMF and the Bank, arguing that they give highest priority to ensuring that LDC debtors adopt liberal-economic policies and repay their loans. According to these critics, a radical restructuring of LDC debtor economies is required to promote their economic development, but IMF conditionality precludes such possibilities. Although some liberal economists concede that IMF and Bank conditionality has contributed to economic dislocation in LDC debtor countries, they nevertheless argue that the liberalization of debtor country policies has "laid the foundations for subsequent sustainable growth." However, critics of the debt strategies believe

> . . . there is some reason to be skeptical about the view that the Third World economies are now "leaner and fitter" to face the world ahead beyond the debt crisis. They are certainly leaner but whether they are fitter remains to be seen.[69]

It is important to note that DC policies in other areas such as trade sometimes counteract the North's efforts to assist the South through debt relief strategies. For LDCs to both succeed in development and repay their debts, they require access to DC markets for their exports. LDCs have a comparative advantage in the production of agricultural goods, textiles, and other products that do not require large amounts of sophisticated machinery and technology. However, the DCs currently impose some of their highest tariffs on these products because of domestic pressures from their workers. Although the North gives preferential treatment to some Southern exports, this treatment often does not extend to exports where the South has a comparative advantage (see Chapter 8). The foreign debt strategies would be far more effective if the North were more willing to open its markets to Southern exports.[70]

To this point, the chapter has discussed the effects of the debt crisis only on the LDCs. However, many transition states in Eastern Europe and the FSU were also major foreign debtors in the 1980s–1990s.

TRANSITION ECONOMIES AND FOREIGN DEBT

The Soviet bloc countries contended with many of the same economic problems as the South during the 1980s debt crisis, including growing balance-of-payments deficits, declining terms of trade, and stagnating economic growth. The increased need for financing also caused Soviet bloc countries to look to the IMF and the Bank for support. Thus, Hungary and Poland joined these institutions during the 1980s, partly in efforts to deal with their growing debt problems.[71]

Eastern Europe

During the 1970s, Eastern Europeans borrowed heavily on international financial markets to finance industrial investment. However, the oil price shocks, poor investment decisions, economic inefficiency, lack of export competitiveness, and high interest rates on their foreign debt created severe economic problems. Indeed, "Eastern

Europe experienced a debt crisis similar and prior to that of Latin America."[72] As early as 1981 an acute foreign exchange shortage forced Poland to negotiate a rescheduling of its debt with official and private creditors. Poland had financed an ambitious program of industrial investment with external funding, but its economic performance and export levels were insufficient to service its debt. Like the South, Eastern European countries have followed different development strategies with major implications for their foreign debt. The two basic strategies were often referred to as the Polish and Czech-Hungarian models.

The Polish model involved large debt buildup followed by repeated debt reschedulings and eventually official debt reduction, partly based on political considerations. Poland's net debt to the Western DCs increased from $7.6 billion in 1975 to $22.1 billion in 1980, and in 1981 it had the highest debt and debt service ratio in the Soviet bloc. Because the Soviet Union seemed unwilling to assist Poland and the Soviet bloc was not implementing effective adjustment measures, Western creditors sharply reduced further credits to all Eastern European states. Poland's growing economic problems resulted in severe economic austerity measures and the formation of the Solidarity Movement. When the Polish government responded by imposing martial law in December 1981, the West imposed trade sanctions and suspended debt repayment talks. Although private banks agreed to refinance some Polish debt, Western governments did not resume rescheduling negotiations on official debts until Poland ended martial law in August 1983.

Poland had seven reschedulings of its commercial bank debt and five reschedulings of its official debt from 1981 to 1990. When a democratically elected government replaced the communist government in late 1989 and adopted a program to promote macroeconomic stabilization and structural change in early 1990, the West offered to provide assistance under the Brady Plan. Indeed, Western governments, which held two-thirds of Poland's debt, offered a 50 percent forgiveness of its official bilateral debt at Paris Club negotiations in 1991. Although Poland had requested 80 percent forgiveness, the Paris Club's 50 percent offer was exceptionally high; it had previously offered a maximum forgiveness of 33 percent to low-income countries. Under pressure from the G-7, commercial banks also reached an agreement with Poland in March 1994 to reduce its private debt by 45 percent. Bulgaria in many respects followed the Polish model, and the private banks agreed in principle to a substantial reduction of Bulgaria's debt in late 1993 (most of Bulgaria's debt was private). The former Czechoslovakia and Hungary were also deeply affected by the 1980s debt crisis, but unlike the Polish-Bulgarian model they followed more restrained and prudent economic policies in efforts to maintain their creditworthiness. For example, in 1981 Hungary had the highest per capita debt in the Soviet bloc, and its debt service ratio was second highest after Poland. Nevertheless, Hungary joined the IMF and the Bank in 1982 and instituted ambitious economic reforms. As a result of their more prudent policies, Hungary and the former Czechoslovakia did not require the debt relief measures that were offered to Poland and Bulgaria.[73]

As with the LDCs, the differing debt strategies of transition economies stemmed partly from domestic economic and political factors. For example, Poland's model of large debt buildup resulted from political events that prevented the Polish government from taking decisive action to deal with its looming debt problems. After

Wladyslaw Gomulka was removed as first secretary of the Polish Communist party in 1970, policies were adopted that led to decentralization of the party and divisions within the top political leadership. When high oil prices and declining exports contributed to serious economic problems in the late 1970s, workers were able to resist austerity moves (that would have been made at their expense) because Poland's political leadership was so fractured. When the leaders attempted to raise prices and hold down wages as part of an economic austerity program, massive strikes by workers forced them to reverse these moves. It was not until December 1981, when the military took control in Poland and dominated strong societal groups such as Solidarity, that an austerity program was introduced (which contributed to hardship and eventually to further protests).[74]

In contrast to Poland, domestic political developments contributed to more prudent economic policies in Hungary. Although Hungary instituted some austerity measures, it also adopted a series of reforms to increase economic efficiency and to give profits and prices a larger role in resource allocation. The suppression of the 1956 revolt in Hungary had led to a number of developments that contributed to these economic reforms. For example, Hungary turned from one-person to collective leadership, which supported the introduction of a limited market mechanism and a more balanced development strategy based on specific Hungarian conditions. Unlike reformers elsewhere, Hungarian supporters of economic reform also "sought not to weaken the [Communist] party but to use it to pursue their particular economic goals."[75] When Hungary confronted debt problems, its earlier reforms and political ability to institute change enabled it to meet its debt service obligations far more effectively than Poland.

Despite the different development strategies followed by Eastern Europeans, their debt problems (as was the case for LDC debtors) also resulted from external events largely beyond their control. All Eastern Europeans, for example, suffered economically from their increased dependence on imports from nonsocialist states to promote economic growth and investment, from the collapse of the Soviet bloc's CMEA in 1991, and from deterioration in their terms of trade as the Soviet Union ended subsidized oil exports. Bulgaria is a prime example of a state affected by external events: The breakup of CMEA had major consequences for Bulgaria because of its export dependence on the Soviet Union, the Gulf War adversely affected Bulgaria's exports to Iraq, and the war in Yugoslavia seriously disrupted Bulgarian export routes to Western Europe. The structural transition to market-oriented economies produced further instability, and domestic output in Eastern Europe fell by almost 25 percent in 1990–1991. Thus, a combination of internal and external factors contributed to Eastern Europe's foreign debt problems.

Russia

The Soviet Union also had external debt problems, which were greatly exacerbated by the breakup of the country. In mid-1992, Russia began negotiations with the other FSU states on "zero-option" agreements, in which Russia assumed responsibility for the entire FSU external debt while taking control of some of the FSU's foreign assets. Russia was willing to assume the entire FSU debt for several reasons: it had the strongest resource base for servicing the debt, the division of assets such as embassies seemed to make little sense, and the assumption of the debt could help preserve Russia's hegemonic role in the region. By assuming the FSU debt, Russia's received assets including gold and foreign exchange, embassies abroad, and a portfolio of loans to countries such as India, Cuba, Libya, and Vietnam. However, the collapse of the Russian economy severely undercut the country's debt-servicing capacity, and Russia had to seek IMF loans and negotiate Paris and London Club reschedulings. In April 1996, the Paris Club agreed to the largest debt rescheduling in its history by postponing $40 billion of Russian debt. (Russia's strategic importance was a major factor in this decision.) In late 1997, Russia's foreign debt totalled $123.5 billion, including $91.4 billion of the FSU's debt Russia had assumed. However, a fourfold increase in Russia's trade surplus between 1998 and 2000 contributed to a large current account surplus and an easing of the debt problem. A major factor in this turnaround has been strong world oil prices, a commodity that constitutes about 20 percent of Russia's exports. In the longer term, Russia's debt situation will depend on its ability and willingness to accelerate economic reforms; restructure enterprises; improve the investment climate, tax system, and banking system; encourage transparency in business financial reportings; counter crime and corruption; institute social and political reforms; and improve the poor socioeconomic conditions of a large share of the population.[76]

THE DEBT CRISIS AND CHANGING ROLES OF THE IMF AND WORLD BANK

A major new element in the 1980s debt crisis was the central role of the international financial institutions—the IMF and the World Bank. The debt crisis also altered the relationship between these two institutions as they adopted new functions that overlap in significant respects. The problem of overlap was recognized when the two institutions were created, and the Bretton Woods negotiators deliberately excluded specific references to the South in the IMF Articles of Agreement because the development function was assigned to the Bank. Thus, the IMF was to provide short-term loans to *any* country with balance-of-payments problems, whereas the Bank was to provide long-term loans for reconstruction and development. (References to the South were later included in the second amendment to the IMF Articles of Agreement.) The only direct linkage between the two organizations was that membership in the IMF was a prerequisite for membership in the Bank.[77]

Despite their separate functions, in the 1960s the Bank began to infringe directly on the IMF's territory. Diverging from its practice of providing loans for specific development projects, the Bank provided large-scale *program lending* to India for general balance-of-payments support. The Bank also linked this support with general conditions for policy reform by the Indian government.[78] The Bank justified its actions by arguing that India's balance-of-payments deficit resulted from long-term development problems. However, IMF officials countered that the Bank's balance-of-payments funding with conditionality attached directly infringed on IMF functions. In 1966 the two organizations signed an agreement in efforts to avoid further overlap problems, but the agreement did not fully clarify the differences in their responsibilities.[79]

Several changes during the 1970s contributed to a marked increase in overlap between IMF and World Bank functions. First, the IMF became less involved with exchange rate stabilization when the Bretton Woods system of pegged exchange rates collapsed. The IMF's other major function of providing loans, in which there is potential overlap with the Bank, therefore became more prominent. Second, the IMF initially provided loans to all countries, but by the late 1970s it was lending almost exclusively to LDCs—the same group of countries receiving Bank loans. Third, although the Bank's Articles of Agreement (Article 3, Section 4) state that it should provide loans for specific projects "except in special circumstances," Bank officials confronted situations in which LDCs could not obtain needed funding for their development programs by borrowing only for specific projects. In 1971, the Bank's executive directors therefore decided that program lending of the type they had provided to India in the 1960s was appropriate under certain circumstances. The Bank's program lending to finance commodity imports has distinct similarities with IMF lending for balance-of-payments purposes.[80]

The most important reason for increased overlap related to the 1980s foreign debt crisis. Indeed, the IMF and the Bank developed some remarkably similar new lending programs for indebted LDCs. The IMF found that its traditional short-term loans for balance-of-payments problems with 3- to 5-year repayment periods were not adequate for LDCs with protracted payments problems. To deal with the debt crisis, the IMF therefore also provided *medium-term* SALs with repayment periods of 5.5 to 10 years. As for the Bank, its long-term loans for development projects with repayment periods of 15 to 20 years (and in some cases 40 years) were also not the type of funding LDC debtors required to deal with more immediate balance-of-payments problems. Like the IMF, the Bank therefore developed medium-term SALs for the debtor countries. Although the IMF still provided short-term balance-of-payments loans and the Bank provided long-term development loans, they *both* were now providing medium-term SALs to indebted LDCs and transition economies.[81]

The greater overlap of IMF and Bank functions has increased both the potential for conflict and the need for collaboration between the two IOs. The overlapping functions also raise questions as to whether two institutions continue to be necessary, and the *Economist* predicted in 1991 that a merger between the two "makes sense, and in time it will happen."[82] Despite this prediction, there are several reasons for maintaining the two as distinctive IOs. First, the Bank group is composed of five institutions, and it is already too large by itself for efficient management (see Chapter 11). Joining the Bank and the IMF would simply compound the problems related to size. Second, development issues are exceedingly complex, and it is important that a range of institutions provide advice and conditions for loans. Although historical structuralists argue that IMF and Bank policies are virtually identical, liberal economists can point to IMF-Bank disputes as an indication of competing perspectives. Third, IMF and Bank responsibilities extend well beyond providing loans to LDCs. Although the IMF's monetary role declined when the pegged exchange rate regime collapsed, the IMF continues to advise states on monetary issues, and it could play a more important role in future monetary and financial issues. As discussed in Chapter 11, the Bank is an important source of economic expertise on development issues. Finally, the disintegration of the Soviet bloc, the financial crises, and the dire economic circumstances in sub-Saharan Africa provide sufficient economic challenges for both institutions, helping to restore a differentiation of their functions. Whereas the IMF has had the lead role in dealing with Eastern European and FSU debt problems and with the Asian financial crisis, the Bank has been coordinating aid efforts in sub-Saharan Africa.[83]

The IMF, World Bank, and Debtor Countries

Although new efforts at IMF-Bank collaboration are partly designed to avert institutional conflict, the South is highly suspicious of these moves. Historical structuralists and LDC debtors often criticize IMF conditionality as an unwarranted infringement on LDC sovereignty, and they argue that the liberal-economic conditions on IMF and World Bank loans hinder rather than facilitate development.[84] With moves toward IMF-Bank collaboration, the South is concerned about the increased likelihood of *cross-conditionality*, in which the IMF's decision that a loan applicant is uncreditworthy prevents the applicant from receiving Bank as well as IMF funding. Thus, the South fears that the conditions placed on official loans will become even more onerous. Although the IMF and the Bank have ruled out cross-conditionality in a formal, legal sense, they sometimes engage in this practice on an informal basis.[85]

Critics also charge that IMF and Bank SALs put the onus of adjustment on LDC debtors—and on the most vulnerable groups within LDCs—even though the North and the South shared responsibility for the debt crisis. SALs have pressured LDC debtors to reduce the role of the state and increase the role of the market, with little concern for the social and distributional effects of these policies. Because SALs are intended to improve LDC balance of payments by reducing spending for social services, lowering wages, emphasizing production for export over local consumption, and ending subsidies for local industries, it is the poorer, more vulnerable individuals in LDCs who are often the most severely affected.

Historical structuralists and some interventionist liberals argue that it is necessary to be aware of the negative distributional effects of IMF and Bank SALs. Poorer women in LDCs, who do unpaid work in managing the household, are the most severely affected by IMF and Bank pressures for a reduction in LDC funding for public services. Because women have primary responsibility for household cooking, cleaning, and health care, public sector services such as clean water supplies, waste disposal, public transport, and health facilities lighten their work and enable them to gain education and skills so they can enter the paid work force. Thus, the burden on poorer women increases as IMF and Bank SALs require cutbacks in social expenditures on health and nutrition. As the government provides fewer of these services, women must make up the difference by providing them through the home. The school dropout rate of young girls also increases as a result of SALs because girls must help with the household labor and often work in sweatshops to supplement the family's income. Furthermore, children and pregnant and lactating mothers are the groups most seriously affected by IMF and Bank pressures to remove food subsidies for LDC consumers. In sum, the informal sector in LDCs grows because of structural adjustment programs, and poorer women pay the price through increased unpaid work and a deterioration of health and nutrition.[86]

In response to these criticisms, the Bank has taken some measures to ameliorate the effects of SALs on the poor while retaining its concerns for promoting efficiency and liberal-economic growth. For example, the Bank continues to view cuts in food subsidies as desirable in terms of efficiency, but it attempts to ameliorate the negative effects on the poor through school lunches, food stamps, and food aid.[87] IMF and Bank officials argue that structural adjustment programs aimed at market efficiency and decreased public sector involvement can be compatible with distributional and social welfare goals, but they have not convinced some of their critics. (Chapter 11 has a more detailed discussion of this issue.)

THE 1990s FINANCIAL CRISIS

This section briefly discusses the 1990s East and Southeast Asian financial crisis (or the Asian financial crisis). Of particular interest are the challenges the crisis posed to the IMF and international financial stability, and the proposals that emerged for improving the "international financial architecture." Chapter 11 discusses the 1990s financial crisis in more detail in the context of international development.

As discussed, international bank lending to LDCs declined precipitously during the 1980s as a result of the foreign debt crisis. In the 1990s, however, there was a renewal of private capital flows to middle-income LDCs. Whereas syndicated bank lending was of primary importance in the 1970s–1980s, **portfolio investment,** or the purchase of stocks, bonds, and money market instruments by foreigners to realize a financial return, was far more important in the 1990s. (**Foreign direct investment,** or the ownership or control of assets in one country by residents of another country, also increased during the 1990s; see Chapter 10.) The sources of the portfolio investment were highly diverse, including institutional investors such as pension funds and life insurance companies, securities traders, and managed funds; and unlike the bank lending of the 1970s, most of the portfolio flows went to private borrowers. The reasons for the revival of capital flows in the 1990s included higher interest rates in the South, economic reforms in LDCs as a result of the debt crisis, a degree of success with Brady Plan debt reductions, and a gradual freeing of capital controls with less regulatory restrictions on investment in LDCs. In the early 1990s, however, some economists expressed concerns that these capital flows were volatile and "could be reversed easily."[88] Their concerns were soon realized when capital inflows to Mexico rather suddenly halted in March 1994 after the assassination of a presidential candidate, resulting in a Mexican currency crisis in 1994–1995. This section devotes primary attention to the 1997–1999 Asian financial crisis because "it was the sharpest financial crisis to hit the developing world since the 1982 debt crisis."[89]

The Asian financial crisis developed in several stages, beginning in Thailand and spreading to other Asian countries. Thailand began receiving capital inflows in the early 1990s, which rose dramatically by the mid-1990s despite a deterioration of economic and financial conditions. Indications of problems included Thailand's growing current account deficit, the foreign currency debt of Thai banks, and the fall in property prices. The Thai *baht*, like other East Asian currencies, was pegged to the U.S. dollar, and Thai exports became less competitive when the exchange rate of the dollar began rising against the Japanese yen in the mid-1990s. A full-blown crisis developed in July 1997 when Thailand had to allow its *baht* to float. After the *baht* began to depreciate, other Asian countries had to float their currencies as they came under severe downward pressure. When foreign investors lost confidence in the currencies of these countries, there was a massive reversal of capital flows, and a number of Asian countries had to seek IMF and World Bank loans to bolster their currencies and economies.[90] Whereas the main concerns of the 1980s debt crisis related to the overall indebtedness and high debt-service ratios of debtor states, the main concerns of the Asian financial crisis related to short-term debt levels and outflows of portfolio investment. In response to the Mexican and Asian financial crises, the major DC governments proposed a number of reforms to strengthen the international financial architecture, or global governance in finance.[91]

The annual G-7 summits played an important role in the architecture exercise, which began in 1995 in response to the Mexican financial crisis, and subsequently evolved in response to the Asian crisis and a financial crisis in Russia.[92] The architecture exercise led to the creation of new IMF lending facilities, encouraged international efforts to strengthen the financial infrastructure in LDCs and transition economies, and resulted in a vigorous debate regarding the role of the IMF and its conditionality requirements. Two major objectives of the architecture exercise were to develop better strategies to prevent financial crises and to resolve financial crises. Of special interest in terms of crisis prevention were developing procedures to identify vulnerable countries before they experienced crises and to foster compliance of countries with international standards and codes designed to produce financial stability. Of interest in terms of crisis resolution were efforts to reform IMF policies and practices and efforts to involve private-sector creditors in resolving financial problems of LDCs and transition economies.[93] Not surprisingly, prescriptions for the best measures to reform the international financial architecture depend on one's theoretical perspective. The following discussion compares the views of four groups: (1) orthodox liberals, (2) those combining orthodox and institutional liberalism, (3) those combining interventionist and institutional liberalism, and (4) historical structuralists.[94]

As discussed in Chapter 4, orthodox liberals promote "negative freedom," or freedom of the market to function with minimal interference from the state. Orthodox liberals such as Milton Friedman believe that the problems with international finance stem from inadequate domestic institutions and inappropriate domestic policies rather than from a freeing of capital flows. The 1994–1995 Mexican peso crisis from this perspective resulted from an overvalued exchange rate and inadequate attention to the country's trade and budget deficits and foreign debt; and the 1997–1998 Asian financial crisis stemmed from poorly capitalized banks offering questionable loans to businesses with political connections, poor financial reporting, and fixed or semi-fixed exchange rates. The financial problems did not develop from freer global capital flows, which maximize efficiency by entering countries that have good regulatory practices such as balanced budgets, market stabilization, and low inflation rates. International regulation to limit risky behavior in capital markets would be harmful, and virtually all capital controls should be abolished.

Some economists believe that financial markets require *a lender of last resort* for states with financial difficulties and propose that the IMF should have more financial resources to serve this purpose. A lender of last resort "is an institution that is willing and able to supply unlimited amounts of short-term credit to financial institutions when they are threatened by a creditor panic."[95] However, orthodox liberals argue that the best way to prevent capital flight and speculative attacks on a state's currency is to eliminate the problem of *moral hazard*. If a lender of last resort exists, states facing financial crises are more likely to engage in risky and irresponsible behavior because they can always count on the lender to rescue them. Some orthodox liberals would abolish the IMF and World Bank because they contribute to moral hazard by providing development assistance, debt bailouts, and balance-of-payments support.

The second group combines orthodox and institutional liberalism. Like orthodox liberals, this group believes that inadequate domestic institutions and inappropriate national policies are the main factors increasing a country's vulnerability to financial crises. As with the first group, this second group believes that the Asian financial crisis stemmed more from "crony capitalism" or overly close connections between business groups and governments than from financial contagion. Unlike the first group, however, this second group thinks there is an important role for international financial institutions such as the IMF and World Bank in ensuring that LDCs and transition economies follow transparent, liberal-economic policies. To the extent that this group is interested in revamping the international financial architecture, it favors stronger IMF conditionality requirements to ensure that states are subject to the discipline of the marketplace and IMF policies "to legitimize financial liberalization by blocking tendencies to move toward increased state regulation of international financial flows."[96]

The third group combines interventionist and institutional liberalism. As liberals, members of this group believe that the failure of countries to follow liberal-economic policies interferes with efficiently functioning markets. As *interventionist* (or *embedded*) liberals, however, they feel that *unrestrained* markets are not necessarily beneficial and that measures must be taken to protect society (see Chapter 4). In regard to finance, currency traders often buy and sell for profit without taking account of fundamental economic conditions, and this produces unnecessary volatility in foreign exchange markets and capital flows. Thus, financial markets according to this group are likely to perform better when regulated. The third group also emphasizes the need for a well-funded international lender of last resort. Without such a lender, financial crises are likely to increase and detract from both global economic efficiency and development in LDCs and transition economies.[97]

Many theorists in this group have been actively involved in the debate regarding changes to the international financial architecture. For example, some members of this group responded to the Asian financial crisis with proposals to implement the *Tobin tax*, which Nobel Laureate James Tobin first proposed in 1972. Tobin's proposal called for "an internationally uniform tax on all spot conversions of one currency into another, proportional to the size of the transaction."[98] Although Tobin referred to a tax of only 1 percent on currency exchange transactions, he believed it would discourage short-term speculative capital flows and would also generate substantial revenue that could be used for global priorities such as combatting international poverty. Many supporters of the Tobin tax argue that it would help reduce the risk of global financial crises and provide the international community with some of the profits flowing from international capital mobility. However, critics of the Tobin tax range from orthodox liberals who insist there is nothing wrong with financial markets, to others who maintain that such a tax would be not be feasible or effective. Whereas currency traders in times of crisis would disregard a small tax, a larger tax would seriously interfere with financial markets.[99] As institutional as well as interventionist liberals, the third group proposes numerous reforms in IMF (and World Bank) transparency and accountability and in conditionality requirements. They also often support the idea that the IMF should become a lender of last resort.[100]

Finally, the fourth group are historical structuralists who argue that the Asian financial crisis is another example of the corrupting power of international capital. Unlike interventionist liberals, this group thinks that the IMF and the Bank are unreformable, and—ironically—like some orthodox liberals, the group therefore favors the abolition of these institutions. For example, one study concludes that "the international financial institutions require Third World countries to adopt policies that harm the interests of working people," and sees little evidence that the IMF is willing or able to reform its policies.[101] In view of the return of orthodox liberalism or neoliberalism, the second group (orthodox and institutional liberals) currently has considerable influence in discussions of the international financial architecture. However, if international financial crises become frequent and severe enough, it is possible that the third group (interventionist and institutional liberals) will gain in influence.[102]

CONCLUSION

What is the relevance of the IPE theoretical perspectives and the major themes of the text—globalization, North-North relations, and North-South relations—for foreign debt issues? The 1980s foreign debt crisis is a prime example of the effects of growing interdependence and globalization on the policies of indebted LDCs and transition economies. The origins of the debt crisis stemmed back to the 1970s, when commercial banks extended a large volume of loans to LDCs after the OPEC price increases. These private loans were attractive to borrowers because of their low interest rates and lack of conditionality. Although orthodox liberals emphasize imprudent borrowing behavior and inefficient domestic policies of LDCs as major causes of the debt crisis, historical structuralists focus instead on the long-term dependency of LDCs and the irresponsible behavior of commercial banks and creditor governments. Despite these differences of view, most would agree that unexpected changes resulting from global interdependence, such as the food and oil crises of the 1970s, should be included among major factors causing the debt crisis.

There is also broad agreement that the IMF and the Bank have used SALs to induce debtors to adopt liberal-economic policies, thus opening their economies to the forces of globalization. For example, after Mexico declared that it could no longer service its foreign debt in 1982, Mexican governments have steadily moved toward economic liberalization policies. These moves include Mexico's shift from ISI to export-led growth policies, its withdrawal of public subsidies in most economic sectors, its domestic economic changes to attract foreign investment, and the opening of its economy to international trade. In the trade area, Mexico joined GATT in 1986 and NAFTA in 1993. Mexico is of course not alone, and there are similar changes throughout the South. Thus, the average import tariffs in Latin America declined from 56 percent in 1985 to 16 percent in 1992, largely as a result of unilateral trade liberalization, and Latin American states signed at least 31 trade liberalization agreements during 1990–1996.[103]

Although these LDC policy changes resulted partly from evidence that previous import substitution policies had been unsuccessful, pressure from DCs, the IMF, and the Bank were also critical factors in the decision of indebted states to open their economies. There are sharp differences of view, however, regarding the effects of these liberal-economic policies on indebted states. Liberal economists often argue that the debt strategies have been quite successful, preventing the collapse of the international banking system and restoring capital market access for many indebted states. Liberals assume that though the policy changes required of debtors have caused hardship for some groups and individuals, the long-term effects of the shift to economic openness will be beneficial for LDCs and transition economies. Realists and historical structuralists, by contrast, argue that liberals largely ignore the effect of political and economic inequality among states on the debt issue. Although globalization has facilitated the *transmission* of liberal values to the DCs, these values have been *imposed on* the LDC debtor states. Liberals also consider the IMF and the Bank to be politically neutral institutions, whereas realists and historical structuralists view them as conduits for imposing policies favored by the most powerful DCs and private actors on the least powerful.[104] Furthermore, historical structuralists argue that the debt strategies required far more sacrifice from LDC debtors than from international banks and that IMF and World Bank conditionality requirements meet the needs of international capital rather than those of indebted states. Indeed, IMF requirements that debtors reduce social expenditures, increase exports, remove restrictions on capital flows, and devalue their currencies have the most negative impact on the poorest and weakest societal groups.

This chapter tells a good deal not only about the themes of globalization and North-South inequality but also about North-North relations. Although the United States has declined as a hegemon in some economic areas, it took a leadership position in helping to manage the debt crisis. U.S. leadership was a reflection of its dominant position in the financial and monetary areas "well into the 1980s because of the relative attractiveness of U.S. financial markets, the pre-eminence of U.S. financial institutions and the dollar in global markets, and the relative size of the U.S. economy."[105] Even in this area, however, there was a gradual shift from U.S. to collective leadership. Thus, Northern-dominated institutions including the IMF, World Bank, BIS, G-7/G-8, and Paris and London Clubs had a major role in collective debt management.

The largest international banks played a major role in managing LDC debt problems through private creditor committees (the London Club) until the Mexican debt crisis in 1982. Thereafter, realists point out that it was the most powerful industrial states and international institutions they supported such as the IMF and the Bank that managed the debt crisis. Only states could mobilize sufficient resources to deal with the crisis, and only official pressures could induce banks to continue lending to debtors, and debtors to meet conditionality requirements. However, liberal interdependence theorists and historical structuralists point out that there were definitive limits to the industrial state capacities for economic management. The prolongation of the debt crisis despite the Baker Plan, Brady Plan and HIPC initiative support the liberal contention that states today have only limited control over market transactions, capital flows, and the behavior of private institutions such as international banks. Historical structuralists have pointed to the fact that the debt management strategies were far more successful in protecting the international banks and restoring capital market access than in ensuring a return to economic growth in debtor LDCs. Finally, civil society groups such as Jubilee 2000 had some role in pressuring the DCs and international institutions to alleviate the debt problems of the poorest LDCs. Although these civil society groups opposed the impact of globalization on the debtors, they used the accoutrements of globalization such as the World Wide Web to communicate their ideas and exert influence.

Growing interdependence and globalization were factors contributing to the 1990s Asian financial crisis as well as the 1980s debt crisis. Furthermore, assessments of the 1990s Asian financial crisis, like the 1980s debt crisis, depend on one's theoretical perspective. Orthodox liberals attributed the Asian financial crisis mainly to inefficient domestic policies, and they strongly opposed any international controls on capital flows. Whereas some extreme orthodox liberals believe that the IMF and the Bank should be abolished because they contribute to moral hazard, others encourage these institutions to strengthen their conditionality requirements to ensure that LDCs and transition economies are subject to market discipline. Interventionist liberals by contrast believe that some degree of control over capital flows is necessary and argue for institutional reforms making the IMF and the Bank more transparent and accountable. The harshest critics of international capital flows are historical structuralists, who argue that the IMF and the Bank should be abolished because they are representatives of international capital and are unreformable. However, those most active in trying to develop a new international financial architecture are interventionist liberals who seek IMF and Bank reform.

NOTES

1. William R. Cline, *International Debt Reexamined* (Washington, DC: Institute for International Economics, 1995), p.1.
2. Rudiger Dornbusch and Stanley Fischer, "Third World Debt," *Science* 234, November 14, 1986, p.836; Stuart Corbridge, *Debt and Development* (Oxford: Blackwell, 1993), p.15.
3. Miles Kahler, "Politics and International Debt: Explaining the Crisis," *International Organization* 39–3 (Summer 1985), p.357.
4. See Albert Fishlow, "Lessons from the Past: Capital Markets During the 19th Century and the Interwar Period," *International Organization* 39–3 (Summer 1985), pp.383–439; Barbara Stallings, *Banker to the Third World: U.S. Portfolio Investment in Latin America, 1900–1986* (Berkeley: University of California Press, 1987); Barry Eichengreen and

Richard Portes, "Dealing with Debt: The 1930s and the 1980s," in Ishrat Husain and Ishac Diwan, eds., *Dealing with the Debt Crisis: A World Bank Symposium* (Washington, DC: World Bank, 1989), pp.69–86; and Barry Eichengreen and Peter H. Lindert, eds., *The International Debt Crisis in Historical Perspective* (Cambridge: MIT Press, 1989).

5. Corbridge, *Debt and Development,* p.25; Cline, *International Debt Reexamined,* p.6.

6. Stallings, *Banker to the Third World,* pp.313–314.

7. John T. Cuddington, "The Extent and Causes of the Debt Crisis of the 1980s," in Husain and Diwan, eds., *Dealing with the Debt Crisis,* p.15; World Bank, *World Debt Tables 1992–1993, Vol. 1* (Washington, DC: IBRD, 1992), pp.41–45. For a historical structuralist perspective on early signs of a debt crisis see Cheryl Payer, *Lent and Lost: Foreign Credit and Third World Development* (London: Zed Books, 1991), pp.83–89.

8. *World Bank Annual Report—1983* (Washington, DC: IBRD, 1983), p.34.

9. William R. Cline, "International Debt: Analysis, Experience and Prospects," *Journal of Development Planning* 16 (1985), p.26.

10. Theodore H. Cohn, *Canadian Food Aid: Domestic and Foreign Policy Implications* (Denver: University of Denver, Graduate School of International Studies, 1979), pp.25–26.

11. Charles Lipson, "The International Organization of Third World Debt," *International Organization* 35–4 (Autumn 1981), p.611; Benjamin J. Cohen, "Balance-of-Payments Financing: Evolution of a Regime," in Stephen D. Krasner, ed., *International Regimes* (Ithaca: Cornell University Press, 1983), p.329.

12. Albert Fishlow, "Lessons from the Past," p.433.

13. Kahler, "Politics and International Debt," pp.358–359.

14. John Loxley, "International Capital Markets, the Debt Crisis and Development," in Roy Culpeper, Albert Berry, and Frances Stewart, eds., *Global Development Fifty Years After Bretton Woods: Essays in Honour of Gerald K. Helleiner* (New York: St. Martin's Press, 1997), pp.138–142. Some analysts argue that the share of the OPEC surplus recycled through banks was actually quite small and that low interest rates were the main reason for the increase in bank loans to LDCs. See Edwin M. Truman, "U.S. Policy on the Problems of International Debt," *Federal Reserve Bulletin* 75–11 (November 1989), p.728.

15. Stallings, *Banker to the Third World,* pp.184–186; Ricardo Ffrench-Davis, "External Debt, Adjustment, and Development in Latin America," in Richard E. Feinberg and Ricardo Ffrench-Davis, eds., *Development and External Debt in Latin America: Bases for a New Consensus* (Notre Dame: University of Notre Dame Press, 1988), p.40.

16. Ethan B. Kapstein, *Governing the Global Economy: International Finance and the State* (Cambridge: Harvard University Press, 1994), pp.60–69.

17. *IMF Annual Report—1997* (Washington, DC: IMF, 1977), pp.40–41.

18. Robert D. Putnam, "Diplomacy and Domestic Politics: The Logic of Two-level Games," *International Organization* 42–3 (Summer 1988), p.457.

19. James Raymond Vreeland, "Why Do Governments and the IMF Enter into Agreements? Statistically Selected Cases," *International Political Science Review* 24–3 (2003), pp.338–339.

20. Cline, *International Debt Reexamined,* pp.2–3; Jeffrey Sachs, "External Debt and Macroeconomic Performance in Latin America and East Asia," in William C. Brainard and George L. Perry, eds., *Brookings Papers on Economic Activity* 2 (Washington, DC: Brookings Institution, 1985), pp.523–535.

21. Lewis W. Snider, "The Political Performance of Third World Governments and the Debt Crisis," *American Political Science Review* 84–1 (December 1990), pp.1263–1280.

22. Sachs, "External Debt and Macroeconomic Performance in Latin America and East Asia," p.526.

23. Cheryl Payer, *The Debt Trap: The IMF and the Third World* (Middlesex: Penguin, 1974), pp.45–49.

24. Peter Körner, Gero Maass, Thomas Siebold, and Ranier Tetzlaff, *The IMF and the Debt Crisis: A Guide to the Third World's Dilemma,* translated by Paul Knight (London: Zed Books, 1986), pp.30–31; Peter Evans, *Dependent Development: The Alliance of Multinational, State, and Local Capital in Brazil* (Princeton: Princeton University Press, 1979).

25. Payer, *The Debt Trap,* p.48. See also Robert E. Wood, *From Marshall Plan to Debt Crisis: Foreign Aid and Development Choices in the World Economy* (Berkeley: University of California Press, 1986), pp.233–241.

26. Jesús Silva-Herzog, "The Costs for Latin America's Development," in Robert A. Pastor, ed., *Latin America's Debt Crisis: Adjusting to the Past or Planning for the Future?* (Boulder: Rienner, 1987), p.33.

27. Peter H. Lindert and Peter J. Morton, "How Sovereign Debt Has Worked," in Jeffrey D. Sachs, ed., *Developing Country Debt and Economic Performance, Vol. 1: The International Financial System* (Chicago: University of Chicago Press, 1989), pp.66–77. On the debt regime see "International Financial Negotiations and Adjustment Bargaining: An Overview," in Thomas J. Biersteker, ed., *Dealing with Debt: International Financial Negotiations and Adjustment Bargaining* (Boulder: Westview Press, 1993), pp.1–15.

28. Vinod K. Aggarwal uses the "nesting" terminology in *Liberal Protectionism: The International Politics of Organized Textile Trade* (Berkeley: University of California Press, 1985). See also Theodore H. Cohn, "The Changing Role of the United States in the Global Agricultural Trade Regime," in William P. Avery, ed., *World Agriculture and the GATT, International Political Economy Yearbook, Vol. 7* (Boulder: Rienner, 1993), pp.17–38.

29. Benjamin Cohen discusses the balance-of-payments financing regime in Cohen, "Balance-of-Payments Financing," pp.315–336.

30. Cohen, "Balance-of-Payments Financing," pp.319–323.

31. Valerie J. Assetto, *The Soviet Bloc in the IMF and the IBRD* (Boulder: Westview Press, 1988), pp.186–187; Jozef M. van Brabant, *The Planned Economies and International Economic Organizations* (Cambridge: Cambridge University Press, 1991), p.126.

32. Harold K. Jacobson and Michel Oksenberg, *China's Participation in the IMF, the World Bank, and GATT: Toward a Global Economic Order* (Ann Arbor: University of Michigan Press, 1990), pp.46–52; William Feeney, "Chinese Policy in Multilateral Financial Institutions," in Samuel S. Kim, ed., *China and the World: Chinese Foreign Policy in the Post-Mao Era* (Boulder: Westview Press, 1984), pp.266–271; Samuel S. Kim, "Whither Post-Mao Chinese Global Policy?" *International Organization* 35–3 (Summer 1981), pp.455–457.

33. Klaus Schröder, "The IMF and the Countries of the Council for Mutual Economic Assistance," *Intereconomics* 2 (March/April 1982), pp.88–90; Marie Lavigne, "Eastern European Countries and the IMF," in Béla Csikós-Nagy and David G. Young, eds., *East-West Economic Relations in the Changing Global Environment* (London: Macmillan, 1986), pp.300–304.

34. Leah A. Haus, *Globalizing the GATT: The Soviet Union's Successor States, Eastern Europe, and the International Trading System* (Washington, DC: Brookings Institution, 1992), p.104; "Sorting Out Russia," *The Economist*, September 26, 1992, pp.97–98.

35. Aziz Ali Mohammed, "The Role of International Financial Institutions," in John P. Hardt and Richard F. Kaufman, eds., *East-Central European Economies in Transition* (Armonk: Sharpe, 1995), pp.192–195.

36. Assetto, *The Soviet Bloc in the IMF and the IBRD*, p.50.

37. Jacobson and Oksenberg, *China's Participation in the IMF, the World Bank, and GATT*, p.128; Feeney, "Chinese Policy in Multilateral Financial Institutions," p.274; Richard W. Stevenson, "In Borrowing from the I.M.F., Did Yeltsin Get a Sweetheart Deal?" *New York Times,* March 3, 1996, p.A5.

38. Alexis Rieffel, *The Role of the Paris Club in Managing Debt Problems* (Princeton: Princeton University, Essays in International Finance, no. 161, December 1985); Alexis Rieffel, "The Paris Club, 1978–1983," *Columbia Journal of Transnational Law* 23–1 (1984),

pp.83–110; and Christine A. Kearney, "The Creditor Clubs: Paris and London," in Bier-steker, ed., *Dealing with Debt*, pp.61–76.

39. Rieffel, *The Role of the Paris Club in Managing Debt Problems*, pp.4–14.

40. Michael G. Kuhn with Jorge P. Guzman, *Multilateral Official Debt Rescheduling: Recent Experience, World Economic and Financial Surveys* (Washington, DC: IMF, November 1990), p.7.

41. Charles Lipson, "International Debt and International Institutions," in Miles Kahler, ed., *The Politics of International Debt* (Ithaca: Cornell University Press, 1986), pp.222–226; and Charles Lipson, "Bankers' Dilemmas: Private Cooperation in Rescheduling Sovereign Debts," in Kenneth A. Oye, ed., *Cooperation Under Anarchy* (Princeton: Princeton University Press, 1986), pp.200–225.

42. See Payer, *Lent and Lost*, pp.52–56.

43. James, *International Monetary Cooperation Since Bretton Woods*, p.347.

44. Benjamin J. Cohen, "International Debt and Linkage Strategies: Some Foreign-policy Implications for the United States," *International Organization* 39–4 (Autumn 1985), p.722; Nicholas Bayne, *Hanging in There: The G7 and G8 Summit in Maturity and Renewal* (Aldershot: Ashgate, 2000), p.64.

45. Paul Krugman, "LDC Debt Policy," in Martin Feldstein, ed., *American Economic Policy in the 1980s* (Chicago: University of Chicago Press, 1994), pp.692–694; Age F. P. Bakker, *International Financial Institutions* (New York: Longman, 1996), pp.95–96.

46. William R. Cline, *International Debt and the Stability of the World Economy* (Washington, DC: Institute for International Economics, 1983), p.74.

47. Lipson, "Bankers' Dilemmas: Private Cooperation in Rescheduling Sovereign Debts," p.223; Lipson, "International Debt and International Institutions," pp.220–227.

48. Kapstein, *Governing the Global Economy*, p.82.

49. Dornbusch and Fischer, "Third World Debt," p.838.

50. William R. Cline, "The Baker Plan and Brady Reformulation: An Evaluation," in Husain and Diwan, eds., *Dealing with the Debt Crisis*, p.177.

51. Corbridge, *Debt and Development*, p.65.

52. Edwin M. Truman, "U.S. Policy on the Problems of International Debt," *Federal Reserve Bulletin* 75-11 (November 1989), p.730; Richard E. Feinberg and Delia M. Boylan, "Modular Multilateralism: North-South Economic Relations in the 1990s," in Brad Roberts, ed., *New Forces in the World Economy* (Cambridge: MIT Press, 1996), p.45.

53. Payer, *Lent and Lost*, p.97.

54. Paul R. Krugman, "Debt Relief is Cheap," *Foreign Policy* 80 (Fall 1990), pp.141–152. Some economists viewed the debt problem as a symptom rather than a cause of slow economic growth. See Jeremy Bulow and Kenneth Rogoff, "Cleaning Up Third World Debt Without Getting Taken to the Cleaners," *Journal of Economic Perspectives* 4–1 (Winter 1990), pp.31–42.

55. "Debtor's Prison" in a Survey of Third-World Finance, *The Economist*, September 25, 1993, pp.11–12; Bayne, *Hanging in There*, p.64.

56. Ross P. Buckley, "The Facilitation of the Brady Plan: Emerging Markets Debt Trading from 1989 to 1993," *Fordham International Law Journal* 21–5 (1998), p.1805.

57. Jeffrey Sachs, "Making the Brady Plan Work," *Foreign Affairs* 68–3 (Summer 1989), pp.87–92.

58. Fred Rosen, "Back on the Agenda: Ten Years After the Debt Crisis," *NACLA Report on the Americas* 31–3 (1997), p.22; William Cline, "Managing International Debt," *The Economist*, February 18, 1995, pp.17–19.

59. Bichaka Fayissa, "Foreign Debt, Capital Inflows, and Growth: The Case of the Sub-Sahara African Countries (SSACs)," *Scandinavian Journal of Development Alternatives and Area Studies* 16–3&4 (September & December 1997), p.253; Bayne, *Hanging in There*, p.123.

60. The list of eligible countries has changed slightly over time. See U.S. General Accounting Office, "Debt Relief Initiative for Poor Countries Faces Challenges," GAO/NSIAD-00-161, June 2000, p.11, fn. 6.

61. U.S. General Accounting Office, "Status of the Heavily Indebted Poor Countries Debt Relief Initiative," GAO/NSIAD-98-229, September 1998, pp.5–8 and 27.

62. Gerardo Esquivel, Felipe Larraín, and Jeffrey D. Sachs, "Central America's Foreign Debt Burden and the HIPC Initiative," *Bulletin of Latin American Research* 20–1 (January 2001), p.2.; David Malin Roodman, "Ending the Debt Crisis," in Lester R. Brown et al., eds., *State of the World 2001* (New York: Norton, 2001), pp.144–146.

63. U.S. GAO, "Debt Relief Initiative for Poor Countries Faces Challenges," p.9. See also Martin Dent and Bill Peters, *The Crisis of Poverty and Debt in the Third World* (Aldershot: Ashgate, 1999); Bayne, *Hanging in There*, pp.169–187; John Davies and Mariette Maillet, "The Debt Crisis: Perspectives of a Bilateral Donor," *International Journal* 55–2 (Spring 2000), pp.270–280.

64. Cline, *International Debt Reexamined*, p.70.

65. Cline, *International Debt Reexamined*, pp.70–76; Bakker, *International Financial Institutions*, p.94.

66. See "Summary of Discussion on LDC Debt Policy," in Feldstein, ed., *American Economic Policy in the 1980s*, p.737; Stallings, *Banker to the Third World*, pp.313–315; Theodore H. Cohn, "The United States and Latin America: Ambivalent Ties," *The Canadian Review of American Studies* 20–2 (Fall 1989), pp.255–263.

67. Ffrench-Davis, "External Debt, Adjustment, and Development," p.31.

68. Richard E. Feinberg, "Latin American Debt: Renegotiating the Adjustment Burden," in Feinberg and Ffrench-Davis, eds., *Development and External Debt in Latin America*, pp.57–58; Corbridge, *Debt and Development*, p.85. William Cline argues from a liberal-economic perspective that the debt strategies did not favor the banks over the debtor countries. See Cline, *International Debt Reexamined*, pp.255–262.

69. H. W. Singer, "Beyond the Debt Crisis," *Development* 1 (1992), p.36.

70. Denise Froning, "Will Debt Relief Really Help?" *Washington Quarterly* (Summer 2000), pp.202–204.

71. Valerie J. Assetto, *The Soviet Bloc in the IMF and the IBRD* (Boulder: Westview Press, 1988), pp.189–190.

72. Cline, *International Debt Reexamined*, p.360.

73. Cline, *International Debt Reexamined*, pp.360–367; Assetto, *The Soviet Bloc in the IMF and the IBRD*, pp.163–179.

74. Matthew Evangelista, "Domestic Structure and International Change," in Michael W. Doyle and G. John Ikenberry, eds., *New Thinking in International Relations Theory* (Boulder: Westview Press, 1997), pp.212–214; Kazimierz Poznanski, "Economic Adjustment and Political Forces: Poland Since 1970," *International Organization* 40–2 (Spring 1986), pp.455–488.

75. Ellen Comisso and Paul Marer, "The Economics and Politics of Reform in Hungary," *International Organization* 40–2 (Spring 1986), p.422. See also Laura D'Andrea Tyson, "The Debt Crisis and Adjustment Responses in Eastern Europe: A Comparative Perspective," *International Organization* 40–2 (Spring 1986), pp.239–285.

76. Cline, *International Debt Reexamined*, pp.346–360; E. Iasin and E. Gavrilenkov, "The Problem of Settling Russia's Foreign Debt," *Problems of Economic Transition* 43–5 (September 2000), pp.86–95.

77. Joseph Gold, "The Relationship Between the International Monetary Fund and the World Bank," *Creighton Law Review* 15 (1982), pp.509–510; Richard E. Feinberg, "The Chang-

ing Relationship Between the World Bank and the International Monetary Fund," *International Organization* 42–3 (Summer 1988), p.547.

78. On the Bank's 1960s program lending to India, see Michael Lipton and John Toye, *Does Aid Work in India? A Country Study of the Impact of Official Development Assistance* (London: Routledge, 1990), ch. 3.

79. Jacques Polak, "The World Bank and the IMF: The Future of Their Coexistence," in *Bretton Woods: Looking to the Future* (Washington, DC: Bretton Woods Commission, July 1994), p.C–149; Edward S. Mason and Robert E. Asher, *The World Bank Since Bretton Woods* (Washington, DC: Brookings Institution, 1973), pp.551–554.

80. Hiroyuki Hino, "IMF-World Bank Collaboration," *Finance & Development* 23–3 (September 1986), p.11.

81. Jacques J. Polak, *The World Bank and the International Monetary Fund: A Changing Relationship*, Brookings Occasional Papers (Washington, DC: Brookings Institution, 1994); Paul Mosley, Jane Harrigan, and John Toye, *Aid and Power: The World Bank and Policy-based Lending, Vol. 1* (London: Routledge, 1991); Stanley Please, "The World Bank: Lending for Structural Adjustment," in Richard E. Feinberg and Valeriana Kallab, eds., *Adjustment Crisis in the Third World* (New Brunswick: Transaction Books, 1984), pp.83–98.

82. "Survey: The IMF and the World Bank," *The Economist*, October 12, 1991, p.48.

83. James, *International Monetary Cooperation*, p.326; Polak, *The World Bank and the IMF: A Changing Relationship*, pp.44–45; Jeffrey Sachs, "Beyond Bretton Woods: A New Blueprint," *The Economist*, October 1, 1994, p.23.

84. Some stronger critiques of IFIs and the debt crisis include Kevin Danaher, ed., *Fifty Years Is Enough: The Case Against the World Bank and the International Monetary Fund* (Boston: South End Press, 1994); Payer, *Lent and Lost;* Martin Honeywell, ed., *The Poverty Brokers: The IMF and Latin America* (London: Latin America Bureau, 1983); and Körner, et al., *The IMF and the Debt Crisis.*

85. Feinberg, "The Changing Relationship Between the World Bank and the International Monetary Fund," pp.552–556; Polak, *The World Bank and the IMF: A Changing Relationship*, pp.16–17.

86. Diane Elson, "From Survival Strategies to Transformation Strategies: Women's Needs and Structural Adjustment," in Lourdes Benería and Shelley Feldman, eds., *Unequal Burden: Economic Crises, Persistent Poverty, and Women's Work* (Boulder: Westview Press, 1992), pp.26–48; Gita Sen and Caren Grown, *Development, Crises, and Alternative Visions: Third World Women's Perspectives* (New York: Monthly Review, 1987), pp.62–63.

87. Marc Williams, *International Economic Organisations and the Third World* (New York: Harvester Wheatsheaf, 1994), p.127.

88. Stijn Claessens and Sudarshan Gooptu, "Can Developing Countries Keep Foreign Capital Flowing In?," *Finance and Development* 31–3 (September 1994), p.64; Susan Schadler, "Surges in Capital Inflows: Boon or Curse?," *Finance and Development* 31–1 (March 1994), pp.20–23.

89. Steven Radelet and Jeffrey Sachs, "The Onset of the East Asian Financial Crisis," in Paul Krugman, ed., *Currency Crises* (Chicago: University of Chicago Press, 2000), p.105.

90. Stephan Haggard, *The Political Economy of the Asian Financial Crisis* (Washington, D.C.: Institute for International Economics, 2000), pp.3–7.

91. U.S. Secretary of the Treasury Robert Rubin was the first to use the "architecture" term in April 1998. See Peter B. Kenen, *The International Financial Architecture: What's New? What's Missing?* (Washington, D.C.: Institute for International Economics, 2001), p.1.

92. On the G-7 role see Karl Kaiser, John J. Kirton, and Joseph P. Daniels, eds., *Shaping a New International Financial System: Challenges of Governance in a Globalizing World* (Aldershot: Ashgate, 2000); Michele Fratianni, Paolo Savona, and John J. Kirton, eds., *Governing Global Finance: New Challenges, G7 and IMF Contributions* (Aldershot: Ashgate, 2002).

93. Kenen, *The International Financial Architecture*, pp.87–123.

94. This section uses different categories but draws extensively upon Leslie Elliott Armijo, "The Political Geography of World Financial Reform: Who Wants What and Why?," *Global Governance* 7–4 (October–December 2001), pp.379–396; and Leslie Elliott Armijo, ed., *Debating the Global Financial Architecture* (Albany: State University of New York Press, 2002).

95. Kenen, *The International Financial Architecture*, p.57.

96. Susanne Soederberg, "The Emperor's New Suit: The New International Financial Architecture as a Reinvention of the Washington Consensus," *Global Governance* 7–4 (October-December 2001), p.460.

97. Armijo, "The Political Geography of World Financial Reform," pp.385–390.

98. James Tobin, "A Proposal for Monetary Reform," *Eastern Economic Journal* 4 (1978), p.155.

99. For arguments for and against the Tobin tax see Barry Eichengreen, *Toward a New International Financial Architecture* (Washington, D.C.: Institute for International Economics, 1999), pp.88–90; and Alex C. Michalos, *Good Taxes* (Toronto: Dundurn Press, 1997).

100. Examples of the voluminous literature on this subject include Shelendra D. Sharma, "Constructing the New International Financial Architecture: What Role for the IMF?," *Journal of World Trade* 34–3 (2000), pp. 47–70; Ngaire Woods, "Making the IMF and the World Bank More Accountable," *International Affairs* 77 (2001), pp.83–100; Tony Porter, "The Democratic Deficit in the Institutional Arrangements for Regulating Global Finance," *Global Governance* 7–4 (October–December 2001), pp.427–439; Graham Bird and Joseph P. Joyce, Remodeling the Multilateral Financial Institutions," *Global Governance* 7–1 (January–March, 2001), pp.75–93.

101. Vincent Lloyd and Robert Weissman, "How International Monetary Fund and World Bank Policies Undermine Labor Power and Rights," *International Journal of Health Services* 32–3 (2002), pp. 433–442.

102. Armijo, "The Political Geography of World Financial Reform," pp.389–393.

103. Gerardo Otero, "Neoliberal Reform and Politics in Mexico: An Overview," in Gerardo Otero, ed., *Neoliberalism Revisited: Economic Restructuring and Mexico's Political Future* (Boulder: Westview Press, 1996), pp.6–7; Sebastian Edwards, "Latin American Economic Integration: A New Perspective on an Old Dream," *The World Economy* 16–3 (May 1993), p.325; "Mercosur: The End of the Beginning," *The Economist*, October 12, 1996, pp.3–4.

104. See Anthony Hurrell and Ngaire Woods, "Globalisation and Inequality," *Millennium* 24–3 (1995), pp.447–470.

105. Eric Helleiner, *States and the Reemergence of Global Finance: From Bretton Woods to the 1990s* (Ithaca: Cornell University Press, 1994), p.13.

C H A P T E R   8

Global Trade Relations

Trade relations have aroused strong positive and negative emotions among societies from the earliest times. On one hand, some early Christian philosophers argued that trade was divinely ordained and a part of the natural order, and proposals for world peace stemming from at least the seventeenth century drew linkages between free trade and the achievement of peaceful conditions.[1] On the other hand, trade conflicts have been common since the latter part of the Middle Ages, when the number of sovereign entities was increasing. Although these conflicts are often limited in scope, they sometimes escalate to the point of becoming major trade wars.[2] The high degree of controversy surrounding trade stems from the fact that interest groups and the broader public view their welfare as being more affected by trade policy than by monetary, investment, or financial policy. Thus, business, labor, agricultural, consumer, environmental, and cultural groups have strong vested interests in policies promoting trade liberalization or protectionism, and they regularly attempt to influence government trade policies.

The forces of globalization have had a major effect on trade relations. From 1948 to 1997, real economic output grew at an average annual rate of 3.7 percent while trade increased at an annual rate of 6 percent. From 1985 to 1997, the ratio of trade to GDP rose from 16.6 to 24.1 percent in the DCs and from 22.8 to 38 percent in the LDCs.[3] Although foreign investment flows have increased even faster than trade flows, the two are closely related. MNCs have growing influence on trade issues, and *intrafirm trade* within MNCs or related partners now accounts for about 40 percent of total world trade. As a former WTO director general has stated, "businesses now trade to invest and invest to trade—to the point where both activities are increasingly part of a single strategy to deliver products across borders."[4]

As global interdependence has increased, societal groups have expressed strong views regarding freer trade. On one hand, internationalist firms that have become dependent on exports, imports, and multinational production, pressure for global and regional trade liberalization agreements. On the other hand, domestically oriented firms, threatened by surging import competition, may oppose these trade agreements (see discussion of the business conflict model in Chapter 5).[5] A number of labor, environmental, cultural, and human rights groups also oppose regional free trade agreements such as NAFTA and efforts to expand the authority of the WTO. To these groups the

221

WTO and NAFTA are negative agents of globalization that force states to lower their environmental and labor standards to the "lowest common denominator."

This chapter discusses the characteristics of the postwar global trade regime and the changing role of the DCs, LDCs, and transition economies in the regime. A major theme relates to the competing pressures for trade liberalization and protectionism.

TRADE THEORY

The promotion of freer trade is a central tenet of liberal theorists, who view trade as a positive-sum game that provides mutual benefits to states. Realists, by contrast, view trade in more competitive terms, with each state striving to increase its exports (especially of high-value-added goods) and decrease its imports. Historical structuralists view trade as a form of unequal exchange in which advanced capitalist states in the core export manufactured and high-technology goods and import raw materials and low-technology goods from the periphery. Of the three main IPE perspectives, liberal theories of trade have been the most influential among DC economists.

Although liberal trade theory has evolved considerably over time, the ideas of Adam Smith and David Ricardo still form a central part of the justification for freer trade. Smith argued that the gains from free trade result from *absolute advantage*, in which all states benefit if they specialize in the goods they produce best and trade with each other. For example, if France produces wine more cheaply than England and England produces cloth more cheaply than France, both states can benefit from specialization and trade. Ricardo's theory of *comparative advantage* is a less intuitive and more powerful theory because it indicates that trade is beneficial even if absolute advantage does not exist. In his 1817 study *Principles of Political Economy and Taxation*, Ricardo argued that England and Portugal could gain from trading wine for cloth even if Portugal produced *both* goods more cheaply than England.[6] The following tables use arbitrary figures to demonstrate Ricardo's theory of comparative advantage.

Table 8.1 gives the amount of labor required (e.g., worker-days) in Portugal and England to produce one bottle of wine and one bolt of cloth. As the table shows, Portugal can produce *both* wine and cloth with fewer labor inputs than England. Nevertheless, the two countries can gain from specialization and trade because England has less of a cost disadvantage in cloth than in wine production. In other words, England has a *comparative* advantage in cloth, and Portugal has a *compara-*

Table 8.1

LABOR REQUIRED TO PRODUCE ONE BOTTLE OF WINE AND ONE BOLT OF CLOTH

	Wine	Cloth
England	6	5
Portugal	2	4

tive advantage in wine. To demonstrate this, we assume that England shifts 30 labor units from wine to cloth production and that Portugal shifts 12 labor units from cloth to wine production. The total amount of labor used in the two countries remains constant, but this reallocation of labor causes the production changes given in Table 8.2.

As Table 8.2 shows, the shift of 30 labor units from wine to cloth in England raises cloth production by 6 bolts (30 divided by 5) and reduces wine production by 5 bottles (–30 divided by 6). The shift of 12 labor units from cloth to wine in Portugal raises wine production by 6 bottles (12 divided by 2) and reduces cloth production by 3 bolts (–12 divided by 4). Table 8.2 shows that with England specializing in cloth and Portugal specializing in wine, the two countries together produce one more bottle of wine and three more bolts of cloth. Liberals therefore argue that two countries enjoy mutual (but not necessarily equal) benefits from specialization and trade even if one of the countries has an absolute advantage in producing *all* the products traded.

Although Ricardo's theory provided a powerful liberal argument in favor of free trade, his assumption that comparative advantage results only from differences in labor productivity is far too limiting. In reality, comparative advantage also results from other factors of production such as capital and natural resources. In the 1920s–1930s, liberal economists therefore turned to a more elaborate theory to explain comparative advantage: the **Heckscher-Ohlin theory,** developed by the Swedish economists Eli Heckscher and Bertil Ohlin. According to this theory, a country's comparative advantage is determined by its relative abundance and scarcity of capital and labor; i.e., it has a comparative advantage in producing goods that involve intensive use of the factor it has in abundance. Thus, more advanced economies such as capital-rich states will specialize in the production and export of capital-intensive goods, whereas LDCs with an abundant supply of cheap labor will specialize in labor-intensive goods. As was the case for Ricardo, the Heckscher-Ohlin theory makes certain simplifying assumptions; for example, the theory assumes that technology and tastes do not differ among countries.[7]

Building on the Heckscher-Ohlin theory, during the 1940s two U.S. economists (Wolfgang Stolper and Paul Samuelson) developed the *Stolper-Samuelson theory,* which helps explain why some domestic groups in a state are free trade oriented and others are protectionist. According to the Stolper-Samuelson theory, trade liberalization benefits abundantly endowed factors of production and hurts poorly endowed factors of production. For example, if a state is rich in labor and productive land but poor in capital, freer trade is beneficial to workers and farmers but detrimental to the owners of capital. Owners of abundant factors of production therefore support freer trade and owners of scarce factors oppose it. The Stolper-Samuelson theory helps explain

Table 8.2

CHANGES IN PRODUCTION OF WINE AND CLOTH

	Bottles of Wine	Bolts of Cloth
England	–5	+6
Portugal	+6	–3
Total	+1	+3

why U.S. and Canadian blue-collar labor opposed NAFTA (Mexico is more abundantly endowed with less skilled workers) and why French wheat farmers have opposed agricultural trade liberalization in the GATT/WTO (the United States, Canada, Australia, and Argentina are better endowed with land for wheat production).[8]

The Heckscher-Ohlin and Stolper-Samuelson models are controversial in certain respects. For example, one researcher found that the United States was highly successful in exporting labor-intensive goods during the 1950s, a period when it was the most capital-rich country.[9] Nevertheless, these theories continue to have considerable influence. The Stolper-Samuelson theory is also of interest because it points to the political reality that there are inevitably both winners and losers as a result of freer trade. Although liberals concede that freer trade may produce job losses in some sectors, they argue that trade liberalization is nevertheless desirable because gains in *overall* efficiency are greater than any losses. Thus, the winners (owners of abundant factors) can compensate the losers (owners of scarce factors) and still be better off as a result of freer trade. Realists and historical structuralists, by contrast, believe the losers will not be adequately compensated and will suffer as a result of their disadvantaged position.

Although liberal theories extending from Ricardo's comparative advantage to the Heckscher-Ohlin theory are still important for explaining interindustry trade, they do not explain the rapid increase in *intraindustry* and *intrafirm trade.* The Heckscher-Ohlin assumption that trade is most beneficial between countries with different factor endowments does not provide an adequate explanation for intraindustry trade, which most often occurs among DCs with similar factor endowments. Whereas traditional trade theory assumes that goods are homogeneous, in intraindustry trade differentiated products are traded within the same industry group. For example, the United States, Japan, and Germany all produce automobiles and trade with one another because consumers value product differentiation and do not consider different types of automobiles to be perfectly interchangeable. Liberals have therefore developed new theories postulating that intraindustry trade provides benefits such as economies of scale, the satisfaction of variegated consumer tastes, and the production of specialized and sophisticated manufactured products. For example, because of economies of scale countries can benefit from producing large quantities of a smaller number of goods and engaging in trade.[10]

The Stolper-Samuelson theory explaining why groups oppose or favor freer trade is also not as applicable to intraindustry trade. It is less common to find owners of scarce factors opposing intraindustry trade, which usually occurs among advanced industrial states with similar factor endowments and in products that use similar factor intensities. Thus, trade liberalization negotiations have been most successful for manufactured products in which DCs are engaging in intraindustry trade. Trade barriers are more persistent for agricultural and other primary products, often traded between DCs and LDCs, where factor endowments still play a major role. Much present-day trade is also *intrafirm* trade between parent companies of MNCs and their subsidiaries. Chapter 10 discusses the fact that theories of the firm best explain why trade occurs between MNC's affiliates.

Realists often argue that liberal assumptions about comparative advantage are overly static, underestimating the ability of a state to upgrade its advantages in trade. The growing amount of intraindustry and intrafirm trade among states with similar factor endowments has added force to these arguments. Thus, realists question whether Ricardo's advice to Portugal in fact served its long-range interests. Portugal might have gained some short-term advantages from specializing in wine; but it would have been less competitive than England over the long term because cloth production was a high-growth, high-technology industry at the time. According to realists, Portugal would have been better off *creating* a comparative advantage for itself in cloth through government assistance to the cloth industry, even if it had a "natural" comparative advantage in wine.[11] **Strategic trade theory** emphasizes the creation of comparative advantage through industrial targeting. Strategic trade theorists justify and even promote the idea of government intervention in the economy and often prefer the term *competitive advantage* to comparative advantage. Although efforts to gain competitive advantage in trade are not new, the growing emphasis on high-technology industries provides "a fertile breeding ground for interventionist policies."[12]

Strategic trade theorists have produced a wide range of studies to demonstrate that interventionist policies can improve a country's position in manufacturing and technology, and they have often pointed to Japan and the East Asian NIEs as examples of states that mobilize a limited amount of resources to create competitive advantage. However, liberal theorists argue that the risks of strategic trade policy outweigh the benefits. According to strategic trade theory, each country wants its firms to capture a larger share of international export markets; but it is increasingly difficult to identify the nationalities of firms because of the proliferation of joint ventures, strategic partnerships, and foreign stock ownership (see Chapter 10). If a government wants to target particular firms for assistance in exporting, how can it determine exactly which are its firms? Strategic trade theorists also do not devote sufficient attention to the possible reaction of foreign governments. Although a country might attempt to increase its competitive advantage at the expense of others according to *individual* rationality, other countries are likely to retaliate and everyone will be worse off as a result (see discussion of prisoners' dilemma in Chapter 4).[13] Despite these liberal warnings, the temptation to engage in strategic trade policy remains strong in an age of global competition.

GLOBAL TRADE RELATIONS BEFORE WORLD WAR II

Countries have alternated between periods of trade liberalization and protectionism throughout modern history. Thus, mercantilist trade restrictions gave way to a period of freer trade when Britain lowered its import duties in 1815 and then repealed its Corn Laws and opened its borders to food imports in 1846. Following the British lead, Latin America's newly independent republics adopted liberal trade policies; Prussia moved Germany to lower its trade barriers; and France and Britain signed the Cobden-Chevalier Treaty in 1860, which resulted in a network of commercial treaties lowering tariff barriers between Britain and France and throughout Europe. After 1875, however, the enthusiasm for free trade waned somewhat because of Britain's declining hegemony, France's defeat in the 1870 Franco-Prussian War, and the 1873–1896 depression. With the outbreak of World War I, the network of European trade and commercial treaties was completely disrupted.[14]

After World War I, renewed efforts to remove trade restrictions were largely unsuccessful as countries reacted to harsh economic conditions by increasing their tariffs. Tariffs were rising not only in European states recovering from the war but also in the United States, which had emerged from the war as a net creditor nation and the world's largest industrial power. Thus, the U.S. Congress enacted the Fordney-McCumber Tariff in 1922, which increased import duties to an average of 38 percent, well above the levels of the 1913 Underwood Tariff. After the 1929 stock market crash, Congress passed the 1930 Smoot-Hawley Tariff Act, which increased average U.S. ad valorem rates on dutiable imports to 52.8 percent, "the highest American tariffs in the twentieth century."[15] The question arises as to why the United States as the top economic power in the interwar period did not act forthrightly to limit the rise of trade protectionism. Hegemonic stability theorists argue that the United States was able but unwilling to become the hegemonic leader until its position became more firmly established after World War II.[16] However, some analysts question whether the United States in fact had the ability to establish an open economic system during the interwar period. Although the United States was the top economic state, its share of world trade and investment was well below Britain's during the latter part of the nineteenth century.[17]

Others look to domestic politics rather than the U.S. global position in explaining U.S. protectionism. Although the United States emerged as the largest industrial power during the interwar period, a number of U.S. industries were fearful of renewed European competition, and U.S. agricultural groups were dismayed by a rapid decrease in agricultural prices. In pressuring for trade protectionism, these domestic groups benefited from the fact that the U.S. Constitution gives Congress the sole power to regulate commerce and impose tariffs. Because members of Congress do not have national constituencies, they are more susceptible than the president to protectionist pressures. Producers and workers seeking to limit imports were also politically organized and concentrated in specific industries, and by joining together they were able to convince Congress to enact the Smoot-Hawley tariff. Consumer groups benefiting from freer trade, by contrast, were far more diffuse in nature and had little influence. Party politics also played a role in the Smoot-Hawley tariff because the Republicans—who were more protectionist than the Democrats—had a Senate majority at the time.[18]

Regardless of the reasons for the U.S. Smoot-Hawley tariff, it had disastrous consequences as other countries rushed to retaliate with their own import restrictions.[19] Between 1929 and 1933, world trade declined from $35 billion to $12 billion, and U.S. exports fell from $488 million to $120 million. In efforts to reverse this damage, the U.S. Congress passed the Reciprocal Trade Agreements Act (RTAA) in 1934. The RTAA in effect transferred tariff-setting authority from Congress to the president, who could lower tariffs by up to 50 percent from Smoot-Hawley levels in trade negotiations with other countries.[20] Although Congress authorized the president to conduct only bilateral (not multilateral) tariff negotiations, the RTAA marked a significant turning point because it directly linked the setting of tariffs to international negotiations. Instead of having Congress set tariffs on a unilateral, statutory basis, the president was given authority to establish "bargaining tariffs" through bilateral agreements.

In introducing bargaining tariffs, the United States recognized that it would gain greater access to foreign markets only by opening its own market to imports.[21] From the 1934 approval of the RTAA to 1945, the United States concluded bilateral trade agreements with 27 countries and lowered its tariff rates by an average of 44 percent. Tariff rates were so high in the early 1930s, however, that these agreements mainly served to correct earlier excesses. The Roosevelt administration's decision to lower tariffs only in exchange for similar concessions by other countries (hence the name *Reciprocal* Trade Agreements Act) also limited the scope of the agreements. Furthermore, many countries were unwilling to lower their tariffs, and the RTAA agreements did not stimulate a worldwide movement toward trade liberalization. Thus, protectionism continued to affect trade relations throughout the interwar period.[22]

GATT AND THE POSTWAR GLOBAL TRADE REGIME

The United States and Britain wanted to ensure that the devastating effects of protectionism during the interwar period were not repeated, and they began holding bilateral discussions in 1943 to lay the groundwork for postwar trade negotiations. In fall 1945 the U.S. State Department issued a document on trade and employment, which formed the basis for multilateral negotiations resulting in the Havana Charter, or charter for an international trade organization (ITO) in March 1948. The charter was unusually broad in scope, dealing not only with commercial policy but also with economic development, full employment, international investment, international commodity arrangements, restrictive business practices, and the administration and functions of an ITO.[23] In view of the protracted nature of the Havana Charter negotiations, some governments decided to begin negotiating a lowering of tariffs before the charter was approved and ratified. These negotiations were concluded in October 1947 when 23 governments signed the final act of the GATT.

It was assumed that GATT would simply be folded into a new ITO, but the U.S. Congress never ratified the Havana Charter, and GATT therefore became permanent by default. The reasons for the U.S. failure to ratify the charter are complex and ironic because the United States had originally proposed the creation of an ITO.[24] In drafting the ITO charter, the trade negotiators were sensitive to the problems of many countries, such as the Europeans recovering from the war. However, in trying to meet everyone's demands, the negotiators satisfied neither protectionists nor free traders. Whereas U.S. protectionists argued that the ITO would lead to low-cost imports and threaten U.S. ability to form its own trade policy, free traders believed that the charter's numerous escape clauses and exceptions would interfere with trade liberalization. President Harry S. Truman agreed not to submit the charter to Congress for ratification because of its limited domestic support, and the ITO was never formed.[25]

With the failure to establish the ITO, GATT became the permanent global trade organization by default. GATT did not even require ratification by the U.S. Congress because it was simply a trade agreement. Thus, countries that signed GATT were referred to as *contracting parties* rather than members. (This chapter uses the less accurate term *GATT members* for the sake of brevity.) Unlike the ITO, which would have become a UN specialized agency on a par with the IMF and World Bank, GATT never attained specialized agency status. GATT continued to be primarily a written code of behavior on international trade, and it had more limited legal obligations and dispute settlement procedures than the planned ITO. GATT also lacked the Havana Charter's provisions relating to investment, employment, commodity agreements, and restrictive business practices.

Despite its informal origins, GATT gradually developed some characteristics of an IO; for example, it had a small secretariat and a number of committees and working parties, and it made decisions that were binding on members.[26] Some analysts even argue that GATT became a more effective organization than the IMF and World Bank because of its informality:

> Many observers would now conclude that the GATT was the more effective arrangement. The strength of a formal arrangement such as the IMF is its rigidity; that of an informal, ideas-based institution such as the GATT is its adaptability. The greater success of the GATT thus illustrates the importance for postwar economic performance of an adaptable institutional framework.[27]

Indications of GATT's strengths included its success in reducing tariffs, its negotiation of disciplines for nontariff barriers, and its steadily growing membership. However, GATT's informality and flexibility were also a source of weakness in several respects. First, some trade sectors such as agriculture and textiles were largely exempted from GATT regulations. Agriculture was treated as an exception to GATT restrictions on import quotas and export subsidies; and the DCs imposed textile import quotas contravening the spirit and rules of GATT, first through bilateral export restraints and then through the multilateral Multi-Fiber Arrangement. Second, GATT was more of a club than a formal organization, and its members could easily waive its regulations and overlook violations. For example, some countries circumvented the GATT ban on import quotas by imposing **voluntary export restraints,** through which they pressured others to "voluntarily" decrease their exports. Third, when countries had conflicts over trade-distorting practices, GATT's rather weak dispute settlement procedures were often inadequate to deal with them. Fourth, burgeoning U.S. balance-of-trade deficits during the 1980s caused the United States to charge others with being unfair traders and to turn more often to trade unilateralism. Only by enhancing the trade regime's authority could the United States be assured that unilateral measures to ensure fair trade were unnecessary. And fifth, GATT's inadequacies became more evident as globalization increased and the United States in particular demanded that the scope of GATT activities be extended beyond trade in goods to trade in services, intellectual property, and investment.

By the mid-1980s, a number of trade experts therefore warned that GATT would become irrelevant if it did not tighten its regulations, improve its dispute settlement procedures, and extend its discipline to older areas such as agriculture and textiles and to newer areas such as services, intellectual property, and investment.[28] Although the Uruguay Round of negotiations began with plans to simply upgrade GATT, the decision was made during the round to replace it with a new WTO. (GATT continues to exist as the largest trade agreement under the WTO.)

PRINCIPLES OF THE GLOBAL TRADE REGIME

In some respects the GATT-based trade regime was not really new; its principles and rules codified past commercial practices, and its basic approach—that trade policy should be made through international negotiation—was established by the 1934 U.S. RTAA. However GATT marked a turning point in one critical respect,: it relied on *multilateral* negotiation. The postwar trade arrangements also reflected the interventionist-liberal compromise. Although the major trading nations approved measures to liberalize trade, they also supported safeguards and exemptions to protect countries' social policies and balance of payments.[29] Despite its informal origins, GATT provided the basis for a highly developed regime in terms of principles, norms, rules, and decision-making procedures. The sections that follow discuss the main trade regime principles.

Trade Liberalization

GATT promoted *liberalization* as a central trade regime principle, first by lowering tariffs and then by regulating NTBs. *Tariffs,* or taxes levied on products passing through customs borders, are usually imposed on imports but may also be applied to exports. Although GATT explicitly permitted tariffs, it sought to lower them through successive rounds of multilateral trade negotiations (MTNs). As Table 8.3 shows, eight MTN rounds were held under GATT auspices. During the first five rounds, members

Table 8.3

ROUNDS OF GATT AND WTO NEGOTIATIONS

Name	Years	Subjects Covered	Countries Participating
Geneva	1947	Tariffs	23
Annecy	1949	Tariffs	13
Torquay	1951	Tariffs	38
Geneva	1956	Tariffs	26
Dillon	1960–61	Tariffs	26
Kennedy	1964–67	Tariffs and antidumping measures	62
Tokyo	1973–79	Tariffs, nontariff measures, plurilateral agreements	102
Uruguay	1986–93	Tariffs, nontariff measures, rules, services, intellectual property, dispute settlement, trade-related investment, textiles, agriculture, creation of World Trade Organization	123
Doha (WTO)	1999–	Agriculture, services, tariffs, nontariff measures, intellectual property, dispute settlement	146

Source: WTO Focus Newsletter, no. 30, May, 1998, p.2, and other WTO information. By permission of the World Trade Organization.

negotiated tariff reductions on an item-by-item basis. However, item-by-item negotiations became more complex and time consuming as GATT membership increased, and the sixth round (the Kennedy Round) therefore shifted to linear or across-the-board tariff reductions on industrial products. These linear cuts resulted in an average tariff reduction of 35 percent in the Kennedy Round for OECD countries.[30] GATT has always preferred tariffs to import quotas because tariffs (at reasonable levels) permit efficient producers to continue increasing their sales, whereas quotas provide no reward for efficiency and set an arbitrary limit on imports. Thus, GATT Article 11 called for the "general elimination of quantitative restrictions" or import quotas. GATT permitted a number of exceptions to Article 11, however, relating to balance-of-payments problems, infant industry protection for LDCs, enforcement of health standards, and national security. Members could also impose import quotas on agricultural products when such regulations were needed to enforce domestic supply management measures.[31]

Because the first five GATT rounds dealt only with the reduction of tariffs, member countries turned increasingly to NTBs as an alternative means of protecting their producers. NTBs include an incredibly large array of measures that restrict imports, assist domestic production, and promote exports, and they are often more restrictive, ill defined, and inequitable than tariffs. NTB negotiations are also more problematic than tariff negotiations because it is difficult to quantify and measure the impact of NTBs, and countries tend to view NTBs as adjuncts to their domestic policies (and therefore as not subject to international regulation).[32] The Kennedy Round was the first to go beyond tariff negotiations and begin the process of negotiating NTBs. The Tokyo Round NTB negotiations were far more extensive and resulted in a number of NTB codes dealing with technical barriers to trade, government procurement, subsidies and countervailing duties, customs valuation, and import licensing. The use of codes resulted partly from the fact that LDCs opposed the extension of GATT discipline to NTBs. Thus, the NTB codes were *plurilateral* rather than multilateral agreements that bound only the signatories, and most LDCs did not participate. The Uruguay Round was the most complicated GATT round because it widened the agenda to include not only trade in goods but also trade in services, intellectual property, and trade-related investment measures, and it began applying global trade rules to sensitive areas such as agriculture and textiles.

The effects of globalization on trade were evident in both the broader scope of the Uruguay Round and the increased number of participants. Table 8.3 shows that the number of participating countries rose from 23 during the first GATT round (Geneva) to 123 in the eighth round (Uruguay). Table 8.3 also shows that after the Dillon Round, the negotiating rounds became more lengthy and complicated. The Uruguay Round involved seven years of difficult negotiations, and there were concerns that the negotiators would never reach a final agreement. However, the Uruguay Round *was* completed, and it resulted in the establishment of a new WTO with jurisdiction over a much wider array of trade and related areas than the GATT.

One question IPE scholars have asked is *why* the trade liberalization principle not only endured but was expanded, despite the decline in U.S. trade hegemony. In 1953 the United States accounted for almost 30 percent of all manufactured exports; but by the late 1970s the United States had fallen to second place as an exporter of manufactures, accounting for only 13 percent. West Germany had moved into first place with 16 percent, and Japan was close behind the United States with 11 percent. Although there was an increase in the "new protectionism" of NTBs during the late 1970s, trade liberalization was *not* as seriously threatened as it had been in the 1920s when Britain's trade hegemony was declining. Indeed, the GATT Tokyo Round (1973–1979) reduced weighted-average industrial tariffs to extremely low levels (to 5, 4, and 3 percent in the EC, United States, and Japan, respectively) and resulted in some regulation of NTBs.[33] Some scholars believe that the difference between the 1920s and 1970s demonstrates the role of regimes in upholding principles and norms that states eventually internalize. In contrast to the 1920s, the GATT-centered global trade regime upheld the trade liberalization principle during the 1970s even as U.S. trade hegemony was declining. Other scholars point to domestic politics to explain the different outcomes in the 1920s and 1970s. As discussed, the U.S. Congress has the power to regulate commerce and impose tariffs under the Constitution, and in the 1920s Congress responded to interest group pressures with dramatically increased tariffs. By the 1970s, however, Congress was regularly transferring its tariff-making authority to the president, who was more insulated from interest group pressures (this transfer to the president had begun with the RTAA in 1934). Thus, changes in the domestic structure of trade policymaking in the United States help to account for the vitality of the trade liberalization principle.

Another domestic factor of importance stems from the forces of globalization. Many industries in the United States and other countries during the 1920s had few international ties and supported trade protectionism to limit external competition. By the 1970s, however, "the increased economic integration of advanced industrial states into the world economy . . . altered the domestic politics of trade."[34] Thus, there were more internationalist firms than during the 1920s, and these firms were highly dependent on multinational production, exports, imports, and intrafirm trade. Despite the decline in the U.S. trade position, the resistance of industries and firms to protectionist forces was therefore much greater in the 1970s than during the 1920s. Domestic as well as international factors account for the resilience of the trade liberalization principle in the post–World War II era.

Nondiscrimination

Nondiscrimination is another basic trade regime principle. Indeed, the first GATT director general referred to nondiscrimination as "the fundamental cornerstone" of the global trade organization.[35] The nondiscrimination principle has two dimensions, one external (most-favored-nation treatment) and the other internal (national treatment). The unconditional **most-favored-nation (MFN)** principle in Article 1 of the General Agreement stipulates that every trade advantage or privilege a GATT member gives to any country must be extended, immediately and unconditionally, to all other GATT members. By requiring equal treatment of imports from different origins, the MFN principle helps to ensure that imports come from the lowest cost foreign suppliers and that comparative advantage determines trading patterns. Unconditional MFN treatment extends back to fifteenth-century Europe and to the 1860 Cobden-Chevalier Treaty. However, unlike these earlier periods, the GATT-centered MFN principle was based on *multilateral* commitments and regular multilateral consultations and negotiations.[36]

Despite the importance GATT negotiators extended to MFN treatment, GATT permitted exceptions to MFN on the basis of colonial preferences, regional integration agreements, balance of payments, and national security and allowed exceptions as a response to "unfair" trade actions. Of these exceptions, the proliferation of free trade agreements and customs unions such as NAFTA and the EU has posed the greatest threat to the MFN principle in recent years. The members of these RTAs abolish tariff barriers among themselves, giving each other more favorable treatment than they give to other GATT/WTO members. (Chapter 9 discusses the relationship between RTAs and GATT/WTO.)

Whereas MFN treatment is designed to prevent discrimination at a country's border, **national treatment** seeks to prevent internal discrimination. The national treatment provisions in GATT Article 3 require member countries to treat foreign products—once they have been imported—at least as favorably as domestic products with regard to internal taxes and regulations. This provision is designed to prevent countries from using domestic measures to limit foreign competition as their tariffs and other external trade barriers decline. The importance of the national treatment provision is seen by the frequency with which it has been tested in GATT dispute settlement cases. In a 1988 case, for example, a GATT panel found that pricing and listing practices of Canadian provincial liquor boards, which discriminated against foreign wines, were inconsistent with Canada's national treatment obligations.[37]

Reciprocity

Reciprocity, the idea that a country benefiting from another country's trade concessions should provide roughly equal benefits in return, is a fundamental principle in MTNs and in the admission of new members to the GATT/WTO. By ensuring that agreements are reached through a balanced exchange of concessions, the reciprocity principle limits free riding under the unconditional MFN principle. Liberal economists argue that a country gains by liberalizing its trade unilaterally as well as through negotiation. However, protectionist forces in specific industries are often well organized and able to mobilize sufficient domestic opposition to prevent unilateral trade liberalization policies. In reaching agreement on *reciprocal* trade concessions, by contrast, governments can depend on support from export-oriented domestic industries that expect to gain from the agreement. New members of the WTO obtain all the benefits of market access resulting from earlier negotiating rounds, and they are therefore expected to provide reciprocal benefits. Thus, an applicant wishing to join the WTO must first agree to liberalize access to its market in negotiations with WTO members.

In practice, the reciprocity principle ensures that tariff negotiations reflect the interests of the major trading powers. WTO members benefiting from others' tariff reductions must be able to offer reciprocal concessions, and those members with large domestic markets and high trade volumes have the greatest concessions to offer and thus the most leverage. The United States and the EU are the leading powers in the GATT/WTO because they have the largest reciprocal concessions to offer. Thus, the GATT Kennedy Round was not completed successfully until the United States and

Table 8.4

Leading World Merchandise Traders (Excluding Intra-EU Trade), 2002 (U.S.$ billions)

Rank	Exporters	Value	Rank	Importers	Value
1	EU	939.0	1	United States	1202.5
2	United States	693.5	2	EU	931.3
3	Japan	416.0	3	Japan	336.4
4	China	325.6	4	China	295.2
5	Canada	252.5	5	Canada	227.6

Source: Derived from World Trade Organization Secretariat, *World Trade Report—2003* (Geneva: WTO), Appendix Table 1A.2, p.69.

the EC reached a compromise on various sectoral issues. The Tokyo Round negotiations were also a pyramidal process, in which the United States and the EC usually initiated agreements and other states were then involved in discussions to reach a broader consensus. LDCs had more influence during the Uruguay Round than in previous rounds, but even in this case U.S. agreements with the EC and Japan on agriculture were critical to ultimate success. Other than China, the most important traders in terms of reciprocal concessions to offer are DCs. Thus, Table 8.4 shows that Japan, China, and Canada ranked third, fourth, and fifth below the United States and EU in 2002 as merchandise exporters and importers. A similar hierarchy exists in services trade; during 2002, all the most important traders in commercial services were DCs, except for China and Hong Kong, China.[38] Even among the LDCs there was a pecking order, with more important states such as Brazil, Mexico, and India taking priority. Although pyramidal negotiations realistically give priority to those with the power to veto an agreement, such negotiations limit the ability of smaller states to affect the outcome or protect their interests.[39]

Although the GATT/WTO is of course the main IO in the global trade regime, a number of other formal and informal institutions also have important roles in the regime. Reflecting the hierarchy in trading power, DC-led institutions are at the top of the global trade regime pyramid. For example, the OECD regularly conducts studies and pressures for changes in the trade regime of interest to the North. During the Uruguay Round the OECD had a major role in ensuring that services trade, which is of particular interest to the North, be subject to GATT/WTO principles and rules. At critical junctures in MTNs beginning with the Tokyo Round the G-7 has also intervened at the highest political level to ensure that negotiations are successfully completed. However, the G-7's primary economic focus has been on monetary, financial, and macroeconomic policies, and it has also become increasingly involved in a wide range of political-security and social issues. In 1981–1982 the trade ministers of the United States, EC, Japan, and Canada therefore established the **Quadrilateral Group** or **Quad** to act as an informal group providing leadership in the global trade regime. (Germany, Britain, and France do not have separate places in the Quad as they do in the G-7 because the European Commission is responsible for trade and commercial policy.) Although the U.S., EC, Japanese, and sometimes the Canadian trade ministers had met informally in earlier years, the formation of the Quad represented a move toward collective consultation in view of declining U.S. trade hegemony. The Quad had an important role during the Uruguay Round in managing trade disputes, promoting trade liberalization, and strengthening the multilateral trade regime.[40] Although the Quad has been less important in recent years, the North continues to predominate in the global trade regime, largely because of the concessions it is able to offer in terms of the reciprocity principle.

Reciprocity may be either specific or diffuse in nature. *Specific reciprocity* refers to "situations in which specified partners exchange items of equivalent value in a strictly delimited sequence;" *diffuse reciprocity* has a less precise definition of equivalence because "one's partners may be viewed as a group rather than as particular actors, and the sequence of events is less narrowly bound."[41] Whereas diffuse reciprocity can coexist with *unconditional* MFN treatment, specific (or aggressive) reciprocity is more akin to *conditional* MFN treatment. In conditional MFN, two countries granting concessions to each other extend these concessions to a third country *only if* it promptly offers equivalent concessions. Realists concerned with relative gains have a preference for specific reciprocity, whereas liberals concerned with absolute gains are satisfied with diffuse reciprocity.

Liberal economists argue that diffuse reciprocity is more conducive to cooperation than specific reciprocity because of the difficulty in determining whether concessions are exactly equivalent. If countries always demanded specific reciprocity, it would be virtually impossible to conduct multilateral negotiations. Nevertheless, the United States responded to its declining trade hegemony and its balance-of-trade deficits since 1971 with claims that specific reciprocity is sometimes necessary to prevent others from acting as free riders. The United States has been particularly inclined to demand specific reciprocity from countries such as Japan with which it has large trade deficits. From the U.S. perspective, Japan has numerous hidden trade barriers and does not genuinely provide reciprocal access to its market. Thus, the United States has often demanded "results-oriented" agreements, in which it gains access to a specified share of the Japanese market for certain products in return for Japan's access to the U.S. market. Japan argues, by contrast, that its trade surpluses are due to its competitive advantages and not to unfair trading practices.[42]

Safeguards and Contingent Trade Measures

Safeguards refer to government actions to limit imports that may cause harm to a country's industry or economy. The safeguard principle is an essential part of trade liberalization agreements; countries would not agree to commitments if rigid adherence was necessary in all situations. Safeguard actions are usually temporary, but Table 8.5 shows that a government may also impose permanent trade barriers under certain circumstances. The most prominent temporary safeguard mechanism is the *general escape clause* (GATT Article 19), which permits a country to counter unforeseen "import surges" that cause, or are likely to cause, *serious* injury to a domestic industry. Such safeguard actions must be applied to all WTO members, and affected countries can request compensation. In view of these stringent requirements, countries do not often use the escape clause. In addition to escape clause actions, Table 8.5 shows that

Table 8.5

SAFEGUARDS AND CONTINGENT TRADE MEASURES

SAFEGUARDS

Temporary	Permanent
Import surges	General exceptions
Balance-of-payments problems	National security
Infant industries	Tariff renegotiations
General waivers	

Contingent Trade Measures

Antidumping duties (ADDs)
Countervailing duties (CVDs)

Sources: Bernard M. Hoekman and Michel Kostecki, *The Political Economy of the World Trading System: From GATT to WTO,* 2nd ed. (Oxford: Oxford University Press, 2001), pp.303–345; John II. Jackson, *The World Trading System: Law and Policy of International Economic Relations* (Cambridge: MIT Press, 1989), pp.149–187.

a country may impose temporary import restrictions to safeguard its balance of payments and infant industries, and it may seek a general waiver from a specific obligation. Furthermore, a country may apply permanent safeguard measures under GATT clauses relating to general exceptions (e.g., to safeguard public morals, health, and natural resources), national security, and tariff renegotiations.[43]

Whereas safeguard provisions are permissible even when other countries engage in fair trade, *contingent trade measures* are taken to counter allegedly unfair trade practices. The two main types of contingent trade measures are antidumping and countervailing duties (see Table 8.5). **Dumping** occurs when a firm sells a product in an export market at a lower price than it charges in the home market or below the cost of production. The WTO permits a country to impose **antidumping duties (ADDs)** if foreign goods are dumped and the dumping causes or threatens material injury to its domestic producers. A country may also impose **countervailing duties (CVDs)** against imports benefiting from *trade-distorting subsidies* that produce or threaten material injury to domestic producers. Unlike safeguard actions, a country imposes contingent trade measures in response to *material* injury (which is less than *serious* injury), and targets specific countries charged with engaging in unfair trade.[44]

Contingent trade measures may be a legitimate response to unfair trade or a justification for trade protectionism. Thus, ADD and CVD actions are highly controversial, and GATT/WTO and NAFTA dispute settlement panels have often examined complaints about such actions. The United States was the first country to use CVDs, and it has been the largest user of CVDs in the post-World War II period. With the U.S. balance-of-trade deficits since 1971 and the decline of tariffs resulting from GATT negotiations, the U.S. Congress responded to domestic pressures by changing the rules and procedures so that CVDs could be imposed more easily. Thus, the United States was responsible for about 58 percent of all CVD investigations launched from 1980 to 1992, and the United States initiated the largest number of antidumping investigations during this period. Other frequent initiators of antidumping investigations include Australia, the EU, Canada, and Mexico.[45]

Development

The failed Havana Charter contained a number of provisions on economic development that did not become part of the 1947 General Agreement, and GATT had little involvement with development issues during the 1940s–1950s.[46] As more LDCs joined GATT, however, a "development principle" began to emerge. Several GATT provisions were added that gave LDCs special treatment and thus diverged from the nondiscrimination and reciprocity principles. However, development remains a less central trade regime principle because the major trading nations have agreed to only limited concessions to promote LDC interests.[47] The WTO Doha Round, which began in 2001, has also been called the Development Round, but the degree to which LDCs achieve their objectives in the round remains to be seen. This chapter later examines the role of development issues in the global trade regime.

FORMATION OF THE WTO

By the early 1980s, the trade regime principles discussed earlier were all in a state of flux, and many GATT achievements in promoting freer trade seemed to be in jeopardy. In terms of the liberalization principle, previous GATT rounds had lowered tariffs, but countries were resorting to NTBs such as voluntary export restraints that were not even covered by GATT rules. Furthermore, liberalization did not extend to major areas such as textiles and agriculture, and GATT procedures for dealing with trade disputes were inadequate. The nondiscrimination principle was also increasingly threatened by RTAs that did not adhere to MFN treatment. As for the reciprocity and safeguard principles, the United States and EC were demanding specific rather than diffuse reciprocity from some of their trading partners, and countries dissatisfied with the GATT safeguards were resorting to unilateral protectionist actions. Finally, in regard to the development principle, LDCs were only marginally involved in the GATT, and most of them refused to sign the Tokyo Round NTB codes.

In view of GATT's shortcomings, the United States in particular pressured for a new round of trade negotiations. With its balance-of-trade deficits increasing rapidly during the 1980s, the United States wanted the trade regulations extended to areas such as services and agriculture, where it continued to have a comparative advantage.[48] The trade regime inadequacies were also evident to other GATT members, and they agreed to begin the Uruguay Round negotiations in 1986. The negotiators at first focused on extending GATT's jurisdiction, but in April 1990 Canada's trade minister proposed that GATT should be replaced by a more formal WTO, and the EC supported this idea.[49] American negotiators, however, believed that the U.S. Congress would have concerns over loss of sovereignty as it had with the ITO in the 1940s, and that plans to create a new trade organization would take time away from substantive negotiations during the Uruguay Round. In the end, the United States altered its view, and the WTO replaced GATT in January 1995 as the main global trade organization.[50]

In contrast to GATT, the WTO is a formal, legally constituted organization like the IMF and World Bank. GATT has not disappeared but has reverted to its original status as an agreement for trade in goods. The WTO oversees trade rules in various treaties, including GATT and several new treaties negotiated during the Uruguay Round: the *General Agreement on Trade in Services (GATS)*, the *Agreement on Trade-Related Intellectual Property Rights (TRIPs)*, and the *Agreement on Trade-Related Investment Measures (TRIMs)*. GATT is the most important agreement under WTO auspices because trade in goods is the largest aspect of international trade.[51] The highest authority in the WTO is the *Ministerial Conference,* which includes all member countries and can take decisions on all matters under the multilateral trade agreements (see Figure 8.1). Although the sessions of the GATT contracting parties occasionally met at ministerial level, GATT ministerials were normally held only to launch or conclude new rounds of trade negotiations (the 1982 GATT ministerial was an exception). The WTO Ministerial Conference, by contrast, meets every two years and is designed to strengthen guidance of the WTO at the higher political levels. However, a number of subsidiary bodies are responsible for the WTO's daily operations. The most important of these is the *General Council,* which is composed of all WTO members and oversees the activities of the *Councils for Trade in Goods, Trade-Related Aspects of Intellectual Property Rights,* and *Trade in Services* (relating to the GATT, TRIPs, and GATS agreements).

The General Council also convenes as the *Trade Policy Review Body* and the *Dispute Settlement Body* when necessary. The Trade Policy Review Body conducts regular reviews of WTO members' trade policies and ensures that others are promptly notified of policies that may interfere with trade. By increasing the transparency of members' policies, the review body helps to promote trust that agreements are being enforced. The Dispute Settlement Body establishes panels to investigate complaints and adjudicate trade disputes. A member country may invoke the dispute settlement procedures if another member has broken a WTO regulation or reneged on previously negotiated concessions. Dispute settlement procedures are more binding and timely under the WTO than they were under GATT. Whereas a single GATT member (including a party to a dispute) could block the adoption of a GATT panel report, a consensus of member states is required to block WTO panel reports, a highly unlikely possibility. A WTO member may appeal a dispute settlement decision against it to the *Appellate Body* (see Figure 8.1), but if the Appellate Body agrees with the panel report, the member must implement the panel's recommendations or pay compensation. If a country refuses to implement a panel report or provide adequate compensation, the Dispute Settlement Body can authorize the complainant to take retaliatory action.[52]

The director general is the chief administrative officer of the GATT/WTO. Although a tacit agreement in the 1940s provided that the World Bank president would always be American and the IMF managing director would always be European, there was no similar agreement for GATT. For years the selection of GATT directors general generated little controversy, but the issue became contentious when the WTO was formed. Recent conflict over the selection process resulted partly from the higher profile of the WTO and from the propensity to appoint politicians for the WTO post unlike the officials previously appointed for the GATT post. In addition, conflict over the WTO selection process reflected greater U.S. assertiveness in response to its

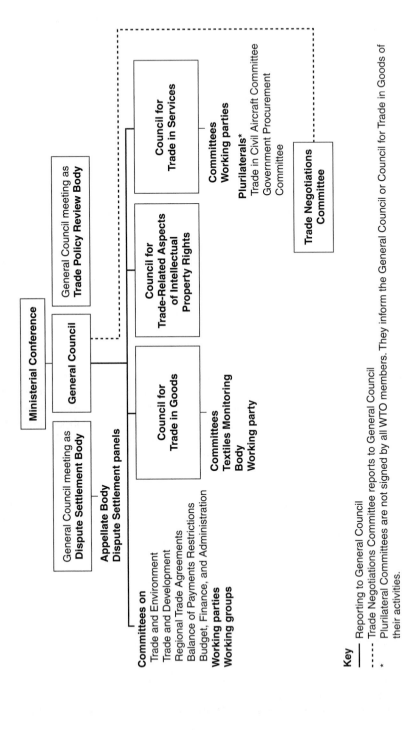

Figure 8.1 Structure of the World Trade Organization

Source: Adapted from WTO Organization Chart, May 20, 2003. Retrieved from WTO website: <www.wto.org/english/thewto_e/whatis_e/tif_e/organigram_e.pdf>.

Table 8.6

DIRECTORS GENERAL OF GATT* AND WTO

	Years in Office	Nationality-Country
Eric Wyndham-White	1948–1968	Britain
Olivier Long	1968–1980	Switzerland
Arthur Dunkel	1980–1993	Switzerland
Peter Sutherland	1993–1995	Ireland
Renato Ruggiero	1995–1999	Italy
Mike Moore	1999–2002	New Zealand
Supachai Panitchpakdi	2002–	Thailand

*The name of GATT's chief administrative officer was changed from *secretary general* to *director general* in 1965.

declining trade hegemony; growing trade rivalry among Europe, the United States, and Japan; and more assertiveness of LDCs. As Table 8.6 shows, all GATT directors general from 1948 to 1995 were Europeans. When it came time to select the first WTO director general, the United States supported a former Mexican president, Japan and most Asian countries supported the South Korean trade minister, and the EU supported former Italian foreign trade minister Renato Ruggiero. Although Ruggiero was clearly the favorite among GATT members, the major trading nations sought a consensus to avoid a divisive vote on the issue. The United States finally agreed to the selection of Ruggiero as director general, partly because its own candidate was indirectly linked to political scandals. However, the United States insisted that Ruggiero serve only one four-year term and that the next WTO head should be non-European. When it came time to select the next WTO director general, the conflict was renewed. This time most DCs other than Japan supported Mike Moore of New Zealand, and most LDCs supported Supachai Panitchpakdi of Thailand. After a protracted dispute, the WTO General Council members finally agreed that Moore should be director general for a three-year term starting in September 1999, and that Supachai should succeed him for a three-year term starting in September 2002.[53]

In contrast to the IMF and World Bank voting systems, the WTO system (like GATT's before it) is based on the one-nation, one-vote principle. Depending on the issue, WTO votes require a simple majority, a special majority of two-thirds or three-quarters, or unanimity. The one-nation, one-vote system has given LDCs less influence than one might expect because most decisions are made by consensus.[54] Furthermore, groups dominated by the North such as the G-7/G-8, Quad, and OECD have a major role in setting the agenda for MTNs.

THE WTO AND THE GLOBAL TRADE REGIME

The WTO was designed to be a more effective and authoritative organization than GATT, and in some respects it has succeeded. Unlike GATT, the WTO is a formal IO with a status comparable to the IMF and World Bank. Member states are also using the WTO's binding dispute settlement system far more frequently than they used the GATT dispute settlement procedures. Furthermore, the WTO is becoming a more genuinely global trade organization, with 146 members as of September 2003. (Major nonmembers include Russia, Ukraine, and Saudi Arabia.) In addition, the WTO not only oversees trade in goods, but also trade in services and trade-related intellectual property rights and investment measures. Finally, the WTO has made greater efforts to integrate LDCs and transition economies into the global trade regime, and it has begun a dialogue with a number of NGOs.

Nevertheless, the WTO has also demonstrated some serious shortcomings, and the organization faces a number of obstacles in maintaining the momentum of global trade liberalization. Many problems that plagued GATT continue to adversely affect the WTO, and it was unrealistic to assume that a new, more formal organization would easily resolve the underlying sources of conflict. After the GATT Uruguay Round, liberal economists argued that a new WTO round was essential to the vitality of the global trade regime for several reasons. First, liberals believe that *the bicycle must keep moving.* Forward momentum is essential to avoid backsliding into protectionism and mercantilism."[55] Second, the Uruguay Round negotiators agreed to conduct further negotiations for trade in services and agriculture after the round was concluded. However, self-standing negotiations on specific issue areas rarely succeed because tradeoffs across issues are needed to satisfy the large number of participants in MTNs. A comprehensive WTO round was therefore necessary. Third, despite the improved WTO dispute settlement procedures, further negotiations were required to deal with lingering problems. For example, U.S.-EU conflicts over bananas, beef hormones, and the U.S. Foreign Sales Corporation program demonstrated the need to improve the Dispute Settlement Understanding's compliance provisions. Fourth, further negotiations were considered necessary to ensure that the growing number of RTAs were compatible with multilateral trade liberalization. In sum, additional negotiations were required to strengthen the WTO-based trade regime.[56]

The initial plans were to launch a new round at the Third WTO ministerial meeting in Seattle, Washington, in November 1999. However, pressures of globalization, combined with the broad scope of WTO activities, elicited a strong negative reaction from civil society groups. Prenegotiations were also inadequate, and the WTO negotiators came to Seattle with widely divergent views on some critical issues. Although anti-WTO protestors in the streets caused some disruption, policy differences among WTO delegates were the decisive factor contributing to the failure of the meeting. The Quad members all wanted a new MTN, but they strongly disagreed over which issues should be negotiated. For example, the United States favored deep cuts in agricultural subsidies but opposed efforts to reform antidumping rules (which the United States used most frequently). Europe and Japan opposed further agricultural reforms but sought new talks on competition and investment policy; and Canada wanted special exemptions for its cultural industries. Because the Quad members differed among themselves, they could not provide leadership in forging a consensus in the WTO. There were also major North-South differences, with LDCs arguing that the DCs should fulfill earlier promises in such areas as textiles and agriculture before they agreed to negotiations on the *Singapore issues:* investment, competition policy, government procurement, and trade-facilitating measures such as customs procedures. (The name derives from the first WTO ministerial in Singapore in December 1996 where the EU and Japan first proposed that these issues be negotiated.) The LDCs also wanted additional time to fulfill commitments they had agreed to during the Uruguay Round.

The DCs were determined to hold a new WTO round, and after the failure in Seattle they planned to launch the round at the fourth WTO ministerial in Doha, Qatar, in November 2001. A major factor in the decision to hold the meeting in Doha related to the ability to prevent disruptive demonstrations of the type that occurred in Seattle. In view of serious divisions, the delegates reached agreement at Doha to launch a new round only after major compromises were made on all sides. For example, the EU accepted a commitment to discuss phasing out farm export subsidies, the United States agreed to negotiations to improve rules for using countervailing and antidumping duties, the North agreed to a (nonbinding) declaration that intellectual property rules should not prevent the South from gaining access to cheaper medicines for serious illnesses such as AIDs, and the South consented reluctantly to commit to future negotiations on foreign investment, competition, and environmental issues. Furthermore, the North agreed to address issues of concern to the South because of the South's disillusionment with the Uruguay Round (see discussion below), and the "name coined for the entire work programme" at the Doha ministerial "was the Doha Development Agenda."[57]

Although the agreement to launch the new WTO Doha Round was a major achievement, there were indications that "this first step . . . [was] in fact the smallest one."[58] Despite the promises of the United States and EU to make major concessions, they seemed unwilling to assume a leadership position comparable with their trading power. With its decline of trade hegemony and its large balance of trade deficits, the United States was more often turning to unilateralism and seeking bilateral trade agreements instead of offering the more difficult concessions required to reach multilateral agreements; and the EU was unwilling to offer sufficient concessions in the critical area of agriculture. The fifth WTO ministerial in Cancún, Mexico, in September 2003 was to mark the halfway point of the Doha Round, which was scheduled for completion in January 2005. As the halfway point, the Cancún meeting was to assess progress in the negotiations, provide political guidance, and make any necessary decisions. However, the Cancún Minsterial ended in failure, mainly because of North-South divisions. In the end, a new bloc of LDCs refused to accept a WTO proposal to make meager cuts in U.S., EU, and Japanese farm subsidies in return for LDC willingness to launch controversial talks on the Singapore issues. If the Doha Round is to succeed both DCs and LDCs will have to make more concessions; most importantly, more leadership must be forthcoming from the United States, the EU, and Japan.[59]

THE SOUTH AND GLOBAL TRADE ISSUES

The DCs were the main participants in GATT negotiations after World War II, and LDCs were largely uninvolved. This lack of involvement related partly to the nature of GATT and partly to LDC policies. The Havana Charter gave some attention to Southern issues in areas such as finance for economic development, preferential agreements among LDCs, and commodity agreements; but when the charter was not approved, most of these provisions were not incorporated into GATT. LDCs were also wary of participating in GATT because they thought it did not take account of their need for special and differential (S&D) treatment.[60] For many years the South therefore sought exemptions from some trade regime principles and rules as well as special access to DC markets. In the 1980s, however, the South became more accepting of GATT's liberal-economic orientation and more interested in participating in the global trade regime. Liberals and historical structuralists have very different views regarding the South's need for special treatment, the reasons why Southern policies changed in the 1980s, and the effects of the trade regime on Southern interests. The discussion that follows identifies five stages of Southern participation in the postwar trade regime:

1. *The 1940s to early 1960s.* LDCs had only limited involvement in GATT.
2. *The early 1960s to early 1970s.* LDCs increased their GATT membership and sought S&D treatment.
3. *The early 1970s to 1980.* North-South confrontation increased, along with LDC demands for a NIEO.
4. *1980 to 1995.* LDCs were more willing to accept GATT's liberal-economic principles.
5. *1995 to the present.* LDCs were disillusioned with the Uruguay Round results, and their commitment to the WTO is uncertain.

The 1940s to Early 1960s: A Period of Limited LDC Involvement

LDCs were largely uninvolved in the global trade regime during the early postwar years because of their limited numbers (many were still colonial territories), their protectionist trade policies, and GATT's inattention to their development problems. Most LDCs in the 1950s adopted protectionist ISI policies, which were designed to replace industrial imports with domestic production. Raúl Prebisch, an Argentinian economist, was the most influential figure supporting ISI in the postwar period. Prebisch argued that structural inequality between DCs in the core and LDCs in the periphery was a major characteristic of the capitalist world economy. As long as LDCs were dependent on exports of primary products, they could not achieve high economic growth rates. Prebisch therefore advised LDCs to pursue ISI policies to increase their production of manufactures.[61]

LDCs influenced by Prebisch's arguments (especially in Latin America) emphasized industrial over agricultural development, production for the domestic market over production for export, and protection of local industry through import barriers. With this focus on inward-looking policies, most LDCs did not seek to actively participate in GATT. Thus, only 10 of the original 23 GATT members were LDCs. Although 20 LDCs had joined GATT by 1960, only seven participated in the Dillon Round (see Table 8.3).[62] As discussed, when the ITO was not formed, the GATT devoted little attention to LDCs. The only major provision in the General Agreement dealing directly with Southern trade problems was GATT Article 28, which gave LDCs some flexibility in imposing import quotas to protect their infant industries and alleviate balance-of-payments problems. The LDCs insisted that GATT should be doing more to give them S&D treatment, but their influence during the 1950s was extremely limited.[63]

The Early 1960s to Early 1970s: Growing Pressures for Special Treatment

Two major changes occurred in the 1960s–1970s, contributing to growing LDC pressures for special treatment. First, some LDCs began to modify their ISI policies or shift to export-oriented growth policies, and second, the South's bargaining power increased. By the 1960s, many LDCs following ISI were experiencing serious economic problems, including a slowdown in the growth of exports, dependence on intermediate imports for the production of industrial goods, and growing balance-of-payments problems. (Chapter 11 discusses LDC development strategies.) As LDCs turned to more outward-looking policies, they demanded special treatment to promote their exports. LDCs also were better able to press their demands as the North-South balance shifted because of decolonization. Thus, in 1961 the UN General Assembly declared the 1960s to be the UN Development Decade, and UNCTAD I, the first major North-South conference on development issues, convened in 1964. The South also established the G-77 at this time, which became a vehicle for expressing its economic interests vis-à-vis the North.[64]

UNCTAD never posed a serious challenge to GATT as the main global trade organization, but it did have some influence in directing attention to Southern issues. Thus, GATT members added a new Part IV to the General Agreement in February 1965, calling for special treatment for LDCs. Although Part IV called on the DCs to reduce their import barriers to LDC goods, this was not a legally binding obligation, and Part IV was largely symbolic in nature. Indeed, during the 1960s the North was actually raising its trade barriers to some products for which the South had a comparative advantage. Textiles and clothing were prime examples of DC protectionism vis-à-vis LDCs. To protect their textile producers in the 1950s, some DCs (e.g., the United States and Britain) violated GATT Article 11, which outlaws import quotas, and imposed "voluntary" restraints on textile/clothing exports from Japan, Hong Kong, India, and Pakistan. The North then sought to legalize these restrictions through multilateral agreements. In 1961, a Short-Term Arrangement on Cotton Textiles was negotiated, and this was succeeded by several Long-Term Arrangements and Multi-Fiber Arrangements (MFAs). In marked contrast to GATT, these multilateral textile agreements endorsed DC protectionism and restricted LDC exports.[65]

GATT Part IV was largely symbolic; but the South gained a more concrete concession in 1971 when GATT permitted DCs to establish a generalized system of preferences (GSP) for LDCs through a 10-year renewable waiver from the MFN clause.[66] The United States and some other DCs had at first strongly opposed the GSP idea, but their position gradually softened. The GSP lowers DC tariff rates for certain imports from LDCs. Although some LDCs have benefited from these preferences, the benefits have been limited. Thus, the North refused to accept any legal obligation to provide preferences or to bind itself to an internationally agreed GSP plan. Instead, each state established its own GSP, often limited the amount of imports that could enter at lower duties, excluded sensitive products such as textiles from preferential status, and often reduced or eliminated its GSP for LDCs that were especially successful in increasing exports. In view of the complexities of different GSP schemes, more competitive LDCs such as the East Asian NIEs have benefited most, and the GSP has offered very few benefits to poorer LDCs. One study, for example, found that three economies—Hong Kong, South Korea, and Taiwan—accounted for 44 percent of the total gains from GSP tariff reductions.[67]

The Early 1970s to 1980: Increased North-South Confrontation

OPEC's success in increasing oil prices in 1973–1974 was a major factor encouraging the South to issue calls for a NIEO in the UN General Assembly.[68] To bring about a NIEO, the South sought a wide range of concessions from the North such as LDC sovereignty over their natural resources, increased control over foreign investment, more assistance for LDC debt and development problems, greater LDC influence in the international economic organizations, improved LDC access to DC markets, and increased prices for LDC commodity exports.[69] We focus here on a central trade-related demand of LDCs—the negotiation of an *Integrated Program for Commodities (IPC)*.

For a number of years, Prebisch as the first UNCTAD secretary general had insisted that commodity agreements were necessary to redress the problems of unstable earnings and declining terms of trade for LDC commodity exports. In 1976 the UNCTAD IV conference finally approved a resolution to establish the IPC, with the goal of establishing agreements for 18 commodities accounting for a substantial share of LDC primary product exports. The two most important elements of the IPC were to be the creation of international buffer stocks and a common fund that would be used to acquire the stocks. By enlarging the stockpiles of commodities with declining prices and selling stockpiles of commodities with increasing prices, the IPC would prevent excessive price fluctuations and ensure producers of remunerative returns.

Despite UNCTAD's passage of the IPC resolution, implementation of the IPC proved to be difficult for several reasons. First, some major DCs opposed an IPC on liberal-economic grounds because of its strong emphasis on market intervention to stabilize prices. Because DCs were to be the largest contributors to the common fund, their opposition did not bode well for implementation. Second, the South's ability to influence the North declined abruptly in the 1980s with the foreign debt crisis. Third, some assumptions of the IPC were defective, and doubts were raised about the possible effects of raising commodity export prices. The South and the North are not neatly divided into commodity exporters and importers, and raising commodity prices would benefit some DC exporters and hurt some LDC importers.

In view of the North's opposition, the agreement to establish a common fund was not ratified until 1989; and since 1989, DCs have contributed only limited amounts to the common fund. Furthermore, the International Natural Rubber Agreement was the only new agreement instituted under the IPC, and the International Tin Agreement collapsed in 1985. The IPC gave UNCTAD an opportunity to raise its profile as a negotiating forum, and the North's willingness to negotiate (albeit reluctantly) represented something of a success for the South. Nevertheless, the IPC's failure to meet Southern expectations demonstrates the aversion most DCs have to nonmarket solutions and points to their ability to prevent successful implementation of North-South agreements.[70]

Although the South was confronting the North in the UN during the 1970s, it was also participating in the 1973–1979 GATT Tokyo Round. One result of the Tokyo Round was the approval of the *enabling clause*, which "established for the first time in trade relations . . . a permanent legal basis for preferences in favour of developing countries."[71] The clause gave permanent legal authorization for the GSP and for preferential trade agreements among LDCs. To gain approval of the enabling clause, LDCs had to support the "graduation" principle for countries that demonstrated notable progress in development. Because some exports from more advanced LDCs (e.g., South Korea, Taiwan, and Brazil) were threatening U.S. producers, the U.S. government demanded that the countries give up special treatment and accept greater GATT discipline.[72] Another significant development in the Tokyo Round was the creation of NTB codes for government procurement, subsidies, technical barriers to trade, import licensing, and antidumping duties. The DCs negotiated the codes among themselves because most LDCs were unwilling to participate. Only a small number of LDCs signed the codes, and some DCs threatened to deny the benefits to nonsignatories. However, LDC attitudes toward participation in such agreements were to change markedly in the 1980s–1990s.

1980s to 1995: More LDC Participation in GATT

Initially, LDCs opposed the idea of a new round of negotiations in the 1980s. They were dissatisfied with inequities in the global trade regime and with efforts to include services, intellectual property, and investment in GATT, in which the DCs had a competitive advantage. The South's opposition gradually softened, however, partly because the North agreed to include issues of interest to LDCs such as trade in textiles and tropical agriculture. In contrast to previous rounds, the South participated actively in the Uruguay Round. The South functioned less as a bloc in the Uruguay Round, and a series of North-South coalitions were formed. For example, one coalition was the *De La Paix Group,* named after the Hôtel De La Paix in Geneva where it often met. The De La Paix Group included small and middle-size DCs and LDCs that shared an interest in a strong rules-based multilateral trade regime that would make a power-based system less justifiable. The De La Paix Group's efforts contributed to the launching of the Uruguay Round and to negotiations on dispute settlement, tariffs and NTBs, antidumping, and the functioning of the GATT system. The most important North-South coalition was the Cairns Group of agricultural exporters that first met in Cairns, Australia, in August 1986. The Cairns Group added a powerful new voice, ensuring that the GATT—and the EC, the United States, and Japan—would have to deal with agriculture. The founding members of the Cairns Group included 13 DCs and LDCs, and one Eastern European country. Although Cairns Group members had little influence individually, they were collectively important, with more agricultural exports than the EC and United States combined. The Cairns Group continues to function, and it currently has 18 members.[73]

In addition to their active participation, LDCs were more willing to accept the reciprocity principle during the Uruguay Round. Most significantly, the South agreed to treat the Uruguay Round agreements as a *single undertaking:* acceptance of the Uruguay Round accord meant acceptance of *all* its agreements. The single undertaking was a marked contrast to the Tokyo Round's NTB codes, in which most LDCs did not participate.[74] LDCs continued receiving S&D treatment during the Uruguay

Round, but the single undertaking principle demonstrated that they were willing to accept "a dilution of special and differential treatment in exchange for better market access and strengthened rules."[75] The types of special treatment the South received in the Uruguay Round included greater flexibility in fulfilling commitments, longer transition times for implementing agreements, and technical assistance from the North.

The South's more active role in the Uruguay Round was directly related to the decision of many LDCs to liberalize their trade policies during the 1980s. Liberal economists and historical structuralists cite different reasons for this dramatic policy shift. According to liberals, LDCs became increasingly aware of the advantages of adopting liberal-economic policies, for several reasons. First, the tariff preferences that LDCs received through the GSP were eroding as tariffs on trade among DCs were falling with each round of trade negotiations. Thus, LDCs were gaining fewer advantages from S&D treatment. Second, the North viewed LDCs as free riders receiving special treatment, and the South was therefore marginalized in trade negotiations. Many products of interest to the South, such as textiles and tropical agriculture, were either excluded from GATT negotiations or subjected to special protectionist rules. And third, liberals attributed the shift in LDC policies to the failure of inward-looking ISI policies and to the notable success of East Asian export-led growth strategies.[76]

Historical structuralists strongly disagree with liberals as to the reasons why LDCs shifted their trade policies in the 1980s. According to historical structuralists, LDCs were *forced* to alter their policies. In response to the 1980s foreign debt crisis, the IMF and World Bank provided SALs to LDCs only on the conditions that they decrease government spending, liberalize their trade, and privatize their economies. Because DCs and private lenders would not extend loans to LDC debtors without the IMF's stamp of approval, debtor countries had no choice but to liberalize their trade policies. Thus, one writer argues that "the current rush toward free trade follows on the heels of 10 years of structural adjustment, a logical 'next step' in the overhaul of the global economy."[77]

1995 to the Present: Uncertainty over LDC Participation in the WTO

Liberals and historical structuralists also disagree in their assessment of the effects of the Uruguay Round on the South. Liberals concede that the South had to make concessions to the North in such areas as intellectual property, services trade, and investment. However, they argue that these were short-term concessions and that LDCs will benefit in the long term from liberalizing their policies. Liberals also point to advantages LDCs gained from participating in the Uruguay Round in such areas as textiles and tropical agriculture. Finally, liberals note that LDCs still benefit from S&D treatment in some areas; for example, LDCs have lower levels of obligation and more flexible implementation timetables, and they benefit from technical assistance and training and special provisions for LLDCs. Many liberals acknowledge that DCs should be doing more to open their markets to LDC exports, but on balance they argue that the Uruguay Round was beneficial to the South.[78]

Historical structuralists (and some interventionist liberals to a lesser degree), by contrast, argue that the South gave up far more than it received from the Uruguay Round. The inclusion of trade in services and intellectual property ensures that income will be transferred from poor to rich countries because LDCs cannot compete effectively in these areas. As for "concessions" to LDCs, the agreement to phase out the protectionist MFA on textiles was backloaded so that almost one-half of the DC import quotas are to be removed only at the end of a 10-year transition period. Even after MFA quotas are eliminated, LDCs will face significant DC tariffs on their textile and clothing exports, and the misuse of safeguards and other protectionist measures will prolong DC restrictions on textiles trade.[79] As for the critical issue of agricultural trade, historical structuralists argue that poor countries cannot compete with the continuing subsidies to agriculture in the rich countries, and that the ability of LDC farmers to produce basic foodstuffs is therefore in jeopardy.

Both the liberals and the historical structuralists have a point. Although LDCs received some "fairly significant benefits from the Uruguay Round," they also realized belatedly "that they had accepted fairly weak commitments in agriculture and textiles while making substantially stronger ones, especially in new areas such as intellectual property."[80] The disillusionment of LDCs with the Uruguay Round results were evident at the third, fourth, and fifth WTO ministerial meetings in Seattle, Doha, and Cancún. India almost blocked the decision to launch a new MTN round at Doha, and LDCs remained "deeply suspicious of the rich world's commitment to truly freer trade."[81] Although the Doha Round was launched, the fifth WTO ministerial in Cancún, which was supposed to be the mid-point of the round, broke up in serious disarray in September 2003 over North-South differences. The major sources of dispute at Cancún were over agriculture and the Singapore issues.

As for agriculture, there was widespread dissatisfaction with the results of the Uruguay Round agreement "among all categories of developing countries, whether they are agricultural exporters, food importers, single-commodity exporters, predominantly agrarian economies, or small-island developing states."[82] The South wanted the North to phase out its excessive agricultural subsidies, lower tariffs on LDC agricultural exports, stop using sanitary and phytosanitary standards to restrict market access, and permit LDCs to protect their agriculture from damaging import surges. At Cancún, the South was dissatisfied with the agricultural concessions the EU, United States, and Japan were willing to make. As for the Singapore issues, LDCs would not agree to DC (especially EU) demands that a commitment be made to negotiate investment, competition policy, government procurement, and trade-facilitating measures. In stark contrast to the North-South coalitions at the Uruguay Round, during Cancún a group of 22 LDCs headed by China, India, and Brazil confronted the DCs, and the Cairns Group was hardly visible.

Although liberals strongly support the Doha Round, many of them acknowledge that DCs must do more to remove their barriers to LDC exports if the round is to succeed:

> Europe and America must quickly open up their markets for farm products and textiles. They must show that environmental concerns are not going to become a backdoor excuse for renewed protectionism. They must reform their oft-abused system of anti-dumping rules. And they must deliver on promises to beef up poorer countries' capacity to deal with the intricate procedures in the world trading system.[83]

LDCs must also of course be willing to make concessions from a liberal perspective. For example, tariff rates on agricultural goods are often higher in LDCs than in

DCs, and the World Bank has indicated that LDCs would benefit from "reductions in tariff and nontariff barriers in both industrial and developing countries."[84] However, the nature and degree of Southern involvement in the WTO will depend largely on whether or not it believes the North is addressing LDC interests and concerns.

THE TRANSITION ECONOMIES AND GLOBAL TRADE RELATIONS

The South only gradually increased its involvement in GATT, but most CPEs were not even GATT members for many years after World War II. As was the case for LDCs, the General Agreement also largely ignored issues of concern to CPEs.[85] The lack of attention to state trading and central planning was not surprising; the Soviet Union had turned down an invitation to attend the Havana Charter negotiations (see Chapter 2), and it was simply assumed that GATT members would be free market economies. Indeed, one of GATT's major functions was to limit government actions that interfered with market forces.

As Table 8.7 shows, Czechoslovakia was a founding member of GATT and remained a member even after it became Communist, but its membership became largely inactive. Other Eastern European countries (Yugoslavia, Poland, Romania, and Hungary) joined GATT in the 1960s–1970s. Lower tariffs do not necessarily increase access to CPE markets, because CPEs exclude foreign products through administrative controls over pricing and purchasing. Thus, GATT admitted these Eastern Euro-

Table 8.7

MEMBERSHIP OF THE TRANSITION ECONOMIES IN GATT/WTO

	GATT/WTO
1948	Czechoslovakia and China (founding members)
1950	Republic of China (Taiwan) withdraws from GATT
1966	Yugoslavia
1967	Poland
1971	Romania
1973	Hungary
1990	East Germany accedes to GATT by virtue of German reunification
1993	Czech Republic, Slovak Republic
1994	Slovenia
1996	Bulgaria
1998	Kyrgyz Republic
1999	Latvia, Estonia
2000	Albania, Croatia, Georgia
2001	Lithuania, Moldova, China
2002	Taiwan
2003	Armenia, Macedonia

Source: General Agreement on Tariffs and Trade, *GATT Activities* (Geneva: GATT, various years); WTO web site.

pean countries under special provisions. In the late 1980s–1990s, however, the requirements for membership became more rigorous, and nonmarket economies were expected to institute specific reforms as a condition for admission. The more stringent requirements resulted from concerns about the possible admission of China and the Soviet Union (later Russia), the revival of orthodox liberalism, and the fact that the WTO was a more formal organization than GATT.

Although relations between GATT and its Eastern European members were often difficult, the problems were limited because these countries had a relatively small effect on the global trade regime. This would not be the case for China and Russia, whose membership could have significant economic and political consequences. China and Russia were readily admitted to the IMF and World Bank because they are loan recipients and have little influence in these weighted-voting institutions.[86] The GATT/WTO, by contrast, does not have weighted voting, and the major trading nations were concerned that these two countries could shift the political and economic balance of power in the organization. Furthermore, if economies as large as China and Russia were admitted before they evolved sufficiently toward developing market economies, there were fears that trade protectionism in the WTO could increase.[87] The following sections examine GATT/WTO relations with Eastern Europe, China, and the FSU countries.

Eastern Europe and the GATT/WTO

Czechoslovakia was a founding member of GATT, the IMF, and the World Bank. Although Czechoslovakia was ousted from the IMF and World Bank shortly after it became a nonmarket economy, it was able to remain an inactive member of GATT for many years because it was an informal IO. Table 8.7 shows that four other Eastern European states (Yugoslavia, Poland, Romania, and Hungary) joined GATT in the 1960s–1970s. Although some of these states were becoming more market oriented, the decision to admit them also resulted from the Western policy of *differentiation.* Designed to contain the Soviet Union, the differentiation strategy rewarded Eastern European states for adopting more independent foreign or domestic policies. The strong U.S. support for Romanian accession to GATT, for example, stemmed mainly from Romania's conflict with the Soviet Union over foreign policy issues. The GATT secretariat also exerted pressure to admit Eastern European states because it aspired to the goal of universal membership.[88]

In accordance with the West's differentiation policy, GATT imposed a diverse range of conditions for admission of the Eastern Europeans. After its break with the Soviet bloc in 1948, Yugoslavia sought to redirect its trade to the West. When Yugoslavia first explored GATT affiliation in 1950, it was a full CPE, but it began to engage in economic decentralization in 1952. Yugoslavia did not become a GATT member until 1966 because major reforms were required to move it from CPE protection toward the GATT model. This experience showed that a CPE could participate in GATT under conditions very similar to those for a market economy if it adopted an economic decentralization policy. Unlike Yugoslavia, both Poland and Romania applied for accession to GATT when they were not yet moving toward market reform. Tariffs have little influence over the import decisions of CPEs, so Poland and Romania had to commit to increasing their imports in return for GATT membership. When Poland joined GATT in 1967, it agreed to increase its total value of imports from GATT members by 7 percent per year, and in return it received limited MFN treatment. However, Poland's 7 percent import commitment was based on an estimate that its exports to GATT members would increase by the same amount. Poland had to decrease its exports to other GATT countries because it did not meet the 7 percent import requirement. Some analysts therefore argue that the 7 percent requirement served as a *disincentive* to Polish trade in GATT.[89]

GATT agreed to classify Romania as an LDC when it applied for membership, and it was therefore subject to less rigid requirements than Poland. Instead of making a specific commitment, Romania expressed a "firm intention" to increase its imports from GATT members by at least as much as its total imports from all countries were increasing. Although this approach avoided the problems encountered with Poland, the Romanian undertakings were so vague that they were unenforceable.[90] The conditions for Hungary's admission to GATT (in 1973) were in between those for Yugoslavia on one hand and Poland and Romania on the other. Because Hungary had been instituting some liberal economic reforms under its New Economic Mechanism, GATT members permitted it to provide tariff concessions as an alternative to commitments to increase its imports. In contrast to other Eastern European states, Bulgaria was rebuffed for many years in its attempts to join GATT. Bulgaria's efforts failed because it was a close Soviet ally during the Cold War and because of fears that its admission would create a precedent for admission of the Soviet Union. With the decline of the Cold War, the strategic rationale for denying Bulgaria WTO membership became less important, but the Bulgarian case continued to be enmeshed with the issue of WTO membership for Russia and China. It was not until 1996 that the WTO finally approved the entry of Bulgaria.[91]

Despite GATT's openness to the admission of Eastern European states, the acceptance of these states was clearly conditional. For example, the accession agreements for Poland, Romania, and Hungary permitted the EC to continue imposing discriminatory quantitative restrictions on imports from these states. Trade between the CPEs and the United States was also subject to special restrictions under U.S. law. Thus, in some respects the Eastern Europeans were second-class citizens in GATT. With the breakup of the Soviet bloc, there were strong pressures to normalize the terms of participation for the Eastern Europeans. The EU agreed to dispense with its quantitative restrictions on Eastern European exports, and the WTO extended virtually the same treatment to Poland and Hungary as it does to market economies.[92] The EU is currently completing negotiations for the admission of 10 Central and Eastern European states, and the membership of these states in the EU should also result in their increased involvement in the WTO (see Chapter 9).

China

China's decision to seek membership in GATT marked a significant departure from its previous policies. In the early 1960s, China had followed a policy of self-reliance, which emphasized import substitution, and its policies became even more autarkic in

1966–1969 during the Cultural Revolution. During the early 1970s, however, China occupied the "China seat" in the UN General Assembly (which had been held by Taiwan) and moved to expand its commercial contacts with the West. After Mao Zedong's death in 1976 and the imprisonment of Cultural Revolution leaders, China began to gradually liberalize its economy in 1978 and it sought to establish contacts with GATT. In 1982, China was given observer status in GATT, permitting it to attend the annual meetings of the contracting parties, and in 1984 China was given special observer status allowing it to attend GATT Council meetings. In 1986 China indicated that it wanted to "rejoin" GATT as a full member, and it renewed its application in 1995 when the WTO was formed.[93]

Compared with China's relatively easy takeover of the China seat in the IMF and World Bank (in 1980), China's accession to GATT/WTO was a protracted affair. The delay in reconciliation stemmed partly from the fact that China had a more ambivalent attitude toward GATT than the IMF and World Bank. To participate in the IMF and World Bank, China would have to provide economic data on itself and pay its subscription, but the benefits of receiving external financing and economic advice from these organizations greatly outweighed the drawbacks. As a full participant of GATT, by contrast, the requirements of China would be greater (e.g., submitting to GATT rules and opening its market) and the benefits more uncertain. Furthermore, China received *de facto* MFN treatment from most states even without being a GATT member. The only major exception was the United States, where Congress held an annual vote on the issue, but even in this case Congress had always voted to renew MFN status for China.[94]

Despite its reticence about GATT membership, China decided to seek full participation in GATT beginning in 1986. Overall, the Chinese leadership believed that the benefits of membership outweighed the costs. Membership would consolidate China's past liberalization measures and provide motivation for further reforms, give it a legal right of access to its export markets, give it access to the GATT dispute settlement system to protect its trading rights, and permit it to participate in GATT's rule-making process. China's commitment to joining the GATT/WTO also increased as the ratio of imports and exports to its GDP rose from less than 10 percent in 1978 to 30 percent in 1996.[95] China was a founding member of GATT in 1948, and it indicated that it would seek a resumption of membership rather than a new membership. However, it was in the midst of a civil war during the early years of GATT, and in 1950 the Chiang Kai-shek government (which had fled to Taiwan) sent a cable withdrawing China from GATT membership. China maintained that the 1950 cable had no legal effect because Chiang Kai-shek was no longer leading the legally constituted government. China also argued that it had reoccupied the China seat without having to apply as a new member in the UN, the Food and Agriculture Organization, and the IMF and World Bank. Thus, China's desire to join GATT should be regarded as a resumption of membership rather than a new membership issue. However, a number of GATT members noted that China had not participated in GATT negotiations or abided by GATT obligations for 35 years. Conditions had to be placed on China's membership because it still had many characteristics of a CPE. Thus, China eventually had to accept the fact that detailed negotiations would precede its accession, and that the procedures would be similar to those for new members.[96] The admission process to the WTO (and to GATT before it) has involved four stages:

1. A fact-finding stage, during which a WTO working party collects information on the applicant's trade policies.
2. A negotiations stage, during which the applicant holds bilateral talks with WTO members and multilateral talks with a WTO working party.
3. A decision stage, during which the WTO General Council decides whether to admit the applicant. Although the General Council normally decides by consensus, it could decide to admit the applicant by a two-thirds majority.
4. An implementation stage, during which the applicant must make internal policy adjustments in accordance with the accession package.[97]

The discussion that follows outlines three issues that were central to China's negotiations for admission to the GATT/WTO.

Requirements That China Should Liberalize Its Economy   As discussed, China has introduced a wide range of market reforms since 1978. Nevertheless, China's trade policies lack transparency, and government intervention in the economy continues to produce significant trade distortions. For example, China limits imports in specific sectors with high tariffs, import quotas, import licenses, and other barriers. The United States has reacted strongly to these trade distortions because the U.S. trade deficit with China increased from $17.8 billion in 1989 to $68.7 billion in 1999. U.S. labor groups argue that many jobs have been lost because of the trade deficit with China, and they exerted strong pressure on the U.S. government to insist that China commit to more economic liberalization and enforceable labor rights as a price for WTO membership.[98] Thus, there has been considerable pressure on China to offer specific commitments to liberalize its trade policies and make them more transparent.[99]

China's Status in the WTO   Another major issue in the accession negotiations was China's status in the WTO. Should China be categorized as an industrial country or an LDC, and should it be viewed as a CPE? The answers to these questions had major implications for the conditions and terms of Chinese membership.

China regularly indicated that it expected "the same differential and more favourable treatment" in the WTO that was "accorded to developing countries at similar stages of economic development."[100] Romania was given developing country status when it was admitted to the GATT, and China wanted similar conditions. With this status, China would be eligible for the special treatment granted to other LDCs, such as protection for infant industries, the generalized system of preferences, and longer transition periods in implementing WTO agreements. Many WTO members, however, argued that China should be treated as a DC because of its size and status as a world exporter. From this perspective, China should be expected to meet the same reciprocity conditions as other industrial states. Even IOs offer conflicting views regarding China's level of development. For example, although the World Bank continues to categorize China's economy as "developing," it now has the second largest (PPP adjusted) GDP after the United States.[101]

A second issue related to whether China should be viewed as a CPE. China argued that the imposition of special conditions for its accession to the WTO was unnecessary because it had become more market oriented. Thus, a Chinese member of the UNCTAD secretariat stated that "China expects unconditional most favoured-nation treatment equivalent to that accorded to all other Contracting Parties."[102] Major trading countries in the WTO, by contrast, maintained that the Chinese government continued to depend on strategic trade rather than comparative advantage as a basis for its policies. Although some Eastern European countries joined GATT as CPEs, China's sheer size and huge trading capacity made the imbalance in market access a much greater concern. The terms for admitting China to the WTO were therefore of considerable importance, and in some respects the major trading powers would not accord China the same terms in the WTO that they gave to market economies. For example, the United States and China concluded their bilateral negotiations for China's accession to the WTO in November 1999. In the bilateral agreement the United States reserves the right to treat China as a nonmarket economy in some respects and to use safeguard mechanisms that would unilaterally restrict Chinese exports. On the other hand, the WTO is permitting China to adopt a phase-in approach for many areas of its trade policy in recognition of the fact that China is a transitional economy.[103]

China's Implementation of Agreements   A third issue in the accession negotiations related to China's past record in implementing agreements. For example, in 1992 the U.S. Bush administration reached an agreement with China to improve protection of intellectual property. Despite the agreement, piracy of computer programs and music recordings became a thriving industry in southern China, and Chinese-made copies of pirated U.S. films, computer programs, and recordings were sent to Eastern Europe, Canada, and elsewhere. Although some argue that China's protection for intellectual property has improved, pirated intellectual property continues to be readily available in major Chinese cities.[104] Concerns about China's commitment and ability to implement agreements therefore became an issue of concern during the accession negotiations.

Despite these contentious issues, China reached bilateral agreements on market access with the United States and the EU in 1999–2000 as a prelude to its accession to the WTO. The United States also had to address the issue of providing permanent MFN status to China. The United States had provided China MFN status on an annual basis since 1980, and extension of MFN was not a major issue until the Tiananmen Square massacre in 1989. Each year after Tiananmen, the U.S. Congress used the annual MFN review to raise a number of concerns with China, ranging from human rights to arms sales and trading practices. Despite opposition from a number of labor and human rights groups, the U.S. Congress voted to grant permanent MFN status or "permanent normal trade relations" to China, and in October 2000 President Clinton signed the legislation. (Although the term "normal trade relations" replaced the MFN term in U.S. law, the MFN term continues to be used in WTO and other trade agreements.)[105]

In November 2001, the delegates at the Doha ministerial finally agreed to admit China and Taiwan ("Chinese Taipei") to the WTO. Thus, China and Taiwan became WTO members in December 2001 and January 2002, respectively. Analysts had widely divergent views of the possible impact of China's membership on China, the WTO, and other trading partners. Some analysts warned that "China's complex and opaque system of bureaucrats, provincial governments, and state-run enterprises, combined with its lack of a rule of law" would have a negative effect on the WTO.[106] Others warned that WTO membership would have painful effects on the Chinese people and economy; for example, China's auto industry, agricultural sector, and financial services could all suffer as a result of freer trade. Some analysts, however, took a more positive view, asserting that China's WTO membership was "in the interests of both China and its major trading partners" because it would liberalize China's economy and eventually its society and polity.[107] China's chief negotiator at the WTO negotiations also argued that "if China wants to develop from a large economic country to an economic power, it must become part of the mainstream of the world economy, otherwise, it will . . . face the danger of marginalization."[108]

Although it is too early for a longer-term assessment of the effects of China's accession to the WTO, one issue is certain: China's membership is having a major impact on the WTO and some of its most important members. As Table 8.4 shows, China was the world's fourth largest trader in 2002 after the United States, the EU, and Japan. Thus, the U.S. Commerce Department has announced plans to create a special China Office in Import Administration to deal with the "different and complex" questions posed by China's transition economy.[109] A major source of tension stems from the large U.S. trade deficit with China. The United States argues that China's undervalued currency (the *yuan* or *renminbi*) gives its exports an unfair competitive advantage, and U.S. officials have pressured China to permit market forces to play a greater role in setting its exchange rates. However, China maintains that the United States is simply trying to divert attention from its own economic problems.[110] Although China has a large trade surplus with the United States, it has trade deficits with some Asian countries and (as an oil importer) with the Persian Gulf states. China has also made its presence felt in WTO negotiations. For example, China joined Brazil and India in leading the group of 22 LDCs demanding more concessions from the DCs at the Cancún ministerial meeting of the Doha Round. According to one trade delegate, "India and Brazil coordinating in the WTO was not new," but "what was new [at Cancún] was the participation of China."[111] In sum, China's membership is certain to have a major effect on the future shape of the WTO.

Russia and Other FSU Countries

After avoiding participation in GATT for more than three decades, in the early 1980s the Soviet Union sought observer status and quietly explored the possibility of membership. However, some important GATT members strongly opposed these efforts. Undeterred, the Soviets in August 1986 asked for observer status during the Punta del Este meetings launching the Uruguay Round, and announced plans to introduce extensive economic reforms. The Soviet Union's change in policy should not have been surprising because a sharp drop in oil prices was posing a serious threat to Mikhail Gorbachev's five-year plan to restructure and modernize the economy. However, invitations to the Uruguay Round were limited to GATT members and to countries that had given formal notification of their intent to join GATT. This decision was designed to permit China's participation in the round but to exclude the Soviet Union and Bulgaria. U.S. officials in particular expressed strong opposition to Soviet participation, arguing that the Soviet economic system was incompatible with the trade regime principles and rules. The major trading nations were also concerned that the Soviet Union would benefit more than the West from accession to GATT and that the Soviets would politicize the GATT, making it difficult to conduct trade negotiations.[112]

The West was far more open to the accession issue after the breakup of the Soviet Union in December 1991, and WTO membership negotiations are ongoing with the FSU states. Serious economic problems in the FSU states and their halting steps toward establishing market economies pose obstacles to their accession. However, as Table 8.7 shows, from 1998 to 2003 seven FSU states were admitted to the WTO (the Kyrgyz Republic, Latvia, Estonia, Georgia, Lithuania, Moldova, and Armenia), and others are certain to follow. Russia entered negotiations for accession in July 1995, and WTO directors general have strongly encouraged Russian membership. Russia is much less important as a trader than China. If the EU is considered as a single trader, Russia ranked only 11th as an exporter and 15th as an importer in world merchandise trade in 2002 (compared with China's fourth-ranked position). Nevertheless, Russia has a large market capacity for goods, services, and investment, and some Russian exports can significantly influence world commodity markets.[113]

In 2000, Russia's newly-elected president Vladimir Putin indicated that WTO membership was a government priority, and this objective was bolstered by renewed Russian cooperation with the United States after the World Trade Center attack on September 11, 2001. However, Russia is far less prepared than China for membership in the WTO. The breakup of the Soviet Union severed economic linkages that had been formed over decades, resulting in serious economic problems. Thus, it is not surprising that a wide range of interests in Russia are either uncertain or opposed to WTO membership. For example, many Russians believe that WTO accession will increase unemployment and that higher tariffs are necessary to increase inward foreign direct investment; also, a strong lobby protecting the financial sector in Russia describes itself as an "infant industry" that would suffer from liberalization.[114]

As a result, the Putin government lowered accession as a priority and began to take a more hardline position in negotiations. The most important obstacle to Russian membership at present relates to its natural gas policies. The EU demands that Russia institute reforms in the natural gas sector to reduce government interference and make the transition to market principles. However, there is strong opposition in Russia to carrying out this reform. Other contentious negotiating issues relate to financial and telecommunications services, agricultural subsidies, tariffs, and membership in the civil aviation agreement. For example, the United States and EU are pressuring Russia to sign the civil aviation agreement, but Russia refuses on the basis that government support is necessary if it is to eventually compete with the leading aircraft producers. Although the major traders would like to see Russia join the WTO by the end of the Doha Round, major obstacles remain. Nevertheless, a number of factors favor Russia's eventual inclusion in the WTO. As long as countries as important as Russia, Ukraine, and Saudi Arabia are not included, the WTO cannot claim to be a truly global trade organization. These countries are more likely to liberalize their economies from within than outside the WTO, and they are more likely to follow disruptive economic policies as long as they remain outsiders. Finally, Russia is a member of the G-8 and is too important in security terms to remain outside the WTO.[115]

CIVIL SOCIETY AND GLOBAL TRADE RELATIONS

Civil society groups protested against the WTO even before it began operations in January 1995, but the third WTO ministerial in Seattle in late 1999 marked a turning point during which protests reached new levels. A major reason the WTO is a target relates to the fact that it is the most important KIEO. Unlike GATT, which dealt only with trade in goods, the WTO mandate also includes trade in services, intellectual property, and trade-related investment measures. Furthermore, the WTO dispute settlement system is considerably stronger than GATT's because parties to a dispute can no longer veto panel decisions against them. In view of the WTO's importance, many civil society groups demand a role in WTO decision making and have strong views about what the WTO should or should not be doing.[116]

WTO agreements establish formal rights and obligations only for member governments, and WTO dispute settlement is formally open only to state actors. This limitation rests on the realist assumption that sovereign states are the key international actors. According to this perspective, the WTO functions best "when governments can speak clearly to each other without a cacophony of other voices."[117] All sessions of the WTO General Council, committees, dispute settlement panels, and appellate body panels are closed to the public, and minutes of these meetings are not released. Although private parties have limited formal roles in some WTO dispute settlement cases, they have no *legal right* to these roles—it is always at the discretion of others. For example, WTO dispute settlement panels have the authority to consider advice or submissions from any private individual or group, but panels can choose whether or not to accept private party submissions.[118] NGOs point to the important informal role business groups sometimes have in WTO dispute settlement cases and argue that they should also have a role in these cases commensurate with their interests; for example, environmental NGOs demand involvement in dispute settlement cases relating to the environment.

Civil society groups also have strong opinions regarding the role of the WTO. Not surprisingly, the views of this wide array of groups are sometimes inconsistent. On one hand, NGOs often portray the WTO as a major vehicle of globalization that has too much power to override the will of governments. On the other hand, a number of NGOs argue that the WTO should contribute to fair trade by exerting pressure on delinquent governments to upgrade their labor, environmental, and human rights standards. In this area, NGO views often diverge from the position of LDCs, which argue that such standards would infringe on their sovereignty and provide DCs with an excuse to impose protectionist trade barriers on LDC exports. In assessing competing views on the proper role for NGOs in the WTO, students should refer to the growing amount of literature on the subject.[119]

CONCLUSION

This chapter demonstrates that the forces of globalization strongly affect international trade. Changes are evident in the growing importance of international trade to national economies and domestic groups, in the closer linkages between trade and other international issues, and in the increased membership in the WTO. Internationalist firms have a major stake in an open trading system because of their reliance on multinational operations, exports, imports, and intrafirm trade. GATT was designed to deal almost exclusively with trade in tangible goods, but this coverage proved to be too narrow. Thus, the WTO is addressing a wide range of additional areas such as services, foreign investment, intellectual property, labor standards, and the environment, which have become closely intertwined with trade issues. Foreign direct investment and trade, for example, are highly complementary because about 40 percent of trade is conducted among affiliates of international firms. (Although some accords such as TRIPS extend beyond the trade area, internationalist firms are pleased to have them included in the WTO.) Finally, membership in the WTO is for the first time becoming truly global. For many years LDCs did not fully participate in GATT negotiations, and a number of LDCs did not even join the organization. The foreign debt crisis that began in 1982 marked a turning point in LDC participation, and Table 8.8 shows that 39 LDCs joined GATT from 1982 to 1994 (the year before the WTO was formed). Another major turning point

Table 8.8

NEW LDC ACCESSIONS TO GATT, 1982–94 (dates of accession)

Angola	1994	Maldives	1983
Antigua and Barbuda	1987	Mali	1993
Bahrain	1993	Mexico	1986
Belize	1983	Morocco	1987
Bolivia	1990	Mozambique	1992
Botswana	1987	Namibia	1992
Brunei	1993	Papua New Guinea	1994
Costa Rica	1990	Paraguay	1993
Djibouti	1994	Qatar	1994
Dominica	1993	St. Kitts and Nevis	1994
El Salvador	1991	St. Lucia	1993
Fiji	1993	St. Vincent and Grenadines	1993
Grenada	1994	Solomon Islands	1994
Guatemala	1991	Swaziland	1993
Guinea, Republic of	1994	Thailand	1982
Guinea-Bissau	1994	Tunisia	1990
Honduras	1994	United Arab Emirates	1994
Hong Kong	1986	Venezuela	1990
Lesotho	1988	Zambia	1982
Macao	1991		

Source: Bernard Hoekman and Michel Kostecki, *The Political Economy of the World Trading System: From GATT to WTO* (Oxford: Oxford University Press, 1995) pp.275–276.

was the breakup of the Soviet Union in the early 1990s, which led to a wave of transition countries seeking membership in GATT/WTO. As of September 2003 there were 146 members in the WTO and a number of observer governments.

Liberals, realists, and historical structuralists have very different reactions to these changes in the global trade regime. Liberal economists believe that DCs, LDCs, and transition economies are all benefiting from trade liberalization. Thus, one liberal researcher argues that "in one country after another, farsighted leaders have recognized that they themselves have the means to invigorating their economies by opening their borders."[120] Orthodox liberals applaud the moves by many LDCs in recent years to liberalize their trade barriers unilaterally, arguing that the main benefits go to those who liberalize. As for the Uruguay Round agreements on services, investment, and intellectual property, liberals believe they should "mark only the beginning, not the completion, of new liberalization."[121] Many realists, by contrast, point to the fact that states are not uniformly moving toward trade liberalization. They also argue that "triadization" is more prevalent than globalization, with the three most developed regions of the world—Western Europe, North America, and East Asia—having the most interactions. The greatest amount of trade occurs between and within these three regions, and trade flows with other regions are relatively small. Triadization is evident not only from statistics but also from general attitudes. Thus, Western Europeans, Japanese, and North Americans believe that the "world that counts is their world in which is located the scientific power, technological potentials and supremacy, military hegemony, economic wealth [and] cultural power."[122] Realists point out that the decline of U.S. trade hegemony has led to growing competition among these three major blocs. In this increasingly competitive world, strategic trade policies involving selective intervention by governments can greatly improve a country's trade position. Thus, realists believe that states can create their own competitive advantage as an alternative to relying on static views of comparative advantage.

Historical structuralists, like realists, point to a hierarchy among states in which the North clearly dominates the global trade regime. However, historical structuralists are more concerned than realists with the consequences for the South. In the view of historical structuralists, LDCs have become more active participants in the global trade regime by necessity rather than choice. IMF and World Bank SALs since the 1980s have been linked with LDC commitments to engage in trade liberalization, privatization, and deregulation, and LDC debtors have had to comply with these conditions to receive international financing. The Uruguay Round agreement, from this perspective, was an unequal agreement in which the North received concrete gains in areas such as intellectual property and services trade while LDCs had to settle for the promise of possible future gains in textiles trade and agriculture.

The TRIPs agreement is a prime example of the differing views of liberals and historical structuralists. The Uruguay Round agreement requires all signatories to provide intellectual property rights protection; for example, WTO members must develop legislation that provides patent protection for at least 20 years. Liberals argue that most innovation occurs privately and groups and individuals will have little incentive to engage in R&D if they are not rewarded with sufficient patent protection. Thus, intellectual property rights are essential for the development of inventions and innovations. Historical structuralists, by contrast, maintain that many of the TRIPs measures "are not explicitly related to trade—except in the name of the agreement."[123] Although the South in the Uruguay Round had wanted the TRIPs discussions to be limited to trade-related measures, the North used these discussions to develop measures they wanted that were outside the competence of GATT. More than 80 percent of patents in the South are owned by foreigners, mainly MNCs with headquarters in the North. Thus, the TRIPs agreement, according to historical structuralists, limits and distorts trade, hinders the transfer of technology to the South and leads to a net transfer of resources in rents from the South to the North.[124]

Liberals, realists, and historical structuralists in fact all point to important trends in the global trade regime. On one hand, trade interdependence has been increasing and there are strong pressures for further trade liberalization. If one considers the current role of transnational actors, it would seem that the forces for trade liberalization are inexorable. Nevertheless, realists point out that this growing interdependence and the decline of U.S. trade hegemony have led to increased competitiveness and greater temptations to resort to strategic trade policy. Historical structuralists argue that the North has been the main beneficiary of trade liberalization, with the South occupying a peripheral position. Both realists and historical structuralists can also point to the wide range of civil society groups that have reacted against WTO policies they associate with globalization. In sum, the pressures for trade liberalization have increased in recent years, but opposing forces have also gained strength and should not be underestimated.

NOTES

1. Jacob Viner, *Studies in the Theory of International Trade* (New York: Augustus M. Kelly, Reprint of Economic Classics, 1965), p.100; David A. Baldwin, *Economic Statecraft* (Princeton: Princeton University Press, 1985), pp.75–76.
2. A trade war is an "intense international conflict where states interact, bargain, and retaliate primarily over economic objectives directly related to the traded goods or service sectors of their economies, and where the means used are restrictions on the free flow of goods or services." (John A. C. Conybeare, *Trade Wars: The Theory and Practice of International Commercial Rivalry,* New York: Columbia University Press, 1987, p.3.)
3. World Trade Organization, *Annual Report—1998* (Geneva.: WTO, 1998), p.5.
4. Renato Ruggiero, "Charting the Trade Routes of the Future: Towards a Borderless Economy," address delivered to the International Industrial Conference, San Francisco, September 29, 1997, *WTO Press Release,* Geneva, Press/77, p.4.
5. Helen V. Milner, *Resisting Protectionism: Global Industries and the Politics of International Trade* (Princeton: Princeton University Press, 1988), pp.290–291.
6. David Ricardo, *The Principles of Political Economy and Taxation* (Homewood: Irwin, 1963). See also Cletus C. Coughlin, K. Alec Chrystal, and Geoffrey E. Wood, "Protectionist Trade Policies: A Survey of Theory, Evidence, and Rationale," *Federal Reserve Bank of St. Louis Review* 70–1 (January–February, 1988), pp.12–13.
7. Beth V. Yarbrough and Robert M. Yarbrough, *The World Economy: Trade and Finance,* 3rd ed. (Fort Worth: Harcourt Brace, 1994), pp.78–82.

8. Wolfgang F. Stolper and Paul A. Samuelson, "Protection and Real Wages," *Review of Economic Studies* 9–1 (November 1941), pp.58–73; Ronald Rogowski, *Commerce and Coalitions: How Trade Affects Domestic Political Alignments* (Princeton: Princeton University Press, 1989).

9. See Wassily Leontief, "Domestic Production and Foreign Trade: The American Capital Position Re-examined," *Proceedings of the American Philosophical Society* 97–4 (September 1953), pp.332–349.

10. Elhanan Helpman and Paul R. Krugman, *Market Structure and Foreign Trade: Increasing Returns, Imperfect Competition, and the International Economy* (Cambridge: MIT Press, 1985), p.3; Robert Gilpin with Jean M. Gilpin, *The Political Economy of International Relations* (Princeton: Princeton University Press, 1987), pp.175–178.

11. Bruce R. Scott, "National Strategies: Key to International Competition," in Bruce R. Scott and George C. Lodge, eds., *U.S. Competitiveness in the World Economy* (Boston: Harvard Business School Press, 1985), pp.93–95.

12. Laura D'Andrea Tyson, *Who's Bashing Whom? Trade Conflict in High-Technology Industries* (Washington, DC: Institute for International Economics, November 1992), p.4; F. M. Scherer and Richard S. Belous, *Unfinished Tasks: The New International Trade Theory and the Post-Uruguay Round Challenges*, Issues Paper no. 3 (Washington, DC: British–North American Committee, May 1994), p.42.

13. Klaus Stegemann, "Policy Rivalry Among Industrial States: What Can We Learn from Models of Strategic Trade Policy?" *International Organization* 43–1 (Winter 1989), p.99; Yarbrough and Yarbrough, *The World Economy*, pp.271–274.

14. Edward John Ray, "Changing Patterns of Protectionism: The Fall in Tariffs and the Rise in Non-Tariff Barriers," *Northwestern Journal of International Law & Business*, 8 (1987), pp.294–295; Rogowski, *Commerce and Coalitions*, pp.168–169.

15. Robert A. Pastor, *Congress and the Politics of U.S. Foreign Economic Policy, 1929–1976* (Berkeley: University of California Press, 1980), p.78.

16. The classic statement of this position is in Charles P. Kindleberger, *The World in Depression 1929–1939* (Berkeley: University of California Press, 1973), pp.291–307.

17. Stephen D. Krasner, "State Power and the Structure of International Trade," *World Politics* 28–3 (April 1976), p.338.

18. E. E. Schattschneider, *Politics, Pressures and the Tariff: A Study of Free Private Enterprise in Pressure Politics, as Shown in the 1929–1930 Revision of the Tariff* (Hamden: Archon Books, 1963, same as 1935 ed.); Pastor, *Congress and the Politics of U.S. Foreign Economic Policy*, pp.80–84.

19. For the effects of the 1930 U.S. tariff, see Joseph M. Jones, Jr., *Tariff Retaliation: Repercussions of the Hawley-Smoot Bill* (Philadelphia: University of Pennsylvania Press, 1934).

20. For the reasons Congress passed the RTAA, see I. M. Destler, *American Trade Politics*, 2nd ed. (Washington, DC: Institute for International Economics and Twentieth Century Fund, June 1992), pp.14–15.

21. Jones, *Tariff Retaliation*, pp.303–305; Gilbert R. Winham, *The Evolution of International Trade Agreements* (Toronto: University of Toronto Press, 1992), p.19; Henry J. Tasca, *The Reciprocal Trade Policy of the United States: A Study in Trade Philosophy* (New York: Russell & Russell, 1938), chs. 2–4.

22. John W. Evans, *The Kennedy Round in American Trade Policy: The Twilight of the GATT?* (Cambridge: Harvard University Press, 1971), pp.5–7.

23. Robert E. Hudec, *The GATT Legal System and World Trade Diplomacy* (New York: Praeger, 1975), pp.7–18; Simon Reisman, "The Birth of a World Trading System: ITO and GATT," in Orin Kirshner, ed., *The Bretton Woods–GATT System: Retrospect and Prospect After Fifty Years.* (Armonk: Sharpe, 1996), pp.83–85. For the early U.S.-U.K.

trade discussions, see E. F. Penrose, *Economic Planning for Peace* (Princeton: Princeton University Press, 1953), pp.87–115.

24. William Diebold, Jr., *The End of the I.T.O.*, Essays in International Finance no. 16 (Princeton: International Finance Section, Department of Economics and Social Institutions, Princeton University, October, 1952), p.2; Richard N. Gardner, *Sterling-Dollar Diplomacy in Current Perspective: The Origins and Prospects of Our International Economic Order* (New York: Columbia University Press, expanded ed., 1980), pp.348–380.

25. For studies favoring the ITO charter, see Clair Wilcox, *A Charter for World Trade* (New York: Macmillan, 1949); and William Adams Brown, Jr., *The United States and the Restoration of World Trade: An Analysis and Appraisal of the ITO Charter and the General Agreement on Tariffs and Trade* (Washington, DC: Brookings Institution, 1950). For a highly critical study, see Philip Cortney, *The Economic Munich: The I.T.O. Charter, Inflation or Liberty, The 1929 Lesson* (New York: Philosophical Library, 1949).

26. John H. Jackson, *World Trade and the Law of GATT* (Indianapolis: Bobbs-Merrill, 1969), pp.120–121.

27. Barry Eichengreen and Peter B. Kenen, "Managing the World Economy Under the Bretton Woods System: An Overview," in Peter B. Kenen, ed., *Managing the World Economy: Fifty Years After Bretton Woods* (Washington, DC: Institute for International Economics, September 1994), p.7.

28. Bernard M Hoekman and Michel M. Kostecki, *The Political Economy of the World Trading System: From GATT to WTO* 2nd ed. (Oxford: Oxford University Press, 2001), pp.1–3; Richard N. Gardner, "The Bretton Woods–GATT System After Fifty Years: A Balance Sheet of Success and Failure," in Kirshner, ed., *The Bretton Woods–GATT System: Retrospect and Prospect After Fifty Years,* p.199.

29. John Gerard Ruggie, "International Regimes, Transactions, and Change: Embedded Liberalism in the Postwar Economic Order," in Stephen D. Krasner, ed., *International Regimes* (Ithaca: Cornell University Press, 1983), p.212.

30. Item-by-item negotiations continued during the Kennedy Round for agricultural goods and some other sensitive products. See Hoekman and Kostecki, *The Political Economy of the World Trading System,* pp.127–129; Robert E. Hudec, *Enforcing International Trade Law: The Evolution of the Modern GATT Legal System* (Salem: Butterworth Legal Publishers, 1993), pp.12–13.

31. Jock A. Finlayson and Mark W. Zacher, "The GATT and the Regulation of Trade Barriers: Regime Dynamics and Functions," in Krasner, ed., *International Regimes,* pp.282–286; Hoekman and Kostecki, *The Political Economy of the World Trading System,* pp.31–33.

32. Theodore H. Cohn, *The International Politics of Agricultural Trade: Canadian–American Relations in a Global Agricultural Context* (Vancouver: University of British Columbia Press, 1990), pp.141–42.

33. Milner, *Resisting Protectionism,* p.8; Marc L. Busch and Helen V. Milner, "The Future of the International Trading System: International Firms, Regionalism, and Domestic Politics," in Richard Stubbs and Geoffrey R. D. Underhill, eds., *Political Economy and the Changing Global Order* (Toronto: McClelland & Stewart, 1994), p.264.

34. Milner, *Resisting Protectionism,* p.290. The Milner volume focuses on a number of case studies to demonstrate the difference in domestic firms' trade preferences during the 1920s and the 1970s.

35. Eric Wyndham-White, "Negotiations in Prospect," in C. Fred Bergsten, ed., *Toward a New World Trade Policy: The Maidenhead Papers* (Lexington: Heath, 1975), p.322.

36. Charles Lipson, "The Transformation of Trade: The Sources and Effects of Regime Change," in Krasner, ed., *International Regimes,* p.242.

37. Winham, *The Evolution of International Trade Agreements,* pp.46–48; Hoekman and Kostecki, *The Political Economy of the World Trading System,* pp.29–31.

38. WTO, *World Trade Report—2003* (Geneva: WTO, 2003), p. 70.

39. Finlayson and Zacher, "The GATT and the Regulation of Trade Barriers," pp.286–290; Ernest Preeg, *Traders and Diplomats: An Analysis of the Kennedy Round of Negotiations Under the General Agreement on Tariffs and Trade* (Washington: Brookings Institution, 1970), p.195; Gilbert Winham, *International Trade and the Tokyo Round Negotiations* (Princeton: Princeton University Press, 1986), pp.172–175; Theodore H. Cohn, "NAFTA, GATT and Canadian–U.S. Agricultural Trade Relations," *The North-South Agenda Papers,* no. 10 (Coral Gables: North-South Center, University of Miami, November 1994), pp.5–8.

40. For a detailed discussion of the role of the G-7, Quad, OECD, and UNCTAD in the global trade regime, see Theodore H. Cohn, *Governing Global Trade: International Institutions in Conflict and Convergence* (Aldershot: Ashgate, 2002).

41. Robert O. Keohane, "Reciprocity in International Relations," *International Organization* 40-1 (Winter 1986), p.4.

42. Carolyn Rhodes, "Reciprocity in Trade: The Utility of a Bargaining Strategy," *International Organization* 43-2 (Spring 1989), p.276; Keohane, "Reciprocity in International Relations," p.24; Tyson, *Who's Bashing Whom?*.

43. John Whalley and Colleen Hamilton, *The Trading System After the Uruguay Round* (Washington, DC: Institute for International Economics, 1996), pp.49–50; John H. Jackson, *The World Trading System: Law and Policy of International Economic Relations* (Cambridge: MIT Press, 1989), p.149.

44. Hoekman and Kostecki, *The Political Economy of the World Trading System,* pp.303–304; Winham, *The Evolution of International Trade Agreements,* pp.50–51; Finlayson and Zacher, "The GATT and the Regulation of Trade Barriers," pp.290–293.

45. J. Michael Finger and Julio Nogues, "International Control of Subsidies and Countervailing Duties," *The World Bank Economic Review* 1 (1987), pp.713–714; Hoekman and Kostecki, *The Political Economy of the World Trading System,* p.307. For a comparison of U.S. and Canadian contingent trade measures, see Theodore H. Cohn, "Emerging Issues in Canada–U.S. Agricultural Trade Under the GATT and FTA," *Canadian–American Public Policy,* no. 10 (Orono: University of Maine, June 1992), pp.18–22.

46. For a discussion of economic development provisions in the Havana Charter and ITO, see Wilcox, *A Charter for World Trade,* pp.140–152.

47. Finlayson and Zacher, "The GATT and the Regulation of Trade Barriers," pp.293–296.

48. Jeffrey J. Schott with Johanna W. Buurman, *The Uruguay Round: An Assessment* (Washington, DC: Institute for International Economics, 1994), pp.4–5.

49. Minister for International Trade, "Canada Proposes Strategy for Creation of a World Trade Organization," *News Release* no. 077, External Affairs and International Trade Canada, April 11, 1990.

50. John Croome, *Reshaping the World Trading System: A History of the Uruguay Round* (Geneva: World Trade Organization, 1995), pp.271–274 and 358–361; Ernest H. Preeg, *Traders in a Brave New World: The Uruguay Round and the Future of the International Trading System* (Chicago: University of Chicago Press, 1995), pp.113–114 and 124–126.

51. Hoekman and Kostecki, *The Political Economy of the World Trading System,* p.1.

52. Hoekman and Kostecki, *The Political Economy of the World Trading System,* pp.74–98; Preeg, *Traders in a Brave New World,* p.42.

53. David E. Sanger, "Yielding, U.S. Bows to Europe on Trade Chief," *New York Times,* March 21, 1995, p.C1; "New Zealand's Moore Heads WTO," *WTO Focus Newsletter,* no. 41, July–August 1999, pp.1–2; Hoekman and Kostecki, *The Political Economy of the World Trading System,* pp.55–56.

54. Gardner Patterson and Eliza Patterson, "The Road from GATT to MTO," *Minnesota Journal of Global Trade* 3–1 (Spring 1994), p.37.

55. C. Fred Bergsten, "Fifty Years of Trade Policy: The Policy Lessons," *World Economy* 24–1 (January 2001), p.1.

56. Jeffrey J. Schott, "The WTO after Seattle," in Jeffrey J. Schott, ed., *The WTO After Seattle* (Washington, DC: Institute for International Economics, 2000), pp.8–17.

57. WTO, *World Trade Report— 2003*, p. 122.

58. "Beyond Doha," *The Economist,* November 17, 2001, p.11.

59. On the divisions leading up to the Cancún ministerial see "The Cancun Challenge," *The Economist,* September 6, 2003, pp.59–61.

60. Martin Wolf, "Two-Edged Sword: Demands of Developing Countries and the Trading System," in Jagdish N. Bhagwati and John Gerard Ruggie, eds., *Power, Passions, and Purpose: Prospects for North-South Negotiations* (Cambridge: MIT Press, 1984), p.202.

61. Raúl Prebisch, "The Economic Development of Latin America and Its Principal Problems," *Economic Bulletin for Latin America* 7–1 (February 1962), pp.1–59; Albert O. Hirschman, "The Political Economy of Import-Substituting Industrialization in Latin America," *Quarterly Journal of Economics* 82–1 (February 1968), pp.1–32; Hollis Chenery, "The Structuralist Approach to Development Policy," *American Economic Review* 65–2 (May 1975), pp.310–316.

62. Marc Williams, *Third World Cooperation: The Group of 77 in UNCTAD* (London: Pinter, 1991), p.23.

63. Kenneth W. Dam, *The GATT: Law and International Economic Organization* (Chicago: University of Chicago Press, 1970), pp.227–228; Robert E. Hudec, *Developing Countries in the GATT Legal System* (Aldershot: Gower, for the Trade Policy Research Centre, 1987), pp.23–24.

64. Karl P. Sauvant, *The Group of 77: Evolution, Structure, Organization* (New York: Oceana Publications, 1981), p.3; Williams, *Third World Cooperation,* pp.89–90.

65. Vinod K. Aggarwal, *Liberal Protectionism: The International Politics of Organized Textile Trade* (Berkeley: University of California Press, 1985), p.8.

66. For UNCTAD's role in pressuring GATT to develop the GSP, see Anindya K. Bhattacharya, "The Influence of the International Secretariat: UNCTAD and Generalized Tariff Preferences," *International Organization* 30–1 (Winter 1976), pp.75–90.

67. Anne O. Krueger, *Trade Policies and Developing Nations* (Washington, DC: Brookings Institution, 1995), pp.40–42; Rolf J. Langhammer and André Sapir, *Economic Impact of Generalized Tariff Preferences,* Thames Essay no. 49 (Aldershot: Gower, 1987).

68. The LDC demands were contained in documents submitted to the General Assembly in 1974: the Declaration on the Establishment of a New International Economic Order (NIEO), the Program of Action on the Establishment of a NIEO, and the Charter of Economic Rights and Duties of States.

69. Jeffrey A. Hart, *The New International Economic Order: Conflict and Cooperation in North-South Economic Relations, 1974–77* (New York: St. Martin's Press, 1983), ch. 2.

70. Hart, *The New International Economic Order,* pp.36–40; Williams, *Third World Cooperation,* pp.133–159; Alfred Maizels, "Reforming the World Commodity Economy," in Michael Zammit Cutajar, ed., *UNCTAD and the South-North Dialogue: The First Twenty Years* (Oxford: Pergamon Press, 1985), pp.101–121; Jock A. Finlayson and Mark W. Zacher, *Managing International Markets: Developing Countries and the Commodity Trade Regime* (New York: Columbia University Press, 1988).

71. Olivier Long, *Law and Its Limitations in the GATT Multilateral Trade System* (Dordrecht: Nijhoff, 1985), p.101.

72. Hudec, *Developing Countries in the GATT Legal System,* pp.70–91.

73. Colleen Hamilton and John Whalley, "Coalitions in the Uruguay Round," *Weltwirtschaftliches Archiv* 125–3 (1989), pp.547–561; Richard A. Higgott and Andrew Fenton Cooper, "Middle Power Leadership and Coalition Building:Australia, the Cairns Group, and the Uruguay Round of Trade Negotiations," *International Organization* 44–4 (Autumn 1990), pp.589–632; Rod Tyers, "The Cairns Group and the Uruguay Round of International Trade Negotiations," *Australian Economic Review* 93–101 (1993), pp.49–60; Cohn, *Governing Global Trade,* ch. 6.

74. Robert Wolfe, "Global Trade as a Single Undertaking: The Role of Ministers in the WTO," *International Journal* 51–4 (Autumn 1996), pp.690–709; Robert Wolfe, *Farm Wars: The Political Economy of Agriculture and the International Trade Regime* (London: Macmillan, 1998), pp.91–97.

75. Quoted in Mari Pangestu, "Special and Differential Treatment in the Millennium: Special for Whom and How Different?" *World Economy* 23–9 (September 2000), p.1291. See also Edwini Kwame Kessie, "Developing Countries and the World Trade Organization: What Has Changed?" *World Competition* 22–2 (June 1999), pp.98–110; and John Whalley, "Special and Differential Treatment in the Millennium Round," *World Economy* 22–8 (August 1999), pp.1065–1093.

76. John Whalley, "Recent Trade Liberalisation in the Developing World: What Is Behind it and Where Is it Headed?" in David Greenaway, Robert C. Hine, Anthony P. O'Brien, and Robert J. Thornton, eds., *Global Protectionism* (London: Macmillan, 1991), pp.225–253; Krueger, *Trade Policies and Developing Nations,* pp.48–50.

77. John Gershman, "The Free Trade Connection," in Kevin Danaher, ed., *Fifty Years Is Enough: The Case Against the World Bank and the International Monetary Fund* (Boston: South End Press, 1994), p.24.

78. See Bernard R. Hoekman, "Developing Countries and the Multilateral Trading System After the Uruguay Round," in Roy Culpeper, Albert Berry, and Frances Stewart, eds., *Global Development Fifty Years After Bretton Woods: Essays in Honour of Gerald K. Helleiner* (New York: St. Martin's Press, 1997), pp.252–279.

79. For historical structuralist arguments, see Chakravarthi Raghavan, *Recolonization: GATT, the Uruguay Round and The Third World* (London: Zed Books, 1990); and Chakravarthi Raghavan, "A New Trade Order in a World of Disorder?" in Jo Marie Griesgraber and Bernhard G. Gunter, eds., *World Trade: Toward Fair and Free Trade in the Twenty-first Century* (London: Pluto Press, 1997), pp.1–31.

80. Jayashree Watal, "Developing Countries' Interests in a 'Development Round,' " in Schott, ed., *The WTO after Seattle,* pp.71–72.

81. "Beyond Doha," p.11.

82. Shishir Priyadarshi, "Reforming Global Trade in Agriculture: A Developing-Country Perspective," *Trade, Environment, and Development,* issue 2, Carnegie Endowment for International Peace, September 2002, p. 1.

83. "Beyond Doha," p.11.

84. World Bank, *World Development Report, 2002—Building Institutions for Markets* (Washington, D.C.: World Bank, 2002), p.143.

85. M. M. Kostecki, *East-West Trade and the GATT System* (London: Macmillan, for the Trade Policy Research Centre, 1979), p.2; Zdenek Augenthaler, "The Socialist Countries and GATT," in Frans A. M. Alting von Geusau, ed., *Economic Relations After the Kennedy Round* (Leyden: Sijthoff-Leyden, 1969), p.81.

86. In 2002, China and Russia together accounted for 5.71 percent of the IMF votes and 5.58 percent of the World Bank votes. (*IMF Annual Report—2002* (Washington, DC: IMF, 2002), p.148; *World Bank Annual Report—2002* (Washington, DC: World Bank, 2002), p.121.

87. Jackson, *The World Trading System,* pp.283–286.
88. Leah A. Haus, *Globalizing the GATT: The Soviet Union's Successor States, Eastern Europe, and the International Trading System* (Washington, DC: Brookings Institution, 1992), pp.15, 28; Bohdan Laczkowski, "Poland's Participation in the Kennedy Round," in Geusau, ed., *Economic Relations After the Kennedy Round,* pp.83–93.
89. Eliza R. Patterson, "Improving GATT Rules for Nonmarket Economies," *Journal of World Trade Law* 20–2 (March/April 1986), p.188; Jozef M. van Brabant, *The Planned Economies and International Economic Organizations* (Cambridge: Cambridge University Press, 1991), pp.199–201.
90. Patterson, "Improving GATT Rules for Nonmarket Economies," p.189; Paul D. McKenzie, "China's Application to the GATT: State Trading and the Problem of Market Access," *Journal of World Trade* 24–5 (October 1990), pp.141–143.
91. "Preparations Intensify for Singapore; Membership of Bulgaria and Panama Approved," World Trade Organization, *WTO Focus Newsletter* no. 12, August–September, 1996, pp.1–2.
92. Laszlo Lang, "International Regimes and the Political Economy of East-West Relations," *Occasional Paper Series 13* (New York: Institute for East-West Security Studies, 1989), pp.35–36; Haus, *Globalizing the GATT,* ch. 3.
93. McKenzie, "China's Application to the GATT," pp.144–145; Robert E. Herzstein, "China and the GATT: Legal and Policy Issues Raised by China's Participation in the General Agreement on Tariffs and Trade," *Law and Policy in International Business* 18–2 (1986), pp.373–374.
94. Harold K. Jacobson and Michel Oksenberg, *China's Participation in the IMF, the World Bank, and GATT: Toward a Global Economic Order* (Ann Arbor: University of Michigan Press, 1990), pp.83–92.
95. Hiddo Houben, "China's Economic Reforms and Integration into the World Trading System," *Journal of World Trade* 33–3 (June 1999), pp.4–5.
96. Chung-chou Li, "Resumption of China's GATT Membership," *Journal of World Trade Law* 21–4 (1987), p.26; Herzstein, "China and the GATT," pp.404–405; Jackson, *The World Trading System,* pp.287–288.
97. U.S. General Accounting Office, "China Trade: WTO Membership and Most-Favored-Nation Status," Statement by JayEtta Z. Hecker before the Subcommittee on Trade, Committee on Ways and Means, U.S. House of Representatives, GAO/T-NSIAD-98-209, June 17, 1998, pp.4–8.
98. Robert E. Scott argues that "in 1996, the U.S. trade deficit with China eliminated over 600,000 jobs, most of them in high-paying manufacturing industries." See Scott's "WTO Accession: China Can Wait," *WorkingUSA* (September/October 1999), p.82.
99. U.S. General Accounting Office, "China Trade," pp.2–3; "The Storm after the Storm: China's WTO Accession and the US-China Trade Relationship," *Stanley Foundation Policy Bulletin,* October 26–28, 2000, p.2.
100. Li, "Resumption of China's GATT Membership," p.30.
101. "China and World Markets: The Debate over Trade Status," *Congressional Digest* 79 (June–July 2000), p.161; U.S. General Accounting Office, "China Trade," p.3.
102. Li, "Resumption of China's GATT Membership," p.30.
103. McKenzie, "China's Application to the GATT," pp.144–145; Herzstein, "China and the GATT," pp.375–377; Yongzheng Yang, "China's WTO Accession: The Economics and Politics," *Journal of World Trade* 34–4 (2000), p.80.
104. Greg Mastel, "China and the World Trade Organization: Moving Forward without Sliding Back," *Law and Policy in International Business* 31–3 (Spring 2000), pp.988–991.
105. U.S. General Accounting Office, "China's Membership Status and Normal Trade Relations Issues," GAO/NSIAD-00-94, March 2000, p.4, fn 1; "China and World Markets: The Debate over Trade Status," pp.161–192.

106. Mastel, "China and the World Trade Organization," p.997.

107. Yang, "China's WTO Accession," p.92.

108. Statement by Long Yongtu quoted in Steven Chase and Miro Cernetig, "WTO Opens Door to China," *Globe and Mail,* November 12, 2001, pp.B1 and B5. See also Minxin Pei, "Future Shock: The WTO and Political Change in China," *Carnegie Endowment Policy Brief* 1–3 (February 2001), pp.1–7.

109. Quoted in "China Update," *Inside U.S. Trade,* September 5, 2003, p. 24.

110. Keith Bradsher, "China Insistent on Bolstering Currency," *New York Times,* September 19, 2003, p. W1.

111. "Cancún Collapse," Bridges Daily Update on the Fifth Ministerial Conference—Issue 6, September 2003.

112. Brabant, *The Planned Economies and International Economic Organizations,* pp.1–6; Lang, "International Regimes and the Political Economy of East-West Relations," pp.53–60.

113. WTO, *World Trade Report—2003,* p. 69; Leonid Sabelnikov, "Russia on the Way to the World Trade Organization," *International Affairs* 72–2 (1996), pp.345–355.

114. Ksenya Yudaeva, "Effects of WTO Accession on the Russian Economy," presentation at the Carnegie Endowment Moscow Center, May 28, 2003, pp.1–6.

115. See Ksenya Yudaeva, "Joining the WTO: Is a Political Decision the only Hope?," Carnegie Endowment Briefing Paper, June 2003, pp.1–6.

116. Jan Aart Scholte with Robert O'Brien and Marc Williams, "The WTO and Civil Society," *Journal of World Trade* 33–1 (February 1999), pp.107–123; David Robertson, "Civil Society and the WTO," *World Economy* 23–9 (September 2000), pp.1119–1134.

117. Daniel C. Esty, "Non-Governmental Organizations at the World Trade Organization: Cooperation, Competition, or Exclusion," *Journal of International Economic Law* 1–1 (March 1998), p.140.

118. "Understanding on Rules and Procedures Governing the Settlement of Disputes," Article 13–1 in World Trade Organization, *The Results of the Uruguay Round of Multilateral Trade Negotiations—The Legal Texts* (Geneva.: WTO, 1995), p.416; Gabrielle Marceau and Peter N. Pedersen, "Is the WTO Open and Transparent?" *Journal of World Trade* 33–1 (February 1999), pp.32–36.

119. In addition to the sources mentioned, see Robert O'Brien, Anne Marie Goetz, Jan Aart Scholte, and Marc Williams, *Contesting Global Governance: Multilateral Economic Institutions and Global Social Movements* (Cambridge: Cambridge University Press, 2000); Jeffrey L. Dunoff, "The Misguided Debate over NGO Participation at the WTO," *Journal of International Economic Law* 1–3 (September 1998), pp.433–456; and G. Richard Shell, "The Trade Stakeholders Model and Participation by Nonstate Parties in the World Trade Organization," *University of Pennsylvania Journal of International Economic Law* 17–1 (1996), pp.359–381.

120. Jim Powell, "Self-Determination Through Unilateral Free Trade," in Doug Bandow and Ian Vásquez, eds., *Perpetuating Poverty: The World Bank, the IMF, and the Developing World* (Washington, DC: CATO Institute, 1994), p.345.

121. Whalley and Hamilton, *The Trading System After the Uruguay Round,* p.2; Hoekman and Kostecki, *The Political Economy of the World Trading System,* pp.268–271.

122. Riccardo Petrella, "Globalization and Internationalization: The Dynamics of the Emerging World Order," in Robert Boyer and Daniel Drache, eds., *States Against Markets: The Limits of Globalization* (London: Routledge, 1996), p.77.

123. Whalley and Hamilton, *The Trading System After the Uruguay Round,* p.52.

124. For contending views on this issue, see Krueger, *Trade Policies and Developing Countries,* pp.52–54; Raghavan, *Recolonization: GATT, the Uruguay Round and the Third World,* pp.114–141; and Croome, *Reshaping the World Trading System,* pp.130–138.

C H A P T E R   9

Regionalism and the Global Trade Regime

The formation of GATT after World War II was an indication of strong support for multilateral trade liberalization. However, regionalism also emerged as a significant force with the creation of a number of regional trade agreements. As noted in Chapter 2, RTAs exist at various stages of integration, ranging from a free trade area to a customs union, a common market, and an economic union (see Figure 2.3). There have been two major waves of regionalism during the postwar period, the first in the 1950s–1960s and the second since the mid–1980s. The second wave has been especially significant, with the EU broadening and deepening the integration process and the United States reversing its longstanding policy of refusing to join RTAs. Of the 109 regional agreements reported to GATT from 1947 to 1994, 33 were concluded from 1990 to 1994, and RTAs "have proliferated at an astonishing pace since the WTO agreement took effect in 1995."[1] 139 of the 259 RTAs notified to the GATT/WTO by the end of 2002 were notified after January 1995 (about 176 of the 259 RTAs are currently in force). These figures do not include the large number of RTAs not yet notified to the WTO and currently being negotiated.[2] Table 9.1 shows the wide range of reciprocal and nonreciprocal RTAs in force as of January 1995. (Preferences are not reciprocal in some RTAs between DCs and LDCs.)

Under some circumstances, multilateralism and regionalism are competing approaches to trade. Whereas multilateralism contributes to global trade liberalization, regionalism may act as a balkanizing force that divides the world into competing trade blocs. However, "open regionalism" can break down national trade barriers and serve as a stepping-stone rather than an obstacle to global free trade. RTAs following open regionalism abolish barriers on substantially all trade within the RTA and lower trade barriers to outsiders. States and MNCs often consider open regionalism and multilateralism to be complementary strategies, that they can use simultaneously to promote market forces and increase their competitiveness in the global economy.

The three IPE perspectives have very different views of RTAs. Liberal economists consider multilateralism to be the best possible route to trade liberalization because it breaks down regional as well as national barriers. However, liberals support open RTAs as a second-best route to trade liberalization when negotiating difficulties in the

Table 9.1

REGIONAL TRADE AGREEMENTS NOTIFIED TO GATT AND IN FORCE AS OF JANUARY 1995

RECIPROCAL RTAS

Europe

European Community (EC)

Austria	Germany	Netherlands
Belgium	Greece	Portugal
Denmark	Ireland	Spain
Finland	Italy	Sweden
France	Luxembourg	United Kingdom

EC Free Trade Agreements with

Estonia	Latvia	Norway
Iceland	Liechtenstein	Switzerland
Israel	Lithuania	

EC Association Agreements with

Bulgaria	Hungary	Romania
Cyprus	Malta	Slovak Rep.
Czech Rep.	Poland	Turkey

European Free Trade Association (EFTA)

Iceland	Norway	Switzerland
Liechtenstein		

EFTA Agreements with

Bulgaria	Israel	Slovak Rep.
Czech Rep.	Poland	Turkey
Hungary	Romania	

Norway Free Trade Agreements with

Estonia	Latvia	Lithuania

Switzerland Free Trade Agreements with

Estonia	Latvia	Lithuania

Czech Republic and Slovak Republic Customs Union

Central European Free Trade Area

Czech Rep.	Poland	Slovak Rep.
Hungary		

Czech Republic and Slovenia Free Trade Agreement

Slovak Republic and Slovenia Free Trade Agreement

North America

Canada-United States Free Trade Agreement (CUSFTA)

North American Free Trade Agreement (NAFTA)

Latin America and the Caribbean

Caribbean Community and Common Market (CARICOM)

Central American Common Market (CACM)

Latin American Integration Association (LAIA)

Andean Pact

Southern Common Market (Mercosur)

Middle East

Economic Cooperation Organization (ECO)

Gulf Cooperation Council (GCC)

Asia

Australia-New Zealand Closer Economic Relations Trade Agreement (CER)

Bangkok Agreement

ASEAN Preferential Trade Arrangement

Lao People's Dem. Rep. and Thailand Trade Agreement

Other

Israel-United States Free Trade Agreement

NONRECIPROCAL RTAS

Europe

EEC-Association of Certain Non-European Countries and Territories (EEC-PTOM II)

EEC Cooperation Agreements with

Algeria	Lebanon	Syria
Egypt	Morocco	Tunisia
Jordan		

ACP-EEC Fourth Lomé Convention

Asia

Australia-Papua New Guinea Agreement

South Pacific Regional Trade and Economic Cooperation Agreement (SPARTECA)

Source: WTO Secretariat, *Regionalism and the World Trading System,* April 1995, p.26, Table 1. By permission of the World Trade Organization.

WTO pose obstacles to freer multilateral trade. Although liberals acknowledge that some groups such as displaced workers may lose as a result of RTAs, they argue that the gains in efficiency from open regionalism outweigh any costs incurred. Liberals do not view power disparities as a major problem for smaller states in RTAs because they assume that all members benefit in the long term from open RTAs. Indeed, liberals argue that small states benefit more than large states from RTAs because of economies of scale and increased demand for their exports.[3]

In contrast to liberals, realists and historical structuralists believe that RTAs have important distributional effects, with some states and groups benefitting *at the expense of* others. Realists, for example, argue that the larger partner in an RTA either will not permit the smaller partner to receive greater benefits or will expect "side payments" in return. These side payments will exceed any economic benefits the smaller partner receives from gains in market access and economies of scale. For example, Canada and Mexico sought free trade with the United States partly to gain more assured access to the large U.S. market. The United States, however, expected side payments in such areas as foreign investment, services trade, and access to natural resources—especially energy.[4] In the long term, realists expect the distribution of benefits in RTAs to reflect the asymmetries of power, wealth, and technology among member states. In the historical structuralist view, MNCs and other sources of transnational capital are the main beneficiaries of RTAs, and the main losers are the working class and poorest groups in the North and the South. From this perspective, MNCs use RTAs to locate their production facilities in member states with the lowest wages, environmental standards, and taxes and then to export freely to other states within the region. Historical structuralists also believe that RTAs permit states in the core (often in association with transnational capital) to exploit states in the periphery. For example, they argue that EU trade linkages with 71 African, Caribbean, and Pacific (ACP) associate members consolidate "the vertical economic relationship of the colonial period."[5]

This chapter begins with a discussion of regionalism and its relationship to globalization. It then examines the historical development of RTAs, competing views as to why states form RTAs, the institutional relationship between the WTO and RTAs, and trade regionalism in Europe, the Western Hemisphere, and East Asia.

REGIONALISM AND GLOBALIZATION

Regionalism is a difficult term to define because it usually connotes not only geographic proximity but also a sense of cultural, economic, political, and organizational cohesiveness. Efforts by IR specialists to precisely define and identify regions have therefore usually resulted in frustration.[6] To compound the confusion, about one-third of the free trade agreements (FTAs) currently being negotiated are cross-regional, and the WTO includes these in its list of RTAs. For example, the EU has concluded FTAs with Mexico, Chile, South Africa, many Middle Eastern countries, and the ACP countries, and the United States has signed FTAs with Israel, Jordan, and Singapore.[7] Furthermore, Japan and the East Asian countries have close regional economic ties that extend beyond their involvement in RTAs (Japan now has an RTA with Singapore).

This chapter therefore includes discussion of some cross-regional RTAs and of trade regionalism that is not limited to RTAs.

Globalization and regionalism are both increasing, and these two processes have a complex relationship. In some respects, globalization limits the growth of regionalism. As interdependence increases, many problems such as financial crises, trade wars, and environmental degradation take on worldwide dimensions and require multilateral management at the global level. Thus, multilateral institutions such as the WTO, IMF, and World Bank are better equipped than regional organizations to deal with many problems resulting from globalization. Globalization also promotes growing linkages among regions as well as states, and in this sense it can undermine both national and regional cohesiveness. Despite these contradictions, globalization may also stimulate the rise of regionalism. States must often rely on institutions above the national level to deal with problems arising from global interdependence. However, IOs with large, diverse memberships have high transaction and information costs that interfere with the ability to identify common interests and sanction defectors.[8] Thus, globalization sometimes leads to shifts from national to regional institutions composed of like-minded states that are better at problem solving than larger, more diverse multilateral institutions. Globalization also contributes to an increase in the intensity and scope of competition, and states and MNCs often can improve their global competitiveness by organizing regionally. Finally, globalization has been closely associated with the revival of orthodox liberalism, which favors a shift in authority from the state to the market. The heightened market pressures weaken state barriers and contribute to the growth of institutions at both the regional and global levels. Thus, regionalism may complement as well as conflict with globalization.[9]

A HISTORICAL OVERVIEW OF RTAS

Regional integration is not a new phenomenon. From the seventeenth century to World War II there were many RTA proposals involving colonies, provinces, and states, and some of the more successful agreements resulted in political as well as commercial unions. Examples of early integration efforts in Europe and North America include a proposal in 1665 for commercial union among Austria, Bavaria, Spain, and some German principalities; an 1826 CU between England and Ireland; an 1833 customs treaty establishing a single German *Zollverein* among German splinter states; and an 1854 Reciprocity Treaty removing all import tariffs on natural products between the United States and Canada. In the Southern Hemisphere, early agreements included a 1910 South African Customs Union among the Union of South Africa, Bechuanaland, Basutoland, and Swaziland, and a 1917 customs union between the British colonies of Kenya and Uganda, which was extended to include Tanganyika in 1927.[10]

Despite these early attempts to establish RTAs, regional integration in its modern form did not develop until after World War II with the creation of the European Economic Community. This chapter deals with the two major waves of regionalism during the postwar period, the first in the 1950s–1960s, and the second since the mid–1980s.

The First Wave of Regionalism

In 1949, the Soviet Union signed a treaty with Bulgaria, Czechoslovakia, Hungary, Poland, and Romania, establishing the *Council for Mutual Economic Assistance (CMEA)*. Although CMEA members engaged in technical cooperation and joint planning, the state-centered orientation of these CPEs precluded any genuine moves toward regional economic integration.[11] As a result, most writers view the first wave of regionalism as beginning with the formation of the EC in 1957 and the European Free Trade Association in 1960.[12] These European agreements provided a stimulus for the spread of regionalism throughout Latin America and Africa during the early 1960s. However, the RTAs in the South were formed for very different reasons from those in Western Europe. Because the small domestic markets of LDCs interfered with their efforts to pursue import substitution policies, they looked to RTAs as a means of providing larger markets—and economies of scale—for their production of industrial goods. Thus, the South's RTAs during the 1950s–1960s were quite inward looking and designed to pursue import substitution at the regional level.

By the early 1970s the first wave of regionalism had proved to be largely unsuccessful outside Europe, for several reasons. First, numerous problems arose with the South's RTAs because of the fundamental "contradiction between the idea of giving impetus to integration via trade liberalization and the protectionist logic of . . . import substitution."[13] Only a limited number of industries were willing to locate in Southern regions, so competition among LDC members of RTAs for these industries was fierce, and most of these industries located in the larger and more advanced LDCs. In the East African Common Services Union, for example, Tanzania and Uganda were resentful that the major industries were concentrated in Kenya. Thus, the benefits of Southern RTAs were often distributed very unequally, leading to numerous disputes among member states. To counter such inequities, some Southern RTAs tried to allocate industries among the members by bureaucratic means rather than relying on the market, but this practice led to economic inefficiencies and political conflicts. A second reason for the failure of the first wave of regionalism outside Europe was that the United States as global hegemon firmly supported multilateralism and generally did not endorse RTAs. Although the United States made an exception in supporting the EC largely for political-security reasons, it made vigorous efforts to open up the European integration process in the GATT Dillon and Kennedy Rounds. In the second wave of regionalism, by contrast, the United States would become an active participant in RTAs.[14]

The Second Wave of Regionalism

The second wave of regionalism started during the mid-1980s, and this time regionalism seems to be more durable in non-European as well as European areas. The EC moved to widen and deepen its integration during the 1980s, and the United States shifted from its position as the key defender of the postwar multilateral trade order and began to participate in RTAs in the mid-1980s. During the 1990s, the collapse of CMEA caused the Central and Eastern European states to realign themselves toward the EU, and about a third of the new RTAs for goods in force since 1990 were signed among transition economies. The last major country to join the trend toward regionalism was Japan, which signed an FTA with Singapore in January 2002. Finally, there has been a revival of RTAs in the South, and 30 to 40 percent of RTAs currently in force are among LDCs. Although the Southern RTAs are more open to global market forces than the agreements of the 1960s, they generally have long transition periods and are often more declarations of intent than agreements producing rapid trade liberalization.[15]

EXPLANATIONS FOR THE RISE OF REGIONALISM

Although there is widespread agreement on some of the reasons for the rise of regionalism, realists, liberals, and historical structuralists emphasize different factors in their theoretical explanations. Whereas realists usually look to security issues and changing power relationships as explanations, liberals focus on the growth of interdependence, and historical structuralists emphasize the influence and demands of transnational capital.

Realist Explanations

Realists explain the development of Western European integration during the first wave (the 1950s–1960s) as a response to changing security and power relationships. Indeed, the initial impulse to form the *European Coal and Steel Community (ECSC)* in 1951–1952 was the desire to consolidate regional peace and security. In 1951, six countries (Belgium, France, West Germany, Italy, Luxembourg, and the Netherlands) formed the ECSC primarily to prevent France and Germany from renewing their age-old rivalries. Seven years later, the six ECSC member countries expanded the integration process by forming the EC. In global terms, realists argue that "the emergence of the Russian and American superpowers created a situation that permitted wider ranging and more effective cooperation among the states of Western Europe."[16] After World War II, Western Europe could focus more on promoting economic integration because the United States and Soviet Union assumed the main responsibilities in the security sphere. Changing global power relationships also provided an incentive for Europeans to form the EC. With the United States and Soviet Union emerging as superpowers, European states facing the eventual loss of their colonies realized that integration was necessary if they were to retain their influence on the global scene.

Although the United States generally opposed RTAs during the 1950s–1960s, it viewed a speedy economic recovery in Western Europe as essential to meet the security threat of the Soviet Union, and it therefore supported Western European integration. Indeed, American insistence that the Europeans develop a common recovery program to jointly administer U.S. Marshall Plan aid resulted in the formation of the *Organization for European Economic Cooperation (OEEC)* in 1948. In addition to developing an economic reconstruction program and organizing a fair distribution of Marshall Plan funds, the OEEC oversaw the moves toward convertibility of European currencies and the liberalization of European trade. Furthermore, the OEEC contributed to the rapid integration of West Germany in Western Europe, laying the foundations for the eventual formation of the EC.[17]

Realists also attribute the second wave of regionalism during the 1980s–1990s to shifting balances in strategic and economic power. For example, they view the change from a bipolar to a multipolar international system as highly significant. In the postwar bipolar system, Western Europe and Japan were willing to accept American leadership because of their dependence on U.S. nuclear deterrence and economic assistance. With the demise of the Soviet Union and the breakdown of bipolarity, U.S. allies have been more inclined to act independently of the United States, and a multilateral system has emerged centered in three major regional economic blocs in Europe, North America, and Japan/East Asia.[18] Another important factor during the second wave, according to realists, has been the decline of U.S. economic hegemony. After World War II, the United States as global hegemon used its power and resources to help develop an open and integrated world economy. As its economic hegemony declined, the United States was less willing to provide public goods to maintain an open multilateral trade regime, and it sought to regain some of its economic leverage by joining RTAs.[19]

It is important to note that theorists' predictions regarding the rise and fall of regionalism are of course not always accurate or even consistent. For example, in the early 1990s some realists predicted that the removal of a major external threat to Western Europe with the breakup of the Soviet Union would increase concerns about relative gains among EU member states and place a significant check on the future progress of European integration. Recent changes such as the formation of the EMU in January 1999 and the preparations for membership of a number of Central and Eastern European states in the EU have raised serious doubts about this prediction.[20]

Liberal Explanations

In the liberal view, the creation of a liberal-economic order at the end of World War II required international institutions, and this helps account for the formation of regional as well as global institutions during the 1940s–1960s. Liberals attribute the revival of regionalism in the 1980s–1990s to the dramatic growth of interdependence. As interdependence increased, states turned to economic liberalization to promote their exports, attract foreign investment, and upgrade their technological capabilities. However, the multilateral GATT-based trade regime had numerous problems in the 1980s (see Chapter 8), and regionalism therefore served as a second-best route to establish trade linkages.[21] Regional trade negotiations, which involved small groups of like-minded states in geographically focused areas, were easier to conduct than multilateral negotiations. RTA members also had objective similarities, such as comparable levels of income and development, which often facilitated negotiations. (Mexico's membership in NAFTA was a notable exception.) Trade negotiations in the larger, more diverse GATT were by contrast more complicated and difficult. Thus, liberals note approvingly that Canada and the United States negotiated issues in their 1988 free trade agreement (such as trade in services and agriculture) that had not yet been dealt with globally.[22]

The growth of interdependence, according to liberals, also led to increased demands by societal groups such as industries and firms for RTAs, and states in the 1980s were willing to supply these domestic groups with agreements. Along with the trend toward globalization, a growing number of firms became highly dependent on trade, and they shifted their operations from the national to the multinational level. These internationalist firms pressured for a freeing of economic relationships at *both* the global and the regional levels. Regionalism often improves the competitiveness of international firms, which can benefit from "the larger regional markets as their base rather than just the home market."[23]

As GATT/WTO negotiations have reduced tariffs on a multilateral basis, one might expect that RTAs would provide fewer relative advantages to states. However, liberals point to the reasons WTO members continue to establish new RTAs at a rapid rate. In sectors where tariffs remain high or where a small tariff advantage is competitively significant, the elimination of tariffs in an RTA continues to provide advantages to members. Furthermore, the members of some RTAs benefit from the phasing out of nontariff barriers and from exemptions from their regional partners' use of safeguards such as ADDs and CVDs. Some RTAs also contribute to deeper integration such as the harmonization of legal regulations governing commerce.[24] Whereas liberals support open RTAs as a second-best option, they have a negative view of more protectionist RTAs. Liberals are concerned about a recent trend toward forming bilateral FTAs, which seems to result from frustration with conflict at the WTO Doha Round and with slow progress toward liberalization in some of the larger RTAs. For example, the United States, the EU, Singapore, Mexico, Canada, and even Japan are actively involved in negotiations for bilateral FTAs. A patchwork of diverse bilateral RTAs "carries the risk that some provisions are mutually inconsistent and may hamper trade."[25]

Historical Structuralist Explanations

Historical structuralists, like liberals, believe that MNCs and other sources of transnational capital played a central role in the revival of regionalism during the 1980s. Unlike liberals, however, historical structuralists view this as a highly negative development. RTAs such as NAFTA, from this perspective, permit MNCs to become more competitive by locating their production facilities in states and regions with the lowest taxes, wages, and environmental standards. Whereas the capitalist class benefits from this growth of regionalism, domestic labor suffers because capital can move more easily to lower-wage regions and countries. Historical structuralists also explain the revival of regionalism in terms of the desire of powerful states to seek regional hegemony. As its economic hegemony declined globally, the United States sought to recoup its losses by establishing its hegemony more firmly on a regional basis. Thus, some critics charge that NAFTA was "designed to fit Canada and Mexico into the American model of development, on terms amenable to American corporations."[26]

GATT/WTO AND RTAS

The United States as global hegemon at the end of World War II strongly opposed preferential agreements and any other type of discrimination in international trade that would interfere with an open multilateral trade regime. Britain, however, wanted to preserve its discriminatory imperial preferences, and a number of states wanted to have the prerogative to establish RTAs. Thus, John Maynard Keynes strongly opposed U.S. pressure for an end to imperial preferences, referring to "all the old lumber, most-favored-nation clause and the rest which was a notorious failure and made such a hash of the old world."[27] U.S. views on this issue largely prevailed, and GATT Article 1 called for unconditional MFN treatment. Nevertheless, GATT also permitted regional exceptions to unconditional MFN treatment: GATT Article 24 permits countries to form CUs and FTAs that discriminate against other members, as long as these RTAs meet specific conditions.[28] An examination of the reasoning behind Article 24 is crucial to understanding the relationship between the WTO and regional agreements.

Liberals consider global free trade to be the best possible route to maximizing welfare, and this was the approach taken by GATT as a liberal-economic institution. Because RTAs discriminate against outsiders, they are clearly inferior to multilateral agreements which liberalize trade without discrimination. However, liberals believe that RTAs may offer a second-best route to trade liberalization when there are obstacles to freer trade at the global level.[29] GATT Article 24 therefore sanctions the formation of CUs and FTAs, but it seeks to ensure that they are more trade creating than trade diverting.[30] Before discussing the Article 24 provisions, it is necessary to describe the ways in which RTAs may be trade creating and trade diverting.

Trade Diversion

RTAs inevitably produce some trade diversion because the reduction or elimination of trade barriers on intraregional trade shifts some imports from more efficient outside suppliers to less efficient regional suppliers. Furthermore, competition increases within member countries' markets as trade within an RTA is liberalized. This competition can lead to adjustment pressures for inefficient industries, which try to shift some of the adjustment burden onto third countries by lobbying for increased external barriers. Thus, trade diversion can result when RTAs raise protectionist barriers against outsiders. Outside countries may also be harmed by investment diversion when MNCs set up branch plants inside an RTA to produce locally instead of producing in the least-cost location and shipping goods to the region.

A CU may be more trade diverting in some respects than an FTA. (As Figure 2.3 shows, a CU has a common external tariff.) Even if external tariffs do not increase on the average when a CU is formed, protectionism may increase because of contingent trade actions; that is, a CU may impose ADDs and CVDs in response to pressure from import-competing industries. The EU's experience shows that such duties can pose formidable trade barriers to outsiders because they limit exports to the entire CU area. ADDs and CVDs pose less of a problem for outsiders in an FTA because FTAs have no common external tariff and industries cannot pressure for areawide protection (each FTA member levies its own duties).[31] Whereas contingent trade actions are a special problem in CUs, **rules of origin** may have serious trade-diverting effects in FTAs. Because each FTA member has its own external tariffs, FTAs must have rules of origin to prevent importers from bringing goods in through the lowest-duty member and then shipping them to other members whose duties are higher. The rules of origin determine whether goods crossing borders within the FTA should qualify for duty-free treatment. These rules are difficult to develop because so many goods are manufactured with components originating in a number of countries. The rules of origin determine whether the products have undergone sufficient processing within the FTA to qualify for the trade preferences. Domestic firms in an FTA often pressure for stiffer rules of origin, which become a form of trade protectionism against outsiders. Although some CUs apply rules of origin, they are a less significant issue for CUs because of the common external tariff.[32]

Trade diversion depends not only on internal political dynamics but also on the reaction of nonmembers to RTAs. When an RTA is formed, nonmember states may have the incentive to establish their own RTAs in efforts to "better defend themselves against the discriminatory effects of *other* regional groups."[33] Furthermore, regional trade blocs such as the EU can become larger as pressure from disadvantaged nonmember firms triggers "membership requests from countries that were previously happy to be nonmembers."[34] This proliferation of regionalism can increase trade conflicts and lead to fragmentation of the global trade regime. From this perspective, regionalism by its very nature causes trade diversion.

Trade Creation

The main source of trade creation in RTAs is the increased trade among members, which shifts demand from less efficient domestic production to more efficient partner country production. To the degree that firms within the region become more competitive as a result of the RTA, they are likely to be more supportive of freer trade at the global as well as regional levels. Furthermore, RTAs often achieve a deeper level of integration than multilateral agreements because negotiations occur among a smaller number of like-minded partners. RTAs may therefore provide a positive demonstration effect and contribute to more effective MTNs. For example, the inclusion of agriculture, services, intellectual property, and investment provisions in the NAFTA provided a stimulus for negotiating these issues during the GATT Uruguay Round.

GATT Article 24 and RTAs

GATT Article 24 is designed to ensure that RTAs result in as much trade creation and as little trade diversion as possible. To increase trade creation, Article 24 stipulates that FTAs and CUs are to eliminate tariffs and other trade restrictions on "substantially all" trade among the members within a "reasonable" period. (GATT occasionally granted waivers from the substantially all trade requirement for sectoral FTAs; notable examples were waivers for the ECSC in 1952 and the Canada–U.S. Auto Pact in 1965.) This condition may seem ironic because maximum preferential liberalization diverges more from MFN treatment and can be more injurious to nonmembers than partial liberalization, but it is included for several reasons. First, the GATT founders believed that a rigorous requirement to remove all tariff barriers in RTAs would prevent the proliferation of preferential agreements with only partial trade liberalization among members. Preferential arrangements of this nature had contributed to trade discrimination and protectionism during the 1930s. Second, genuine FTAs or CUs are more likely to facilitate trade liberalization at the global level. When RTAs involve deeper integration (i.e., the removal of all tariffs), they can serve as stepping-stones to multilateral free trade. Preferential agreements with only partial trade liberalization do not have this positive demonstration effect. To minimize trade diversion, Article 24 stipulates that an RTA when it is formed should not raise tariffs on the average to countries outside the agreement. Whereas individual member states in an FTA are not to raise their average level of duties, the common external tariff of a CU may not "on the whole" be higher than the member countries' separate duties were before the CU was established. These provisions are designed to limit reductions in imports from nonmembers as a result of the RTA.[35]

Although GATT Article 24 seems to provide a mechanism for regulating RTAs, in reality the GATT/WTO has often had only limited influence in this area. It is therefore necessary to examine the effectiveness of Article 24.

The Effectiveness of GATT Article 24

When countries form an RTA, the GATT/WTO establishes a working party to determine whether the RTA meets the requisite conditions. Although Article 24 has permitted the working parties to exert some influence over RTAs, their influence in practice has been quite limited. GATT's regulations for RTAs were drafted with smaller agreements in mind, such as the Benelux CU negotiated by Belgium, the Netherlands, and Luxembourg in 1944. This situation changed dramatically in 1957, when the Treaty of Rome establishing the EC was notified to GATT. In view of its size and importance, the EC was simply not willing to wait for GATT approval under Article 24 before proceeding with economic integration. Negotiating the Treaty of Rome had been a difficult and sensitive process, and EC members indicated they would not readjust the treaty to satisfy GATT.[36]

In the end, GATT acceded to the EC's demands and never completed its examination of the Treaty of Rome, even though GATT members had reached no consensus regarding the treaty's consistency with Article 24. GATT's acquiescence in this case had a detrimental effect on its ability to exert authority over subsequent RTAs. Thus, GATT working parties had little success in bringing about changes in RTAs after the member states in the region negotiated them. Whereas early agreements such as the EC and the Latin American Free Trade Association (LAFTA) were notified to GATT before they entered into force, later RTAs were sometimes notified to GATT belatedly. For example, two agreements that entered into force *before* working parties were even established to examine them were NAFTA in January 1994 and the accession of Austria, Finland, and Sweden to the EU in January 1995.[37]

It is not surprising that GATT working parties had little influence over RTAs after they were negotiated. Governments had already engaged in extensive bargaining and were reluctant to reopen negotiations in response to outside criticism. The most GATT working parties could accomplish was to embarrass RTA members with allegations of noncompliance and thus encourage countries to comply with GATT guidelines in the future. Nevertheless, the GATT rules had some influence on national decision making at earlier stages in the process. One authority on international trade points out that GATT Article 24 influenced the EC and CUSFTA at an early stage by setting broad parameters for conducting the regional negotiations:

The diplomats negotiating each of these agreements were operating under instructions to make maximum efforts to comply with GATT rules, and the actual results of these negotiations testify that a quite important degree of GATT compliance was achieved. Except for agriculture . . . and except for the EC's relationship with former colonies, the . . . developed-country agreements . . . were essentially GATT-conforming. To be sure, GATT was unable to do anything further once the agreements were signed and deposited in Geneva for review.[38]

Some analysts point out that GATT was less effective because the conditions it required of RTAs were not clearly specified. Legitimate differences exist over the interpretation of Article 24 requirements that RTAs cover "substantially all" trade, do not become more restrictive "on average," and be fully implemented in a "reasonable length of time." In addition to its imprecise wording, Article 24 does not adequately address such issues as contingent trade measures (ADDs and CVDs) and rules of origin, which may significantly increase regional protectionism toward outside countries.[39] In view of the ambiguous Article 24 requirements, working parties were reluctant to give RTAs their unqualified approval. By the end of 1994, only six of 69 working parties had reached a consensus that particular RTAs conformed with Article 24, and only two of the six approved RTAs are still operative.[40] In the great majority of cases, working parties simply noted that members had divergent views regarding the RTA's conformity with GATT. However, GATT never explicitly concluded that an RTA had *not* met the legal requirements.[41]

In efforts to improve the monitoring and regulation of RTAs, the Uruguay Round agreements include a 1994 Understanding on the Interpretation of Article 24 (UR Understanding), and a GATS article on regional integration in services trade (Article 5) which is similar to GATT Article 24.[42] To address continuing concerns about RTAs, the WTO General Council also established a *Committee on Regional Trade Agreements (CRTA)* with a mandate to develop procedures for improving the RTA examination process. The Uruguay Round agreements and the CRTA have dealt with some of the GATT Article 24 shortcomings, but a number of problems remain. On the positive side, the UR Understanding and CRTA strengthen the WTO review process for RTAs and apply the stronger WTO dispute-settlement procedures to RTAs. Dispute-settlement cases may help resolve some of the issues that continue to be unclear in Article 24. The UR Understanding also improves the methodology for determining whether the level of duties in a CU are higher "on the whole" as a result of the common external tariff. On the negative side, divisions among members persist on the interpretation of key concepts and the admissibility of various RTAs. For example, the UR Understanding makes very little progress in determining whether the "substantially all trade" requirement permits the exclusion of certain sectors, and many RTAs continue to exclude agriculture. Furthermore, the Uruguay Round negotiators reached no agreement on how to deal with restrictive rules of origin in FTAs. It remains to be seen whether the CRTA will address the most challenging issues hindering the WTO's assessment of RTAs.[43]

Special Treatment for LDCs

Although GATT Article 24 was to apply to all RTAs, LDCs over time were given special treatment in this area. Two types of RTAs involving LDCs have been especially prominent: RTAs among LDCs and the EU association agreements with LDCs.

RTAs Among LDCs GATT's examination of RTAs among LDCs was even less stringent than its examination of RTAs among DCs. For example, GATT did not openly object to the formation of the Latin American Free Trade Association in 1960, even though it was quite protectionist and "did not even approach the requirements of total integration."[44] After Part IV on trade and development was added to GATT in 1965, LDCs sometimes invoked it to justify forming preferential RTAs that did not meet the substantially all trade requirement of GATT Article 24. When the 1979 enabling clause "established for the first time in trade relations . . . a permanent legal basis for preferences in favour of developing countries," it became the main legal cover for LDCs forming questionable RTAs.[45] The enabling clause basically removes the requirement that RTAs among LDCs must cover substantially all trade, and it permits LDCs to lower rather than eliminate tariff barriers within RTAs. Mercosur, a South American CU discussed later in this chapter, was notified to GATT under the enabling clause, not under Article 24.[46]

Despite the GATT/WTO's permissiveness with RTAs among LDCs, recent LDC moves toward trade liberalization have inevitably affected their RTAs. The negative experiences of LDCs with inward-looking import substitution policies, combined with IMF and World Bank pressures on LDC debtors to liberalize their policies, have increased the likelihood of LDCs forming more outward-looking RTAs since the 1980s.

The EU Association Agreements with LDCs The North has at times agreed to provide the South with nonreciprocal trade preferences. In Chapter 8, for example, we examined the GSP, which DCs have provided to LDCs since 1971. As discussed, DCs unilaterally establish their GSP provisions without a formal role for LDCs in the decision making. DCs have also unilaterally established nonreciprocal trade schemes on a regional basis. For example, the United States created the *Caribbean Basin Initiative* in 1983, the *Andean Trade Preference Act* in 1991, the *Caribbean Basin Trade Partnership Act* in 2000, and the *African Growth and Opportunity Act* in 2000; and Canada enacted the *Canadian Trade, Investment, and Industrial Cooperation program* for Commonwealth Caribbean countries in 1986. In contrast to these unilaterally established programs, DCs and LDCs have *jointly* negotiated some nonreciprocal regional preference programs; these have included the *Lomé Conventions* between the EU and associate LDCs, and the *South Pacific Regional Trade and Economic Cooperation Agreement (SPARTECA)* between Australia, New Zealand, and 13 island countries. Although these were negotiated agreements, the LDCs have a much weaker negotiating position than the DCs.[47]

This section focuses on the EU agreements with associate LDCs because they provide the world's largest economic and political framework for North-South cooperation. When the EC was formed in 1957, France insisted that trade preferences it was giving to its African Overseas Territories be continued. France wanted to ensure that exports from its territories would have preferential access to the EC and that other EC members would share the costs of providing economic assistance. Despite the opposition of some EC members, the French were adamant, and Part 4 of the Treaty of Rome provided associate status to overseas territories that had "special relations" with a member state. Although Belgian, Dutch, and Italian colonial territories were also involved, French colonial territories predominated. Part 4 called for the gradual removal of tariffs between EC members and the associates, but the associates could protect their infant industries and retain some tariffs for revenue purposes, and the EC provided aid to the associates through a European Development Fund (EDF). When most of the associate territories gained their independence in the early 1960s, new arrangements were necessary. The EC structured them through two *Yaoundé Conventions,* signed at Yaoundé, Cameroon, in 1963 and 1969 with 18 principally francophone LDCs known as the *Associated African States and Madagascar (AASM).* The Yaoundé Conventions dealt with financial aid, technical assistance, trade preferences, investment, and capital movements. In trade, they established preferential arrangements permitting the AASM states to export the small amount of manufactures they produced to the EC usually at duty free rates; but the EC provided much less preference for AASM agricultural exports because of its protectionist Common Agricultural Policy. In return for EC preferential treatment, the AASM states had to accept a comparable amount of exports from EC members.[48]

The EC's enlargement from six to nine countries when Britain, Denmark, and Ireland joined in 1973 necessitated a change in the Yaoundé Convention because of British efforts to protect its relationship with Commonwealth LDCs. In 1975, the nine EC members concluded the first *Lomé Convention* (Lomé I) at Lomé, Togo, with 46 LDCs in *Africa, the Caribbean, and the Pacific.* This new *ACP* group included the original 18 Yaoundé states and Mauritius, six other African LDCs, and 21 Commonwealth LDCs. Lomé I differed from the previous conventions because of its emphasis on the nonreciprocity principle (which had also been introduced in Part IV of GATT and the GSP—see Chapter 8). Under this principle, the EC offered preferential access for ACP products to its market without requiring reciprocal concessions (other than MFN status) for EC goods. Lomé I also introduced a system for the *Stabilization of Export Earnings (STABEX)* that guaranteed ACP states funds to cover production shortfalls or price fluctuations for certain agricultural commodities exported to Europe. The EC's willingness to provide the ACP states with this preferential treatment in Lomé I resulted in part from the OPEC oil crisis and the South's calls for a NIEO in the 1970s.[49]

Lomé I was followed by three more Lomé Conventions, which were revised in accordance with changing circumstances: Lomé II in 1979 (with 58 ACP states), Lomé III in 1984 (with 65 ACP states), and Lomé IV in 1989 (with 68 ACP states, later extended to 71 ACP states). However, the results of the nonreciprocal preferences in the Lomé Conventions were disappointing, and there were growing external pressures to alter the system. Externally, a number of GATT members argued that the associate system was not a genuine FTA because it was nonreciprocal. GATT Article 24 provides an exception to MFN treatment only for RTAs that follow the reciprocity principle. Thus, the association agreements were in direct conflict with GATT's nondiscrimination principle. Furthermore, the 1979 enabling clause permits DCs to provide trade preferences to LDCs, only if *all* LDCs have access to these preferences. The enabling clause therefore does *not* sanction EU discrimination in favor of its ex-colonies at the expense of other LDCs. Although the EC insisted that the association agreements were coordinate with UN proposals that the North should promote socio-economic development in the South, external events during the 1990s increased pressure on it to change the nonreciprocal preferences. In 1994, Mexico accepted almost the same reciprocal free trade obligations as the two DCs (the United States and

Canada) in the NAFTA; and in 1995 the formation of the WTO "reflected and rein-forced" orthodox liberal pressures for global trade liberalization, and this posed prob-lems for the Lomé Conventions.[50]

In addition to the external pressures, the results of the Lomé Conventions were disappointing for several reasons. First, ACP benefits from the EC trade preferences declined as MFN tariffs were reduced during successive GATT rounds and the EC formed FTAs with more developed regions. Second, EC regulations in effect limited the export of some ACP agricultural products and textiles and clothing. Third, some economists argued that the nonreciprocal preferences enabled ACP states to shield their economies from international competition and maintain inefficient production structures. Thus, the ACP states' share of the EU market fell from 6.7 percent in 1976 to 3 percent in 1998, with more than 60 percent of ACP exports concentrated in only 10 primary products.

Interestingly, historical structuralists as well as orthodox liberals have criticized the EU association agreements. Historical structuralists have described EU nonrecip-rocal preferences "as a form of neocolonialism that perpetuates the production of and trade in products not compatible" with the long-term interests of the ACP states. For example, the Lomé Conventions' trade preferences for bananas from the Windward Islands "have perpetuated the one-product economy of these islands and discouraged them from taking necessary measures to diversify production."[51] Historical structural-ists have also viewed the STABEX system as a mechanism for ensuring that ACP states continue to supply Europe with cocoa, coffee, and other raw commodities.

In view of these pressures for change (especially the orthodox liberal pressures), official negotiations for more WTO compatible EU-ACP agreements began in Sep-tember 1998. After intensive negotiations, the EU and ACP states signed the *Cotonou Agreement* (or *New Partnership Agreement*) in Cotonou, Gabon, in June 2000. Al-though the Cotonou Agreement builds on the Lomé Conventions, it is quite different in some respects. Most significantly, LDCs that are not LLDCs will eventually have to grant reciprocity for EU preferences by reducing their own tariffs on imports from the EU. Under the Cotonou Agreement, the current all-ACP nonreciprocal tariff prefer-ences will continue until December 2007. However, starting from 2008, reciprocal agreements will begin to replace them and will be implemented within 10 to 12 years. Only the LLDCs will be able to retain nonreciprocal trade preferences with the EU. Although supporters of this change argue that the ACP states will benefit in the long term by liberalizing their trade policies, critics argue that EU-ACP nonreciprocal rela-tions must continue because of the lower level of development of ACP economies.[52]

EUROPE

Postwar regional integration has been centered mainly in Europe, with European states as parties to 76 of the 109 RTAs notified to GATT from 1948 to 1994 (62 of these RTAs were still in force in December 1994). In 2000 the EU was a party to 28 of the 91 RTAs in goods notified under GATT Article 24 and to 8 of the 11 RTAs in ser-vices notified under GATS Article 5. The EU is the largest trading bloc in the world, with about 374 million inhabitants (compared with 268 million in the United States) and a GDP of $8.5 trillion in 1997 (compared with a GDP of $7.7 trillion in the United States).[53]

European integration can be traced to a French proposal during the interwar period that a European CU be formed to resolve the continent's political and economic problems. After World War II these plans were realized with U.S. support and encouragement, but only Western Europe was involved because of the Cold War. In 1951, six states (Belgium, France, West Germany, Italy, Luxembourg, and the Netherlands) formed the ECSC and then extended their integration under the Treaty of Rome to establish the EC and the European Atomic Energy Community (Euratom) in 1957. In 1960, seven European states (Austria, Britain, Denmark, Norway, Portugal, Sweden, and Switzerland) responded to the EC by forming the EFTA. Although these "outer seven" states wanted to be included in an FTA, they were not prepared to join the "inner six" EC states. As a CU, the EC required a common external tariff and a degree of policy coordination that threatened Britain's Commonwealth preference system and the nonaligned policies of states such as Sweden and Switzerland. The EFTA did not pose the same threat to their autonomy because it did not require a common external tariff (see Figure 2.3). Since the formation of the EC and EFTA, there has been a gradual deepening and widening of European integration. In 1993 there was a formal name change after the Maastricht Treaty to symbolize the extension of the community from trade and economic matters to a much broader range of activities. Thus, the term "EC" is used when discussing events from 1957 to 1992, and the term "EU" is used when discussing events from 1993 to the present.

The Deepening of European Integration

The European integration process began with considerable enthusiasm, and the EC accelerated its timetable for creating a CU among the original six member states. However, two events during the 1960s marked a setback for the integration process: In 1963, French President Charles de Gaulle unilaterally vetoed Britain's application for EC membership, and in 1965, de Gaulle withdrew France from the work of the Council of Ministers to protest a commission proposal for financing the EC budget. The eventual compromise with France over the budgetary issue limited the EC Commission's power and undermined prospects for further integration during the 1960s. (The European Commission, as the EU's permanent executive, supports the EU's supranational authority. The Council of Ministers, composed of foreign ministers, represents the continuing influence of the member states.) During the 1970s, the EC was buffeted by turbulence in the global economy and the outlook for integration became even dimmer. The collapse of the Bretton Woods monetary regime, the OPEC oil crisis, and the onset of recession all contributed to a slowdown of the integration process. Although three states joined the EC in 1973 (Britain, Denmark, and Ireland), Britain and Denmark opposed the development of strong EC supranational institutions. The EC had some successes such as the launching of the EMS in March 1979 (see Chapter 6). Nevertheless, the 1970s to early 1980s were generally marked by "Eurosclerosis" and a loss of faith in the EC's vitality.[54]

In the early 1980s, EC members became acutely aware of their lack of competitiveness in world markets vis-à-vis the United States and Japan. A major source of this problem was the persistence of differential taxation, border inspections, domestic subsidies, and internal impediments to market access within the EC. A more unified European market would produce more competitive European firms as a result of increased specialization and economies of scale. Thus, the EC launched a major effort to increase the level of integration during the 1980s–1990s. A significant force for change was new EC Commission President Jacques Delors, who pressured for deeper integration. As a result of Delors' efforts, EC members signed the Single European Act (SEA) in 1986, which was designed to complete the freeing of the internal market by the end of 1992. The goals of the SEA included ending nontariff barriers to trade in industrial goods, liberalizing trade in services, and facilitating the free movement of capital and labor throughout the EC.[55] In addition to its trade objectives, the SEA also included a commitment to monetary union, and the European Council established the Delors Committee in June 1988 to propose a plan for this purpose. The committee proposed a three-stage process toward EMU, and negotiations subsequently resulted in the Treaty on European Union or Maastricht Treaty in December 1991. Although the proposed EMU was the centerpiece of the Maastricht Treaty, the treaty also had noneconomic goals to establish a European federal political system with common social, foreign, and security policies. The Maastricht Treaty initially met with a hostile reaction among a large segment of European public opinion, and this forced European governments to confront a problem they had often neglected—legitimizing an integration process in which European bureaucrats were largely removed from the populace.[56] Because the EMU is discussed in Chapter 6, this section briefly focuses on the two other aspects of the Maastricht Treaty designed to deepen European integation: cooperation on foreign and security policy and cooperation on social policy.

The Maastricht Treaty established common foreign and security policy as the second pillar of the EU (the EC was the first pillar), demonstrating the difficulty in separating economic from political security issues. Reflecting divisions within the EU, the Maastricht Treaty "produced a delicate balance between a French view that sought to develop security policy in the Union through the European Commission and a British view that sought to enhance the Western European Union in order to strengthen NATO."[57] The degree of cooperation between the EU's common European Security and Defense Policy (ESDP) and NATO will depend on future negotiations, but it is evident that an ESDP will depend on NATO in the near to medium-term. For example, a European rapid reaction force would have to rely on NATO's transport and intelligence capabilities to function adequately. Divisions within the EU on security issues ranging from the former Yugoslavia to the Middle East and the response to terrorism raise questions as to whether the Europeans can in fact develop a common security policy. The other major Maastricht Treaty area involves social policy, including policy toward organized labor, a welfare state, and migration into the EU. For example, the EU Council of Ministers was given broader authority to make decisions regarding such issues as working conditions and worker health and safety by qualified majority vote. These social issues are highly sensitive because of political divisions in Europe between conservatives and social democrats, and management to this point has occurred more through informal agreements than formal policy decisions. Of the

Maastricht Treaty's broad goals for deepening integration, the objective of forming an EMU has been the most successful (see Chapter 6).[58]

The Widening of European Integration

As discussed in Chapter 2, the EC expanded from six to 15 full members in three successive enlargements (see Figure 2.4). In the first enlargement, Britain, Denmark, and Ireland joined the EC in 1973; in the second enlargement, Greece joined in 1979 and Spain and Portugal joined in 1986; and in the third enlargement, Austria, Finland, and Sweden joined in 1995. While expanding its membership, the EC was also extending associate linkages with the ACP states and other LDCs. The question arose as to whether the EC should be widening the integration process by accepting new members at the same time it was facing many challenges in deepening integration. Whereas deepening of integration has often been a response to "rapidly changing economic conditions," widening was "thrust on the EU by the failure of communism in Europe."[59] This section focuses on issues regarding the accession of a large number of Central and Eastern European countries (CEECs) to the EU.

The Soviet Union was extremely hostile to the EC when it was established in 1957, and the relationship continued to be strained in the 1960s–1970s. The EC in turn did not want to give legitimacy to the Soviet-led CMEA, and it preferred to negotiate bilateral trade agreements with Eastern European states outside CMEA auspices. Although the Soviet Union insisted that CMEA be the vehicle for EC economic contacts, the EC successfully encouraged some Eastern European states to break ranks with the Soviet position. For example, the EC granted the GSP to Romania in 1972, and in 1980 Romania and the EC signed a trade and cooperation agreement. As economic conditions in Eastern Europe worsened during the 1980s and the Eastern bloc became more dependent on economic linkages with the West, the Soviet Union softened its position. After a 1988 EC-CMEA agreement sanctioned the negotiation of trade agreements between the EC and individual Eastern European states, the EC negotiated a number of agreements promoting trade, cooperation, and economic assistance.[60] A major landmark was the breakup of the Soviet bloc, which led to CMEA's dissolution and the EU's negotiation of "Europe agreements" with a number of Central and Eastern European countries (CEECs) in the early 1990s. Although these agreements were similar to the association agreements that helped Greece, Spain, and Portugal join the EU, they provided no timetable for CEEC membership in the EU. However, the EU offered the CEECs fewer trade concessions than they had given to the associate ACP states, and one after another the CEECs applied for full membership in the EU.

In July 1997, the EU Commission produced a report titled *Agenda 2000*, which identified several issues that enlargement negotiations would have to address. First, EU members feared that firms might move eastward after enlargement because of lower labor costs in Eastern Europe; relocation could be most marked in coal mining, agriculture, and traditional industries such as textiles. Second, the EU was concerned about migration pressures from the CEECs because of large wage differentials with Western Europe. Third, the EU Commission feared that enlargement would sharply increase the population eligible for assistance from EU social and economic development funds. All these issues relate to economic development disparities between the

CEECs and most current EU members. Ten CEECs that signed Europe agreements with the EU had only one-fourth of the purchasing power of the present EU average, and about 20 percent of their workers had agricultural jobs compared with only 6 percent of EU workers.[61] These states would increase pressures on the EU's structural funds directed to poorer EU regions and on funds for agricultural subsidies. The Common Agricultural Policy (CAP) already absorbs about half the EU budget and structural funds another 30 percent, so states that contribute most to these funds (e.g., Germany, France, Britain, and the Netherlands) are concerned. The less developed southern European countries in the EU, such as Spain, Portugal, and Greece, also feel threatened by possible EU expansion because they share with CEECs such as Poland and Hungary a comparative advantage in agriculture, traditional manufactures, and resource-intensive products.[62]

Despite these concerns, official EU statements generally described enlargement as "a political necessity and a historic opportunity."[63] Both the CEECs and the EU see a number of possible advantages from enlargement. The CEECs want to join with the EU and NATO to gain security vis-à-vis Russia, and they want access to EU capital, technology, and markets as a means of closing the economic gap with the West. As for EU members, they want stable CEECs as a buffer against political instability in the post-Soviet era, and they believe that enlargement will enhance their influence in Europe and the world. From a realist perspective, the EU believes it will "not be able to withstand competition from the two main strategic areas of America and Asia unless it expands its economic area and market."[64] The EU's Northern more developed states such as Germany, Britain, and France also have a comparative advantage in high-technology manufactures and service exports, and the CEECs will provide these states with cheaper workers and more investment opportunities.[65]

In December 1994, the European Council agreed to prepare some CEECs for accession to full membership in the EU; and in December 2002, the European Council formally closed negotiations with 10 CEECs and approved their accession to the EU. The 10 countries are Estonia, Latvia, Lithuania, Poland, Czech Republic, Slovak Republic, Hungary, Slovenia, Cyprus, and Malta. If the 2003 schedule of conditions is followed (mainly ratifications), these countries are scheduled to join the EU in May 2004. The 10 CEECs will account for 15 percent of the EU population but will add only 5 percent to the EU's GDP because of their lower level of economic development. Accession will also not contribute greatly to an increase in trade with the EU because most of the trade reorientation has already taken place through the FTAs established by the Europe Agreements. Under these agreements, the acceding countries have had duty-free access to the EU for industrial exports, and their share of exports going to the EU increased from 60 to 68 percent from 1995 to 2001. The degree of integration of the acceding countries is also evident from the large increase in foreign investment from the EU.[66]

As discussed, analysts foresee both benefits and drawbacks from EU enlargement to the East. Economic benefits are already being experienced from opening markets as a result of the Europe agreements. However, the EU must confront a series of controversial issues related to extending the costly CAP and Structural Funds to the new members, reconciling the deepening of integration (the EMU) with enlargement, permitting free movement of labor, upholding environmental standards, and controlling crime. In view of current EU problems with establishing confidence in the euro and extending the EMU to important members such as Britain, the enlargement process will be extremely challenging. Furthermore, Europe must address the complexities of balancing EU enlargement with the expansion of NATO. Although EU enlargement is now accepted, disputes over a wide range of political and economic issues will continue long after accession of the CEECs.[67]

Theoretical Perspectives and the EU

Realists often focus on European integration as a means of increasing Europe's power vis-à-vis other major actors. Thus, the post–World War II bipolar system dominated by the United States and the Soviet Union was a major factor in the decision of Western Europeans to embark on economic integration to increase their influence. The United States was willing to support the formation of the EC because it viewed a strong Western Europe as an important component of the Western alliance vis-à-vis the Soviet Union. During the late 1960s, Jean-Jacques Servan-Schreiber's book *The American Challenge* focusing on the increased penetration of U.S. capital into Europe also had a major impact on European thinking. Individual European states lacked the resources to develop firms that could rival U.S. MNCs, Servan-Schreiber argued, and only a united Europe could preserve European autonomy and influence.[68] In the 1980s–1990s, European concerns about U.S. and Japanese technological leadership were similarly a major factor in the signing of the SEA and the Maastricht Treaty.

Liberal economists are primarily concerned with ensuring that the EU is an open integration movement. However, liberals do *not* necessarily agree on whether the EU is more open or closed in nature. Some liberals express concerns about EU protectionism, and their concerns have increased during the moves toward consolidation in the SEA and the EU intransigence on agriculture in the GATT/WTO. In discussions of the EU's inward orientation, liberals point to the reorientation of trade away from non-European countries to other EU members following the creation of the community and the accession of new members. They also focus on specific EU policies, such as the CAP, as examples of extreme protectionism. Liberals often point to the detrimental effects of inward-looking EU policies on members as well as outsiders. For example, one European specialist argues that "the use of protection to avoid industrial restructuring has almost certainly contributed to Europe's falling behind the United States and Japan in hi-tech goods."[69]

Other liberals disagree with these concerns and maintain that the EU is responding to globalization forces with outward-looking policies. For example, they note that the largest industrial firms in Europe were a major force behind the single-market program during the late 1980s–1990s. These firms are global competitors that oppose regional protectionism because of fears of retaliation. The deepening and widening of integration also promises to add considerably to trade creation within the EU and to further integrate the CEECs in the global economy. Although this has the risk of contributing to trade diversion vis-à-vis outsiders, there would also be a substantial amount of trade creation within such a large regional bloc. With accession of the 10 CEECs, the share of the EU in world merchandise exports (including intra-EU flows) will reach 41 percent. As for global trade relations, these liberals point out that the EU eventually approved the Uruguay Round agreement despite dire predictions that European intransigence over agriculture would lead to failure of the round. Although some liberals are more optimistic than others about the EU's openness, they all favor open RTAs.[70]

Interventionist liberals praise the EU for directing more attention to social policy than some other RTAs, such as NAFTA. For example, the EC created a European Social Fund as early as the 1960s with the goal of decreasing socioeconomic disparities among members. Furthermore, Ireland and the poorer Southern European EC states were willing to support the SEA in the 1980s partly because they were promised increased structural funds. Historical structuralists are more inclined to view the European social programs as inadequate solutions to inequality and poverty, and they note that some European states oppose an increase in funding for social purposes. Thus, major disparities in wealth continue to exist between Northern and Southern European states and between different regions within European states.[71]

Interventionist liberals and historical structuralists also differ in their views of EU relations with the ACP states. In the liberal view, the EU has been willing to absorb the short-term economic costs of providing aid and trade preferences to ACP states in the interests of long-term economic and political security. Historical structuralists, by contrast, argue that the EU associate agreements perpetuate the dependence of ACP states on their former colonial masters. Thus, the EU maintains the colonial pattern of trade, with EU members exporting industrial goods and the ACP states exporting primary products. Historical structuralists therefore believe that "prospects for symmetrical EurAfrica relations remain . . . dim despite all the rhetoric to the contrary."[72] Historical structuralists also argue that the CEECs will never become full and equal members of the EU. From this perspective, "the present EU, plus perhaps some new central European members, will be flanked to the east by a tier of excluded states available as sites for low-cost assembly by firms headquartered in the EU."[73]

THE WESTERN HEMISPHERE

The Western Hemisphere is currently characterized by three overlapping regional integration processes: the first is centered in the United States and NAFTA; the second consists of several Latin American RTAs, the most prominent of which is *Mercosur;* and the third is the attempt to negotiate hemispheric integration in a *Free Trade Area of the Americas (FTAA)*. As discussed, the United States was unwilling to participate in RTAs from the 1940s to the early 1970s because of concerns that they detracted from efforts to develop a strong GATT-based multilateral trade regime. However, a reversal of U.S. policies combined with greater openness to free trade in Canada and Mexico resulted in the creation of CUSFTA in the 1980s and NAFTA in the 1990s. Unlike the United States, the countries of Latin America and the Caribbean had established several RTAs during the 1960s–1970s, including LAFTA, the Central American Common Market (CACM), the Andean Community, and the Caribbean Community and Common Market (CARICOM). However, these RTAs were generally inward-looking and did not expose the members to much international competition. Since the mid–1980s there has been a revival of Latin American regionalism, this time on a more open basis. RTAs in Latin America and the Caribbean include CACM, CARICOM, the Andean Group, and the Southern Cone Common Market (Mercosur). NAFTA and Mercosur are the two dynamic poles in current efforts to negotiate an FTAA, and the two most important countries in the FTAA negotiations are the United States (in NAFTA) and Brazil (in Mercosur).[74] This section focuses on CUSFTA, NAFTA, Mercosur, and the proposed FTAA.

The Formation of CUSFTA and NAFTA

Moves toward free trade between the United States and Canada have a remarkably long history even though the two countries did not establish a comprehensive FTA until the 1980s. Indeed, a noted historian has observed that one economic issue in Canada "comes close to rivalling the linguistic and race question for both longevity and vehemence, and this is, of course, the question of free trade with the United States."[75] In 1854, the United States and Canada concluded a Reciprocity Treaty providing for free trade in natural products such as grains, meat, dairy products, and fish. However, the United States abrogated the treaty in 1866 because of an unfavorable trade balance with Canada, increased Canadian duties on U.S. manufactures, and the British role in the American Civil War. Efforts to revive free trade in 1911 and 1948 were unsuccessful, but the two countries concluded the Canada–U.S. Automotive Agreement in 1965, which provided for free trade in automobiles and parts; a GATT waiver was necessary because this agreement did not meet the Article 24 requirement that an FTA should cover substantially all trade. It was not until 1988 that the two countries established a more general FTA, the CUSFTA. In December 1992, Mexico joined the United States and Canada in signing NAFTA, which superseded CUSFTA.

The question arises as to why these FTAs were formed after so many years. The United States first had to reverse its policy on participation in RTAs, and this reversal came with the 1974 U.S. Trade Act, which permitted the president to "initiate negotiations for a trade agreement with Canada to establish a free trade area."[76] However, it was a Canadian and then a Mexican request for free trade negotiations that resulted in CUSFTA and NAFTA. Protectionism increased in the United States during the mid-1980s because of massive balance-of-payments deficits during the Reagan administration. Canada decided an FTA was essential to gain more assured access to the U.S. market because more than 75 percent of its exports were going to the United States. Of particular concern to Canada were U.S. CVDs and trade unilateralism. Another motivation for free trade with the United States was the perceived need to alter Canadian domestic policies. Business leaders in Canada (as in many other countries) were critical of the government's central role in the economy during the 1980s, and they thought that an FTA would force Canadians to rely more on market forces.[77]

Starting from high levels of protectionism, Mexico instituted unilateral measures to ease trade restrictions *before* it sought free trade with the United States. These unilateral moves were impelled by the conditions attached to IMF and World Bank SALs to deal with Mexican debt and by the realization that liberalization was necessary if Mexico was to attract foreign investment. Mexico, like Canada, depended on the United States for more than 70 percent of its exports, and it shared Canada's concerns about gaining more assured access to the U.S. market. The foreign investment issue, however, was even more important to Mexico. Despite Mexico's unilateral liberalization, potential foreign investors were skeptical that this change was permanent because of Mexico's long history of government intervention. An FTA with the United States would help convince foreign investors that Mexico's liberalization policies were permanent.[78]

The United States as a major economic power was more concerned about global than regional trade linkages; its decision to conclude CUSFTA and NAFTA was motivated largely by frustration with the slow pace of the GATT Uruguay Round negotiations. Negotiating regional agreements, in the U.S. view, would induce other major economic powers—especially the EU and Japan—to offer concessions in the MTNs. Regionalism also has a tendency to breed more regionalism, and the EU's enlargement and consolidation in the SEA provided a U.S. incentive to establish FTAs as a counterweight. Because its trade hegemony was declining, the United States was less committed to multilateralism as the sole option and more willing to participate in RTAs. Although regional trade is less important to the United States than it is to Canada and Mexico, it is noteworthy that Canada and Mexico are the largest and second-largest U.S. trading partners. Finally, the United States wanted Canada and Mexico to ease their regulations on foreign investment and natural resources, and it was willing to open its market more widely to Canadian and Mexican goods in return.[79]

The IPE Theoretical Perspectives and NAFTA

CUSFTA was a highly controversial treaty in Canada, and controversy continues to surround NAFTA in all three member countries. U.S. individuals and groups critical of NAFTA stretch across the political spectrum, ranging from liberals to nationalists and historical structuralists. Whereas nationalist critics maintain that NAFTA's environmental and labor side agreements do not provide genuine protection for U.S. jobs and the environment, historical structuralists argue that NAFTA facilitates the ascendancy of the transnational capitalist class over labor. Even U.S., Canadian, and Mexican critics viewing NAFTA from the same theoretical perspective often point to different shortcomings in the agreement. For example, U.S. liberals criticized Canada's failure to include culture and Mexico's unwillingness to include energy-sharing provisions in NAFTA; Canadian liberals criticized the United States for refusing to agree to agricultural export subsidy reductions; and Canadian and Mexican liberals have criticized U.S. persistence in using CVDs and ADDs.[80] Despite this controversy, many liberal supporters argue that all three countries benefit from NAFTA even if they do not benefit equally. Because such a wide array of groups have strong views on NAFTA, this discussion of the theoretical perspectives is illustrative rather than all-inclusive.

The Liberal Perspective   Liberal economists want to ensure that NAFTA contributes to trade openness and serves as a stepping-stone rather than an obstacle to multilateral free trade. Although open RTAs are a second-best option for liberals after global free trade, they have often praised NAFTA for contributing to freer trade. The CUSFTA and NAFTA negotiations demonstrated that the United States might opt for regionalism as an alternative to multilateralism, and the EU and Japan were therefore more willing to compromise during the GATT Uruguay Round. NAFTA also had a positive "demonstration effect" on the WTO in services trade, investment, and intellectual property rights, and it goes beyond the WTO in coverage of these areas. For example, NAFTA follows a "negative list" approach to national treatment for trade in services; that is, all services not itemized on a country's list are automatically included. This approach puts the onus on each NAFTA member to identify services it wants to exclude from national treatment. The GATS, by contrast, takes a "positive list" approach to national treatment; that is, national treatment applies only to sectors specifically included in a member's list of commitments. Thus, NAFTA's services trade provisions are more trade creating than those of GATS.[81] Liberal economists also point positively to NAFTA as the first North-South FTA that does not give S&D treatment to the LDC (Mexico).

Although liberals generally have a positive view of NAFTA, they also point to NAFTA's shortcomings. The United States has been the largest user of CVDs during the postwar period. With the U.S. balance-of-trade deficits since 1971 and the decline of tariffs resulting from GATT negotiations, the U.S. Congress responded to domestic pressures by changing the rules so that CVDs could be imposed more easily. Because of their asymmetrical relations, U.S. CVDs "can have a severe impact" on Canada and Mexico whereas Canadian and Mexican CVDs are normally "little more than another irritant to the United States."[82] Canada wanted CUSFTA and NAFTA to deal with contingent trade actions, and NAFTA (like CUSFTA before it) forms binational panels to assess disputes over each country's CVD and ADD decisions.[83] Unlike the previous system, in which domestic courts provided final review of CVD and ADD decisions, the binational panels ensure that both countries' interpretations of trade law are considered in dispute-settlement cases. However, liberal critics in Canada note that each country retains the right to implement its own contingent trade legislation, and the binational panels can judge only whether a U.S. (or Canadian or Mexican) CVD or ADD decision is made in accordance with U.S. (or Canadian or Mexican) law; that is, the panels cannot assess the fairness of each country's laws.

Another liberal criticism of NAFTA relates to its complex rules of origin. Liberals argue that rules of origin are a common protectionist device in FTAs, and in some respects NAFTA's rules of origin are more restrictive than those of CUSFTA. Examples of highly restrictive rules of origin in NAFTA include the requirements for automobiles, textiles and apparel, and color televisions.[84] A third criticism shows that there are divisions among liberals as there are within the other two perspectives. Whereas orthodox liberals view NAFTA's environmental and labor side agreements as nontrade issues that can be used as an excuse to impose protectionist trade barriers, interventionist liberals believe that these side agreements may be useful to correct imperfections in the market. Despite these criticisms, liberals are generally favorable to NAFTA, arguing that it is on average more trade creating than trade diverting. For example, one recent study concludes that NAFTA has "contributed to an explosion of exports and imports between the U.S. and Mexico, producing gains from trade as specified by the theory of comparative advantage."[85]

The Realist and Historical Structuralist Perspectives   Realists and historical structuralists believe that CUSFTA and NAFTA have significant distributional effects resulting from major asymmetries in power and levels of economic development. Thus, realists reject the liberal view that smaller countries often benefit from FTAs more than larger countries because of economies of scale and increased exports. From the realist perspective, the United States as the larger partner expected its benefits from free trade to outweigh those received by Canada and Mexico. For example, Canada sought free trade with the United States to gain more assured access to the U.S. market. In return for granting free trade, the United States expected a number of side payments, including an easing of Canadian regulations on U.S. foreign investment, greater U.S. access to Canadian energy supplies, and an agreement on trade in services. The United States also agreed to free trade with Mexico, but in return Mexico agreed to free trade in agriculture and gave up claims to receive S&D treatment as an LDC in NAFTA.[86] Realists also argue that some NAFTA provisions have a detrimental effect on national sovereignty. For example, NAFTA's Chapter 11 permits investors to resort to binding international arbitration if they believe that a host government is violating NAFTA investment provisions related to national treatment. Whereas liberals view Chapter 11 as an innovative mechanism that permits foreign enterprises to prevent states from discriminating against them, realists view it as "a vehicle for investors to harass governments whose policies they dislike."[87]

In contrast to realists and liberals, historical structuralists focus on transnational capital and class relationships. From their perspective, NAFTA represents a shift of power in favor of the capitalist class and against labor groups. For example, NAFTA enables MNCs to avoid more rigorous labor and environmental standards in Canada and the United States by relocating production in Mexico. As capital leaves the United States and Canada, wages and employment in these countries decline. Some historical structuralists use the terms *core* and *periphery* to designate social position and class rather than geographic location, arguing that NAFTA has relegated many impoverished U.S. and Canadian workers to peripheral status. For example, one study concludes that "the emergence of Mexico as the first-ranked exporter of clothing to the United States as a result of NAFTA has been accompanied by dramatic growth of garment maquiladora employment south of the border and a dramatic decline in garment industry north of the border, especially among manual, direct production workers."[88]

The losses for U.S. and Canadian workers, according to historical structuralists, do not result in comparable gains for Mexican workers. For example, they argue that NAFTA is destroying the livelihoods of Mexican peasants because U.S. corn, which benefits from a range of government subsidies, is being freely exported to Mexico. Historical structuralists thus argue that NAFTA is increasing poverty and inequality between the rich and poor in all three member countries. Some Gramscian theorists discuss the possibility that progressive groups opposing NAFTA could form a counter-hegemonic bloc based on opposition to the domination of corporate capital in North America. This broad-based coalition would consist of labor, environmental, consumer, and women's groups. A counterhegemonic bloc of this nature would seek to replace the current corporate view of liberalization in North America with a more democratic, participatory model.[89]

As is the case with current tensions between the EU and NATO, realists can point to the fact that the 2001 terrorist attacks on the World Trade Center have made it more difficult to separate economic from security issues in NAFTA. Thus, some analysts note that "September 11 added a new dimension to the NAFTA project. If economic borders have been largely dismantled under the banner of free trade, security borders have become more sensitive."[90]

Mercosur

In March 1991 the presidents of Argentina, Brazil, Paraguay, and Uruguay signed the Treaty of Asunción (TOA) with the objective of forming Mercosur, or the Common Market of the South.[91] The TOA set a timetable in three stages, including the formation of an FTA from 1991 to 1994, a CU in 1995, and eventually a common market. This was a surprisingly rapid schedule, and the specificity of commitments were unusual in Latin America, where most previous RTA plans included only vague promises. Mercosur's significance also stemmed from the importance of its two largest members: Brazil and Argentina. In 1999 Mercosur encompassed a population of 213 million, a GDP of almost $1.1 trillion, and an area larger than the continental United States.[92] However, many observers were skeptical that Mercosur would succeed for several reasons. First, efforts to form RTAs in Latin America since the early 1960s had encountered problems because of members' inward-looking development strategies, national security concerns, and unpredictable macroeconomic policies. Second, the relationship between Brazil and Argentina was marked by a 150-year history of suspicion and economic and military rivalry. However, much had changed by the time Mercosur was formed.

At the time the TOA was signed, most Latin American LDCs were changing from import-substitution to export-oriented development strategies, unilaterally reducing their tariffs and NTBs while becoming more active participants in the GATT Uruguay Round. Whereas earlier failed efforts to form RTAs applied an interventionist and inward-looking national model to the regional level, Mercosur's approach placed more emphasis on open regionalism. Furthermore, elected civilian regimes replaced military dictatorships in the Mercosur region during the late 1980s–1990s. Old antagonisms receded and new types of relationships began to develop because political leaders in Brazil and Argentina felt that regional integration would bolster their fledgling democratic governments. The Argentine and Brazilian presidents in the early 1990s also supported integration as a component of their orthodox liberal economic strategies, and a growing number of business and political groups gradually came to depend on integration. The end of the Cold War was an important international change because Latin Americans were concerned that the North would devote little attention to their concerns. Whereas the EC was developing its single-market program and moving toward monetary integration, Mexico was joining with the United States and Canada in NAFTA negotiations. RTAs were beginning to play a more important role in global trade relations, and Argentina and Brazil viewed economic integration as a means of strengthening their position vis-à-vis the world's major trading blocs. Finally, some officials in Brazil's Foreign Ministry and armed forces viewed Mercosur as a means of gaining greater political and economic independence from the United States.[93]

Mercosur integration demonstrated considerable dynamism from 1991 to 1995. When the Mercosur CU was formed in 1995, tariffs on about 90 percent of goods traded among the member states had been eliminated, and 88 percent of dutiable goods were included in the common external tariff. From 1991 to 1995 the share of intraregional trade in the exports of Mercosur countries rose from 8.9 to 20.3 percent, and the share of intraregional trade in the imports of these countries rose from 14.1 to 18.1 percent. Furthermore, increasing numbers of business firms in the Mercosur countries began to organize their production and sales activities on a regional basis. In addition, Chile and Bolivia became associate members by forming FTAs with Mercosur in 1996 and 1997. Finally, Mercosur began to emerge as an important regional actor in the global economy. New initiatives to create an FTAA and an intercontinental FTA between the EU and Mercosur were an indication of the increasing interest of the United States and Europe in Latin America.[94]

However, Mercosur began to encounter growing problems in 1995, when Brazil and then Argentina introduced new import tariffs and NTBs. Intra-Mercosur exports as a share of the group's total exports declined from a 25 percent high in 1998 to only 11 percent in 2002, the lowest share since Mercosur was formed in 1991. Most trade in goods within Mercosur is now duty-free, but Mercosur discipline does not extend to services trade and government purchases, and a number of NTBs and administrative barriers remain. Furthermore, almost none of the deepening of integration associated with a CU has occurred. Mercosur has not agreed on common policies on customs codes, investment subsidies, and competition policy, and most disputes continue to be settled by presidential intervention rather than agreed rules. In some cases, Mercosur countries have not respected treaties they had ratified. For example, both Brazil and Argentina have held trade talks with the Andean countries and Mexico separately from their Mercosur partners, which violates their commitment to the CU. Furthermore, the automotive sector, which accounts for about 25 percent of intra-Mercosur trade, continues to operate according to managed trade in which a Mercosur country can export only as much as it imports from a partner country.[95]

A number of international, regional, and national factors account for the problems confronting Mercosur. First, Mercosur members as LDCs are highly vulnerable to international developments. As discussed in Chapter 7, the Latin American LDCs had the highest debts during the 1980s foreign debt crisis, and indebtedness continues to plague these economies. In 1997, the combined debt of the four Mercosur countries amounted to 29 percent of their $1.13 billion GNP. Mercosur was also affected by the Mexican and East Asian financial crises in the 1990s, which created highly adverse conditions on international financial markets (see Chapters 7 and 11). Financial turbulence during these crises contributed to the loss of important markets for Latin American exports in East Asia and a marked decrease in the prices of primary commodities. In addition, Latin American economies suffered an abrupt downturn following the September 11, 2001 terrorist attacks. Thus, Mercosur countries as LDCs are highly vulnerable to external economic and security changes.[96]

Second, a high degree of asymmetry, with Brazil accounting for about 70 percent of Mercosur's GDP, raises questions about the prospects for deepening integration. Although the Mercosur "integration process has been driven largely by the strategy and needs of Brazil," Brazil (like the United States in NAFTA) has often attached greater importance to its multilateral goals than to its regional goals.[97] This is not surprising because Argentina, Uruguay and Paraguay are far more dependent on the regional market than Brazil. In the late 1990s about 33 percent of Argentina's, 35 percent of Uruguay's, and 40 percent of Paraguay's exports were directed to Brazil.

Although other Mercosur members complain about Brazil's tendency to disregard their concerns, they often can do little to prevent Brazil from acting unilaterally and disregarding their concerns. A third related problem is that Mercosur, unlike NAFTA, does not have a formal dispute-settlement process. Political negotiation is the means of handling all disagreements and conflicts. Brazil has always opposed creating a Mercosur dispute-settlement body, viewing this as a loss of sovereignty.

A fourth obstacle to integration has been the disparity in macroeconomic and monetary policies between the two main Mercosur members, Brazil and Argentina. In 1991 Argentina pegged its peso to the U.S. dollar, a policy that contrasted sharply with Brazil's policy of adjusting the exchange rate to account for inflation. Until 1999 the overvaluation of Brazilian currency, the *real*, had reinforced Argentina's trade surplus with Brazil; but after Brazil devalued its currency in 1999, Argentina's balance of trade with Brazil sharply deteriorated and a number of companies moved operations from Argentina to Brazil. By December 2001, Argentina had accumulated a massive foreign debt and defaulted on its loans because of a wide range of economic problems that were partly related to its policy of pegging the peso to the dollar. Although devaluation of the peso was essential, it threatened to greatly add to Argentina's debt burden, which was denominated in dollars. Argentina finally devalued its currency in January 2002, and this contributed to hopes that it would be able to begin repairing relations with Brazil.[98]

Despite the problems and uncertain prospects of Mercosur, it is the largest Southern RTA measured in GDP terms. Realists view Mercosur as a response to the trend toward regionalization in the global economy, and they point to the fact that Mercosur has contributed to security as well as economic ties. For example, Argentina and Brazil have upgraded their military cooperation, with joint military exercises and annual meetings between their joint chiefs of staff. Some realists also believe that Mercosur members may be willing to "forgo some relative gains in intraregional relations to enhance their bargaining power at the South-North regional level."[99] Liberals have the most positive view of Mercosur and its prospects. They predict that domestic business groups will continue to support Mercosur because of the need to persuade global investors that member states have shifted toward internationalism. Historical structuralists see Mercosur as the result of IMF pressure (via structural adjustment loans) on indebted Latin American states to liberalize their policies. From this perspective, Mercosur "serves the function of more thoroughly incorporating . . . [the members] within the world capitalist system while preserving their subordinate status in the system."[100]

Free Trade Area of the Americas

In June 1990, President George Herbert Bush responded to Latin America's economic problems by announcing a new framework for U.S.–Latin American relations: the *Enterprise for the Americas Initiative (EAI)*. The EAI called for investment promotion and U.S. aid in debt reduction, but the trade provisions (the goal of eliminating trade barriers) were the centerpiece of the EAI. Bush assumed the United States would sign separate FTAs with different regional groups, which would serve as stepping-stones to a larger hemispheric FTA. Although this vision was superseded by NAFTA, which the U.S. came to view as the best route to hemispheric integration, the EAI had an important role in stimulating moves toward hemispheric free trade. In December 1993 U.S. Vice President Al Gore proposed creation of a hemispheric FTA and called for a 1994 summit of the Western Hemisphere states. At the Miami Summit of the Americas in December 1994, the 34 participating states agreed to begin the process of negotiating an FTAA, and "the United States played a key role in orchestrating" this commitment.[101] In March 1998 the trade ministers met in Costa Rica to approve a consensus document on the format of an FTAA; this document formed the basis on which the heads of state at the second hemispheric summit in Santiago, Chile, in April 1998 announced a detailed plan of action to conclude FTAA negotiations no later than 2005. If the FTAA is formed, it will encompass a population of about 730 million, a combined GDP of almost $10 trillion (U.S.), and total exports of more than $1 trillion.[102]

A potential problem is that the Western Hemisphere is not a single "natural" region for an RTA. The United States accounts for 76 percent of the Western hemisphere's total GDP, and it would seem to be the main focal point of trade in the region. However, countries vary greatly in terms of their trade patterns. Whereas more than 80 percent of Canadian and Mexican trade and about 60 percent of Central American and Caribbean trade is with the United States, the southern cone of South America has only about 20 percent of its trade with the United States. For the southern cone, trade agreements with the EU and South American and Asian countries could be as important as concluding an agreement with the United States. Nevertheless, changes in global, regional, and national conditions have contributed to growing interest in an FTAA.

Several factors account for U.S. interest in an FTAA. First is the relative decline of U.S. economic hegemony. After joining CUSFTA and NAFTA, it was natural for the United States to turn to Latin America. Whereas the United States had chronic trade deficits with East Asia and its trade with Europe was stagnant, it had substantial trade surpluses with Latin America. Furthermore, a large share of U.S. exports to Latin America were high value-added goods. U.S. exports to Latin America (excluding Mexico) increased by 52 percent from 1994 to 1999, almost twice as fast as exports to countries outside the Western Hemisphere. Second, the United States views an FTAA as an opportunity to advance a new trade agenda at a time when it is less able to control the multilateral trade agenda and the Doha Round is not going well. Third, the United States is interested in an FTAA for security as well as economic reasons. Issues on the U.S. security agenda for Latin America relate to drugs, terrorism and insurgency, oil and energy, immigration, and the environment. The moves toward an FTAA were also sparked by changes in other countries. Canada had previously been ambivalent about ties with Latin America, but in 1992 it joined the Organization of American States, and in 1993 it joined in forming NAFTA. In Latin America, the shift from import-substitution to export-oriented policies and the consolidation of civilian rule and democracy were additional factors conducive to negotiations for an FTAA. Finally the revival of regionalism on a more open basis than previously in Latin America served as a possible stepping-stone to a broader FTAA.[103]

Despite the interest in an FTAA, a wide diversity of views among countries has made the negotiations protracted and difficult. Only a brief discussion of some of the major disputes is possible here. First, there were disputes over the process of forming an FTAA. The United States wanted to gradually extend NAFTA to include other countries, but some other states led by Brazil argued that an FTAA should be a new initiative negotiated by equal partners. These countries believed that NAFTA focused primarily on issues of interest to the United States, and they were reluctant to comply with the NAFTA requirement to free substantially all trade. The approach that Brazil advocated eventually prevailed, partly because the U.S. Congress refused to grant President Clinton fast-track authority for expanding NAFTA. Second, the United States wanted the negotiations to be conducted by individual countries, but Brazil proposed that the negotiations be held through regional groups such as Mercosur, the Andean Community, and the CACM. Brazil has suspicions about an FTAA and prefers to deepen Mercosur integration before turning to hemispheric integration. The Mercosur members supported Brazil's position to negotiate as a bloc, and the decision was made that each country could choose how it would be represented. Whereas the United States, Canada, and Mexico are representing themselves individually, some others such as the Mercosur members are negotiating as a group.[104] Third, the United States would like the FTAA to be a "WTO-plus" agreement that improves on WTO commitments in services, investment, government procurement, and intellectual property rights. By going beyond the WTO, the United States hopes to provide an impetus to move the MTN agenda forward. However, the Latin Americans have argued that WTO commitments were part of a balanced outcome that should not be altered unless the United States is willing to negotiate the issues of domestic agricultural subsidies and contingent trade measures (ADDs and CVDs). To this point, the United States and Brazil—the co-chairs of the FTAA negotiations—have been unwilling to give way on this issue.

Although the United States is the major market in the hemisphere, it has had difficulty inducing others to accept its views. Of the 34 participants in the negotiations, the United States, Brazil, and Mexico together account for two-thirds of the hemisphere's population and for more than 85 percent of total output. Brazil and Mexico have been the least enthusiastic of the major Latin American states for rapid negotiation of an FTAA, and Brazil has at times been able to gain support from others in conflicts with the United States. However, Brazil's ability to get other Latin Americans to support it has limitations because "its neighbors have become ever more enticed by the idea of improved access to the world's biggest consumer market."[105] The difficulties U.S. presidents encountered in renewing fast-track authority to negotiate trade agreements also slowed the negotiations. The renewal of fast-track authority under George W. Bush's administration removes one obstacle to concluding an FTAA agreement, but other obstacles remain. Partly in response to slow progress in the FTAA talks, the United States has been negotiating bilateral and subregional (e.g., with Central America) FTAs in the region, and it is uncertain whether these agreements will facilitate or impede the broader FTAA negotiations.

In sum, the FTAA talks have made some progress, but there is still "a long distance to traverse between where the negotiations stand now and where they need to be by 2005."[106] From an orthodox liberal perspective, an FTAA can be a second-best option in moving toward freer trade *if* it is more trade creating than trade diverting and preferably goes beyond what the WTO has achieved. As is the case for NAFTA and Mercosur, realists point to the importance of power relationships and expect the United States and to a lesser extent Brazil to achieve much of what they want from an FTAA in the longer term. Historical structuralists are at the opposite pole from orthodox liberals, arguing that an FTAA would perpetuate Latin American dependency with the United States and to a lesser extent Canada. The thousands of protestors at the third Summit of the Americas in Quebec City in April 2001 demonstrate that regional as well as global gatherings are now targets for civil society demonstrations. It is impossible to categorize the Quebec City protestors in terms of a theoretical perspective. Whereas some protestors were protectionists such as U.S. steel workers who wanted limits on Brazilian imports, others viewed the FTAA as a vehicle for MNCs to extend their influence, and still others had environmental concerns. Despite these differences, most protestors had concerns that the proposed FTAA, like the IMF, World Bank, and WTO, would add to pressures for globalization.

EAST ASIA

During the 1980s East Asia emerged as a major center of world production and trade, and its impact on the global economy has grown markedly in recent years. As Table 9.2 shows, East Asia accounted for only 10.8 percent of world trade in 1970, whereas North America accounted for almost twice that amount (20.7 percent) and Western Europe accounted for more than four times that amount (48.2 percent). By 1990, East Asia's share of world trade had almost doubled, reaching 19.4 percent, while the shares of North America and Western Europe declined slightly to 18.1 and 46.8 percent.[107] Despite East Asia's important economic role, it has been a latecomer in the move toward RTAs. East Asia was not involved in the first wave of regional integration among LDCs in the 1960s, and it has been slower than other areas to join in the current wave of regionalism. In 2000, preferential trade arrangements accounted for only 5.6 percent of merchandise imports in Asia as a whole, compared with 64.7 percent for Western Europe, 41.4 percent for North America, 37.2 percent for Africa, and 18.3 percent for Latin America (excluding Mexico).[108] However, since the 1997 financial crisis, some East Asian states such as Singapore and Japan have been actively negotiating bilateral FTAs, and the *Association of Southeast Asian Nations (ASEAN)* has accelerated tariff reductions.

Table 9.2

REGIONAL SHARES OF WORLD TRADE (PERCENT)

	1970	1990
East Asia	10.8	19.4
North America (United States, Canada, Mexico)	20.7	18.1
Western Europe (European Union and European Free Trade Association)	48.2	46.8
Other countries	20.5	15.7

Source: Derived from Soogil Young, "East Asia as a Regional Force for Globalism," in Kym Anderson and Richard Blackhurst, eds., *Regional Integration and the Global Trading System* (New York: Harvester Wheatsheaf, 1993), p.130, Table 6.1.

Although East Asians have been slow to develop formal institutional initiatives to promote regional integration, trade and investment among East Asian countries have demonstrated impressive growth rates. Thus, the East Asian case shows that countries can develop strong regional linkages even without formal institutions.[109] A major reason for the rise in intraregional trade is that dynamic, rapidly growing economies (like those in East Asia in the 1970s–1980s) are likely to trade with one another. Indeed, neighboring provinces of some East Asian countries have developed close trade and investment linkages even though relations among the central governments are not particularly friendly. Another stimulus for trade is the wide diversity of Asian economies in terms of size, per capita income, and natural resources, which provides opportunities for specialization. In addition to being informal and market oriented, East Asian regional linkages are designed to increase the competitiveness of the region's firms in global markets. Thus, the internationalization of the East Asian production process has contributed to the region's ability to market high-quality goods at competitive prices. Whereas Japan has provided capital and high-technology goods, East Asian NIEs have provided goods and services with increasing levels of sophistication, and low-wage countries such as China, Indonesia, and Vietnam have provided labor-intensive assembly operations. (Chapter 11 discusses the Japan-led production system in East Asia.)[110]

Although East Asia is currently showing more interest in developing formal regional trade and financial linkages, East Asian regional relationships are unlikely to become as institutionalized as those of Europe and the Western Hemisphere. One reason for the delay of East Asian economies in establishing RTAs relates to the advantages they see in the WTO: it helps reduce trade barriers such as voluntary export restraints that have restricted the access of East Asian goods to DC markets, it provides S&D treatment for East Asian LDCs (although the NIEs are in the process of "graduating" to more DC status), and it offers smaller East Asian states some protection from the pressures of major regional powers such as Japan and China. A second related obstacle is that persistent hostility and suspicion among East Asian states has limited formal integration, with a number of countries having memories of Japan's military conquest in the 1930s and concerns about dominance by China. Yet another obstacle is the protectionist and interventionist industrial policies in many Asian countries. Finally, the United States continues to have considerable military and economic influence in the region, and it strongly opposes the establishment of an RTA limited to East Asians. Despite these obstacles to the development of formal institutions, the East Asian economies are concerned about the protectionist and exclusionary aspects of the EU and NAFTA and are showing more interest in developing formal regional arrangements.[111]

The sections that follow examine the movement toward trade liberalization in East Asia through ASEAN, the Asia-Pacific Economic Cooperation forum (APEC), and bilateral FTAs.

ASEAN

Indonesia, Malaysia, the Philippines, Singapore, and Thailand agreed to establish ASEAN in 1967, with the stated goals of promoting peace, stability, and economic growth in the region. ASEAN was largely a political organization for many years, with only a few programs to promote economic linkages. It was not until 1977 that the

ASEAN countries signed an Agreement on Preferential Trading Arrangements, which had only limited product coverage and little effect on intra-ASEAN trade. The *ASEAN Free Trade Area (AFTA)* was formed in 1992 by ASEAN's five founding members and Brunei (which had joined ASEAN in 1984). As ASEAN expanded its membership, new countries joined AFTA: Vietnam in 1995, Lao PDR and Myanmar in 1997, and Cambodia in 1999.

AFTA has a Common Effective Preferential Tariff (CEPT) scheme, which was designed to decrease tariffs on manufactured and processed agricultural products to a range of 0–5 percent by 2008. In 1994 the time frame was advanced to 2003; and in 1998 it was advanced again to 2002 as a confidence-building move after the 1997 Asian financial crisis. ASEAN's newer members have a slightly delayed timetable. Under the CEPT scheme, four lists are used to determine the pace and scope of liberalization: an inclusion list, a temporary exclusion list, a sensitive list, and a general exceptions list. The inclusion list consisted of items that were subject to immediate tariff reductions to bring them down to the 0–5 percent range by 2002. The goal is to gradually move items from the other three lists to the inclusion list.[112]

In some respects AFTA has been reasonably successful. ASEAN members have achieved a substantial degree of trade liberalization in some areas; AFTA has broadened its targets to include unprocessed agricultural products in the tariff removal program; an AFTA-plus program has been developed to include preferential liberalization of services and investment, intellectual property cooperation, and the harmonization of product standards; AFTA instituted a goal of eliminating all intra-regional tariffs by 2010; and in October 2003, ASEAN members signed an accord to establish an economic community similar to the EU by 2020. Despite these moves, however, the share of intra-regional trade among AFTA members has not increased significantly since the 1970s for several reasons. First, about 66 percent of the tariff lines within AFTA have the same MFN and CEPT preferential rates, and for many other items the difference between the MFN and CEPT rate is small. Second, many products with strong potential for intra-regional trade (e.g., sugar, rice, and automobiles) are politically sensitive, and AFTA members have delayed their liberalization to a later date.

Third, AFTA members are at very different stages of development ranging from high-income Singapore to upper-middle-income Malaysia, to lower-middle income Thailand, the Philippines, and Indonesia, to the newest members (Lao PDR, Cambodia, Myanmar, and Vietnam), which are low-income. The advantages from market expansion depend on ASEAN's ability to provide S&D treatment and assistance to the low-income members. When Vietnam, Laos, Myanmar, and Cambodia joined ASEAN, they were given more time to adjust to trade liberalization in AFTA as well as assistance to move toward market reform. Nevertheless, the 1997 financial crisis exacerbated ASEAN's problems as a two-tiered organization because the founding members have become less willing and able to offer the newer members S&D treatment and assistance to promote economic reform and development. Finally, "the ASEAN approach towards trade liberalization has always been too cautious and ambivalent and entangled in indigenous, ethnic and particularistic factors." Although ASEAN's emphasis on informal procedures may contribute to solidarity, it results in a lack of political commitment to "formal trade liberalization."[113]

As a small, open economy, Singapore has been frustrated by the slow pace of AFTA and has sought to conclude bilateral FTAs. For example, it is in various stages of negotiating FTAs with Japan, Australia, New Zealand, the European Free Trade Area, the United States, and Mexico; and it is also considering FTA negotiations with Canada, the EU, India, and Chile. ASEAN itself is involved in broader negotiations in efforts to revitalize the free trade process. For example, in November 2002 China and ASEAN signed a framework agreement beginning negotiations for an FTA within 10 years; and ASEAN is considering free trade pacts with Australia and New Zealand, China, Japan, the United States, and India. ASEAN Plus Three meetings (including Japan, China, and South Korea) could also result in broader moves for regional free trade. In sum, a patchwork of trade agreements is developing in East Asia that offers possibilities of greater free trade. However, there is a danger that the confusing array of agreements may contain inconsistent provisions that in effect hinder regional free trade.[114]

APEC

The largest regional initiative involving East Asia is APEC, which was inaugurated at a ministerial meeting in Canberra, Australia, in 1989. As Table 9.3 shows, APEC emphasizes open regionalism, with its 21 members from Asia, Australasia, and North and South America. In view of its broad geographic reach on both sides of the Pacific, one could view APEC as a transregional rather than a regional group. APEC's potential importance stems from the influence of its members: they include the world's three largest national economies (the United States, China, and Japan), and three of the five permanent members of the UN Security Council (China, Russia, and the United States). Economically, the APEC members together account for almost one-half of total world trade. In 1993 APEC established a permanent secretariat in Singapore and began to hold summit meetings of heads of government and state. Currently, almost 300 projects to promote economic and technical cooperation are operating under APEC auspices, and future APEC targets include establishing a free trade and investment area. APEC refers to its members as economies rather than countries.[115]

Despite the promise of APEC, there is a notable lack of consensus among the members as to the group's main objectives. Indeed, the lack of agreement is evident in the term "APEC," which does not even specify whether it is an organization, forum, or

Table 9.3
MEMBERS OF ASIA-PACIFIC ECONOMIC COOPERATION (APEC)

Year of Joining	Member
1989	Australia, Brunei, Canada, Indonesia, Japan, Republic of Korea, Malaysia, New Zealand, Philippines, Singapore, Thailand, United States
1991	China, Hong Kong, Taiwan
1993	Mexico, Papua New Guinea
1994	Chile
1998	Peru, Russia, Vietnam

other entity. APEC has in fact served more as a forum for exchanging ideas than as an organization producing substantive outcomes. Most APEC members value a large open regional or transregional group in the Asia-Pacific, but for different reasons. The United States wanted to secure political-security and economic access to the region and did not want to be excluded from an East Asian trading bloc (East Asia overtook the EC as North America's largest foreign market region in the early 1980s); Japan wanted to limit U.S. unilateralism and prevent the Western Hemisphere from erecting protectionist barriers toward Asia; and China as an emerging power viewed APEC as a useful forum for cooperation with other Asia-Pacific economies. Furthermore, China had not yet been accepted into the GATT/WTO, and APEC seemed to be one route to establish its respectability. Smaller East Asian economies also support APEC because it addresses their concerns regarding access to the large U.S. market and prevents dominance by any of the three largest economies.[116]

When the Australian prime minister proposed that APEC be established, he wanted to model it after the OECD, which disseminates information about members' economic policies and promotes coordination of their policies. Thus, APEC was not originally intended to be a forum for trade negotiations. In 1993, however, trade liberalization became a central agenda item at the APEC summit in Seattle because of pressure from the United States, Canada, Australia, and New Zealand. Most Asian members were less committed to promoting trade liberalization and more interested in emphasizing trade facilitation and economic and technical cooperation. The Asian members' lack of enthusiasm for trade liberalization stemmed partly from concerns that the United States would use APEC to pressure them to open their markets.[117] Despite the ambivalence of most Asian members, the 1994 APEC Summit in Bogor, Indonesia, agreed to the goal of establishing a free and open trade and investment area for DCs by 2010 and for LDCs by 2020. The 1995 APEC Summit in Osaka, Japan, adopted an "action agenda" to begin implementing this free trade commitment by January 1997.

In view of the different objectives of APEC members, the agreement to establish free trade is ambiguous in several respects. For example, the agreement does not clearly specify whether trade liberalization in services and agriculture is to be included and whether some APEC members are to be categorized as DCs or LDCs. China is reluctant to commit to free trade along with more developed economies by 2010, but most APEC members would not classify the industrial parts of China along with the LDCs. The 1994 Bogor Summit also did not specify how a free and open investment area was to be established, and it left the details for discussion at future meetings. APEC in this respect "is very Asian with its broad consensus style, and very unlike North American and European regional pacts with their detailed liberalization schedules."[118] Because the Asian members dislike the WTO method of bargaining negotiations, liberalization in APEC is to occur instead through concerted unilateral action. Under this process, each APEC economy independently develops its own plans for liberalization to attain free trade by the specified date. Thus, liberalization depends on enlightened self-interest and peer pressure rather than negotiations. The trade liberalization is also to occur through open regionalism, in which concessions to APEC members would be granted to *all* WTO members on an unconditional MFN basis. Since APEC proposes to liberalize trade on a nondiscriminatory basis, it is not an RTA in terms of the WTO.[119]

Implementing free trade under APEC is proving to be difficult. Most APEC members other than Canada, Australia, Hong Kong, New Zealand, Singapore, and the United States have tariffs averaging above 10 percent, with levels of more than 30 percent for some products, and these members are unlikely to significantly lower their tariffs on a unilateral basis. To this point, "the process of voluntary, unilateral trade liberalization" has "left the most politically sensitive and hence heavily protected sectors largely untouched."[120] Furthermore, U.S. policies could pose obstacles to APEC free trade plans for several reasons. First, the United States would be unwilling to extend its APEC concessions to Europe and other non-APEC areas on a nonreciprocal basis. Second, U.S. producer groups would strongly oppose free trade with countries such as Japan, South Korea, and China without substantial domestic opening of their economies. In the U.S. view, domestic policies and societal factors rather than tariffs are the main source of its trade problems with these countries. Phasing out tariffs in APEC will not result in reciprocal concessions unless domestic policy issues are also addressed.[121]

The size and diversity of the APEC membership could also interfere with plans for free trade. In December 1990, Malaysian Prime Minister Mahathir Mohamad criticized the size and regional scope of APEC, and proposed that an East Asian economic grouping be formed for this purpose. The Malaysian proposal was aimed not only at economic liberalism but also at countering the political power of the United States and Europe. In response to harsh criticism from the United States, an informal East Asian Economic Caucus was formed instead *within* APEC. If APEC's free trade objectives do not materialize, it is possible that the idea of a regional FTA limited to East Asian countries could re-emerge in the future.[122]

The IPE Perspectives and East Asian Regionalism

Liberal economists are often highly supportive of APEC as an example of open regionalism that is likely to serve as a stepping-stone to global trade liberalization. APEC includes countries in a huge area spanning more than one continent, and liberals sometimes compare it favorably with the EU, which is more discriminatory. Liberals realize there are obstacles to promoting free trade in a forum as diverse as APEC, but they are hopeful that this brand of open regionalism will succeed in the long term. Thus, a prominent liberal who was chair of APEC's eminent persons' group from 1992 to 1995 has argued that APEC could become "the first big international institutional success of the post–Cold War era."[123]

Realists view APEC in political as well as economic terms as an effort by non-Asian countries such as Australia and the United States to prevent the formation of a regional trading bloc limited to Asians (as proposed by Malaysia's prime minister). From this perspective, the United States uses APEC "as a forum to maintain U.S. power, [and] embrace the exclusionary East Asian identity within an inclusionary "Asia-Pacific" identity."[124] Realists also argue that ASEAN emphasizes security as much as trade and finance. This explains the acceptance of Vietnam, Cambodia, Lao PDR, and Myanmar in ASEAN, which have a minor economic role but can pose a major risk to security in the region.[125] Realists place less emphasis than liberals on the institutional aspects of Asian regionalism and point to the central role of Japan in establishing its own brand of regionalism. Instead of establishing an RTA, "Japan is using its

Asian production alliance in part as a platform from which to continuing supplying high-technology products to Western markets."[126] Thus, realists point to the competitive challenge that Japan, China, and East Asian NIEs pose to the West.

Historical structuralists are concerned that APEC could eventually lead to "the erosion of social programs, downward harmonization of environmental, labour and health standards, and a permanent shift of political and economic power to large corporations."[127] Because some East Asian states provide minimal protection for the environment, labor, and human rights, the freeing of trade and foreign investment in APEC could force other states to sacrifice their own standards to remain competitive. As in the case of NAFTA, APEC members would be forced into a "competitive race to the bottom."[128] In line with this view, civil society demonstrators at the 1997 APEC summit in Vancouver protested what they viewed as the abuse of human rights in APEC countries and the globalizing effects of the APEC agenda. Historical structuralists also focus on the noninstitutional aspects of East Asian regionalism. In their view, Japan and its MNCs have acted as the core economic power in the region, supplying high-technology products and keeping most of the R&D at home. East Asian NIEs have acted as a semiperiphery supplying high- to medium-technology inputs, and Southeast Asian countries and China have performed the role of a periphery, supplying medium- to low-technology inputs. Thus, Japanese capital is playing a dominant role in bringing about a large degree of informal integration in East Asia.[129]

CONCLUSION

During the postwar period there were two major waves of regionalism, the first in the 1950s–1960s and the second since the mid–1980s. Globalization has clearly acted as a stimulus to the second phase of regionalism, and it is likely to be more enduring than the first wave. Regional institutions are developing to deal with problems of global interdependence that states are unable to deal with individually. States are also joining in regional groups to improve their competitiveness as global competition increases. Furthermore, internationalist firms that have expanded their foreign investment and trade have pressured for free market exchange at both the regional and global levels. It is important to note, however, that not all regionalism is outward looking. For example, the United States, Japan, and others are actively involved in negotiating a series of bilateral and subregional FTAs. RTAs also cannot substitute in some respects for global trade negotiations. For example, the United States has indicated that it cannot offer major concessions on agricultural export subsidies and antidumping actions at the FTAA talks until it reaches agreement on these issues with its main competitors (the EU and Japan) in WTO negotiations.

The revival of regionalism stems not only from globalization pressures but also from changes in North-North and North-South relations. Most significantly, the United States changed from a position of refusing to participate in RTAs to openly supporting them during the 1980s. One factor explaining the change in U.S. policy was the decline in its trade hegemony. As long as the United States was undisputed hegemon in the global trade regime, it was firmly committed to multilateral trade liberalization. However, the United States was less willing and able to provide the public goods to maintain an open multilateral trade regime as its economic leverage declined, and it sought to regain its economic influence through joining RTAs. The LDCs also turned to regionalism in the 1980s, but they generally supported a more open regionalism than they had during the 1960s. The 1980s foreign debt crisis had induced LDCs to adopt orthodox liberal reforms, reflected in their new approach to regionalism. For example, Mexico unilaterally liberalized its trade policies and then joined GATT and NAFTA.

The three IPE perspectives differ in their approach to RTAs. Liberals believe that multilateralism is the best route to trade liberalization, but they generally support open RTAs as a second-best option. Until recently, most liberals have had a positive view of the current phase of regionalism, assuming that it is serving as a stepping-stone rather than an obstacle to multilateral free trade. However, liberals are concerned that the recent propensity to form bilateral FTAs is creating a patchwork of agreements with inconsistent provisions. Liberals are also critical of some Southern RTAs such as Mercosur that are encountering problems in promoting trade liberalization. Liberals assume that all member states benefit from open RTAs, and they often argue that smaller states gain more benefits than larger states in terms of market shares and economies of scale.

Realists believe that the underlying power relationships between states are evident in RTAs and that the more powerful states gain more from RTAs than the less powerful. Although RTAs give smaller members access to larger members' markets, the larger members demand side payments in return. For example, in CUSFTA, the United States gained concessions from Canada in energy sharing, foreign investment, and trade in services; and in NAFTA, Mexico gave up any claim to S&D treatment that LDCs often receive in international trade agreements. Brazil similarly has expected side payments from the smaller members of Mercosur. Realists also point to the interaction between security and economics in RTAs and note that "security has played a formative role as a catalyst in the EU, ASEAN, and MERCOSUR for regional market integration."[130] Historical structuralists have a far more negative view than liberals of RTAs such as NAFTA. In the historical structuralist view, transnational capital is the main beneficiary of such agreements, and the working class and poorest people in member states are the main losers. Because RTAs permit MNCs to locate production facilities in states with the lowest wages and environmental standards, they have a negative effect on labor, environmental, health and safety, public service, and consumer protection standards.

Chapters 8 and 9 have focused mainly on international trade issues. Trade and investment are closely related, and their relationship has intensified in recent years. Indeed, a former WTO director general has stated that "businesses now trade to invest and invest to trade—to the point where both activities are increasingly part of a single strategy to deliver products across borders."[131] Although international trade has been increasing dramatically, foreign direct investment of MNCs has been increasing at a faster rate. It is to the issue of MNCs that this book now turns.

NOTES

1. Robert E. Hudec and James D. Southwick, "Regionalism and WTO Rules: Problems in the Fine Art of Discriminating Fairly," in Miguel Rodriguez Mendoza, Patrick Low, and

Barbara Kotschwar, eds., *Trade Rules in the Making: Challenges in Regional and Multilateral Negotiations* (Washington, DC: Brookings Institution, 1999), p.47.

2. World Trade Organization Secretariat, *World Trade Report 2003* (Geneva: WTO), p.46.
3. Gerald K. Helleiner, "Considering U.S.–Mexico Free Trade," in Ricardo Grinspun and Maxwell A. Cameron, eds., *The Political Economy of North American Free Trade* (Montreal: McGill-Queen's University Press, 1993), p.50.
4. Helleiner, "Considering U.S.-Mexico Free Trade," pp.50–51.
5. Vincent A. Mahler, "The Lomé Convention: Assessing a North-South Institutional Relationship," *Review of International Political Economy* 1–2 (Summer 1994), p.246.
6. Andrew Hurrell, "Explaining the Resurgence of Regionalism in World Politics," *Review of International Studies* 21 (1995), p.333. For the difficulty in defining a region, see Bruce M. Russett, *International Regions and the International System: A Study in Political Ecology* (Chicago: Rand McNally, 1967).
7. WTO Secretariat, *World Trade Report 2003*, p.51.
8. Mancur Olson, *The Logic of Collective Action: Public Goods and the Theory of Groups* (Cambridge: Harvard University Press, 1965).
9. Hurrell, "Explaining the Resurgence of Regionalism in World Politics," pp.345–347; Andrew Wyatt-Walter, "Regionalism, Globalization, and World Economic Order," in Louise Fawcett and Andrew Hurrell, eds., *Regionalism in World Politics: Regional Organization and International Order* (Oxford: Oxford University Press, 1995), p.77.
10. For the early attempts to establish RTAs, see Fritz Machlup, *A History of Thought on Economic Integration* (New York: Columbia University Press, 1977), pp.105–115.
11. Michael Kaser, *Comecon: Integration Problems of the Planned Economies* (London: Oxford University Press, 1965).
12. The 1957 agreement was in fact called the European Economic Community, but the name was later changed to European Community. The latter term is used in this book. Britain was the leading force behind the EFTA, which also included Austria, Denmark, Norway, Portugal, Sweden, and Switzerland.
13. Lia Valls Pereira, "Toward the Common Market of the South: Mercosur's Origins, Evolution, and Challenges," in Riordan Roett, ed., *Mercosur: Regional Integration, World Markets* (Boulder: Lynne Rienner, 1999), p.8.
14. Jagdish Bhagwati, "Regionalism and Multilateralism: An Overview," in Jaime de Melo and Arvind Panagariya, eds., *New Dimensions in Regional Integration* (Cambridge: Cambridge University Press, 1993), pp.28–29.
15. Bhagwati, "Regionalism and Multilateralism: An Overview," pp.29–31; WTO Secretariat, *World Trade Report 2003*, p.46.
16. Kenneth N. Waltz, *Theory of International Politics* (Reading: Addison-Wesley, 1979), p.70.
17. In 1960, the OEEC was converted into the OECD, which also includes non-Europeans as members. On the U.S. role in the formation of the OEEC, see Philip E. Jacob, Alexine L. Atherton, and Arthur M. Wallenstein, *The Dynamics of International Organization* rev. ed. (Homewood: Dorsey Press, 1972), pp.337–347.
18. See Joanne Gowa, "Bipolarity, Multipolarity, and Free Trade," *American Political Science Review* 83–4 (December 1989), pp.1245–1256; Lawrence Krause, "Trade Policy in the 1990s I: Good-bye Bipolarity, Hello Regions," *The World Today* 46–5 (May 1990), pp.83–86.
19. Hurrell, "Explaining the Resurgence of Regionalism in World Politics," pp.341–342.
20. Mark A. Pollack, "International Relations Theory and European Integration," *Journal of Common Market Studies* 39–2 (June 2001), pp.222–223; John J. Mearsheimer, "Back to the Future: Instability in Europe After the Cold War," *International Security* 15–1 (1990), pp.47–48.

21. For one view of GATT's problems in the 1980s–1990s, see Clyde V. Prestowitz, Jr., Alan Tonelson, and Robert W. Jerome, "The Last Gasp of GATTism," *Harvard Business Review* 69-2 (March–April 1991), pp.130–138.

22. Bernard M. Hoekman and Michel M. Kostecki, *The Political Economy of the World Trading System: The WTO and Beyond* (Oxford: Oxford University Press, 2nd ed., 2001), pp.347–352.

23. Marc L. Busch and Helen V. Milner, "The Future of the International Trading System: International Firms, Regionalism, and Domestic Politics," in Richard Stubbs and Geoffrey R. D. Underhill, eds., *Political Economy and the Changing Global Order* (Toronto: McClelland & Stewart, 1994), p.270.

24. Hudec and Southwick, "Regionalism and WTO Rules," pp.47–48.

25. WTO Secretariat, *World Trade Report 2003*, p.52.

26. Duncan Cameron, "Introduction," in Duncan Cameron and Mel Watkins, eds., *Canada Under Free Trade* (Toronto: Lorimer, 1993), p.xxi.

27. Quoted in Dean Acheson, *Present at the Creation: My Years in the State Department* (New York: Norton, 1969), p.30.

28. General Agreement on Tariffs and Trade, *Text of the General Agreement* (Geneva: GATT, July, 1986), Article 24.

29. See R. G. Lipsey and Kelvin Lancaster, "The General Theory of Second Best," *The Review of Economic Studies* 24-1 (1956–1957), pp.11–32; and J. E. Meade, *Trade and Welfare* (London: Oxford University Press, 1955).

30. Jacob Viner coined the terms *trade creation* and *trade diversion* after GATT Article 24 was written. However, these terms clearly summarize the intent of Article 24. See Jacob Viner, *The Customs Union Issue* (New York: Carnegie Endowment for International Peace, 1950), pp.41–55.

31. Hoekman and Kostecki, *The Political Economy of the World Trading System*, pp.350–363.

32. Robert Z. Lawrence, *Regionalism, Multilateralism, and Deeper Integration* (Washington, DC: Brookings Institution, 1996), pp.41–42.

33. Gardner Patterson, *Discrimination in International Trade, The Policy Issues: 1945–1965* (Princeton: Princeton University Press, 1966), pp.146–147. See also C. Michael Aho, "More Bilateral Trade Agreements Would Be a Blunder: What the New President Should Do," *Cornell International Law Journal* 22-1 (Winter 1989), p.25.

34. Richard E. Baldwin, "A Domino Theory of Regionalism," in Richard Baldwin, Pertti Haaparanta, and Jaakko Kiander, eds., *Expanding Membership of the European Union* (Cambridge: Cambridge University Press, 1995), p.45.

35. Bhagwati, "Regionalism and Multilateralism: An Overview," pp.25–26; World Trade Organization Secretariat, *Regionalism and the World Trading System* (Geneva: WTO, advance copy, April 1995), p.7.

36. Robert E. Hudec, *The GATT Legal System and World Trade Diplomacy* (New York: Praeger, 1975), pp.195–196; J. Michael Finger, "GATT's Influence on Regional Arrangements," in Melo and Panagariya, eds., *New Dimensions in Regional Integration*, pp.136–37.

37. WTO Secretariat, *Regionalism and the World Trading System*, pp.12–13.

38. Robert E. Hudec, "Discussion," in Melo and Panagariya, eds., *New Dimensions in Regional Integration*, p.152.

39. Gary Clyde Hufbauer and Jeffrey J. Schott, *NAFTA: An Assessment*, rev. ed. (Washington, DC: Institute for International Economics, 1993), p.112.

40. The only two active agreements are the Caribbean Community and Common Market (CARICOM) and the Czech and Slovak Republics Customs Union.

41. WTO Secretariat, *Regionalism and the World Trading System*, pp.16–17; Jeffrey J. Schott, "More Free Trade Areas?" in Jeffrey J. Schott, ed., *Free Trade Areas and U.S. Trade Policy* (Washington, DC: Institute for International Economics, 1989), pp.24–25.

42. "Understanding on the Interpretation of Article XXIV of GATT 1994," and GATS Article V, in WTO, *The Results of the Uruguay Round of Multilateral Trade Negotiations—The Legal Texts* (Geneva: WTO, 1994), pp.31–34 and 331–332.

43. Hudec and Southwick, "Regionalism and WTO Rules," pp.49–74; Sam Laird, "Regional Trade Agreements: Dangerous Liaisons?," *World Economy* 22–9 (1999), pp.1192–1197.

44. Hudec, *The GATT Legal System and World Trade Diplomacy*, pp.205–206; John H. Jackson, *World Trade and the Law of GATT* (Indianapolis: Bobbs-Merrill, 1969), pp.590–591. The Havana Charter had a special article for RTAs among LDCs, which was not incorporated into GATT.

45. Olivier Long, *Law and Its Limitations in the GATT Multilateral Trade System* (Dordrecht: Nijhoff, 1985), p.101.

46. Laird, "Regional Trade Agreements," p.1196; World Trade Organization Secretariat, *Regionalism and the World Trading System*, pp.18–19.

47. On these regional schemes, see Bonapas Francis Onguglo, "Developing Countries and Trade Preferences," in Rodriguez Mendoza, Low, and Kotschwar, eds., *Trade Rules in the Making*, pp.109–133; and Jon D. Haveman and Howard J. Shatz, "Developed Country Trade Barriers and the Least Developed Countries," United Nations University discussion paper no. 2003/46, June 1003, pp.1–9.

48. Martin Holland, *The European Union and the Third World* (London: Palgrave, 2002), pp.25–32; Enzo R. Grilli, *The European Community and the Developing Countries* (Cambridge: Cambridge University Press, 1993), pp.7–8.

49. On STABEX see John Ravenhill, *Collective Clientilism: The Lomé Conventions and North-South Relations* (New York: Columbia University Press, 1985), ch. 3.

50. Matthew McQueen, "ACP-EU Trade Cooperation after 2000: An Assessment of Reciprocal Trade Preferences," *Journal of Modern African Studies* 36–4 (1998), p.669; Richard Gibb, "Post-Lomé: The European Union and the South," *Third World Quarterly* 21–3 (2000), pp.457–467.

51. Onguglo, "Developing Countries and Trade Preferences," p.119.

52. Francis A. S. T. Matambalya and Susanna Wolf, "The Cotonou Agreement and the Challenges of Making the New EU-ACP Trade Regime WTO Compatible," *Journal of World Trade* 35–1 (2001), pp.123–144; Gibb, "Post-Lomé," pp.465–478; Holland, *The European Union and the Third World*, pp.196–219.

53. WTO Secretariat, *Regionalism and the World Trading System*, pp.27–29; André Sapir, "EC Regionalism at the Turn of the Millennium: Toward a New Paradigm?," *World Economy* 23–9 (September 2000), p.1135; Thomas C. Fischer, *The United States, the European Union, and the "Globalization" of World Trade* (Westport: Quorum Books, 2000), p.75.

54. Stephen George and Ian Bache, *Politics in the European Union* (Oxford: Oxford University Press, 2001), pp.87–104; Andrew Moravcsik, "Negotiating the Single European Act," in Robert O. Keohane and Stanley Hoffmann, eds., *The New European Community: Decisionmaking and Institutional Change* (Boulder: Westview Press, 1991), p.41.

55. Stephen George, "The European Union, 1992 and the Fear of 'Fortress Europe,' " in Andrew Gamble and Anthony Payne, eds., *Regionalism and World Order* (New York: St. Martin's Press, 1996), pp.21–54.

56. Fischer, *The United States, the European Union, and the "Globalization" of World Trade*, p.97.

57. Stuart Croft, "Guaranteeing Europe's Security? Enlarging NATO Again," *International Affairs* 78–1 (January 2002), p. 101. On the EU and security policy see Robert E. Hunter, *The European Security and Defense Policy: NATO's Companion or Competitor?* (Santa Monica: RAND, 2002); David M. Wood and Birol A. Yeşilada, *The Emerging European Union* (New York: Longman, 3rd ed., 2004), ch. 12.

58. Michael H. Abbey and Nicholas Bromfield, "A Practitioner's Guide to the Maastricht Treaty," *Michigan Journal of International Law* 15–4 (Summer 1994), pp.1329–1357; Fischer, *The United States, the European Union, and the "Globalization" of World Trade,* pp.94–116.

59. Fischer, *The United States, the European Union, and the "Globalization" of World Trade,* p.136.

60. Grilli, *The European Community and the Developing Countries,* pp.296–316.

61. The 10 countries are Poland, Hungary, the Czech Republic, Slovakia, Bulgaria, Romania, Estonia, Latvia, Lithuania, and Slovenia.

62. Erik Faucompret and Jozef Konings, "The Integration of Central and Eastern Europe in the European Union," *Journal of World Trade* 33–6 (December 1999), pp.121–127; Pier Carlo Padoan, "The Changing European Political Economy," in Stubbs and Underhill, eds., *Political Economy and the Changing Global Order,* pp.340–342.

63. Quoted in "Arguments for Enlargement," *The Economist,* August 3, 1996, p.41.

64. EC Economic and Social Council document, quoted in Wood and Yeşilada, *The Emerging European Union,* p.118.

65. Fischer, *The United States, the European Union, and the "Globalization" of World Trade,* pp.136–142; Wood and Yeşilada, *The Emerging European Union,* pp.117–122.

66. WTO, *World Trade Report 2003,* pp.16–17.

67. Susan Senior Nello, "Preparing for Enlargement in the European Union: The Tensions between Economic and Political Integration," *International Political Science Review* 23–3 (July 2002), pp.291–317; Fritz Breuss, "Benefits and Dangers of EU Enlargement," *Empirica* 29–3 (2002), pp.245–279; Howard J. Wiarda, "The Politics of Enlargement: NATO, the EU, and the New U.S.-European Relationship," *World Affairs* 164–4 (Spring 2002), pp.178–197.

68. J. J. Servan-Schreiber, *The American Challenge,* translated from the French by Ronald Steel (New York: Atheneum, 1979). The book was first published in 1967.

69. L. Alan Winters, "The European Community: A Case of Successful Integration?" in Melo and Panagariya, eds., *New Dimensions in Regional Integration,* p.208.

70. J. M. C. Rollo, "The EC, European Integration and the World Trading System," in Vincent Cable and David Henderson, eds., *Trade Blocs? The Future of Regional Integration* (London: Royal Institute of International Affairs, 1994), pp.57–58; WTO, *World Trade Report 2003,* p.16.

71. Stephen R. Sleigh, "The Social Dimensions of Economic Integration," in Jo Marie Griesgraber and Bernhard G. Gunter, eds., *World Trade: Toward Fair and Free Trade in the Twenty-first Century* (London: Pluto Press, 1997), pp.40–44.

72. Ralph I. Onwuka, "Beyond Lomé III: Prospects for Symmetrical EurAfrican Relations," in Ralph I. Onwuka and Timothy M. Shaw, eds., *Africa in World Politics: Into the 1990s* (London: Macmillan, 1989), pp.83–84; Mahler, "The Lomé Convention," pp.244–248.

73. John Agnew, "How Many Europes? The European Union, Eastward Enlargement and Uneven Development," *European Urban and Regional Studies* 8–1 (2001), p.35.

74. Stephan Haggard, "The Political Economy of Regionalism in the Western Hemisphere," in Carol Wise, ed., *The Post-NAFTA Political Economy: Mexico and the Western Hemisphere* (University Park: Pennsylvania State University Press, 1998), pp.303–305.

75. J. L. Granatstein, "Free Trade Between Canada and the United States," in Dennis Stairs and Gilbert R. Winham, eds., *The Politics of Canada's Economic Relationship with the United States,* Royal Commission on the Economic Union and Development Prospect for Canada, (Toronto: University of Toronto Press, 1985) vol. 29, p.11.

76. "U.S. Trade Act of 1974, as amended (Public Law 93-618)," Title VI, section 612, in *Legislation on Foreign Relations Through 1989* (Washington, DC: U.S. Government Printing Office, 1990), p.456.

77. On the CUSFTA negotiations see G. Bruce Doern and Brian W. Tomlin, *Faith and Fear: The Free Trade Story* (Toronto: Stoddart, 1991); and Michael Hart with Bill Dymond and Colin Robertson, *Decision at Midnight: Inside the Canada-US Free-Trade Negotiations* (Vancouver: University of British Columbia Press, 1994).

78. Lawrence, *Regionalism, Multilateralism, and Deeper Integration,* pp.67–68; Helleiner, "Considering U.S.-Mexico Free Trade," pp.47–48.

79. John Whalley, "Regional Trade Arrangements in North America: CUSTA and NAFTA," in Melo and Panagariya, eds., *New Dimensions in Regional Integration,* pp.352–353.

80. Theodore H. Cohn, "The Intersection of Domestic and Foreign Policy in the NAFTA Agricultural Negotiations," *Canadian-American Public Policy* no. 14 (Orono: University of Maine, September 1993).

81. Bernard Hoekman and Pierre Sauvé, "Liberalizing Trade in Services," *World Bank Discussion Papers* no. 243 (Washington: World Bank, 1994).

82. Rodney de C. Grey, *Trade Policy in the 1980s: An Agenda for Canadian-U.S. Relations* (Montreal: C.D. Howe Institute, 1981), pp.56–57.

83. Some NAFTA dispute-settlement panels are trinational, but dispute settlement panels for CVDs and ADDs are binational. If two countries complain about a third country's ADDs or CVDs, two binational panels are formed. See Jon R. Johnson, *The North American Free Trade Agreement: A Comprehensive Guide* (Aurora: Canada Law Book, 1994), p.522.

84. Hudec and Southwick, "Regionalism and WTO Rules," p.56.

85. Willem Thorbecke and Christian Eigen-Zucchi, "Did NAFTA Cause a 'Giant Sucking Sound'?," *Journal of Labor Research* 23–4 (Fall 2002), p.647.

86. Helleiner, "Considering U.S.-Mexico Free Trade," pp.50–51.

87. Johnson, *The North American Free Trade Agreement,* p.512; Mark MacKinnon, "NAFTA Members to Talk Reform," *Toronto Globe and Mail,* April 10, 2001, p.B1.

88. David Spener and Randy Capps, "North American Free Trade and Changes in the Nativity of the Garment Industry Workforce in the United States," *International Journal of Urban and Regional Research* 25–2 (June 2001), p.320. See also Robert W. Cox, *Production, Power, and World Order: Social Forces in the Making of History* (New York: Columbia University Press, 1987), p.345; Ricardo Grinspun and Robert Kreklewich, "Consolidating Neoliberal Reforms: 'Free Trade' as a Conditioning Framework," *Studies in Political Economy* 43 (Spring 1994), p.45.

89. Mark E. Rupert, "(Re) Politicizing the Global Economy: Liberal Common Sense and Ideological Struggle in the US NAFTA Debate," *Review of International Political Economy* 2–4 (Autumn 1995), pp.679–681; Herman E. Daly, "Free Trade: The Perils of Deregulation," in Jerry Mander and Edward Goldsmith, eds., *The Case Against the Global Economy: For a Turn Toward the Local* (San Francisco: Sierra Club, 1996), p.234.

90. Gary Clyde Hufbauer and Gustavo Vega-Cánovas, "Whither NAFTA: A Common Frontier?," in Peter Andreas and Thomas J. Biersteker, *The Rebordering of North America: Integration and Exclusion in a New Security Context* (New York: Routledge, 2003), p.129.

91. Mercosur is the acronym for Mercado Común del Sur (Spanish) or Mercado Común del Sul (Portuguese).

92. José Manuel Salazar-Xirinachs, Theresa Wetter, Karsten Steinfatt, and Danila Ivascanu, "Customs Unions," in José Manuel Salazar-Xirinachs and Maryse Robert, eds., *Toward Free Trade in the Americas* (Washington, D.C.: Brookings Institution, 2001), p.76.

93. Jeffrey Cason, "On the Road to Southern Cone Economic Integration," *Journal of Interamerican Studies and World Affairs* 42–1 (2000), pp.23–28; Heinz G. Preusse, "Mercosur—Another Failed Move Towards Regional Integration?," *World Economy* 24–7 (July 2001), pp.911–914; Riordan Roett, "Introduction," in Riordan Roett, ed., *Mercosur: Regional Integration, World Markets* (Boulder: Lynne Rienner, 1999), pp.1–5.

94. Preusse, "Mercosur—Another Failed Move Towards Regional Integration?," pp.915–916.

95. Preusse, "Mercosur—Another Failed Move Towards Regional Integration?," pp.915–921; Mario E. Carranza, "Can Mercosur Survive? Domestic and International Constraints on Mercosur," *Latin American Politics and Society* 45–2 (Summer 2003), p.94.

96. Rafael A. Lecuona, "Economic Integration: NAFTA and Mercosur, a Comparative Analysis," *International Journal of World Peace* 16–4 (December 1999), pp.41–42; Carranza, "Can Mercosur Survive?," p.95.

97. Cason, "On the Road to Southern Cone Economic Integration," p.24.

98. Lia Valls Pereira, "Toward the Common Market of the South," pp.7–13; Cason, "On the Road to Southern Cone Economic Integration," pp.24–29; Nicola Phillips, "Regionalist Governance in the New Political Economy of Development: 'Relaunching' the Mercosur," *Third World Quarterly* 22–4 (August 2001), pp.565–569; Michael Mecham, "Mercosur: A Failing Development Project?," *International Affairs* 79–2 (March 2003), pp.377–379.

99. Carranza, "Can Mercosur Survive?," p.74.

100. Donald G. Richards, "Dependent Development and Regional Integration: A Critical Examination of the Southern Cone Common Market," *Latin American Perspectives* 24–6 (November 1997), p.133.

101. Haggard, "The Political Economy of Regionalism in the Western Hemisphere," p.303.

102. Gary Clyde Hufbauer and Jeffrey J. Schott, with Diana Clark, *Western Hemisphere Economic Integration* (Washington, D.C.: Institute for International Economics, 1994), p.1; Jeffrey J. Schott and Gary C. Hufbauer, "Whither the Free Trade Area of the Americas?," *World Economy* 22–6 (August 1999), pp.767–769; Paulo S. Wrobel, "A Free Trade Area of the Americas in 2005?," *International Affairs* 74–3 (July 1998), pp.548–549.

103. Nicola Phillips, "Hemispheric Integration and Subregionalism in the Americas," *International Affairs* 79–2 (March 2003), pp.330–336; Schott and Hufbauer, "Whither the Free Trade Area of the Americas?," pp.774–776; Wrobel, "A Free Trade Area of the Americas in 2005?," pp.550–554.

104. Haggard, "The Political Economy of Regionalism in the Western Hemisphere," pp.310–314 and 334–335; Wrobel, "A Free Trade Area of the Americas in 2005?," pp.555–556.

105. "Trade in the Americas," *The Economist,* 21 April 2001, p.19.

106. José Manuel Salazar-Xirinachs, "The FTAA Process: From Miami 1994 to Quebec 2001," in Salazar-Xirinachs and Robert, eds., *Toward Free Trade in the Americas,* p.300.

107. Soogil Young, "East Asia as a Regional Force for Globalism," in Anderson and Blackhurst, eds., *Regional Integration and the Global Trading System,* pp.127–128.

108. WTO, *World Trade Report 2003,* p.48.

109. Miles Kahler, *International Institutions and the Political Economy of Integration* (Washington, DC: Brookings Institution, 1995), pp.107–108.

110. Lawrence, *Regionalism, Multilateralism, and Deeper Integration,* pp.80–83.

111. Lawrence, *Regionalism, Multilateralism, and Deeper Integration,* pp.83–86.

112. Emiko Fukase and Will Martin, "Free Trade Area Membership as a Stepping Stone to Development: The Case of ASEAN," *World Bank Discussion Paper* no. 421 (Washington, DC: World Bank, 2001), pp.10–11; WTO, *World Trade Report 2003,* p.54.

113. Linda Low, "Multilateralism, Regionalism, Bilateral and Crossregional Free Trade Arrangements: All Paved with Good Intentions for ASEAN?," *Asian Economic Journal* 17–1

(2003), p.67; Herman Joseph S. Kraft, "ASEAN and Intra-ASEAN Relations: Weathering the Storm?," *Pacific Review* 13–3 (2000), pp.453–472; Joshua Kurlantzick, "Is East Asia Integrating?," *Washington Quarterly* 24–4 (Autumn 2001), pp.19–28; "ASEAN: A Holiday in Bali," *The Economist,* October 11, 2003, p.46.

114. Low, "Multilateralism, Regionalism, Bilateral and Crossregional Free Trade Arrangements," pp.74–84; WTO, *World Trade Report 2003,* pp.51–52.

115. John Ravenhill, "APEC Adrift: Implications for Economic Regionalism in Asia and the Pacific," *Pacific Review* 13–2 (2000), p.320.

116. Johnny Chi-Chen Chiang, "Conceptualizing the APEC Way: International Cooperation in a Non-Insitutionalized Regime," *Issues & Studies* 36–6 (November/December 2000), pp.183–187; Fred Bergsten, "The Case for APEC," *The Economist,* 6 January 1996, p.62; Shuji Miyazaki, "APEC: The First Seven Years and the Road to Manila," *World Economic Affairs* 1–1 (Summer 1996), p.20.

117. Ravenhill, "APEC Adrift," pp.321–323.

118. Gary Hufbauer and Jeffrey J. Schott, "Toward Free Trade and Investment in the Asia-Pacific," in Brad Roberts, ed., *New Forces in the World Economy* (Cambridge: MIT Press, 1996), pp.217–218.

119. Peter J. Lloyd and Hyun-Hoon Lee, "Subregionalism in East Asia and Its Relationship with APEC," *Journal of the Korean Economy* 2–2 (Fall 2001), p.219.

120. John Ravenhill, *APEC and the Construction of Pacific Rim Regionalism* (Cambridge: Cambridge University Press, 2001), p.185. See also Philipp von Carlowitz and Tim Goydke, "APEC and Its Open Regionalism: Success or Failure?," *Aussenwirtschaft* 56–1 (March 2001), pp.69–97.

121. Hufbauer and Schott, "Toward Free Trade and Investment in the Asia-Pacific," pp.219–220.

122. Richard Higgott and Richard Stubbs, "Competing Conceptions of Economic Regionalism: APEC Versus EAEC in the Asia Pacific," *Review of International Political Economy* 2–3 (Summer 1995), pp.522–526.

123. Bergsten, "The Case for APEC," p.63.

124. Glenn Hook, "Japan and the Construction of Asia-Pacific," in Gamble and Payne, eds., *Regionalism and World Order,* p.193.

125. Eul-Soo Pang, "AFTA and MERCOSUR at the Crossroads: Security, Managed Trade, and Globalization," *Contemporary Southeast Asia* 25–1 (April 2003), p.129.

126. Walter Hatch and Kozo Yamamura, *Asia in Japan's Embrace: Building a Regional Production Alliance* (Cambridge: Cambridge University Press, 1996), p.36.

127. Grinspun and Kreklewich, "Consolidating Neoliberal Reforms," p.41.

128. Ralph Nader, "Introduction: Free Trade and the Decline of Democracy," in *The Case Against 'Free Trade': GATT, NAFTA, and the Globalization of Corporate Power* (San Francisco: Earth Island Press, 1993), p.6.

129. Hatch and Yamamura, *Asia in Japan's Embrace,* chs. 1 and 2.

130. Pang, "AFTA and MERCOSUR at the Crossroads," p.124.

131. Renato Ruggiero, Director General of the World Trade Organization, "Charting the Trade Routes of the Future: Towards a Borderless Economy," address delivered to the International Industrial Conference, San Francisco, 29 September 1997, *World Trade Organization Press Release* (Geneva; Press/77), p.4.

C H A P T E R 1 0

Multinational Corporations and Global Production

$\cancel{K FOI}$

The largest MNCs are in many respects the main agents of globalization. They produce and distribute goods and services across national boundaries; plan their operations on a global scale; and spread ideas, tastes, and technology throughout the world. MNCs are most commonly considered to be firms that control productive assets in more than one country. Parent firms in the home countries of MNCs acquire foreign assets by investing in affiliate or subsidiary firms in host countries. This type of investment involves management rights and control and is referred to as *foreign direct investment (FDI). Portfolio investment,* by contrast, is investment without control; i.e., it involves the purchase of bonds, money market instruments, or a small amount of equity securities or stocks of a firm simply to realize a financial return.

The growing presence of MNCs in the world economy testifies to their role as agents of globalization. In 2002, about 64,000 MNCs controlled 870,000 foreign affiliates; and world FDI stock was valued at $7.1 trillion, an increase of more than 10 times since 1980. Foreign affiliates also employed about 53 million workers in 2002, 2.5 times more workers than in 1982. The world's largest MNCs, based almost exclusively in the North, dominate this picture. For example, the top 100 nonfinancial MNCs in 2000 accounted for more than half of the total sales and employment of foreign affiliates. Despite variations in different years, FDI has generally increased more rapidly than trade. From 1973 to 1995, annual FDI outflows multiplied more than 12 times (from $25 billion to $315 billion), whereas the value of merchandise exports multiplied by 8.5 times. Almost a third of world exports of goods and services takes place within the networks of foreign affiliates. The years 2001 and 2002 were unusual, with global FDI inflows declining due to slow economic growth in most parts of the world, falling stock market valuations, lower corporate profitability, and the slowing of privatization rates in some countries. Since 1970 there were three previous downturns in FDI inflows—in 1976, 1982–1983, and 1991; these downturns were all associated with periods of slow growth in the world economy. The current downturn has not changed the importance of MNCs in integrating global production.[1]

The growing importance of MNCs has caused some analysts to argue that the critical problem in the current study of IPE "is the tension between states and multinationals, not states and markets."[2] Nevertheless, MNCs receive less attention than they should in IPE literature because many theorists continue to place primary emphasis on relations among governments. A major obstacle to the study of MNCs is the limited amount of reliable data. As private enterprises, MNCs are reluctant to provide information about themselves, and they are adept at obscuring their activities. This problem is compounded by the fact that no international organization oversees foreign investment the way organizations monitor monetary relations, trade, and development assistance. Furthermore, the study of MNCs is highly controversial, and an analyst's view of "the facts" is often colored by his or her general perspective. Thus, it is not uncommon in debates about MNCs for "anecdote to replace data" and for "the witty phrase to replace analysis."[3]

Liberals, realists, and historical structuralists have differing views regarding the power of MNCs and their impact on states and societies. Orthodox liberals traditionally have devoted little attention to MNCs because of their inattention to institutions and because the oligopolistic behavior of MNCs points to problems with depending only on the market. However, institutional liberals believe that the mobility of MNCs gives them a major advantage over national governments, which are bound to specific territories. In the current age of interdependence, MNCs and private banks have therefore become "the major weavers of the world economy."[4] Historical structuralists also refer to the growing power of MNCs, but unlike liberals they argue that corporate managers constitute a transnational class that maintains and defends the capitalist system. Writers from this perspective often assert that managers of major corporations have a predominant influence over the conduct of U.S. foreign policy.[5] Realists, by contrast, argue that the most powerful states have considerable control over their MNCs and that MNCs retain close ties with their home governments.[6]

Although institutional liberals and historical structuralists agree that the influence of MNCs has increased, they strongly differ over the effects of this change. Liberals believe that FDI contributes to increased efficiency in the use of the world's resources by stimulating innovation, competition, economic growth, and employment. MNCs also provide countries with numerous benefits, such as capital, technology, managerial skills, and marketing networks. Historical structuralists, by contrast, view MNCs as predatory monopolists that overcharge for their goods and services, limit the flow of technology, and create dependency relationships with host countries in the South.[7] MNCs can also have a negative impact on home countries, critics argue, by exporting jobs and imposing downward pressures on labor and environmental standards.

DEFINITIONS AND TERMINOLOGY

Controversy exists not only over the importance and effects of MNCs but even over definitions and terminology.[8] MNCs are usually defined as firms that control assets in at least two countries, but some writers believe that MNCs must have more of an international presence. For example, a classic study of MNCs argues that only enterprises with manufacturing subsidiaries in at least six countries are "entitled to" the MNC label.[9] Those who favor more restrictive definitions of this type believe that the important investment issues relate to the largest firms, which establish a number of foreign affiliates as part of a global strategy. However, restrictive definitions are problematic because they exclude enterprises on a rather arbitrary basis. This chapter therefore adopts the more expansive definition of MNCs as firms that operate in two or more countries. An enterprise is of course not an MNC simply because it does business in more than one country. To qualify, a firm must possess at least one FDI project in which it has management rights or control. A firm can undertake FDI in a host country in two ways: *greenfield investment,* or the creation of new facilities and productive assets by foreigners; and *mergers and acquisitions (M&As),* or the purchase of stocks in an existing firm by foreigners with the purpose of participating in its management. In a cross-border merger, the assets and operations of two firms belonging to different countries are combined to establish a new legal entity. In a cross-border acquisition, a local firm becomes an affiliate or subsidiary of a foreign firm. During the past decade, most growth in international production has occurred through M&As rather than greenfield investment, and the data on M&As show that acquisitions are far more common than mergers.[10]

Although the definition of FDI may seem straightforward, there are differences of view over what constitutes "control." Until the 1960s, the U.S. Department of Commerce defined FDI as involving control over at least 25 percent of the equity of a foreign business. However, the department subsequently lowered this figure to 10 percent, and international organizations such as the IMF and OECD use the 10 percent figure for statistical purposes. In reality, the share of equity required for control varies in different circumstances. On one hand, a foreign investor may gain managerial control of an enterprise by owning less than 10 percent of the stock if ownership is widely dispersed. On the other hand, 49 percent ownership may not confer control if a single individual or firm owns the other 51 percent. The important point is that a shareholder may have considerable control over a company's operations even without holding a majority of shares. Foreign affiliates can be minority-owned (10 to 50 percent of equity capital), majority-owned (greater than 50 percent but less than 100 percent), or wholly-owned (100 percent) subsidiaries.[11]

Differences exist not only over definitions but also over the use of the term MNC itself. The UN and a number of scholars prefer the term *transnational* to multinational because the ownership and control of most firms is not really multinational. Instead, a firm normally extends its operations from a single home country across national frontiers.[12] It is true that most MNCs are *ethnocentric* or home country oriented, with directives flowing from the headquarters to the affiliates and much of the MNCs' R&D located in the home country. Nevertheless, a small but growing number of MNCs are more *geocentric* or *stateless;* that is, they adopt a worldwide approach and are not as closely tied to any single state. Strategic alliances among MNCs from different states further complicate the task of associating an MNC with a specific home government. These alliances can take the form of production-sharing agreements, collaborative research and networking arrangements, and other types of cooperation. Finally, host states in some cases may induce an MNC to engage in activities attuned to the hosts' requirements. For example, MNCs can sometimes gain entry into a foreign country only by agreeing to form *joint ventures* with local firms. Joint ventures involving two or more firms are increasingly common in LDCs and transition states.[13]

The term transnational accurately reflects the fact that the home country continues to be significant for most international firms. Nevertheless, the existence of stateless firms, strategic alliances, and joint ventures demonstrates that corporations differ in the degree to which their nationality has significance. This text uses the more common term MNC, simply to signify that a firm has ongoing managerial and productive activities in more than one country.[14]

WHY DO FIRMS BECOME MNCs?

To understand why firms become MNCs, it is important to distinguish between horizontal and vertical integration. A *horizontally integrated MNC* extends its operations abroad by producing the same product or product line in its affiliates in different countries. A *vertically integrated MNC* produces goods and services at different stages of the production process, with the outputs of some affiliates serving as inputs to other affiliates.

Firms may engage in **horizontal integration** to defend or increase their market share. Although a firm's exports from the home country may initially meet the demand for products and services in a foreign market, the firm may have to set up a subsidiary to compete with new local suppliers that enter the foreign market. By establishing a presence in the foreign market, the MNC can compete more effectively with local firms by lowering costs such as transportation and by becoming more aware of the market's special characteristics. If the market is large enough, it may be economically feasible for the firm to produce goods and services specifically attuned to the tastes of its consumers. If a firm is producing for LDC markets, producing directly in the LDCs will lower labor costs. Another reason firms engage in horizontal integration relates to foreign government policies. When governments impose tariffs and NTBs that interfere with a firm's exports from its home country, the firm may establish foreign operations to get behind the external barriers. For example, Honda had the largest stake of the Japanese automakers in exports to the U.S. market in the early 1980s. When the United States imposed voluntary export restraints on Japanese auto imports in 1981–1985, Honda responded by becoming the first Japanese firm to produce automobiles in the United States. National and subnational governments also provide direct and indirect investment incentives to encourage firms to locate production facilities in their territories, and the efforts of subnational governments have been especially notable since the early 1970s. Only 10 U.S. states had committed budgetary resources to attract foreign investment before 1969, but 47 states had developed active investment programs by 1979.[15]

Firms engage in **vertical integration** to avoid uncertainty and reduce transaction costs. Instead of depending on uncertain "arm's length transactions" with different owners at various stages of the production process, vertically integrated MNCs gain control of these transactions by *internalizing* them within the firm. Vertically integrated firms opt for *backward integration* when raw materials and other inputs they require for production are not readily available or involve high transaction costs. Examples of backward integration include steel firm investments in iron ore operations, oil company investments in the extraction of crude oil, and rubber manufacturer investments in natural rubber plantations. Backward integration also enables MNCs to gain control over the quality of inputs. It is no accident that three vertically integrated MNCs accounted for 60 percent of the export trade in bananas during the 1980s; bananas are highly perishable and require specific handling and ripening conditions. When the growers, shippers, and distributors are not vertically integrated, independent firms at each stage of the production process have more incentive to compromise quality control. The motivations for *forward vertical integration* are similar to those for backward integration: to reduce uncertainty and transaction costs and to ensure the quality of goods and services that reach the consumer.[16]

Another reason firms engage in vertical integration is to limit competition. When a small number of MNCs control the inputs such as raw materials for an industry, they can impose substantial barriers to the entry of new rival firms. As private firms, MNCs also engage in vertical integration to limit governmental scrutiny of their activities. For example, MNCs sometimes manipulate their transfer prices without detection by governments. **Transfer prices,** the prices an MNC's affiliates charge each other for internal sales of goods and services, help the MNC efficiently manage its internal operations and monitor the performance of its affiliates. However, an MNC can shift its reported profits from high-tax to low-tax countries (and thus avoid paying some taxes) by artificially raising or lowering the prices each affiliate charges. In 1993, for example, the U.S. Internal Revenue Service ruled that Nissan Motor Company had used transfer prices to seriously underreport its U.S. income, and Nissan was required to pay the United States about $150 million.[17]

Firms that become MNCs must have the ability as well as the incentive to make this transition. Innovations in communications, transportation, and technology have enabled firms to internationalize their production more easily, and they are likely to multinationalize successfully if they can "think globally" and "act locally." On one hand, large MNCs have numerous advantages resulting from their worldwide presence, such as economies of scale, access to global financing, special access to raw materials and other inputs, and brand name reputation. On the other hand, MNCs operate in a world of states in which they must adhere to national laws and cater to the demands and tastes of local consumers.[18]

THE HISTORICAL DEVELOPMENT OF FDI

Although the rapid expansion of MNCs is a post–World War II phenomenon, FDI and MNCs have a much longer history.[19] Some scholars trace the MNC's origins to transborder business operations of medieval banks such as the Medici bank in fifteenth century Florence. During the sixteenth to eighteenth centuries, international trading companies such as the English, Dutch, and French East India Companies and the Hudson's Bay Company coordinated large amounts of cross-border business activity. During the nineteenth century, firms that are commonly considered MNCs became involved with more sustained, longer term investments in a wider array of activities and countries. Thousands of these MNCs existed by the time of World War II.

Despite the general growth of MNCs and FDI over time, a number of factors have affected the rapidity of growth—and sometimes the contraction—of MNC activity during different periods. First, MNC activity increases more rapidly when there are major advances in communications, transportation, and technology. These advances have facilitated the establishment and expansion of MNC control over foreign operations. Second, rapid economic growth often stimulates the expansion of MNCs, whereas depressed economic conditions have the opposite effect. Third, MNCs expand their operations more rapidly when national governments and the international system are receptive to such activity. Internationally, for example, the development of rules protecting private property encouraged FDI, whereas major wars had a depressing effect. Fourth, capital liberalization leads to increased FDI, whereas capital and exchange controls discourage such activity. Finally, it is ironic that FDI often expands during periods of trade protectionism because MNCs shift production abroad to circumvent the trade barriers.[20] The historical discussion that follows is divided into three broad periods: before World War II, from the mid–1940s to mid–1980s, and since the mid–1980s.

The Period Before World War II

Most economists traditionally maintained that long-term capital flows during the nineteenth and early twentieth centuries were composed mainly of portfolio investment rather than FDI. However, data on foreign investment for this early period were extremely limited, and there was confusion as to how investments should be categorized. As economists refined their definitions, they concluded that a larger share of total foreign investment was FDI than was earlier assumed. Indeed, some studies estimate that FDI accounted for as much as 45 percent of British foreign investment in 1913–1914.[21] As global hegemon and the first country to industrialize, Britain was the main force behind the dramatic growth of FDI during the nineteenth century. Although there were no government guarantees or international institutions to provide safeguards, investments were fairly secure for several reasons. First, economic risk was lower under the pre–World War I gold standard because currencies were convertible, dividends could be remitted easily, and exchange rates were reasonably stable. Second, political risk was lower because a large share of European investment was in colonial territories that operated under home country rules. Third, the lack of restrictions on capital flows facilitated the growth of FDI; and fourth, wars during this period were limited in scope. The nineteenth century was also a period of rapid advances in rail and sea transport and communications (e.g., the telegraph), which facilitated the task of managing FDI over long distances.[22]

As Table 10.1 shows, British firms were the leading source of FDI before World War II, accounting for 45 percent of the total in 1914 and 40 percent in 1938. The United States was an important host country for European FDI during the nineteenth century, and it was also beginning to establish its own MNCs. Singer Manufacturing Company was the first major U.S. manufacturing MNC, with plants in four countries by the 1880s, and resource-based U.S. firms such as Standard Oil Company also estab-

Table 10.1

SHARE OF OUTWARD STOCK OF FDI (percentages)

	1914	1938
Britain	45	40
United States	14	28
Germany	14	1
France	11	9
Netherlands	5	10
Other Western Europe	5	3
Rest of World	6	9

Source: Geoffrey Jones, *The Evolution of International Business: An Introduction* pp.30 and 42. Copyright © 1996 by Geoffrey Jones. First published 1996 by Routledge. By permission of International Thomas Publishing Services Ltd.

Table 10.2

SHARE OF INWARD STOCK OF FDI (percentages)

	1914	1938
Latin America	33	31
Asia	21	25
United States	10	7
Eastern Europe	10	2
Western Europe	8	7
Canada	6	10
Africa	6	7
Rest of World	6	11

Source: Geoffrey Jones, *The Evolution of International Business: An Introduction,* pp.31 and 43. Copyright © 1996 by Geoffrey Jones. First published 1996 by Routledge. By permission of International Thomas Publishing Services Ltd.

lished extensive offshore operations. Thus, Table 10.1 shows that the U.S. share of outward FDI increased from 14 percent in 1914 to 28 percent in 1938. Western Europe and the United States accounted for more than 90 percent of outward FDI before World War II.

Table 10.2 shows that in marked contrast to the home countries, the largest recipients of FDI in 1914 and 1938 were LDCs in Latin America and Asia. Indeed, 63 percent of the world's FDI was directed to Latin America, Asia, and Africa in 1938. Other major recipients in 1938 were Canada (10 percent), the United States (7 percent), and Western Europe (7 percent). Whereas most FDI in manufacturing was concentrated in Western Europe and North America, the FDI in LDCs was mainly in natural resources and services (FDI in natural resources was also directed to Eastern Europe, Canada, and the United States).[23]

The rapid growth of FDI during the nineteenth century continued into the twentieth century and the interwar period. After World War I, however, the increase in global economic and political instability hindered foreign investment. For example, a number of host countries began to impose restrictions on inward FDI, the Soviet Union nationalized foreign property, and the gold exchange standard was suspended. As a result of the Great Depression and World War II, there was a severe contraction in MNC activities. Thus, MNCs accounted for a much smaller share of world economic activity in 1949 than in 1929. It was not until after World War II that the vigorous growth of MNCs and FDI would resume.[24]

The Mid–1940s to Mid–1980s

Britain was the leading source of FDI in the nineteenth and early twentieth centuries, but U.S. MNCs took over the leadership after World War II. As Table 10.3 shows, U.S. firms accounted for more than half (53.8 percent) of outward stocks of FDI in 1967. Under U.S. leadership, FDI entered a period of rapid expansion because of several changes during the postwar period. First, the North experienced a sustained period of economic growth from 1950 to 1973, which was conducive to the expansion of MNC activity. Second, there were major improvements in international transportation and communications: faster jet and ocean transport, telex and satellite communications, and the fax machine all contributed to the flow of capital. Third, most DCs relaxed their controls over FDI after the return to convertibility of their currencies. (A notable exception was Japan, which continued to restrict foreign investment flows.)

Although U.S. MNCs accounted for the largest share of outward FDI during the postwar period, their share has declined steadily since the late 1960s. A major reason for the declining U.S. share was the rapid economic growth in Japan, Germany, and other Western European states as they recovered from the war. Thus, Table 10.3 shows that the U.S. share of total outward stocks of FDI fell from 53.8 percent in 1967 to 36.6 percent in 1985, whereas Japan's share rose from 1.4 to 6.5 percent, and West Germany's share rose from 2.8 to 8.7 percent. Table 10.3 also shows that the developed market economies were the source of almost all outward FDI flows: 99 percent in 1960 and 96.9 percent in 1985. Nevertheless, MNCs based in the South increased their share of outward FDI from only 1 percent in 1960 to 3 percent in 1985. Most of this FDI came from OPEC states and more prosperous LDCs in Asia and Latin America.

Whereas the U.S. share of outward FDI was declining, Table 10.4 shows that the U.S. share of inward stocks of FDI increased from 11.2 percent in 1975 to 25.1 percent in 1985. Japan was the only DC that maintained an extremely low share of inward FDI, at 0.6 percent in 1985, largely because of governmental, societal, and cultural factors that limited investment flows. Thus, the developed market economies were the largest recipients as well as providers of FDI, accounting for about 75 percent of inward stocks from 1975 to 1985. Although the South had received well over 60 percent of total FDI before World War II, this figure fell to about 30 percent during the immediate postwar period as FDI activities shifted from primary products to manufacturing. From the mid–1970s, the LDC share of inward FDI declined even further to about 25 percent because of LDC demands for more control over their natural resources, growing LDC external debts, and an increase in technology-related investment in the North.

Among the LDCs, the most prosperous and resource-rich states received by far the most FDI. Thus, Table 10.4 shows that the share of FDI directed to Africa, which contains many LLDCs, declined from 6.7 percent in 1975 to only 3.7 percent in 1985.

Table 10.3

OUTWARD STOCKS OF FDI, THE GROUP OF SEVEN (U.S.$ billions)

	1960 Value	1960 %	1967 Value	1967 %	1975 Value	1975 %	1980 Value	1980 %	1985 Value	1985 %	1990 Value	1990 %	2001 Value	2001 %
United States	31.9	47.1	56.6	53.8	124.2	44.0	220.0	42.9	251.0	36.6	435.2	25.8	1381.7	21.9
Japan	0.5	0.7	1.5	1.4	15.9	5.7	18.8	3.7	44.3	6.5	204.7	12.2	300.1	4.7
Germany*	0.8	1.2	3.0	2.8	18.4	6.5	43.1	8.4	59.9	8.7	151.6	9.0	553.3	8.8
Britain	12.4	18.3	17.5	16.6	37.0	13.1	80.4	15.7	100.3	14.6	230.8	13.7	906.5	14.3
France	4.1	6.1	6.0	5.7	10.6	3.8	23.6	4.6	37.1	5.4	110.1	6.5	489.4	7.7
Italy	1.1	1.6	2.1	2.0	3.3	1.2	7.3	1.4	16.3	2.4	56.1	3.3	182.4	2.9
Canada	2.5	3.7	3.7	3.5	10.4	3.7	22.6	4.4	40.9	6.0	78.9	4.7	244.6	3.9
Total G-7†	53.3	78.7	90.4	85.8	219.8	77.9	416.0	81.0	549.8	81.0	1267.4	75.3	4058.0	64.2
Total DMEs‡	67.0	99.0	—	—	275.4	97.7	507.5	98.8	664.2	96.9	1614.6	95.9	5487.6	86.8
Total	67.7	100.0	105.3	100.0	282.0	100.0	513.7	100.0	685.6	100.0	1684.1	100.0	6318.9	100.0

* The 1960 to 1985 data are for West Germany.

† G-7: Group of Seven

‡ DMEs: developed market economies

Source: Centre on Transnational Corporations, *Transnational Corporations in World Development: Trends and Prospects* (New York: UN, 1988), Table 1.2, p.24 (1960 and 1975 data); UN Economic and Social Council, *International Corporations in World Development: A Re-Examination*, E/C. 10/38 (New York: UN, 1978), Table III-32, p.236 (1967 data); UNCTAD, *World Investment Report 1996* (New York: UN, 1996), Annex Table 4. pp.245–247 (1980–1990 data); UNCTAD, *World Investment Report 2003* (New York: UN, 2003), Annex Table B.4, p.262 (2001 data).

Table 10.4
INWARD STOCKS OF FDI (U.S.$ billions)

	1975		1980		1985		1990		2001	
	Value	%	Value	%	Value	%	Value	%	Value	%
DMEs*	185.3	75.1	373.5	77.5	538.0	73.2	1,373.3	80.0	4,277.2	64.7
Western Europe	100.6	40.8	200.3	41.6	244.8	33.3	758.7	44.2	2,544.4	38.5
United States	27.7	11.2	83.0	17.2	184.6	25.1	394.9	23.0	1,321.1	20.0
Japan	1.5	0.6	3.3	0.7	4.7	0.6	9.9	0.6	50.3	0.8
Other	57.0	23.1	86.9	18.0	103.9	14.1	209.8	12.2	361.4	5.5
LDCs†	61.5	24.9	108.3	22.5	196.8	26.8	341.7	19.9	2,173.8	32.9
Africa	16.5	6.7	20.3	4.3	27.0	3.7	41.6	2.4	157.8	2.4
Asia	13.0	5.3	38.0	7.9	91.8	12.5	175.9	10.2	1,306.3	19.8
Latin America and Caribbean	29.7	12.0	48.0	10.0	76.3	10.4	121.3	7.1	705.7	10.7
Other	2.3	0.0	1.5	0.3	1.7	0.2	2.9	0.2	4.0	0.1
Central and Eastern Europe	—	—	0.09	0.0	0.2	0.0	1.8	0.1	155.7	2.4
Total	246.8	100.0	481.9	100.0	734.9	100.0	1,716.9	100.0	6,606.9	100.0

* DMEs: developed market economies
† LDCs: less developed countries

Source: Centre on Transnational Corporations, *Transnational Corporations in World Development: Trends and Prospects* (New York: UN, 1988), Table 1.3, p.25 (1975 data); UNCTAD, *World Investment Report 1996* (New York: UN, 1996), Annex Table 3. pp.239–243 (1980–1990 data); UNCTAD, *World Investment Report 2003* (New York: UN, 2003), Annex Table B.3, pp.257–260 (2001 data).

Table 10.5

SHARE OF INWARD AND OUTWARD FDI STOCK AS A PERCENT OF GDP*

	1980	1985	1990	1995	2002
DCs[†]					
Inward	4.9	6.2	8.2	8.9	18.7
Outward	6.2	7.3	9.6	11.3	24.4
United States					
Inward	3.0	4.4	6.9	7.3	12.9
Outward	7.8	5.7	7.5	9.5	14.4
Japan					
Inward	0.3	0.3	0.3	0.6	1.5
Outward	1.8	3.2	6.6	4.5	8.3
Germany					
Inward	3.9	5.1	7.1	7.8	22.7
Outward	4.6	8.4	8.8	10.5	29.0
Britain					
Inward	11.8	14.1	20.6	17.6	40.8
Outward	15.0	22.0	23.2	26.9	66.1
France					
Inward	3.8	6.9	7.1	12.3	28.2
Outward	3.6	7.1	9.1	13.2	45.8
Italy					
Inward	2.0	4.5	5.3	5.8	10.6
Outward	1.6	3.9	5.2	8.8	16.4
Canada					
Inward	20.4	18.4	19.6	21.1	30.4
Outward	8.9	12.3	14.7	20.3	37.6

* GDP: gross domestic product
[†] DCs: developed countries
Source: UNCTAD, *World Investment Report 2003* (New York: UN, 2003), Annex Table B.6, pp.278–279.

Asian and Latin American LDCs, by contrast, received 12.5 and 10.4 percent of total inward FDI stocks in 1985 (the decline of the Latin American share from 12 percent in 1975 was partly due to the foreign debt crisis). The Central and Eastern European socialist states (including the Soviet Union) received almost no FDI from 1975 to 1985. Thus, by the mid–1980s developed market economies were directing most FDI to each other, and the LDCs were increasingly marginalized.

The 1980s to the Present

As discussed, there have been periodic downturns in FDI flows, with downturns occurring in 1982–1983 and 2001–2002. Nevertheless, FDI flows since the 1980s have increased *on average* at a faster rate than at any time since the late nineteenth century. Table 10.5 shows that inward and outward FDI as a share of the GDPs of developed economies increased from 4.9 percent and 6.2 percent in 1980 to 18.7 percent and 24.4 percent in 2002. A number of factors account for the rapid growth of FDI since the early 1980s. Most important, many restrictions on international business were phased out with the re-emergence of orthodox liberalism. An end to restrictions on capital flows, along with deregulation and privatization in much of the North and the South, gave MNCs more freedom to expand their activities. Furthermore, the shift of the transition economies to market-oriented reforms after the breakup of the Soviet bloc opened up large new areas for FDI. Another factor in the expansion of FDI was the problems with international trade. The protracted GATT Uruguay Round negotiations, combined with the use of NTBs, caused many MNCs to extend their activities abroad to circumvent trade barriers. Finally, significant advances in information and transportation technologies enabled MNCs to extend their global network.[25]

A remarkable feature of current FDI is the degree to which it is concentrated in the "triad"—the United States, EU, and Japan. From 1985 to 2002, the triad accounted for about 80 percent of the world's outward FDI stock, and for 50 to 60 percent of the world's inward stock. U.S. firms have shown a strong preference for investing in Europe, intra-European investment has accelerated, and Japan and Western European countries have invested heavily in the United States. Until the late 1970s, Western European integration occurred largely through the expansion of trade, but during the 1980s the growth of intra-European FDI was even more significant than the growth of trade. Table 10.6 shows that the nine largest host countries for FDI from 1985 to 1995 were also included among the largest home countries for FDI, and all but one of these nine (China) is an advanced industrial state. The only important home country for FDI that is not also an important host country is Japan. Although Japan has eased some of its formal impediments to inward FDI, a number of informal barriers remain. As shown in Table 10.4, Japan accounted for only 0.8 percent of the total inward stocks of FDI in 2001—a strikingly small figure compared with other G-7 countries.[26]

Despite the continued predominance of DCs in outward and inward FDI flows, several changes during the 1980s–1990s are especially noteworthy. First, the United States lost its dominant position as a source of FDI. As Table 10.3 shows, the U.S. share of outward FDI stocks fell from 42.9 percent in 1980 to 21.9 percent in 2001. Second, there were erratic changes in Japan's share of FDI outflows. As Table 10.3 shows, Japan's share of outward FDI rose dramatically from 6.5 percent in 1985 to 12.2 percent in 1990. A strong Japanese yen as a result of the 1985 Plaza accord, combined with rising trade barriers such as voluntary export restraints on Japanese goods, forced Japanese corporations to invest and produce more abroad.[27] However, Table 10.3 shows that Japan's share of outward FDI returned to a lower level of 4.7 percent in 2001. Persistent economic recession and the financial problems of major Japanese banks (see Chapter 11) "led to changes in the corporate strategies of a number of Japanese . . . [MNCs] faced with a reduced ability to expand abroad."[28] Table 10.5 shows that Japan's outward FDI stock accounted for only 8.3 percent of its GDP in 1998, the lowest share of any G-7 country. Third, LDCs have increased their share of outward FDI stocks since the late 1990s. (As Table 10.3 shows, the DC share of outward FDI stocks fell from 95.9 percent in 1990 to 86.8 percent in 2001.) In 2000 for the first time, five firms headquartered in LDCs were on the list of the world's largest 100 MNCs.[29]

Fourth, the DC share of inward FDI has declined, and the LDC share has increased in recent years. Table 10.4 shows that the developed market economy share of

Table 10.6

LEADING HOST ECONOMIES FOR FOREIGN DIRECT INVESTMENT (Cumulative Inflows, 1985–1995)*

Rank	Country	FDI (U.S.$ billions)
1	**United States**	477.5
2	**United Kingdom**	199.6
3	**France**	138.0
4	**China**	130.2
5	**Spain**	90.9
6	**Belgium-Luxembourg**	72.4
7	**Netherlands**	68.1
8	**Australia**	62.6
9	**Canada**	60.9
10	Mexico	44.1
11	**Singapore**	40.8
12	**Sweden**	37.7
13	**Italy**	36.3
14	Malaysia	30.7
15	**Germany**	25.9
16	**Switzerland**	25.2
17	Argentina	23.5
18	Brazil	20.3
19	**Hong Kong**	17.9
20	**Denmark**	15.7

* Economies in bold are also among the 20 leading home economies for FDI.
Source: World Trade Organization Annual Report 1996, Vol. 1, *Trade and Foreign Direct Investment*, p.47, Table 4.1. Copyright © World Trade Organization 1996. By permission of the World Trade Organization.

inward FDI fell from 80 percent in 1990 to 64.7 percent in 2001, whereas the LDC share rose from 19.9 percent to 32.9 percent during the same period. As Table 10.6 shows, a small group of rapidly growing LDCs, including China, Mexico, Singapore, Malaysia, Argentina, Brazil, and Hong Kong, were among the 20 leading host economies for FDI between 1985 and 1995. China's position is especially notable because it now accounts for more than one-third of all FDI directed to the LDCs.[30] In contrast to the more prosperous LDCs, sub-Saharan African LDCs are becoming increasingly marginalized. Table 10.4 shows that Africa accounted for only 2.4 percent of inward FDI stocks in 2001, compared with 19.8 percent for Asia and 10.7 percent for Latin America and the Caribbean. Fifth, FDI has become a significant part of the privatization process in the transition economies in Eastern Europe and the former Soviet Union.[31]

A sixth development is the proliferation of firms engaging in FDI as well as in new forms of investment activity. Indeed, the number of MNCs headquartered in 15 major DCs almost quadrupled between 1968 and 1993, from about 7,000 to 27,000. There has also been a marked shift in FDI from manufacturing and petroleum to service industries. Deregulation of the financial and telecommunications sectors in DCs and privatization in LDCs have stimulated this shift to services. New forms of FDI involving nonequity arrangements such as joint ventures, management contracts, technology licensing, and turnkey projects have also become more important. With these nonequity investments, firms provide certain benefits such as management skills or access to technology in return for royalties, fees, or revenue from sales.[32]

Although MNCs are having a growing impact on all states, they have a qualitatively different relationship with home and host states. The following sections therefore examine home and host states separately. LDCs are normally host rather than home states for MNCs, so considerable discussion of host state-MNC relations is devoted to the LDCs. The discussion of home state-MNC relations, by contrast, focuses mainly on the advanced industrial states.

MNC-HOST COUNTRY RELATIONS: THEORETICAL APPROACHES

In the orthodox liberal view, LDCs require capital inflows, imported technology, and the replacement of traditional social values with modern ideas to further their development. MNCs help their host countries achieve faster development because they provide all these resources: external capital, new technologies, and modern values. Thus, LDCs with a stronger MNC presence will be better off. Liberal explanations for the positive effect of FDI stem partly from liberal theories of trade. In accordance with the Heckscher-Ohlin theory (see Chapter 8), liberals assume that states have different factor endowments and that foreign investment flows to areas where it is most needed or in shortest supply. Thus, inward FDI provides external finance to compensate for inadequate local savings, export earnings, and foreign aid; tax revenues from MNC profits supplement local taxes; and managerial skills and technology are transferred. Although some liberals acknowledge that a stronger MNC presence may initially result in more income inequality, they attribute this to the positive effect of MNCs on income growth in general. Thus, this inequality is a temporary price to be paid for economic success. In the longer term liberals predict economic convergence between DCs and LDCs.[33]

The first major challenge to orthodox liberal views came from two economists, Stephen Hymer (a Marxist) and Charles Kindleberger (a liberal). Hymer and Kindleberger argued that FDI cannot simply be equated with the movement of capital from the home to the host country. Instead, MNCs often get financing for FDI from other sources, including borrowing funds in the host country. Although FDI supporters espoused the benefits of free markets, Hymer and Kindleberger (and others such as Raymond Vernon) pointed to the fact that MNCs are oligopolistic by nature. MNCs lack certain advantages that local firms possess, but they can gain competitiveness by creating an oligopolistic environment. For example, an MNC can raise barriers to the entry of firms through its use of new technologies, its economies of scale, and its privileged access to global finance. Thus, Hymer wrote that "the industries in which there is much foreign investment tend to be concentrated industries, while the industries in which there is little or no foreign investment tend to be unconcentrated."[34]

Hymer's critique of the MNC provided many ideas that were adopted in revised form by Marxists and dependency theorists. According to dependency theorists, MNCs prevent LDCs from achieving autonomous development. For example, MNCs prevent local firms and entrepreneurs from participating in the most dynamic sectors of the economy, appropriate local capital rather than bringing in new capital, increase income inequalities in the host country, and use inappropriate capital-intensive technologies that contribute to unemployment. MNCs also undermine the host country's government, culture, and society by co-opting local business and government elites, imposing political and economic pressures on the host country (often with the help of the MNC's home country), and altering consumer tastes and attitudes. Although Latin American and East Asian NIEs are industrializing, dependency theorists believe that MNCs prevent these states from achieving genuine autonomous development. Thus, one study claims that MNCs in Brazil keep "the innovative side of their businesses as close to home as possible" and ensure that "the industrialization of the periphery will remain partial."[35]

Many studies indicate that the effects of MNCs on host states are neither as positive nor as negative as orthodox liberal and dependency theorists maintain and that a host state's options vary under different circumstances. For example, one factor affecting a host state's options is the amount of competition among investors; i.e., a host state has greater leverage if it has more investors to choose from. Although states have become more dependent on investment in recent years, the sources of investment have become more diverse and numerous. As discussed, U.S. MNCs are no longer as dominant, and there are growing numbers of European, Japanese, and even Southern MNCs. Another factor affecting a host state's options is the "obsolescing bargain," which causes host state-MNC relations to change over time. Before an MNC enters a country, the host state is in a weak bargaining position because the MNC can pursue other options and the host state must provide significant incentives to attract the initial investment. The MNC's bargaining power stems from its sophisticated technology, brand name identification, access to capital, product diversity, and ability to promote exports. Thus, the initial investment agreement strongly favors the MNC. After the investment is made, however, the bargaining leverage shifts toward the host state because the MNC commits itself to immobile resources. The host state can treat these resources as a "hostage," and it gains bargaining, technological, and managerial skills through spinoffs from the foreign investment. Thus, the host state is likely to demand a renegotiation of the original bargain and gain more favorable terms with the MNC.[36]

A number of studies indicate that the obsolescing bargain is more applicable in some cases than in others. For example, it is more likely to apply in projects that require large fixed investments. Such projects give foreign investors considerable leverage initially, but several years later the large fixed investments can become hostage to the host state. MNCs with smaller fixed investments, by contrast, can more easily threaten to withdraw from the host state. Another factor is the type of technology an MNC uses in a project. Foreign investors using new and sophisticated technologies that are unavailable to the host state may be less vulnerable to aggressive host state policies at a later date. A third factor is the importance of marketing or product differentiation through advertising. When a firm's sales are determined to a large degree by brand identification and consumer loyalty, the firm is in a stronger position vis-à-vis the host state. These three factors—fixed investments, new technologies, and brand identification—help predict whether an industry will be subject to the obsolescing bargain. For example, the obsolescing bargain is less applicable to sophisticated manufacturing industries that are less dependent on resources in specific host states, rely on more advanced technologies, and manufacture differentiated products with brand names familiar to consumers. The obsolescing bargain is more applicable to natural resource industries that involve large fixed investments and familiar technologies, and it is not surprising that LDC nationalizations in the past were more common in natural resource industries. Studies of natural resource projects confirm that host states have often been successful in their demands for higher taxes, more processing of goods, joint marketing, and the employment of local people in management.[37]

Although an MNC's investments may be subject to uncertainties due to the obsolescing bargain, political unrest in the host state, and other factors, the MNC can employ a variety of strategies to offset these risks. Vertical integration is an important strategy open to large MNCs. By placing the various stages of production in different host states and maintaining control over the different stages, an MNC can decrease its vulnerability to particular host states. Another strategy is selecting local private partners for joint ventures or other types of arrangements. Evidence indicates that MNCs often avoid strong pressures from a host state by establishing alliances with the local private sector. When an MNC becomes more firmly established in a host state, it can also build a political and economic base of support for itself by creating linkages with local suppliers, distributors, and consumers. One indication that MNCs have been successful in countering risks is the fact that current host state actions are often more circumscribed than they were in the past. For example, there have been virtually no nationalizations of MNC affiliates in host states since the mid–1980s.

State-to-state interactions can also affect the bargaining relationship between host states and MNCs. Thus, one analyst argues that "the traditional bargaining model of MNC-host developing country relations has become obsolete," and should be replaced with "a two-tier, multi-party bargaining process."[38] The first-tier bargaining occurs between governments of the host and home states bilaterally or through multilateral institutions. This tier has a major effect on the second-tier bargaining between MNCs and host states. For example, in recent years DC home states have induced LDC host states to liberalize their policies toward FDI through bilateral investment agreements (discussed later in this chapter) and through conditions attached to IMF and World Bank structural adjustment loans. As a result of first-tier bargaining, host states have been more amenable to MNC pressures in the second-tier bargaining. In assessing MNC-host state bargaining relationships, one must therefore also consider the role of other actors such as home states, international organizations, and NGOs.

HOST COUNTRY POLICIES TOWARD MNCS

Host state policies toward MNCs have varied widely, ranging from nationalization of FDI operations on one hand to efforts to attract MNCs with concessions and incentives on the other. Many governments welcome FDI in some sectors while limiting or blocking it in others (e.g., in defense industries); and host governments often impose obligations such as performance requirements on MNCs to ensure that their benefits are maximized. Whereas some federal governments follow restrictive policies toward foreign investment, their subnational governments (e.g., states or provinces) may at the same time compete with one another to attract FDI. Some governments even have an "attraction-aversion dilemma" that leads them to both invite and restrict FDI. Although they seek the capital, technology, and organizational skills that MNCs provide, they also try to preserve large segments of the domestic market for local firms. The issue becomes even more complicated when a host state's verbal statements courting FDI differ from the experiences of foreign investors.[39] Because there are extensive differences between host government policies in the South and the North, the following sections discuss these two groups separately.

The South

Before World War I, there were very few restrictions on MNCs in the South. Colonial territories were of course open to foreign investment from the imperial powers, and states that had gained their independence—for example, in Latin America—generally accepted the liberal view that foreign investment was necessary for their economic modernization and development. Russia's nationalization of its oil industry after the Russian Revolution in 1917 had a major impact on LDC attitudes, and some LDCs shifted to more nationalist policies during the interwar period. (*Nationalization* or *expropriation* refers to the forced takeover of FDI, with or without compensation.) Although confrontations with foreign oil companies followed in Iran, Argentina, Venezuela, and Bolivia, very few LDCs actually expropriated foreign assets. However, Mexico nationalized most of its foreign oil industry in 1938 and avoided Western retaliation, partly because of the outbreak of World War II.

After World War II, the change to restrictive policies in the South was far more notable. In extreme instances, the spread of communism to China, North Korea, North Vietnam, and Cuba resulted in the nationalization of Western assets. In other parts of the South, many newly independent states viewed limits on FDI as essential to their national sovereignty. FDI often bred hostility because it involved foreign control over LDCs' natural resources and public utilities and was often associated with the former colonial powers. Nevertheless, the ability of LDCs to pressure for a greater share of the benefits from FDI was limited because they lacked experience in dealing with MNCs, their sources of external finance were limited, and they were often preoccupied with security concerns. From 1946 to 1959, U.S. MNCs accounted for more than two-thirds of all new foreign-owned subsidiaries in the South, and LDCs had few alternative sources of FDI.[40]

In the 1960s–1970s, several factors contributed to an increase in LDC leverage and activism vis-à-vis MNCs. The development of more non-U.S. MNCs gave the LDCs alternatives in seeking outside finance; FDI was often concentrated in natural resources, which were subject to the obsolescing bargain; dependency theory was highly influential in the South during the 1960s, and this encouraged LDCs to exert more pressure on MNCs; and LDCs developed more managerial, administrative, and technical capabilities for regulating MNC behavior. As a result of increased LDC assertiveness, nationalization of foreign firms became widespread in the petroleum and mining industries in the late 1960s–1970s. After OPEC succeeded in raising oil prices in 1973, LDCs also posed a major challenge to liberal-economic views of FDI in the UN. In the 1950s–1960s, the liberal regime for FDI had emphasized national treatment, adequate compensation to MNCs for infringement of their rights and privileges, and the right of MNCs to seek support from their home countries. By the late 1960s, LDCs were pressuring instead for agreements to restrict the rights of MNCs, permit discrimination between national and multinational firms, and give host states' legal institutions the authority to resolve investment disputes.[41] In the UN General Assembly, Southern views of MNCs were embodied in resolutions that the G-77 majority passed over the objections of the North. For example, the 1974 Declaration on the Establishment of a New International Economic Order indicated that host states should unilaterally determine what rules to apply to MNCs operating in their territories. Although the G-77 was successful in winning approval for symbolic resolutions of this nature, it was unable to reach authoritative agreements acceptable to the North. For example, the G-77 failed to reach a UN agreement on a comprehensive code of behavior for MNCs (see discussion later in this chapter).[42]

By the late 1970s, the South shifted to more a conciliatory position toward MNCs, and the number of nationalizations declined for a number of reasons. First, the nationalization of large-scale petroleum and mining industries was largely completed. Second, the experience of many LDCs with nationalization of their natural resource industries was disappointing. Problems included declining productivity, failure to introduce new technologies, and continued dependence on MNCs for marketing their products. Third, LDC militancy on foreign investment issues during the 1970s caused many MNCs to be reticent about investing in the South. MNCs often preferred to invest in DCs with natural resources such as Australia, Canada, and the United States. Finally, the 1979 oil price increase, followed by the 1980s foreign debt crisis and world recession, led to severe cutbacks in commercial bank lending to LDCs. Fears about exploitation by MNCs were therefore largely replaced by concerns that the South's share of inward FDI was declining.[43]

A number of LDCs therefore adopted more open policies toward MNCs during the 1980s. Mexico, for example, liberalized its policies toward FDI and participated in drafting the NAFTA provisions for freer foreign investment activities. A number of other Latin American states, such as Argentina, Chile, Colombia, and Venezuela, also took unilateral steps to liberalize their investment policies. The most significant turnaround, however, was in the policies of emerging CPEs, especially China. Although China was largely closed to FDI during the 1950s–1970s, it passed laws in the late 1970s–1980s that were more welcoming to FDI in some sectors, and it even granted foreign investors special treatment not available to domestic firms. MNCs that transfer advanced technology to China or export a substantial share of their output have received especially favorable treatment. Thus, China soon became the largest LDC host country for FDI.[44]

Although LDCs shifted to more welcoming policies, some governments have imposed performance requirements on MNCs, such as local content and export requirements, and have pressured MNCs to enter into joint ventures with local firms. The East Asian NIEs, for example, have welcomed investment, but have also attached a number of conditions to inward FDI. Nevertheless, even the East Asians are liberalizing their foreign investment policies as a result of the TRIMs agreement in the GATT Uruguay Round and because of concerns that the North may impose trade restrictions on host states with performance requirements for foreign investors.

In the 1990s, LDC policies became even more open to FDI. Indeed, most LDCs, DCs, and transition economies are seeking to attract FDI in recognition of the fact that MNCs have a growing role in the global economy. Of the 1,035 changes in FDI laws of countries from 1991 to 1999, 974 were more favorable and only 61 were less favorable to FDI. Most new measures by LDCs and transition economies reduced sectoral restrictions to foreign entry or liberalized operations in industries that were previously closed or restricted to FDI. LDCs also offered additional incentives—mainly tax incentives—to promote investment in priority industries. Thus, Table 10.4 shows that the LDC share of inward stocks of FDI rose from 19.9 percent in 1990 to 32.9 percent in 2001. FDI has become the largest source of external finance for LDCs, and during financial crises in recent years, LDCs have found FDI inflows to be more stable than other capital flows. Whereas access to bank lending and portfolio investment is influenced by investment ratings and short-term financial considerations, FDI responds more to underlying economic fundamentals.[45]

It is important to note that the poorest LDCs are finding it difficult to attract FDI even when they liberalize their investment policies. For example, most sub-Saharan African LDCs adopted policies to encourage FDI, partly under pressure from IMF and World Bank SAL programs. Nevertheless, low economic growth rates, civil conflicts, political crises, and high levels of indebtedness have had a depressing effect on their FDI inflows. As Table 10.4 shows, Africa's share of inward stocks of FDI declined from 6.7 percent in 1975 to 2.4 percent in 2001.[46]

The North

Host states in the North are generally in a different position vis-à-vis MNCs than host states in the South. Whereas FDI in the South has historically been involved in natural resource extraction and lower technology manufacturing, investment in the North is usually based on higher technology production. MNCs also loom larger in LDC economies and create more LDC dependence than is the case for most DCs. Furthermore, DCs are often major home as well as host countries for FDI, so they are reluctant to restrict incoming foreign investment. Despite these differences, DC as well as LDC policies toward incoming FDI have shifted over time.

During the nineteenth century, Western European countries, the United States, and Canada imposed very few controls on foreign-owned firms. This openness to

MNCs resulted from the liberalism of the period, which was fostered by British hegemony. After World War I, Western European countries followed more open policies toward inward FDI than the United States, which restricted foreign ownership in a number of sectors, including banking, shipping, and petroleum. However, countries in Western Europe followed a "national champions" strategy to promote the development of local enterprises in key sectors of the economy. At the end of World War II, the United States as the new global hegemon adopted more liberal policies toward FDI than Western Europe. The shift of European countries to more restrictionist policies toward FDI was especially noticeable during the 1960s. At that time, Europeans were concerned that U.S. MNCs were contributing to the Americanization of the developed world. A French writer, Jean-Jacques Servan-Schreiber, expressed these concerns forcefully in his book *The American Challenge.*[47]

Servan-Schreiber attributed the American challenge to the dynamism of U.S. society, and he called on Europe to respond by reforming its educational system, industrial policy, and social structure and by establishing its own MNCs. European governments responded partly by upgrading their policies of promoting national champions in key industries through subsidizing research, encouraging mergers, and increasing preferential procurement from national firms. However, Europeans also responded to the American challenge by imposing requirements on foreign MNCs in such areas as job creation and export promotion. France in particular screened inward FDI carefully, and its rejection rate for FDI proposals in the late 1970s was much higher than elsewhere in Europe. When takeovers were proposed—even from other EC countries—the French government often tried to find a French buyer instead. Canada also adopted a screening process in the 1970s because 50 percent of its manufacturing output and 70 percent of its oil production was foreign (i.e., largely U.S.) controlled. As Table 10.5 shows, inward FDI accounted for 20.4 percent of Canada's GDP in 1980, compared with only 11.8 percent for Britain, 3.8 percent for France, 3 percent for the United States, and 0.3 percent for Japan. This high level of FDI contributed to concerns about Canadian dependence on U.S. foreign investment, and a number of special commissions and task forces during the 1960s–1970s produced studies on the issue. In 1974 the Canadian government established the Foreign Investment Review Agency (FIRA) to determine whether foreign takeovers were of "significant benefit" to the country, and in 1980, Canada developed an interventionist National Energy Program (NEP) that was partly designed to increase Canadian ownership in the oil and gas industry. These policies produced significant tensions with the United States.[48]

Japan, however, had the most interventionist policy of the DCs. Table 10.4 shows that Japan's inward FDI accounted for only 0.7 percent of total inward FDI stocks in 1980, compared with 41.6 percent for Western Europe and 17.2 percent for the United States. Although this low level of inward investment resulted partly from the fact that Western MNCs had not adapted to Japan's cultural and linguistic differences, Japanese investment restrictions also played a critical role. Dating back to at least the sixteenth century, Japan's controls on international economic interactions resulted from fear of foreign intervention and national pride in its distinct economy, polity, and society. During the 1930s, Japan developed strategies aimed to extract the benefits of foreign investment, such as access to capital and technology, while avoiding the drawbacks of foreign control. During the postwar period, Japan enacted its restrictive 1950

Foreign Investment Law, and it continued to impose restrictions on FDI inflows in the 1960s–1970s.[49]

Although DCs often restricted or imposed conditions on FDI during the 1970s, in most cases they liberalized their policies and shifted emphasis to attracting FDI in the mid-to-late 1980s. Several factors accounted for this policy change. First, the phasing out of controls on global capital flows and the re-emergence of orthodox liberalism under the leadership of U.S. President Reagan and British Prime Minister Thatcher caused countries to question the legitimacy of imposing FDI restrictions. Second, the increase in global competitiveness, along with economic problems such as unemployment in the North, generated pressures on states to seek rather than restrict FDI. Governments placed considerable value on the jobs FDI could provide because the average unemployment rate in OECD countries rose from 3.3 percent in 1973 to 8.6 percent in 1983. DCs began to view inward FDI as a vehicle for enhancing their competitiveness, and they provided financial incentives and tax concessions to attract MNCs.[50]

A third factor in the shift to more open FDI policies was the change in the country composition of FDI. As other DCs in addition to the United States became important home countries for FDI, they were more likely to favor policies that eased restrictions on MNCs. Traditionally, the EC opposed international rules on investment, and it was ambivalent about a 1981 U.S. proposal that GATT should compile an inventory of trade-related investment measures in host countries. However, during the 1980s the EC began to favor greater discipline over host countries, and it supported the U.S. position at the TRIMs negotiations in the GATT Uruguay Round. This change resulted from the fact that European MNCs greatly increased their outward investment during the 1980s. European firms wanted to encourage the United States to retain its liberal policy on incoming FDI because much of their FDI was directed to the United States.[51]

Japan also felt pressure to ease its inward restrictions on FDI as the disparity between its growing outward investment and its restrictions on inward investment increased. By the 1980s Japan had removed most of its legal obstacles to inward FDI, but intangible barriers to entry continue to limit the role of foreign firms. Foreign M&As are less common in Japan because shareholders that have close linkages with the firms' management and members of *keiretsus* (groups with extensive cross-shareholdings) hold a large share of the stock of Japanese firms. For example, of the 584 M&As involving Japan in 1992, 165 were Japanese firms acquiring other Japanese firms, 165 were Japanese firms acquiring foreign firms, and only 32 were foreign firms acquiring Japanese firms. Inward FDI in Japan has usually occurred through greenfield investments or joint ventures rather than M&As. However, it is also difficult to develop new FDI production projects because of the high cost and complexities of doing business in Japan, the exclusionary business practices of the *keiretsu*, the complex distribution systems, the bureaucratic practices that discriminate against foreign firms, and the high cost of land. The situation is changing to some degree because the Japanese government is adopting policies to encourage greater openness, and foreign takeovers of Japanese firms are increasing. Nevertheless, Table 10.5 shows that inward FDI accounted for only 1.5 percent of Japan's GDP in 2002.[52]

A fourth reason for the shift to more open investment policies is related to pressures imposed by the United States. The two U.S. neighbors, Canada and Mexico, felt these pressures most strongly. For example, U.S. protests and a U.S. challenge in GATT were major factors explaining the Canadian Liberal government's decision to loosen the controls on inward FDI it had instituted through the FIRA and NEP. (Canada was also concerned about declining inward foreign investment at the time.) The Progressive Conservative government of Brian Mulroney, which was elected in 1984, rescinded the NEP and replaced the FIRA with a new institution called Investment Canada. Unlike the FIRA, Investment Canada was more involved with encouraging than reviewing inward FDI. Subsequently, the CUSFTA and NAFTA led to further liberalization of Canadian (and Mexican) foreign investment regulations. It is important to note that Canada's position on inward FDI changed not only because of U.S. pressure but also because Canada (like the EC and Japan) was becoming a more important *source* of FDI. A growing segment of Canadian business interests believed that investment rules were necessary to protect their FDI abroad and that opening Canada to inward FDI was a necessary trade-off. As Table 10.5 shows, in 2002 outward FDI accounted for a higher percentage of Canada's GDP (37.6 percent) than inward FDI (30.4 percent).[53]

The United States was the main advocate of liberalized foreign investment policies and was highly critical of host government interventionism in the 1970s to early 1980s. It is therefore ironic that the United States shifted somewhat toward more restrictive policies in the 1980s–1990s. This policy shift resulted largely from the relative decline of U.S. economic hegemony and the increased U.S. role as a host as well as a home country for FDI. Table 10.5 shows that inward FDI accounted for only 3 percent of U.S. GDP in 1980 and 4.4 percent in 1985. However, U.S. inward FDI rose to 6.9 percent in 1990 and to 12.9 percent by 2002. Some congressional leaders were concerned that foreign investors were acquiring U.S.-owned high technology firms and that the U.S. military was becoming too dependent on foreign-controlled suppliers. As a result, U.S. policies began to shift toward greater interventionism.

The more interventionist approach in the U.S. Congress was evident in a number of proposed and actual legislative changes. The most important was the Exon-Florio amendment to the 1988 Omnibus Trade and Competitiveness Act, sponsored by Senator James Exon (D–Nebraska) and Representative James Florio (D–New Jersey). This amendment enables the president to block foreign mergers or acquisitions of U.S. firms when there is a possible danger to national security. The authority to implement Exon-Florio rests with an interagency Committee on Foreign Investment in the United States (CFIUS), which was created as an oversight body in 1975. Some more extreme proposals were not passed in the U.S. Congress, and the Exon-Florio amendment represents a compromise between internationalist interests of the executive branch and nationalist pressures in the Congress. The CFIUS and U.S. presidents have implemented the Exon-Florio amendment with considerable moderation. For example, during an active period of inward FDI from 1988 to 1992, CFIUS received 700 cases it judged worthy of review. However, it subjected only 13 of those cases to an extended review and referred only nine of them to the president for a final decision. The president took action on only one of the cases. Nevertheless, an administration could limit inward FDI in the future if it chose to liberally interpret the national security clause in Exon-Florio.[54]

Despite the Exon-Florio amendment, the United States continues to strongly support liberalized foreign investment policies in international forums. For example, the

United States was the main force behind the TRIMs negotiations during the GATT Uruguay Round and behind negotiations for an MAI in the OECD. The North in general continues to support liberalization. Thus, 95 percent of the new DC policy measures in 2001 and 2002 were more favorable to FDI. They involved tax incentives, investment guarantees, the removal or relaxation of restrictions on entry, and the establishment of investment promotion agencies.[55]

MNC-HOME COUNTRY RELATIONS

The number of major home countries for MNCs has always been small. At least 80 percent of FDI before World War I originated in Western Europe, and Britain accounted for the largest share. Between World War I and 1980, only three DCs accounted for 65 to 75 percent of the outward FDI stock—the United States, Britain, and the Netherlands. Although the sources of FDI became more diverse after 1980, six DCs accounted for about 75 percent of the total in the early 1990s—the United States, Britain, Germany, France, Japan, and the Netherlands. Some LDCs have become more important as sources of FDI, and there have been three "waves" of FDI from MNCs in the South. The first wave emanated mainly from Latin American MNCs in the 1960s–1970s, operating under import substitution policies. East Asian firms, by contrast, led the second wave of outward FDI beginning in the 1980s, and Latin American FDI lost ground. The Asian FDI was directed not only to other Asian countries, but also to North America and Europe. Since the late 1980s Latin America has been the source of a third wave of outward FDI. However, most of this FDI has been concentrated in other Latin American states, and unlike Asian MNCs, very few Latin American MNCs operate in high-technology industries.[56] Despite the increase in FDI from LDCs, Table 10.3 shows that the DCs still accounted for 86.8 percent of outward FDI stock in 2001. This discussion of FDI-home country relations therefore focuses mainly on the North.

The effects of FDI on the home country depend on both the characteristics of the home country and the characteristics of its MNCs. Realists often focus on the home country's characteristics, differentiating between rising and declining hegemons. When Britain and the United States first emerged as hegemons in the nineteenth and twentieth centuries, outward FDI seemed to have numerous benefits and few costs to the home country because no powerful domestic groups viewed it as hurting their interests. As a hegemonic state declines, however, some important domestic groups begin to perceive outward FDI as having detrimental effects. In the United States, for example, domestic labor groups experienced rising unemployment during the 1970s, and they began to argue that U.S. FDI was exporting jobs and adversely affecting their interests.[57]

Whereas some theorists focus on the home state's characteristics, others examine the MNC's characteristics as the source of changing MNC-home state relations. Those who focus on the MNC often present evidence that a growing number of MNCs are becoming "denationalized" or "stateless" and are developing interests that diverge from the interests of their home countries. American oil companies, for example, became less closely identified with the U.S. national interest after the 1973 energy crisis, when they were accused of aiding the Arab oil embargo; and European oil companies refused to give their home markets preferential deliveries during the embargo, despite the requests of the home governments. In recent years, increasingly mobile capital is limiting the ability of home states as well as host states to affect the behavior and activities of MNCs.

Whether policymakers focus on the characteristics of the state or the MNC as a causal factor, questions about the costs as well as benefits of FDI to home countries have increased in recent years. This section begins with a discussion of home country policies toward their MNCs. It then examines two contentious questions in regard to home country-MNC relations: (1) What are the costs and benefits of FDI for labor groups in the home country? and (2) What is the relationship between the competitiveness of a home country and the competitiveness of its MNCs?

Home Country Policies Toward Their MNCs

Although government policies toward outward FDI have been less extensive than those toward inward FDI, it is possible to identify a range of home country policies. Home governments normally view outward FDI as an indication of economic and political strength, and as beneficial to their competitiveness. Thus, home governments usually give their MNCs favored treatment and try to protect them from hostile actions by foreigners, particularly when the MNCs operate in strategic industries. On some occasions, however, governments attempt to monitor, control, or even restrain outward FDI in the interests of the home economy. For example, home governments sometimes view their MNCs as tools of foreign policy and are willing to coerce them if necessary to affect their behavior. Furthermore, home governments sometimes associate outward FDI with a decrease in home country exports, a decline in the country's industrial base, and losses in domestic employment. In such circumstances, home countries may attempt to stem the flow of outward FDI.

The Pre–World War II Period   During the nineteenth and early twentieth centuries, home countries adopted policies to support their corporations and protect them when they encountered difficulties abroad. For example, in the colonial period European states sometimes intervened militarily to ensure that their trading and producing companies could develop and prosper. During the interwar years, European home governments provided subsidies and other types of assistance to support airlines, shipping firms, and oil companies that were closely tied to their strategic interests. In the 1930s, the Japanese army occupied Chinese plants and gave Japanese companies control over their management. The United States was also willing to support the interests of its companies in Latin America with military force, but the use of military force was not automatic. On certain occasions, governments took actions to limit outward FDI. For example, after the Nazis came to power the German government had to approve all new FDI, and it was willing to approve investments only in exceptional cases. Although the U.S. government expressed concerns as early as the 1920s that outward FDI could transfer technology and export employment to foreign countries, it adopted no policies to restrict FDI outflows during the pre–World War II period.[58]

Early Postwar Period   In the 1950s–1970s, the United States as hegemonic power assertively protected its MNCs and pressured them for political and economic reasons. For example, the U.S. Congress responded to corporate lobbying by passing the Hickenlooper Amendment in 1962, which threatened to withhold development assistance from LDCs that nationalized American MNC affiliates without providing adequate compensation. The United States also viewed its MNCs as tools of foreign policy vis-à-vis certain communist countries. For example, the U.S. government used its Trading with the Enemy Act and Foreign Assets Control Legislation in the 1960s–1970s to limit the trade of U.S. subsidiaries with China, Cuba, North Vietnam, and North Korea. Host governments for U.S. subsidiaries in Canada, Europe, and Latin America considered these policies an infringement on their sovereignty, and they often adopted laws to counter the U.S. legislation. The United States also took actions to control corporate behavior in response to its growing balance-of-payments deficit. During the 1960s, the U.S. government called on its MNCs to limit the outflow of capital to their foreign affiliates; and in the 1970s, the government created the Domestic International Sales Corporation (DISC) program, which provided tax incentives to MNCs to encourage them to export from the United States rather than from abroad.[59]

European governments recovering from World War II were concerned that outward FDI would adversely affect their balance of payments. However, they did little to either encourage or restrict outward FDI in the 1950s–1960s. Japan was the only major economy that systematically restricted outward FDI for about two decades after World War II. In its efforts to keep scarce capital at home for postwar reconstruction, the Japanese government scrutinized every possible FDI project and approved only those that would increase exports, provide access to necessary raw materials, and pose no threat to Japanese producers. Thus, Table 10.3 shows that Japan accounted for only 0.7 percent of outward stocks of FDI in 1960 and 1.4 percent in 1967. Japan did not begin to liberalize its controls on outward FDI until the late 1960s, when its balance-of-trade surpluses were rapidly increasing.[60]

1980s to the Present   Although the United States devoted less effort to limiting dealings with communist countries with the decline of the Cold War, it sometimes acted in response to international events and domestic political pressures. In the early 1980s, for example, Western Europe and the Soviet Union agreed to construct a natural gas pipeline, in which Western European firms were to provide equipment needed for the pipeline's construction in return for future deliveries of Soviet natural gas. After Poland declared martial law in December 1981, the United States retaliated against the Soviet Union by imposing an embargo on materials produced by U.S. companies that were destined for use in constructing the pipeline. The United States not only prohibited subsidiaries of U.S. MNCs from exporting foreign-produced equipment and technology to the Soviet Union but also ordered foreign companies not to export goods produced with technology acquired under licensing agreements with U.S. companies. The Reagan administration's opposition to the pipeline stemmed from concerns that Western Europe would become overly dependent on Soviet gas supplies and that the gas exports would provide the Soviet Union with hard currency needed to strengthen its economy.

However, planning for the pipeline was already at an advanced stage when the Reagan administration tried to impede the project, and Europeans argued that the

U.S. actions represented a new level of extraterritorial interference. Britain, France, West Germany, and Italy reacted harshly by ordering their resident firms to ignore the U.S. restrictions and provide the needed goods and technology to the Soviet Union. A number of firms, such as Dresser-France (a U.S. subsidiary) and licensees of General Electric in Britain, Italy, and West Germany, complied with the European counter-orders. Initially, the United States retaliated by imposing penalties on these firms. However, when it became evident that the Europeans would not back down, the Reagan administration removed most of its sanctions on the supply of equipment for the Siberian gas pipeline, and the European sales proceeded.[61] Since the breakup of the Soviet Union, U.S. extraterritorial actions of this nature have been aimed mainly at Cuba. For example, the controversial 1996 Helms-Burton Act penalizes *foreign* companies for doing business in Cuba if they use assets or property of U.S. MNCs (or individuals) that were nationalized after the 1959 Cuban Revolution. Foreign governments reacted angrily to this legislation and indicated that their resident companies would not abide by it.[62]

Other home countries have been less inclined (and less able) than the United States to take such blatant political actions to control the behavior of their MNCs. In *economic* areas, however, Japan and the Western European countries have been more willing than the United States to establish close linkages with their MNCs to achieve common purposes. Indeed, the United States has been more inclined than other DCs to maintain an arm's length relationship between business and the government (the U.S. defense and oil industries have been exceptions). Realists have argued that the United States should develop its own industrial policy to support its MNCs and counter the actions of Japan and Europe, especially in high-technology areas. Such a policy would involve the establishment of institutional mechanisms to assess competitive trends in high-technology industries, and a shift of federal R&D funds from military uses to dual-use and economic areas. The United States has pursued some limited industrial policy initiatives but not to the same extent as Japan and some European countries. The adoption of industrial policy measures poses a realist challenge to liberal support for dependence on the market and on firms that are the lowest cost suppliers, regardless of their nationality.[63]

The Effects of MNCs on Labor Groups in Home Countries

The effects of MNCs on labor is one of the most contentious issues in home countries. The most common concerns relate to the effects of outward FDI on home country workers' employment, wages, and position in industrial relations. In the 1970s, when the United States was mainly a home country for MNCs, organized labor began to strongly oppose outward FDI. American union leaders called for restraints on foreign investment, tax incentives to encourage U.S. MNCs to produce at home for export rather than producing abroad, and adjustment assistance for workers. In 1971, the AFL-CIO supported the ill-fated Burke-Hartke Bill, which would have ended the tax credit MNCs received for foreign income taxes and given the president authority to block new outward FDI. In the early 1990s, U.S. labor groups opposed NAFTA because of concerns that U.S. MNCs would shift their operations to Mexico; and more recently, some U.S. labor groups have attributed the rising wage gap between skilled and unskilled labor to outward FDI. Unemployment has risen in several DCs in recent years, fueling concerns among labor groups about the growing FDI outflows. For example, a 1993 report to the French Senate argued that FDI was a major cause of unemployment among factory workers; Japanese policymakers expressed concerns that unemployment resulted from the relocation of Japanese plants to other Asian countries; and Germany was concerned about the employment effects of German industries relocating in Eastern Europe.[64]

Although there are differences of view among liberals, they have been more inclined to focus on the positive effects of FDI on home country employment. Realists and historical structuralists, by contrast, have usually emphasized the negative effects. Major concerns about the negative effects of outward FDI on home country employment relate to export substitution and intra-firm imports. Export substitution results when production of a foreign affiliate in country B substitutes for exports from the parent firm in country A, or when exports from the foreign affiliate to a third country (C) substitute for goods and services formerly supplied by the parent firm to C. Intra-firm imports involve goods and services that the home country imports from foreign affiliates of parent firms.[65] Realists often argue that both export substitution and intra-firm imports can reduce production and employment in the home country. Historical structuralists argue that the mobility of capital and MNCs puts immobile workers at a distinct disadvantage. Whereas MNCs can increase their flexibility and competitiveness by extending production to many countries, labor unions are largely limited to organizing themselves on a national or even local basis. The transfer of MNC activities to subsidiaries in LDCs with lower wages and standards will produce a deterioration of working conditions in the home country. The geographical fragmentation of production by MNCs in different industrial states can also put labor at a disadvantage because of its difficulty in organizing on a multi-country basis.[66]

Liberals by contrast often argue that the effect of outward FDI on home country employment is generally positive. Thus, they present evidence to demonstrate that MNCs have a better record than domestic firms in regard to job creation, worker salaries, export performance, and technological innovations in the home country.[67] Liberals also reject the idea that home country workers will suffer as a result of the transfer of MNC activities to subsidiaries in LDCs with lower wages and standards. For example, one liberal study argues that foreign investment by U.S. firms in Mexico as a result of NAFTA "creates U.S. jobs, both in the short run, by boosting U.S. exports of capital goods, and in the long run, by establishing channels for the export of U.S. intermediate components, replacement parts, and associated goods and services."[68]

Beyond the national level, labor unions have been interested in developing a system of multinational collective bargaining since the early 1970s. The goal is to increase the ability of unions from different countries to bargain together with MNCs. Initiatives that international unions are taking to achieve this objective include holding world congresses of workers from the same MNC and putting all of an MNC's collective agreements into a single database to increase awareness of arrangements in different plants. Multilateral collective bargaining, however, has definite limitations, and even in the EU national structures continue to dominate unions. Furthermore, the NAFTA experience demonstrates that labor in DC home countries such as the United States may have very different perspectives from labor in LDC host states such as Mexico.[69]

Competitiveness and Home Country–MNC Relations

As a growing number of MNCs have organized their operations on a global level, questions have arisen as to whether they have worldwide interests that differ from the interests of their home countries. Robert Reich suggests that residents of a nation-state must ask, "Who is *us*?" Does *us* include our MNCs?[70] Phrased another way, is the competitiveness of a nation-state closely linked with the competitiveness of its MNCs? Realists argue that the nationality of firms and the amount of foreign ownership can have a major impact on a state's competitiveness. From this perspective, "a nation's standard of living in the long term depends on its ability to attain a high and rising level of productivity in the industries in which its firms compete."[71] Thus, some realists argue that a country such as Canada has a good standard of living but can never have the best because of the high degree of foreign ownership in its manufacturing industry. The best jobs, and most of the R&D, are usually located in the home country.[72]

Liberals, by contrast, often argue that MNCs seek profitable opportunities around the world and that "they are becoming disconnected from their home nations."[73] A country's competitiveness, from this perspective, is no longer closely linked with the competitiveness of its MNCs. Thus, liberals maintain that the economic future of the United States depends more on U.S. workers' education and skills than on U.S. corporate ownership. If Americans have the requisite technical training, foreign as well as U.S. corporations will employ U.S. workers in growing numbers. Some liberals go even further and assert that we are entering a "borderless world" in which a corporation's nationality will no longer make a difference.[74] The position analysts take on either side of this competitiveness debate obviously affects their prescriptions for policymaking. Thus, realists argue that governments should pursue active industrial policies to promote their own MNCs in high-technology areas. Interventionist liberals, by contrast, believe that governments should focus more on upgrading the technological skills and sophistication of the working population than on helping their MNCs. In other words, governments must make their countries attractive so that global firms—regardless of their nationality—will want to do business, invest, and pay taxes there.[75]

Some evidence indicates that large MNCs are in fact becoming more global in their operations and outlook and less closely tied to their home countries. For example, the sales of foreign affiliates of U.S. firms were about four times greater than the exports of goods from the United States between 1988 and 1990; foreign affiliates of U.S. MNCs accounted for 43 percent of their parent companies' total profits in 1990; and U.S. firms increased their foreign R&D spending by 33 percent compared with a spending increase of only 6 percent in the United States from 1986 to 1988. Furthermore, national boundaries are becoming blurred as some MNCs have spread their head office functions and listed their shares in stock exchanges in several countries. For example, Shell and Unilever have headquarters in Britain and the Netherlands, and Astra-Zeneca has its corporate headquarters in one country and conducts most of its R&D in another country. Another example of an MNC with blurred national boundaries is Asea Brown Boveri (ABB), which was formed from a merger of Sweden's ASEA and Switzerland's Brown Boveri. ABB moved its headquarters from Stockholm to Zurich, which is more centrally located vis-à-vis major European markets. Although the ABB managers are Swiss, German, and Swedish, the company does its business in English and keeps its financial records in dollars.

The increase of cross-border M&As and conglomerate cross-holding of shares are additional complications in defining an MNC's nationality. Furthermore, the growth of integrated production systems makes it more difficult to determine a product's origins. MNCs can insulate themselves from national policies and conditions by sourcing inputs, information, and personnel from around the world. For example, an automobile manufactured by Ford may be assembled in Britain from inputs coming from all over Europe, from designs produced in the United States and Europe, and from stages of processing in many different locations. Thus, liberals argue that home government policies must change as the national origins, loyalties, and culture of some MNCs become increasingly blurred. In this age of globalization, the highest priority should be "to provide competitive conditions for businesses in general in the country rather than only for the country's firms in particular."[76]

Despite the blurring of nationalities, realists are correct that *most* MNCs continue to be home-country based and that an MNC's competitiveness can affect the competitiveness of its home state. R&D is a major factor in promoting competitiveness, and there is evidence that MNCs in the North keep much of their R&D activity at home. In 1984, for example, the ratio of R&D to sales for industrial machinery and equipment firms in Canada was only about 40 percent of the ratio in the United States, and much of this difference resulted from the high degree of foreign ownership in the Canadian industry. Although American MNCs are more willing than Japanese MNCs to invest in R&D abroad, even U.S. companies spent only 8.6 percent of their R&D funding in foreign countries in 1988.[77] One factor in a country's competitiveness is its ability to maintain a favorable trade balance, and there is evidence that U.S. affiliates of Japanese firms have a higher propensity than American firms to import goods and services into the United States. R&D funding is also essential for the development of new technologies, and ownership and control of technologically sophisticated industries can have significance for a country's long-term national security.[78]

Although the competitiveness of a state can be tied to the competitiveness of its firms, there are important national differences in the operation of MNCs headquartered in different countries. For example, there is some evidence that U.S. MNCs favor their home country less than Japanese and German MNCs. Studies have shown that U.S. MNCs are more interested in the financial returns on investments, whereas Japanese MNCs place more emphasis on market share; U.S. MNCs are more willing to invest in overseas R&D activities than their Japanese counterparts; and German and Japanese MNCs place more emphasis on exporting from the home country than U.S. MNCs. Thus, Reich's question as to whether "our MNCs" look after "our national interests" may be more relevant for U.S. MNCs than for Japanese and German MNCs.[79]

Some liberal theorists argue that the term *competitiveness* has more meaning when applied to MNCs than to states. A corporation may go out of business if it is not competitive, but states normally continue to exist. Furthermore, companies such as Coca-Cola and Pepsi Co. are rivals involved in a zero-sum game, whereas the DCs are each other's major trading partners even when they are in competition. International trade is not a zero-sum game; a prosperous European economy provides U.S. exporters with larger markets and offers U.S. consumers higher quality goods at lower prices than a weaker European economy.[80] A number of economists, however, present counterarguments to demonstrate that in an age of globalization, competitiveness is as much of a concern for states as it is for MNCs.[81]

A REGIME FOR FDI: WHAT IS TO BE REGULATED?

Although MNCs have a central role in the global economy, the principles, norms, and rules regulating foreign investment are far more rudimentary than those in many other areas, such as trade and monetary relations. Furthermore, no international organization has a role in a "foreign investment regime" comparable with that of the WTO in the global trade regime. Most government policies related to MNCs are formulated at the national level, but the transnational nature of MNCs makes these policies inadequate. The main obstacle to forming a foreign investment regime is the lack of consensus on what should be regulated—the MNC, the host state, or the home state. The prominent role of private actors (MNCs, multinational banks, etc.) as sources of investment capital also makes international regulation a difficult and contentious issue.

According to orthodox liberals, investment agreements should regulate host state behavior so investors can function freely in the global marketplace. Thus, agreements should provide maximum protection for MNCs against nationalization, performance requirements, and other impediments. Home countries should have the right to intervene on behalf of their MNCs, in the orthodox liberal view, if the purpose is to counter host government actions that inhibit investment flows. Realists and historical structuralists, by contrast, see some government limitations on foreign investment as legitimate. From a realist perspective, states understandably want to ensure that MNC activity does not conflict with national interest or national security. From a historical structuralist perspective, investment agreements should regulate MNCs and protect host governments. Labor in both host and home countries is at a distinct disadvantage because investors can easily move their assets across international borders. LDC host countries also require special protection because they are in a highly dependent position vis-à-vis MNCs. Thus, international rules should limit the power of MNCs and the major home countries that support them.

In the 1950s–1960s, the United States as global hegemon provided much of the regulatory activity in the foreign investment area. American policy during this period was mainly aimed at protecting FDI flows against hostile actions of host states (such as nationalization) and ensuring that MNC behavior did not conflict with U.S. and Western objectives in the Cold War. European states also concluded *bilateral investment treaties (BITs)* in the 1960s, which provided some protection for their investments in LDCs (BITs are discussed later in this chapter). In the 1970s, attention shifted to developing an international regulatory framework for FDI, and several economists proposed that "a General Agreement for the International Corporation" be established, similar to GATT.[82] A number of developments in the 1970s contributed to sentiments that an international framework should regulate the behavior of MNCs. For example,

MNCs engaged in currency speculation when the Bretton Woods pegged exchange rate regime was faltering; some DCs such as France and Canada became concerned about the influence of U.S. MNCs and established mechanisms to screen foreign investment; and LDCs pressured for the international regulation of MNCs as part of their demands for a NIEO.[83] A number of scholars supported these policy changes in the 1970s. For example, one noted author argued that "global corporations must be regulated to restore sovereignty to government" because the MNC is "not accountable to any public authority that matches it in geographical reach."[84]

Despite widespread sentiments during the 1970s to exert some control over MNC behavior, the South took the main initiatives in this direction. Arguing that the customary rules of international law regarding foreign investment did not take sufficient account of Southern needs and interests, the G-77 pressured for UN regulation of MNCs rather than host states. As a result of this LDC activism, the UN Economic and Social Committee set up a Commission on Transnational Corporations in 1974 with a mandate to develop a binding Code of Conduct for MNCs. LDCs also engaged in a series of nationalizations in the 1960s–1970s, and OPEC actions to gain greater control over oil pricing and production posed a threat to the international oil companies. To counter these developments, the OECD ministers at the urging of the U.S. government decided to develop their own policy on MNCs, which sought to achieve a greater balance than the UN in recognizing the responsibilities of host states as well as MNCs. Thus, the OECD adopted a Declaration and Decisions on International Investment and Multinational Enterprises in 1976 that included some guidelines for MNC behavior but also sought to improve the foreign investment climate in host states.[85]

By the late 1970s, it was evident that the OECD would not agree to LDC demands for a UN Code of Conduct for MNCs, and several factors contributed to a shift of the pendulum back to emphasis on controlling the behavior of host states. Most significantly, the South's share of inward FDI was declining because of the foreign debt crisis, concerns about LDC political and economic stability, and the emphasis on high-technology investment in the North. As the needs of LDCs for capital inflows increased, they gradually abandoned their interventionist policies toward MNCs. The increased bargaining power of the DCs enabled them to begin forging a consensus during the 1980s that a stronger regime was necessary to facilitate increased flows of FDI and that the behavior of host countries—not MNCs—was in need of regulation. Although BITs had been the predominant source of foreign investment rules, the feeling grew stronger during the 1980s that multilateral rules were required. Before examining the multilateral efforts to regulate investment, the next section provides some background on BITs.

BILATERAL INVESTMENT TREATIES

Countries have been concluding bilateral treaties to promote and protect foreign investment for more than 40 years. Known generically as BITs, these treaties impose obligations on the contracting parties with regard to the treatment of foreign investment and provide dispute resolution mechanisms to enforce these obligations. However, BITs were not the first bilateral treaties to provide protection for foreign investment. As early as the late eighteenth century, the United States, and to a lesser extent

Japan and a few Western European countries, concluded Friendship, Commerce, and Navigation (FCN) treaties; Treaties of Establishment; and Treaties of Amity and Commerce. Unlike the BITs of the post–World War II period, these treaties dealt with many issues in addition to investment such as trade, maritime, and consular relations. However, these treaties also included property protection provisions related to investment, such as restrictions on a host country's right of expropriation. A significant number of these FCN treaties remain in force today.[86]

After World War II, bilateral trade agreements became less significant because of the establishment of the GATT-based multilateral trade regime. Thus, investment protection became the main purpose of the BITs. In 1959 West Germany negotiated the first two BITs, with Pakistan and the Dominican Republic. However, most BITs in the 1960s were concluded between Western European and African states. Other major DCs, including the United States and Japan, soon joined Western Europe in concluding BITs with the LDCs. It is interesting that the negotiation of BITs increased dramatically during the 1970s. Although LDCs were actively calling for an NIEO in the 1970s, this did not prevent them from concluding BITs that contained provisions they were actively opposing in the UN. The LDCs wanted to alter the international principles and norms for foreign investment, but they were prepared to participate in BITs for pragmatic reasons to attract FDI. Some centrally planned economies, such as Romania and Yugoslavia, also signed their first BITs with the DCs during the 1970s.

As discussed in Chapter 7, LDCs depended heavily on private bank lending for their development needs during the 1970s. However, the onset of the foreign debt crisis in 1982 resulted in a sharp reduction in commercial bank exposure, and the LDC debtor countries therefore became highly dependent on foreign investment for development finance. As a result, many more LDCs and transition economies concluded BITs in the 1980s. For example, China negotiated its first BIT in 1982, and by the end of the 1980s China had concluded 25 BITs. The total number of BITs signed increased from 167 at the end of the 1970s to 385 in 1989. The number of BITs increased even more rapidly during the 1990s, partly because LDCs required more foreign investment as a result of a steady decline in DC foreign aid. Thus, 176 countries had concluded 2,181 BITs by 2002. Although the predominant number of BITs were traditionally between DCs and LDCs, more BITs are being concluded between LDCs, and between LDCs and transition economies. This change results from the fact that some LDCs and transition economies are now home countries as well as host countries for FDI. Currently BITs are the most widely used international agreement for protecting FDI.[87]

The BITs generally uphold MFN and national treatment, under which an MNC is assured of treatment at least as favorable as that granted to domestic firms or to MNCs from third countries. The treaties also often prohibit host country performance requirements that commit MNCs to export goods produced in the host country or to purchase goods and services locally. Furthermore, the BITs require payment of prompt and adequate compensation in the event of nationalization. From the South's perspective, BITs with the North are one-sided because they impose "obligations on the host state for the protection of foreign investment, without any corresponding obligations on the part of the home country or the foreign investor."[88] The DCs also view the BITs as inadequate, but for very different reasons. They are particularly concerned that the variation in their terms seriously limits the effectiveness of these bilateral agreements in international law.

Because both the South and the North are dissatisfied with BITs, the question arises as to why they continue to be so important. From the North's perspective, BITs have provided a "second best solution in the absence of a universal investment agreement."[89] Other than some regional agreements such as NAFTA, BITs continue to be the best means for regulating the treatment of foreign investors by LDC host countries. From an LDC host country perspective, joining in BITs with DCs is necessary if they want to attract FDI. With the foreign debt crisis and the decline in foreign aid, LDC ideological views against BITs gave way to a more pragmatic approach. Thus, "whether BITs are one-sided agreements in favor of the capital-exporting country became less relevant than in past decades as developing countries made special efforts to create conditions favourable to attracting FDI."[90]

With the rapid increase in the number of BITs in recent years, there is a risk that growing reliance on them will "produce a wide range of non-uniform and inconsistent arrangements that could become increasingly inefficient, complex, and non-transparent."[91] However, wide differences among countries on the issue of what is to be regulated—the MNC, the home state, or the host state—have to this point precluded the development of a multilateral foreign investment regime. A number of international and regional organizations have provisions dealing with foreign investment. The sections that follow focus on five efforts to establish foreign investment regulations at the multilateral and regional levels: the United Nations, the WTO, regional agreements such as the EU and NAFTA, the OECD, and private actors such as NGOs and business groups.

UNITED NATIONS

As discussed, the late 1960s–1970s was a period when LDCs and some DCs such as France and Canada raised concerns about the effects of MNCs on the national sovereignty of host states. A high-profile case in the early 1970s involving the International Telephone and Telegraph Corporation (ITT) and Chile heightened LDC criticisms and brought the issue of regulating MNCs to UN attention. The importance of this case stemmed from the fact that ITT was one of the world's largest and most successful MNCs. ITT was concerned that the Marxist candidate in the 1970 Chilean presidential election, Salvador Allende, would nationalize its Chilean affiliate without compensation. As a result, ITT engaged in a series of attempts from 1970 to 1972 to prevent Allende's election, and after Allende was elected to have him removed from power. ITT also tried to involve the U.S. Central Intelligence Agency (CIA) and U.S. Information Agency (USIA) in its clandestine activities. ITT's actions became public in March 1972 when a syndicated columnist, Jack Anderson, published documents on the issue, and there were serious repercussions. In the United States, a subcommittee of the U.S. Senate Committee on Foreign Relations conducted an investigation and released a report titled *The International Telephone and Telegraph Company and Chile.*[92] Internationally, the UN secretary general appointed a Group of Eminent Persons in 1972 to examine the impact of MNCs. In 1974 the group issued a report strongly condemning "subversive political intervention" by MNCs such as ITT in Chile, and recommending that a commission be established to develop a code of conduct for governments and MNCs.[93] In response, the UN established a *Commission on Transnational Corporations* to exchange views on MNCs, develop a comprehensive information system on MNC activities, and help establish a code of conduct. The commission met only on an annual basis, and a *UN Center on Transnational Corporations (UNCTC)* served as its secretariat.

The development of a comprehensive code of conduct for MNCs was a priority objective of the UN commission, and the South strongly supported this objective. An intergovernmental working group began preparing a draft text of the code and submitted its report to the commission in 1982. However, a long period of negotiations on the report followed because of fundamental disagreements among member states. For example, there was no consensus on whether the code should have the force of law or simply provide a set of voluntary guidelines. Most LDCs and socialist states supported the draft code because it sought to prevent MNC tax evasion, restrictive business practices, and transfer pricing. The DCs as leading home states for MNCs, by contrast, strongly opposed the draft UN code, arguing that it did not adequately address the issue of host state treatment of MNCs. In 1992, after years of sporadic negotiations, the UN finally abandoned its efforts to form a consensus on a code of conduct for MNCs. One year later the UNCTC was dissolved and replaced by a less proactive Division on Transnational Corporations and Investment located within UNCTAD.[94]

UNCTAD has developed its expertise on foreign investment issues, and its annual publications titled *World Investment Report* and *Trade and Development Report* are highly regarded. However, it is highly unlikely that the North would ever agree to have UNCTAD host negotiations for multilateral investment rules. Thus, the UN's efforts since 1993 have been directed to promoting purely voluntary standards of behavior for MNCs. At the 1999 World Economic Forum in Davos the UN Secretary General Kofi Annan proposed that a Global Compact be established. The compact comprises principles on human rights, labor standards, and the environment, and urges MNCs to act on those principles in their corporate management practices. Participating MNCs are to work with the UN in partnership projects and to notify the UN of concrete steps they have taken to act on the compact's principles. Although the International Chamber of Commerce has pledged to work with UN agencies to implement the Global Compact and some MNCs have lent their support, the response of MNCs and NGOs has been highly uneven. Unlike a regulatory instrument or code of conduct, the compact is voluntary, and one can raise serious questions about its ability to alter MNC behavior.[95]

GATT/WTO

The WTO is a natural institution to deal with FDI issues because of the close interaction between foreign investment and trade. A growing percentage of trade is intrafirm trade, and a number of current regional as well as multilateral trade agreements contain investment provisions. FDI has nevertheless been referred to as the "neglected twin" of trade; trade rather than investment was the focus of multilateral negotiations and institution building during the postwar period.[96] Indeed, investment was virtually "a forbidden subject" in GATT for many years because a number of governments were reluctant to accept limits on their control of FDI within their territorial boundaries.[97]

The United States for years had wanted GATT to regulate host country controls on foreign investment, but GATT members did not seriously consider negotiating investment issues until the 1980s during preparations for the Uruguay Round. Although the Uruguay Round included negotiations on trade-related investment measures, Brazil, India, and most other LDCs strongly opposed the TRIMs talks. As a result, TRIMs were very narrowly defined to accommodate governments that opposed any discipline over such issues, and the final TRIMs agreement deals with only the most obvious violations of existing GATT articles. The TRIMs agreement does prohibit host countries from imposing local content requirements on FDI; i.e., requirements that a certain share of an investor's inputs or value added must be of domestic origin. However, the agreement does not address many other issues, such as a host country's export performance requirements; i.e., requirements that a certain share of an investor's output be exported from the host country. In addition to TRIMs, TRIPs and GATS have provisions related to FDI because intellectual property and services issues involve foreign investment as well as trade. Thus, the provisions on foreign investment are scattered throughout the agreement, and they do not constitute a comprehensive body of rules for foreign investment.[98] Most liberal economists view the TRIMs and other WTO investment provisions as only "a tentative first step toward a multilateral investment regime,"[99] but the TRIMs and NAFTA agreements created a precedent for conducting far more extensive multilateral negotiations on investment in the OECD (see the following discussion).[100]

REGIONAL APPROACHES: THE EU AND NAFTA

Liberal economists have viewed RTAs as a second-best approach to dealing with FDI because multilateral institutions such as the GATT/WTO have failed to develop a strong foreign investment regime. Most RTAs include investment as well as trade provisions, at least in principle. The general aim is to liberalize trade and FDI flows within regions. This section focuses on two of the most important examples: the EU and NAFTA. The EU's advanced stage of economic integration is reflected in its system for regulating FDI. As a common market, the EU provides for the free movement of capital and protection of FDI among the member states. Thus, the European Commission has legal authority to monitor and regulate MNC activities, with the ultimate goal of developing a "level playing field." The EU has been concerned that European MNCs are not large enough to compete with American and Japanese MNCs. Thus, the EU's policy toward MNCs "is two-edged, encouraging multinational activity in a transnational European market, while seeking to remedy the concerns caused by this activity by specific binding measures of containment."[101] In view of the high level of EU integration, its method of dealing with FDI is less likely to serve as a model for future efforts to develop a multilateral foreign investment regime. This section therefore devotes more attention to NAFTA.

The investment provisions in Chapter 11 of NAFTA "carry forward on a trilateral basis all of the key provisions of U.S. bilateral investment treaties."[102] For example, NAFTA commits its three members to provide MFN and national treatment to foreign investors; to ban all new export performance, local content, and technology transfer requirements; and to phase out most existing performance requirements within 10 years. NAFTA also provides for binding arbitration of investment disputes in an international forum rather than in national courts. Most significantly, private investors may submit complaints against a NAFTA government directly to a three-member tribunal that has the authority to make final decisions and award damages. In the WTO, by contrast, only governments have "standing" in dispute settlement cases, and investors must be represented by governments in settling their claims. Although many BITs have investor-state dispute settlement provisions, the NAFTA provisions go beyond the bilateral level and may lead to the development of similar provisions in a multilateral investment agreement.

Although the NAFTA provisions are groundbreaking, members may claim numerous exceptions to the Chapter 11 obligations. For example, the United States excludes its maritime industry, Canada exempts its cultural industries, and Mexico shields its energy and rail sectors from the investment provisions. The NAFTA rules of origin also include complex procedures for determining local content, which may disadvantage outside firms wishing to enter North America. Despite the limitations of the NAFTA provisions, they go much further than multilateral agreements in liberalizing investment flows and have been a source of considerable controversy. Most liberal economists believe that "open investment policies should be the norm, with limited . . . exceptions allowed only when justified in the name of national security or some other overriding principle."[103] Liberals therefore generally applaud NAFTA for its significant advances in freeing investment flows. Liberal criticisms of the NAFTA provisions stem from the sectoral exceptions that have prevented NAFTA from "completely liberalizing the North American investment regime."[104] Realists and historical structuralists, by contrast, view the NAFTA investment provisions as a threat to national sovereignty and to the ability of labor groups in all three countries to protect their interests. In the historical structuralist view, the NAFTA rules increase capital mobility and give the capitalist class even greater advantages vis-à-vis labor. Thus, MNCs can now easily transfer their operations from the United States and Canada to Mexico to benefit from lower labor costs and environmental standards, contributing to a competitive "race to the bottom."[105] Realists argue that NAFTA's limits on the use of performance requirements prevent host countries from gaining positive spinoffs from foreign investment. Canada and Mexico have imposed performance requirements to encourage investment in depressed regions and in certain sectors of the economy to ensure that foreign investment contributes to local employment and the growth of exports. By preventing these measures, NAFTA makes it difficult for host countries to channel foreign investment to further their development objectives.

Liberals and realists have differing views of NAFTA's Chapter 11 investment dispute-resolution provisions, which permit private investors to obtain relief directly from governments for alleged NAFTA violations. In the liberal view, "these procedures have the merit of distancing investment disputes from the political arena. An investor who feels that it has suffered damage by reason of a measure taken by a NAFTA country can pursue its claim without having to involve its government." Realists by contrast believe the dispute resolution provisions "provide a vehicle for investors to harass governments whose policies they dislike."[106] By giving MNCs legal standing in investment disputes with governments, realists argue that the NAFTA provisions pose a direct threat to national sovereignty. Despite the controversy over the NAFTA provisions, they establish important precedents, and in many respects served as a model for OECD negotiations on a multilateral investment agreement.[107]

THE OECD

In September 1995, the OECD members began negotiations to establish an MAI. The OECD seemed to be a natural venue for developing a multilateral investment agreement with legally binding obligations because OECD countries account for about 87 percent of FDI outflows and 65 percent of FDI inflows. Furthermore, the OECD has had long-term experience in dealing with foreign investment issues. In 1961 the OECD adopted two codes to liberalize capital flows, and in 1976 it adopted a Declaration on International Investment and Multinational Enterprises. The OECD developed the 1976 declaration to provide an alternative to the draft UN code of conduct that would have focused only on MNC behavior. For example, the OECD declaration contains both a national treatment instrument designed to provide MNCs with treatment no less favorable than local firms and voluntary guidelines for responsible MNC behavior. Unlike the WTO, which seeks to achieve its goals through negotiating rounds, the OECD relies on unilateral liberalization and peer persuasion. In some respects the peer review process has contributed to investment liberalization, but it is uncertain whether the OECD guidelines have had much effect on MNC behavior. For example, although the guidelines call on MNCs to refrain from using transfer pricing to avoid paying taxes, the U.S. Internal Revenue Service maintains that this admonition has not induced MNCs to pay their "fair share of taxes in the United States."[108]

The United States wanted a comprehensive and binding MAI, and it had been frustrated by LDC opposition to even the limited TRIMs agreement negotiated in the GATT Uruguay Round. Most OECD members are DC capital exporters, and the United States had good reason to expect they would agree on an MAI. However, there was no DC consensus that the OECD was the best venue for the negotiations. The EU Commission preferred the WTO as the venue because this was the only IO where it could represent all the EU members as a united front. Furthermore, the EU Commission wanted an MAI that would bind non-OECD countries which were a growing destination for EU-based FDI. Canada also favored the WTO as a venue because NAFTA already dealt with its most important investment relationship, and it wanted an MAI to benefit Canadian MNCs in Latin America and Africa. Despite these differences of view, the MAI negotiations began in the OECD for several reasons. First, there was no WTO consensus to address the investment issue because of opposition from many LDCs. Second, some EU members were reluctant to expand the Commission's mandate by going to the WTO and preferred to negotiate for themselves in the OECD. To allay concerns about the exclusivity of the MAI negotiations, the OECD indicated that non-OECD countries would be consulted.[109]

From September 1995 to April 1997 the OECD negotiating group made remarkable progress, and the emerging MAI was to focus on three aspects of rule making: protection for foreign investors, liberalization of investment, and dispute-settlement procedures. The investment-protection provisions would deal with such issues as compensation for expropriation of property, freedom of investors to transfer profits and dividends out of the host country, and fair and equitable treatment for foreign investors. The investment-liberalization provisions would obligate host countries to provide MFN and national treatment for foreign investors and to limit performance requirements. The dispute-settlement procedures would permit investors as well as states to submit complaints for binding dispute settlement at the international level. Although a number of these provisions were already included in the BITs and NAFTA, the MAI would be multilateral in scope and more comprehensive in coverage than previous agreements.

Despite progress in the negotiations, significant differences remained, and in May 1997 the negotiating group had to request a one-year extension of its mandate. The remaining differences were in three main areas: labor and the environment, liberalization and exceptions, and extraterritoriality. For example, the EU and Canada resented the Helms-Burton law that the United States used to sanction foreign companies for investing in Cuba, Iran, and Libya; France and Canada wanted to exempt culture from the agreement to protect their arts and media sectors; and OECD members had differing views regarding the extent to which environmental and labor measures should be included. The prolongation of negotiations because of the differences within the OECD gave outside critics such as civil society groups and LDCs the opportunity to organize opposition to an agreement.

LDCs led by India, Egypt, Pakistan, and Malaysia expressed strong hostility to an MAI because it was being negotiated in the OECD without their participation. Although most LDCs had become more open to foreign investment after the 1982 foreign debt crisis, they were concerned that an MAI would impose more obligations on host governments than on MNCs. Indeed, most OECD members seemed "to agree that an MAI should not impose any obligations on firms but that it should be binding on governments."[110] This OECD consensus resulted partly from the negative experiences of DCs in the 1970s–1980s with LDC efforts to develop a UN code of conduct for MNCs. Even more important was the revival of orthodox liberalism, which was evident in changing attitudes toward the freeing of foreign investment and capital flows. In the LDC view, the Asian financial crisis of the late 1990s indicated that capital and foreign investment should be regulated rather than given free reign, and that the MAI threatened the autonomous development of LDCs.[111]

The most effective opposition to the MAI was launched by a wide-ranging coalition of civil society NGOs. These NGOs argued that the MAI would threaten protection of human rights, labor and environmental standards, and LDCs. A particular concern was that the MAI would result in a race to the bottom among countries willing to lower their labor and environmental standards to attract foreign investment. A crucial turning point occurred when Ralph Nader and his consumer advocacy group acquired a copy of an OECD draft MAI agreement and put it on the Internet. Using a variety of Web sites, NGOs mobilized a strong and diverse opposition composed of human rights groups, labor and environmental groups, and consumer advocates. Gramscian theorists would argue that the NGOs representing disaffected groups organized a counter-hegemony, which used an electronic information tool—the Internet—"with incredible effectiveness to derail a planned . . . pact designed to increase globalization."[112] Within the OECD, sensitivity to cultural domination proved to be "the decisive stumbling block" to the MAI negotiations.[113] On October 14, 1998, France withdrew from the negotiations because of concerns about culture and the threat to national sovereignty. At that point, the OECD had no option but to suspend the negotiations.

The unsuccessful efforts to negotiate an MAI demonstrate that it is better for the OECD to provide policy advice and analysis and to conclude nonbinding accords than to negotiate binding and enforceable agreements on sensitive issues. A number of analysts consider the WTO a better venue for negotiating a foreign investment agreement because of its almost universal membership and because of the close linkages between trade and investment issues. As discussed, the WTO already has agreements (TRIMs, TRIPs, and GATS) that deal with some aspects of FDI. After the MAI negotiations collapsed, a WTO working group on the relationship between trade and investment became the only forum where multilateral investment issues were still being discussed. However, enthusiasm for negotiating multilateral investment rules since the MAI debacle has dissipated, and the only major actors to include investment in their negotiating positions at the 1999 WTO ministerial meeting in Seattle were the EU and Japan.[114]

A major obstacle to the negotiation of an MAI under the WTO is the wide divergence of views on the issue. Liberal economists want an MAI to regulate host state behavior, establish a level playing field for foreign investors with uniform and equitable rules for market access, facilitate the efficient use of scarce economic resources, and eliminate distortions in investment flows. Realists and historical structuralists, by contrast, strongly oppose regulations on host states. In their view, an MAI would enable MNCs to move operations to countries with lower environmental, labor, and consumer safety standards; ban performance requirements that countries use to promote their development; prevent restrictions on the repatriation of profits and removal of capital from the host country; and restrict the ability of host countries to sanction irresponsible MNC behavior. In view of these divergent perspectives, governments have been unable to establish an effective foreign investment regime. As a result, private actors have begun to play a greater role in regard to FDI issues.

PRIVATE ACTORS

In view of the lack of multilateral mechanisms to regulate MNCs, many consumer groups, other NGOs, IOs, and sometimes MNC managers are focusing on social responsibility and self-regulation by MNCs. For example, environmental and labor activists have joined with IOs and national regulatory agencies in pressuring MNCs to implement voluntary certification arrangements such as codes of conduct, monitoring standards, and production guidelines. The UN Secretary General's Global Compact proposal discussed earlier is also attuned to the dynamic interplay between NGOs and MNCs, and seeks "to bring about convergence in corporate practices around universally shared values."[115] The efforts to promote MNC social responsibility target several activities, including the outsourcing of MNC production to low-wage countries with inferior labor and environmental conditions; MNC cooperation with, or implicit support for, oppressive regimes; and the environmental damage resulting from some MNC operations.[116]

NGOs employ a variety of strategies to target MNCs. While they have used some strategies such as consumer boycotts and exposure of corporate misconduct for many years, other strategies such as shareholder activism and the creation of stewardship councils are of more recent origin. NGOs can be categorized as conformers, reformers, and radicals in terms of their goals and preferred strategies.[117] Conformers largely endorse MNC behavior and do not favor restrictions on their activities, reformers believe that MNCs can be reformed with some regulations, and radicals believe that MNCs are not reformable. In some respects, conformers are similar to orthodox liberals, reformers to interventionist liberals and realists, and radicals to historical structuralists. Of particular interest are NGOs that pressure for some regulation of MNCs: reformist liberals and more critical radicals or historical structuralists.

NGO reformers prefer to promote responsible MNC behavior rather than engage in ideological confrontation. For example, liberal strategies in the environmental area include ecoconsumerism, project collaboration, codes of conduct, and the development of private regimes. Ecoconsumerism refers to NGO campaigns to reward ecologically minded firms by purchasing products that have a less damaging effect on the environment. Project collaboration refers to environmental partnerships between NGOs and business firms to make production methods more environmentally responsible. Codes of conduct call on business firms to voluntarily decrease the release of pollutants, use sustainable energy sources, and appoint people with a commitment to the environment to their boards of directors. Private regimes bring MNCs and environmental groups together to develop accreditation procedures for good corporate conduct. They are more institutionalized than codes of conduct and provide ongoing opportunities for dialogue and review.[118]

Critical NGO strategies are more oppositional and provide less scope for compromise and dialogue. Unlike liberal strategies, the primary purpose of critical strategies is to expose and punish allegedly irresponsible corporate behavior. Examples of critical NGO strategies include consumer boycotts, MNC monitors, counterinformation, and shareholder activism. Consumer boycotts are more extreme than ecoconsumerism because they are designed to expose and punish alleged environmental abuses in the public arena. MNC monitors include groups such as the Multinationals Resource Center in the United States and Corporate Watch in Britain, which monitor MNCs and disseminate information about their allegedly destructive activities. Counterinformation aims at refuting the claims a company makes about itself and encouraging consumers to boycott the company's products. NGOs engaging in shareholder activism encourage their supporters to purchase a small number of shares in an MNC in attempts to influence decision making at shareholders' annual meetings. In the extreme, NGOs following historical structuralist strategies aim to develop a counterhegemony to "confront the hegemonic formation of globalization," which includes MNCs.[119]

It is important to note that some NGOs employ liberal and critical strategies simultaneously. For example, Greenpeace has worked with companies to develop ozone-friendly refrigerators at the same time as it has encouraged consumers to boycott Shell Oil Company over its alleged involvement with state suppression in Nigeria. In efforts to avoid negative NGO campaigns and government regulations, many MNCs have become more proactive in responding to environmental and other concerns with their own regulatory frameworks. Companies often benefit from collaboration with reformist NGOs. For example, MNCs that engage in project collaboration with environmental groups may gain a reputation for being environmentally responsible and may draw on the expertise of environmental NGOs in reforming their practices. Instead of binding commitments at the international level, business firms and associations have supported voluntary agreements as an alternative. For example, the International Chamber of Commerce endorsed 16 principles on the environment known as the *Business Charter on Sustainable Development* before the 1992 UN Conference on Environment and Development in Rio de Janeiro, Brazil.

Despite the numerous examples of liberal and critical NGO efforts to alter MNC behavior, the question arises as to how effective these activities have been in practice. MNCs clearly have different levels of vulnerability to NGO strategies. Oil companies, for example, are less vulnerable to NGO pressure because governments depend on MNCs' access to oil technology, expertise, and distribution networks. Furthermore, NGOs have limited monitoring capabilities. Although NGOs direct their campaigns and protests at certain high-profile companies, they permit other companies to be free riders and thus undermine the efforts to reform MNC behavior. Overall, it is likely that MNCs have not changed significantly as a result of NGO activities and that NGOs do not substitute for adequate multilateral regulation. One can also question how realistic it is to expect MNCs to regulate themselves through voluntary codes of conduct. Governments "are at least formally accountable to their citizens . . . when setting and enforcing standards," whereas "companies are primarily accountable to their own shareholders."[120] MNC self-regulation can supplement but not substitute for the responsibility of governments to set and maintain standards of behavior for business and other groups.

It is important to note that reformist and radical NGOs are themselves the target of numerous criticisms. For example, critics maintain that NGOs are not elected by the public and are not representative of societal attitudes toward MNCs. Furthermore, NGOs tend to focus almost exclusively on the regulation of MNC behavior, whereas the MAI tried to regulate only host state behavior. As discussed, no consensus has developed to this point on the need to achieve a balanced approach to regulation of MNCs, host states, and home states.

CONCLUSION

The postwar economy has been marked by increasing global interdependence among states. Initially, trade liberalization under GATT was the main factor contributing to globalization. However, since the 1980s FDI has become even more important than trade as a force behind the growth of interdependence. Technological advances in communications and transportation enabled firms to extend their operations abroad, and MNCs increased their FDI to gain access to foreign markets, benefit from economies of scale, and gain control over all stages of the production process. Fewer than 200 U.S. firms and a small number of European firms were global in their operations in 1970, but during the 1980s there was a dramatic increase in both the number of global firms and the number of states serving as home countries. Thus, by the early 1990s at least 1,000 firms could be categorized as global, and the home countries included the United States, European states, Japan, East Asian and Latin American NIEs, and some other LDCs.[121]

Despite the rapid globalization of foreign investment, its growth across countries has been very uneven. As Tables 10.3 and 10.4 show, the developed market economies accounted for 86.8 percent of the outward stocks of FDI and 64.7 percent of the inward stocks of FDI in 2001. Thus, a triad including the EU, North America, and Japan/East Asia are the main sources of FDI, and these areas direct most of their FDI to each other. From the 1950s to early 1970s, the United States as the main source of FDI was highly critical of restrictions other DCs were imposing on inward FDI. Nevertheless, Western Europe and Japan liberalized their inward FDI policies as they became more competitive with the United States, and their outward FDI increased. The United States, by contrast, became more sensitive about incoming FDI as its economic hegemony declined. For example, U.S. Congress's Exon-Florio amendment enables the president to block foreign takeovers of U.S. firms that present a possible danger to national security. Despite Exon-Florio, the United States, like other DCs, is basically committed to an open foreign investment regime. As major home countries for MNCs, DCs have a vested interest in removing obstacles to incoming FDI. Thus, it was the OECD countries that attempted to negotiate an MAI.

Unlike the DCs, LDCs are primarily host rather than home countries for foreign investment. As host countries, LDCs are sensitive to the effects of MNCs on their ability to achieve autonomous economic development. During the 1970s, LDCs reacted strongly to the growing impact of MNCs, demanding greater control over their natural resources and the ability to nationalize MNCs as part of their demands for a NIEO. Nevertheless, the oil price increase of 1979 followed by world recession and the 1980s foreign debt crisis led to severe cutbacks in commercial bank lending to the South. LDC fears about exploitation by MNCs were largely replaced by concerns that their share of inward FDI was declining. Currently, many LDCs are unilaterally liberalizing their foreign investment policies and competing for incoming investment.

As discussed, liberals, realists, and historical structuralists have widely divergent views regarding MNCs. Liberals view MNCs as positive agents of global change, which contribute to increased efficiency and stimulate innovation, economic growth, and employment. Liberals also tend to downgrade the importance of an MNC's nationality, and they advise states to upgrade the skills of their populations to attract investment, regardless of the source. Realists, by contrast, believe that an MNC's nationality does make a difference and that the competitiveness of a nation-state is closely linked with the competitiveness of its MNCs. Realists also believe that host states should be able to impose performance requirements and other policies on MNCs to promote industrial development and protect their national interest. Historical structuralists argue that MNCs overcharge for their goods and services, create dependency relationships with LDC host states, and pose a threat to labor groups in home as well as host states. Whereas MNCs can extend their operations to many countries, labor is largely limited to working and organizing on a national basis. Thus, MNCs contribute to a deterioration of working conditions and a competitive race to the bottom by transferring operations to affiliates in countries with lower wages and environmental standards.

Most liberals, realists, and historical structuralists believe that some sort of foreign investment regime is necessary, but they have markedly different views as to what is to be regulated—the MNC, the host state, or the home state. The UN tried to develop a comprehensive code of conduct for MNCs in the 1970s–1980s, but it abandoned these efforts in 1992 because of strong opposition from the major DCs. During the 1990s, the OECD tried to conclude an MAI. Unlike the UN efforts to develop a code of conduct, the MAI was designed to regulate the behavior of host states rather than MNCs. However, divisions within the OECD, as well as strong opposition from LDCs and civil society groups, resulted in a suspension of the MAI talks.

In the absence of a multilateral regime limiting host state restrictions on FDI, the North has pursued second-best options at the bilateral and regional levels. Important examples include the BITs and the investment provisions in the EU and NAFTA. In the absence of a multilateral regime regulating MNCs, NGOs have pressured MNCs to alter their behavior through voluntary agreements and self-regulation. Whereas liberal NGOs have emphasized reform of MNCs, critical NGOs have emphasized ideological confrontation. In sum, regulation of FDI is a patchwork quilt because there is no effective multilateral regime for foreign investment as there is for trade and monetary relations. This situation is unlikely to change until a consensus develops as to *what* is to be regulated: the MNC, the host state, the home state, or all three.

NOTES

1. United Nations Conference on Trade and Development (UNCTAD), *World Investment Report 2003* (New York: UN, 2003), pp.3–31; UNCTAD, *World Investment Report 2002* (New York: UN, 2002), pp.3–22; World Trade Organization, *Annual Report 1996, Vol. 1, Trade and Foreign Direct Investment* (Geneva: WTO, 1996), p.44.
2. Lorraine Eden, "Bringing the Firm Back In: Multinationals in International Political Economy," in Lorraine Eden and Evan H. Potter, eds., *Multinationals in the Global Political Economy* (New York: St. Martin's Press, 1993), p.26.
3. Ethan B. Kapstein, "We Are US: The Myth of the Multinational," *The National Interest* (Winter 1991–1992), p.55.
4. DeAnne Julius, "International Direct Investment: Strengthening the Policy Regime," in Peter B. Kenen, ed., *Managing the World Economy: Fifty Years After Bretton Woods* (Washington, DC: Institute of International Economics, 1994), p.269.
5. Robert W. Cox, *Production, Power, and World Order: Social Forces in the Making of History* (New York: Columbia University Press, 1987), pp.358–359; G. William Domhoff, "Who Made American Foreign Policy 1945–1963?" pp.25–69, and William Appleman Williams, "The Large Corporation and American Foreign Policy," pp.71–104, in David Horowitz, ed., *Corporations and the Cold War* (New York: Monthly Review Press, 1969).

6. See Stephen D. Krasner, "Power Politics, Institutions, and Transnational Relations," in Thomas Risse-Kappen, ed., *Bringing Transnational Relations Back In: Non-State Actors, Domestic Structures and International Institutions* (Cambridge: Cambridge University Press, 1995), p.279.

7. Stephen Hymer, "The Multinational Corporation and the Law of Uneven Development," in George Modelski, ed., *Transnational Corporations and World Order* (San Francisco: Freeman, 1979), p.398.

8. Yair Aharoni, "On the Definition of a Multinational Corporation," *Quarterly Review of Economics and Business* 11–3 (Autumn 1971), pp.27–37; Grazia Ietto-Gillies, *International Production: Trends, Theories, Effects* (Cambridge: Polity Press, 1992), pp.17–20.

9. Raymond Vernon, *Sovereignty at Bay: The Multinational Spread of U.S. Enterprises* (New York: Basic Books, 1971), p.11.

10. UNCTAD, *World Investment Report 2000* (New York: UN, 2000), pp.99–136.

11. Edward M. Graham and Paul R. Krugman, *Foreign Direct Investment in the United States* 3rd ed. (Washington, DC: Institute for International Economics, 1995), pp.9–11; Geoffrey Jones, *The Evolution of International Business: An Introduction* (London: Routledge, 1996), pp.4–6.

12. See, for example, United Nations Centre on Transnational Corporations (UNCTC), *Transnational Corporations in World Development: Third Survey* (New York: UN, 1985).

13. Howard V. Perlmutter, "The Tortuous Evolution of the Multinational Corporation," *Columbia Journal of World Business* 4–1 (January–February 1969), p.11; Wyn Grant, "Perspectives on Globalizational and Economic Coordination," in J. Rogers Hollingsworth and Robert Boyer, eds., *Contemporary Capitalism: The Embeddedness of Institutions* (Cambridge: Cambridge University Press, 1997), pp.322–325.

14. Although most political scientists and U.S. scholars prefer the term *MNC,* economists, business professors, and British scholars often use the term *multinational enterprise (MNE).* MNE is a more accurate term in their view because an "enterprise" includes "a network of corporate and non-corporate entities in different countries joined together by ties of ownership." See United Nations Department of Economic and Social Affairs, *Multinational Corporations in World Development* (New York: UN, 1973), p.4; Eden, "Bringing the Firm Back In," p.55.

15. Laura D'Andrea Tyson, "They Are Not Us: Why American Ownership Still Matters," *The American Prospect* 4 (Winter 1991), p.42; John M. Kline, *State Government Influence in U.S. International Economic Policy* (Lexington: Heath, 1983), p.63.

16. Jean-François Hennart, "The Transaction Cost Theory of the Multinational Enterprise," in Christos N. Pitelis and Roger Sugden, eds., *The Nature of the Transnational Firm* (London: Routledge, 1991), pp.143–151; Mark Casson, *Alternatives to the Multinational Enterprise* (London: Macmillan, 1979), p.45.

17. Graham and Krugman, *Foreign Direct Investment in the United States,* p.83. On transfer pricing see Lorraine Eden, *Multinational Enterprise and Economic Analysis* (Toronto: University of Toronto Press, 1997); Alan M. Rugman and Lorraine Eden, eds., *Multinationals and Transfer Pricing* (London: Croom Helm, 1985); and Wagdy M. Abdallah, *International Transfer Pricing Policies: Decision-Making Guidelines for Multinational Companies* (New York: Quorum Books, 1989).

18. Lorraine Eden, "Thinking Globally—Acting Locally: Multinationals in the Global Political Economy," in Lorraine Eden and Evan H. Potter, eds., *Multinationals in the Global Political Economy* (New York: St. Martin's Press, 1993), pp.1–2; Michael E. Porter, *The Competitive Advantage of Nations* (New York: Free Press, 1990), p.53.

19. Charles Wilson, "The Multinational in Historical Perspective," in Keiichiro Nakagawa, ed., *Strategy and Structure of Big Business* (Tokyo: University of Tokyo Press, 1974),

p.265; Peter Hertner and Geoffrey Jones, "Multinationals: Theory and History," in Peter Hertner and Geoffrey Jones, eds., *Multinationals. Theory and History* (Aldershot: Gower, 1986), p.1.

20. Jones, *The Evolution of International Business*, pp.23–25.
21. Peter Svedberg, "The Portfolio-Direct Composition of Private Foreign Investment in 1914 Revisited," *The Economic Journal* 88 (December 1978), pp.763–777; T. A. B. Corley, "Britain's Overseas Investments in 1914 Revisited," *Business History* 36–1 (January 1994), pp.71–88.
22. Julius, "International Direct Investment," pp.272–273.
23. Jones, *The Evolution of International Business*, pp.28–32.
24. Edward M. Graham, *Global Corporations and National Governments* (Washington, DC: Institute for International Economics, 1996), pp.25–26, 136–140; John H. Dunning, "Changes in the Level and Structure of International Production: The Last One Hundred Years," in Mark Casson, ed., *The Growth of International Business* (London: Allen and Unwin, 1983), p.88.
25. Jones, *The Evolution of International Business*, pp.52–59.
26. Peter J. Buckley and Mark Casson, *The Future of the Multinational Enterprise*, 2nd ed. (London: Macmillan, 1991), p.11; UNCTAD, *World Investment Report 2003*, p.23; United Nations Centre on Transnational Corporations (UNCTC), *World Investment Report 1991* (New York: UN, 1991).
27. Dennis J. Encarnation, *Rivals Beyond Trade: America Versus Japan in Global Competition* (Ithaca: Cornell University Press, 1992), p.5; Kiyoshi Kojima, *Direct Foreign Investment: A Japanese Model of Multinational Business Operations* (New York: Praeger, 1978), pp.1–18.
28. UNCTAD, *World Investment Report 1999* (New York: UN, 1999), p.42.
29. UNCTAD, *World Investment Report 2002*, p.xv.
30. World Trade Organization, *Annual Report—1996, Vol. 1*, p.47.
31. See Kálmán Kalotay and Gábor Hunya, "Privatization and FDI in Central and Eastern Europe," *Transnational Corporations* 9–1 (April 2000), pp.66; and special issue of *Transnational Corporations* 20–3 (December 2001) on "Privatization and Greenfield FDI in Central and Eastern Europe: Does the Mode of Entry Matter?"
32. Graham, *Global Corporations and National Governments*, pp.22–24; Julius, "International Direct Investment," pp.276–277; Ietto-Gillies, *International Production*, pp.25–32.
33. Ietto-Gillies, *International Production*, pp.78–84; Mark Herkenrath and Volker Bornschier, "Transnational Corporations in World Development–Still the Same Harmful Effects in an Increasingly Globalized World Economy?," *Journal of World-Systems Research* 9–1 (Winter 2003), pp.108–109.
34. Stephen Herbert Hymer, *The International Operations of National Firms: A Study of Direct Foreign Investment* (Cambridge: MIT Press, 1976), p.100; Ietto-Gillies, *International Production*, pp.86–90.
35. Peter Evans, *Dependent Development: The Alliance of Multinational, State, and Local Capital in Brazil* (Princeton: Princeton University Press, 1979), p.37; Theodore H. Moran, "Multinational Corporations and Dependency: A Dialogue for Dependentistas and Non-Dependentistas," *International Organization* 32–1 (Winter 1978), pp.79–100; Herkenrath and Bornschier, "Transnational Corporations in World Development," pp.105–139.
36. Vernon, *Sovereignty at Bay*, pp.46–59; Raymond Vernon, "Sovereignty at Bay Ten Years After," *International Organization* 35–3 (Summer 1981), pp.521–523; Ravi Ramamurti, "The Obsolescing 'Bargaining Model'? MNC-Host Developing Country Relations Revisited," *Journal of International Business Studies* 32–1 (2001), p.25.
37. Stephen J. Kobrin, "Testing the Bargaining Hypothesis in the Manufacturing Sector in Developing Countries," *International Organization* 41–4 (Autumn 1987), pp.609–638;

Theodore H. Moran, "Multinational Corporations and the Developing Countries: An Overview," in Theodore H. Moran, ed., *Multinational Corporations: The Political Economy of Foreign Direct Investment* (Lexington: Heath, 1985), pp.3–24.

38. Ramamurti, "The Obsolescing 'Bargaining Model'?," p.23.

39. William A. Stoever, "Attempting to Resolve the Attraction-Aversion Dilemma: A Study of FDI Policy in the Republic of Korea," *Transnational Corporations* 11–1 (April 2002), pp.49–76; On subnational government policies toward FDI, see Douglas M. Brown and Earl H. Fry, eds., *States and Provinces in the International Economy* (Berkeley: Institute of Governmental Studies Press, University of California, 1993); and Peter Karl Kresl and Gary Gappert, eds., *North American Cities and the Global Economy: Challenges and Opportunities*, Urban Affairs Annual Review 44 (Thousand Oaks: Sage, 1995).

40. Jones, *The Evolution of International Business*, pp.288–291.

41. Stephen J. Kobrin, "Expropriation as an Attempt to Control Foreign Firms in LDCs: Trends from 1960 to 1979," *International Studies Quarterly* 28–3 (September 1984), pp.337–342; A. Edward Safarian, "Host Country Policies towards Foreign Direct Investment in the 1950s and 1990s," *Transnational Corporations* 8–2 (August 1999), pp.102–105.

42. Stephen D. Krasner, *Structural Conflict: The Third World Against Global Liberalism* (Berkeley: University of California Press, 1985), pp.176–195; Horst Heininger, "Transnational Corporations and the Struggle for the Establishment of a New International Economic Order," in Alice Teichova, Maurice Lévy-Leboyer, and Helga Nussbaum, eds., *Multinational Enterprise in Historical Perspective* (Cambridge: Cambridge University Press, 1986), pp.351–361.

43. Kobrin, "Expropriation as an Attempt to Control Foreign Firms in LDCs," p.338; Jones, *The Evolution of International Business*, pp.294–295.

44. Graham, *Global Corporations and National Governments*, pp.17–20.

45. UNCTAD, *World Investment Report 2000*, pp.6, 7, 17–18.

46. UNTAD, *World Investment Report 1994* (New York: UN, 1994), pp.91–97; Graham, *Global Corporations and National Governments*, pp.97–100.

47. J. J. Servan-Schreiber, *The American Challenge*, translated from French by Ronald Steel (New York: Atheneum, 1979). The book was first published in 1967.

48. Stephen Clarkson, *Canada and the Reagan Challenge: Crisis and Adjustment, 1981–85* updated ed. (Toronto: James Lorimer & Company, 1985), pp.3–113; C. Fred Bergsten, "Coming Investment Wars? Multinational Corporations in World Politics," *Foreign Affairs* 53–1 (October 1974), pp.136–139; Barbara Jenkins, *The Paradox of Continental Production: National Investment Policies in North America* (Ithaca: Cornell University Press, 1992), pp.113–117.

49. Mark Mason, *American Multinationals and Japan: The Political Economy of Japanese Capital Controls, 1899–1980* (Cambridge: Council on East Asian Studies, Harvard University, 1992), pp.243–247.

50. Jones, *The Evolution of International Business*, pp.280–281.

51. Safarian, "Host Country Policies towards Inward Foreign Direct Investment," p.105; Graham, *Global Corporations and National Governments*, pp.96–97.

52. Paul N. Doremus, William W. Keller, Louis W. Pauly, and Simon Reich, *The Myth of the Global Corporation* (Princeton: Princeton University Press, 1998), pp.77–78; Robert Z. Lawrence, "Japan's Low Levels of Inward Investment: The Role of Inhibitions on Acquisitions," in Kenneth Froot, ed., *Foreign Direct Investment* (Chicago: University of Chicago Press, 1993), pp.85–107; C. Fred Bergsten and Marcus Noland, *Reconcilable Differences? United States–Japan Economic Conflict* (Washington, DC: Institute for International Economics, 1993), pp.79–82; and Encarnation, *Rivals Beyond Trade*, pp.36–41.

53. Jenkins, *The Paradox of Continental Production*, pp.117–121; Clarkson, *Canada and the Reagan Challenge*, pp.83–113; Tom Keating, *Canada and World Order: The Multilateralist Tradition in Canadian Foreign Policy* (Don Mills: Oxford University Press, 2002), pp.195–196.

54. Edward M. Graham and Michael E. Ebert, "Foreign Direct Investment and US National Security: Fixing Exon-Florio," *The World Economy* 14–3 (September 1991), pp.245–268; Edward M. Graham and Paul R. Krugman, *Foreign Direct Investment in the United States* (Washington, DC: Institute for International Economics, 1995), pp.126–132; Doremus, Keller, Pauly, and Reich, *The Myth of the Global Corporation*, pp.76–77.

55. UNCTAD, *World Investment Report 2003*, pp.73–74.

56. John H. Dunning, Roger van Hoesel, and Rajneesh Narula, "Third World Multinationals Revisited: New Developments and Theoretical Implications," in John H. Dunning, ed., *Globalization, Trade and Foreign Direct Investment* (Amsterdam: Elsevier, 1998), pp.255–286; Daniel Chudnovsky and Andrés López, "A Third Wave of FDI from Developing Countries: Latin American TNCs in the 1990s," *Transnational Corporations* 9–2 (August 2000), pp.31–73.

57. Robert Gilpin, *U.S. Power and the Multinational Corporation: The Political Economy of Foreign Direct Investment* (New York: Basic Books, 1975), p.62.

58. UNCTC, *Transnational Corporations in World Development—Trends and Prospects* (New York: UN, 1988), p.240; Jones, *The Evolution of International Business*, pp.219–220.

59. Robert T. Kudrle, "The Several Faces of the Multinational Corporation: Political Reaction and Policy Response," in W. Ladd Hollist and F. LaMond Tullis, eds., *An International Political Economy* (Boulder: Westview Press, 1985), pp.176–177; Jack N. Behrman and Robert E. Grosse, *International Business and Governments: Issues and Institutions* (Columbia: University of South Carolina Press, 1990), pp.82–85; Gilpin, *U.S. Power and the Multinational Corporation*, pp.142–144.

60. Jones, *The Evolution of International Business*, pp.221–222.

61. Gary Clyde Hufbauer and Jeffrey J. Schott, "The Soviet-European Gas Pipeline: A Case of Failed Sanctions," in Moran, ed. *Multinational Corporations*, pp.219–245.

62. Paul Lewis, "Cuba Trade Law: Export of U.S. Ire and Politics," *New York Times*, 15 March, 1996, pp.C1, C3; "Biter Bitten: The Helms-Burton Law," *The Economist*, 8 June, 1996, p.45.

63. Robert B. Reich, "Who Is Us?" *Harvard Business Review* 90–1 (January–February 1990), pp.59–60; Vernon, *Sovereignty at Bay*, pp.214–215; Laura D'Andrea Tyson, *Who's Bashing Whom? Trade Conflict in High-Technology Industries* (Washington, DC: Institute for International Economics, 1992), pp.289–295.

64. Sol C. Chaikin, "Trade, Investment, and Deindustrialization: Myth and Reality," in Moran, ed., *Multinational Corporations*, pp.159–172; Jamuna Prasa Agarwal, "Effect of Foreign Direct Investment on Employment in Home Countries," *Transnational Corporations* 6–2 (August 1997), pp.1–2.

65. Agarwal, "Effect of Foreign Direct Investment on Employment in Home Countries," pp.3–4.

66. Gordon Betcherman, "Globalization, Labour Markets and Public Policy," in Robert Boyer and Daniel Drache, eds., *States Against Markets: The Limits of Globalization* (London: Routledge, 1996), p.258; Ietto-Gillies, *International Production*, pp.136–143.

67. Peter Enderwick, *Multinational Business and Labour* (London: Croom Helm, 1985); Richard E. Caves, *Multinational Enterprise and Economic Analysis* (Cambridge: Cambridge University Press, 1962), pp.131–159; Theodore H. Moran, "Multinational Corporations and the Developed World: An Analytical Overview," in Moran, ed. *Multinational Corporations*, pp.139–146.

68. Gary Clyde Hufbauer and Jeffrey J. Schott, *NAFTA: An Assessment* (Washington, D.C.: Institute for International Economics, revised ed., 1993), p.19.

69. Robert O'Brien, "The Agency of Labour in a Changing Global Order," in Richard Stubbs and Geoffrey R.D. Underhill, eds., *Political Economy and the Changing Global Order*, 2nd ed. (Don Mills: Oxford University Press, 2000), pp.42–44.

70. Reich, "Who Is Us?" pp.53–64; Robert B. Reich, *The Work of Nations: Preparing Ourselves for 21st-Century Capitalism* (New York: Vintage Books, 1991), chap. 25.

71. Porter, *The Competitive Advantage of Nations*, p.2; Tyson, "They Are Not Us," pp.37–49.

72. Lester Thurow, *Head to Head: The Coming Economic Battle Among Japan, Europe, and America* (New York: Morrow, 1992), p.201.

73. Reich, *The Work of Nations*, p.8.

74. Kenichi Ohmae, *The Borderless World: Power and Strategy in the Interlinked Economy* (New York: HarperPerennial, 1991), p.10.

75. Reich, *The Work of Nations*, p.163; Ohmae, *The Borderless World*, p.194.

76. UNCTAD, *World Investment Report 2000*, pp.20–21; Robert B. Reich, "Who Do We Think They Are?" *The American Prospect* 4 (Winter 1991), p.51; Grant, "Perspectives on Globalizational and Economic Coordination," pp.323–324.

77. Fred Lazar, "Corporate Strategies: The Costs and Benefits of Going Global," in Boyer and Drache, eds., *States Against Markets*, p.285; Louis W. Pauly and Simon Reich, "National Structures and Multinational Corporate Behavior: Enduring Differences in the Age of Globalization," *International Organization* 51–1 (Winter 1997), p.13.

78. Richard G. Harris and William G. Watson, "Three Visions of Competitiveness: Porter, Reich and Thurow on Economic Growth and Policy," in Thomas J. Courchene and Douglas D. Purvis, eds., *Productivity, Growth and Canada's International Competitiveness* (Kingston: John Deutsch Institute for the Study of Economic Policy, 1993), pp.254–256; Graham and Krugman, *Foreign Direct Investment in the United States*, p.84.

79. See Pauly and Reich, "National Structures and Multinational Corporate Behavior," pp.1–30; and Doremus, Keller, Pauly, and Reich, *The Myth of the Global Corporation*, chaps. 3–5.

80. Paul Krugman, "Competitiveness: A Dangerous Obsession," *Foreign Affairs* (March/April 1994), pp.31–33; Paul Krugman, "Competitiveness: Does It Matter?" *Fortune* (March 7, 1994), pp.109–115.

81. Clyde V. Prestowitz, Jr., "The Fight over Competitiveness: A Zero-Sum Debate?" *Foreign Affairs* (July/August 1994), p.189.

82. Paul M. Goldberg and Charles P. Kindleberger, "Toward a GATT for Investment: A Proposal for Supervision of the International Corporation," *Law and Policy in International Business* 2 (Summer 1970), pp.295–325.

83. Christopher J. Maule and Andrew Vanderwal, "International Regulation of Foreign Investment," *International Perspectives*, (November/December 1985), p.22.

84. Vernon, *Sovereignty at Bay*, p.249; Richard J. Barnet and Ronald E. Müller, *Global Reach: The Power of the Multinational Corporations* (New York: Simon & Schuster, 1974), p.375.

85. OECD, *International Investment and Multinational Enterprises: Review of the 1976 Declaration and Decisions* (Paris: OECD, 1979); Peter Muchlinski, *Multinational Enterprises and the Law* (Oxford: Blackwell, 1995), pp.578–592; Oswaldo de Rivero B., *New Economic Order and International Development Law* (Oxford: Pergamon Press, 1980), pp.88–92.

86. This section on BITs relies mainly on UNCTAD, *Bilateral Investment Treaties in the Mid-1990s* (New York and Geneva: United Nations, 1998); Paul Bryan Christy, III. "Negotiating Investment in the GATT: A Call for Functionalism," *Michigan Journal of International Law* 12–4 (Summer 1991), pp.754–763; and UNCTAD, *World Investment Report 2003*, pp.89–91. On private international efforts to regulate MNCs, see A. Claire Cutler, "Public Meets Private: The International Harmonization and Unification of Private International Law," *Global Society* 13–1 (January 1999), pp.25–48.

87. UNCTAD, *World Investment Report 2003*, p.89.

88. UNCTC, *Transnational Corporations in World Development: Trends and Prospects*, p.337.

89. UNCTAD, *Bilateral Investment Treaties in the Mid-1990s*, p.4.

90. UNCTAD, *Bilateral Investment Treaties in the Mid-1990s*, p.16.

91. Sherif H. Seid, *Global Regulation of Foreign Direct Investment* (Aldershot: Ashgate, 2002), p.55.

92. U.S. Senate, "The International Telephone and Telegraph Company and Chile, 1970–1971," in George Modelski, ed., *Transnational Corporations and World Order* (San Francisco: W.H. Freeman, 1979), pp.226–244.

93. United Nations, "Report of the Group of Eminent Persons to Study the Impact of Multinational Corporations on Development and on International Relations," in Modelski, ed., *Transnational Corporations and World Order*, pp.323, 330.

94. UNCTC, *The United Nations Code of Conduct on Transnational Corporations* (New York: UN, September 1986), pp.1–6; R. Alan Hedley, "Transnational Corporations and Their Regulation: Issues and Strategies," *International Journal of Comparative Sociology* 40–2 (May 1999), pp.218–221; "Target Practice," *New Internationalist*, (August 1993) p.15.

95. Georg Kell and John Gerard Ruggie, "Global Markets and Social Legitimacy: The Case for the 'Global Compact'," *Transnational Corporations* 8–3 (December 1999), pp.101–120.

96. De Anne Julius, *Foreign Investment: The Neglected Twin of Trade*, Occasional Papers no. 33 (Washington, DC: Group of Thirty, 1991).

97. Christy, "Negotiating Investment in the GATT," p.746.

98. John Croome, *Reshaping the World Trading System: A History of the Uruguay Round* (Geneva: World Trade Organization, 1995), p.138; Graham, *Global Corporations and National Governments*, pp.71–76; Julius, "International Direct Investment," p.281.

99. Jeffrey J. Schott, with Johanna W. Buurman, *The Uruguay Round: An Assessment* (Washington, DC: Institute for International Economics, 1994), p.112.

100. Ernest H. Preeg, *Traders in a Brave New World: The Uruguay Round and the Future of the International Trading System* (Chicago: University of Chicago Press, 1995), pp.195–196.

101. John Robinson, *Multinationals and Political Control* (New York: St. Martin's Press, 1983), p.44.

102. Jon R. Johnson, *The North American Free Trade Agreement—A Comprehensive Guide* (Aurora: Canada Law Book, 1994), p.275.

103. Graham, *Global Corporations and National Governments*, p.47.

104. Alan M. Rugman and Michael Gestrin, "A Conceptual Framework for a Multilateral Agreement on Investment: Learning from the NAFTA," in Sauvé and Schwanen, eds., *Investment Rules for the Global Economy*, p.170.

105. Fred Lazar, "Investment in the NAFTA: Just Cause for Walking Away," *Journal of World Trade* 27–5 (October 1993), pp.28–29; Jim Stanford, "Investment," in Duncan Cameron and Mel Watkins, eds., *Canada Under Free Trade* (Toronto: Lorimer, 1993), pp.164–166.

106. Johnson, *The North American Free Trade Agreement*, p.512.

107. Edward M. Graham and Christopher Wilkie, "Multinationals and the Investment Provisions of the NAFTA," *International Trade Journal* 8–1 (Spring 1994), pp.9–38.

108. Quoted in Hedley, "Transnational Corporations and Their Regulation," p.222. On the OECD's long-term experience with international investment, see OECD, *International Investment Perspectives* (Paris: OECD, 2002), pp.197–205.

109. Elizabeth Smythe, "Your Place or Mine? States, International Organizations and the Negotiation of Investment Rules," *Transnational Corporations* 7–3 (December 1998), pp.85–120.

110. Edward M. Graham and Pierre Sauvé, "Toward a Rules-Based Regime for Investment: Issues and Challenges," in Sauvé and Schwanen, eds., *Investment Rules for the Global Economy*, p.135.

111. Elizabeth Smythe, "The Multilateral Agreement on Investment: A Charter of Rights for Global Investors or Just Another Agreement?," in Fen Osler Hampson and Maureen Appel Molot, eds., *Canada Among Nations 1998: Leadership and Dialogue* (Toronto: Oxford University Press, 1998), pp.239–277.

112. Peter Morton, "MAI Gets Tangled in Web," *The Financial Post,* 22 October 1998, p.3.

113. Marinus W. Sikkel, "How to Establish a Multilateral Framework for Investment?," *Transnational Corporations* 9–2 (August 2000), p.140.

114. David Robertson, "Multilateral Investment Rules," in Bijit Bora, ed., *Foreign Direct Investment: Research Issues* (London: Routledge, 2002), pp.310–324.

115. Kell and Ruggie, "Global Markets and Social Legitimacy," p.104.

116. Ans Kolk, Rob van Tulder and Carlijn Welters, "International Codes of Conduct and Corporate Social Responsibility: Can Transnational Corporations Regulate Themselves?," *Transnational Corporations* 8–1 (April 1999), pp.143–180. On corporate codes of conduct see also Neil Kearney, "Corporate Codes of Conduct: The Privatized Application of Labour Standards," and Petrina Fridd and Jessica Sainsbury, "The Role of Voluntary Codes of Conduct and Regulation—A Retailer's View," in Sol Picciotto and Ruth Mayne, eds., *Regulating International Business: Beyond Liberalization* (London: Macmillan, 1999), pp.205–234; and Gary Gereffi, Ronie Garcia-Johnson, and Erika Sasser, "The NGO-Indus," *Foreign Policy,* 125 (July/August 2001), pp.56–65.

117. Jan Aart Scholte with Robert O'Brien and Marc Williams, "The WTO and Civil Society," *Journal of World Trade* 33–1 (1999), pp.112–116.

118. This discussion of environmental NGOs draws on Peter Newell, "Environmental NGOs, TNCs, and the Question of Governance," in Dimitris Stevis and Valerie J. Assetto, eds., *The International Political Economy of the Environment: Critical Perspectives* (Boulder: Lynne Rienner, 2001), pp.85–107.

119. Robert W. Cox, "Civil Society at the Turn of the Millennium: Prospects for an Alternative World Order," *Review of International Studies* 25 (1999), p.26.

120. Ruth Mayne, "Regulating TNCs: The Role of Voluntary and Governmental Approaches," in Picciotto and Mayne, eds., *Regulating International Business,* p.246; Newell, "Environmental NGOs, TNCs, and the Question of Governance," pp.100–104.

121. Schwanen, "Investment and the Global Economy," pp.2–3; Graham, *Global Corporations and National Governments,* p.27.

CHAPTER 11

International
Development

The Bretton Woods system and its institutions have often been credited with contributing "to almost unprecedented global economic growth and change over the past five decades."[1] However, a substantial percentage of people living in the South have received little benefit from this growth. Poverty, hunger, and disease are prevalent in much of the world, and the gap between the richest and poorest states is growing. According to the World Bank, the average income in the world's richest 20 states is 37 times higher than the average in the poorest 20 states—a gap that has doubled in the past 40 years. About 2.8 billion of the world's 6 billion people live on less than $2 a day, and 1.2 billion live on less than $1 a day. LDCs generally have low levels of economic development, marked by low per capita incomes, inadequate infrastructure facilities (e.g., communications and transportation), and limited access to modern technology. The economic development problems of LDCs often prevent them from fostering social and political development. Thus, many LDCs have inadequate health and educational facilities, low literacy rates, and high infant mortality rates. Politically, many LDCs have difficulty maintaining stable governments with some degree of democratic participation. During the 1990s, 40 states were involved in conflict, mainly civil, and this included over half of the poorest LDCs. These conflicts often destroy past development gains and leave a legacy of mistrust that prevents future gains.[2]

Although severe economic and social problems confront a substantial majority of people in the South, there are major differences in economic development among LDCs. As Table 11.1 shows, East Asian and Latin American NIEs have per capita gross national incomes (GNIs) in the middle- to high-income range, reaching $26,050 in Hong Kong, China, and $24,910 in Singapore. Some OPEC countries such as Kuwait and Saudi Arabia also have per capita GNIs in the high- and upper middle-income range. Indeed, countries such as Singapore, Kuwait, and Saudi Arabia are not eligible to borrow World Bank funds.[3] In stark contrast, Table 11.1 shows that the poorest African and Asian states such as Mozambique, Malawi, Ethiopia, Cambodia, and Nepal have per capita GNIs in the $100 to $270 range. In addition to their higher incomes, Table 2.2 in Chapter 2 shows that East Asia (excluding China) ranks higher than other LDC regions on human development indicators such as infant mortality rates, life expectancy, and adult literacy rates.

Table 11.1

PER CAPITA GNI* OF SOUTHERN ECONOMIES, 2001

HIGHER- AND MIDDLE-INCOME ECONOMIES

East Asian NIEs		OPEC Countries		Latin American NIEs	
Hong Kong, China	$26,050	Kuwait	$18,690	Argentina	$11,690
Singapore	24,910	Saudi Arabia	11,390	Mexico	8,770
South Korea	18,110	Iran	6,230	Brazil	7,450

LOW-INCOME ECONOMIES

Africa		Asia	
Nigeria	$290	Bangladesh	$370
Mozambique	210	Lao PDR	310
Malawi	170	Cambodia	270
Ethiopia	100	Nepal	250

*Gross national income

Source: World Bank, *World Development Report 2003* (New York: Oxford University Press, 2003), pp.234–235.

Table 11.2

GROWTH OF REAL GDP PER CAPITA
(Average Annual Percentage Change)

Group	1965–1973	1973–1980	1980–1989
Industrial countries	3.7	2.3	2.3
Less-developed countries			
Sub-Saharan Africa	2.1	0.4	−1.2
East Asia	5.3	4.9	6.2
South Asia	1.2	1.7	3.0
Europe, Middle East, and North Africa	5.8	1.9	0.4
Latin America and the Caribbean	3.8	2.5	−0.4

Source: World Bank, *World Development Report 1991*, Table 1, p.3. Copyright © 1991 by The International Bank for Reconstruction and Development/The World Bank. By permission of Oxford University Press.

The East Asian NIEs were the most rapidly growing LDCs during the crucial oil and foreign debt crises from 1973 to 1989. Indeed, Table 11.2 shows that the average annual economic growth rate in East Asia increased to 6.2 percent during 1980–1989, a period marked by a global recession and the foreign debt crisis. Sub-Saharan Africa and Latin America and the Caribbean, by contrast, had *negative* economic growth rates (of −1.2 and −0.4 percent) during 1980–1989. Many scholars therefore refer to the 1980s as "a lost decade," with much of the South experiencing a foreign debt crisis, declining prices for raw material exports, declining foreign investment, and capital flight. In 1991, the World Bank reported that the real income gap between the North and all Southern regions except East Asia was widening.[4] During the 1990s, many

LDCs continued to experience problems with economic growth. As in the 1980s, there were major differences among LDC regions. In East Asia, the number of very poor people (those living on less than $1 a day) fell from 420 million in 1987 to 280 million in 1998. Of particular note was the decline in the number of very poor people in China as a result of strong economic growth. In contrast, the number of very poor people has been steadily increasing in sub-Saharan Africa.[5] Thus, Table 2.3 in Chapter 2 shows that 20 of the 44 least developed countries (LLDCs) for which statistics are available had *negative* GDP per capita growth rates from 1990 to 1999. Almost three-quarters of the LLDCs are in Africa, and a substantial number are in the Asia/Pacific. As discussed, even higher-income East and Southeast Asian economies experienced a serious financial crisis during the late 1990s that raised questions about the sustainability of rapid economic development in the region.

In view of its vulnerabilities, the South is ambivalent about its relations with the North. Although LDCs look to the North for trade, foreign investment, development assistance, and technology transfers, they are fearful that these linkages contribute to their dependence on the North and to threats to their autonomy. LDCs are also ambivalent about the IMF, World Bank, and GATT/WTO. The KIEOs have helped the South gain access to external finance and foreign export markets, but LDCs resent the fact that the DCs are the dominant actors in the KIEOs. Furthermore, LDC debtor countries believe that the conditions the IMF and World Bank attach to structural adjustment loans often inhibit rather than further their development efforts.[6] Despite the South's ambivalence about the North, a series of developments has induced LDCs to increase their Northern linkages, adopt liberal-economic policies prescribed by the North, and participate more fully in the global economy.

First, a major turning point was the 1980s foreign debt crisis, when a number of LDCs were unable to meet their debt repayment obligations. As discussed in Chapter 7, the debtor LDCs had to turn to the IMF, the World Bank, and the industrial states for assistance. The failure of inward-looking ISI policies, combined with the conditions of IMF and World Bank SALs, induced LDCs to shift to more open economic policies with an emphasis on trade liberalization, deregulation, and privatization. A second factor inducing LDCs to open their economies was the revival of orthodox liberalism. For example, Chapter 8 discussed the growing Northern opposition to S&D treatment for LDCs in trade and Northern pressure on LDCs to liberalize their trade policies. Most LDCs had refused to become signatories to the NTB codes concluded during the GATT Tokyo Round in the late 1970s, but the Uruguay Round was organized as a single undertaking in which LDCs were expected to be full participants in all the agreements. A third factor causing LDCs to participate more fully in the global economy has been the growing fear that most of the South is becoming increasingly marginalized. Major reasons for this marginalization include the decline of the Cold War and the breakup of the Soviet bloc. Consistent with realist predictions, the decline of the Cold War has deprived the South of a traditional source of leverage it had in extracting concessions from both the East and the West. Thus, Western DCs have been less willing to provide foreign aid. Table 11.3 shows that *Official Development Assistance (ODA)* fell from 0.52 percent of the GNP of OECD donor states at the height of the Cold War in 1960 to 0.37 percent in 1980 and to only 0.22 percent in 2000.[7]

Table 11.3

OFFICIAL DEVELOPMENT ASSISTANCE (ODA) OF OECD MEMBERS AS A PERCENT OF GNP

	1960	1970	1980	1990	2000
Australia	0.38	0.59	0.48	0.34	0.27
Austria	—	0.13	0.23	0.25	0.23
Belgium	0.88	0.48	0.50	0.46	0.36
Canada	0.19	0.43	0.43	0.44	0.25
Denmark	0.09	0.38	0.74	0.94	1.06
Finland	0	0	0.22	0.63	0.31
France	1.38	0.65	0.63	0.60	0.32
Germany	0.31	0.32	0.44	0.42	0.27
Greece	—	—	—	—	0.20
Ireland	0	0	0.16	0.16	0.30
Italy	0.22	0.16	0.17	0.31	0.13
Japan	0.24	0.23	0.32	0.31	0.28
Luxembourg	0	0	0	0.21	0.71
Netherlands	0.31	0.63	0.97	0.92	0.84
New Zealand	0	0	0.33	0.23	0.25
Norway	0.11	0.33	0.87	1.17	0.80
Portugal	1.45	0.45	0	0.25	0.26
Spain	0	0	0	0.20	0.22
Sweden	0.05	0.37	0.78	0.91	0.80
Switzerland	0.04	0.14	0.24	0.32	0.34
United Kingdom	0.56	0.37	0.35	0.27	0.32
United States	0.53	0.31	0.27	0.21	0.10
Total	**0.52**	**0.34**	**0.37**	**0.33**	**0.22**

Source: OECD, *Development Co-operation,* (Paris: OECD, various years).

In addition to the steady decline of aid, the number of aid recipients increased during the 1990s as a result of the breakup of the Soviet bloc and Soviet Union. Whereas the former Soviet Union and some Eastern Europe states had been foreign aid donors, during the 1990s they turned to the West for assistance and became competitors with the South for export markets, development finance, and inward foreign investment. At the 1991 OECD Council meeting, the OECD ministers provided assurances that "their co-operation with developing countries will not be diminished because of their support for central and eastern Europe,"[8] but the statistics on development assistance indicate otherwise. To interpret these statistics, it is necessary to discuss the OECD's terminology for aid giving. *Official development assistance* refers to grants or loans the official or public sector of OECD countries provide to LDCs for development purposes. To qualify as ODA, loans must be concessional rather than commercial; i.e., they must have a *grant element* of at least 25 percent. The grant element refers to the financial terms of a commitment, including the interest rate, maturity period, and grace period (the interval before the first repayment of capital). The grant element ranges from zero for a loan at 10 percent interest to 100 percent for a grant which requires no repayment; and the

Table 11.4

TEN LARGEST RECIPIENTS OF ODA* OR OA†
FROM THE OECD COUNTRIES

1995–1996		1999–2000	
Country	Amount‡	Country	Amount‡
1. China	2,412	1. Indonesia	2,456
2. Indonesia	2,118	2. China	2,097
3. Poland	2,018	3. Russia	1,495
4. Egypt	1,937	4. Egypt	1,442
5. India	1,708	5. India	1,438
6. Israel	1,484	6. Thailand	1,187
7. Russia	1,228	7. Vietnam	1,153
8. Philippines	1,195	8. Israel	1,000
9. Thailand	1,059	9. Philippines	990
10. Bangladesh	849	10. Bangladesh	825

*ODA: Official Development Assistance
†OA: Official Aid
‡Millions of U.S. dollars
Source: OECD, *Development Co-operation Report 1997*, (Paris: OECD, 1998), p.79; OECD, *Development Co-operation Report 2001*, (Paris: OECD, 2002), p.92.

grant element lies between these two limits for a loan at less than 10 percent interest. The OECD categorizes aid to Russia, the Ukraine, and most Eastern European states as *official aid (OA)* rather than ODA because the recipients are transition economies rather than LDCs. OA meets all the requirements for ODA in terms of concessionality, except that the recipients are classified as transition economies. (China and many smaller and poorer FSU countries are categorized as LDCs and receive ODA. FSU countries that are LDCs include Armenia, Azerbaijan, Kazakstan, Kyrgyz Republic, Moldova, Tajikistan, Turkmenistan, and Uzbekistan.)[9]

The important point is that ODA to the South has declined since the end of the Cold War, partly because a considerable amount of OA and ODA is being directed to the former centrally-planned economies (CPEs) in Eastern Europe, the FSU countries, and China. As Table 11.4 shows, in 1995–1996 three former CPEs (China, Poland, and Russia), and in 1999–2000 two former CPEs (China and Russia) were among the 10 largest recipients of ODA and OA from the OECD countries.

This chapter assesses the strategies LDCs have pursued to promote their economic development, such as import substitution, socialism, and export-led growth. In accordance with the revival of orthodox liberalism, LDCs in recent years have shifted to more open economic policies. Current development policies fall short, however, in meeting the needs of the poorest and most disadvantaged (e.g., LDC women and children) and in looking after the needs of the future as well as the present (e.g., in preserving the environment). As background for examining the LDC economic development strategies, this chapter first discusses the three major IPE perspectives and describes the functions of the World Bank, which "enjoys a unique position as a generator of ideas about economic development."[10] During the postwar period, the World

Bank and the United States have had considerable influence over the ideological and operational models used to promote development in the South.

IPE Perspectives and North-South Relations

This section briefly summarizes the main tenets of the three IPE perspectives as they relate to North-South relations. For a more detailed discussion of these perspectives, see Chapters 3 to 5.

Realist writers in the North, preoccupied with the issues of power and influence, tend to ignore the economic interests of poorer countries in the South. In the realist view, "Third World states want power and control as much as wealth,"[11] and it is only when LDCs pose a challenge to the North's economic predominance that most realists take notice. In the 1970s, for example, realists looked at OPEC's increased leverage in raising oil prices and at LDC attempts to gain more power and wealth through calls for an NIEO. During the 1980s–1990s, realists became interested in the challenge that the East Asian developmental state model posed to the North. Despite the lack of realist attention to poverty in the South, realist ideas have had considerable influence on LDC policies. For example, Alexander Hamilton and Friedrich List emphasized state building and argued that the late industrializers of their time (the United States and Germany) required a large degree of government involvement if they were to "catch up" with Britain—the leading state. Major LDC development strategies such as import substitution and export-led growth draw on Hamilton and List's ideas calling for a larger role for the state in promoting economic development.

Liberals believe that the growth of interdependence has widespread benefits, and they often argue that North-South linkages provide even more benefits to the South than to the North. LDC economic problems, from the liberal perspective, stem more from inefficient domestic policies than from their dependent position in the global economy. Thus, LDCs that follow open economic policies and increase their linkages with the North are most likely to achieve successful development. Although all liberals encourage LDCs to follow open, market-oriented policies, interventionist liberals (also called reformist liberals) recognize that North-South inequalities can put LDCs at a distinct disadvantage. Unlike orthodox liberals, who emphasize equal treatment and reciprocity, interventionist liberals call on the North to give more consideration to the special needs of the South. Nevertheless, interventionist liberals believe that the necessary changes can occur within the existing capitalist order, and they share the faith of other liberals in private enterprise and the market.

As historical structuralists, dependency theorists reject the optimism of liberals and the liberal view that LDC economic problems result primarily from inefficient domestic policies. From the dependency view, structural factors related to the global capitalist economy are responsible for constraining LDC development possibilities. Thus, dependency theorists argue that capitalist states in the core of the global economy either "underdevelop" LDCs in the periphery or prevent them from attaining genuine, autonomous development. Dependency theorists are also interested in class linkages, and they maintain that elites in the South (the "comprador" class) collaborate with foreign capitalists in the

North to reinforce the pattern of LDC dependency. Because some LDCs such as the East Asian and Latin American NIEs were successfully industrializing, world-systems theorists modified the classical dependency argument by introducing a third category of countries, the semiperiphery. Countries may move upward (or downward) from the periphery to the semiperiphery and even to the core, but world-systems theorists believe this occurs only rarely. Whereas some historical structuralists call for a redistribution of resources from the core to the periphery, the more extreme theorists believe that the core will never willingly agree to such a transfer of resources. Thus, they call for a domestic social revolution in the South and/or a severing of contacts with the North. The solution for disadvantaged groups, according to Gramscian theorists, is the development of a counterhegemony.

THE WORLD BANK GROUP

It is important to provide some background on the World Bank (or "the Bank") before examining LDC economic development strategies. The Bank's policies have been subject to numerous criticisms, and it currently faces some major stresses and uncertainties as an institution. Nevertheless, the Bank has had a major effect on LDC development strategies, because of its dominant role "as a non-private lender, as a research and idea-generating unit, and as a provider of advice to the Third World."[12] DCs traditionally have preferred to give most of their ODA bilaterally, or directly to recipient countries. However, the share of ODA extended multilaterally through IOs has increased from only 5 percent in 1960–1964 to 20 percent in 1970–1974, 29 percent in 1980–1984, and 33 percent in 1995–1997.[13] The World Bank has benefited from this shift toward multilateral aid because it is the largest lender of multilateral funds for international development.

The World Bank's considerable influence stems not only from the amount of funding it provides, but even more importantly from "its role as a rating agency for others."[14] The Bank's lending decisions, data collection, and country analysis have a powerful influence on bilateral donors, regional development banks, and providers of private portfolio and direct investment. The Bank also has an influential role in the evolution of ideas on economic development, and global "debates on development issues" are often "framed in terms of 'pro or anti' World Bank positions."[15] Thus, the Bank's influence stems partly from its role as an epistemic community on development issues. An **epistemic community** is "a network of professionals with recognized expertise and competence in a particular domain and an authoritative claim to policy-relevant knowledge within that domain or issue-area."[16] Recognized expertise can be a source of power in today's knowledge-based world economy, and several factors account for the Bank's influence in generating ideas on development: the Bank affects the terms under which LDCs gain access to development financing and international capital markets, it has the largest group of development economists and the largest research and policy analysis budget of any development organization, and the global media pay considerable attention to Bank studies and reports. The following discussion examines the Bank's organizational characteristics, and the views of proponents and critics of its policies.

Located in Washington, D.C., the Bank is actually a World Bank group composed of five institutions (see Figure 2.1 under Specialized Agencies in Chapter 2). The first of these institutions, the IBRD, was planned at the Bretton Woods conference. Foreign aid was *not* a central concern of the Western DCs at Bretton Woods. They were mainly interested in establishing the IMF to deal with monetary and balance of payments issues, and the decision to establish the IBRD was "something of an afterthought."[17] The Western DCs also expected the IBRD to give priority to European reconstruction over Southern development, and Harry Dexter White of the U.S. Treasury Department in fact suggested that the new institution should be called the "Bank for Reconstruction."[18] Because of LDC protests, the negotiators decided that the IBRD would devote "equitable" consideration to reconstruction and development; but the first IBRD loans in 1947 went to France, the Netherlands, and Denmark for European reconstruction. It was not until the United States established the European Recovery Program or Marshall Plan for Western Europe in 1948 that the IBRD shifted its focus from reconstruction to development.[19]

As is the case for the IMF, the World Bank is a weighted voting institution. Each member state has a capital subscription (or quota) based on its economic strength, which determines its financial contribution to the Bank and the number of votes it has in the policymaking bodies. The G-5 countries have the largest subscriptions and the greatest number of votes. In June 2002, the G-5 had 37.4 percent of the votes in the IBRD Board of Governors; the United States led with 16.4 percent, followed by Japan, Germany, France, and Britain, with 7.9, 4.5, 4.3, and 4.3 percent of the votes, respectively.[20] Member states in fact pay only 10 percent of their subscriptions to the IBRD and hold the remaining 90 percent as callable capital if needed to meet the IBRD's financial obligations. The IBRD receives the greatest share of its funds for development loans not from these subscriptions, but from its borrowing on world capital markets. In fiscal 2002 the IBRD raised $23 billion at medium- to long-term maturities in international capital markets. The IBRD is able to depend on capital markets for funding because of its good record in LDC repayment of loans and because of its large reserves of members' callable capital. Thus, the principal U.S. bond-rating services have given IBRD bonds a triple-A credit rating.

To make its bonds attractive to purchasers, the IBRD must pay market interest rates on its financial borrowing, and it must therefore in turn charge near-conventional interest rates on loans to LDC borrowers. For example, the interest rate on IBRD loans in 1997 was about 6.8 percent, the grace period was 3 to 5 years, and the maturity period ranged from 15 to 20 years.[21] IBRD loans are not concessional enough (i.e., they have too low a grant element) to qualify as ODA. Thus, the OECD introduced the concept of *Official Development Finance (ODF)* to recognize the developmental value of hard loans from multilateral institutions such as the IBRD. (Hard loans have higher interest rates and shorter repayment periods, whereas soft loans are more concessional with lower interest rates and longer repayment periods.) The IBRD's quasi-commercial loans are considered to be ODF because it extends them for development purposes, it accompanies the loans with economic and technical advice which is often in short supply in the South, and LDCs receive the IBRD loans on better terms than they could obtain from borrowing directly on capital markets (LDCs deemed uncreditworthy find it difficult to even borrow on capital markets).

To be a World Bank member, a country must also be a member of the IMF. This requirement deterred most Communist countries from joining the Bank for many years—even though they would have liked to receive Bank loans—because members must provide the IMF with detailed information about their economies (see Table 2.4 in Chapter 2). As in the IMF, the *board of governors* is theoretically the main World Bank policymaking body. Although every member state has one governor, the governors have different numbers of votes based on the weighted voting system. The governors meet only once a year to review the Bank's operations and policies, admit new members, and amend the Articles of Agreement; they delegate most of their functions to a 24-member *board of executive directors* (or *executive board*). The executive board, which also has weighted voting, is responsible for approving all Bank loan proposals and for developing the Bank's general policies. Whereas the G-5 countries are assured of appointing their own executive directors because of their large number of votes, coalitions of member countries elect the other executive directors every two years. (China, Saudi Arabia, and Russia have also elected their own executive directors, but they have fewer votes than the G-5 countries.) Elected executive directors cannot split their votes; i.e., they must cast the votes of their entire coalition group as a unit.

Early in the Bank's history, the United States and other Western DCs were willing to give the president and staff considerable discretion in daily operations because of the lack of Communist members, the Bank's weighted voting system, and the dominant position of Western DCs on the professional staff. The staff also had a degree of autonomy from governments because of the IBRD's dependence on financial markets for most of its funds (dependence on financial markets of course had other costs). In addition, several factors give the Bank staff a degree of autonomy vis-à-vis the executive board. First, most executive directors do not have the analytical support to monitor the broad range and complexity of issues the staff is dealing with; second, the frequent rotation of executive directors puts them at a distinct disadvantage in relation to Bank staff members, many of whom are career civil servants; and third, although the executive board can turn down a loan proposed by the staff, only the Bank president can decide whether, and when, to bring a loan proposal to the executive board. Despite the staff's prerogatives, there have always been limits to its autonomy, and the United States and some other DCs have scrutinized Bank actions more closely in recent years (see discussion later in this chapter).[22]

The IBRD was the only World Bank group institution until the International Finance Corporation (IFC) was established in 1956 (see Figure 2.1 in Chapter 2). Reflecting the Bank group's liberal-economic orientation, the IFC encourages private business and investment in LDCs, and currently it is the largest multilateral source of loans and equity financing for private-sector projects in the South. To promote private enterprise, the IFC is active in areas where the IBRD cannot operate. IBRD loans are provided only to governments, or with a government guarantee. The IFC by contrast can make loans to private ventures in LDCs without a government guarantee; indeed, it may not even accept a government guarantee. The IFC also invests in equity shares of corporations and acts as a broker bringing foreign and domestic partners together in joint ventures. Furthermore, the IFC has persuaded commercial banks to lend to LDCs, partly through joint financing deals with banks as co-lenders. Like the IBRD, the IFC charges near-commercial rates on its loans. During the 1980s, the U.S. Reagan administration's emphasis on the private sector elevated the IFC's importance in the World Bank group, and the IFC reported net profits of $142 million in fiscal

1992–1993. These profits, combined with the high interest rate on IFC loans, raise questions among critics as to whether the IFC is a money-making or philanthropic institution. Nevertheless, the IFC maintains that it promotes development by providing technical, financial, and environmental advice for development projects.[23]

In 1960, the International Development Association (IDA) became the third institution of the World Bank group. The IDA was formed largely in response to the South's complaints that poorer LDCs could not pay the high interest rates on IBRD hard loans. Even major LDCs such as India and Pakistan were reaching the limits of their borrowing ability on conventional terms in the late 1950s. LDCs also opposed the World Bank's weighted voting system, and throughout the 1950s they demanded a soft-loan agency in which they would have greater control. The DCs finally agreed to create the IDA as a soft-loan agency in 1960, but they insisted that the agency be under World Bank auspices with its weighted voting system. Although the IDA and IBRD are legally and financially distinct, they share the same staff and their projects must meet the same criteria.[24]

The IDA provides soft loans or "credits" to LDC governments with no interest rate, 10-year grace periods, and 35- to 40-year maturities. Unlike IBRD and IFC loans, the highly concessional IDA credits are categorized as ODA. Because IDA credits are reserved for poorer LDCs, a number of LDCs and transition countries with somewhat stronger economies are only eligible for IBRD loans; examples include Argentina, Brazil, Mexico, Malaysia, Thailand, Iran, Egypt, the Czech Republic, Hungary, Russia, the Ukraine, and China. A small middle range group of states with somewhat weaker economies are eligible for a blend of IBRD and IDA funds; examples include India, Pakistan, Indonesia, Nigeria, Bolivia, the Federal Republic of Yugoslavia, Azerbaijan, and Uzbekistan. States with the weakest economies are eligible for IDA credits but not IBRD loans. In 2002, 65 states were in this category; examples include Bangladesh, Nepal, Vietnam, Honduras, Tanzania, Republic of the Congo, Kenya, Ethiopia, Albania, Georgia, Armenia, and Mongolia.[25] Unlike the IBRD and IFC, the interest-free terms of IDA credits give it no basis for borrowing on capital markets. IDA funds therefore depend primarily on replenishments by DC governments after difficult negotiations every three years. Other donors often wait for the United States to pledge funds before making their own pledges, and the U.S. Congress sometimes delays its approval of IDA contributions. Orthodox liberal views that LDCs should rely more on private capital and less on World Bank "handouts" pose a constant threat to IDA's financial viability. Despite the importance of IDA credits to some of the poorest LDCs, non-concessional lending accounts for almost three-fourths of the Bank group's total annual loan agreements and payments.[26]

The fourth and fifth Bank group institutions—the *International Centre for Settlement of Investment Disputes (ICSID)* and the *Multilateral Investment Guarantee Agency (MIGA)*—were established to encourage the flow of private foreign investment to LDCs and transition economies. The ICSID was formed in 1966 to provide international facilities for conciliation and arbitration of disputes over FDI. The need for a neutral international forum arose because foreign investors were concerned that the courts in host countries would not be impartial, and issues of sovereignty and national dignity prevented host countries from submitting disputes to foreign courts. The MIGA was established in 1988 to provide guarantees to foreign investors against losses caused by noncommercial risks such as currency inconvertibility, expropriation, war, and civil disturbances. The MIGA also provides technical assistance to help LDCs and transition economies disseminate information on investment opportunities.[27]

It is important to note that the World Bank has considerable influence over bilateral as well as multilateral aid giving. As a key source of data and analysis on development issues, World Bank reports and publications are highly regarded by government officials. The World Bank also chairs a number of aid consortia and **consultative groups.** Meetings of these groups enable DC donors to coordinate their bilateral aid giving to a particular recipient and avoid needless duplication. From the view of LDCs, however, consultative groups often permit donors to exert collective pressures on a recipient government because only one recipient and many donors attend each meeting.[28] As the most important multilateral development institution, the World Bank has also provided a model for regional development banks, including the Inter-American Development Bank (established in 1960), the African Development Bank (1964), the Asian Development Bank (1966), and the European Bank for Reconstruction and Development or EBRD (1991). Like the World Bank, regional development banks usually raise funds on international capital markets and lend at near-commercial interest rates. The regional banks can borrow and lend money at favorable rates of interest because their credit ratings are backed by member states' subscriptions (most of which are callable rather than paid in capital). These banks also have IDA-type soft-loan affiliates, which must raise funds from government subscriptions. Whereas the World Bank directs most of its funding to larger projects and programs, the regional banks usually support smaller development projects at the regional level.[29]

The United States is the most important member of the World Bank, and there are several indicators of its influence. First, the United States has more votes than any other member. Second, English is the Bank's only working language, reflecting U.S. influence and the Bank's location in Washington, D.C. The U.S. view that a single working language contributes to efficiency contrasts with the view of many other countries that cultural and ethnic diversity dictates the need for more than one working language in IOs.[30] Third, the World Bank president has always been American, and the executive directors accept the U.S. government's nominee for the position. Whereas the U.S. Treasury Department handles most matters related to U.S. involvement in the Bank, the White House nominates the Bank presidents and "invariably chooses candidates with connections to the U.S. political establishment."[31] The Bank president has considerable influence in setting the agenda as well as determining policies regarding personnel, financial controls, and budgetary procedures.

Some data would seem to indicate that U.S. influence has declined, however. In earlier years, the IBRD was extremely dependent on the U.S. capital market for funds, but the share of the World Bank's outstanding securities held in the United States has steadily decreased. U.S. voting power in the Bank has also fallen from about 40 percent of the total to less than 17 percent. Nevertheless, the United States continues to have predominant influence in the Bank for several reasons. First, despite the decline in U.S. voting power, it is the only country with a veto over formal amendments to the Bank Articles of Agreement and over decisions to increase the Bank's capital. In 1989 an amendment to the Bank's articles increased the voting majority for approving a capital increase from 80 to 85 percent so the United States could retain its veto power in this area. Second, the ratio of U.S. bilateral aid to World Bank lending has declined dramatically, largely because of the end of the Cold War. The use of Bank resources has therefore become far more important to the United States in framing its policies toward the South. Third, other Bank members have done little to challenge U.S. leadership. Other DCs have often been "happy that the United States was taking the lead—and the heat—for doing what they wanted anyway," and they are unwilling to jeopardize their bilateral relations with the United States by challenging it openly.[32] This is especially the case for Japan, whose financial contributions to the Bank have increased substantially since the 1980s. The Europeans also have felt that their interests are better served by insitutions under their control, which explains their decision to form the EBRD. As for LDCs, divisions within the South and the South's dependence on Bank loans continues to limit their influence. Fourth, the United States continues to have a considerable amount of structural or soft power in the Bank; i.e., it is often successful in getting "other countries to *want* what it wants."[33] This soft power depends partly on a range of U.S.-based civil society actors such as academics, think tanks, and NGOs with ready access to the Bank in Washington, D.C. Soft power also results from the fact that a large majority of World Bank economists have at least some post–graduate education in a North American university, and this affects their perception of development issues. Fifth, the creation of IDA in 1960 gave the United States (and other DCs) a source of influence that they did not have over the IBRD. Indeed, the U.S. threat to withhold IDA replenishments may be its most important source of pressure, and in some cases this threat is explicitly linked with U.S. objections to specific Bank policies.

Despite the high degree of U.S. influence in the Bank, it is important to note that the Bank sometimes asserts its autonomy on particular issues (e.g., in its loans to public sector institutions under Bank President Robert McNamara) and relies on its expertise to influence foreign aid officials in the United States and other DCs. Thus, the United States and the World Bank "have had a complex, evolving relationship that is part symbiosis, part two-way influence, and part struggle over the Bank's autonomy of action."[34]

It is impossible to detail here the numerous arguments in favor of, and against, World Bank policies. Instead, this chapter provides a brief outline of some salient issues raised by critics and supporters. The strongest critics are often historical structuralists on the left and orthodox liberals on the right. Historical structuralists accuse the Bank of "prying state control of its Third World member countries out of the hands of nationalists and socialists who would regulate international capital's inroads."[35] Historical structuralists also argue that Bank loans enrich DC exporters and MNCs at the expense of the poorest people and LDCs. Some orthodox liberals, by contrast, charge that IOs such as the Bank "have an evident interest in ever-increasing multinational aid" and suggest that the Bank should "impose a greater check on the staff's tendency to be 'state enthusiasts.' "[36] Defenders often view the Bank as adopting interventionist or reformist liberal policies as a development institution and consider it inevitable "that the Bank should be subjected to severe criticism from the ideologues of both left and right."[37]

As this chapter discusses, the Bank has in fact often been too ready to disregard challenges to its liberal free market approach to development problems, and it has been more willing to accept studies emphasizing government failure than studies emphasizing market failure.[38] During the 1980s–1990s, the Bank became a stronger supporter of orthodox liberal policies and pressured LDCs to adopt these policies through its SALs. Only recently has the Bank become more aware of the problems resulting if measures are not taken to cushion vulnerable groups and states from unrestrained market pressures. Other criticisms of the Bank range from its dismissive and patronizing attitude toward other institutions such as the United Nations Development Program (UNDP), UNICEF, and the regional development banks; its highly centralized structure in Washington, D.C., with too little staff time spent in the field; and its practice of giving priority to large-project commitments with fast-disbursing loans over project supervision, implementation, and evaluation.

In fairness to the World Bank, one should note that as the largest multilateral development institution it is sometimes a target of criticism regardless of the policies it adopts. For example, some critics charge that the Bank is too slow to alter its approach to development in response to civil society pressures and changing LDC requirements. However, when the Bank alters its policies, others charge that "under pressure from NGOs and other interest groups" the Bank rushes "to embrace the latest fads in development thinking regardless of their substantive merits."[39] Furthermore, the Bank, like all IOs, is to a large degree a creature of its most important member states. Ultimately, the Bank's ability to provide increased IDA funds for the poorest LDCs in Asia and sub-Saharan Africa depends on the willingness of the North to provide IDA replenishments. Having provided some background on the World Bank group, the discussion turns to LDC development strategies.

IMPORT-SUBSTITUTING INDUSTRIALIZATION

During the early postwar period, the ideas of several major economists had considerable influence on Southern development strategies. First, development strategies drew on the interventionist liberal ideas of John Maynard Keynes. Although Keynes called for a greater governmental role in welfare and job creation in DCs, his ideas contributed to the view that LDC governments should also have a major role in promoting economic development. Second, Southern development strategies drew on the ideas of Raúl Prebisch and Hans Singer. In 1950, Prebisch and Singer separately published studies arguing that there was a growing income gap between the North and the South because of a long-term decline in the prices of primary products (raw materials and agricultural goods). To close the income gap, LDCs would have to alter the structures of their economies, decreasing their emphasis on the production of primary products and focusing first and foremost on industrialization.[40]

In arguing that LDCs were disadvantaged because of their role as primary product exporters, Prebisch and Singer contradicted the liberal economic view that free trade based on comparative advantage benefits all states. According to the Prebisch-Singer thesis, the demand for industrial goods such as automobiles and televisions rises as individual incomes increase, but the same does not apply to agricultural products and raw materials. Indeed, the demand for raw materials may even decline in DCs as technological advances lead to the discovery of substitute products (such as synthetic rubber for natural rubber). Thus, LDCs that depend on primary product exports suffer from declining terms of trade. When LDCs raise their production of primary products in attempts to garner more revenue, they are faced with lower prices and more abject levels of poverty as surplus stocks accumulate. Prebisch therefore argued that an ISI strategy would permit LDCs to produce manufactured goods at home that they had previously imported. In the 1950s Prebisch began to use the terms "center" and "periphery," and his classic work formed the core of Latin American structuralist policies in the 1950s–1960s. Although Prebisch's structuralism was a precursor (along with Marxism) to dependency theory, it was *not* dependency theory. Latin American structuralism was reformist and was more optimistic than dependency theory that the South could catch up with the North through protectionism and state-promoted industrialization.[41]

Realists such as Hamilton and List had supported policies similar to ISI for late industrializers during the eighteenth and nineteenth centuries, and some Latin American and Middle Eastern LDCs had developed ISI policies as a short-term response to the Great Depression during the interwar period. However, it was not until after World War II that the South adopted ISI as a long-term development strategy. Central to ISI was the argument that LDCs should protect and support their infant industries through tariff and nontariff barriers to industrial imports and through subsidies and other incentives to promote industrial growth. Only by emphasizing industrial development (and de-emphasizing agriculture) would LDCs be able to compete with the DCs. An alliance of government, local industrialists, and foreign capital was necessary to begin the industrialization process.

In the 1950s–1960s, LDCs in Latin America, Asia, and Africa followed ISI policies, and import substitution "emerged as the new gospel for Third World industrialization."[42] Although ISI is a realist development strategy with strong nationalist overtones, the World Bank was generally supportive of ISI policies during the 1950s. The Bank has always been interested in promoting private enterprise in LDCs, but it was affected by postwar interventionist liberal views that the state had an important role to play in the development process. The Bank's approach to development placed considerable emphasis on industrialization, which normally meant ISI in the 1950s. Because of the infant industry problem for LDCs, the Bank accepted the fact that ISI would involve some degree of trade protectionism. Furthermore, the Bank provided funding for major infrastructure projects such as transportation and communications facilities, power projects, and port developments, which LDCs needed to promote industrialization.[43]

Initially, ISI policies seemed to provide major gains for LDCs. For example, Latin America registered healthy industrial growth rates in the 1940s–1950s, and the Mexican economy grew at an average annual rate of 6.5 percent until 1970. India's steel production increased by six times during its first three 5-year plans from 1951 to 1966, and some African states such as Ghana also registered industrial gains. International economic conditions were highly favorable to the success of ISI in the 1950s and early 1960s, with LDCs benefiting from prosperity and growth in North America and Western Europe. Furthermore, the South's output of agricultural products generally did not suffer during the 1960s even though ISI policies downgraded the role of agriculture because the Rockefeller Foundation-supported "green revolution" led to the development of dwarf strains of high-yielding grains. The green revolution exacerbated differences between rich and poor farmers in the South because only the rich could afford the irrigation, fertilizer, and other inputs required to grow the new high-yielding grains. Nevertheless, increased agricultural output in India and other Asian states masked the fact that ISI was promoting industrialization at the expense of agriculture.[44]

Despite the initial success of ISI policies, external problems and internal distortions started to become evident in LDCs employing ISI during the 1960s–1970s. International economic changes such as the food and oil crises of the 1970s were especially important in exposing the weaknesses of ISI. Inclement weather, Soviet crop shortfalls, and other unexpected events in the early 1970s led to greatly increased demand for food imports, and global food stocks in 1972–1973 fell to their lowest levels in 20 years. Many LDCs lacked *effective demand,* or demand backed by purchasing power, so they had less ability than countries such as the Soviet Union and Japan to purchase foodstuffs on global markets at inflated prices. Thus, the global food crisis of the early 1970s had its severest effects on the South.[45] When OPEC managed to limit supplies and drastically raise oil prices in 1973, a number of LDC oil importers such as India were doubly hit by the food and energy crises. These new external stresses exposed a number of weaknesses in ISI as a development strategy.

First, the global food crisis of the early 1970s pointed to the pitfalls for LDCs in overemphasizing industrialization at the expense of agriculture. The neglect of agriculture under ISI contributed to poverty in the countryside, the need for foodgrain imports, and the stagnation of agricultural exports. The LDC share of world agricultural exports fell from 44 percent in 1955 to 32 percent in 1970, and the resultant decline in revenue simply exacerbated LDC balance-of-payments deficits and lack of funding for investment. Second, despite the emphasis of the ISI strategy on promoting self-sufficiency, ISI ironically increased the South's dependence on the North. In view of their shortages of capital and foreign exchange, LDCs considered foreign investment to be a necessary evil to promote industrialization, and they therefore encouraged inward FDI as part of their ISI policies. As a result, MNCs were able to set up subsidiaries behind the LDC trade barriers; this helps explain why the U.S. government supported ISI as part of "its vigorous efforts to secure favorable conditions for U.S. foreign direct investment."[46] U.S. policies were less consistently pro-free trade during the postwar period than many hegemonic stability theorists have indicated.

The most serious weakness of ISI was its inability to accomplish what it was supposed to be best at: promoting industrial competitiveness. Industrialization seemed to proceed well under an "easy" first stage of ISI, but the second stage of ISI was far more difficult. In the first stage, LDCs replaced imports of nondurable consumer goods such as shoes, household products, and clothing with domestic production. These are labor-intensive goods that do not require large amounts of capital investment, advanced technology, or a network of component suppliers, and there is a sizable domestic market in LDCs for these goods. However, LDCs had to move on to a second stage of ISI to maintain high industrial growth rates, replacing imports of intermediate goods (e.g., petrochemicals and steel) and producer and consumer durables (e.g., refrigerators and automobiles) with domestic production. These second-stage products were more difficult for LDCs to produce because they are capital intensive and depend on economies of scale and higher levels of technology. LDC producers had to import technology and inputs required to produce these goods, and the cost of the imported inputs outweighed any savings from producing the final goods locally. Finally, the emphasis on capital-intensive production under ISI concentrated development gains in a small percentage of the population in industrial enclaves, and unemployment emerged as a major problem for most people outside these enclaves. ISI therefore simply exacerbated the income inequalities within LDCs.[47]

Those LDCs pursuing the second stage of ISI suffered from a slowdown in the growth of primary product exports, dependence on imports for the production of second-stage goods, and a failure to increase manufactured exports. In response to their balance-of-payments problems, these LDCs sought external loans, aid, and investment and turned increasingly to trade protectionism. By the 1960s, liberal economists were therefore arguing that "an import substitution policy tends to be less and less successful the longer it continues,"[48] and the World Bank was changing its views and beginning to oppose ISI. For example, the Bank began to sponsor a series of studies in 1965 that demonstrated the high cost of ISI in LDC automotive industries and in the production of heavy electrical and manufacturing equipment. By the late 1960s, "the financing of profitable import-substituting industry by IFC and Bank-financed development finance companies, without much regard for the relation of domestic to international prices" was giving way "to a more discriminating policy of industrial financing."[49] Even Prebisch expressed concerns that "the proliferation of industries of every kind in a closed market has deprived the Latin American countries of the advantages of specialization and economies of scale."[50] In efforts to revive ISI, Prebisch hoped that RTAs would provide the necessary economies of scale so that Latin American LDCs could continue to industrialize. As discussed in Chapter 9, however, Latin American regionalism during the 1970s was unsuccessful.

Despite the problems with second-stage ISI, many Latin American and South Asian states continued following an ISI strategy because domestic groups with vested interests in trade protectionism limited the ability of governments to institute policy change.[51] It was not until the 1980s foreign debt crisis that most LDCs finally dispensed with ISI and shifted to a more outward-oriented development strategy (see the following discussion). Although many LDCs persisted with ISI during the 1960s–1970s, some sought alternatives. A second group of LDCs adopted a more extreme inward-looking strategy than ISI, turning to socialist central planning based on the Soviet Union model. However, LDC experiments with socialism encountered a number of problems. A third group, the East Asian NIEs, changed from ISI to export-led growth strategies at a fairly early stage, and they experienced far more impressive economic growth rates than other LDCs. As a result, the development community began to look positively at export-led growth as an alternative strategy to promote economic development.

Socialist Development Strategies

During the 1960s scholars challenged ISI from both the right and the left, and many left-leaning scholars turned to dependency theory (see the discussion of dependency theory in Chapter 4).[52] According to dependency theorists, ISI did not adequately restructure the peripheral LDC economies or increase their leverage vis-à-vis the DCs in the core. The South could promote autonomous development, dependency theorists argued, only by turning to socialism and severing linkages with the North. Although most LDCs continued with ISI, a small number such as China, North Korea, Cuba, Ethiopia, Mozambique, Vietnam, Laos, Cambodia, and Burma eventually opted for socialist central planning strategies. China was the only one of these LDCs with the size and resources to be able to reap major economic benefits from socialist central planning.[53]

The socialist development strategies were patterned after the Soviet model, which involved the abolition of the capitalist market economy and private ownership as well as the establishment of state control over the economy and its resources. Thus, state central planning largely replaced market signals in economic decisions concerning the allocation of resources and investment and the setting of production targets, wages, and prices. LDCs opting for the socialist route were more concerned than nonsocialist LDCs about the redistributional aspects of economic development. Thus, they often registered more gains than nonsocialist LDCs in reducing economic and social inequities by providing better access to health care and education, improving the status of women, and opening parks and other facilities for public use. Despite the advances of some socialist LDCs in social areas such as health and education, these countries encountered a number of economic problems.

A major problem with the socialist strategy was that LDCs other than China were too small and lacking in resources to engage in central planning on the Soviet/Eastern European model. For example, LDCs lacked the communications and transportation infrastructure essential for central planning and a well-trained technocratic bureaucracy necessary to design and monitor the plans. LDCs also encountered many of the same problems that plagued the Soviet Union and Eastern Europe. Thus, central planners were more successful in setting production targets and increasing the quantity of output than they were in ensuring the quality of output and the efficient use of resources. Although LDCs were ill equipped to employ socialist central planning, Western aid and investment policies did not make their task easier. For example, World Bank and U.S. Agency for International Development (AID) officials believed that foreign aid should be designed at least partly to promote private enterprise. Thus, most LDCs following a socialist development model were not major beneficiaries of Western development assistance programs.

A prime example of the problems facing LDCs that pursued a socialist model was Mozambique. Shortly after gaining independence in 1975, a Marxist government in Mozambique tried to loosen its linkages with South Africa's apartheid government and follow a socialist development path. However, the state had to intervene massively in the economy to achieve its egalitarian and socialist objectives, and this was beyond the Mozambique government's capacity. In agriculture, for example, Mozambique established communal villages and about 2,000 state farms to supply most of the country's food supplies. Nevertheless, agricultural production fell drastically after 1975 because farmers preferred family plots over farming on a communal basis, and the government could devote only limited resources to the state farms and communal villages. Although Mozambique tried to promote cooperative ties with the West as well as with socialist states, the U.S. Congress maintained a ban on U.S. foreign aid to Mozambique (often over the U.S. executive branch's objections) from 1975 to 1984. Mozambique was also the target of a destabilization campaign launched by the South African government, partly because of its support for refugees and liberation movements in southern Africa. By the end of 1983, Mozambique was facing a severe economic crisis marked by a lack of foodstuffs for the population, a shortage of foreign exchange, and a serious decline in local production. As a result, the Mozambique government defaulted on its debts and became a major recipient of international aid. In response to assistance and debt-rescheduling negotiations with the IMF, World Bank, and the Paris and London Clubs, Mozambique introduced orthodox liberal reforms.[54]

Mozambique's experiences were repeated with some variations in a number of other LDCs seeking to pursue socialist economic objectives, and when the Soviet bloc collapsed in the late 1980s–1990s, the socialist LDCs could no longer look to the "Second World" for economic and military support. Thus, very few LDCs currently follow socialist strategies, and even the few holdouts such as Cuba are seeking to establish closer ties with the capitalist world.[55]

EXPORT-LED GROWTH

The experience of the East Asian NIEs—South Korea, Taiwan, Singapore, and Hong Kong—was very different from that of most other LDCs. The East Asian NIEs adopted export-led growth strategies, and they registered impressive growth rates and improvement in their economic performance. Export-led growth strategies were far more successful than either the socialist or ISI strategies in the 1970s–1980s. In examining the effects of export-led growth on economic development, it is best to discuss the experience of South Korea and Taiwan because Singapore and Hong Kong have a unique status in the South. Both are so small geographically that they are more akin to city-states, and Hong Kong was a British crown colony before it was incorporated into mainland China. Hong Kong was also the only East Asian NIE that never followed ISI policies.

Taiwan and South Korea adopted ISI in the 1950s and experienced serious economic problems. Both economies had large balance-of-payments deficits, which were covered mainly by foreign aid, and their exports consisted almost entirely of primary commodities. During the 1960s, Taiwan and South Korea followed the example of Japan and shifted from ISI to a policy encouraging the growth of manufactured exports. While maintaining a moderate degree of trade protection of the domestic market, they promoted exports with tax incentives, export credits, export targets, and duty-free imports of inputs required by exporters and their suppliers. Taiwan and South Korea also abandoned minimum wage legislation and imposed only minimal taxes on the employment of labor so that employment in export-oriented industries could rapidly increase. During the early 1980s, Southeast Asian economies such as Malaysia, Indonesia, and Thailand followed the path taken by Japan and the East Asian NIEs and switched to export-led growth strategies. Thus, analysts sometimes refer to Hong Kong, Singapore, South Korea, and Taiwan as "first-tier" and to Malaysia, Indonesia, and Thailand as "second-tier" Asian NIEs.

The change from ISI to export-led growth had a dramatic effect on the economic performance of the East Asian NIEs. For example, South Korea's GDP grew at an average annual rate of more than 8 percent throughout the 1960s, and its exports rose

Table 11.5

GDP* PER CAPITA AND EXPORT/GDP RATIOS

	GDP PER CAPITA		EXPORT/GDP RATIOS	
	1963	**1988**	**1963**	**1988**
East Asian NIEs[†]				
Hong Kong	$2,247	$11,952	39.0	51.1
South Korea	747	4,094	2.3	35.4
Singapore	1,777	11,693	124.5	164.2
Taiwan	980	4,607	15.3	51.8
Latin American NIEs				
Argentina	$2,949	$3,474	10.0	10.2
Brazil	1,400	3,424	6.0	9.5
Chile	3,231	3,933	11.6	31.9
Mexico	2,312	3,649	5.1	11.9

*GDP: Gross Domestic Product
[†]NIES: Newly Industrializing Economies
Source: Bela Balassa, *Policy Choices for the 1990s* (London: Macmillan, 1993), pp.57 and 59.

from about $31 million in 1960 to $882 million in 1970. Of significance was not only the dramatic growth of South Korean and Taiwanese exports but also the change in their composition. In the 1960s to early 1970s, most of their rapidly growing exports were industrial products that required large amounts of unskilled labor and relatively little capital. Over time industrial wages increased, and there was a structural transformation in the two economies as they began to produce sophisticated industrial goods that required more highly skilled labor. Thus, by the late 1980s Taiwan and South Korea were the tenth and thirteenth largest world exporters of manufactures.[56]

The East Asian economic successes of the 1960s–1980s were often compared with the less favorable economic fortunes of the Latin American NIEs—Argentina, Brazil, Chile, and Mexico.[57] Although the Latin American NIEs instituted some reforms to provide incentives for exports in the 1960s, their policies continued to be based primarily on ISI. Thus, the first two columns of Table 11.5 show that per capita GDP growth rates were much higher for the East Asian NIEs than for the Latin American NIEs. For example, whereas South Korea's GDP per capita of $747 was well *below* the per capita GDPs of all four Latin American NIEs in 1963, by 1988 South Korea's per capita GDP of $4,094 was *above* the figures for the Latin American NIEs. The change was even more dramatic for Hong Kong and Singapore: their GDPs soared to more than $11,000 by 1988. The last two columns of Table 11.5 show that the export-to-GDP ratios were also higher for the East Asian NIEs. South Korea again provides a striking example. Whereas the South Korean export-to-GDP ratio of 2.3 was well below the figures for the Latin American NIEs in 1963, its export-led growth policies resulted in an export-to-GDP ratio of 35.4 in 1988, exceeding the ratios of all the Latin American NIEs. The export-to-GDP ratios in 1988 for Singapore (164.2), Taiwan (51.8), and Hong Kong (51.1) were much higher than the ratios for the Latin American NIEs. Finally, there were striking differences in the composition as well as level of exports. By the late 1980s, Taiwan, South Korea, and Hong Kong were *each* producing more manu-factured exports than all of Latin America.[58]

The East Asian NIEs had a few years of reduced growth during the 1980s debt crisis, but they did not have to seek debt rescheduling and soon adjusted their economies and returned to a pattern of rapid growth. Although the East Asian NIEs had about the same ratios of debt obligations to GDP as other oil importers, their ratios of debt obligations to exports were much lower. Their relatively healthy export positions, combined with large infusions of foreign investment (especially from Japan), enabled them to garner sufficient revenue to continue their debt payments without depending on IMF and World Bank SALs. The Latin American NIEs following ISI strategies, by contrast, were more severely affected by the debt crisis and had to seek substantial IMF and World Bank funding.[59]

As discussed later, the East and Southeast Asian economies began to encounter some economic problems during the late 1980s, and these problems became starkly evident in the late 1990s. Nevertheless, just as ISI had been viewed as the "gospel for Third World industrialization" in the 1950s,[60] so the Asian export-led growth strategy emerged as the new gospel for many development specialists from the 1970s to the early 1990s. Although there was a general consensus that export-led growth policies were more successful than ISI, there was a wide divergence of views as to the reasons for the East Asians' success.

IPE Perspectives and the East Asian Experience

Liberals, realists, and historical structuralists offered widely differing explanations for the success of the East Asian export-led growth strategy in the 1960s–1980s. According to liberal economists, the strong East Asian economic performance resulted from the fact that the export-led growth strategy was "outward-oriented," as opposed to the "inward-oriented" ISI strategy of Latin American NIEs.[61] From this perspective, the East Asians were successful because they did not have "the mistrust of markets and private entrepreneurship that motivates large-scale doctoring in other Asian countries and in African and South American countries."[62] Thus, the East Asians encouraged the growth of free markets, competition, and private entrepreneurship through the liberalization of trade, foreign investment, and exchange rate policies. In sum, liberals attributed the success of the East Asian NIEs to their willingness to follow the example of Western DCs in adopting open market policies.

In contrast to the liberals, realists argued that the key to East Asian economic growth (with the possible exception of Hong Kong) was the existence of a strong *developmental state,* which had "a fundamental role in engineering economic growth, development and success in these countries."[63] As early as the eighteenth and nineteenth centuries, Hamilton and List had argued that late industrializers required state intervention if they were to catch up with more advanced nations (see Chapter 3). However, it was not until the early 1980s that Chalmers Johnson first used the phrase *developmental state* in his seminal works on Japan and the East Asian NIEs.[64] According to realists, the East Asian developmental state had several characteristics. First, the state provided extensive guidance to the market, strictly controlling investment flows, promoting the development of technology, and protecting selected infant industries. Second, the state identified development as its top objective, encouraging citizens to increase investment rather than current consumption and using repression if necessary to enforce its priorities. Third, the state invested heavily in education to ensure that the population had the skills to meet the standards of global competitiveness. And fourth, the state depended on a highly skilled, technocratic bureaucracy that was committed to instituting economic reforms. Although ISI and export-led growth both depended on a large degree of government intervention, realists argued that the policies differed in two critical respects: First, the East Asian developmental state focused primarily on developing the country's export industries, whereas ISI sought to build an industrial base mainly to meet domestic demand. Second, ISI generally protected all local industries, whereas the East Asian developmental state supported a small number of key industries considered to be "winners."[65]

In marked contrast to liberals and realists, dependency and world-systems theorists argued that the NIEs were not in fact achieving genuine economic development. Although the Latin American and East Asian NIEs had ascended to a semiperiphery, which was somewhere above the level of LDCs in the periphery, they were simply "more advanced exemplars of dependent development," still dependent on the industrial states in the core.[66] Thus, André Gunder Frank argued that when the NIEs "produce end products such as shirts, radios or even cars they are simply increasing their dependent integration into a worldwide division of labor . . . in which they are allocated the least remunerative and technologically obsolete contribution."[67]

In addition to the three main IPE perspectives, a fourth perspective explained the success of the East Asian NIEs in terms of domestic social factors, referred to collectively as *political culture*. Political culture can be defined as widely shared social values that affect a state's political economy. Those who emphasized political culture as the key to the East Asians' success argued that the realist focus on the role of the state was insufficient because "the nature of . . . society is important in determining whether or not state policies are effective."[68] The East Asian NIEs and China and Japan all have political cultures that are strongly influenced by Confucianism.[69] Confucianism is a secular philosophy that emphasizes respect for authority, the role of government in promoting the public good, the importance of education, and the value of strong kinship ties in creating incentives for family-based entrepreneurship. Thus, Confucian philosophy is highly supportive of an economic development model based on collective values, hard work and enterprise, and a benevolent state staffed by the most educated individuals. According to theorists focusing on political culture, Confucianism was a major factor explaining the success of Japan and the East Asian NIEs in promoting economic development. (Political culture theorists argue that the Southeast Asians lack "a unifying cultural force comparable to Confucianism in East Asia."[70])

Of the four perspectives, most analysts opted for the realist model of the strong developmental state as the best explanation for the rapid economic growth in East and Southeast Asia. However, the Asian financial crisis of the late 1990s raised serious questions about the realist and other models and demonstrated "how rapidly an informed consensus can change."[71]

The Asian Financial Crisis

In 1993 the World Bank issued a report titled *The East Asian Miracle*, which examined the region's "remarkable record of high and sustained economic growth" from 1965 to

1990 (the report is discussed later in this chapter), and a number of policymakers and academics began to refer to the East Asians as "miracle economies."[72] The widely divergent perspectives discussed earlier indicated that economists could not agree on a satisfactory explanation for the East Asian successes, and the choice of the term "miracle" implied that "the phenomenon was beyond purely scientific explanation."[73] Although rapid growth continued in East Asia during the early 1990s, questions arose about the vigor of these economies in 1996 when export growth slowed, earnings declined, and surplus capacity developed in many industries. Analysts expressed increasing concerns in 1997 when problems emerged in Thailand's real estate and financial sector, several large South Korean enterprises or *chaebol* failed, and the Japanese economy continued to stagnate. Then a full-blown financial crisis started in July 1997 when Thailand allowed its *baht* currency to float. Subsequently, a number of Asian economies permitted their currencies to float, and they depreciated sharply. The four economies affected most by the crisis were Thailand, Indonesia, Malaysia, and South Korea. Foreign investors lost confidence in the currencies of these economies, and eventually the most severely affected economies had to seek large IMF and World Bank loans to bolster their currencies and economies.[74]

The 1990s Asian financial crisis was different from the 1980s foreign debt crisis in two major respects. First, during the 1980s crisis governments in Latin America, sub-Saharan Africa, and Eastern Europe held a significant share of the debt, while the lenders were mainly banks and other private institutions. The East Asian NIEs affected by the 1990s financial crisis in contrast had relatively small states, and their debts were held largely by the private sector. Second, the main concerns in the debt crisis related to the overall indebtedness and high debt-service ratios of the debtor states, whereas the main concerns in the East Asian financial crisis related to short-term debt levels and outflows of portfolio investment. Despite these differences, both the debt and financial crises were preceded by large volumes of private capital inflows and resulted in a sudden reversal of these flows. By early 1999, the worst part of the Asian financial crisis was over, and although the Japanese economy remained weak, other Asian economies began to recover as U.S. and European demand for their exports increased. Recovery continued throughout 1999, and by 2000 there was growing confidence in the future of East Asian economic growth. Nevertheless, the Asian economies have been slow to institute some needed economic reforms, and they continue to be vulnerable to changing economic conditions.[75] The following discussion examines the reasons for the East Asian shift from "miracle" to "meltdown" status and the effects of the Asian financial crisis on international development strategies. (Chapter 7 discusses the effects of the Asian financial crisis on debates over the IMF's role and the need for a new international financial architecture.)

The emergence of serious East Asian economic problems in 1997 caused some analysts to question whether the "miracle" was over or even whether it had ever occurred, and whereas economists "had struggled to find a fully convincing explanation" for the rapid East Asian growth, they "now struggled to explain the 'meltdown.'"[76] Historical structuralists had questioned whether the East Asian economies were achieving genuine, autonomous development, and they believed that the financial crisis added weight to their arguments. The East Asian NIEs grew far more rapidly than LDCs in other regions for most of the 1970s–1980s, but their development was more fragile and dependent in some respects than was earlier assumed. Although the existence of strong developmental states contributed to East Asian economic growth, this growth was highly dependent on U.S. and Japanese policies. Economies such as Taiwan and South Korea, with strategic geographic positions vis-à-vis the Soviet Union and China, had special linkages with the United States extending back to the 1950s. Thus, the United States provided South Korea and Taiwan with substantial military and economic aid and opened its market to their exports while permitting them to follow protectionist policies. East Asian economic growth also stemmed from special linkages with Japan. Japanese colonialism had created the social foundations for industrialization in East Asia, but also the foundations for dependency relations. When the value of the Japanese yen increased as a result of the 1985 Plaza Agreement (see Chapter 6), Japanese companies made huge investments in subsidiary plants throughout East Asia to take advantage of cheaper costs of production. These Japanese investments helped East Asia avoid the worst effects of the debt crisis that ravaged Latin America and Africa during the 1980s.

Beginning in the late 1980s, however, it became evident that East Asia's dependence on the United States and Japan could have major costs as well as benefits. For example, in response to its growing balance-of-payments deficits the United States became more protectionist and accused some East Asian economies of being unfair traders. After the passage of new U.S. trade legislation in 1988, South Korea and Taiwan offered concessions they had previously resisted because the United States threatened to retaliate against their "unfair" trade practices. With the breakup of the Soviet bloc and the decline of the Cold War, the United States was also less willing to continue supplying large amounts of aid and other support to South Korea and Taiwan. In sum, changes in the United States' economic and strategic position made it less willing to provide the East Asian NIEs with the economic and military support it had given them from the 1950s to the mid–1980s.[77]

East Asian economic development was also fragile because of the region's dependent relationship with Japan. Although East Asian economies were exporting increasing amounts of industrial goods to the West, these goods were often produced by Japanese subsidiaries and designed in Japan, included imported Japanese components, and depended on Japanese technology. For example, South Korea seems to have successfully developed an automobile industry, but the industry is highly dependent on Japanese auto parts and advanced technology. When a large Korean industrial conglomerate (called Samsung) received government approval to enter the auto industry in 1994, it indicated that it would "import all of the advanced technology it needs from Nissan" in Japan.[78] The dependence of East Asians on Japan had negative effects on their balance of trade and payments. Whereas the East Asians generally had large trade surpluses with the West, their trade deficits with Japan were growing steadily. The depreciation of the Japanese yen relative to the U.S. dollar from 1995 put growing downward pressure on East Asian currencies, many of which were pegged (at least in part) to the U.S. dollar. As Japanese exports became more competitive and Japanese markets absorbed a declining share of East Asian exports, problems of indebtedness and lack of competitiveness in the region increased. The financial crisis began when Thailand had to begin floating its *baht* currency in July 1997 (the *baht* had previously been pegged to a basket of currencies, with the U.S. dollar having predominant weight).[79]

Although historical structuralists were correct in pointing to East Asian dependence on the United States and Japan as one source of the financial crisis, realists and liberals consider the historical structuralists to be unduly negative. As discussed, by 2000 East Asia had largely recovered from the financial crisis and there was renewed confidence in economic growth in the region. Even if the East Asian NIEs had not been miracle economies, they *had* developed rapidly for several decades, and many expected their economic development to resume. It is therefore important to discuss the liberal and realist perspectives on the crisis. As early as 1968, Samuel Huntington had argued that authoritarian governments provided needed stability and order in developing societies and that democratic practices were a luxury that should be introduced only later.[80] For a number of years, the authoritarian governments of East Asia strictly limited individual freedoms and assumed a strong role in providing guidance to the developmental state. Although individual freedoms were limited, realists pointed out that these governments oversaw some marked improvements in economic growth and prosperity. However, liberals by contrast attributed the East Asian financial crisis to the pervasive role of governments and government-business linkages in the region.

In the liberal view, the 1990s financial crisis revealed that authoritarian developmental states were not as efficient and immune to political pressures as realist writers on the East Asian "miracle" often implied. For example, the one-party authoritarian states and close government-business linkages in these economies contributed to widespread nepotism, and the operation of banks and access to credit depended more on political connections than on market forces. With weak financial regulation, lenders and foreign investors expanded credit without sufficient safeguards to risky borrowers. Huge sums were spent for questionable building and real estate projects, without regard for their necessity or how they would be financed.[81] These inefficiencies challenged the realist contention that East Asian authoritarian states facilitated the development process.

Whereas liberals questioned the benefits of authoritarian developmental states, realists questioned liberal claims that the East Asians benefited from global economic interdependence. Indeed, realists (and also historical structuralists) maintained that "the process of deeper financial integration constituted a necessary condition" for the East Asian financial crisis to occur.[82] Most East Asian economies had opened their capital accounts, and the region experienced a dramatic increase of international capital inflows during the early 1990s. Thus, the financial crisis resulted from the vulnerability of these economies to the subsequent massive reversal of capital flows. Furthermore, realists argued that deeper financial integration contributed to a contagion effect in which creditors engaged in speculative attacks on currencies, not because of economic fundamentals but because of the actions of other creditors.[83] Realists, historical structuralists, and some liberals also charged that the liberal-economic emphasis on composite statistics such as the growth in GDP and per capita GDP led to an overestimation of East Asian development. In the mid-1990s some economists were already maintaining that East Asian economic growth resulted largely from physical and human capital accumulation rather than from increases in total factor productivity. In other words, increased labor and capital inputs rather than increased efficiency explained much of the rapid East Asian economic growth in the 1980s and early 1990s. Thus, the noted economist Paul Krugman has argued in reference to the East Asian economies that:

sustained growth in a nation's per capita income can only occur if there is a rise in output *per unit of input.* Mere increases in inputs, without an increase in the efficiency with which those inputs are used—investing in more machinery and infrastructure—must run into diminishing returns; input-driven growth is inevitably limited.[84]

Environmentalists have also maintained that the East and Southeast Asian recipe for rapid economic growth is not sustainable in the long term. In Indonesia, for example, logging practices are contributing to a deforestation rate of 2.4 million hectares per year; in the Malaysian state of Sarawak, loggers have removed 30 percent of the forest area in 23 years; and in Vietnam, resources are being exported with little concern for social and environmental consequences.[85] Of particular importance in this regard is the concept of *sustainable development,* which was popularized by NGOs in the early 1980s and received multilateral approval in the 1987 report of the World Commission on Environment and Development (the Brundtland Report). The Brundtland Report describes sustainable development as a policy that "meets the needs of the present without compromising the ability of future generations to meet their own needs."[86] Sustainable development is a controversial concept because LDCs have argued that they cannot afford to divert resources from their immediate development to pay the costs of following environmentally friendly policies. The LDCs also point out that DCs did not adopt sustainable policies when they were developing and that the North currently produces more global pollutants than the South. Nevertheless, East Asians will not be able to sustain their economic growth rates in the long term if they disregard the effects of environmental degradation.

The export-led growth model undoubtedly has a number of strengths, and the East Asian developmental state outperformed other LDCs according to most economic indicators in the 1970s–1980s. However, the financial crisis demonstrated some serious weaknesses in their export-led growth strategy. Another development strategy was strongly supported by the IMF, World Bank, and most industrial states in response to the 1980s foreign debt crisis, and more recently in response to the 1990s Asian financial crisis: the orthodox liberal model.

THE REVIVAL OF ORTHODOX LIBERALISM

Development specialists have discussed a number of factors that are likely to prevent other LDCs from adopting the positive aspects of the East Asian developmental state model. Two characteristics of the developmental state are critical to its effective functioning: a highly skilled technocratic bureaucracy and close cooperation among major economic groups such as agriculture, business, and labor. However, most LDCs "still lack the highly professional merit-based bureaucracies and the tradition of cooperation between key economic actors that would permit them to replicate the East Asian model."[87] Developmental states also have usually been authoritarian or semiauthoritarian in order to guide the economy and control labor, business, and other private groups. However, current globalization pressures are causing democracy (in a political sense) to spread throughout the world, and this raises questions as to whether other LDCs could replicate the rapid economic growth rates of the East Asians. The most important constraint on replicating the East Asian developmental state model in other LDCs was evident much earlier—in the late 1970s–1980s—with the return of orthodox liberalism. In line with the new orthodoxy the IMF and World Bank adopted the view that "the market rational/market ideological approach is the only correct course for development."[88]

When British Prime Minister Thatcher and U.S. President Reagan led a shift to the right with the revival of orthodox liberalism in the late 1970s–1980s, the IMF, World Bank, and others launched a strong attack on realist or statist development strategies in the South. In response to the 1980s foreign debt crisis, the IMF and World Bank were powerful advocates of what later became known as the *Washington consensus.* Strongly endorsed by the Reagan administration, the U.S. Treasury, the Federal Reserve, and the international financial institutions in the 1980s, the Washington consensus refers to the orthodox liberal belief that "the combination of democratic government, free markets, a dominant private sector and openness to trade is the recipe for prosperity and growth."[89] (Ironically, this is not what John Williamson meant by the term when he coined it in 1989.[90]) In applying the Washington consensus to the 1980s debt crisis, the IMF and World Bank imposed a range of conditions on their SALs, including requirements that recipient LDCs control inflation, decrease government spending, balance their budgets, privatize state-owned enterprises, deregulate financial and labor markets, and liberalize their trade and investment policies. As discussed in Chapter 7, the IMF and World Bank ruled out cross-conditionality in a formal, legal sense, but there is no doubt that they sometimes engaged in this practice on an informal basis to jointly impose the Washington consensus on LDC borrowers.[91]

Structural Adjustment and the Theoretical Perspectives

During the 1980s, a large number of LDC debtor countries implemented World Bank and IMF-financed structural adjustment programs (SAPs), and the South became "a laboratory for a huge experiment" in promoting economic development through orthodox liberalism.[92] Perceptions of the effects of SAPs have varied widely. For example, three studies of the effects of SAPs in sub-Saharan Africa presented strikingly different conclusions. The first study concluded that "the performance of poor compliers deteriorates over time and is significantly worse than the performance of countries that comply" with the structural adjustment policy conditions;[93] the second study found that countries that followed World Bank structural adjustment policy conditions most closely "failed to grow as quickly as several less compliant African economies during the same period";[94] and the third study argued that structural adjustment policies "followed over the past decade are leading to the destruction of the [African] continent . . . with the failure of the state being an immediate outcome and environmental deterioration being devastating in the long run."[95] In view of these starkly different perceptions, this section briefly discusses SAPs and the three main theoretical perspectives.

Historical structuralists believe that SAPs are not "simply an innocuous remedial package for sustained growth and development." Instead, they are "an almost deliberate scheme for the perpetuation of export dependency . . . and reproduction of existing conditions of global inequality."[96] Furthermore, SAPs subordinate peripheral states to MNCs, international banks, and core states, and increase income inequalities between classes. It is unrealistic to expect that the World Bank, IMF, and other Northern-dominated institutions will ever design SAPs to alleviate the South's problems because they caused the LDC debt problems in the first place.[97] Whereas historical structuralists are the harshest critics of structural adjustment, orthodox liberals are the strongest supporters. They believe that SAPs provide the necessary prescriptions and discipline based on the Washington consensus to deal with LDC debt problems. Interventionist liberals agree with orthodox liberals that SAPs are often necessary to combat domestic inefficiencies and corruption in LDC debtor economies. However, they are more receptive than orthodox liberals to state interventionism and argue that the World Bank and IMF should do more to focus on the human development aspects of adjustment. From this perspective, the Bank should be more sensitive to the implications of its adjustment policies for the poorest groups and states in the South.[98] From a realist perspective, the World Bank and IMF's emphasis on downsizing government through privatization, deregulation, and trade liberalization is misguided. Realists argue that late industrializers, whether they be the United States and Germany in the nineteenth century, the East Asian NIEs in the 1950s–1980s, or other present-day LDCs, *require* a large degree of government interventionism to catch up with the leading powers. A strong state in the realist view is essential for LDC economic development.

Despite these differing perceptions, many analysts would agree that there were some serious problems with SAPs in the 1980s–1990s. After referring to some strengths of the SAPs, a discussion of their problems follows.

Structural Adjustment and Questions About Orthodox Liberalism

The World Bank's SALs were generally most effective in middle-income LDCs that export manufactures, such as Brazil, Morocco, the Philippines, South Korea, Thailand, and Uruguay. These countries had more developed institutions for bringing about policy reforms as well as better resilience in dealing with the disruptions and sacrifices resulting from structural adjustment policies. Thus, liberal studies indicate that SAPs in middle-income LDCs often contributed to reduced government budget deficits, increased export earnings, increased financing available for private investment, and enhanced economic growth and efficiency. However, the effects of SAPs on the poorest and most highly indebted LDCs and on the poorest groups *within* LDCs were a far more contentious issue.

Although SAPs were not designed to deal with poverty or promote equity, the World Bank endorsed liberal-economic views holding that benefits from the efficient allocation of resources under freer markets would naturally trickle down to the poor. However, a number of critics rejected this trickle-down theory and argued that the poorest groups had to bear a disproportionate share of the adjustment burdens. The persistence or exacerbation of poverty in low-income LDCs and in vulnerable groups within LDCs gave credence to these criticisms and eventually forced the Bank to rethink its approach.[99] In addition to the effects of SAPs on the poor, critics also charged that the emphasis of SAPs on privatization, deregulation, and openness gave inadequate attention to the need for effective LDC governments, and that the World Bank's "top-down" approach to structural adjustment did not give sufficient attention to the need for local participation in "owning" policies and implementing reforms. Furthermore, critics argued that SAPs were designed in the 1980s for LDCs with large public sectors and substantial public debts, and that they were inappropriate for the East Asian NIEs, whose problems were substantially different during the 1990s financial crisis.

The sections that follow examine these criticisms by focusing on one LDC region and one group within LDCs in which the effects of SAPs have been most controversial: the sub-Saharan African states and LDC women. We then turn to a discussion of World Bank attempts to address the problems with its structural adjustment policies.

Structural Adjustment and Sub-Saharan Africa

Some of the strongest criticisms of SAPs have related to their effects on sub-Saharan Africa. (In this section, the term *Africa* refers to sub-Saharan Africa.) The decade of the 1980s, when more than two-thirds of African states were receiving IMF and World Bank SALs, was generally considered to be a lost decade for Africa. During this period, economic growth and industrial production stagnated, agricultural output lagged behind population growth, per capita incomes and investment declined, and unemployment increased. Each year the United Nations Development Program ranks countries according to a human development index, which includes such factors as per capita incomes, adult literacy rates, education, and life expectancy (see Chapter 2). In 1999, the 28 lowest ranked countries in terms of the human development index were African; and in 2001, 19 of the 31 poorest countries in the world in terms of per capita GNP were African.[100] A 1988 study by the United Nations Program of Action for African Recovery and Development concluded that although SAPs had registered a few gains, "for the majority of African states, there has not been even a hint of recovery."[101]

Liberal-economic supporters of structural adjustment argue that SAPs are often blamed for problems caused by general economic deterioration. Thus, the World Bank and IMF were simply reacting to the foreign debt crisis, which had resulted from both inefficient LDC economic policies and unfavorable global economic changes stemming from the 1970s oil crisis. Furthermore, liberals maintain that many problems in Africa, such as political instability, civil wars, and famine, have been unusually resistant to solution and that African economic conditions would be even worse without IMF and World Bank SAPs. The World Bank and IMF market-led prescriptions are the best strategies for bringing about adjustment and growth, according to liberals, because state-led strategies such as ISI were clearly unsuccessful.[102]

Critics, by contrast, argue that IMF and World Bank SAPs in Africa place too much emphasis on market-oriented policies, do not contribute to economic growth, and impose the largest costs on the poorest groups and countries. The strongest criticisms relate to IMF and World Bank demands that LDC debtors downgrade the role of the government and emphasize privatization so that market forces can operate. A downgrading of the government's role increases unemployment and underemployment because the public sector provides a critical source of employment for Africans.

As governmental capacity declines, crucial infrastructure such as transportation and communications as well as services such as health care and education suffer. Furthermore, the emphasis on privatization does not take account of the fact that private firms are often unwilling or unable to supply essential public goods required for development. LDCs must therefore rely heavily on their governments to provide the resources for technical and scientific education of the populace and for other aspects of human capital necessary for industrialization and competitiveness.

Critics also oppose the emphasis that IMF and World Bank SAPs place on trade liberalization. Middle-income Latin American and East Asian countries may reap some benefits from freer trade, but the benefits are far more dubious for lower income African and Asian LDCs. Domestic industries in Latin America and East Asia may presently be able to compete with growing imports because many of these countries have had lengthy periods of sheltering their industrial producers. Most African LDCs, by contrast, are only beginning to embark on the path to industrialization, and they require continued protection for their infant industries. Critics charge that World Bank and IMF market-based prescriptions have harmed African economic development because most African LDCs are at an early stage of development and continue to require a substantial role for the government.[103]

Structural Adjustment and LDC Women

A major criticism of IMF and World Bank SAPs is that they have disregarded gender issues. Almost all societies (DCs as well as LDCs) are characterized in varying degrees by gender inequality and the exploitation of women. Critics argue that it is therefore not possible for SAPs to be gender neutral. By disregarding the subsidiary role of women, these programs often reinforce male bias and exacerbate the socio-economic problems confronting LDC women.

The positions of LDC women vary widely as a result of diverse cultural values, historical factors, levels of economic development, and types of government. Women in the same society may also occupy vastly different positions depending on their social class and ethnicity. Nevertheless, it is possible to identify some general characteristics of the position of LDC women:

- In the household, women spend much more time than men, on the average, on unpaid subsistence work involving child care, food production and preparation, health care, and education.
- In work outside the home, women are overrepresented relative to men in the informal sector of the economy. Unlike formal-sector employment, work in the informal sector is largely unaffected by government regulations and standards. About three-fourths of those in the informal sector are service providers such as roadside food stall operators, market traders, messengers, and shoe shiners. Informal-sector earnings on the average are well below those of the formal sector.
- In the formal sector, women are more concentrated in the lower skilled, lower wage occupations, and they often receive lower salaries than men for doing the same work.

- Compared with men, women are more important in agricultural labor and less important in industry. In Africa, for example, women produce about 90 percent of the food, but they are less important in the production of export crops.
- If one combines women's lower wages in the formal sector with their overrepresentation in agriculture, the informal sector, and work in the household, women's incomes are normally significantly less than those of men. Thus, households in which women are the sole breadwinners are among the poorest groups in LDC societies.[104]

The position of LDC women as outlined in this text should be considered in any SAPs. However, World Bank policy prescriptions are based on macroeconomic concepts, which view the economy as a whole rather than looking at individual firms or households. The World Bank gives little attention to the effect of its structural adjustment policies on women's work time because much of women's time is spent doing unpaid subsistence work in the household, which does not appear in production statistics. For example, SAPs usually call for cutbacks in government spending, leading to decreases in the provision of public goods in areas such as health, education, and water and sanitation facilities. As a result of these cutbacks, much of the burden of health care and education shifts to the community and household, where women have most of the responsibilities.

World Bank and IMF policy prescriptions that raise the cost of basic foodstuffs simply add to the problems of LDC women. Structural adjustment usually requires LDCs to lower government deficits by phasing out food subsidies and to provide incentives to farmers by raising the prices they receive for their tradeable goods. Because of the higher food costs, women must use cheaper foods that take longer to prepare, such as coarse grain and root crops rather than wheat products, and they must rely on home baking rather than purchasing bread. Hospitals, too, may cut their costs per patient largely by shifting costs of care to the unpaid economy of the household. Whereas the World Bank views cutbacks in government spending and subsidies as an indication of increased efficiency, the costs are simply being shifted from the paid to the unpaid economy, where women do most of the work.[105]

Even if women worked only in the household, the off-loading of government services and subsidies would place unreasonable new burdens on them. The need for income, however, "has forced women into the labour force to protect their families' survival."[106] Thus, women as a proportion of the total labor force rose in Asia from 29 percent in 1950 to 33.8 percent in 1985, and in Latin America from 18 percent to 24.2 percent. Women have often fared poorly as members of the formal and informal labor forces under SAPs. In sub-Saharan Africa, for example, farmers were paid higher prices to encourage them to produce more crops for the export market. Cash crops, however, tend to be men's crops, whereas subsistence food crops are more often women's crops. Men also tend to market most of the crops produced by both women and men, and women do not benefit from the increased prices because men often keep most of the revenue for their own use.[107]

Critics thus argue that SAPs affect women adversely in their multiple roles as mothers, household managers, community leaders, and workers in the formal and informal sectors. To fully confront the problems that SAPs pose for LDC women, it is necessary to dispense with the myth that such programs are gender neutral.

ANOTHER SHIFT IN DEVELOPMENT STRATEGY?

In the late 1980s–1990s, the World Bank became more responsive to criticisms of its structural adjustment policies and began to take a second look at its orthodox liberal approach to development. The question therefore arises as to whether the Bank's re-assessment of its SALs is an indication of another shift in development strategy. To answer this question, it is necessary to discuss three areas of concern to the Bank: its approach to the role of the state in development, to the poorest LDCs and groups within LDCs, and to the "top-down" imposition of conditionality based on the Washington consensus. The Bank's reassessment can be divided into two major periods: from the late 1980s to 1994 and from 1995 to the present.

The Late 1980s to 1994

In the late 1980s to 1994, the Bank began to reassess its approach to the role of the state in development and to the poorest LDCs and most vulnerable groups. Protracted economic and political problems in the least developed countries (LLDCs) in Africa and Asia led to a gradual recognition by the Bank that the state had a significant role to play in economic development. At the same time, however, the Bank did not wish to veer too far from orthodox liberal views favoring the unfettered market. The evolution in Bank thinking was evident throughout the 1990s. In its 1991 *World Development Report,* the Bank acknowledged that "governments need to do more in those areas where markets cannot be relied upon" such as health, education, nutrition, family planning, and poverty alleviation. Nevertheless, the 1991 report basically adhered to the orthodox liberal position that to have a positive developmental impact any state intervention had to be market conforming, and that "governments need to do less in those areas where markets work, or can be made to work."[108]

Japan, as an increasingly important aid donor and foreign investor, reacted negatively to the 1991 report and the liberal orthodoxy that had come to dominate Bank thinking during the 1980s. The Japanese government could "hardly be expected to fund a set of policies, and an underlying ideology" that denied "its own experience of having been heavily interventionist."[109] Thus, Japan insisted that the World Bank give more recognition to the value of the Japanese and East Asian developmental state model, and it called on the Bank to commission a study of the issue. As a result, the Bank published a policy research report in September 1993 titled *The East Asian Miracle: Economic Growth and Public Policy* (henceforth, "the report"), which sought to determine why East Asia had such "a remarkable record of high and sustained economic growth."[110] The report made some concessions to the value of government intervention in specific circumstances, noting that Japanese, Korean, and Taiwanese government policies of allocating credit to high-priority activities "may have been beneficial."[111] (Some observers claim that this was a necessary concession to Japan's Ministry of Finance, which financed the report.[112]) Most of the report, however, questioned the value of government-directed industrial policy, indicated that the East Asian model would not necessarily be successful elsewhere, and cautioned that the

East Asian successes should not "be taken as an excuse to postpone needed market-oriented reform."[113] Furthermore, the report claimed that the Southeast Asian economies of Malaysia, Thailand, and Indonesia (unlike the Northeast Asian economies) achieved rapid growth without industrial policy, and that other LDCs would be better off emulating the Southeast Asians. In sum, the Bank's approach to the role of the state in development did not change significantly during the early 1990s. Although the report gave more recognition than previous Bank studies to governmental involvement in East Asian development, it attributed the East Asians' success primarily to their liberal market-friendly approach.[114]

The Bank also began to address the issue of the poorest LDCs and most vulnerable groups during the late 1980s–1990s. To understand the Bank's view on poverty in that time period, it is necessary to provide some historical background. It is possible to identify four major phases in Bank thinking (and in the thinking of the foreign aid community in general) on poverty reduction.[115] In the first phase from 1945 to the late 1960s, the Bank focused on large economic infrastructure projects to provide LDCs with transportation and communication facilities, port development, power projects, and other public utilities. Bank officials believed that large transfers of capital and technology would contribute to industrial development, employment, and a reduction of poverty. This is the trickle-down approach to development aid, which assumes that prosperity will "eventually trickle down from the top, alleviating the problem of poverty at the bottom."[116] Although LDCs achieved rapid economic growth rates in the 1960s, the large capital-intensive projects bypassed the neediest and contributed to a worsening of income distribution within LDCs. Thus, Bank President McNamara ushered in the second phase in the 1970s, with an explicit commitment to give more attention to poverty reduction. For example, the Bank developed more basic human needs projects, which provided basic health, educational, and family-planning services to the poor; increased the involvement of women; and gave special attention to the poorest LDCs. Although these declared intentions to focus on basic needs were only partly fulfilled in practice, the Bank did increase its lending in the 1970s for agricultural and rural development, low-cost urban housing and slum rehabilitation, and primary and nonformal education.[117]

However, alleviating poverty by directly targeting the poorest was a more difficult and complex task than had been anticipated, and orthodox liberals argued that the basic needs approach distracted attention from the need to promote economic growth. Thus, disillusionment with the basic needs approach along with significant global changes in the 1980s—the foreign debt crisis and the return of orthodox liberalism—ushered in the third phase of the Bank's approach to poverty. In some respects, the third phase in the 1980s was similar to the first phase in the 1950s–1960s when the Bank relied on trickle-down theories of poverty reduction; but the third phase placed more emphasis than the first phase on orthodox liberal reforms. World Bank SALs during the 1980s were conditioned on the implementation of orthodox liberal policies such as privatization, deregulation, and liberalization in trade and finance, and the basic needs of vulnerable groups were largely forgotten. Indeed, the previous discussion of sub-Saharan Africa and LDC women shows that the poorest and most vulnerable groups in the South often bore a disproportionate share of the burden of IMF and Bank structural adjustment policies.

Throughout the 1980s, there were growing pressures on the Bank because it was the main multilateral development agency to devote attention to the distributional effects of structural adjustment. For example, in a 1987–1988 two-volume study titled *Adjustment with a Human Face,* the United Nations Children's Fund (UNICEF) indicated that it was necessary to include a "poverty alleviation dimension" in adjustment programs.[118] These pressures eventually resulted in a fourth phase of Bank thinking on poverty, which began in the late 1980s and currently continues. The fourth phase has similarities to the second phase in which the Bank devoted more explicit attention to basic human needs and poverty reduction. For example, in 1989 the Bank shifted its position somewhat when it acknowledged that "sub-Saharan Africa has now witnessed almost a decade of falling per capita incomes and accelerating ecological degradation" and that there was a need for "special measures . . . to alleviate poverty and protect the vulnerable."[119] Most significantly, the Bank devoted its 1990 *World Development Report* to poverty and began to redesign its SAPs to decrease adverse effects on the poor.[120]

Despite the Bank moves in the late 1980s and early 1990s to devote more attention to poverty reduction and the role of the state in development, tension continued to exist between pressures for orthodox liberal reforms on one hand and concerns with the state and poverty on the other. Thus, the Bank's strategies to reduce poverty and promote state effectiveness continued to have major limitations. In December 1994 the Bank had to confront the shortcomings of its development approach more directly when Mexico—a country the Western policy establishment had viewed as a model of economic management—encountered a serious financial crisis and had to appeal for emergency loans.[121] Mexico had implemented an economic strategy based largely on the Bank model, had lowered its trade barriers, and had signed the NAFTA with the United States and Canada. The Bank was also subject to other criticisms during that time, including charges that it was more interested in loan approval than in development effectiveness and accountability; that it was lending to corrupt governments such as the Suharto regime in Indonesia; and that it was devoting too little attention to the social and environmental effects of its projects. For example, in 1991–1992 international controversy flared over the environmental and social effects of the Bank-financed Narmada River Sardar Sarovar dam in India.[122]

On the fiftieth anniversary of the Bretton Woods agreements in 1994, NGOs launched a "Fifty Years is Enough" campaign which strongly criticized the Bank for failing to alleviate poverty and promote environmentally sustainable development. At the same time, the Bank was facing a crisis of relevance in regard to its financial influence. Whereas private capital flows to LDCs increased from $40.9 billion in 1990 to $256 billion in 1997, multilateral and bilateral development assistance during the same period declined in relative importance from 57 percent to only 15 percent of all net financial flows to LDCs. Thus, it was evident that the Bank "had no option but to modify its approach to development" if it was to continue to be an effective development institution.[123] The new Bank President James Wolfensohn was appointed in June 1995 with the task of rebuilding the Bank's confidence and legitimacy.

1995 to the Present

From the first day he took office, Wolfensohn "promised to revolutionize the Bank and finish the unfinished business of internal reform long overdue."[124] A highly significant development was Wolfensohn's appointment of Joseph Stiglitz in late 1996 as chief economist of the Bank. Stiglitz was a prestigious U.S. economist who had formerly been chair of the U.S. Council of Economic Advisors. He had written earlier about the limits of privatization and the need for a stronger role for the state in development, and his appointment signified a shift away from the Bank's adherence to the Washington consensus.[125] Policy statements and decisions indicated that the Bank's approach was changing in regard to poverty reduction, the state's role in development, and the top-down imposition of conditionality based on the Washington consensus. Although some critics (including historical structuralists) have argued that Stiglitz was merely repackaging orthodox liberal ideas, most analysts believe that Stiglitz was seeking changes ranging from modest reforms to a fundamental shift in Bank policy.[126]

Regarding the role of the state in development, the Bank focused its 1997 *World Development Report* on "The State in a Changing World." The report rejected orthodox liberal preferences for a minimalist state and argued that state minimalism "is at odds with the evidence of the world's development success stories."[127] Thus, the report maintained that "development requires an effective state, one that plays a catalytic, facilitating role, encouraging and complementing the activities of private businesses and individuals."[128] The 1997 report also indicated that most sub-Saharan African states lacked critical capabilities, and it identified the need to "rebuild state effectiveness" in the region "through an overhaul of public institutions, reassertion of the rule of law, and credible checks on abuse of state power."[129] Although the report warned against the dangers of stateless development, however, it also opposed state-dominated development. In the case of South Asia, for example, the report considered overregulation to be "both a cause and effect of bloated public employment and the surest route to corruption." Thus, the report called for "a contraction of the role of the state" in South Asia.[130]

Regarding poverty, Wolfensohn's October 1998 annual address to the Bank board of governors described poverty as the "other crisis" along with the 1997 financial crisis, and he signaled that the Bank would devote increased attention to the poorest individuals in LDCs. There was strong support "to make poverty reduction the core issue in the Bank's agenda at the beginning of the new century," and an important Bank initiative was its *Voices of the Poor* study in which it consulted about 60,000 poor people in more than 50 countries. Furthermore, the main theme of the Bank's 2000–2001 *World Development Report* was "Attacking Poverty."[131] The report proposed a three-pronged strategy for attacking poverty: promoting opportunity, facilitating empowerment, and enhancing security. The Bank's discussion of empowerment departed from its traditional focus on economic issues and emphasized the need to strengthen the participation of poor people in political processes.

Potentially most significant was Wolfensohn's introduction of a *Comprehensive Development Framework (CDF)* in January 1999. The CDF is designed to take a much broader holistic approach to development than structural adjustment, emphasizing the linkages among the financial, social, and institutional aspects of development. Furthermore, the CDF is an attempt to alter Bank lending practices. Unlike the coercive conditionality of structural adjustment policy, the CDF emphasizes partnership between the Bank and recipient government, and between the government and civil society. Thus, the CDF is designed to employ a consultative rather than a top-down framework for providing development finance.[132]

Despite the Bank's expressed intentions to move away from the Washington consensus, there are reasons to question whether it is in fact shifting to policies that will more effectively promote socio-economic development. First, it is easier for Bank officials to verbally support a number of new objectives such as meeting basic human needs and supporting poverty reduction than it is to convert these objectives into practice. In efforts to satisfy a wide array of critics, the Bank has broadened its objectives to include poverty reduction, governance, democratic development and human rights, women in development, environmental considerations, and corruption. Although each of these objectives is positive in itself, the results have been to severely overload the Bank's agenda and to divert the Bank from devoting sufficient attention to its traditional areas of expertise.[133] Second, international events have constrained the Bank's ability to alter its development strategies. For example, the Bank's 1997 *World Development Report* on the need for an effective state was released several months before the East Asian financial crisis. Orthodox liberals subsequently argued that the financial crisis demonstrated the weaknesses in East Asia's strong developmental state model, and Japan's continued economic problems add weight to their arguments (as discussed, realists of course interpret these events differently).

A third reason for constraints on the Bank relates to the reaction of its major members, especially the United States. The Bank's chief economist Stiglitz was the strongest advocate of the proposed changes, and he openly criticized the IMF for its handling of the 1997–1998 Asian financial crisis. Stiglitz also called on a professor of development economics—Ravi Kanbur—to oversee the writing of the Bank's 2000–2001 *World Development Report* on attacking poverty. The draft report was highly controversial within the IMF and the Bank as well as the United States. For example, the draft report's empowerment section "attracted immediate criticism," and some of the Bank's own leading economists charged that the draft devoted too little emphasis to economic growth. Critics were especially concerned that the empowerment section in the draft report preceded the sections on security and opportunity, and Kanbur eventually agreed to put the section on opportunity first.[134] Furthermore, critics charged that the Bank's CDF, which Stiglitz strongly supported, represented "a capitulation to NGOs."[135] In response to pressures on the Bank president, Stiglitz and Kanbur left the Bank "in controversial circumstances."[136]

In sum, it is uncertain whether the Bank is significantly altering its approach to development because the strongest supporter of a new approach—the Bank's chief economist—was retired from his position. As realists would point out, ultimately the Bank and other international economic organizations cannot diverge too far from the policy preferences of their most important members. For example, the World Bank's stated objectives in its 2000–2001 *World Development Report* on attacking poverty can only be realized if its members are willing to support this objective with meaningful policy changes. As discussed, globalization pressures and the end of the Cold War diminished the North's concerns about poverty and discontent in the South.

A prime example of the growing marginalization of the poorest states and individuals is the degree to which foreign aid has declined in recent years. In 1969, a Commission on International Development (the Pearson Commission), which had been formed at the suggestion of the Bank to study foreign aid, recommended that every advanced industrial state should devote at least 0.7 percent of its GNP to development assistance.[137] Table 11.3 shows that despite this recommendation, OECD members have *decreased* rather than increased the percentage of their GNP devoted to ODA in recent years. The OECD countries' net ODA as a share of GNP declined from 0.52 percent in 1960 to 0.37 percent in 1980 and to 0.22 percent in 2000. Table 11.3 shows that the ODA of the two largest bilateral aid donors, Japan and the United States, amounted to only 0.28 percent and 0.10 percent of their GNPs in 2000. The Bank and the DCs have become more aware of the need to adopt development programs that recognize the important role of the state in LDCs and are attuned to the needs of the poorest, most vulnerable groups. Nevertheless, in the current environment of global competitiveness and orthodox liberalism, the commitment to these objectives is inevitably limited.

CONCLUSION

The postwar period has generally been marked by prosperity and economic growth for DCs of the North, but this has not been the case for the poorer LDCs and peoples in the South. Indeed, other than a small number of NIEs and the OPEC states, the income gap between the North and the South has been growing. This chapter examines some of the strategies LDCs have used in attempts to promote their economic development and discusses the important role the World Bank group has played as the largest multilateral development organization in framing debates on these strategies. The discussion of ISI, socialist, export-led growth, and orthodox liberal models provides some basis for drawing conclusions about the most appropriate development strategies.

First, all of the development strategies followed over the years have shortcomings, and one is unlikely to find the "perfect" development strategy. Development is clearly a more difficult and complex process than Walt Rostow had indicated in his widely read 1960 book on *The Stages of Economic Growth*.[138] Rostow claimed that societies move through five stages on their way to modernity, and his predictions regarding LDC growth were overly optimistic. For example, Rostow argued that an LDC reaching the takeoff stage would be transformed in such a way that its growth would become self-sustaining. Such predictions raised false hopes that LDC economic development was a readily achievable and irreversible process. Whereas Rostow's liberal prescriptions for economic growth placed major emphasis on the need for domestic changes (i.e., modernization), historical structuralists place primary emphasis on the need for altering international relations (e.g., relations of dependency). In reality, economic development is a complex process that requires *both* domestic and international changes. Only a small number of LDCs such as the East Asian NIEs have been fortunate enough to meet both the domestic and international requirements for rapid economic development. However, even the East Asian economies had to confront a financial crisis in the late 1990s, which demonstrated how difficult it currently is to avoid serious setbacks on the path to development.

Second, the same development strategy is not necessarily feasible or desirable for all LDCs. Although a number of East and Southeast Asian LDCs achieved impressive economic growth rates through an export-led growth strategy, it is unlikely that many other LDCs could emulate their experience. The East Asian NIEs' success resulted from a confluence of favorable external and domestic circumstances, such as U.S. and Japanese support and the presence of highly skilled, technocratic government bureaucracies. These characteristics are often lacking in poorer African and Asian LDCs. Indeed, many sub-Saharan African states with ongoing economic and political crises would find it impossible to follow the developmental state model of the East Asian NIEs. The return to liberal orthodoxy in the 1980s has also precluded many LDCs from following state-led growth policies. Instead, IMF and World Bank SAPs have pressured LDC debtors to engage in deregulation, privatization, and other measures to downsize the role of the state.[139]

Third, negative experiences with IMF and World Bank SAPs have pointed to the pitfalls of focusing on the economic aspects of development without looking sufficiently at the social and human aspects. Thus, the United Nations Development Program began to publish an annual *Human Development Report* in 1990 to emphasize the fact that "there was no automatic link between growth and human development."[140] The human development approach assesses development not only in terms of a country's per capita GDP growth but also in terms of such factors as life expectancy, health and sanitation facilities, education, employment, the income gap between rich and poor, the gender gap, and the rural-urban gap. In thinking about human development, for example, it is necessary to understand how women's unpaid subsistence work in the household puts them at a disadvantage in markets.[141] Although economic growth should continue to be a major objective of development strategies, human factors must also be included because the main purpose of economic development is to improve human well-being.

Fourth, an economic development strategy should strike a realistic balance "between the state and the market so as to stimulate a positive and dynamic interaction between them."[142] Whereas ISI policies emphasize state intervention and give too little consideration to market signals, orthodox liberal approaches disregard the fact that late industrializers often require an active role for the state. East Asian governments were particularly adept at using state-market interactions to their advantage, and this enabled them to register some striking economic gains, even during the 1980s foreign debt crisis. However, the East Asians have also too often substituted "political whim . . . for proper risk assessment for commercial activities," and their failure to provide sufficient banking regulations was a major factor contributing to the 1990s financial crisis.[143] The mixed record of the East Asian governments indicates that it is not government regulation per se that should concern us but finding the amount and type of regulation that will ensure economic stability, confidence, and the proper functioning of market signals.

Finally, an economic development strategy should take account of the difference in wealth and power between the North and the South. Except in a small number of East Asian NIEs, the North-South income gap has continued to widen, and the 1980s foreign debt crisis was a reminder of the degree to which the South is still dependent on the North. Although Northern linkages in trade, foreign investment, and other economic areas are critical to the South, development strategies should provide the South with some special and differential treatment, and permit the South to act somewhat independently (within the limits of current global interdependence). One possible route to greater self-sufficiency is through establishing more South-South economic linkages. South-South trade linkages can enable LDCs to foster new comparative advantages and can contribute to their production and export of industrial goods. Indeed, about 60 percent of the goods traded among LDCs are manufactures.[144]

All three theoretical perspectives—realism, liberalism, and historical structuralism—have something important to say regarding the most appropriate development strategies. Furthermore, there seems to be no single best development strategy for all LDCs because of major differences among these states and their positions in the world. A variety of development strategies therefore will be, and should be, pursued in the future, as they have been in the past.

Notes

1. Bretton Woods Commission, *Bretton Woods: Looking to the Future* (Washington, DC: Bretton Woods Committee, 1994), p.B3.
2. World Bank, *World Development Report 2000/2001* (New York: Oxford University Press, 2001), p.3; World Bank, *World Development Report 2003* (New York: Oxford University Press, 2003), pp.1–4; Howard Handelman, *The Challenge of Third World Development* (Upper Saddle River: Prentice Hall, 1996), pp.3–10.
3. *World Bank Annual Report 2002* (Washington, DC: World Bank, 2002), vol. 1, pp.82–83.
4. World Bank, *World Development Report 1991* (New York: Oxford University Press, 1991), p.2.
5. World Bank, *World Development Report 2000/2001*, p.3.
6. Stephan Haggard, *Developing Nations and the Politics of Global Integration* (Washington, DC: Brookings Institution, 1995), p.1.
7. See Tomohisa Hattori, "Reconceptualizing Foreign Aid," *Review of International Political Economy* 8–4 (Winter 2001), p.646.
8. Organisation for Economic Co-operation and Development, *Development Co-operation—1994 Report* (Paris: OECD, 1995), p.86.
9. For a list of LDCs qualifying for ODA and transition economies qualifying for OA, see OECD, *Development Co-operation Report 2002* (Paris: OECD, 2003), p.327.
10. Robert Wade, "Japan, the World Bank, and the Art of Paradigm Maintenance: The East Asian Miracle in Political Perspective," *New Left Review* 217 (May/June 1996), p.5.
11. Stephen D. Krasner, *Structural Conflict: The Third World Against Global Liberalism* (Berkeley: University of California Press, 1985), p.3.
12. Gustav Ranis, "The World Bank Near the Turn of the Century," in Roy Culpeper, Albert Berry, and Frances Stewart, eds., *Global Development Fifty Years After Bretton Woods* (New York: St. Martin's Press, 1997), p.73.
13. Hattori, "Reconceptualizing Foreign Aid," p.644.
14. Ranis, "The World Bank Near the Turn of the Century," p.73.
15. Wade, "Japan, the World Bank, and the Art of Paradigm Maintenance," p.5.
16. Peter M. Haas, "Introduction: Epistemic Communitites and International Policy Coordination," *International Organization* 46–1 (Winter 1992), p.3.
17. Barry Eichengreen and Peter B. Kenen, "Managing the World Economy under the Bretton Woods System: An Overview," in Peter B. Kenen, ed., *Managing the World Econ-*

omy: Fifty Years After Bretton Woods (Washington, D.C.: Institute for International Economics, 1994), p.6.

18. Victor L. Urquidi, "Reconstruction vs. Development: The IMF and the World Bank," paper presented to "Bretton Woods Revisited: An International Conference," Bretton Woods, New Hampshire, October 15–17, 1994, revised text, November 11, 1994, p.11.

19. Edward S. Mason and Robert E. Asher, *The World Bank Since Bretton Woods* (Washington, DC: Brookings Institution, 1973), pp.52–53; Robert E. Wood, *From Marshall Plan to Debt Crisis: Foreign Aid and Development Choices in the World Economy* (Berkeley: University of California Press, 1986), p.29. Chile was the first LDC to receive an IBRD loan in 1948, and Mexico and Brazil received loans in early 1949.

20. *World Bank Annual Report 2002* (Washington, DC: World Bank, 2002), vol. 2, pp.47–50.

21. *World Bank Annual Report 1997* (Washington, DC: World Bank, 1997), pp.134–137.

22. Devesh Kapur, "The Changing Anatomy of Governance of the World Bank," in Jonathan R. Pincus and Jeffrey A. Winters, *Reinventing the World Bank* (Ithaca: Cornell University Press, 2002), pp.54–59.

23. *IFC Annual Report 1995* (Washington, DC: IFC, 1995), pp.5–6; "Hey, Big Lender," *The Economist,* April 23, 1994, pp.81–82.

24. See Ronald T. Libby, "International Development Association: A Legal Fiction Designed to Secure an LDC Constituency," *International Organization* 29–4 (Autumn 1975), pp.1065–1072.

25. *World Bank Annual Report 2002,* vol. 1, pp.131–132.

26. John Degnbol-Martinussen and Poul Engberg-Pedersen, *Aid: Understanding International Development Cooperation* (London: Zed Books, 1999), p.105; Paul Lewis, "Clinton Backs Funds for World Bank Agency," *New York Times,* October 12, 1995, p.C4; "Aid for the World's Poorest," *New York Times,* October 18, 1995, p.A18.

27. On the MIGA, see Ibrahim F. I. Shihata, *MIGA and Foreign Investment: Origins, Operations, Policies and Basic Documents of the Multilateral Investment Guarantee Agency* (Dordrecht: Nijhoff, 1988).

28. Anne O. Krueger, Constantine Michalopoulos, and Vernon W. Ruttan, with Keith Jay, *Aid and Development* (Baltimore: Johns Hopkins University Press, 1989), pp.106–108; John White, *Pledged to Development: A Study of International Consortia and the Strategy of Aid* (London: Overseas Development Institute, 1967).

29. See John White, *Regional Development Banks: A Study of Institutional Style* (London: Overseas Development Institute, 1970); and a five-volume series published in association with the North-South Institute in Ottawa, Canada: E. Phillip English and Harris M. Mule, *The African Development Bank;* Nihal Kappagoda, *The Asian Development Bank;* Chandra Hardy, *The Caribbean Development Bank;* Diana Tussie, *The Inter-American Development Bank;* and Roy Culpeper, *Titans or Behemoths?* (Boulder: Rienner, 1995–1997).

30. Theodore Cohn, "Developing Countries in the International Civil Service: The Case of the World Bank Group," *International Review of Administrative Sciences* 41–1 (1975), pp.47–56.

31. Stephen Fidler, "Who's Minding the Bank?," *Foreign Policy* 126 (September/October 2001), p.41.

32. Kapur, "The Changing Anatomy of Governance of the World Bank," pp.58–64.

33. Joseph S. Nye, Jr., "Soft Power," *Foreign Policy* 80 (Fall 1990), p.166. See also Susan Strange, "The Persistent Myth of Lost Hegemony," *International Organization* 41–4 (Autumn 1987), pp.551–574.

34. William Ascher, "The World Bank and U.S. Control," in Margaret P. Karns and Karen A. Mingst, eds., *The United States and Multilateral Institutions* (Boston: Unwin Hyman, 1990), p.115. See also Robert Hunter Wade, "US Hegemony and the World Bank: The Fight over People and Ideas," *Review of International Political Economy* 9–2 (May 2002), pp.201–229.

35. Cheryl Payer, *The World Bank: A Critical Analysis* (New York: Monthly Review Press, 1982), p.20.

36. P. T. Bauer, *Reality and Rhetoric: Studies in the Economics of Development* (London: Weidenfeld and Nicolson, 1984), p.70; Kalman Mizsei, "The Role of the Bretton Woods Institutions in the Transforming Economies," in *Bretton Woods: Looking to the Future*, p.C–103.

37. Robert L. Ayres, *Banking on the Poor: The World Bank and World Poverty* (Cambridge: MIT Press, 1983), p.15.

38. Ranis, "The World Bank Near the Turn of the Century," p.76.

39. Fidler, "Who's Minding the Bank?," p.45. See also Ranis, "The World Bank Near the Turn of the Century," p.84.

40. Raúl Prebisch, *The Economic Development of Latin America and Its Principal Problems* (New York: UN Economic Commission for Latin America, 1950) 7–1, pp.1–59; H. W. Singer, "The Distribution of Gains Between Investing and Borrowing Countries," *American Economic Review* 40–2 (May 1950), pp.473–485.

41. On Latin American structuralism see Anil Hira, *Ideas and Economic Policy in Latin America: Regional, National, and Organizational Case Studies* (Westport: Praeger, 1998), ch. 3.

42. Ozay Mehmet, *Westernizing the Third World: The Eurocentricity of Economic Development Theories* (London: Routledge, 1995), p.78; John Rapley, *Understanding Development: Theory and Practice* (Boulder: Rienner, 1996), pp.27–34.

43. Luiz Carlos Bresser Pereira, "Development Economics and the World Bank's Identity Crisis," *Review of International Political Economy* 2–2 (Spring 1995), pp.215–217; Devesh Kapur, John P. Lewis, and Richard Webb, *The World Bank: Its First Half Century*, Volume 1 (Washington, DC: Brookings Institution, 1997), p.451; Mason and Asher, *The World Bank Since Bretton Woods*, pp.150–153.

44. See Rapley, *Understanding Development*, pp.27–36.

45. Theodore Cohn, *Canadian Food Aid: Domestic and Foreign Policy Implications* (Denver: University of Denver Graduate School in International Studies, 1979), pp.25–27.

46. Sylvia Maxfield and James N. Nolt, "Protectionism and the Internationalization of Capital: U.S. Sponsorship of Import Substitution Industrialization in the Philippines, Turkey and Argentina," *International Studies Quarterly* 34–1 (March 1990), p.50.

47. Anne O. Krueger, *Trade Policies and Developing Nations* (Washington, DC: Brookings Institution, 1995), pp.3–10, 33–44; Rapley, *Understanding Development*, pp.33–44; Stephan Haggard, *Pathways from the Periphery: The Politics of Growth in the Newly Industrializing Countries* (Ithaca: Cornell University Press, 1990), pp.9–14.

48. Anne O. Krueger, "The Effects of Trade Strategies on Growth," *Finance and Development* 20–2 (June 1983), p.8.

49. Mason and Asher, *The World Bank Since Bretton Woods*, pp.378–379.

50. Raúl Prebisch, *Towards a Dynamic Development Policy for Latin America* (New York: United Nations, 1963), p.71. See also Raúl Prebisch, "Five Stages in My Thinking on Development," in Gerald M. Meier and Dudley Seers, eds., *Pioneers in Development* (New York: Oxford University Press, 1984), p.181.

51. See Bela Balassa, "The Process of Industrial Development and Alternative Development Strategies," in Bela Balassa, ed., *The Newly Industrializing Countries in the World Economy* (New York: Pergamon Press, 1981), pp.5–16.

52. Joseph L. Love, "The Origins of Dependency Analysis," *Journal of Latin American Studies* 22 (February 1990), pp.143–160.

53. This section draws partly on Rapley, *Understanding Development*, pp.44–47.

54. James H. Mittelman and Mustapha Kamal Pasha, *Out from Underdevelopment Revisited: Changing Global Structures and the Remaking of the Third World*, 2nd ed. (London: Macmillan, 1997), pp.181–214.

55. David Slater, "The Political Meanings of Development: In Search of New Horizons," in Frans J. Schuurman, ed., *Beyond the Impasse: New Direction in Development Theory* (London: Zed Books, 1993), pp.101–105.

56. John M. Page, "The East Asian Miracle: An Introduction," *World Development* 22–4 (1994), p.619; Robert Wade, *Governing the Market: Economic Theory and the Role of Government in East Asian Industrialization* (Princeton: Princeton University Press, 1990), p.34.

57. Arnold C. Harberger, "Growth, Industrialization and Economic Structure: Latin America and East Asia Compared," in Helen Hughes, ed., *Achieving Industrialization in East Asia* (Cambridge: Cambridge University Press, 1988), pp.164–194; Haggard, *Pathways from the Periphery*, chs. 3–7; and Bela Balassa, *Policy Choices for the 1990s* (London: Macmillan, 1993), pp.56–67.

58. Wade, *Governing the Market*, p.34.

59. Krueger, *Trade Policies and Developing Nations*, pp.20–23.

60. Mehmet, *Westernizing the Third World*, p.78.

61. Bela Balassa, *The Newly Industrializing Countries in the World Economy* (New York: Pergamon Press, 1981), pp.6–24.

62. Staffan Burenstam Linder, *The Pacific Century: Economic and Political Consequences of Asian-Pacific Dynamism* (Stanford: Stanford University Press, 1986), p.31.

63. Ronen Palan and Jason Abbott, with Phil Deans, *State Strategies in the Global Political Economy* (London: Pinter, 1996), p.78.

64. Chalmers Johnson, "Introduction—The Taiwan Model," in James C. Hsiung et al., eds., *Contemporary Republic of China: The Taiwan Experience 1950–1980* (New York: Praeger, 1981), pp.9–18; Chalmers Johnson, *MITI and the Japanese Miracle: The Growth of Industrial Policy, 1925–1975* (Stanford: Stanford University Press, 1982).

65. Rapley, *Understanding Development*, pp.124–127; Adrian Leftwich, "Bringing Politics Back In: Towards a Model of the Developmental State," *Journal of Development Studies* 31–3 (February 1995), pp.401–403.

66. Peter Evans, *Dependent Development: The Alliance of Multinational, State, and Local Capital in Brazil* (Princeton: Princeton University Press, 1979), p.33.

67. Quoted in William Nester, "The Development of Japan, Taiwan and South Korea: Ends and Means, Free Trade, Dependency, or Neomercantilism?," *Journal of Developing Societies* 6 (1990), p.206.

68. Cal Clark and Steve Chan, "MNCs and Developmentalism: Domestic Structure as an Explanation for East Asian Dynamism," in Thomas Risse-Kappen, ed., *Bringing Transnational Relations Back In: Non-State Actors, Domestic Structures and International Institutions* (Cambridge: Cambridge University Press, 1995), p.125.

69. On Confucian political culture in East Asia, see Lucian W. Pye with Mary W. Pye, *Asian Power and Politics: The Cultural Dimensions of Authority* (Cambridge: Belknap Press, 1985), ch. 3.

70. Pye, *Asian Power and Politics*, p.90; Clark and Chan, "MNCs and Developmentalism," pp.120–123.

71. Christopher Lingle, "What Ever Happened to the 'Asian Century'?", *World Economic Affairs* 2–2 (Spring 1998), p.32.

72. World Bank, *The East Asian Miracle: Economic Growth and Public Policy:* Oxford University Press, 1993), p.1.

73. Graham Bird and Alistair Milne, "Miracle to Meltdown: A Pathology of the East Asian Financial Crisis," *Third World Quarterly* 20–2 (1999), p.421.

74. Stephan Haggard, *The Political Economy of the Asian Financial Crisis* (Washington, DC: Institute for International Economics, 2000), p.3.

75. James Busumtwi-Sam, "International Financial Institutions, International Capital Flows and Financial Liberalization in Developing Countries," in Stephen McBride and John Wiseman, eds., *Globalization and Its Discontents* (London: Macmillan, 2000), pp.88–90; Shahid Yusuf, "The East Asian Miracle at the Millennium," in Joseph E. Stiglitz and Shahid Yusuf, eds., *Rethinking the East Asian Miracle* (Oxford: Oxford University Press, 2001), pp.1–4.

76. Bird and Milne, "Miracle to Meltdown," p.422. See also Seth Mydans, "An 'Asian Miracle' Now Seems Like a Mirage," *New York Times,* October 22, 1997, pp.A1, A8.

77. Walden Bello and Stephanie Rosenfeld, *Dragons in Distress: Asia's Miracle Economies in Crisis* (San Francisco: Institute for Food and Development Policy, 1990), pp.3–10; I. M. Destler, *American Trade Politics,* 2nd ed. (Washington, DC: Institute for International Economics, 1992), pp.131–133.

78. Walter Hatch and Kozo Yamamura, *Asia in Japan's Embrace: Building a Regional Production Alliance* (Cambridge: Cambridge University Press, 1996), p.37.

79. Jim Glassman and Pádraig Carmody, "Structural Adjustment in East and Southeast Asia: Lessons from Latin America," *Geoforum* 32–1 (February 2001), pp.79–80.

80. Samuel P. Huntington, *Political Order in Changing Societies* (New Haven: Yale University Press, 1968).

81. Edward A. Gargan, "Currency Assault Unnerves Asians," *New York Times,* July 29, 1997, pp.A1, C15; Joseph Stiglitz, "How to Fix Asian Economies," *New York Times,* October 31, 1997, p.A19.

82. Haggard, *The Political Economy of the Asian Financial Crisis,* p.4.

83. Stephan Haggard and Andrew MacIntyre, "The Political Economy of the Asian Economic Crisis," *Review of International Political Economy* 5–3 (Autumn 1998), p.405; Haggard, *The Political Economy of the Asian Financial Crisis,* pp.5–6.

84. Paul Krugman, "The Myth of Asia's Miracle," *Foreign Affairs* 73–6 (November/December 1994), p.67. See also Alwyn Young, "The Tyranny of Numbers: Confronting the Statistical Realities of the East Asian Growth Experience," *Quarterly Journal of Economics* 110–3 (August 1995), pp.641–680.

85. Walden Bello, "Overview of Current Economic, Strategic and Political Developments in Southeast and South Asia," *Focus Files* (Bangkok, Thailand, October 1997), p.3.

86. World Commission on Environment and Development, *Our Common Future* (Oxford: Oxford University Press, 1987), p.8.

87. Handelman, *The Challenge of Third World Development,* p.228.

88. Palan and Abbott, *State Strategies in the Global Political Economy,* p.99.

89. Christopher L. Gilbert and David Vines, "The World Bank: An Overview of Some Major Issues," in Christopher L. Gilbert and David Vines, eds., *The World Bank: Structures and Policies* (Cambridge: Cambridge University Press, 2000), p.16.

90. See John Williamson, "Democracy and the 'Washington Consensus,' " *World Development* 21–8 (August 1993), pp.1329–1336.

91. Ngaire Woods, "The Challenges of Multilateralism and Governance," in Gilbert and Vines, eds., *The World Bank: Structures and Policies,* p.141; Richard E. Feinberg, "The Changing Relationship Between the World Bank and the International Monetary Fund," *International Organization* 42–3 (Summer 1988), pp.552–556; Jacques J. Polak, *The World Bank and the International Monetary Fund: A Changing Relationship* (Washington, DC: Brookings Institution, 1994), pp.16–17.

92. Rapley, *Understanding Development,* p.76.

93. Farhad Noorbakhsh and Alberto Paloni, "Structural Adjustment and Growth in Sub-Saharan Africa: The Importance of Complying with Conditionality," *Economic Development and Cultural Change* 49–3 (April 2000), pp.479–509.

94. Cited in Bob Milward, "The Heavily Indebted Poor Countries and the Role of Structural Adjustment Policies," in *Developments in Economics: An Annual Review* (Lancashire: Causeway Books, 2001), p.38.

95. J. Barry Riddell, "Things Fall Apart Again: Structural Adjustment Programmes in Sub-Saharan Africa," *Journal of Modern African Studies* 30–1 (1992), p.67.

96. Gloria Thomas-Emeagwali, "Introductory Perspectives: Monetarists, Liberals and Radicals: Contrasting Perspectives on Gender and Structural Adjustment," in Gloria Thomas-Emeagwali, ed., *Women Pay the Price*, p.5.

97. Glassman and Carmody, "Structural Adjustment in East and Southeast Asia," p.82.

98. Gloria Thomas-Emeagwali, "Introductory Perspectives," pp.3–4.

99. James H. Weaver, "What Is Structural Adjustment?," in Daniel M. Schydlowsky, ed., *Structural Adjustment: Retrospect and Prospect* (Westport: Praeger, 1995), pp.12–13; Barend A. de Vries, "The World Bank's Focus on Poverty," in Jo Marie Griesgraber and Berhard G. Gunter, eds., *The World Bank: Lending on a Global Scale* (London: Pluto Press, 1996), pp.68–69.

100. UN Development Program, *Human Development Report 2001* (New York: Oxford University Press, 2001), pp.141–144; World Bank, *World Development Report 2003* (New York: Oxford University Press, 2003), pp.234–235.

101. Quoted in Julius O. Ihonvbere, "Economic Crisis, Structural Adjustment and Africa's Future," in Gloria Thomas-Emeagwali, ed., *Women Pay the Price: Structural Adjustment in Africa and the Caribbean* (Trenton: Africa World Press, 1995), p.137.

102. For a strong defense of World Bank SAPs in Africa, see Elliot Berg, "African Adjustment Programs: False Attacks and True Dilemmas," in Schydlowsky, ed., *Structural Adjustment*, pp.89–107.

103. Rapley, *Understanding Development*, pp.83–92; Riddell, "Things Fall Apart Again: Structural Adjustment Programmes in Sub-Saharan Africa," pp.53–68.

104. Frances Stewart, "Can Adjustment Programmes Incorporate the Interests of Women?," in Haleh Afshar and Carolyne Dennis, eds., *Women and Adjustment Policies in the Third World* (New York: St. Martin's Press, 1992), pp.22–24.

105. Diane Elson, "Male Bias in Macro-Economics: The Case of Structural Adjustment," in Diane Elson, ed., *Male Bias in the Development Process* (Manchester: Manchester University Press, 1991), pp.175–178.

106. Stewart, "Can Adjustment Programmes Incorporate the Interests of Women?," p.27.

107. Elson, "Male Bias in Macro-Economics," p.173; Stewart, "Can Adjustment Programmes Incorporate the Interests of Women?," p.22.

108. World Bank, *World Development Report 1991*, p.9.

109. Ben Fine, "Neither the Washington nor the Post-Washington Consensus: An Introduction," in Ben Fine, Costas Lapavitsas, and Jonathan Pincus, eds., *Development Policy in the Twenty-First Century: Beyond the Post-Washington Consensus* (London: Routledge, 2001), p.12.

110. World Bank, *The East Asian Miracle: Economic Growth and Public Policy* (New York: Oxford University Press, 1993), p.1.

111. World Bank, *The East Asian Miracle*, p.274.

112. K. S. Jomo, "Rethinking the Role of Government Policy in Southeast Asia," in Stiglitz and Yusuf, eds., *Rethinking the East Asian Miracle*, p.462.

113. World Bank, *The East Asian Miracle*, p.26.

114. Jomo, "Rethinking the Role of Government Policy in Southeast Asia," pp.461–463; Wade, "Japan, the World Bank, and the Art of Paradigm Maintenance," pp.3–36.

115. Ravi Kanbur and David Vines, "The World Bank and Poverty Reduction: Past, Present and Future," in Gilbert and Vines, eds., *The World Bank: Structures and Policies*, pp.87–107; and Kapur, Lewis, and Webb, *The World Bank: Its First Half Century*.

116. Mohammed H. Malek, "Towards an Integrated Aid and Development Programme for Europe," in Mohammed H. Malek, ed., *Contemporary Issues in European Development Aid* (Aldershot: Avebury, 1991), p.142.

117. OECD, *Twenty-five Years of Development Co-operation: A Review—1985 Report* (Paris: OECD, November 1985), p.49; Ayres, *Banking on the Poor*, pp.4–6; Anthony Bottrall, "The McNamara Strategy: Putting Precept into Practice," *ODI Review* 1 (1974), pp.70–80; Paul Dickson, "A Fresh Look at the World Bank," *Vista* 8–6 (June 1973), pp.24–49. The basic human needs approach was not really new in the 1970s because basic human needs had been emphasized as early as 1961 under the Charter of the U.S.-Latin American Alliance for Progress.

118. Giovannia Andrea Cornia, Richard Jolly, and Frances Stewart, eds., *Adjustment with a Human Face, Vol. 1: Protecting the Vulnerable and Promoting Growth* (Oxford: Clarendon Press, 1987), p.7.

119. World Bank, *Sub-Saharan Africa: From Crisis to Sustainable Growth, a Long-Term Perspective Study* (Washington DC: World Bank, 1989), pp.17, xi. See also Ihonvbere, "Economic Crisis, Structural Adjustment and Africa's Future," pp.138–147.

120. See World Bank, *World Development Report 1990, "Poverty"* (New York: Oxford University Press, 1990).

121. On the 1994–1995 Mexican financial crisis see Peter B. Kenen, *The International Financial Architecture: What's New? What's Missing?* (Washington, D.C.: Institute for International Economics, 2001), pp.19–26.

122. Bruce Rich, "The World Bank under James Wolfensohn," in Pincus and Winters, eds., *Reinventing the World Bank*, pp.27–29.

123. John Pender, "From 'Structural Adjustment' to Comprehensive Development Framework: Conditionality Transformed?," *Third World Quarterly* 22–3 (2001), p.402; Rich, "The World Bank under James Wolfensohn," p.28. See also Kevin Danaher, ed., *50 Years is Enough: The Case Against the World Bank and the International Monetary Fund* (Boston: South End Press, 1994).

124. Rich, "The World Bank under James Wolfensohn," p.26.

125. Pender, "From 'Structural Adjustment' to Comprehensive Development Framework," pp.402–403.

126. For critiques of Stiglitz's ideas see the articles in Fine, Lapavitsas, and Pincus, eds., *Development Policy in the Twenty-first Century;* and Guy Standing, "Brave New Words? A Critique of Stiglitz's World Bank Rethink," *Development and Change* 31–4 (2000), pp.737–763.

127. World Bank, *World Development Report 1997*, Foreword, p.iii. The Bank's views on state minimalism reflected views of others at the time that it was necessary to re-examine the role of the state in development. See Paul Streeten, "Markets and States: Against Minimalism," *World Development* 21–8 (August 1993), pp.1281–1298; and the symposium articles on "The State and Economic Development" in *Journal of Economic Perspectives* 4–3 (Summer 1990).

128. World Bank, *World Development Report 1997*, p.iii.

129. World Bank, *World Development Report 1997*, p.14.

130. World Bank, *World Development Report 1997*, p.14.

131. Kanbur and Vines, "The World Bank and Poverty Reduction," p.88. See also World Bank, *World Development Report 2000/2001;* and Pender, "From 'Structural Adjustment' to Comprehensive Development Framework," pp.404–406.

132. World Bank, *World Development Report 1999/2000* (New York: 2000), pp.21–23; Paul Collier, "Conditionality, Dependence and Coordination: Three Current Debates in Aid Policy," in Gilbert and Vines, eds., *The World Bank: Structures and Policies*, p.323.

133. Kapur, "The Changing Anatomy of Governance of the World Bank," p.69.
134. Robert Wade, "Showdown at the World Bank," *New Left Review* 7 (January/February 2001), p.132; Wade, "US Hegemony and the World Bank," p.212.
135. Fidler, "Who's Minding the Bank?," p.46.
136. Pender, "From 'Structural Adjustment' to Comprehensive Development Framework," p.407.
137. *Partners in Development,* Report of the Commission on International Development, chaired by Lester B. Pearson (New York: Praeger, 1969), p.152.
138. W. W. Rostow, *The Stages of Economic Growth: A Non-Communist Manifesto* (Cambridge: Cambridge University Press, 1960).
139. Rapley, *Understanding Development,* pp.135–154.
140. United Nations Development Program, *Human Development Report 1996,* p.1.
141. Diane Elson, "Economic Paradigms Old and New: The Case of Human Development," in Culpeper, Berry, and Stewart, eds., *Global Development Fifty Years After Bretton Woods,* p.60.
142. Cristóbal Kay, "For a Renewal of Development Studies: Latin American Theories and Neoliberalism in the Era of Structural Adjustment," *Third World Quarterly* 14–4 (1993), p.695.
143. Lingle, "What Ever Happened to the 'Asian Century'?," p.33.
144. Rapley, *Understanding Development,* pp.155–157. See also Elizabeth Parsan, *South-South Trade in Global Development* (Aldershot: Avebury, 1993).

P A R T   I V

Concluding
Comments

The last three decades of the twentieth century and the beginning of the twenty-first century have been marked by a series of unexpected and disruptive developments in global politics and economics. Some of the most notable developments were the food and oil crises in the 1970s, the foreign debt crisis in the 1980s, the breakup of the Soviet bloc and Soviet Union during the 1980s–1990s, the Asian financial crisis of the late 1990s, and the terrorist attacks on New York and Washington, D.C., in September 2001. As globalization has increased, economic and security events in one part of the world are having a greater impact on distant areas, and predictions about the future of the global economy have become more hazardous. Nevertheless, the historical discussion in this book enables us to speculate about current and possible future changes in the twenty-first century. Relying on the major themes of this book, Chapter 12 examines contemporary trends in the global political economy.

CHAPTER 12

Current Trends
in the Global
Political Economy

This book provides a comprehensive approach to the study of IPE, introducing
students to the major theoretical perspectives and substantive issue areas. The
three perspectives of realism, liberalism, and historical structuralism have
evolved and influenced each other over time, and some theoretical approaches such as
hegemonic stability theory, regime theory, and the business conflict model draw on
more than one of the three major perspectives. Approaches that focus on domestic-
international linkages and economic-security linkages are becoming more common
and contributing to further changes in the study of IPE.

To help link theory and practice, this book focuses on three themes central to the
study of IPE: globalization, North-North relations, and North-South relations. Issues
surrounding Eastern Europe and the former Soviet Union are subsumed under these
three themes because the Cold War has virtually ended and the transition economies
are becoming increasingly integrated in the capitalist global economy. Whereas the
more developed former Eastern bloc states such as the Czech Republic and Hungary
have levels of development almost comparable with some Northern DCs, the poorer
states such as Moldova and Tajikistan face economic problems comparable with those
of LDCs in the South. It is useful in this concluding chapter to examine where we currently are with these three themes of globalization, North-North relations, and North-
South relations and to speculate about the future.

GLOBALIZATION

Globalization is a process that involves both the broadening and deepening of interdependence among societies and states throughout the world. *Broadening* refers to the
geographic extension of linkages to encompass virtually all major societies and states,

411

and *deepening* refers to an increase in the frequency and intensity of interactions. This book has *not* adopted an extreme view of globalization that we are entering a "border-less world" where MNCs are losing their national identities and nation-states are losing their distinctiveness.[1] In fact, globalization affects some states and regions more than others, threatens the state's autonomy in some respects but does not prevent it from making policy choices, and contributes to fragmentation and conflict as well as unity and cooperation. Although there was a high degree of economic interdependence among states and societies during the nineteenth and early twentieth centuries, globalization is more encompassing today than it was at any time in the past. Advances in technology, communications, and transportation are facilitating the globalization process as never before; the role of the MNC in generating FDI, trade, and technology is unprecedented; with the breakup of the Soviet bloc, the capitalist economic system is spreading throughout the globe; and international economic organizations are for the first time becoming truly universal in membership.

Realists, liberals, and historical structuralists have widely divergent views of globalization. Realists emphasize the continuing importance of the nation-state and often question whether there is in fact a significant increase in globalization. Although realists may acknowledge that global interdependence is increasing in some areas, they believe this occurs only with the permission or encouragement of the most powerful states that continue to dictate the terms and limits of such transactions. Because realists prioritize security over economic issues, they also believe that states have the incentive to limit the growth of global interdependence. Liberals, by contrast, believe there is a significant level of globalization that is eroding state control, and they view the growth of global interdependence as a positive development. Whereas realists believe that globalization occurs at the whim of the state, liberals attach far more importance to such factors as technological change and advances in communications and transportation that are beyond state control. Liberals also argue that globalization is increasing as a result of the demands of domestic and transnational societal actors such as internationalist firms.[2]

Historical structuralists, like liberals, see globalization as having a significant impact, but unlike liberals, they believe that globalization has extremely negative consequences for poorer states and classes in the periphery of the global economy. Some Gramscian theorists argue that globalization is leading to the development of a "transnational historic bloc" composed of the largest MNCs, international banks, international economic organizations, and international business groups in the most powerful capitalist states. A crucial element of this transnational historic bloc is the power and mobility of transnational capital, which is putting national groups such as labor unions on the defensive. The only way to counter such a transnational historic bloc, according to Gramscians, is to develop a counterhegemonic bloc composed of the disadvantaged and disaffected such as labor, human rights, environmental, consumer, development, and women's groups. A counterhegemonic bloc of this nature would be committed to replacing the current corporate view of liberalization with a more democratic, participatory model based on socialism.[3]

Globalization and Triadization

Globalization is in many respects more akin to "triadization." The integrative processes are most intense among three major regions that contain most of the world's developed market economies: Western Europe, North America, and Japan/East Asia.[4] Countries in these three regions are the main sources of foreign direct investment, and they direct most of their FDI to each other. In 2001, for example, the developed market economies accounted for 86.8 percent of the outward stocks of FDI and for 64.7 percent of the inward stocks of FDI. Western Europe, North America, and Asia also dominate international trade flows, and they trade much more with each other than with other parts of the world. In 1998, the industrial states in Europe and North America accounted for 72 percent of world trade, East Asia accounted for 12.2 percent, and all other parts of the globe accounted for only 15.8 percent.[5]

Although some LDCs have increased their share of inward FDI, the distribution of this investment has been very uneven. On one hand, 10 LDCs located mainly in East Asia and Latin America (Singapore, Brazil, Mexico, China, Hong Kong, Malaysia, Egypt, Argentina, Thailand, and Colombia) received about three-fourths of total FDI inflows to the South during the 1980s. On the other hand, the LLDCs—most of which are in sub-Saharan Africa—received only 1.5 percent of the FDI inflows to the South during 1980–1984, and their share fell to 0.7 percent in 1985–1989. (The UN has designated 49 LDCs as "least developed.") Many of the poorest LDCs have also received little benefit from the expansion of world trade. Although the Asian countries' share of world trade grew from 4.6 percent to 12.5 percent between 1970 and 1991, the share for other LDC regions declined. The LLDCs, with about 10 percent of the world's people, accounted for only 0.3 percent of world trade in 1997—which was about half of their share two decades earlier.[6] Historical structuralists have warned against Southern dependence on the North, but an even greater problem for the poorer LDCs is the threat of marginalization. The breakup of the Soviet bloc and the decline of the Cold War decreased the South's leverage in gaining economic concessions from both East and West. This marginalization of the poorer LDCs is likely to continue because the triad of the EU, North America, and Japan is primarily interested in increasing economic linkages with the more prosperous LDCs and transition economies of Eastern Europe and the FSU.[7]

Despite the continuing importance of triadization, conflict within the triad on a wide range of security and economic issues has increased in recent years. This conflict and its implications for the global political economy are discussed later in this chapter (under North-North relations).

Globalization and the Nation-State

Liberals, historical structuralists, and even some realists would agree that with the rise of globalization the state has had to share authority in IPE with other entities, including MNCs, international institutions, and NGOs. Domestically, central governments are increasingly sharing authority with regional and local governments. Thus, "state authority has leaked away, upwards, sideways, and downwards."[8] For example, globalization has constrained the ability of DCs to continue providing the social welfare benefits that citizens came to expect during the 1950s–1970s, and the revival of orthodox liberalism has made such social expenditures seem less legitimate. Globalization has also limited the ability of the state to regulate the national economy. For example, the massive growth of international capital flows has contributed to volatility and misalignment in currency exchange rates. Major fluctuations in exchange rates interfere with the state's ability to promote economic regulation and stability.

Liberal economists generally view the increase in capital flows as a favorable development because financial markets impose necessary discipline on states, and global savings and resources move to their most productive locations. Historical structuralists, by contrast, view increased capital mobility as a highly negative development because the fear of capital outflows can force governments to adopt policies that adversely affect the poorest and weakest in society. If governments do not adopt capital-friendly policies, MNCs and international banks can readily shift their funds to more welcoming locations. Thus, MNCs tend to locate their production facilities in states with the lowest wages, taxes, and environmental standards. Realists believe that the increase in global financial flows has occurred with the permission or even encouragement of the most powerful states and that these states continue to dictate the terms for such transactions. From the realist perspective, states are *competition states* involved in supporting research and development (R&D) in high-technology sectors, restructuring industry, and deregulating financial markets.[9] The impressive economic growth rates of some states seem to be closely related to their success in fostering a symbiotic relationship with the competitive marketplace. Although the United States, Britain, and others adopted policies that contributed to the globalization of finance, this globalization "has had unintended consequences for those who promoted it," and realists overlook the fact that it may be extremely difficult for states to regain control over the global market forces they have unleashed.[10]

LDCs are especially vulnerable to the freeing of capital flows, as the Asian financial crisis of the late 1990s demonstrated. East and Southeast Asian countries had opened their economies to freer capital flows in the years leading up to the crisis, and a surge of bank lending and portfolio investment contributed to risky and ill-advised investments in the region. When weaknesses in the economies of these countries became evident, there was a "rush of international capital out of the region in 1997—a movement that was more frenzied than its mad rush to get into the area in earlier years."[11] Although domestic political and economic factors in the Asian economies contributed to the financial crisis, a major external factor was the volatility of capital flows or contagion. "Contagion" refers to "the spread of currency and asset market problems from one market to another."[12] As investor concern spreads from country to country, even sound financial institutions can be adversely affected. Thus, one Asian currency after another was depreciated sharply, countries experienced severe liquidity crises, and the IMF became deeply involved in providing finance.

Even the IMF's first deputy managing director acknowledged that the "factors contributing to contagion suggest it has been excessive—and that a way should be found to moderate it."[13] There is also a consensus developing that LDCs and transition economies should not open their capital markets too rapidly because it may be difficult for them to make adequate adjustments. In 1993, the G-7 released a study that examined possible multilateral approaches to dealing with the negative effects of international capital mobility, but it is difficult for the G-7 countries to coordinate their policies for several reasons. First, states often give priority to their own national concerns over the need for coordination. Second, it is questionable whether governments have the will to regain control over capital and foreign investment movements in the present climate of orthodox liberalism. Third, although there is general agreement that LDCs must be more careful in liberalizing capital flows, that is about all the experts agree on. Many analysts blame the IMF for mishandling the Asian financial crisis, but there is a notable lack of consensus on proposals for reform (see Chapter 7). Thus, some aspects of globalization such as the freeing of capital flows pose a major challenge to the ability of states (especially Southern states) to regulate global market forces.

Globalization and Inequality

Many liberals recognize that globalization may contribute to inequalities in the short to medium-term, but they nevertheless believe that "globalization . . . has improved the lot of hundreds of millions of poor people around the world." In view of efficiency gains, liberals argue that "poverty can be reduced even when inequality increases."[14] Some liberals also differentiate the short from the long term, arguing that globalization is likely to reduce inequalities over time. For example, one liberal writer asserts that in a globalized world where LDCs are closely integrated in the global economy "the late-comers to modern economic growth tend to catch up with the early-comers;" and another liberal writer maintains that "the economic gap between South Korea and industrialized countries . . . has diminished in part because of global markets."[15] The poorest LDCs such as North Korea and Myanmar, according to liberals, have never become rich by isolating themselves from global markets. Realists and historical structuralists, by contrast, believe there will be long-term losers as well as winners from globalization. From the realist perspective, the most powerful states have considerable control over the pace and direction of globalization, and they can use the globalization process "to reinforce their position and their relative power." For less powerful states, by contrast, globalization "is a process which is happening to them and to which they must respond."[16] Historical structuralists also believe that globalization benefits the most powerful capitalist states and nonstate actors such as MNCs in the core at the expense of peripheral states and vulnerable societal groups.

Although the statistics are sometimes conflicting, it does seem that globalization and liberalization in combination have contributed to greater inequalities both among and within states. As discussed in Chapter 11, the World Bank reports that the average income in the richest 20 countries is 37 times higher than the average income in the poorest 20 countries—a gap that has doubled in the past 40 years. The growing inequalities among countries are of course most evident between the North and the South. About 1.2 billion of the world's 6 billion people live on less than $1 a day, and almost 44 percent of these people live in South Asia. Although the number of people living on less than $1 a day declined in East Asia between 1987 and 1998, the numbers of poor people in South Asia, Latin America, sub-Saharan Africa, and the transition countries of Europe and Central Asia increased during this period.[17]

In many DCs, globalization has contributed to an increase in *overall* income, but also to a rise in unemployment. In 1995, 7.5 percent of the work force or 34 million people in the OECD countries were unemployed, and from 1979 to 1997, unemployment in the EU more than doubled to 11 percent. In the United States, the employment picture was healthier in the late 1990s, but there is evidence that the income gap between the rich and poor was widening. Globalization has also contributed to greater inequalities within a number of LDCs and former Soviet bloc countries. For example, in 1997 the United Nations Development Program reported that a falling share of national income was going to the poorest 20 percent of people in several Latin American states (Argentina, Chile, the Dominican Republic, Ecuador, Mexico, and Uruguay) and that income distribution had worsened and poverty had increased in 16 of 18 states in Eastern Europe and the FSU (excluding Estonia, Latvia, and Lithuania).[18]

Mexico, an LDC that has been something of a pacesetter in liberalizing its economic policies since the mid-1980s, provides a prime example of the fact that there are both winners and losers from globalization. On one hand, policies such as the privatization of state industries and the 1992 land reform permitting investors to purchase land from smallholders were highly beneficial to owners of capital and to large commercial farms. On the other hand, the share of Mexicans living in absolute poverty rose from 19 percent in 1984 to 24 percent in 1989, and in rural areas the number of poor people increased from 6.7 million to 8.8 million. Although large commercial fruit and vegetable producers in Mexico are benefiting from free trade in agriculture under NAFTA, many Mexican corn and bean subsistence farmers who must compete with U.S. producers who benefit from advanced production methods and U.S. government subsidies could lose what little they have.[19]

It is important to note that there are variations among countries, indicating that the domestic policies of governments (and their positions in the global economy) can make a difference. For example, there is evidence that some Asian LDCs, such as China, India, Bangladesh, and Vietnam, have liberalized their trade and investment policies while also reducing poverty to some extent. Variations among LDCs in the concentration of land ownership, the degree to which production is labor intensive, and other factors can influence the way in which globalization affects the distribution of wealth in society. In the North, some Scandinavian countries have liberalized while still maintaining a substantial social safety net. In the short to medium term, then, globalization contributes to inequalities within and among a number of states, but the policies of states can ameliorate these effects. As for the long term, it is difficult to either prove or disprove the liberal claim that globalization will eventually contribute to a decrease in inequalities.

Globalization and Democracy

Many liberals note that globalization is helping to promote stable democratic governments throughout the world. Indeed, they can point to the spread of liberal democratic practices in southern Europe during the 1970s, in Africa and Latin America during the 1980s, and in the transition economies of Eastern Europe and the FSU during the late 1980s–1990s. Thus, liberal democratic practices such as constitutional guarantees, freedom of speech, open elections, and a multiparty system have spread to a number of countries throughout the world. Nevertheless, historical structuralists point out that the poorest individuals in the South often lack employment, education, sanitation and health facilities, and enough food to eat. To these people, the economic right to an adequate standard of living is far more important than Northern-oriented political rights such as free speech and democratic elections. It is difficult to argue that globalization has genuinely contributed to democracy in the South because of increased economic inequalities. Even in the North, globalization critics argue, political rights mean little to the poorest individuals in society who lack employment, housing, and other basic amenities. Furthermore, income inequalities resulting from globalization contribute to growing disparities in political influence that decrease the opportunities for democratic policymaking.[20]

Critics also argue that globalization is transferring control from democratically accountable governments to MNCs, international banks, and IOs. For example, decisions and policies adopted in the IMF, World Bank, and WTO are having a growing effect on individuals and groups within states. Whereas these groups and individuals could previously ensure accountability of their national governments through periodic elections, they must now deal with international institutions where an increasing number of policies are being formulated. Thus, the questions are often being asked today, "to whom are" IOs such as the IMF, World Bank, and WTO "accountable and are they accountable to those whom they directly affect?."[21] Liberal supporters of globalization argue that democratization has occurred in the KIEOs in some important respects. For example, transparency has increased in the KIEOs through the publication of minutes, decisions, and documents; and all three KIEOs have upgraded their relations with NGOs. Critics by contrast argue that genuine accountability of the KIEOs has not increased, and they often refer to the gap between national and international governance as a "democratic deficit."[22]

Globalization and Civil Society

As discussed throughout this book, globalization has contributed to the growth of civil society groups committed to social change. There are in fact three types of civil society groups in terms of objectives and strategies: conformers, reformers, and radicals (also called critical groups). Conformers largely endorse the behavior of the KIEOs and private actors such as MNCs. Reformers accept the existence of and sometimes the need for the KIEOs and MNCs but believe that they should and can be reformed. Radical or critical groups believe that the KIEOs and MNCs are not reformable, and they seek to decrease their influence or even to abolish them. Reformers are more inclined to rely on cooperative strategies to alter the behavior of the KIEOs and MNCs, whereas radical or critical groups prefer to engage in ideological—and sometimes physical—confrontation. Conformers and reformers are similar to liberals, with reformers committed to a reintroduction of embedded liberalism that takes account of the social effects of the market. Radicals, like historical structuralists, are committed to a transformation of the capitalist system. Whereas these three groups are pure models, some NGOs in fact employ reformer and critical strategies simultaneously. For example, Greenpeace worked with companies to develop ozone-friendly refrigerators at the same time as it encouraged consumers to boycott Shell Oil over its alleged involvement with state suppression in Nigeria.[23]

In recent years reformers and radicals have been increasingly vocal in protesting against international institutions and MNCs that they view as promoting globalization. For example, this book has discussed civil society protests against the OECD's unsuccessful attempt to establish an MAI and against the WTO, APEC, the proposed

FTAA, and MNCs as purveyors of globalization. In opposing globalization, civil society groups ironically are able to benefit from some of the effects of globalization such as the World Wide Web. As discussed in Chapter 10, the Web was particularly useful to protestors against the MAI. The Web has been helpful to civil society protestors because it "facilitates networked sociopolitical relationships in important new ways, it (potentially) increases NGOs' organizational effectiveness and political significance, and it helps to foster more broadly participatory (transnational) political processes."[24]

The question arises as to whether a "global civil society" is likely to develop a counterhegemony in opposition to the forces of globalization in Gramscian terms.[25] Civil society groups have had some influence in particular cases such as their opposition to the proposed MAI, and a number of international institutions and MNCs have responded to civil society pressures by establishing communication channels and procedures with NGOs. Nevertheless, it is highly unlikely that a global civil society will establish a counterhegemony for several reasons. First, most civil society groups are conformers; i.e., a "silent majority." Although conformers may be dissatisfied with some features of the global economic order, they are not sufficiently dissatisfied to attempt to institute major changes. Many conformer groups are also beneficiaries of the current global order. Second, civil society groups have a strikingly diverse range of objectives, and it is often easier for them to agree on what they are against than on what type of alternative world order they favor. For example, labor and environmental groups tend to be closely linked with Northern interests that are often quite different from the perceived interests of the South. About 87 percent of the 738 NGOs accredited to the WTO ministerial in Seattle in 1999 were based in the North, and there is concern that these NGOs further magnify the North's disproportionate influence in the KIEOs.[26] A third obstacle to the development of a counterhegemony relates to differences in strategies and tactics. Thus, reformers and radicals may have widely divergent views regarding the legitimacy of violent protests. In sum, civil society groups have had some influence in inducing international institutions and MNCs to adopt bottom-up as well as top-down modes of decision making, but one should not overestimate the effect that civil society groups are likely to have on the global political economy.

Globalization and 'Newer Issues': Migration, Health, and Illegal Activity

Most IPE theorists associate globalization with the liberalization of trade, foreign investment, and capital flows. However, it is difficult to separate these explicitly economic processes from the effects of globalization on a variety of "newer" socioeconomic processes and issues. This section briefly examines the effects of globalization on three of these issues: migration, health, and illegal activity.

It is quite common for individuals, societal groups, and states to support some aspects of globalization from which they benefit and at the same time to oppose other aspects of globalization that pose a real or presumed threat to them. Whereas many states and societal groups support the freeing of trade and capital flows, they are far more resistant to the cross-border movement of people. Indeed, there are growing signs of anti-immigrant sentiment in a number of DCs. An EU public opinion survey in 1993 found that 52 percent of respondents thought there were too many immigrants, and a 1993

New York Times/CBS national telephone survey reported that 61 percent of Americans favored a decrease in the number of immigrants, compared with 42 percent in a 1977 Gallup poll.[27] The September 11, 2001, terrorist attacks on the World Trade Center and the Pentagon added greatly to U.S. concerns about migration.

Although citizens and states may wish to regulate cross-border migration because of valid concerns about illegal immigration and terrorism, societal groups may also seek to impose limits for more questionable reasons. For example, labor groups are often sensitive about immigration because of the gradual shift in demand away from less skilled workers in DCs. There is no conclusive empirical evidence of a linkage between increased unemployment among semi-skilled and unskilled workers in DCs on one hand and immigration from LDCs on the other. Indeed, some analysts argue that migrants often enter low-wage occupations that do not attract the local population, that many migrants are self-employed and create their own jobs, and that migration can stimulate growth and thus reduce unemployment.[28] Nevertheless, concerns about the effects of migration on employment remain. Hostility to immigrants is also heightened by groups with less legitimate objectives linked with extreme nationalism, racism, and suspicion of those who are different.

Despite these negative societal attitudes, the politics of immigration is complex and there are also countervailing tendencies. For example, the market demand for certain types of foreign workers sometimes makes it difficult for political leaders to limit immigration. Newly naturalized immigrants can also form an important voting constituency, and the Clinton administration adopted a "Citizenship USA" plan in 1996 under which more than 1 million people became citizens. These new citizens provided Clinton with an important source of votes for his re-election.[29] Most IPE scholars who write about globalization do not even discuss migration because "no other issue remains so much under the thrall of states and so resistant to globalizing effects."[30] Nevertheless, as globalization increases migration pressures will grow along with the pressures for other types of international interactions.

The linkages between globalization and health have become increasingly evident in recent years because of growing concerns about the threat that health issues can pose to human security. With the acceleration of global travel and trade, health problems can spread more rapidly and over a broader geographic area and be more resistant to treatment. For example, a study of the seven cholera pandemics (epidemics over a wide geographic area) from the nineteenth century to the present reveals that the seventh pandemic which began in 1963, has spread more rapidly, lasted longer (it still continues), and encompassed more countries than the previous six pandemics. The growth of international trade has also resulted in local epidemics in previously protected areas (e.g., cyclospora in the United States through imported fruits and vegetables) and has caused unprecedented health fears (e.g., over bovine spongiform encephalitis or mad cow disease). Furthermore, new environmental threats ranging from global warming to acid rain, ozone depletion, and toxic wastes also have major implications for global health. The more rapid spread of health problems over time and space serve as a reminder of the persistent and growing inequalities in health conditions within and across countries. For example, the average life expectancy ranges from 78 years in higher-income countries to 43 years in the poorest countries; and many people in the South lack access to sanitary facilities, clean water, and modern health services.[31]

It is only possible here to briefly discuss a few examples of the effects of global governance on health issues. First, IMF and World Bank structural adjustment loans sometimes exacerbate deficiencies in LDC health delivery services by requiring loan recipients to institute major cuts in social expenditures and to privatize basic services such as health care. Chapter 11 outlines more recent efforts by the World Bank to incorporate social and human concerns into structural adjustment programs. These efforts are of particular importance because in a development context "nutritional imbalances are . . . as crucial as trade imbalances, and high infant mortality rates require the same immediate action as high rates of inflation."[32] Second, the WTO's trade-related intellectual property rights (TRIPs) agreement became a flash point for North-South conflict when a transnational alliance of NGOs stepped up their campaign to increase access to anti-retroviral (ARV) drugs for HIV/AIDS sufferers, especially in Africa. Although the TRIPs agreement requires members to provide 20 years protection for the exclusive sale of patented products or processes, it contains several measures that LDCs could use to increase their access to affordable medicines. However, pressures from some DCs and pharmaceutical companies made it politically unviable to adopt these measures. In August 2003, WTO members finally broke the deadlock with an agreement to allow LDCs "to make full use of the flexibilities in the WTO's intellectual property rules."[33] Nevertheless, it is uncertain whether this agreement will give many of the poorest people more access to necessary medicines.

In addition to migration and health, it is necessary for IPE specialists to address the effects of globalization on illegal activity. Indeed, one analyst refers to "the five wars of globalization" as "the fights against the illegal trade in drugs, arms, intellectual property, people, and money."[34] For example, the annual trade in illicit drugs is estimated at $400 billion or about 8 percent of world trade, illicit trade accounts for about 20 percent of the total small arms trade, the piracy rate of business software is as high as 60 percent in Greece and South Korea, and estimates of the volume of global money laundering (hiding, moving, and investing assets obtained by criminal activity) range from 2 to 5 percent of the world's GNP. Although states have often benefited from more rapid communication and transportation as well as stronger economic and political linkages, so have criminal networks. Furthermore, state moves to privatize, deregulate and decentralize, and to create a more open environment for international trade and investment have made it more difficult to control global criminal activity. Governments must develop the skills, the laws, and the institutions to address these issues and must also address the social factors that contribute to global criminal activity. In sum, IPE specialists must develop an understanding of globalization's effect on a much broader range of issues including migration, health, and illegal activities.

North-North Relations

The second theme of this book relates to the interactions among DCs of the North. The issue of international economic management is primarily a North-North issue because only the Northern states have the wealth and power to look after the management of the global economy. This book has discussed two factors contributing to international economic management: hegemony and international institutions.

The Current State of U.S. Hegemony

Part III of this book provides a mixed picture of the current state of U.S. economic hegemony. On one hand, the United States continues to demonstrate a number of strengths as a global hegemon. With the breakup of the Soviet bloc, the United States has emerged as the unchallenged military power in the world. As long as the threat of violent conflict persists, a state with hegemony in security matters will also have a degree of power over economic and other nonsecurity areas.[35] The U.S. dollar continues to serve as the main international currency, and in the weighted-voting Bretton Woods institutions (the IMF and World Bank), the United States continues to have the most votes. The United States has also had a considerable amount of co-optive power (also referred to as structural or soft power): it is often successful in getting "other countries to *want* what it wants."[36] For example, Part III shows that the United States played a crucial role in setting the agenda for the GATT Uruguay Round negotiations and in guiding DC policies on a range of issues extending from liberalized capital flows to the foreign debt crisis and international development.

On the other hand, Part III also provides a number of indications of U.S. hegemonic decline. The U.S. dollar shifted from top-currency to negotiated-currency status in the 1960s, the United States has had chronic balance-of-trade deficits since 1971, it has become more dependent on FDI inflows in recent years and has accounted for a declining share of outward FDI, and Japan surpassed the United States for the first time in 1989 as the largest single-country donor of ODA. Furthermore, there are indications of a decline in U.S. soft or structural power in recent years. Although U.S. military predominance increased with the breakup of the Soviet bloc, even traditional U.S. allies at times seem to resent the *ability* of the United States to act unilaterally on security issues. This resentment has increased in response to the Bush administration's penchant toward unilateralism and its dismissive approach to states and international organizations that disagree with its policies. These U.S. unilateral tendencies increased after the understandable outrage against the September 11, 2001, terrorist attacks on U.S. territory. The Bush administration has also diverged from the customary U.S. role of being a prime supporter of liberalization in some key economic areas such as trade. As a result of this shift in U.S. international posture, its co-optive or soft power seems to be decreasing. This has important implications for managing trade disputes, the Doha Round, the negotiation of an FTAA, and many other economic issues.[37]

Despite the conflicting signals about the status of U.S. hegemony, almost all analysts agree that U.S. economic power has declined *in a relative sense* since 1945. U.S. predominance at the end of World War II was so great that its relative position was bound to decline as a result of economic reconstruction in Europe and Japan. It is therefore useful to examine whether another country or group of countries could replace the United States as global hegemon.

Is There a Candidate to Replace the United States as Global Hegemon?

In the late 1980s, some academics and policymakers took a positive view of Japan's hegemonic prospects. For example, one scholar wrote that "if any country surpasses the United States as the world's leading economic power, it will be Japan."[38] By the early to mid-1990s, however, most analysts were arguing that Japan lacked the military power and ideological appeal of a hegemon, and that it would be unwilling to assume the global responsibility of leadership. During the late 1990s, the Asian financial crisis raised further questions about Japan's hegemonic potential. Many hoped that Japan would set an example of reform because it shared some economic problems with other East and Southeast Asian states such as failing banks, questionable bookkeeping methods, and corrupt interlocking corporate relationships.[39] Political indecisiveness and inflexible economic and social practices, however, prevented Japanese leaders from adopting bold policies to reform the economy. Despite Japan's economic strengths, it is highly unlikely that it will replace the United States as a global hegemon.

Some writers speculate that the EU could become the top power, and one economist has even predicted that "future historians will record that the twenty-first century belonged to the House of Europe."[40] However, the EU will not have the ability and willingness to lead unless it becomes a more cohesive unit. In May 1997, the EU heads of government agreed that 11 EU members would form an economic and monetary union and replace their national currencies, and Greece later joined this group. In view of the combined strength of these countries' economies, the euro is becoming an important currency and could eventually supplant the U.S. dollar as the key currency in the global monetary regime. The expansion of the EU with the pending admission of 10 Central and Eastern European countries will further increase its global reach. Nevertheless, continued divisions among EU countries over a wide range of economic and political issues could prevent the EU from assuming hegemonic responsibilities.

A third possibility is that an LDC, China, could eventually become the global hegemon. One indication of China's growing influence is its effects on the major DCs. In 2003, China's trade surplus with the United States amounted to about $120 billion, and this has been a source of growing friction between the two countries. Also in 2003, the EU complained that China was refusing to permit its currency—the yuan—to rise against the U.S. dollar, and that the euro was therefore bearing an unfair share of the burden of dollar depreciation. As for Japan, it has been concerned about China's growing economic influence in Asia at the same time as it has looked more to China as a growing market for its exports. In October 2003 China also became the third country after the Soviet Union and the United States to put an astronaut in space. China anticipates that its space launches will help its military missile and satellite programs, and it has been modernizing its nuclear force for some time. Despite the impressive changes in China, as an LDC it is still an aid recipient and it continues to be more vulnerable than the major DCs to economic and political instabilities. In the short to medium-term it is therefore highly unlikely that China will assume hegemonic status.[41]

A fourth possibility is that global leadership is becoming more collective in nature and that the United States would lead this collectivity because its strength is so multidimensional; that is, it encompasses military, political, economic, scientific, cultural, and ideological power resources.[42] The most obvious candidates for collective leadership in the core would be the triad: the United States, the EU, and Japan. However, the possibilities that such a collective leadership will succeed is highly questionable in view of ongoing disputes among these three actors, the growing U.S. tendencies to act unilaterally, and the difficulties the EU has in reaching agreement among its own member states. Even if the triad reached agreement on major issues, it is uncertain that it could retain hegemony because a number of NIEs, along with major powers such as China and India, are gaining economic influence.[43] A final possibility is the Gramscian idea that MNCs and internationally mobile capital may be vying with the nation-state today for global hegemony.[44]

The Role of International Institutions

International institutions—both international regimes and IOs—are discussed under North-North relations because the DCs have clearly assumed the largest role in setting the principles, norms, and rules for these institutions. Three KIEOs have performed major functions in overseeing economic management: the IMF, World Bank, and GATT/WTO. As discussed, the three main IPE perspectives present widely differing views of these organizations. Whereas liberals believe the KIEOs are beneficial organizations that seek to promote economic efficiency and openness, realists view the KIEOs as rather passive creatures of their most powerful member states, and historical structuralists consider the KIEOs to be a mechanism by which the capitalist core states exploit weaker states in the periphery. Instead of attempting to decide which of these views is most accurate (all three perspectives in fact have some validity), this section provides an assessment of the current and possible future influence of the KIEOs.

The KIEOs have all been adaptable in altering their functions to meet changing economic circumstances, and it is likely they will continue to have important roles in global economic management. As discussed in Chapter 6, the IMF lost one of its two main functions—looking after the pegged exchange rate system—when the major economic powers shifted to floating exchange rates in 1973. The IMF also became a less essential source of loans for more creditworthy LDCs in the 1970s when private banks recycled large sums of petrodollars to the South. During the 1980s, however, the IMF regained its stature when it took the lead role (along with the United States) in managing the LDC foreign debt crisis. With the breakup of the Soviet Union, the IMF also became an essential source of funding for Russia and other transition economies. During the Asian financial crisis of the late 1990s the IMF again assumed the lead responsibility for dealing with the crisis. Furthermore, the IMF is currently seeking to establish a role for itself in promoting the orderly liberalization of capital movements.[45]

IMF conditionality on its loans has long created resentment in the South, and this resentment increased as the IMF attached more intrusive conditions to its SALs to highly indebted countries during the 1980s–1990s. Nevertheless, the IMF maintained its influential position because it retained the confidence of the advanced industrial states. The 1990s financial crisis marked somewhat of a turning point as DC economists and policymakers began to attack the IMF's stabilization programs in countries such as South Korea, Indonesia, and Russia. For example, critics charged that the IMF imposed the same conditions on loans to South Korea that it had imposed on foreign debtors in the 1980s, even though South Korea had fundamentally different economic problems. South Korea's foreign debt and current account deficit were both low, and its problems were related to a temporary lack of liquidity resulting from short-term debts rather than from insolvency. In Indonesia and Russia, serious economic problems persisted despite the IMF's involvement, and the IMF was accused of simply bailing out governments and foreign investors without providing long-term economic solutions. Thus, one noted economist strongly criticized the IMF programs as being "too flawed to be a standard of good or bad performance."[46]

Despite strong criticisms of the IMF, most DC analysts believe that abolishing the organization is not the answer and that emphasis should be placed instead on "refocusing the IMF."[47] The IMF serves an important function as a source of official financing, and if it were dismantled another organization like it would probably be reinvented. The IMF also performs a useful function in deflecting the South's anger over the conditionality on loans; without the IMF, this anger would be aimed more directly at the United States, Germany, Japan, and other DCs. Although the IMF is uncertain about the proper current macroeconomic solutions, it is certainly not alone in lacking definitive answers. Most analysts who referred to the East and Southeast Asian states as miracle economies did not predict that the fortunes of these states would change so drastically, and the policy prescriptions of different experts for dealing with the current problems are often contradictory. It is therefore likely that the IMF will continue to play a central role and will adapt its functions to meet changing circumstances as it has in the past. In view of the Asian financial crisis, the G-7 leaders and their finance ministers have begun to address the IMF's shortcomings and to discuss proposals for creating a new international financial architecture. As discussed in Chapter 7, ideas for the new architecture are still evolving.

Of the three KIEOs, the World Bank group is probably in the most uncertain position. The IBRD or the Bank initially provided long-term loans for European reconstruction and LDC development. When the Bank lost its reconstruction function, it shifted its attention almost solely to the South. The Bank's importance has stemmed partly from the fact that it is the largest source of multilateral financing for LDC development. In recent years, however, "public support and public resources for official development assistance have declined."[48] The decline in development assistance has resulted from a variety of factors: aid agencies have not succeeded in promoting economic development, the end of the Cold War removed the security rationale for providing aid, and states want to cut spending in an increasingly competitive global environment. "Aid fatigue" in the North has of course had adverse effects on the Bank's functioning. For example, the United States and other donors have often been reluctant to replenish funding for the Bank group's soft-loan affiliate, the IDA (see Chapter 11).

The 1980s foreign debt crisis gave the Bank as well as the IMF new functions to perform. However, both the IMF and the Bank began to provide SALs to LDC debtors, and the IMF rather than the Bank was given responsibility for coordinating the response to the foreign debt crisis. As the IMF and Bank functions increasingly overlapped, questions were raised about whether the Bank was redundant. Still another problem confronting Bank officials has been the high degree of controversy surrounding the current Bank president's efforts to alter the institution's policy outlook and mode of operation (see Chapter 11). The Bank, however, has been highly adaptable, and it will probably continue to function as a separate institution. As discussed in Chapter 11, sub-Saharan Africa is currently facing a development crisis, and the Bank is the only multilateral organization with the economic resources and technical expertise to deal with the crisis. The Bank has also managed to carve out for itself "a unique position as a generator of ideas about economic development."[49] In its 1997 *Annual*

Report the Bank indicated that it was placing greater emphasis on "building a sound knowledge base to support nonlending (as well as lending) activities."[50] The Bank's influence as a disseminator of ideas depends on the expertise of its operating staff as well as on its important position as a source of development finance. Thus, it seems likely that the Bank will continue to operate as a KIEO.

Of the three KIEOs, the WTO is in a number of respects the most important. Unlike the IMF and the Bank, which impose conditions only on LDC and transition economy borrowers, the WTO establishes rules for almost all the world's major trading nations. The WTO moved much closer to becoming a universal membership organization recently when China became a new member, and Russia is certain to become a member in the future. The WTO's importance is ironic because its predecessor, the GATT, became a permanent organization only by default when the proposed ITO did not receive final approval. Nevertheless, the informal nature of GATT permitted it to be highly adaptable. Although GATT negotiations were initially designed to lower tariff barriers, the trade organization also began to negotiate NTB reductions during the Kennedy Round in the 1960s, and it expanded these NTB negotiations at the Tokyo Round in the 1970s. The Uruguay round in the 1980s–1990s was the most complex and ambitious GATT negotiation. Thus, the new WTO oversees regulations not only for trade in goods but also for trade in services, intellectual property, and trade-related investment measures.

Despite the WTO's importance, there are some major threats to its legitimacy. Whereas the GATT oversaw eight rounds of trade negotiations, major differences among members prevented the WTO from launching its first round in Seattle in 1999 (see Chapter 8). Although the Doha Round was finally launched during the fourth WTO ministerial, it is in serious trouble at the time of this writing. Another challenge to the WTO relates to dispute settlement. The WTO has a much stronger dispute settlement system than the GATT, but it is still uncertain whether major trading powers such as the United States and the EU would accept a series of major dispute settlement decisions against them. A third challenge relates to the increase in regional trade agreements. Although some RTAs such as the EU and NAFTA are more likely to be stepping-stones than obstacles to global free trade, the recent increase in a wide range of bilateral FTAs threatens to fragment the global trade regime. In sum, the WTO like the IMF and the Bank faces serious governance challenges.

NORTH-SOUTH RELATIONS

The population of the South accounted for almost 65 percent of the total world population in 1950, and by 1996 the South's population had climbed to almost 80 percent of the world total. Furthermore, a number of transition economies are now receiving foreign debt and development finance from the advanced industrial states and thus have characteristics in common with the South. Despite their significant numbers, however, this book has shown that Southern countries and their populations have had relatively little influence in setting the agenda and making decisions regarding the global political economy.

In addition to the weak economic and political positions of most LDCs, there are major divisions within the South that prevent it from taking unified actions. For example, poverty is spread very unevenly among LDC geographic regions. The United Nations has identified 49 LDCs as "least developed" because they have extremely low per capita incomes and literacy rates and are poorly endowed with natural resources. Almost all of these LLDCs are in sub-Saharan Africa and South Asia. Poverty also has a differential impact on societal groups in the South, with women and children most severely affected. Furthermore, there are indications that globalization is marginalizing the weakest states and societal groups, even as it is contributing to growth in many of the stronger states. For example, the poorest LDCs, which contain 20 percent of the world's population, saw their share of world trade fall from about 4 percent in 1960 to less than 1 percent in 1990. Private investment flows to LDCs increased from $5 billion in 1970 to $173 billion in 1994, but about 75 percent of this investment went to only 10 countries, mainly in East and Southeast Asia and Latin America.[51] The statistics on the poorest LDCs and societal groups indicate that development strategies over the years have had only limited success—especially if one believes that a degree of equity is necessary for development to be considered successful. The following discussion examines how the concept of development is changing and considers whether there is a demonstrated best path to development.

Changing Concepts of Development

During the 1950s–1960s, economic development was usually equated with material economic growth, and the essential indicators of development were a country's GDP and per capita income. In the orthodox liberal view, Western industrial states with high per capita incomes had achieved successful development, and LDCs could acquire similar wealth if they simply followed the same path set by the developed states. Orthodox liberals were not concerned about redistributing wealth to the poorest LDCs and groups because they believed that benefits from the efficient allocation of resources under freer markets would "eventually trickle down from the top, alleviating the problem of poverty at the bottom."[52]

Although the South experienced unprecedented economic growth during the 1960s, unemployment, poverty, and the gap between the rich and the poor were increasing. Thus, a number of development specialists rejected the orthodox liberal view that growth would naturally trickle down to the poor, and they proposed that conscious efforts should be made to redistribute income to the poor and meet their basic human needs for health, education, food, and clean water. From this perspective, GDP and per capita income are not the only important indicators of economic development, and human development indicators must also be considered. These human development indicators include such measures as life expectancy, health and sanitation, literacy rates, education, employment, malnourishment, the position of women and children, and rural-urban disparities. The human development approach demonstrates that development must be measured "through investment in people and not just in machinery, buildings, and other physical assets."[53]

Another change in the concept of development came from those who are concerned about environmental degradation. Of particular importance in this regard was the concept of *sustainable development,* which was popularized by some NGOs in the early 1980s and received multilateral approval in the 1987 report of the World Commission on Environment and Development (the Brundtland Report). The Brundtland Report describes sustainable development as a policy that "meets the needs of the present without compromising the ability of future generations to meet their own needs."[54] Sustainable development is a controversial concept because LDCs often argue that they cannot afford to divert resources from their immediate development needs to pay the costs of following environmentally friendly policies. The LDCs also point out that the advanced industrial states did not adopt sustainable policies when they were developing and that the North produces more pollutants than the South. If the North expects the South to follow more environmentally friendly policies, from this perspective, it must be willing to compensate the South with financial resources.[55]

The prevailing concepts of development have a major effect on policymaking, so it is essential that we opt for a broad rather than narrow concept of development for two reasons. First, recent decades of experience have shown that rapid economic growth does not necessarily enrich people's lives and may even enhance income gaps and poverty under some circumstances. A broader concept of development includes not only economic growth but also human development, poverty reduction, and environmental protection. Second, as interdependence increases, the form that development takes can have major implications for the entire globe. For example, the World Bank estimates that more than 2 million people in China die each year from the effects of air and water pollution and that this pollution may extend far beyond the boundaries of China. Aside from the United States, China is the largest source of greenhouse gases that are linked to global warming, and China and India are the two fastest growing sources of these gases.[56] In an age of globalization, we can no longer afford to adopt a narrow concept of development that is limited to economic growth. Thus, the North must provide assistance to LDCs that lack the capacity to transfer scarce resources from economic growth to other crucial development objectives such as sustainability and the reduction of poverty.

Is There a "Best" Development Strategy?

Chapter 11 discussed several major development strategies, including import substitution, socialist development models, export-led growth, and orthodox liberalism. Liberals, realists, and historical structuralists disagree as to which strategy is best to follow, and they even sometimes disagree as to the type of strategy a state is actually following. For example, when the East Asian export-led growth model was experiencing its greatest success during the 1970s–1980s, liberals attributed the success of these countries to their outward market orientation. Realists, by contrast, attributed the East Asians' success to the existence of a strong developmental state that promoted an effective industrial policy, and historical structuralists argued that the East Asians were following a strategy based on dependency, which was not as successful as the realists and liberals assumed. The experience with different development strategies indicates that *none* of these strategies is necessarily the best and that *every* strategy has strengths and weaknesses. Furthermore, in view of the diverse nature of the South, the best strategy for one LDC may not even be feasible for another. A brief recounting of the strengths and weaknesses of various development strategies will help reinforce these points.

As discussed in Chapter 11, ISI was a commonly used development strategy among LDCs during the 1950s–1960s. The easier first stage of ISI resulted in economic growth and industrialization in a number of LDCs. However, those states in Latin America and elsewhere that continued on to a second stage of ISI encountered increasing problems with balance-of-payments deficits, uncompetitive industries, and increased dependence on external finance. When problems arose with ISI, some Southern states adopted more extreme inward-looking policies and attempted to follow the socialist planning model of the Soviet Union. Central planning contributed to increases in industrial production in some countries, but even larger LDCs such as China were plagued by inefficiencies, low-quality production, and lack of competitiveness. For smaller LDCs lacking in resources such as North Korea, Cuba, Ethiopia, Mozambique, Vietnam, and Burma, the attempts at central planning were even more ineffective. Nevertheless, these states did register some gains in social areas, such as providing better access to health care and education, improving the status of women, and adopting measures to reduce social and economic inequalities.[57]

The East Asian NIEs, which followed the Japanese model and turned from import substitution to export-led growth policies in the 1960s were by far the most successful group of LDCs in increasing their economic growth during the 1960s–1980s. Although liberals and realists often agreed that other LDCs should learn from the East Asian example, they had widely differing interpretations of the reasons for these countries' successes. The realists in fact were probably more accurate in their interpretations: the East Asian NIEs (other than Hong Kong) had strong developmental states that provided extensive guidance to the market, controlled investment flows, promoted the development of technology, and protected selected infant industries. A financial crisis during the 1990s, however, demonstrated that the developmental state was not as efficient and immune to political pressures as was earlier assumed. Thus, the crisis stemmed partly from the failure of governments to develop adequate regulations for banking and other financial institutions. It also became evident that the East Asians had benefited from a unique set of circumstances in which the United States and Japan gave them favored treatment in terms of military and economic aid, trade, and foreign investment. The cost of this special treatment was the development of dependent linkages, and when U.S. and Japanese policies changed in the 1990s, the East Asian states were highly vulnerable. In addition, environmentalists raised questions about the sustainability of rapid economic growth in East Asia, where little action was being taken to prevent environmental degradation. By the late 1990s, few analysts were still claiming that the export-led growth model was the answer to LDC development problems.

During the 1980s, the debt crisis and IMF and World Bank SALs ushered in yet another Southern development strategy based on orthodox liberalism. In marked contrast to import substitution and export-led growth, the orthodox liberal strategy emphasized decreased government spending, privatization, deregulation, and liberal policies toward trade and foreign investment. In middle-income LDCs the SAPs had some positive effects in reducing government budget deficits, increasing export earnings, and enhancing economic efficiency and growth. However, IMF and World Bank SALs also had some negative effects on the poorest LDCs in sub-Saharan Africa and Asia and on vulnerable groups in LDCs, such as women and children. Critics argued that the SAPs underestimated the need for involving the state in development and for maintaining social, health, and educational programs for vulnerable groups despite their financial costs. Supporters of orthodox liberalism, however, asserted that LDCs would benefit most from liberalizing their economies and following in the path of Western Europe and North America.[58]

In view of the global spread of orthodox liberalism, the question arises as to whether we have reached the "end of history" for Southern development strategies and whether liberalism has become the only acceptable path to follow.[59] This is not likely to be the case. As discussed, even the World Bank has acknowledged that SAPs will succeed only if they take account of the need for strong, stable LDC governments and include some distributional goals vis-à-vis the poorest and most vulnerable groups. The problems with SAPs also serve as a reminder that development strategies for the future should avoid the "northern ethnocentrism which permeated much of orthodox development thinking" with its "false claim of universality."[60] As realists have noted, strategies that provide an active role for the government, such as import substitution and export-led growth, may be necessary for Southern countries at various stages in their development if they are to catch up with the leading states. Both import substitution and export-led growth strategies have encountered some problems, but this could mean that we need to find the correct regulatory regime rather than simply opting for deregulation and privatization. As for historical structuralists, they have pointed out correctly that we must be concerned with the distributional effects of development strategies and with overdependence on the North as a possible hindrance to Southern development.

We have *not* reached the end of history in terms of development strategies. The best development strategy is likely to include realist and historical structuralist as well as liberal characteristics, and again, the best strategy for some LDCs may not necessarily be the best strategy for others.

A FINAL WORD ON THEORY AND PRACTICE

This book has combined theory and practice in the study of IPE and has focused on three major theoretical perspectives: realism, liberalism, and historical structuralism. Significant changes have occurred in recent years, including the breakup of the Soviet Union and the end of the Cold War, the pressures of globalization, and the emergence of common threats to humanity such as environmental degradation. These changes have revealed a need for "new theoretical categorizations."[61] One approach to the shortcomings of the three main IPE perspectives is to develop new theories and models that draw on more than one theoretical perspective. This book has focused on several of these hybrid theories, particularly hegemonic stability theory and regime theory. Another approach is to develop new theoretical perspectives in IPE that focus on approaches (e.g., constructivism) and issues (e.g., feminism and environmentalism) that the three traditional perspectives largely ignore.[62]

As discussed in Chapter 1, IPE as a university discipline only began to develop in the 1970s, and IPE theorists have made great strides since that time. In focusing on IPE issues, however, these theorists have often ignored security issues just as security theorists have ignored IPE. It is time that theorists devote more attention to the important linkages between IPE and security issues. The globalization phenomenon points to yet another direction theorists should follow: the development of theories that explore domestic-international interactions in the global political economy. With globalization, the sensitivity of national economies to changes in capital, foreign investment, and trade flows has dramatically increased, as the 1990s Asian financial crisis clearly demonstrates. As states become more interdependent, policies that were traditionally considered to be domestic can have a major impact on outsiders. This book has focused on a number of issues that involve domestic-international interactions, but a more systematic examination of such issues is essential to understanding IPE.

Although no country can escape the fact of growing international interdependence, a country's openness to outside influences also depends on domestic factors such as the position and influence of socioeconomic groups and the nature of the country's political institutions. As a country becomes more involved in foreign trade and investment, domestic conflict may increase between societal groups that benefit from greater international openness and groups that depend on protectionism and economic closure. The extent to which the government adopts more open economic policies depends not only on the relative influence of these societal groups but also on the country's domestic political institutions. Existing institutions can exert strong pressures on governments either to accede to the forces of globalization or to resist these forces with more protectionist economic policies. The reluctance that the U.S. Congress had to give President Clinton fast-track approval to expand NAFTA and to negotiate other trade liberalization agreements is one example of the important role of domestic institutions. All three of the traditional IPE perspectives have devoted too little attention to domestic variables, and the study of IPE will benefit from increased attention to domestic-international interactions.[63]

Students have been introduced to a range of theoretical approaches in this book and have seen how these theories are applied to substantive IPE issue areas. As one noted international relations theorist has stated, "to think theoretically one must be constantly ready to be proven wrong,"[64] and this book has shown that all theoretical perspectives have been partly correct and partly incorrect in their assessments of a wide range of IPE issues. It is only through formulating and reformulating our theories that we can address anomalies and increase our understanding of the global political economy.

NOTES

1. The "borderless world" terminology derives from Kenichi Ohmae's *The Borderless World: Power and Strategy in the Interlinked Economy* (New York: HarperPerennial, 1990).
2. Helen V. Milner, *Resisting Protectionism: Global Industries and the Politics of International Trade* (Princeton: Princeton University Press, 1988).
3. Stephen Gill and David Law, "Global Hegemony and the Structural Power of Capital," in Stephen Gill, ed., *Gramsci, Historical Materialism and International Relations* (Cambridge: Cambridge University Press, 1993), pp.93–124; Mark E. Rupert, "(Re) Politicizing the

Global Economy: Liberal Common Sense and Ideological Struggle in the US NAFTA Debate," *Review of International Political Economy* 2–4 (Autumn 1995), pp.679–681.

4. Riccardo Petrella, "Globalization and Internationalization: The Dynamics of the Emerging World Order," in Richard Boyer and Daniel Drache, eds., *States Against Markets: The Limits of Globalization* (London: Routledge, 1996), pp.77–78.

5. UNCTAD, *World Investment Report 2003* (New York: United Nations, 2003), pp.257–262; Bernard M Hoekman and Michel M. Kostecki, *The Political Economy of the World Trading System: The WTO and Beyond* (Oxford: Oxford University Press, 2nd ed., 2001), pp.9–10.

6. United Nations Development Programme, *Human Development Report—1997* (New York: Oxford University Press, 1997), pp.83–84.

7. United Nations Centre on Transnational Corporations, *World Investment Report 1991: The Triad in Foreign Direct Investment* (New York: United Nations, 1991), pp.9–15.

8. Susan Strange, "The Defective State," *Daedalus* 124 (Spring, 1995), p.56.

9. Philip G. Cerny, *The Changing Architecture of Politics: Structure, Agency and the Future of the State* (London: Sage, 1990), pp.228–229.

10. Ethan B. Kapstein, *Governing the Global Economy: International Finance and the State* (Cambridge: Harvard University Press, 1994), p.6.

11. Walden Bello, "East Asia: On the Eve of the Great Transformation?," *Review of International Political Economy* 5–3 (Autumn 1998), p.426.

12. Stephan Haggard and Andrew MacIntyre, "The Political Economy of the Asian Economic Crisis," *Review of International Political Economy* 5–3 (Autumn 1998), p.383.

13. Stanley Fischer, "Lessons from a Crisis," *The Economist*, October 3, 1998, p.27.

14. Joseph S. Nye, Jr., "Globalization's Democratic Deficit: How to Make International Institutions More Accountable," *Foreign Affairs* 80–4 (July/August 2001), p.3.

15. W. W. Rostow, *Why the Poor Get Richer and the Rich Slow Down* (Austin: University of Texas Press, 1980), p.259; Nye, "Globalization's Democratic Deficit," p.3.

16. Andrew Hurrell and Ngaire Woods, "Globalisation and Inequality," *Millennium* 24–3 (1995), p.458.

17. World Bank, *World Development Report 2000/2001: Attacking Poverty* (New York: Oxford University Press, 2001), p.3.

18. United Nations Development Programme, *Human Development Report—1997*, pp.88–89.

19. United Nations Development Programme, *Human Development Report—1997*, p.88. On the effects of NAFTA on Mexican agriculture, see Theodore H. Cohn, "The Intersection of Domestic and Foreign Policy in the NAFTA Agricultural Negotiations," *Canadian-American Public Policy*, no. 14 (Orono: University of Maine, September 1993), pp.24–33.

20. Ian Robinson, "Globalization and Democracy," *Dissent* (Summer 1995), pp.374–377. For a detailed examination of globalization and democracy, see David Held, *Democracy and the Global Order: From the Modern State to Cosmopolitan Governance* (Cambridge: Polity Press, 1995).

21. Ngaire Woods and Amritar Narlikar, "Governance and the Limits of Accountability: The WTO, the IMF, and the World Bank," *International Social Science Journal* 170 (December 2001), p.569. See also Ngaire Woods, "Making the IMF and the World Bank More Accountable," *International Affairs* 77–1 (2001), pp.83–100.

22. For a range of views on this issue see Tony Porter, "The Democratic Deficit in the Institutional Arrangements for Regulating Global Finance," *Global Governance* 7 (2001), pp.427–439; Woods and Narlikar, "Governance and the Limits of Accountability"; Nye, "Globalization's Democratic Deficit"; and Stephen Gill, "Globalization, Democratization, and the Politics of Indifference," in James H. Mittleman, ed., *Globalization: Critical Reflections* (Boulder: Lynne Rienner, 1996), pp.213–218.

23. Jan Aart Scholte with Robert O'Brien and Marc Williams, "The WTO and Civil Society," *Journal of World Trade* 33–1 (1999), pp.107–123; Peter Newell, "Environmental NGOs,

TNCs, and the Question of Governance," in Dimitris Stevis and Valerie J. Assetto, eds., *The International Political Economy of the Environment: Critical Perspectives* (Boulder: Lynne Rienner, 2001), pp.85–107.

24. Craig Warkentin and Karen Mingst, "International Institutions, the State, and Global Civil Society in the Age of the World Wide Web," *Global Governance* 6–2 (April–June, 2000), p.240.

25. Robert W. Cox, "Civil Society at the Turn of the Millennium: Prospects for an Alternative World Order," *Review of International Studies* 25 (1999), pp.3–28.

26. Woods and Narlikar, "Governance and the Limits of Accountability," p. 581.

27. Myron Weiner, *The Global Migration Crisis: Challenge to States and to Human Rights* (New York: HarperCollins, 1996), p.3.

28. Keith Griffin, "Nine Good Reasons to Love Labor Migration," *UC Mexus News*, of California Institute for Mexico and the United States, p.2.

29. "Immigration: Suspicious Minds," *The Economist*, July 4, 1998, p.25.

30. Malcolm Waters, *Globalization* (London: Routledge, 1995), p.89.

31. Kelley Lee and Richard Dodgson, "Globalization and Cholera: Implications for Global Governance," *Global Governance* 6–2 (April–June, 2000), pp.213–236; Lincoln C. Chen, Tim G. Evans, and Richard A. Cash, "Health as a Global Public Good," in Inge Kaul, Isabelle Grunbert, and Marc A. Stern, eds., *Global Public Goods: International Cooperation in the 21st Century* (Oxford: Oxford University Press, 1999), pp.284–304; Kelley Lee, Kent Buse, and Suzanne Fustukian, eds., *Health Policy in a Globalising World* (Cambridge: Cambridge University Press, 2002).

32. Fantu Cheru, "Debt, Adjustment and the Politics of Effective Response to HIV/AIDS in Africa," *Third World Quarterly* 23–2 (2002), p.309.

33. WTO Press Release, "Intellectual Property Decision Removes Final Patent Obstacle to Cheap Drug Imports," September 4, 2003; Caroline Thomas, "Trade Policy and the Politics of Access to Drugs," *Third World Quarterly* 23–2 (2002), pp.251–164; Gauri Sreenivasan and Ricardo Grinspun, "Trade and Health" Focus on Access to Essential Medicines," Canadian Council for International Cooperation, June 2002.

34. Moisés Naím, "The Five Wars of Globalization," *Foreign Policy* (January/February, 2003), p.29. See also Nigel Morris-Cotterill, "Money Laundering," *Foreign Policy* (May/June, 2001), pp.16–22; and Michel Schiray, "Introduction: Drug Trafficking, Organized Crime, and Public Policy for Drug Control," *International Social Science Journal* 53–169 (2001), pp.351–358.

35. Susan Strange, *States and Markets* (London: Pinter, 2nd ed., 1994), p.29.

36. Joseph S. Nye, Jr., "Soft Power," *Foreign Policy* 80 (Fall 1990), p.166; Susan Strange, "The Persistent Myth of Lost Hegemony," *International Organization* 41–4 (Autumn 1987), pp.551–574.

37. On the changing U.S. position on international trade see Theodore H. Cohn, *Governing Global Trade: International Institutions in Conflict and Convergence* (Aldershot: Ashgate, 2002).

38. Ronald A. Morse, "Japan's Drive to Pre-Eminence," *Foreign Policy* no. 69 (Winter 1987–1988), pp.3–21. See also articles by Philip J. Meeks and Kojui Taira in Tsuneo Akaha and Frank Langdon, eds., *Japan in the Posthegemonic World* (Boulder: Rienner, 1993); and by Alan Rix in Richard Higgott, Richard Leaver, and John Ravenhill, eds., *Pacific Economic Relations in the 1990s* (Boulder: Rienner, 1993).

39. "Japan on the Brink," *The Economist*, April 11, 1998, pp.15–17; Ron Bevacqua, "Whither the Japanese Model? The Asian Economic Crisis and the Continuation of Cold War Politics in the Pacific Rim," *Review of International Political Economy* 5–3 (Autumn 1998), pp.410–423.

40. Lester Thurow, *Head to Head: The Coming Economic Battle Among Japan, Europe, and America* (New York: Morrow, 1992), p.258.

41. "Congratulations, China," *The Economist*, October 18, 2003; "Tilting at Dragons," *The Economist*, October 25, 2003, pp.65–66; "Learning to Love a Growing China," *The Economist*, November 29, 2003, pp.38–39.

42. Nye, "Soft Power," pp.154–155; Samuel Huntington, "The U.S.—Decline or Renewal?," *Foreign Affairs* 67–2 (Winter 1988–89), p.90.

43. Aaron Segal, "Managing the World Economy," *International Political Science Review* 11–3 (1990), p.362.

44. Stephen Gill, "Global Finance, Monetary Policy and Cooperation among the Group of Seven, 1944–1992," in Philip G. Cerny, ed., *Finance and World Politics: Markets, Regimes and States in the Post-hegemonic Era* (London: Elgar, 1993), p.105.

45. See Stanley Fischer, "Capital Account Liberalization and the Role of the IMF," paper released by the IMF, September 1997, p.12.

46. Jeffrey Sachs, "Global Capitalism: Making it Work," *The Economist,* September 12, 1998, p.25.

47. See Martin Feldstein, "Refocusing the IMF," *Foreign Affairs* 77–2 (March/April 1998), pp.20–33; Jagdish Bhagwati, "The Capital Myth: The Difference between Trade in Widgets and Dollars," *Foreign Affairs* 77–3 (May/June 1998), p.11.

48. OECD, *Development Co-operation—1996* (Paris: OECD, 1997), p.1.

49. Robert Wade, "Japan, the World Bank and the Art of Paradigm Maintenance: The East Asian Miracle in Political Perspective," *New Left Review* 217 (May/June 1996), p.5.

50. World Bank, *Annual Report 1997* (Washington, DC: World Bank, 1997), p.7.

51. World Bank, *World Development Report 1990* (New York: Oxford University Press, 1990), pp.1–2; United Nations Development Programme, *Human Development Report 1996* (New York: Oxford University Press, 1996), pp.8–9.

52. Mohammed H. Malek, "Towards an Integrated Aid and Development Programme for Europe," in Mohammed H. Malek, ed., *Contemporary Issues in European Development Aid* (Aldershot: Avebury, 1991), p.142.

53. Wilfred L. David, *The Conversation of Economic Development: Historical Voices, Interpretations, and Reality* (Armonk: Sharpe, 1997), p.177.

54. World Commission on Environment and Development, *Our Common Future* (Oxford: Oxford University Press, 1987), p.8.

55. See Maurice F. Strong, "Achieving Sustainable Global Development," in the South Centre, *Facing the Challenge: Responses to the Report of the South Commission* (London: Zed Books, 1993), pp.305–313.

56. Nicholas D. Kristof, "Across Asia, a Pollution Disaster Hovers," *New York Times,* November 28, 1997, pp.A1, A10.

57. John Rapley, *Understanding Development: Theory and Practice in the Third World* (Boulder: Rienner), 1996, pp.44–47.

58. See Walter Russell Mead, "Asia Devalued," *New York Times Magazine,* May 31, 1998, pp.38–39.

59. See Francis Fukuyama, "The End of History?," *The National Interest* 16 (Summer 1989), pp.3–18.

60. Cristóbal Kay, "For a Renewal of Development Studies: Latin American Theories and Neoliberalism in the Era of Structural Adjustment," *Third World Quarterly* 14–4 (1993), p.697.

61. Thomas J. Biersteker, "Evolving Perspectives on International Political Economy: Twentieth-Century Contexts and Discontinuities," *International Political Science Review* 14–1 (January 1993), p.27.

62. On constructivism see Kurt Burch and Robert A. Denemark, eds., *Constituting International Political Economy* (Boulder: Lynne Rienner, 1997).

63. Robert O. Keohane and Helen V. Milner, eds. *Internationalization and Domestic Politics* (Cambridge: Cambridge University Press, 1996); and Helen V. Milner, *Interests, Institutions, and Information: Domestic Politics and International Relations* (Princeton: Princeton University Press, 1997).

64. James N. Rosenau, "Thinking Theory Thoroughly," in James N. Rosenau, *The Scientific Study of Foreign Policy* rev. ed. (London: Pinter, 1980), p.30.

Glossary

absolute advantage A condition in which a country is able to produce a good more efficiently and at a lower cost than another country (or countries). Liberal-economic trade theorists maintain that countries benefit by specializing in the production of goods for which they have an absolute advantage. See *comparative advantage.*

antidumping duties (ADDs) Duties a country may impose on imported goods if it determines that the goods are being dumped and that this is causing or threatening material injury to its domestic producers. See *dumping.*

Asia-Pacific Economic Cooperation (APEC) An "open" regional initiative that includes the three largest national economies (the United States, Japan, and China) and has members from Asia, Australasia, and North and South America. Initially, foreign and economic ministers attended APEC meetings, but in 1993 the forum began to hold annual summit meetings of heads of state. Although APEC's economic activities to this point have been rather limited, the goal has been established to form a free trade area, and there are possibilities for agreements on competition policies, product standards, dispute settlement, and private investment.

Association of Southeast Asian Nations (ASEAN) Established in 1967 with the objectives of promoting peace, stability, and economic growth in the region, ASEAN currently has 10 Southeast Asian countries as members. ASEAN was largely a political organization for many years, but in 1977 the members signed a preferential trade agreement, and the members have a stated goal of establishing an ASEAN Free Trade Area (AFTA).

Baker Plan A plan proposed by U.S. Secretary of the Treasury James A. Baker III in 1985 to deal with the LDC foreign debt crisis. The plan emphasized the postponement of some debt payments, the provision of new IMF and World Bank loans as an incentive for continued lending by private banks, and structural changes in debtor country policies.

balance of payments A summary record of all international economic transactions that a country has, normally over a one-year period. The most important components of the balance of payments are the *current account* and the *capital account.*

Bank for International Settlements (BIS) The oldest of the international financial institutions, formed in 1930 to oversee German war reparations. The BIS is located in Basel, Switzerland, and is the main forum for cooperation and consultation among central bankers in the OECD countries. It helps to deal with exchange rate problems and provides credit to central banks that lack liquidity. In response to the 1980s debt crisis, the BIS provided "bridging" finance until IMF and World Bank loans were available and adopted measures to increase confidence in the international banking system.

basic human needs A foreign aid approach that focuses on the poorest people among and within LDCs. The basic human needs (or basic needs) approach was prominent in the 1970s and marked a shift from the emphasis on GNP growth in the 1960s. Aid programs, according to this approach, should emphasize basic health, education, family planning, rural development, and services to the poor; the increased involvement of women in development programs; and special attention to the problems of the least developed countries.

bilateral aid A type of foreign assistance that flows directly from a donor to a recipient government. The largest percentage of official development assistance is given bilaterally. See *foreign aid, multilateral aid,* and *official development assistance.*

bilateral investment treaties (BITs) Bilateral treaties that developed countries have been negotiating with LDCs to promote and protect foreign investment. The BITs generally uphold the MFN and national treatment principles, often prohibit host country performance requirements, and require prompt and adequate compensation in the event of nationalization.

Brady Plan   A plan proposed by U.S. Secretary of the Treasury Nicholas Brady in 1988 after it became evident that the Baker Plan was insufficient to deal with the foreign debt crisis. The Brady Plan introduced the idea that debt relief or reduction was necessary for some LDCs with severe and protracted debt problems in exchange for structural adjustment of the debtors' economies.

Bretton Woods system   Bretton Woods, New Hampshire, was the location of meetings during July 1944 that culminated in the creation of the postwar economic order. The IMF and International Bank for Reconstruction and Development (or World Bank) were established at Bretton Woods, as was the monetary regime of pegged exchange rates. This monetary regime ended in 1973, when major countries shifted to flexible exchange rates.

Canada-U.S. Free Trade Agreement (CUSFTA)   Concluded in 1988, the CUSFTA resulted from a change in U.S. policy in which it agreed to participate in RTAs, and from Canada's desire to gain more assured access to the U.S. market. The NAFTA replaced the CUSFTA in 1994. See *North American Free Trade Agreement.*

capital   A factor of production, along with land and labor. Capital consists of physical assets such as equipment, tools, buildings, and other manufactured goods that are capable of generating income, and it consists of financial assets such as stocks, which presumably reflect a firm's physical assets. Marxists view capital in social and political as well as economic terms and emphasize capital's exploitation of labor in the capitalist system.

capital account   A major item in the balance of payments, which records the amounts a country lends to and borrows from nonresidents. Countries often finance their current account deficits with a net inflow of capital or a surplus in their capital accounts. The transactions in the capital account include *foreign direct investment* and *portfolio investment.*

capital market   A capital market consists of all those institutions in a country (e.g., the stock exchange, banks, and insurance companies) that match supply with demand for long-term capital. Unlike a capital market, a money market deals with shorter term loanable funding. The World Bank floats bonds on the capital markets of developed states to acquire much of its funding for lending purposes.

central bank   The public authority responsible for managing a country's money supply and for regulating and controlling its monetary and financial institutions and markets. All developed countries and most LDCs rely on a central bank for such regulatory activities.

civil society   A wide range of nongovernmental, noncommercial organizations outside official circles that seek to reinforce or alter existing norms, rules, and social structures.

common market   The third stage of regional integration, which has the characteristics of a customs union *plus* the free mobility of factors of production (i.e., capital and labor). See *customs union, economic union,* and *free trade area.*

comparative advantage   A country has a comparative advantage in producing good A if it can produce A at a *relatively* lower cost than other goods, even if it does not have an absolute advantage in producing any good. Comparative advantage is a powerful liberal-economic theory justifying specialization and free trade.

competitiveness   A frequently cited definition of competitiveness, developed by the U.S. President's Commission on Industrial Competitiveness, is "the degree to which . . . [a nation] can, under free and fair market conditions, produce goods and services that meet the tests of international markets while simultaneously expanding the real income of its citizens." Wide disagreement exists, however, over the most important factors determining competitiveness and over the relationship between the competitiveness of states and firms.

concessional loans (or *soft loans*)   Loans that have lower interest rates, longer grace periods, and longer repayment periods than *commercial* or *hard loans.*

conditionality   A concept that is most closely associated with the IMF but is also associated with World Bank SALs. As a condition for receiving IMF loans above a certain level, borrowers must explicitly commit themselves to follow a prescribed set of policies. These policies typically include decreased government spending, increased government revenues, devaluation, deregulation, and privatization.

consultative group   A group that brings together donor states that provide development assistance to a particular recipient. In using consultative groups, donors seek to coordinate their bilateral aid giving and to exert collective pressure on recipient states.

countervailing duties (CVDs)   Duties a country may impose on imported goods if it determines that the goods are benefiting from trade-distorting subsidies in the exporting country and that this is causing or threatening material injury to domestic producers.

current account A major item in the balance of payments, which records a country's trade in goods and services with foreigners, investment income and payments, and gifts and other transfers paid to and received from foreigners.

customs union (CU) The second stage of regional integration in which the member countries eliminate tariffs on all (or substantially all) their trade with each other and develop a common external tariff toward outside countries.

debt service ratio (or **debt-to-export ratio**) The ratio of a country's interest and principal payments on its debt to its export income; often used to assess a country's ability to repay its foreign debt. The East Asian NIEs had stronger export positions than the Latin American NIEs and were better able to service their foreign debts during the 1980s.

dependency theory A historical structuralist development theory that argues that the world is hierarchically organized, with the leading capitalist states in the core of the global economy dominating and exploiting the poorer states in the periphery.

devaluation A reduction in the official rate or value at which one currency is exchanged for another. When a country devalues its currency, the prices of its imported goods and services increase while its exports become less expensive to foreigners. A country can therefore gain certain trade advantages through devaluation of its currency.

developmental state A term first used by Chalmers Johnson in the early 1980s to describe Japan and the East Asian NIEs. According to realists, the East Asian developmental state provided extensive guidance to the market, identified development as its primary objective, invested heavily in education, and depended on a highly skilled technocratic bureaucracy. Questions about the efficacy of the developmental state have become more common since the East Asian financial crisis of the late 1990s.

dollarization The likelihood that a country will replace its own currency with the currency of another country, usually within the same region.

dumping Selling a product in an export market at a lower price than charged in the home market, or below the cost of production.

economic union The fourth stage of regional integration, which has the characteristics of a common market and harmonizes the industrial, regional, fiscal, monetary, and other economic policies of member countries. A full economic union also involves the adoption of a common currency by the members.

economism An overemphasis on the importance of the economic sphere along with a corresponding underemphasis on the autonomy of the political sphere.

endogenous growth theory Posits that technological change is not simply the result of fortunate breakthroughs in the quest for new knowledge that are exogenous to the basic factors of production determining economic growth. Instead, technological knowledge is an important endogenous factor of production along with labor and capital that provides developed countries and their firms major advantages over LDCs.

epistemic community A group of professionals with acknowledged expertise and a recognized claim to policy-relevant knowledge in a particular issue area.

Eurocurrencies National currencies traded and deposited in banks outside the home country, frequently (but not necessarily) in Europe. The most common form of Eurocurrencies are U.S. dollars or Eurodollars. International firms and national governments often prefer to use the Eurocurrency market for deposits and loans because the transactions in this market are free of most government regulations.

European Coal and Steel Community (ECSC) Six Western European countries (Belgium, France, West Germany, Italy, Luxembourg, and the Netherlands) formed the ECSC in 1951. Although the ECSC integrated the member countries' coal and steel resources, it was created primarily to prevent France and Germany from renewing their age-old rivalries. Seven years later, the six ECSC member countries expanded the integration process by forming the *European Community*.

European Community (EC) A regional integration agreement formed in 1957 among six Western European countries for political as well as economic reasons. In economic terms, the EC goals were to establish a customs union and a common market. The EC also established a complex institutional structure, including a Commission, Council of Ministers, European Court of Justice, and European Parliament. Membership in the EC increased to 12 countries by 1986, and in 1993 the EC was superseded by the *European Union*.

European Union (EU)   The EU became the successor organization to the EC in 1993, largely as a result of the "Europe 92" program. Europe 92 was designed to complete the establishment of a single market by the removal of remaining fiscal, nontariff, technical, and other barriers to trade. The EU has moved to both widen and deepen the integration process in Europe. As for widening, EU membership increased from 12 to 15 countries during 1995, and future membership of East European countries was under consideration. As for deepening, 12 members of the EU have joined in an economic and monetary union (EMU) with a common currency (the euro).

exchange rate   The number of units of one currency that can be exchanged for a unit of another currency. See *fixed exchange rates* and *floating exchange rates.*

export-led growth   An outward-looking economic development strategy that emphasizes the production of industrial goods for export to developed countries. Export-led growth is commonly associated with the economic success of the NIEs in East Asia. See *import-substituting industrialization.*

fast-track authority   Measures first introduced in the 1974 U.S. Trade Act to expedite congressional approval of trade agreements negotiated by the U.S. executive. Under the fast track, the president can assure U.S. trading partners that Congress will vote for or against negotiated agreements without amendments within a fixed period. Such authority is often necessary because other countries are reluctant to negotiate trade agreements with the United States that the U.S. Congress can later seek to amend.

fiscal policy   Fiscal policy affects the economy through changes in taxes and government spending. A government that uses fiscal policy to deal with a balance-of-payments deficit lowers government expenditures and raises taxes to withdraw purchasing power from the public. See *monetary policy.*

fixed exchange rates   In a fixed exchange rate system, currencies are given official exchange rates, and governments regularly take actions to keep the market rates of their currencies close to the official rates.

floating exchange rates or flexible exchange rates   In a floating exchange rate system, the supply of and demand for each currency in the foreign exchange market determine its exchange rate. With *free-floating exchange rates,* governments do not intervene and the market alone determines currency valuations. With *managed floating,* central banks intervene to deal with disruptive conditions such as excessive fluctuations in exchange rates. Although managed floating is considered to be legitimate, the IMF calls on central banks to avoid *dirty floating,* which refers to a government's manipulation of exchange rates to prevent effective balance-of-payments adjustment or to give that country an unfair competitive advantage.

foreign aid   The administered transfer of resources to recipient countries for the stated purpose of promoting their welfare and economic development. The greatest share of foreign aid is official development assistance, but aid is also provided by private or nongovernmental organizations. According to the Development Assistance Committee of the OECD, only grants that do not require repayment and concessional loans with a grant element of at least 25 percent should qualify as foreign aid. See *concessional loans, bilateral aid, multilateral aid,* and *official development assistance.*

foreign direct investment (FDI)   Investment involving the ownership and control of assets in one country by residents of another country. The foreign residents are usually MNCs that have management rights or control in a branch plant or subsidiary. FDI may occur through the creation of new productive assets by foreigners (i.e., greenfield investment) or through the purchase of stock in an existing firm. See *portfolio investment.*

free trade area (FTA)   The first stage of regional integration, in which the member countries are to eliminate tariffs on all (or substantially all) trade with one another. However, each member country can continue to levy its own tariffs and follow its own trade policies toward nonmembers.

General Agreement on Tariffs and Trade (GATT)   A provisional treaty that became the main global trade organization in 1948 by default when a planned International Trade Organization did not receive final approval. As an organization, GATT provided a written code of behavior, a forum for multilateral negotiations, and a venue for dispute settlement on trade issues. When the more formal WTO was formed in 1995, GATT reverted to its original status as a treaty to regulate trade in goods.

General Agreement on Trade in Services (GATS)   A set of concepts, principles, rules, and commitments by members that apply to measures affecting trade in services. The GATS was established as a result of the GATT Uruguay Round agreement and is a treaty under the WTO.

generalized system of preferences (GSP)   During the 1970s, the developed countries agreed to establish a GSP in response to LDC demands. Under the GSP, individual developed countries can waive

MFN treatment and give preferential treatment to imports of specific goods from LDCs. Thus, the import duties for some LDC products are lower than those levied on developed countries' products.

global governance   Efforts to respond in a collective and orderly manner to issues that go beyond the competence of states to deal with individually. See *governance*.

gold standard   A monetary system in which central banks fix the value of their currencies in terms of gold and hold official international reserves in gold. A regime based on the gold standard existed from the 1870s to 1914, and many countries unsuccessfully tried to restore it after World War I. In a *gold exchange standard* (e.g., the Bretton Woods regime), central banks hold their international reserves in two forms—gold and foreign exchange—in any proportion they choose.

governance   Formal and informal processes and institutions that organize collective action.

gross domestic product (GDP)   The total value of goods and services produced within a country's borders during a given year. GDP counts income in terms of where it is earned rather than who owns the factors of production.

gross national income (GNI)   Virtually identical with the GNP. The GNI measures the income produced by the GNP rather than the value of the product itself.

gross national product (GNP)   The total value of goods and services produced by domestically owned factors of production during a given year. GNP counts income according to who owns the factors of production rather than where the income is earned.

Group of Eight (G-8)   The G-8 includes the G-7 members plus Russia. Although Russia is theoretically a full member, serious economic problems prevent it from participating fully in the G-7's economic deliberations.

Group of Five (G-5)   The G-5 includes the finance ministers and central bank governors of the largest developed economies: the United States, Japan, Germany, France, and Britain. It has played a major role at times in coordinating monetary and other economic policies.

Group of Seven (G-7)   The G-5 plus Italy and Canada. The G-7 includes the seven largest industrial democracies, which account for about two-thirds of global output. G-7 heads of state and government hold annual summit meetings to provide leadership in international economic policy.

Group of Seventy-Seven (G-77)   The principal group representing Third World economic interests in negotiations with developed countries. The G-77 derives its name from the 77 LDCs that formed the group in 1964, but well over 100 LDCs are in fact current members of the group.

Group of Ten (G-10)   The G-10 includes the 10 developed countries that established the General Arrangements to Borrow with the IMF in 1962. Eleven countries are in fact current members of the G-10—the G-7 plus the Netherlands, Belgium, Sweden, and Switzerland. In addition to providing supplementary finance, the G-10 regularly meets to discuss important matters related to the international monetary regime.

Group of Twenty-Four (G-24)   The G-24 was formed by the G-77 in 1972 to represent the interests of LDCs on international monetary issues. The G-24 is composed of eight finance ministers or central bank governors from each of the three main LDC regions—Africa, Asia, and Latin America.

Heavily Indebted Poor Countries (HIPC) initiative   An initiative proposed in 1996 to provide debt relief for HIPC. Unlike early plans (e.g., the Baker and Brady plans), the HIPC initiative was designed to permit rescheduling of debts of low-income LDCs to the IMF and World Bank. An enhanced HIPC initiative was established in 1999. See *Baker Plan* and *Brady Plan*.

Heckscher-Ohlin theorem   A theory named after two Swedish economists that postulates that comparative advantage is determined by the relative abundance and scarcity of factors of production (land, labor, and capital). Thus, capital-rich countries (usually the more advanced nations) should specialize in capital-intensive production, whereas countries with an abundance of cheap labor (many LDCs) should specialize in labor-intensive production.

hegemonic stability theory   A theory asserting that a relatively open and stable international economic system is most likely to exist when a hegemonic state is willing and able to provide leadership. The hegemonic state may manage the global economic system through coercive tactics, the provision of public goods, or both. See *hegemony* and *public goods*.

hegemony   Leadership, preponderant influence, or dominance in the international system, usually (but not always) associated with a particular nation-state. Gramscian theorists use the term hegemony in a cultural sense to connote not only the dominance of a single world power but also the complex of "ideas" that social groups use to legitimize their authority.

horizontal integration   A horizontally integrated MNC extends its operations abroad by producing the same product or product line in plants located in different countries. Firms often engage in horizontal integration to defend or increase their market share. See *multinational corporation* and *vertical integration.*

human development index (HDI)   The UNDP's measure of human development based on life expectancy at birth; the adult literacy rate; primary, secondary, and tertiary school enrolments; and the PPP-adjusted per capita GDP.

import-substituting industrialization (ISI)   A Third World strategy to promote economic development by replacing industrial imports with domestic production through trade protectionism and government assistance to domestic firms. Import substitution is most commonly associated with the economic problems of a number of Latin American LDCs.

infrastructure   The underlying framework of basic facilities, equipment, institutions, and installations that are crucial for the growth and functioning of an economy. Examples of infrastructure include transportation systems, public utilities, finance systems, laws and law enforcement, education, and research.

instrumental Marxism   A form of Marxism that perceives formal government institutions as responding in a passive manner to the interests and pressures of the capitalist class. See *structural Marxism.*

International Monetary Fund (IMF)   An international financial organization formed in 1944 to uphold the Bretton Woods system of pegged exchange rates (until the move to floating rates in 1973) and to provide countries with short-term loans for balance-of-payments problems. The IMF has had a leading role in dealing with the 1980s foreign debt crisis and the 1990s financial crisis.

liquidity   The ease with which an asset can be used at a known price in making payments. Cash is the most liquid form of an asset.

Lomé Conventions   Trade and aid agreements between the EU and 71 African, Caribbean, and Pacific (ACP) countries. The Lomé Conventions replaced the earlier Yaoundé Conventions and provide the ACP countries with associate status in the EU.

London Club   An informal group of large private commercial banks that have provided credit to Third World countries encountering debt repayment problems. The London Club has no formal structure or specific location for its meetings. Meetings often occur in "creditor committees," in which the largest creditor banks coordinate their positions in debt rescheduling negotiations with individual LDC debtor countries. See *Paris Club.*

macroeconomics   The branch of economics that deals with the behavior of the economy as a whole. For example, macroeconomics is concerned with overall levels of employment, growth, production, and consumption. It examines such issues as monetary and fiscal policy, the banking system, trade, and the balance of payments.

market   a coordinating mechanism where sellers and buyers exchange goods, services, and factors of production at prices and output levels determined by supply and demand.

market economy   An economy in which the market coordinates individual choices to determine the types of goods and services produced and sold as well as the methods of production.

mercantilism   A policy of states from the sixteenth to eighteenth centuries to build up their power and wealth relative to other states, largely by maintaining a balance-of-trade surplus. States that rely on government involvement and trade protectionism to increase their power and wealth are often considered to be *neomercantilist.*

Mercosur   Mercosur was formed in March 1991 when Argentina, Brazil, Paraguay, and Uruguay signed the Treaty of Asunciön to establish a common market according to an agreed timetable. The significance of Mercosur as a Third World RTA stems from the importance of its two largest members, Brazil and Argentina.

monetary policy   Monetary policy influences the economy through changes in the money supply. When a government uses monetary policy to deal with a balance-of-payments deficit, its central bank limits public access to funds for spending purposes and makes such funds more expensive.

most-favored-nation (MFN) treatment   A principle stipulating that every trade advantage, favor, privilege, or immunity a GATT/WTO member gives to any country must be extended to all other member states. A major exception to MFN treatment is provided for regional integration agreements.

multilateral aid   A type of foreign assistance in which donor governments provide funding through international organizations (such as the World Bank) whose policies are collectively determined. See *bilateral aid, foreign aid,* and *official development assistance.*

multinational corporation (MNC)   An enterprise that owns and controls facilities for production, distribution, and marketing in at least two countries. Also referred to as a transnational corporation or multinational enterprise.

national treatment   A principle stating that all GATT/WTO members should treat foreign products—after they have been imported—as favorably as domestic products with regard to internal taxes and other internal charges and regulations.

New International Economic Order (NIEO)   A set of proposals for extensive international economic reform and concessions from the developed countries of the North, which Third World countries presented to the United Nations in the 1970s. These included LDC demands for control over their economies and natural resources, control over foreign investment, greater assistance for economic development, greater access to markets in developed countries, and increased prices for LDC commodity exports. The Northern states ultimately rejected most of these demands for change.

nontariff barriers (NTBs)   An incredibly large array of measures other than tariffs that restrict imports, assist domestic production, and promote exports. As tariffs declined because of successive rounds of GATT negotiations, nontariff barriers became relatively more important. NTBs are often more restrictive, ill defined, and inequitable than tariffs.

North American Free Trade Agreement (NAFTA)   An FTA joining the United States, Canada, and Mexico, which entered into force in January 1994. The importance of NAFTA stems from the inclusion of the United States, the comprehensive nature of the agreement, and the fact that it is the first reciprocal free trade accord among developed countries and an LDC. Unlike the WTO, NAFTA does not give special and differential treatment to the LDC member (Mexico).

official aid (OA)   Flows of foreign aid that meet the same criteria of eligibility as *official development assistance*. The only difference is that recipients of official aid are the more advanced emerging countries (e.g., Russia, Hungary, and Poland) and a small number of advanced Third World countries (e.g., Kuwait and Singapore).

official development assistance (ODA)   Flows of foreign aid to LDCs and multilateral institutions from official government agencies. See *bilateral aid, foreign aid,* and *multilateral aid.*

official development finance (ODF)   Nonconcessional or "hard" loans that the IBRD provides to LDCs and transition economies. Although the IBRD's quasi-commercial loans are not concessional enough to be classified as ODA or OA, they are classified as ODF because the IBRD extends them for development purposes, it accompanies the loans with economic and technical advice, and LDCs receive the IBRD loans on better terms than they could obtain from borrowing directly on capital markets.

optimum currency area   A concept first developed by Robert Mundell, an optimum currency area is a region that maximizes the benefits minus the costs of using a common currency. Regions that are optimum currency areas are subject to common economic shocks, have a high degree of labor mobility, and have a tax-transfer system that relocates resources from economically strong to weak areas.

Organization for Economic Cooperation and Development (OECD)   An organization of 30 mainly developed countries, located in Paris, France. The OECD conducts policy studies on economic and social issues, serves as a forum for the developed countries to discuss members' economic policies as well as promote cooperation and policy coordination, and sometimes serves as a forum for negotiation or prenegotiation.

Organization for European Economic Cooperation (OEEC)   An organization of Western European countries formed in 1948, which was responsible for developing a program for distribution of Marshall Plan funds and for facilitating moves toward convertibility of European currencies and the liberalization of trade in Western Europe. In 1960 the OEEC was replaced by the OECD, which also includes non-European developed countries as full members.

Pareto-optimal outcome   A condition of equilibrium in which no one actor can be made better off without making someone else worse off. A Pareto-suboptimal outcome, by contrast, is one in which all actors prefer another outcome to the equilibrium outcome. See *prisoners' dilemma.*

Paris Club   An informal grouping of creditor governments (members of the OECD) that meets with individual LDC debtor governments to negotiate debt-rescheduling agreements. The Paris Club normally meets in the French Ministry of Finance, but it has no legal status or written rules, no voting procedure, and no formal organizational structure.

politicism   An overemphasis on politics and power and an underemphasis on economic structures and processes.

portfolio investment   The purchase of stocks, bonds, and money market instruments by foreigners for the purpose of realizing a financial return, which does not result in foreign management, ownership, or legal control.

prisoners' dilemma   A game used by theorists (often in international relations) to examine situations in which individual rationality induces each state to "cheat" regardless of the actions taken by others. Such individually rational actions, however, can produce a Pareto-suboptimal outcome; hence the "dilemma" in the prisoners' dilemma. See *Pareto-optimal outcome.*

public goods   Also called *collective goods*, these are goods that are *nonexcludable* (i.e., all states have access to them) and *nonrival* (i.e., any state's use of the good will not decrease the amount available for others). Hegemons often provide public goods, according to the liberal interpretation of hegemonic stability theory. A major problem associated with public goods is the existence of *free riders* because even noncontributing states (or individuals) can benefit from the provision of public goods.

purchasing power parity (PPP)   The number of units of a country's currency needed to buy the same amount of goods and services in the domestic market as a U.S. dollar can buy in the United States.

Quadrilateral Group of Trade Ministers or **Quad**   An informal grouping of trade ministers and trade officials from the United States, the European Commission, Japan, and Canada that helps to resolve differences among the major traders and to help set the agenda for meetings and negotiations in the global trade regime.

reciprocity   The GATT/WTO principle that a country benefiting from another country's trade concessions should provide roughly equal benefits in return. *Specific reciprocity*, the more demanding type, requires concessions of equivalent value between two actors within a strict period. *Diffuse reciprocity* is less demanding, with more flexibility in terms of equivalence of value and the time period for granting reciprocal concessions.

regime   A form of institution dealing with a specific issue area in international relations, in which principles, norms, rules, and decision-making procedures affect actors' expectations and behavior. *International organizations* are more concrete and formal institutions than regimes and are often embedded within regimes. For example, the WTO is embedded within the global trade regime.

rules of origin   Regulations designed to prevent importers from bringing goods into a free trade area through member countries with the lowest duties and then shipping them to partner countries that have higher duties. Rules of origin often provide an excuse for protectionism.

safeguards   Term usually applied to Article 19 of GATT (the general escape clause). This article permits countries to take emergency protection measures to counter unexpected import surges that cause, or are likely to cause, serious injury to domestic industry. Safeguard actions are to be applied on a nondiscriminatory basis, and affected countries can request compensation.

seignorage   The profit and advantages accruing to a "seigneur" or sovereign power from issuing money. The term usually refers to the influence and power a hegemon acquires as a result of its position as the top-currency state.

single undertaking   A single undertaking indicates that acceptance of an agreement requires acceptance of all its parts. The GATT Uruguay round agreement was a single undertaking because it required LDCs to accept all parts of the agreement; this was in marked contrast to the NTB Tokyo Round codes, in which most LDCs did not participate.

special drawing rights (SDRs)   Artificial international reserves created and managed by the G-10 and used among central banks. SDRs have been issued only two times, and efforts to have them supplement (or replace) the U.S. dollar as the main international monetary reserve have been unsuccessful.

state   A sovereign, territorial political unit.

Stolper-Samuelson theory   According to the Stolper-Samuelson theory, trade liberalization benefits abundantly endowed factors of production and hurts poorly endowed factors of production in a state. Building on the Heckscher-Ohlin theory, Stolper-Samuelson helps explain why some domestic groups in a state are free-trade oriented and why other groups are protectionist.

strategic trade theory   A realist theory indicating that a state can successfully intervene through industrial targeting to alter its comparative or "competitive" advantage vis-à-vis other states. In deciding on its intervention strategies, a state tends to favor industries with presumed advantages in research and development, technology, economies of scale, and market power.

structural adjustment loans (SALs)   Medium-term balance-of-payments financing provided by the World Bank and IMF to LDCs. To receive such loans, borrowing countries must agree to institute structural reforms prescribed by the IMF, the World Bank, or both.

structural Marxism   Structural Marxists view the state as relatively autonomous of direct political pressure from particular capitalists, but they believe that the state acts in the long-term interests of the capitalist class.

sustainable development   A policy that recognizes the complementarity between economic development and environmental conservation. Sustainable development was popularized by nongovernmental organizations in the early 1980s and received multilateral approval in 1987 by the Brundtland Commission. According to the Brundtland Commission, sustainable development "meets the needs of the present without compromising the ability of future generations to meet their own needs."

tariffs   Taxes levied on products that pass through a customs border. Although tariffs are usually imposed on imports, they may also be applied to exports. Import tariffs are most commonly used as a means of protectionism, but they may also be valued as a source of revenue for the state.

terms of trade   The relationship between the prices of a country's exports and the prices of its imports. During the late 1940s and early 1950s, structuralists such as Raúl Prebisch argued that relations between the core and periphery were marked by unequal exchange, in which there were deteriorating terms of trade for LDCs in the periphery. LDCs were therefore advised to follow ISI policies.

Trade-Related Intellectual Property Rights (TRIPs)   An agreement that establishes minimum standards of protection for copyrights, patents, and other types of intellectual property; provides for remedies available to members to protect these rights; and extends some basic GATT principles to intellectual property. The TRIPs agreement was concluded during the GATT Uruguay round and is part of the WTO.

Trade-Related Investment Measures (TRIMs)   The TRIMs is a rather weak and narrowly defined agreement to impose some discipline over trade-related investment issues. The TRIMs agreement prohibits host countries from imposing local content requirements on FDI, but the agreement does not address many other issues such as a host country's export performance requirements.

transfer prices   Prices used by a business firm for the internal sale of goods and services among its divisions (i.e., for intrafirm trade). Although transfer prices help an MNC to efficiently manage its internal operations, an MNC may artificially raise or lower its transfer prices to shift its reported profits from high-tax to low-tax countries.

Triffin dilemma   Named after Robert Triffin, the Triffin dilemma described the position of the United States as the top-currency state. Continued balance-of-payments deficits would create a "confidence" problem in the U.S. dollar, but if the United States moved to reduce its payments deficit, there would be a shortage of U.S. dollars for liquidity purposes. The Triffin dilemma therefore refers to the conflict between the liquidity and confidence functions of a top-currency state.

United Nations Conference on Trade and Development (UNCTAD)   A permanent organ of the United Nations General Assembly, created in 1964 as a result of Third World dissatisfaction with existing international economic organizations such as GATT. UNCTAD is primarily concerned with promoting international trade, economic development, and the interests of LDCs.

vertical integration   A vertically integrated MNC controls and coordinates production of goods and services at different stages of the production process. When an MNC is vertically integrated, the outputs of some of its affiliates serve as inputs to other affiliates. Firms often engage in vertical integration to avoid uncertainty, reduce transaction costs, and limit competition. See *horizontal integration.*

voluntary export restraints   A practice by which countries have circumvented the GATT Article 11 ban on import quotas by pressuring other countries to "voluntarily" decrease their exports of specific products.

Washington consensus   A term referring to the orthodox liberal belief that countries can best achieve economic growth through free markets, a dominant private sector, democratic government, and trade liberalization. (Ironically, this is not what John Williamson meant by the term when he coined it in 1989.)

World Bank group   The largest multilateral group of institutions providing international development financing for Third World countries and emerging centrally planned economies. The group consists of five institutions, including the International Bank for Reconstruction and Development (formed at Bretton Woods in the 1940s), the International Finance Corporation (formed in 1956), the International Development Association (created in 1960), the International Centre for the Settlement of Investment Disputes (established in 1966), and the Multilateral Investment Guarantee Agency (established in 1988).

world-systems theory   Like dependency theory, world-systems theory rejects the view of modernization theorists that countries in the periphery have problems because they follow traditional practices. World-systems theorists argue that problems in the periphery stem from capitalism, a global system for organizing economic activities that has existed since the "long sixteenth century." To explain the fact that some countries in the periphery have experienced some development, world-systems theorists introduced the concept of the semiperiphery.

World Trade Organization (WTO)   The main global trade organization, established as the successor to GATT in 1995 by the signatories to the GATT Uruguay round agreement. Under the WTO are various agreements, including the General Agreement on Tariffs and Trade (GATT), the General Agreement on Trade in Services (GATS), the Agreement on Trade-Related Intellectual Property Rights (TRIPs), and the Agreement on Trade-Related Investment Measures (TRIMs).

Selected
Bibliography

Topics

I. General Studies—International Political Economy

Baldwin, David A., ed. *Neorealism and Neoliberalism: The Contemporary Debate*. New York: Columbia University Press, 1993.

Biersteker, Thomas J. "Evolving Perspectives on International Political Economy: Twentieth-Century Contexts and Discontinuities." *International Political Science Review* 14-1 (January 1993): 7–33.

Boyer, Robert, and Daniel Drache, eds. *States Against Markets: The Limits of Globalization*. London: Routledge, 1996.

Burch, Kurt, and Robert A. Denemark, eds. *Constituting International Political Economy*. Boulder: Rienner, 1997.

Caporaso, James A. "Global Political Economy." In *Political Science: The State of the Discipline II*, ed. Ada Finifter, 451–481. Washington, DC: American Political Science Association, 1993.

Cerny, Philip G., ed. *World Politics: Markets, Regimes and States in the Post-Hegemonic Era*. London: Elgar, 1993.

Cox, Robert W. *Production, Power, and World Order: Social Forces in the Making of History*. New York: Columbia University Press, 1987.

Crane, George T., and Abla Amawi, eds. *The Theoretical Evolution of International Political Economy: A Reader*. New York: Oxford University Press, 2nd ed., 1997.

Doyle, Michael W., and G. John Ikenberry. *New Thinking in International Relations Theory*. Boulder: Westview Press, 1997.

Frieden, Jeffry A., and David A. Lake, eds. *International Political Economy: Perspectives on Global Power and Wealth*. New York: St. Martin's Press, 3rd ed., 1995.

Gerschenkron, Alexander. *Economic Backwardness in Historical Perspective*. Cambridge: Harvard University Press, 1962.

Gilpin, Robert, with Jean Gilpin. *The Political Economy of International Relations*. Princeton: Princeton University Press, 1987.

———. *Global Political Economy: Understanding the International Economic Order*. Princeton: Princeton University Press, 2001.

Howlett, Michael, and M. Ramesh. *The Political Economy of Canada: An Introduction*. Toronto, Canada: McClelland & Stewart, 1992.

Kegley, Charles W., Jr., ed. *Controversies in International Relations Theory: Realism and the Neoliberal Challenge*. New York: St. Martin's Press, 1995.

Kenen, Peter B., ed. *Managing the World Economy: Fifty Years After Bretton Woods*. Washington, DC: Institute for International Economics, 1994.

Kindleberger, Charles P. *Power and Money: The Economics of International Politics and the Politics of International Economics*. New York: Basic Books, 1970.

Kresl, Peter Karl, and Gary Gappert, eds. *North American Cities and the Global Economy: Challenges and Opportunities*. Thousand Oaks: Sage, 1995.

Lindblom, Charles E. *Politics and Markets: The World's Political-Economic Systems*. New York: Basic Books, 1977.

Mander, Jerry, and Edward Goldsmith, eds. *The Case Against the Global Economy: For a Turn Toward the Local*. San Francisco: Sierra Club, 1996.

McKinlay, R. D., and R. Little. *Global Problems and World Order*. London: Pinter, 1986.

Murphy, Craig N., and Roger Tooze, eds. *The New International Political Economy*. Boulder: Rienner, 1991.

O'Hara, Phillip Anthony, ed. *Encyclopedia of Political Economy*, vols. 1 and 2. London: Routledge, 1999.

Olson, Mancur. *The Logic of Collective Action: Public Goods and the Theory of Groups*. Cambridge: Harvard University Press, 1965.

Palan, Ronen, ed. *Global Political Economy: Contemporary Theories*. London: Routledge, 2000.

Peterson, V. Spike, and Anne Sisson Runyan. *Global Gender Issues*. Boulder: Westview Press, 2nd ed., 1999.

Polanyi, Karl. *The Great Transformation*. Boston: Beacon Press, 1965.

Schwartz, Herman M. *States versus Markets: History, Geography, and the Development of the International Political Economy*. New York: St. Martin's Press, 2nd ed., 2000.

Staniland, Martin. *What Is Political Economy? A Study of Social Theory and Underdevelopment*. New Haven: Yale University Press, 1985.

Stevis, Dimitris, and Valerie J. Assetto, eds. *The International Political Economy of the Environment: Critical Perspectives*. Boulder: Rienner, 2001.

Strange, Susan, ed. *Paths to International Political Economy*. London: Allen & Unwin, 1984.

———. *States and Markets*. London: Pinter, 1988.

Stubbs, Richard, and Geoffrey R. D. Underhill, eds. *Political Economy and the Changing Global Order*. Toronto: Oxford University Press, 2nd ed., 2000.

Tickner, J. Ann. *Gender in International Relations: Feminist Perspectives on Achieving Global Security*. New York: Columbia University Press, 1992.

Webb, Michael C. *The Political Economy of Policy Coordination: International Adjustment Since 1945*. Ithaca: Cornell University Press, 1995.

Whitworth, Sandra. *Feminism and International Relations: Towards a Political Economy of Gender in Interstate and Non-Governmental Institutions*. London: Macmillan, 1994.

Yarbrough, Beth V., and Robert M. Yarbrough. *The World Economy: Trade and Finance*. Fort Worth: Harcourt Brace, 3rd ed., 1994.

II. Globalization

Burback, Roger, Orlando Núñez, and Boris Kagarlitsky. *Globalization and Its Discontents: The Rise of Post-modern Socialisms*. London: Pluto Press, 1997.

Carnoy, Martin, Manuel Castells, Stephen S. Cohen, and Fernando Henrique Cardoso. *The New Global Economy in the Information Age: Reflections on Our Changing World*. University Park: Pennsylvania State University Press, 1993.

Cohn, Theodore H., Stephen McBride, and John Wiseman, eds. *Power in the Global Era: Grounding Globalization*. London: Macmillan, 2000.

"Globalization." Special issue of *International Journal* 51-4 (Autumn 1996).

Held, David. *Democracy and the Global Order: From the Modern State to Cosmopolitan Governance*. Cambridge: Polity Press, 1995.

Held, David, and Anthony McGrew, eds. *Governing Globalization: Power, Authority and Global Governance*. Oxford: Polity Press, 2002.

Hirst, Paul, and Grahame Thompson. *Globalization in Question*. Cambridge: Polity Press, 1996.

Holm, Hans-Henrik, and Georg Sorensen, eds. *Whose World Order? Uneven Globalization and the End of the Cold War*. Boulder: Westview Press, 1995.

Jones, R. J. Barry. *Globalisation and Interdependence in the International Political Economy: Rhetoric and Reality*. London: Pinter, 1995.

Kapstein, Ethan B. *Governing the Global Market: International Finance and the State*. Cambridge: Harvard University Press, 1994.

Mander, Jerry, and Edward Goldsmith, eds. *The Case Against the Global Economy: For a Turn Toward the Local*. San Francisco: Sierra Club, 1996.

McBride, Stephen, and John Wiseman, eds. *Globalization and Its Discontents*. London: Macmillan, 2000.

Mittelman, James H. *Globalization: Critical Reflections*. Boulder: Rienner, 1996.

Nye, Joseph S., Jr, and John D. Donahue, eds., *Governance in a Globalizing World*. Washington, D.C.: Brookings Institution, 2000.

Ohmae, Kenichi. *The Borderless World: Power and Strategy in the Interlinked Economy*. New York: Harper Perennial, 1990.

Prakash, Aseem, and Jeffrey A. Hart, eds., *Globalization and Governance*. London: Routledge, 1999.

Scholte, Jan Aart. *Globalization: A Critical Introduction*. New York: St. Martin's Press, 2000.

Sklair, Leslie. *Sociology of the Global System*. Hertfordshire: Prentice Hall/Harvester Wheatsheaf, 2nd ed., 1995.

Stiglitz, Joseph E. *Globalization and Its Discontents*. New York: W. W. Norton, 2002.

III. Institutional Framework for Managing the Postwar World Economy

Acheson, A. L. K., J. F. Chant, and M. F. J. Prochowny, eds. *Bretton Woods Revisited*. Toronto: University of Toronto Press, 1972.

Assetto, Valerie J. *The Soviet Bloc in the IMF and the IBRD*. Boulder: Westview Press, 1988.

Bakker, Age F. P. *International Financial Institutions*. New York: Longman, 1996.

Bayne, Nicholas. *Hanging in There: The G7 and G8 Summit in Maturity and Renewal*. Aldershot: Ashgate, 2000.

Bergsten, C. Fred, and C. Randall Henning. *Global Economic Leadership and the Group of Seven*. Washington, DC: Institute for International Economics, 1996.

Blair, David J. *Trade Negotiations in the OECD: Structures, Institutions and States*. London: Kegan Paul, 1993.

Bleicher, Samuel A. "UN v. IBRD: A Dilemma of Functionalism." *International Organization* 42-1 (Winter 1970): 31–47.

Brabant, Jozef M. van. *The Planned Economies and International Economic Organizations*. Cambridge, UK: Cambridge University Press, 1991.

Bretton Woods Commission. *Bretton Woods: Looking to the Future*. Washington, DC: Bretton Woods Committee, 1994.

Camps, Miriam, with C. Gwin. *Collective Management: The Reform of Global Economic Organizations*. New York: McGraw-Hill, 1980.

Cavanagh, John, Daphne Wysham, and Marcos Arruda, eds. *Beyond Bretton Woods: Alternatives to the Global Economic Order*. London: Pluto Press, 1994.

Cutajar, Michael Zammit, ed. *UNCTAD and the North-South Dialogue: The First Twenty Years*. Oxford: Pergamon Press, 1985.

Danaher, Kevin, ed. *50 Years Is Enough: The Case Against the World Bank and the International Monetary Fund*. Boston: South End Press, 1994.

Feeney, William. "Chinese Policy in Multilateral Financial Institutions." In *China and the World: Chinese Foreign Policy in the Post-Mao Era*, ed. Samuel S. Kim, 266–292. Boulder: Westview Press, 1984.

Feinberg, Richard E. "The Changing Relationship Between the World Bank and the International Monetary Fund." *International Organization* 42–3 (Summer 1988): 545–560.

Ferguson, Tyrone. *The Third World and Decision Making in the International Monetary Fund: The Quest for Full and Effective Participation*. London: Pinter, 1988.

Gilbert, Christopher L., and David Vines, eds. *The World Bank: Structures and Policies*. Cambridge: Cambridge University Press, 2000.

Gold, Joseph. "The Relationship Between the International Monetary Fund and the World Bank." *Creighton Law Review* 15 (1982): 499–521.

Hajnal, Peter I., ed. *The Seven Power Summit: Documents from the Summits of Industrialized Countries 1975–1989*. New York: Kraus International Publications, 1989.

———. *The G7/G8 System: Evolution, Role and Documentation*. Aldershot, UK: Ashgate, 1999.

Hart, Jeffrey A. *The New International Economic Order: Conflict and Cooperation in North-South Economic Relations, 1974–77*. London: Macmillan, 1983.

Higgott, Richard A., Geoffrey R. D. Underhill, and Andreas Bieler, eds. *Non-State Actors and Authority in the Global System*. London: Routledge, 2000.

Jacobson, Harold K. *Networks of Interdependence: International Organizations and the Global Political System*. New York: Knopf, 1979.

Jacobson, Harold K., and Michel Oksenberg. *China's Participation in the IMF, the World Bank, and GATT: Toward a Global Economic Order*. Ann Arbor: University of Michigan Press, 1990.

Johnson, Hazel J. *Global Financial Institutions and Markets*. Oxford: Blackwell, 2000.

Kapur, Devesh, John P. Lewis, and Richard Webb. *The World Bank: Its First Half Century, Volume 1: History*. Washington, DC: Brookings Institution Press, 1997.

Karns, Margaret P., and Karen A. Mingst. *The United States and Multilateral Institutions: Patterns of Changing Instrumentality and Influence*. Boston: Unwin Hyman, 1990.

Kirshner, Orin, ed. *The Bretton Woods–GATT System: Retrospect and Prospect After Fifty Years*. Armonk: M. E. Sharpe, 1996.

Kirton, John J., and George M. von Furstenberg, eds. *New Directions in Global Economic Governance: Managing Globalisation in the Twenty-First Century*. Aldershot: Ashgate, 2001.

Laszlo, Ervin, et al. *The Obstacles to the New International Economic Order*. New York: Pergamon Press, 1980.

Mason, Edward S., and Robert E. Asher. *The World Bank Since Bretton Woods*. Washington, DC: Brookings Institution, 1973.

O'Brien, Robert, Anne Marie Goetz, Jan Aart Scholte, and Marc Williams. *Contesting Global Governance: Multilateral Economic Institutions and Global Social Movements*. Cambridge: Cambridge University Press, 2000.

Pincus, Jonathan R., and Jeffrey A. Winters, eds., *Reinventing the World Bank*. Ithaca: Cornell University Press, 2002.

Polak, Jacques J. *The World Bank and the International Monetary Fund: A Changing Relationship*. Brookings Occasional Papers. Washington, DC: Brookings Institution, 1994.

Putnam, Robert D., and Nicholas Bayne. *Hanging Together: Cooperation and Conflict in the Seven-Power Summits*. London: Sage, revised ed., 1987.

Risse-Kappen, Thomas, ed. *Bringing Transnational Relations Back In: Non-State Actors, Domestic Structures and International Institutions*. Cambridge: Cambridge University Press, 1995.

Rochester, J. Martin. "The Rise and Fall of International Organization as a Field of Study." *International Organization* 40-4 (Autumn 1986): 777–813.

Ruggie, John Gerard., ed. *Multilateralism Matters: The Theory and Praxis of an Institutional Form*. New York: Columbia University Press, 1993.

Sauvant, Karl P. *The Group of 77: Evolution, Structure, Organization*. New York: Oceana Publications, 1981.

Shihata, Ibrahim F. I. *MIGA and Foreign Investment: Origins, Operations, Policies and Basic Documents of the Multilateral Investment Guarantee Agency*. Dordrecht: Nijhoff, 1988.

Van Dormael, Armand. *Bretton Woods: Birth of a Monetary System*. London: Macmillan, 1978.

Williams, Marc. *Third World Cooperation: The Group of 77 in UNCTAD*. London: Pinter Publishers, 1991.

———. *International Economic Organizations and the Third World*. New York: Harvester Wheatsheaf, 1994.

World Commission on Environment and Development. *Our Common Future*. Oxford: Oxford University Press, 1987.

Wysham, Daphne, and Marcos Arruda, ed., *Beyond Bretton Woods: Alternatives to the Global Economic Order*. London: Pluto Press, 1994.

IV. The Realist Perspective

Baldwin, David A. *Economic Statecraft*. Princeton: Princeton University Press, 1985.

Evans, Peter B., Dietrich Rueschemeyer, and Theda Skocpol, eds. *Bringing the State Back In*. Cambridge: Cambridge University Press, 1985.

Gilpin, Robert. "The Richness of the Tradition of Political Realism." *International Organization* 38-2 (Spring 1984), pp.287–304.

Grieco, Joseph. *Cooperation Among Nations: Europe, America, and Non-Tariff Barriers to Trade*. Ithaca: Cornell University Press, 1990.

Heckscher, Eli F. *Mercantilism*, vol. 2. London: Allen & Unwin, 1934.

Hirschman, Albert O. *National Power and the Structure of Foreign Trade*. Berkeley: University of California Press, expanded ed., 1980.

Johnson, Chalmers. *MITI and the Japanese Miracle: The Growth of Industrial Policy, 1925–1975*. Stanford: Stanford University Press, 1982.

Keohane, Robert O., ed. *Neorealism and Its Critics*. New York: Columbia University Press, 1986.

Kirshner, Jonatan. "Political Economy in Security Studies After the Cold War." *Review of International Political Economy* 5-1 (Spring 1998): 64–91.

Krasner, Stephen D. *Defending the National Interest: Raw Materials Investments and U.S. Foreign Policy*. Princeton: Princeton University Press, 1978.

———. *Structural Conflict: The Third World Against Global Liberalism*. Berkeley: University of California Press, 1985.

———. *Sovereignty: Organized Hypocrisy*. Princeton: Princeton University Press, 1999.

Lake, David A. "Power and the Third World: Toward a Realist Political Economy of North-South Relations." *International Studies Quarterly* 31-2 (June 1987): 217–234.

List, Friedrich. *The National System of Political Economy*. Translated by Sampson S. Lloyd. London: Longmans, Green, 1916.

Machiavelli, Niccolò. *The Prince and the Discourses*. New York: Modern Library, 1940.

Mastanduno, Michael. "Economics and Security in Statecraft and Scholarship." *International Organization* 52-4 (Autumn 1998): 825–854.

Mastanduno, Michael, David A. Lake, and G. John Ikenberry, "Toward a Realist Theory of State Action." *International Studies Quarterly* 33-4 (December 1989): 457–474.

Morgenthau, Hans. J., revised by Kenneth W. Thompson. *Politics Among Nations: The Struggle for Power and Peace*. New York: Knopf, 6th ed., 1985.

Rothstein, Robert L. *The Weak in the World of the Strong: The Developing Countries in the International System*. New York: Columbia University Press, 1977.

Syrett, Harold C., ed. *The Papers of Alexander Hamilton*, vol. 10. New York: Columbia University Press, 1966.

Thucydides. *The History of the Peloponnesian War*. Translated by Richard Crawley. London: Dent, Everyman's Library, 1963.

Viner, Jacob. "Power versus Plenty as Objectives of Foreign Policy in the Seventeenth and Eighteenth Centuries." *World Politics* 1 (October 1948): 1–29.

·ᴸ· N. *Theory of International Politics*. Reading: Addison Wesley, 1979.

V. Hegemonic Stability Theory

Akaha, Tsuneo, and Frank Langdon, eds. *Japan in the Posthegemonic World*. Boulder: Rienner, 1993.

Calleo, David P. *Beyond American Hegemony: The Future of the Western Alliance*. New York: Basic Books, 1987.

Cowhey, Peter F., and Edward Long. "Testing Theories of Regime Change: Hegemonic Decline or Surplus Capacity?" *International Organization* 37-2 (Spring 1983): 157–188.

Gibbs, David N. "Washington's New Interventionism: U.S. Hegemony and Inter-Imperialist Rivalries" *Monthly Review* 53-4 (September 2001): 15–37.

Gill, Stephen. "American Hegemony: Its Limits and Prospects in the Reagan Era." *Millennium* 15-3 (Winter 1986): 311–336.

Gilpin, Robert. *War and Change in World Politics*. Cambridge: Cambridge University Press, 1981.

Goldstein, Joshua S. *Long Cycles: Prosperity and War in the Modern Age*. New Haven: Yale University Press, 1988.

Huntington, Samuel. "The U.S.—Decline or Renewal?" *Foreign Affairs* 67-2 (Winter 1988–1989): 76–96.

Kennedy, Paul. *The Rise and Fall of the Great Powers: Economic Change and Military Conflict from 1500 to 2000*. New York: Random House, 1987.

Keohane, Robert O. "The Theory of Hegemonic Stability and Changes in International Economic Regimes, 1967–1977." In *Change in the International System*, eds. Ole R. Holsti, Randolph M. Siverson, and Alexander L. George, 131–162. Boulder: Westview Press, 1980.

————. *After Hegemony: Cooperation and Discord in the World Political Economy*. Princeton: Princeton University Press, 1984.

Kindleberger, Charles P. *The World in Depression, 1929–1939*. Berkeley: University of California Press, 1973.

————. "Dominance and Leadership in the International Economy: Exploitation, Public Goods, and Free Rides." *International Studies Quarterly* 25-2 (June 1981): 242–254.

Mead, Walter Russell. *Mortal Splendor: The American Empire in Transition*. Boston: Houghton Mifflin, 1987.

Modelski, George. *Long Cycles in World Politics*. Seattle: University of Washington Press, 1987.

Nau, Henry R. *The Myth of America's Decline: Leading the World Economy into the 1990s*. New York: Oxford University Press, 1990.

Nye, Joseph S., Jr. *Bound to Lead: The Changing Nature of American Power*. New York: Basic Books, 1990.

Olson, Mancur. *The Logic of Collective Action: Public Goods and the Theory of Groups*. Cambridge, MA: Harvard University Press, 1965.

Russett, Bruce. "The Mysterious Case of Vanishing Hegemony; or, Is Mark Twain Really Dead?" *International Organization* 39-2 (Spring 1985): 207–231.

Snidal, Duncan. "The Limits of Hegemonic Stability Theory." *International Organization* 39-4 (Autumn 1985): 579–614.

Stein, Arthur A. "The Hegemon's Dilemma: Great Britain, the United States and the International Economic Order." *International Organization* 38-2 (Spring 1984): 355–386.

Strange, Susan. "The Persistent Myth of Lost Hegemony." *International Organization* 41-4 (Autumn 1987): 551–574.

Thurow, Lester. *Head to Head: The Coming Economic Battle Among Japan, Europe, and America*. New York: Morrow, 1992.

Webb, Michael C., and Stephen D. Krasner. "Hegemonic Stability Theory: An Empirical Assessment." *Review of International Studies* 15 (Spring 1989): 183–198.

Zuckerman, Mortimer B. "A Second American Century." *Foreign Affairs* 77-3 (May/June, 1998): 18–31.

VI. The Liberal Perspective

Arblaster, Anthony. *The Rise and Decline of Western Liberalism*. New York: Basil Blackwell, 1984.

Axelrod, Robert. *The Evolution of Cooperation*. New York: Basic Books, 1984.

Balassa, Bela, ed. *The Newly Industrializing Countries in the World Economy*. New York: Pergamon Press, 1981.

Bauer, P. T., and B. S. Yamey. "Against the New Economic Order." *Commentary* 63-4 (April 1977): 25–31.

Black, C. E. *The Dynamics of Modernization: A Study in Comparative History*. New York: Harper & Row, 1966.

Cooper, Richard N. *The Economics of Interdependence: Economic Policy in the Atlantic Community*. New York: McGraw-Hill, 1968.

Cutler, A. Claire. "The 'Grotian Tradition' in International Relations." *Review of International Studies* 17 (1991): 41–65.

Fox, Annette Baker, Alfred O. Hero Jr., and Joseph S. Nye Jr., eds. *Canada and the United States: Transnational and Transgovernmental Relations*. New York: Columbia University Press, 1976.

Friedman, Milton, ed. *Essays in Positive Economics*. Chicago: University of Chicago Press, 1953.

Friedman, Milton, and Rose Friedman. *Free to Choose: A Personal Statement*. New York: Harcourt Brace Jovanovich, 1980.

Fukuyama, Francis. "The End of History?" *The National Interest* 16 (Summer 1989): 3–18.

Hall, Peter A., ed. *The Political Power of Economic Ideas: Keynesianism across Nations*. Princeton: Princeton University Press, 1989.

Hayek, F. A. *New Studies in Philosophy, Politics, Economics and the History of Ideas*. Chicago: University of Chicago Press, 1978.

Keohane, Robert O., and Joseph S. Nye Jr., eds. *Transnational Relations and World Politics*. Cambridge: Harvard University Press, 1972.

———. *Power and Interdependence: World Politics in Transition*. Boston: Little, Brown, 1977.

Keynes, John Maynard. *The General Theory of Employment, Interest, and Money*. New York: Harcourt, Brace and World, 1935.

Krasner, Stephen D., ed. *International Regimes*. Ithaca: Cornell University Press, 1983.

Lerner, Daniel. *The Passing of Traditional Society: Modernizing the Middle East*. New York: Free Press, 1964.

Moggridge, D. E. *Keynes*. London: Macmillan, 1976.

Moravcsik, Andrew. "Taking Preferences Seriously: A Liberal Theory of International Politics." *International Organization* 51-4 (Autumn 1997): 513–553.

Oye, Kenneth A., ed. *Cooperation Under Anarchy*. Princeton: Princeton University Press, 1986.

Ricardo, David. *The Principles of Political Economy and Taxation*. Homewood: Irwin, 1963.

Risse-Kappen, Thomas, ed. *Bringing Transnational Relations Back In: Non-State Actors, Domestic Structures and International Institutions*. Cambridge: Cambridge University Press, 1995.

Rostow, W. W. *The Stages of Economic Growth: A Non-Communist Manifesto*. Cambridge: Cambridge University Press, 1960.

———. *Why the Poor Get Richer and the Rich Slow Down*. Austin: University of Texas Press, 1980.

Ruggie, John Gerard. "International Regimes, Transactions, and Change: Embedded Liberalism in the Postwar Economic Order." In *International Regimes*, ed. Stephen D. Krasner, 195–231. Ithaca: Cornell University Press, 1983.

Schattschneider, E. E. *Politics, Pressures and the Tariff*. Hamden: Archon Books, 1935. Reprint, 1963.

Smith, Adam. *The Wealth of Nations*. London: Dent & Sons, Everyman's Library, 1910.

von Mises, Ludwig. *Planning For Freedom*. South Holland, IL: Libertarian Press, 1974.

VII. International Institutions and Regime Theory

Cohn, Theodore H. "The Changing Role of the United States in the Global Agricultural Trade Regime." In *World Agriculture and the GATT*, International Political Economy Yearbook, vol. 7, ed. William P. Avery, 17–38. Boulder: Rienner, 1993.

Cutler, A. Claire, and Mark W. Zacher, eds. *Canadian Foreign Policy and International Economic Regimes*. Vancouver: University of British Columbia Press, 1992.

de Senarclens, Pierre. "Regime Theory and the Study of International Organizations." *International Social Science Journal* (November 1993): 45–138.

Haggard, Stephan, and Beth A. Simmons. "Theories of International Regimes." *International Organization* 41-3 (Summer 1987): 491–517.

Hollingsworth, J. Rogers, and Robert Boyer, eds. *Contemporary Capitalism: The Embeddedness of Institutions*. Cambridge: Cambridge University Press, 1997.

Jacobson, Harold K. *Networks of Interdependence: International Organizations and the Global Political System*. New York: Knopf, 1979.

Kahler, Miles. *International Institutions and the Political Economy of Integration*. Washington, DC: Brookings Institution, 1995.

Keohane, Robert O. *After Hegemony: Cooperation and Discord in the World Political Economy*. Princeton: Princeton University Press, 1984.

———. *International Institutions and State Power: Essays in International Relations Theory*. Boulder: Westview Press, 1989.

Krasner, Stephen D., ed. *International Regimes*. Ithaca: Cornell University Press, 1983.

Levy, Marc A., Oran R. Young, and Michael Zürn. "The Study of International Regimes." *European Journal of International Relations* 1-3 (1995): 267–330.

Martin, Lisa, and Beth Simmons. "Theories and Empirical Studies of International Institutions." *International Organization* 52-4 (Autumn 1998): 729–757.

Mearsheimer, John J. "The False Promise of International Institutions." *International Security* 19-3 (Winter 1994–1995): 5–49.

Rittberger, Volker, with Peter Mayer, eds. *Regime Theory and International Relations*. Oxford: Clarendon Press, 1993.

Rosenau, James N., and Ernst-Otto Czempiel, eds. *Governance Without Government: Order and Change in World Politics*. Cambridge: Cambridge University Press, 1992.

Snidal, Duncan, "International Political Economy Approaches to International Institutions." In *Economic Dimensions in International Law*, eds. Jagdeep S. Bhandari and Alan O. Sykes, 477–512. Cambridge: Cambridge University Press, 1997.

Young, Oran R. *The Effectiveness of International Environmental Regimes*. Cambridge: MIT Press, 1999.

———. *Governance in World Affairs*. Ithaca: Cornell University Press, 1999.

Zacher, Mark W., with Brent A. Sutton. *Governing Global Networks: International Regimes for Transportation and Communications*. Cambridge: Cambridge University Press, 1996.

VIII. The Historical Structuralist Perspective

Aglietta, Michel. *A Theory of Capitalist Regulation: The US Experience*. Translated by David Fernbach. London: New Left Books, 1979.

Avineri, Shlomo, ed. *Karl Marx on Colonialism and Modernization: His Dispatches and Other Writings on China, India, Mexico, the Middle East and North Africa*. Garden City: Doubleday, 1968.

Baran, Paul A. *The Political Economy of Growth*. New York: Monthly Review Press, 1962.

Blaney, David L. "Reconceptualizing Autonomy: The Difference Dependency Theory Makes." *Review of International Political Economy* 3-3 (Autumn 1996): 459–497.

Brewer, Anthony. *Marxist Theories of Imperialism: A Critical Survey*. London: Routledge, 2nd ed., 1990.

Caporaso, James. "Dependency Theory: Continuities and Discontinuities in Development Studies." *International Organization* 34-4 (Autumn 1980): 605–628.

Cardoso, Fernando Henrique. "The Consumption of Dependency Theory in the United States." *Latin American Research Review* 12-3 (1977): 7–24.

Cardoso, Fernando Henrique, and Enzo Faletto. *Dependency and Development in Latin America*. Translated by Marjory Mattingly Urquidi. Berkeley: University of California Press, 1979.

Chase-Dunn, Christopher. "Comparing World-Systems: Toward a Theory of Semiperipheral Development." *Comparative Civilizations Review* 19 (Fall 1988): 29–66.

Chase-Dunn, Christopher, and Peter Grimes. "World-Systems Analysis." *Annual Review of Sociology* 21 (1995): 387–417.

Clark, Cal, and Donna Bahry. "Dependent Development: A Socialist Variant." *International Studies Quarterly* 27-3 (September 1983): 271–293.

Cox, Robert W. *Production, Power, and World Order: Social Forces in the Making of History*. New York: Columbia University Press, 1987.

———. "Civil Society at the Turn of the Millennium: Prospects for an Alternative World Order." *Review of International Studies* 25 (1999): 3–28.

De Vroey, Michel. "A Regulation Approach Interpretation of Contemporary Crisis." *Capital & Class* 23 (Summer 1984): 45–66.

dos Santos, Theotonio. "The Structure of Dependence." *American Economic Review* 60-2 (May 1970): 231–236.

Evans, Peter. *Dependent Development: The Alliance of Multinational, State, and Local Capital in Brazil.* Princeton: Princeton University Press, 1979.

———. "After Dependency: Recent Studies of Class, State, and Industrialization." *Latin American Research Review* 20-2 (1985): 149–160.

Frank, André Gunder. *Capitalism and Underdevelopment in Latin America: Historical Studies of Chile and Brazil.* New York: Monthly Review Press, 1967.

Galtung, Johan. "A Structural Theory of Imperialism." *Journal of Peace Research* 8-2 (1971): 81–117.

Gereffi, Gary. *The Pharmaceutical Industry and Dependency in the Third World.* Princeton: Princeton University Press, 1983.

Ghosh, B. N. *Dependency Theory Revisited.* Aldershot: Ashgate, 2001.

Gill, Stephen, ed. *Gramsci, Historical Materialism, and International Relations.* Cambridge: Cambridge University Press, 1993.

Gramsci, Antonio. *Selections from the Prison Notebooks of Antonio Gramsci.* Edited and translated by Quintin Hoare and Geoffrey Nowell Smith. New York: International Publishers, 1971.

Hobson, J. A. *Imperialism: A Study.* Ann Arbor: University of Michigan Press, 1965.

Jessop, Bob. *The Capitalist State: Marxist Theories and Methods.* Oxford: Martin Robertson, 1982.

Laclau, Ernesto. "Feudalism and Capitalism in Latin America." *New Left Review* 67 (May/June 1971): 19–38.

Lenin, V. I. *Imperialism: The Highest Stage of Capitalism.* Revised translation. New York: International Publishers, 1939.

Lipietz, Alain. *Towards a New Economic Order: Postfordism, Ecology and Democracy.* Translated by Malcolm Slater. New York: Oxford University Press, 1992.

Love, Joseph L. "The Origins of Dependency Analysis." *Journal of Latin American Studies* 22 (February 1990): 143–168.

Marx, Karl, and Frederick Engels. *Selected Works.* New York: International Publishers, 1968.

McGowan, Pat, and Stephen G. Walker. "Radical and Conventional Models of U.S. Foreign Economic Policy Making." *World Politics* 33-3 (April 1981): 347–382.

Miliband, Ralph. *The State in Capitalist Society.* New York: Basic Books, 1969.

O'Leary, Brendan. *The Asiatic Mode of Production: Oriental Despotism, Historical Materialism and Indian History.* Oxford: Basil Blackwell, 1989.

Owen, Roger, and Bob Sutcliffe, eds. *Studies in the Theory of Imperialism.* Burnt Mill, Harlow Essex, UK: Longman, 1981.

Prebisch, Raúl. *Towards a Dynamic Development Policy for Latin America.* New York: United Nations, 1963.

Sassoon, Anne Showstack, ed. *Approaches to Gramsci.* London: Writers and Readers Publishing Cooperative Society, 1982.

Shannon, Thomas Richard. *An Introduction to the World System Perspective.* Boulder: Westview Press, 2nd ed., 1996.

Skocpol, Theda. "Wallerstein's World Capitalist System: A Theoretical and Historical Critique." *American Journal of Sociology* 82-5 (March 1977): 1075–1090.

Smith, Tony. "The Underdevelopment of Development Literature: The Case of Dependency Theory." *World Politics* 31-2 (January 1979): 247–288.

Valenzuela, J. Samuel, and Arturo Valenzuela. "Modernization and Dependency: Alternative Perspectives in the Study of Latin American Development." *Comparative Politics* 10 (July 1978): 535–557.

Wallerstein, Immanuel. *The Modern World System: Capitalist Agriculture and the Origins of the European World-Economy in the Sixteenth Century.* New York: Academic Press, 1974.

———. *The Capitalist World-Economy.* New York: Cambridge University Press, 1979.

———. *The Politics of the World-Economy: The States, the Movements and the Civilizations.* London: Cambridge University Press, 1984.

Warren, Bill. *Imperialism: Pioneer of Capitalism.* London: New Left Books, 1980.

IX. Domestic-International Interactions

Avery, William P. *World Agriculture and the GATT.* Boulder: Rienner, 1993.

Cohn, Theodore H., and Patrick J. Smith. "Subnational Governments as International Actors: Constituent Diplomacy in the Pacific Northwest." *BC Studies* 110 (Summer 1996): 25–59.

Coleman, William D., and Grace Skogstad. *Policy Communities and Public Policy in Canada: A Structural Approach*. Mississauga: Copp Clark Pitman, 1990.

Comisso, Ellen, and Laura D'Andrea Tyson, eds. *Power, Purpose, and Collective Choice: Economic Strategy in Socialist States*. Special issue of *International Organization* 40-2 (Spring 1986).

Cox, Ronald W. *Power and Profits: U.S. Policy in Central America*. Lexington: University Press of Kentucky, 1994.

Eichengreen, Barry. *The Gold Standard and the Great Depression, 1919–1939*. New York: Oxford University Press, 1992.

Evangelista, Matthew. "Domestic Structure and International Change." In *New Thinking in International Relations*, eds. Michael W. Doyle and G. John Ikenberry. Boulder: Westview Press, 1997.

Evans, Peter B., Harold K. Jacobson, and Robert D. Putnam, eds. *Double-Edged Diplomacy: International Bargaining and Domestic Politics*. Berkeley: University of California Press, 1993.

Friman, H. Richard. "Side-Payments versus Security Cards: Domestic Bargaining Tactics in International Economic Negotiations." *International Organization* 47-3 (Summer 1993): 387–410.

Gibbs, David N. *The Political Economy of Third World Intervention: Mines, Money, and U.S. Policy in the Congo Crisis*. Chicago: University of Chicago Press, 1991.

Gourevitch, Peter. "The Second Image Reversed: The International Sources of Domestic Politics." *International Organization* 32-4 (Autumn 1978): 881–912.

———. *Politics in Hard Times: Comparative Responses to International Economic Crises*. Ithaca: Cornell University Press, 1986.

———. "Squaring the Circle: The Domestic Sources of International Cooperation." *International Organization* 50-2 (Spring 1996): 349–373.

Ikenberry, G. John, David A. Lake, and Michael Mastanduno, eds. *The State and American Foreign Economic Policy*. Special issue of *International Organization* 42-1 (Winter 1988).

Katzenstein, Peter J. "International Relations and Domestic Structures: Foreign Economic Policies of Advanced Industrial States." *International Organization* 30-1 (Winter 1976): 1–45.

———, ed. *Between Power and Plenty: Foreign Economic Policies of Advanced Industrial States*. Special issue of *International Organization* 31-4 (Autumn 1977).

Keohane, Robert O., and Helen V. Milner, eds. *Internationalization and Domestic Politics*. Cambridge: Cambridge University Press, 1996.

Kresl, Peter, Karl Kresl, and Gary Gappert. *North American Cities and the Global Economy: Challenges and Opportunities*. Thousand Oaks: Sage, 1995.

Milner, Helen V. *Interests, Institutions, and Information: Domestic Politics and International Relations*. Princeton: Princeton University Press, 1997.

Nowell, Gregory P. *Mercantile States and the World Oil Cartel, 1900–1939*. Ithaca: Cornell University Press, 1994.

Putnam, Robert D. "Diplomacy and Domestic Politics: The Logic of Two-Level Games." *International Organization* 42 (Summer 1988): 427–460.

Risse-Kappen, Thomas, ed. *Bringing Transnational Relations Back In: Non-State Actors, Domestic Structures and International Institutions*. Cambridge: Cambridge University Press, 1995.

Rogowski, Ronald. *Commerce and Coalitions: How Trade Affects Domestic Political Alignments*. Princeton: Princeton University Press, 1989.

Rosenau, James N. *Along the Domestic-Foreign Frontier: Exploring Governance in a Turbulent World*. Cambridge: Cambridge University Press, 1997.

Simmons, Beth A. *Who Adjusts? Domestic Sources of Foreign Economic Policy During the Interwar Years*. Princeton: Princeton University Press, 1994.

Stolper, Wolfgang F., and Paul A. Samuelson. "Protection and Real Wages." *Review of Economic Studies* 9-1 (November 1941): 58–73.

X. International Monetary and Financial Relations

Bergsten, C. Fred, and John Williamson, eds. *Dollar Overvaluation and the World Economy*. Washington, D.C.: Institute for International Economics, 2003.

Bird, Graham. "The Political Economy of the SDR: The Rise and Fall of an International Reserve Asset." *Global Governance* 4-3 (1998): 355–379.

Cerny, Philip G., ed. *Finance and World Politics: Markets, Regimes and States in the Post-Hegemonic Era.* London: Elgar, 1993.

Cohen, Benjamin J. *Organizing the World's Money: The Political Economy of International Monetary Relations.* New York: Basic Books, 1977.

———, ed. *The International Political Economy of Monetary Relations.* Aldershot: Elgar, 1993.

———. *The Geography of Money.* Ithaca: Cornell University Press, 1998.

Dam, Kenneth W. *The Rules of the Game: Reform and Evolution in the International Monetary System.* Chicago: University of Chicago Press, 1982.

Dell, Sidney. "On Being Grandmotherly: The Evolution of IMF Conditionality." *Essays in International Finance no. 144.* Princeton: Princeton University, October 1981.

Eichengreen, Barry. *International Monetary Arrangements for the 21st Century.* Washington, DC: Brookings Institution, 1994.

Eichengreen, Barry, and Jeffry Frieden, eds. *The Political Economy of European Monetary Unification.* Boulder: Westview Press, 1994.

Eijffinger, Sylvester C.W., and Jakob de Haan. *European Monetary and Fiscal Policy.* Oxford: Oxford University Press, 2000.

Ferguson, Tyrone. *The Third World and Decision Making in the International Monetary Fund: The Quest for Full and Effective Participation.* London: Pinter, 1988.

Frankel, Jeffrey A., and Shang-Jun Wei. "Is a Yen Bloc Emerging?" in Symposium on "Economic Cooperation and Challenges in the Pacific." *Joint U.S.-Korea Academic Studies* 5 (1995): 145–175.

Gardner, Richard N. *Sterling-Dollar Diplomacy in Current Perspective: The Origins and Prospects of Our International Economic Order.* New York: Columbia University Press, expanded ed., 1980.

Gowa, Joanne. *Closing of the Gold Window: Domestic Politics and the End of Bretton Woods.* Ithaca: Cornell University Press, 1983.

Helleiner, Eric. *States and the Reemergence of Global Finance: From Bretton Woods to the 1990s.* Ithaca: Cornell University Press, 1994.

Henning, C. Randall, and Pier Carlo Padoan. *Transatlantic Perspectives on the Euro.* Washington, DC: Brookings Institution, 2000.

Horsefield, Keith J. *The International Monetary Fund, 1945–1965: Twenty Years of Monetary Cooperation. Vols. I–III.* Washington, DC: International Monetary Fund, 1969.

James, Harold. *International Monetary Cooperation Since Bretton Woods.* Washington, DC: International Monetary Fund, 1996.

Kapstein, Ethan B. *Governing the Global Economy: International Finance and the State.* Cambridge: Harvard University Press, 1994.

Levitt, Malcolm, and Christopher Lord. *The Political Economy of Monetary Union.* London: Macmillan, 2000.

Mann, Catherine L. *Is the U.S. Trade Deficit Sustainable?.* Washington, D.C.: Institute for International Economics, 1999.

McKinnon, Ronald I. "The Rules of the Game: International Money in Historical Perspective." *Journal of Economic Literature* 31-1 (March 1993): 1–44.

Mundell, Robert A. "A Theory of Optimum Currency Areas." *American Economic Review* 51-4 (September 1961): 657–665.

Odell, John S. *U.S. International Monetary Policy: Markets, Power, and Ideas as Sources of Change.* Princeton: Princeton University Press, 1982.

Plumptre, A. F. W. *Three Decades of Decision: Canada and the World Monetary System, 1944–1975.* Toronto: McClelland & Stewart, 1977.

Preeg, Ernest H. *The Trade Deficit, the Dollar, and the U.S. National Interest.* Indianapolis: Hudson Institute, 2000.

Schweitzer, Pierre-Paul. "Political Aspects of Managing the International Monetary System." *International Affairs* 52-2 (April 1976): 208–218.

Solomon, Robert. *The International Monetary System, 1945–1981.* New York: Harper & Row, 2nd ed., 1982.

Strange, Susan. *Sterling and British Policy: A Political Study of an International Currency in Decline.* London: Oxford University Press, 1971.

———. *Casino Capitalism.* Oxford: Basil Blackwell, 1986.

Triffin, Robert. *Gold and the Dollar Crisis: The Future of Convertibility*. New Haven: Yale University Press, revised ed., 1961.

Verdun, Amy, ed. *The Euro: European Integration Theory and Economic and Monetary Union*. Lanham: Rowman & Littlefield, 2002.

Webb, Michael C. *The Political Economy of Policy Coordination: International Adjustment Since 1945*. Ithaca: Cornell University Press, 1995.

Williamson, John. *The Failure of World Monetary Reform, 1971–1974*. Sunbury-on-Thames: Nelson, 1977.

———. *The Exchange Rate System*. Washington, DC: Institute for International Economics, revised ed., June 1985.

XI. Foreign Debt and Financial Crises

Armijo, Leslie Elliott, ed. *Debating the Global Financial Architecture*. Albany: State University of New York Press, 2002.

Biersteker, Thomas J., ed. *Dealing with Debt: International Financial Negotiations and Adjustment Bargaining*. Boulder: Westview Press, 1993.

Cline, William R. *International Debt and the Stability of the World Economy* Washington, DC: Institute for International Economics, 1983.

———. *International Debt Reexamined*. Washington, DC: Institute for International Economics, 1995.

Cohen, Benjamin J. "Balance-of-Payments Financing: Evolution of a Regime." In *International Regimes*, ed. Stephen D. Krasner, 315–336. Ithaca: Cornell University Press, 1983.

Corbridge, Stuart. *Debt and Development*. Oxford: Blackwell Publishers, 1993.

D'Andrea Tyson, Laura. "The Debt Crisis and Adjustment Responses in Eastern Europe: A Comparative Perspective." *International Organization* 40-2 (Spring 1986): 239–285.

Eichengreen, Barry. *Toward a New International Financial Architecture: A Practical Post-Asia Agenda*. Washington, DC: Institute for International Economics, 1999.

Eichengreen, Barry, and Peter H. Lindert, eds. *The International Debt Crisis in Historical Perspective*. Cambridge: MIT Press, 1989.

Elson, Diane. "From Survival Strategies to Transformation Strategies: Women's Needs and Structural Adjustment." In *Unequal Burden: Crises, Persistent Poverty, and Women's Work*, eds. Lourdes Beneria and Shelley Feldman, 26–48. Boulder: Westview Press, 1992.

Feinberg, Richard E., and Ricardo Ffrench-Davis, eds., *Development and External Debt in Latin America: Bases for a New Consensus*. Notre Dame: University of Notre Dame Press, 1988.

Fratianni, Michele, Paolo Savona, and John J. Kirton, eds. *Governing Global Finance: New Challenges, G7 and IMF Contributions*. Aldershot: Ashgate, 2002.

Frieden, Jeff. "Third World Indebted Industrialization: International Finance and State Capitalism in Mexico, Brazil, Algeria, and South Korea." *International Organization* 35-3 (Summer 1981): 407–431.

Honeywell, Martin, ed. *The Poverty Brokers: The IMF and Latin America*. London: Latin America Bureau, 1983.

Husain, Ishrat, and Ishac Diwan, eds. *Dealing with the Debt Crisis: A World Bank Symposium*. Washington, DC: World Bank, 1989.

Kahler, Miles, ed. *The Politics of International Debt*. Ithaca: Cornell University Press, 1986.

Kaiser, Karl, John J. Kirton, and Joseph P. Daniels, eds. *Shaping a New International Financial System: Challenges of Governance in a Globalizing World*. Aldershot: Ashgate, 2000.

Kenen, Peter B. *The International Financial Architecture: What's New? What's Missing?*. Washington, DC: Institute of International Economics, 2001.

Körner, Peter, Gero Maass, Thomas Siebold, and Ranier Tetzlaff. *The IMF and the Debt Crisis: A Guide to the Third World's Dilemma*. Translated by Paul Knight. London: Zed Books, 1986.

Kuhn, Michael G., with Jorge P. Guzman. *Multilateral Official Debt Rescheduling: Recent Experience, World Economic and Financial Surveys*. Washington, DC: IMF, November 1990.

Lipson, Charles. "The International Organization of Third World Debt." *International Organization* 35-4 (Autumn 1981): 603–631.

———. "Bankers' Dilemmas: Private Cooperation in Rescheduling Sovereign Debts." In *Cooperation Under Anarchy*, ed. Kenneth A. Oye, 200–225. Princeton: Princeton University Press, 1986.

Pastor, Robert A., ed. *Latin America's Debt Crisis: Adjusting to the Past or Planning for the Future?* Boulder: Rienner, 1987.

Payer, Cheryl. *The Debt Trap: The IMF and the Third World.* Middlesex: Penguin, 1974.

———. *Lent and Lost: Foreign Credit and Third World Development.* London: Zed Books, 1991.

Rieffel, Alexis. "The Paris Club, 1978–1983." *Columbia Journal of Transnational Law* 23-1 (1984): 63–110.

———. "The Role of the Paris Club in Managing Debt Problems." No. 161, *Essays in International Finance.* Princeton: Princeton University, December 1985.

Sachs, Jeffrey, ed. *Developing Country Debt and Economic Performance, Vol. 1: The International Financial System.* Chicago: University of Chicago Press, 1989.

———. "Making the Brady Plan Work." *Foreign Affairs* 68-3 (Summer 1989): 87–104.

Sharma, Shalenda D. "Constructing the New International Financial Architecture: What Role for the IMF?" *Journal of World Trade* 34-3 (2000): 47–70.

Smith, Gordon W., and John T. Cuddington, eds. *International Debt and the Developing Countries: A World Bank Symposium.* Washington, DC: World Bank, 1985.

Stallings, Barbara. *Banker to the Third World: U.S. Portfolio Investment in Latin America, 1900–1986.* Berkeley: University of California Press, 1987.

XII. Global Trade Relations

Aggarwal, V. K. *Liberal Protectionism: The International Politics of Organized Textile Trade.* Berkeley: University of California Press, 1985.

Bhagwati, Jagdish. *The World Trading System at Risk.* New York: Harvester Wheatsheaf, 1991.

Brown, William Adams, Jr. *The United States and the Restoration of World Trade.* Washington, DC: Brookings Institution, 1950.

Cameron, James, and Karen Campbell, eds. *Dispute Resolution in the World Trade Organization.* London: Cameron, 1998.

Cline, William R., ed. *Trade Policy in the 1980s.* Washington, DC: Institute for International Economics, 1983.

Cohn, Theodore H. *The International Politics of Agricultural Trade: Canadian-American Relations in a Global Agricultural Context.* Vancouver: University of British Columbia Press, 1990.

———. *Governing Global Trade: International Institutions in Conflict and Convergence.* Aldershot: Ashgate, 2002.

Conybeare, John A. C. *Trade Wars: The Theory and Practice of International Commercial Rivalry.* New York: Columbia University Press, 1987.

Cortney, Philip. *The Economic Munich: The I.T.O. Charter, Inflation or Liberty, The 1929 Lesson.* New York: Philosophical Library, 1949.

Croome, John. *Reshaping the World Trading System: A History of the Uruguay Round.* Geneva: World Trade Organization, 1995.

Curzon, Gerard. *Multilateral Commercial Diplomacy.* London: Michael Joseph, 1965.

Dam, Kenneth W. *The GATT: Law and International Economic Organization.* Chicago: University of Chicago Press, 1970.

Destler, I. M. *American Trade Politics.* Washington, DC: Institute for International Economics and The Twentieth Century Fund, 2nd ed., 1992.

Evans, John W. *The Kennedy Round in American Trade Policy: The Twilight of the GATT?* Cambridge: Harvard University Press, 1971.

Finlayson, Jock A., and Mark W. Zacher. "The GATT and the Regulation of Trade Barriers: Regime Dynamics and Functions." In *International Regimes,* ed. Stephen D. Krasner, 273–314. Ithaca: Cornell University Press, 1983.

———. *Managing International Markets: Developing Countries and the Commodity Trade Regime.* New York: Columbia University Press, 1988.

Greenaway, David, Robert C. Hine, Anthony P. O'Brien, and Robert J. Thornton, eds. *Global Protectionism.* London: Macmillan, 1991.

Griesgraber, Jo Marie, and Bernhard G. Gunter, eds. *World Trade: Toward Fair and Free Trade in the Twenty-first Century.* London: Pluto Press, 1997.

Haus, Leah A. *Globalizing the GATT: The Soviet Union's Successor States, Eastern Europe, and the International Trading System.* Washington, DC: Brookings Institution, 1992.

Higgott, Richard A., and Andrew Fenton Cooper. "Middle Power Leadership and Coalition Building: Australia, the Cairns Group, and the Uruguay Round of Trade Negotiations." *International Organization* 44-4 (Autumn 1990): 589–632.

Hirschman, Albert O. *National Power and the Structure of Foreign Trade*. Berkeley: University of California Press, 1945.

Hoekman, Bernard M., and Michel M. Kostecki. *The Political Economy of the World Trading System: The WTO and Beyond*. Oxford: Oxford University Press, 2nd ed., 2001.

Hudec, Robert E. *The GATT Legal System and World Trade Diplomacy*. New York: Praeger, 1975.

———. *Developing Countries in the GATT Legal System*. Thames Essay no. 50. Aldershot: Gower, for the Trade Policy Research Institute, 1987.

———. *Enforcing International Trade Law: The Evolution of the Modern GATT Legal System*. Salem: Butterworth Legal Publishers, 1993.

Jackson, John H. *World Trade and the Law of GATT*. Indianapolis: Bobbs-Merrill, 1969.

———. *The World Trading System: Law and Policy of International Economic Relations*. Cambridge: MIT Press, 2nd ed., 1997.

Kock, Karin. *International Trade Policy and the GATT, 1947–1967*. Stockholm: Almqvist & Wiksell, 1969.

Kostecki, M. M. *East-West Trade and the GATT System*. London: Macmillan, 1979.

Krasner, Stephen D. "State Power and the Structure of International Trade." *World Politics* 28 (April 1976): 317–347.

Krueger, Anne O., ed. *The WTO as an International Organization*. Chicago: University of Chicago Press, 1998.

Lake, David A., *Power, Protection, and Free Trade: International Sources of U.S. Commercial Strategy, 1887–1939*. Ithaca: Cornell University Press, 1988.

Long, Olivier. *Law and Its Limitations in the GATT Multilateral Trade System*. Dordrecht: Nijhoff, 1985.

Milner, Helen V. *Resisting Protectionism: Global Industries and the Politics of International Trade*. Princeton: Princeton University Press, 1988.

Odell, John S., and Thomas D. Willett. *International Trade Policies: Gains from Exchange Between Economics and Political Science*. Ann Arbor: University of Michigan Press, 1990.

Organisation for Economic Co-operation and Development. *Integration of Developing Countries into the International Trading System*. Paris: OECD, 1992.

Preeg, Ernest. *Traders and Diplomats: An Analysis of the Kennedy Round of Negotiations Under the General Agreement on Tariffs and Trade*. Washington, DC: Brookings Institution, 1970.

———. *Traders in a Brave New World: The Uruguay Round and the Future of the International Trading System*. Chicago: University of Chicago Press, 1995.

Raghavan, Chakravarthi. *Recolonization: GATT, the Uruguay Round and The Third World*. London: Zed Books, 1990.

Runge, C. Ford, with François Ortalo-Magné and Philip Vande Kamp. *Freer Trade, Protected Environment: Balancing Trade Liberalization and Environmental Interests*. New York: Council on Foreign Relations Press, 1994.

Schattschneider, E. E. *Politics, Pressures and the Tariff*. Hamden: Archon Books, 1963, unaltered from the 1935 edition.

Schott, Jeffrey J., assisted by Johanna W. Buurman. *The Uruguay Round: An Assessment*. Washington, DC: Institute for International Economics, 1994.

———, ed. *The WTO after Seattle*. Washington, DC: Institute for International Economics, 2000.

Stegemann, Klaus. "Policy Rivalry Among Industrial States: What Can We Learn from Models of Strategic Trade Policy?" *International Organization* 43-1 (Winter 1989): 73–100.

Tyson, Laura D'Andrea. *Who's Bashing Whom? Trade Conflict in High-Technology Industries*. Washington, DC: Institute for International Economics, 1992.

Viner, Jacob. *Studies in the Theory of International Trade*. New York: Augustus M. Kelly, Reprint of Economic Classics, 1965.

Whalley, John, ed. *Developing Countries and the Global Trading System*, vol. 1. Ann Arbor: University of Michigan Press, 1989.

Whalley, John, and Colleen Hamilton. *The Trading System After the Uruguay Round*. Washington, DC: Institute for International Economics, July 1996.

Wilcox, Clair. *A Charter for World Trade*. New York: Macmillan, 1949.

Winham, Gilbert. *International Trade and the Tokyo Round Negotiations*. Princeton: Princeton University Press, 1986.

———. *The Evolution of International Trade Agreements*. Toronto, Canada: University of Toronto Press, 1992.

Wolfe, Robert. "Global Trade as a Single Undertaking: The Role of Ministers in the WTO." *International Journal* 51-4 (Autumn 1996): 690–709.

———. *Farm Wars: The Political Economy of Agriculture and the International Trade Regime*. London: Macmillan, 1998.

XIII. Regionalism and Globalism

Anderson, Kym, and Richard Blackhurst, eds. *Regional Integration and the Global Trading System*. Hertfordshire: Harvester Wheatsheaf, 1993.

Andreas, Peter, and Thomas J. Biersteker, eds. *The Rebordering of North America: Integration and Exclusion in a New Security Context*. New York: Routledge, 2003.

Balassa, Bela. *The Theory of Economic Integration*. London: Allen and Unwin, 1962.

Cameron, Duncan, and Mel Watkins, eds. *Canada Under Free Trade*. Toronto, Canada: Lorimer, 1993.

Dinan, Desmond. *Ever Closer Union? An Introduction to the European Community*. Boulder: Rienner, 1994.

Doern, G. Bruce, and Brian W. Tomlin. *Faith and Fear: The Free Trade Story*. Toronto: Stoddart, 1991.

Dosch, Jörn, and Manfred Mols, eds. *International Relations in the Asia-Pacific: New Patterns of Power, Interest, and Cooperation*. New York: St. Martin's Press, 2000.

Fischer, Thomas C. *The United States, the European Union, and the "Globalization" of World Trade*. Westport: Quorum Books, 2000.

Gamble, Andrew, and Anthony Payne, eds. *Regionalism and World Order*. London: Macmillan, 1996.

George, Stephen, and Ian Bache. *Politics in the European Union*. Oxford: Oxford University Press, 2001.

Gibb, Richard, and Wieslaw Michalak, eds. *Continental Trading Blocs: The Growth of Regionalism in the World Economy*. Chichester: Wiley, 1994.

Globerman, Steven, and Michael Walker, eds. *Assessing NAFTA: A Trinational Assessment*. Vancouver, Canada: Fraser Institute, 1993.

Grilli, Enzo R. *The European Community and the Developing Countries*. Cambridge: Cambridge University Press, 1993.

Grinspun, Ricardo, and Maxwell A. Cameron, eds. *The Political Economy of North American Free Trade*. Montreal: McGill-Queen's University Press, 1993.

Haas, Ernst B. *The Obsolescence of Regional Integration Theory*. Berkeley, CA: University of California, Institute of International Studies, 1975.

Hart, Michael, with Bill Dymond and Colin Robertson. *Decision at Midnight: Inside the Canada-US Free-Trade Negotiations*. Vancouver: University of British Columbia Press, 1994.

Hatch, Walter, and Kozo Yamamura. *Asia in Japan's Embrace: Building a Regional Production Alliance*. Cambridge: Cambridge University Press, 1996.

Higgott, Richard, Richard Leaver, and John Ravenhill, eds. *Pacific Economic Relations in the 1990s: Cooperation or Conflict?* Boulder: Rienner, 1993.

Holland, Martin. *The European Union and the Third World*. London: Palgrave, 2002.

Hufbauer, Gary Clyde, and Jeffrey J. Schott. *NAFTA: An Assessment*. Washington, DC: Institute for International Economics, revised ed., 1993.

———. *Western Hemisphere Economic Integration*. Washington, DC: Institute for International Economics, 1994.

Johnson, Jon R. *The North American Free Trade Agreement: A Comprehensive Guide*. Aurora: Canada Law Book, 1994.

Jovanovic, Miroslav N. *International Economic Integration*. London: Routledge, 1992.

Kahler, Miles. *Regional Futures and Transatlantic Economic Relations*. New York: Council on Foreign Relations, 1995.

Kaser, Michael. *Comecon: Integration Problems of the Planned Economies*. London: Oxford University Press, 1965.

Keohane, Robert O., and Stanley Hoffmann. *The New European Community: Decisionmaking and Institutional Change*. Boulder: Westview Press, 1991.

Lawrence, Robert Z. *Regionalism, Multilateralism and Deeper Integration*. Washington, DC: Brookings Institution, 1996.

Lipsey, R. G., and Kelvin Lancaster. "The General Theory of Second Best." *The Review of Economic Studies* 24-1 (1956–1957): 11–32.

Machlup, F. *A History of Thought on Economic Integration*. London: Macmillan, 1977.

Melo, Jaime de, and Arvind Panagariya, eds. *New Dimensions in Regional Integration*. Cambridge: Cambridge University Press, 1993.

Mendoza, Miguel Rodriguez, Patrick Low, and Barbara Kotschwar, eds. *Trade Rules in the Making: Challenges in Regional and Multilateral Negotiations*. Washington, DC: Brookings Institution, 1999.

Nader, Ralph. *The Case Against 'Free Trade': GATT, NAFTA, and the Globalization of Corporate Power*. San Francisco: Earth Island Press, 1993.

Patterson, Gardner. *Discrimination in International Trade. The Policy Issues: 1945–1965*. Princeton: Princeton University Press, 1966.

Ravenhill, John. *Collective Clientilism: The Lomé Conventions and North-South Relations*. New York: Columbia University Press, 1985.

Roett, Riordan, ed. *Mercosur: Regional Integration. World Markets*. Boulder: Rienner, 1999.

Rupert, Mark E. "(Re) Politicizing the Global Economy: Liberal Common Sense and Ideological Struggle in the US NAFTA Debate." *Review of International Political Economy* 2-4 (Autumn 1995): 658–692.

Salazar-Xirinachs, José Manuel, and Maryse Robert, eds. *Toward Free Trade in the Americas*. Washington, DC: Brookings Institution, 2001.

Schott, Jeffrey J., ed. *Free Trade Areas and U.S. Trade Policy*. Washington, DC: Institute for International Economics, 1989.

Smith, Murray G., with C. Michael Aho and Gary N. Horlick. *Bridging the Gap: Trade Laws in the Canadian-U.S. Negotiations*. Toronto: Canadian-American Committee, 1987.

Steger, Debra P. *A Concise Guide to the Canada-United States Free Trade Agreement*. Toronto: Carswell, 1988.

Stone, Frank. *The Canada-United States Free Trade Agreement and the GATT*. Ottawa: Institute for Research for Public Policy, November 1988.

Viner, Jacob. *The Customs Union Issue*. New York: Carnegie Endowment for International Peace, 1950.

Wilcox, Clair. *A Charter for World Trade*. New York: Macmillan, 1949.

Wise, Carol, ed. *The Post-NAFTA Political Economy: Mexico and the Western Hemisphere*. University Park: Pennsylvania State University Press, 1998.

Wise, Mark, and Richard Gibb. *Single Market to Social Europe: The European Community in the 1990s*. Essex: Longman, 1993.

World Trade Organization. *Regionalism and the World Trading System*. Geneva, Switzerland: World Trade Organization, 1995.

XIV. Multinational Corporations and Global Production

Barnet, Richard J., and Ronald E. Müller. *Global Reach: The Power of the Multinational Corporations*. New York: Simon & Schuster, 1974.

Behrman, Jack N., and Robert E. Grosse. *International Business and Governments: Issues and Institutions*. Columbia: University of South Carolina Press, 1990.

Bergsten, C. Fred, and Marcus Noland. *Reconcilable Differences? United States-Japan Economic Conflict*. Washington, DC: Institute for International Economics, 1993.

Bora, Bijit, ed. *Foreign Direct Investment: Research Issues*. London: Routledge, 2002.

Buckley, Peter J., and Mark C. Casson. *The Future of the Multinational Enterprise*. London: Macmillan, 2nd ed., 1991.

Casson, Mark, ed. *The Growth of International Business*. London: Allen and Unwin, 1983.

Caves, Richard E. *Multinational Enterprise and Economic Analysis*. Cambridge: Cambridge University Press, 2nd ed., 1996.

Cutler, A. Claire. "Public Meets Private: The International Harmonization and Unification of Private International Law." *Global Society* 13-1 (January 1999): 25–48.

Doremus, Paul N., William W. Keller, Louis W. Pauly, and Simon Reich. *The Myth of the Global Corporation*. Princeton: Princeton University Press, 1998.

Dunning, John H. *Multinational Enterprises and the Global Economy*. Wokingham: Addison-Wesley, 1993.

———, ed. *Globalization, Trade and Foreign Direct Investment*. Amsterdam: Elsevier, 1998.

Eden, Lorraine. *Taxing Multinationals*. Toronto: University of Toronto, 1997.

Eden, Lorraine, and Evan H. Potter, eds. *Multinationals in the Global Political Economy*. New York: St. Martin's Press, 1993.

Encarnation, Dennis S. *Rivals Beyond Trade: America versus Japan in Global Competition*. Ithaca: Cornell University Press, 1992.

Enderwick, Peter. *Multinational Business and Labour*. London: Croom Helm, 1985.

Froot, Kenneth, ed. *Foreign Direct Investment*. Chicago: University of Chicago Press, 1993.

Gilpin, Robert. *U.S. Power and the Multinational Corporation: The Political Economy of Foreign Direct Investment*. New York: Basic Books, 1975.

Graham, Edward M. *Global Corporations and National Governments*. Washington, DC: Institute for International Economics, 1996.

Graham, Edward M., and Paul R. Krugman. *Foreign Direct Investment in the United States*. Washington, DC: Institute for International Economics, 3rd ed., 1995.

Hertner, Peter, and Geoffrey Jones. *Multinationals: Theory and History*. Aldershot: Gower, 1986.

Hymer, Stephen Herbert. *The International Operations of National Firms: A Study of Direct Foreign Investment*. Cambridge: MIT Press, 1976.

Ietto-Gillies, Grazia. *International Production: Trends, Theories, Effects*. Cambridge: Polity Press, 1992.

Jenkins, Barbara. *The Paradox of Continental Production: National Investment Policies in North America*. Ithaca: Cornell University Press, 1992.

Jones, Geoffrey. *The Evolution of International Business: An Introduction*. London: Routledge, 1996.

Julius, De Anne. *Foreign Investment: The Neglected Twin of Trade*. Occasional Papers no. 33. Washington, DC: Group of Thirty, 1991.

Kindleberger, Charles P. *American Business Abroad: Six Lectures on Direct Investment*. New Haven: Yale University Press, 1969.

Kindleberger, Charles P., and David B. Audretsch, eds. *The Multinational Corporation in the 1980s*. Cambridge: MIT Press, 1983.

Kojima, Kiyoshi. *Direct Foreign Investment: A Japanese Model of Multinational Business Operations*. London: Croom Helm, 1978.

Krugman, Paul. "Competitiveness: A Dangerous Obsession." *Foreign Affairs* (March/April 1994): 28–44.

———. "Competitiveness: Does It Matter?" *Fortune* (March 7, 1994): 109–115.

Mason, Mark. *American Multinationals and Japan: The Political Economy of Japanese Capital Controls, 1899–1980*. Cambridge: Council on East Asian Studies, Harvard University, 1992.

Mason, Mark, and Dennis Encarnation, eds. *Does Ownership Matter? Japanese Multinationals in Europe*. Oxford: Clarendon Press, 1994.

Modelski, George, ed. *Transnational Corporations and World Order: Readings in International Political Economy*. San Francisco: Freeman, 1979.

Moran, Theodore H., ed. *Multinational Corporations: The Political Economy of Foreign Direct Investment*. Lexington: Heath, 1985.

Muchlinski, Peter. *Multinational Enterprises and the Law*. Oxford: Blackwell, 1995.

Ohmae, Kenichi. *The Borderless World: Power and Strategy in the Interlinked Economy*. New York: Harper Perennial, 1991.

Pauly, Louis W., and Simon Reich. "National Structures and Multinational Corporate Behavior: Enduring Differences in the Age of Globalization." *International Organization* 51-1 (Winter 1997): 1–30.

Picciotto, Sol, and Ruth Mayne, eds. *Regulating International Business: Beyond Liberalization*. London: Macmillan, 1999.

Pitelis, Christos N., and Roger Sugden, eds. *The Nature of the Transnational Firm*. London: Routledge, 1991.

Porter, Michael E. *The Competitive Advantage of Nations*. New York: Free Press, 1990.

"Privatization and FDI in Central and Eastern Europe: Does the Mode of Entry Matter?" Special issue of *Transnational Corporations* 20-3. December 2001.

Reich, Robert B. *The Work of Nations: Preparing Ourselves for Twenty-First Century Capitalism*. New York: Vintage Books, 1991.

Robinson, John. *Multinationals and Political Control*. New York: St. Martin's Press, 1983.

Rugman, Alan M., and Lorraine Eden, eds. *Multinationals and Transfer Pricing*. London: Croom Helm, 1985.

Sauvé, Pierre, and Daniel Schwanen. *Investment Rules for the Global Economy: Enhancing Access to Markets*. Toronto: Howe Institute, 1996.

Servan-Schreiber, J. J. *The American Challenge*. Translated by Ronald Steel. New York: Atheneum, 1979.

Smythe, Elizabeth. "The Multilateral Agreement on Investment: A Charter of Rights for Global Investors or Just Another Agreement." In *Canada Among Nations—1998: Leadership and Dialogue*, eds. Fen Osler Hampson and Maureen Appel Molot, 239–277. Toronto: Oxford University Press, 1998.

Stopford, John M., and Susan Strange, with John S. Henley. *Rival States, Rival Firms: Competition for World Market Shares*. Cambridge: Cambridge University Press, 1991.

Teichova, Alica, Maurice Lévy-Leboyer, and Helga Nussbaum. *Multinational Enterprise in Historical Perspective*. Cambridge: Cambridge University Press, 1986.

Tyson, Laura D'Andrea. *Who's Bashing Whom? Trade Conflict in High-Technology Industries*. Washington, DC: Institute for International Economics, 1992.

Vernon, Raymond. *Sovereignty at Bay: The Multinational Spread of U.S. Enterprises*. New York: Basic Books, 1971.

Waldmann, Raymond J. *Regulating International Business through Codes of Conduct*. Washington, DC: American Enterprise Institute for Public Policy Research, 1980.

XV. International Development

Afshar, Haleh, and Carolyne Dennis, eds. *Women and Adjustment Policies in the Third World*. New York: St. Martin's Press, 1992.

Amsden, Alice H. "Why Isn't the Whole World Experimenting with the East Asian Model to Develop? Review of the East Asian Miracle." *World Development* 22-4 (1994): 627–633.

Ayres, Robert L. *Banking on the Poor: The World Bank and World Poverty*. Cambridge: MIT Press, 1983.

Balassa, Bela, ed. *The Newly Industrializing Countries in the World Economy*. New York: Pergamon Press, 1981.

Baldwin, David A. "The International Bank in Political Perspective." *World Politics* 18-1 (October 1965): 68–81.

Bauer, P. T. *Reality and Rhetoric: Studies in the Economics of Development*. London: Weidenfeld and Nicolson, 1984.

Bello, Walden. "East Asia: On the Eve of the Great Transformation?" *Review of International Political Economy* 5-3 (Autumn 1998): 424–444.

Bello, Walden, and Stephanie Rosenfeld. *Dragons in Distress: Asia's Miracle Economies in Crisis*. San Francisco: Institute for Food and Development Policy, 1990.

Benería, Lourdes, and Shelley Feldman. *Unequal Burden: Economic Crises, Persistent Poverty, and Women's Work*. Boulder: Westview Press, 1992.

Bhagwati, Jagdish N., and John Gerard Ruggie. *Power, Passions, and Purpose: Prospects for North-South Negotiations*. Cambridge: MIT Press, 1984.

Chilcote, Ronald H., and Dale L. Johnson, eds. *Theories of Development: Mode of Production or Dependency?* Beverly Hills: Sage, 1983.

Cohn, Theodore H. "Politics in the World Bank Group: The Question of Loans to the Asian Giants." *International Organization* 28-3 (Summer 1974): 561–571.

———. "Developing Countries in the International Civil Service: The Case of the World Bank Group." *International Review of Administrative Sciences* 41-1 (1975): 47–56.

———. *Canadian Food Aid: Domestic and Foreign Policy Implications*. Denver: University of Denver Graduate School of International Studies, 1979.

Cornia, Giovannia Andrea, Richard Jolly, and Frances Stewart, eds. *Adjustment with a Human Face. Vol. 1: Protecting the Vulnerable and Promoting Growth*. Oxford: Clarendon Press, 1987.

Culpeper, Roy. *The Multilateral Development Banks. Vol. 5: Titans or Behemoths?* Boulder: Rienner, 1997.

Culpeper, Roy, Albert Berry, and Frances Stewart, eds. *Global Development Fifty Years After Bretton Woods*. New York: St. Martin's Press, 1997.

Dorraj, Manochehr, ed. *The Changing Political Economy of the Third World*. Boulder: Rienner, 1995.

Elson, Diane, ed. *Male Bias in the Development Process*. Manchester: Manchester University Press, 1991.

English, E. Philip, and Harris M. Mule. *The Multilateral Development Banks. Vol. 1: The African Development Bank*. Boulder: Rienner, 1996.

Evans, Peter. *Dependent Development: The Alliance of Multinational, State, and Local Capital in Brazil*. Princeton: Princeton University Press, 1979.

Fine, Ben, Costas Lapavitsas, and Jonathan Pincus, eds. *Development Policy in the Twenty-First Century: Beyond the Post-Washington Consensus*. London: Routledge, 2001.

Gilbert, Christopher L., and David Vines, eds. *The World Bank: Structures and Policies*. Cambridge: Cambridge University Press, 2000.

Gold, Thomas B. *State and Society in the Taiwan Miracle*. Armonk: M. E. Sharpe, 1986.

Gran, Guy. *Development by People: Citizen Construction of a Just World*. New York: Praeger, 1983.

Griesgraber, Jo Marie, and Bernhard G. Gunter, eds. *The World Bank: Lending on a Global Scale*. London: Pluto Press, 1996.

Haggard, Stephan. *Pathways from the Periphery: The Politics of Growth in the Newly Industrializing Countries*. Ithaca: Cornell University Press, 1990.

———. *Developing Nations and the Politics of Global Integration*. Washington, DC: Brookings Institution, 1995.

———. *The Political Economy of the Asian Financial Crisis*. Washington, DC: Institute for International Economics, August 2000.

Handelman, Howard. *The Challenge of Third World Development*. Upper Saddle River: Prentice-Hall, 1996.

Hardt, John P., and Richard F. Kaufman, eds. *East-Central European Economies in Transition*. Armonk: M. E. Sharpe, 1995.

Hatch, Walter, and Kozo Yamamura. *Asia in Japan's Embrace: Building a Regional Production Alliance*. Cambridge: Cambridge University Press, 1996.

Hira, Anil. *Ideas and Economic Policy in Latin America: Regional, National, and Organizational Case Studies*. Westport: Praeger, 1998.

Hsiung, James. C., et al., eds. *Contemporary Republic of China: The Taiwan Experience 1950–1980*. New York: Praeger, 1981.

Hughes, Helen, ed. *Achieving Industrialization in East Asia*. Cambridge: Cambridge University Press, 1988.

Johnson, Chalmers. *MITI and the Japanese Miracle: The Growth of Industrial Policy, 1925–1975*. Stanford: Stanford University Press, 1982.

Kappagoda, Nihal. *The Multilateral Development Banks. Vol. 2: The Asian Development Bank*. Boulder: Rienner, 1995.

Kapur, Devesh, John P. Lewis, and Richard Webb. *The World Bank: Its First Half Century, Volume 1: History*. Washington, DC: Brookings Institution Press, 1997.

Krasner, Stephen D. *Structural Conflict: The Third World Against Global Liberalism*. Berkeley: University of California Press, 1985.

Krueger, Anne O. *Trade Policies and Developing Nations*. Washington, DC: Brookings Institution, 1995.

Krueger, Anne O., Constantine Michalopoulos, and Vernon W. Ruttan, with Keith Jay. *Aid and Development*. Baltimore: Johns Hopkins University Press, 1989.

Kuczynski, Pedro-Pablo, and John Williamson, eds., *After the Washington Consensus: Restarting Growth and Reform in Latin America*. Washington, D.C.: Institute for International Economics, 2003.

Mason, Edward S., and Robert E. Asher. *The World Bank Since Bretton Woods*. Washington, DC: Brookings Institution, 1973.

Mason, Mike. *Development and Disorder: A History of the Third World Since 1945*. Toronto: Between the Lines, 1997.

Mehmet, Ozay. *Westernizing the Third World: The Eurocentricity of Economic Development Theories*. London: Routledge, 1995.

Mittelman, James H., and Mustapha Kamal Pasha. *Out from Underdevelopment Revisited: Changing Global Structures and the Remaking of the Third World*. London: Macmillan, 2nd ed., 1997.

Mosley, Paul, Jane Harrigan, and John Toye. *Aid and Power: The World Bank and Policy-Based Lending*, vol. 1. London: Routledge, 1991.

Otero, Gerardo, ed. *Neoliberalism Revisited: Economic Restructuring and Mexico's Political Future*. Boulder: Westview Press, 1996.

Payer, Cheryl. *The World Bank: A Critical Analysis*. New York: Monthly Review Press, 1982.

Pincus, Jonathan R. and Jeffrey A. Winters, eds., *Reinventing the World Bank*. Ithaca: Cornell University Press, 2002.

Prebisch, Raúl. *The Economic Development of Latin America and Its Principal Problems*. New York: United Nations Economic Commission for Latin America, 1950.

———. *Towards a Dynamic Development Policy for Latin America*. New York: United Nations, 1963.

Pye, Lucian W., with Mary W. Pye. *Asian Power and Politics: The Cultural Dimensions of Authority*. Cambridge: Belknap Press, 1985.

Rapley, John. *Understanding Development: Theory and Practice*. Boulder: Rienner, 1996.

Reynolds, Lloyd G. *Economic Growth in the Third World, 1850–1980*. New Haven: Yale University Press, 1985.

Schuurman, Frans J. *Beyond the Impasse: New Direction in Development Theory*. London: Zed Books, 1993.

Schydlowsky, Daniel M., ed. *Structural Adjustment: Retrospect and Prospect*. Westport: Praeger, 1995.

Sen, Gita, and Caren Grown. *Development, Crises, and Alternative Visions: Third World Women's Perspectives*. New York: Monthly Review, 1987.

Shonfield, Andrew. *The Attack on World Poverty*. New York: Random House, 1960.

Singer, H. W. "The Distribution of Gains Between Investing and Borrowing Countries." *American Economic Review* 40-2 (May 1950): 473–485.

Stiglitz, Joseph E., and Shahid Yusuf, eds. *Rethinking the East Asian Miracle*. Oxford: Oxford University Press, 2001.

Thomas-Eneagwali, Gloria, ed. *Women Pay the Price: Structural Adjustment in Africa and the Caribbean*. Trenton: Africa World Press, 1995.

Tussie, Diana. *The Multilateral Development Banks. Vol. 4: The Inter-American Development Bank*. Boulder: Rienner, 1995.

Wade, Robert. *Governing the Market: Economic Theory and the Role of Government in East Asian Industrialization*. Princeton: Princeton University Press, 1990.

———. "Japan, the World Bank, and the Art of Paradigm Maintenance: The East Asian Miracle in Political Perspective." *New Left Review* 217 (May/June 1996): 3–36.

White, John. *Pledged to Development: A Study of International Consortia and the Strategy of Aid*. London: Overseas Development Institute, 1967.

Wood, Robert E. *From Marshall Plan to Debt Crisis: Foreign Aid and Development Choices in the World Economy*. Berkeley: University of California Press, 1986.

World Bank. *Sub-Saharan Africa: From Crisis to Sustainable Growth, a Long-Term Perspective Study*. Washington, DC: World Bank, 1989.

———. *The East Asian Miracle: Economic Growth and Public Policy*. Policy Research Report. Oxford: Oxford University Press, 1993.

XVI. Documentary Sources

A number of international and regional organizations and national government agencies provide valuable information and data on issues related to international political economy. Below is a selected list of some useful sources from international organizations. (Unless a date is mentioned, most of these sources are serial publications.)

International Finance Corporation (IFC)
Annual Reports
Articles of Agreement

International Monetary Fund (IMF)
Annual Reports
Articles of Agreement
Balance of Payments Statistics Yearbook
Direction of Trade Statistics

Finance and Development Journal
Government Finance Statistics Yearbook
IMF Papers on Policy Analysis and Assessment
IMF Survey newsletter
IMF Working Papers
International Financial Statistics
Summary Proceedings of the Board of Governors
World Economic Outlook (a survey of global economic developments)

Multilateral Investment Guarantee Agency (MIGA)
Annual Reports
Convention Establishing the MIGA

Organization for Economic Cooperation and Development (OECD)
Development Co-operation: Efforts and Policies of the Members of the Development Assistance Committee
Economic Surveys
Financing and External Debt of Developing Countries (was *External Debt of Developing Countries* until 1984)
International Direct Investment Statistics Yearbook
International Investment Perspectives (annual publication, began in 2002)
Main Economic Indicators: Sources and Methods
Twenty-Five Years of Development Co-operation: A Review—1985 Report

United Nations Centre on Transnational Corporations (no longer exists)
Transnational Corporations
Transnational Corporations in World Development: Trends and Prospects, 1988
The United Nations Code of Conduct on Transnational Corporations, 1986

United Nations Conference on Trade and Development
Bilateral Investment Treaties in the Mid-1990s. New York: United Nations, 1998.
Handbook of International Trade and Development Statistics
International Monetary and Financial Issues for the 1990s
Report of the Trade and Development Board
The Least Developed Countries—Annual Report
Trade and Development Report
Transnational Corporations
UNCTAD Bulletin
UNCTAD Review
World Investment Report

United Nations Department for Economic and Social Information and Policy Analysis
International Trade Statistics Yearbook
Monthly Bulletin of Statistics
World Economic and Social Survey (*World Economic Survey* before 1995)

United Nations Development Program
Human Development Report

United Nations Industrial Development Organization (UNIDO)
Industry and Development: Global Report

World Bank
Annual Reports
Annual World Bank Conference on Development Economics

Articles of Agreement
Global Economic Prospects
Summary Proceedings of the Board of Governors
World Debt Tables
World Development Report

World Trade Organization (WTO) and General Agreement on Tariffs and Trade (GATT)
Annual World Bank Conference on Development Economics
Basic Instruments and Selected Documents
GATT Activities
GATT Focus newsletter
International Trade Statistics
Results of the Uruguay Round of Multilateral Trade Negotiations: The Legal Texts
Text of the General Agreement on Tariffs and Trade
Texts of the Tokyo Round Agreements
Trade Policy Reviews
WTO Annual Reports
WTO Focus newsletter
WTO Press Releases

Index